Moving Beyond the Page

Moving Beyond the Page

A Reader for Writing and Thinking

Elpida Morfetas   Tanya Ceolin

OXFORD

UNIVERSITY PRESS

OXFORD
UNIVERSITY PRESS

Oxford University Press is a department of the University of Oxford.

It furthers the University's objective of excellence in research, scholarship, and education by publishing worldwide. Oxford is a registered trade mark of Oxford University Press in the UK and in certain other countries.

Published in Canada by
Oxford University Press
8 Sampson Mews, Suite 204,
Don Mills, Ontario M3C 0H5 Canada
www.oupcanada.com

Library and Archives Canada Cataloguing in Publication

Moving beyond the page : a reader for writing and thinking /
[edited by] Elpida Morfetas, Tanya Ceolin.

Includes index.

ISBN 978-0-19-543949-6

1. College readers. 2. English language—Rhetoric. 3. Critical thinking.

I. Morfetas, Elpida, 1969– II. Ceolin, Tanya

PE1122.M69 2011   808'.0427   C2011-904833-7

Cover image: ©iStockphoto.com/Baran Özdemir

This book is printed on permanent acid-free paper ∞

Printed and bound in Canada.

2 3 4 — 15 14 13

Contents

······• Non-Fiction •·······

Fiction

Prologue

If you are reading this sentence, you are most likely one of two people: an instructor curious to see what this book contains and whether or not it may be useful in a composition course, *or* a student who has been instructed to read this section as part of an assignment or as preparation for a quiz on what can be found in this book, something we often give our own students. Either way, you are probably not starting off with excitement and anticipation. One way or another, you are probably being "forced" to read what's on this page—especially if you are a student.

Fair enough.

But take a look at the title of this book: *Moving Beyond the Page*. That is what we hope will happen for you—that the readings in this book will take on a life of their own and leave the confines of paragraphs and pages. We know that when readers learn how to truly engage with what's on a page, the words, even those written hundreds of years ago, take on new life and become very much a part of us.

But here is the real question: how does one become truly "engaged" with words on a page? Actually, it is quite simple. We can start right now. What word at the top of this page names what you are reading? You are reading a PROLOGUE. Do you actually know what a prologue is? Could you properly define it if someone bet you to do so one night at a party? Does it come from a Greek word that means "in favour of logs"? Or is it Greek for "before words"? Ask yourself this: do you know what you know because you absolutely know it? Or have you been "getting by" with guesses, assumptions, and glances?

We don't want students to just get by. We want you to actually get involved and do well in your writing courses. You can do this if you are ready to ask yourself some hard questions and be prepared to answer honestly. The first question is whether or not you believe that writing well is an ability that people (other than you) seem to be born with. The answer is NO! While it is true that some people enjoy writing more than others, it does not mean that they enjoy writing because it comes easily to them. People who do well at writing usually implement some strategies that help them write. What are some of the strategies you implement when you are assigned an essay? How are they working out for you?

The first place to start is acknowledging that reading, writing, and critical thinking are all skills that are interconnected. Moreover, they are all skills that can be learned and used each time you need to sit down and read an article, tackle any type of writing assignment, or analyze and summarize the main point of a speech.

There is no one who knows more about your abilities in reading, writing, and critical thinking than you. Therefore, the survey below will help you gain insight into the why, when, where, and how you approach all of these skills. So before you begin this course, we recommend you fill out this survey to get an honest look at your current methods, habits, and approaches. Simply circle the letter that most closely resembles what you do now or have done in the past when it comes to your academic assignments.

	Always (A)	Sometimes (S)	Rarely (R)	Never (N)

Preparation/Organization

1. When you are assigned a reading, do you do any preliminary research on the writer or the topic? — A S R N
2. Do you bring your textbook and notes to every class? — A S R N
3. Do you try to analyze a reading before the professor explains it in class? — A S R N
4. Do you organize and expand on your notes after a class? — A S R N
5. Do you approach your professor before an assignment is due to discuss your ideas? — A S R N

Reading

1. If the professor assigns a reading, do you read the material well ahead of time and do you read it more than once? — A S R N
2. Do you read actively, by making notes in the margins as you read the material? — A S R N
3. Do you read actively, by looking up any unknown words from the reading? — A S R N
4. Do you read other works from your textbook, in addition to those assigned by your professor? — A S R N
5. Do you read in relative quiet without distractions such as television, the Internet, and music devices? — A S R N

Critical Thinking

1. Are you able to summarize the main points of an assigned reading? — A S R N
2. Are you able to research from other sources and synthesize or see how the additional work you've done enhances or expands an assigned reading? — A S R N
3. Are you able to see bias in a writer's perspective or argument? — A S R N
4. Do you formulate questions as you read through an assigned reading? — A S R N
5. Do you reflect on differences and similarities between the readings assigned throughout the semester? — A S R N

Writing

1. Do you think about your audience before you write an essay? — A S R N
2. Do you give yourself time to come up with ideas or "pre-write" on your assigned topic for an essay? — A S R N
3. Do you prepare more than one draft of your essay before submitting it? — A S R N
4. Do you take the time to edit (organization, structure) and then proofread (grammar, spelling, punctuation) your work? — A S R N
5. Once your professor returns your essay, do you reflect on his or her comments and your own work? — A S R N

If you are expecting to see how to tally your results here, consider this: how many times did you answer "Always" and how many times did you answer "Rarely" or "Never"? Anything other than "Always" means that you have not approached these skills (or your assignments) in a manner that is not only expected of you at the post-secondary level, but more importantly, in a manner that will benefit you in your academic career as well as your entire life.

Many books tell students that writing is a skill like any other and that being a good writer involves being organized, conscientious, and thorough when it comes to facing that "blank page" or any other project you are assigned as a student. If this seems overwhelming and you are unsure where to start, try to choose one question you answered "Never" to in each section and turn it into an "Always." The easiest way to do this is to GET INVOLVED in your reading and writing assignments.

Reading and the Writing Process

Here are some simple and concrete suggestions on ways you can get more involved in your readings and assignments.

- Read the introductory notes for each section. These notes give you clues about the subject and the author's purpose.
- Look at the title. Authors spend a lot of time thinking of good titles. In non-fiction, a title often gives away an author's purpose and is a direct link to the thesis. In fiction, examining the title a writer has given a story can give the work a whole other layer of meaning. However, be aware that writers are also notorious "rule-breakers": sometimes you must read right to the end of a piece of writing to understand what the title means.
- Consider what you know about the author. What is he or she an authority on? What ideas or prejudices can be seen in the person's writing?
- Read the FIRST and LAST paragraphs more than once. Non-fiction writers often present their main idea at the beginning and then restate it at the end.
- Read the FIRST and LAST sentence of each paragraph in a piece of non-fiction (essay or article). This first sentence is often the TOPIC sentence and can give you a summary of the entire paragraph.
- Read ACTIVELY. Ideas and information are not going to leap off the page and into your mind. You have to make an effort. Turn off the TV or stereo and focus on what you are reading! It is also a good idea to read with a pencil and make notes on what you are reading, such as by underlining important words (or unknown ones), main points, and significant passages.
- Look for the MAIN IDEA in a non-fiction reading. Once you find the main idea, ask yourself how the supporting details the writer uses connect to the main idea.
- DECIDE what the author's PURPOSE is: to inform, to persuade, or to entertain? Focus on the details that carry out the writer's purpose.
- Understand the WORDS. Build your vocabulary by reading, and check the dictionary for any unknown words. Challenge yourself by examining the meaning of words that you assume you know. Students often think they know what a word means, but when it comes time to define it, they find they can't.
- Quiz yourself when you have finished a reading. For non-fiction ask yourself, what is the thesis or main idea? What are the main supporting points? Did the writer do a good job of defending an argument or explaining an idea? For fiction, ask yourself, who are the main characters? What is the climax? Is there an atmosphere the writer is working to establish in a story? What themes is the writer communicating through the story?
- Read the material again. Remember, you cannot read the material only once and come to the level of understanding you need for a college or university class.

F.Y.I.: ASSESSMENT

It is crucial for you to be aware of how your essay will be assessed, even before you attack your topic. Essays are often evaluated in college and university using four general categories:

Language (L)   Organization (O)   Content (C)   Style (S)

We can call this the LOCS system. We find that students who do well in essay writing have a clear picture of what their instructor is looking for and plan enough time to see that all four categories are addressed; students do poorly when writing is left to the last minute, which leads to careless errors, illogical statements, and little or no support for ideas.

Before examining the sample essays, familiarize yourself with the LOCS system since your instructors will be reading your paper with the following in mind:

- **CONTENT**: Good content grows organically from good thinking. When students give themselves an adequate amount of time to read the source material and think it over in relation to the topic and their own perspective, then strong content can be provided in the paper. Good content means strong examples, statistics, illustrations, arguments from supporting sources, and quotations from source works, not just regurgitated content that was heard in class.

- **STYLE:** Like one's fashion style, when we speak of a writer's style it refers to the use of appropriate words for any given occasion; a writer's careful consideration of word choice creates an appropriate tone for the paper. Mixing formal and conversational styles distracts the reader from the ideas behind the words. In the editing stage, improving on the quality and variety of words, in addition to eliminating wordiness or excess words, facilitates reader comprehension.

- **ORGANIZATION:** Ideas do not just have to be good, they must appear in the best possible sequence within a paper. Planning the "layout" of your paper (or "blue-printing" your ideas) before you formulate sentences will also help your reader's understanding and will strengthen the points you are making in your paper.

- **LANGUAGE**: Language refers to the correct use of grammar, spelling, and punctuation. Though not a consideration in the early stages of writing an essay, it is what proofreading is all about. Instructors hate coming to the end of a topic sentence for a paragraph and realizing it is a fragment, reading sentences with missing words, or seeing that a student has consistently misspelled the name of a main character or the source writer's name. Such errors can be caught if you give yourself just the right amount of time to proofread your work before your instructor does!

Assessment Guidelines: Check the Thing Before You Wreck the Thing

Although there are many different formats for essays, as professors in a college writing class we typically assign a five-paragraph essay. We do this for the following reasons:

1. It is a classic template for a short essay of about 500 to 1000 words.

2. It has many applications outside of the classroom. For example, the five-paragraph essay form is the basis for many business presentations. Presenters need an introduction, three main points (it is easier to remember things in groupings of three), and a strong closing.

3. It is a manageable form for people who do not do a great deal of writing. Students who do not have a strong background in disciplined essay writing or argument construction are able to work with this streamlined and compact format.

4. It is good for working on critical thinking skills and building an argument. Because the five-paragraph essay is suited for a shorter word-count requirement, students must be able to get to the point, cut-out all filler material, and make certain their logic is sound.

This may come as a shock to students, but a professor can already gauge how successful or effective an essay will be just by taking a 10-second "visual snapshot" of the essay as a whole. Therefore, once a student has written his or her essay, the first step in assessing an essay is looking at it visually. Below are three visual representations of essay assignments we routinely receive:

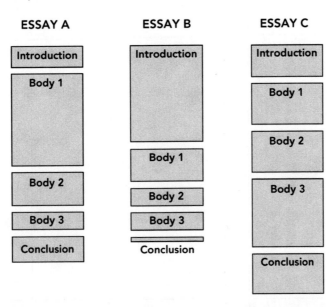

Which essay do you think "looks" like it was properly planned, edited, and proof-read? **Essay A** has a short introductory paragraph, a lengthy first body paragraph, an average length (10–15 sentences) second body paragraph, and a very short third body paragraph. The conclusion is also short. **Essay B** has a very lengthy introduction (over 20 sentences), an average length first body paragraph, very short second and third body paragraphs, and a "tiny" conclusion (1 or 2 sentences). **Essay C** has an average length introduction (5–8 sentences), as well as two body paragraphs of average length

(10–15) and a final body paragraph that is the longest of all. The conclusion is 5 to 10 sentences and preferably a bit longer than the introduction.

If you answered **Essay C**, you would be correct! Visually, it LOOKS like it fulfills the criterion for an effective essay. Students often construct essays that look like A and B. This is usually because they have not done enough effective planning and proofreading. However, there is more to an effective essay than just how it looks on the page.

The following table will help you see how a professor may evaluate your essay:

Criterion Sheet for LOCS Method	UNSATISFACTORY (below 54%)	SATISFACTORY (55%–69%)	ABOVE AVERAGE (70%–79%)	EXCELLENT (above 80%)
Language: Grammar and mechanics are usually broken up into "major" and "minor" errors				
Organization: Effective use of organizational patterns (logical, emphatic, chronological, spatial, and random) and transitions				
Content: A clearly worded thesis in addition to developing the thesis using appropriate writing strategies; the use of specific and logical concrete details and examples; thoughtful and convincing content that discusses the topic				
Style: Tone and diction appropriate to topic and audience; precise and clear language; no slang, no wordiness, no clichés, no jargon, and no conversational words or phrases				

So if you are still here reading this introduction then hopefully we've helped you see writing and reading in a different light. Writing isn't about being born a good writer; it's about allowing yourself the time to write, pushing yourself to examine not just the biases of others but also your own. Many students have "knee-jerk" or immediate reactions to what they read and are unable to separate their own views on a topic from what the author is saying or showing. To do anything well in life requires strong planning, clear focus, continuous practice, and attention to detail. Writing is no exception. So maybe it is time, as Stephen King writes, to reconsider the way you "approach the act of writing."

Features of This Book

This textbook has been written and structured to help you strengthen your reading, writing, and critical thinking skills. Each chapter contains the following:

1. **Author's Biography**: How can you get involved with a reading if you don't even know what was going on in the writer's life at the time the piece was written? Each chapter includes biographical information to help you get a sense of the author as a real person. This section is more than just a listing of published works or awards: we have included information about the writer's early life, influences, mentors, interests, successes, failures, and other factors that contributed to the creation of the chosen selection.

2. **In His/Her Own Words:** To further illuminate their personalities and work, we have let the writers "speak" for themselves by including their own words on a variety of topics such as the writing process, politics, history, media, humour, and aspects of human nature.

3. **Before We Begin:** The questions in this section can be effective for both independent and co-operative learning. Initially, these questions set the stage for topics and themes that will be addressed in the upcoming reading. However, they are also meant to generate ideas that can be used later to answer analysis questions and provide content for writing assignments.

4. **F.Y.I.:** Not just a texting abbreviation, the "For Your Information" section is meant to be much more than simply a list of definitions. Each name, word, or term is included as a mini background lesson about sections of a text that the writer would have assumed the audience was familiar with. Without knowing what a "morass," a "Hussar" or a "gamin" is, how can a reader get a full understanding of a piece of writing that features these terms? As these terms are not readily available as definitions in a dictionary, the F.Y.I. section is meant to demonstrate the necessary additional background research that students should be doing so that they are not only

able to understand a reading fully, but they are also able to effectively discuss and write about that reading in class.

5. **Words to Build on:** It is never a good idea to just assume you know what a word means in a reading. Students can try to guess what a word means by its context, but this is not always possible. Since some of the readings have vocabulary that can have multiple meanings and are not easily defined, we have provided definitions of some of the more challenging words.

6. **Tricks of the Trade:** Here is a list of literary devices that writers use but do not necessarily telegraph to the audience. In each chapter, there is a list of terms that are casually thrown around in an English classroom but don't necessarily get defined or explained all the time.

7. **In Your Words: Comprehension:** These questions are meant to gauge how closely students have read the text and how well they are able to summarize main ideas and recall specific details. Sometimes when students "skim" a reading just before class, they often miss relevant details, such as character names and specific plot developments.

8. **In Your Words: Analysis**: These questions involve a higher level of reasoning and require students to read between the lines and formulate their own ideas on what they have read. The purpose of these questions is to help students synthesize and engage in a level of higher critical reasoning.

9. **Now Write:** These writing topics are not meant to generate narrative essays. Students will be challenged to go beyond the personal point of view. Some topics will require students to compare and contrast different readings in the book, while others will involve research into ideas and themes that go beyond the reading. The topics are formulated to suit both short (500 words) and longer (1000+) writing assignments. Instructors will be able to adapt and revise some of these topics to better suit their classes.

Additional Features

This book also includes an Appendix containing a two-part assessment guideline and a sample of two student essays, a "Writer's Toolbox" in which all the terms found in the Tricks of the Trade section are listed alphabetically and explained in detail, and an Index of Themes. We recommend you read the section on how college and university professors evaluate essays in the prologue before viewing the sample essays and tackling your own writing assignments.

Acknowledgements

The seed of inspiration for this book came from the experiences I had in the classroom using Professor Smaro Kamboureli's *Making a Difference: Canadian Multicultural Literatures in English*. For this reason I would like to thank her for her work and extend this thanks to the students at Seneca College in Toronto to whom I had the pleasure of teaching this material.

My great appreciation goes to Professor John Kay and Professor Linda Hutcheon from the University of Toronto, and Professor Armand Ruffo and Professor Brenda Carr from Carleton University in Ottawa. So much of what I know about literature I learned from them, and what they taught me helped immensely with my contributions to this book.

I would like to express my thanks to my family: the Morfetas, Harding, and Mantzourogianni families, and to my friends—χίλια ευχαριστώ!

To my co-author and colleague Tanya Ceolin: thank you for all of your hard work, your dedication, your insights, and your unique sense of humour.

Elpida Morfetas
Toronto, February 2011

To my parents, Leo and Marie: thank you for giving me an amazing life. It is an absolute truth that without your continual love and support, I would not have been able to do any of this.

To Gino, Meghann, and Mathew: thank you for your interest, questions, and love which all helped a great deal in Auntie's work. All I can say now is bring on "The Scribbler!"

To Michael, Carrie, Benjamin, Luke, and Avery: thanks for hoping that this book "does better than *Harry Potter*!" Your immense love of cereal and all things collectible is a constant inspiration.

To Jacqueline Lacroix and Bill Porter: thank you for not taking radio silence from me to mean that you weren't on my radar. I couldn't ask for truer or more patient friends!

To Derek Cohen: many thanks for being a professor extraordinaire and showing me that the work didn't have to be dry. You always wanted me to cast you in one of my movies. Well, I'm putting your name in my book instead.

To Michael Dempsey: thank you for letting me live vicariously through your life during this time and for writing songs dedicated to me. I also thought you'd get a kick out of seeing your name in a book of learnin'!

To my colleague Elpida Morfetas: thank you for your generosity of spirit as well as time and encouragement, but more importantly, for being my friend

Tanya Ceolin
Toronto, February 2011

Together we would like to thank our editors at Oxford University Press, Jacqueline Mason, Allison McDonald, and Peter Chambers, for their guidance and support. Our deepest gratitude goes to Eric Sinkins and Suzanne Clark for listening to us and for trusting in our ideas—we appreciate all of your input and help with this project. A tremendous thanks to Leanne Rancourt for her work on editing our book. Warmest thanks to our colleagues and office mates at Seneca College, Jeannine Maxfield and Mary Elsisi, for their unwavering support and friendship. Special thanks are due to Pavitra Elliot, who was generous with her teaching materials and thoughts on the readings from Seneca's College Writing Course. Lastly, thanks are extended to author Timothy N. Hornyak for kindly forwarding to us the information we needed for the chapter on his work.

Finally, we would like to extend our sincere appreciation to all the authors who appear in this book.

Non-Fiction

Jonathan Swift

Jonathan Swift (1667–1745) was born in Dublin, Ireland, to Protestant Anglo-Irish parents. His father, Jonathan (a cousin of the influential English poet and playwright John Dryden), died a few months before Swift was born. Much of Swift's childhood is unclear and contradictory, but it is known that after his father's death, his mother was left with virtually no money, and some reports state that when Swift's nurse returned to England, she took the young boy with her. Swift's mother would return to England, her country of birth, while he was still very young, leaving Swift to be raised and educated by an uncle who sent him to Kilkenny College, the best school in Ireland at the time. He went on to Trinity College in Dublin, where he graduated in 1686. Despite the exemplary education he received, many biographies state that Swift was not the greatest of students.

While Swift was studying for his master's degree, Dublin was immersed in political troubles stemming from the Glorious Revolution, and Swift was forced to leave for England in 1688. In 1689, he secured a position as secretary and personal assistant to an English diplomat named Sir William Temple. Through Temple, Swift met many politically influential people of the time, which would play a role in his ideas and work. It was also during this time that he began to exhibit symptoms of an illness known as Ménière's disease, an imbalance of the inner ear that causes nausea and vertigo. Physicians suggested that Swift return to Ireland to recuperate. However, he did not stay long and soon came back to England and his position with Sir William. In 1692, not only did Swift finish his master's degree at Oxford, his first poem was published. His father's famous cousin John Dryden's review of the poem was to the point: "Cousin Swift, you will never be a poet."

Swift would venture back and forth between Ireland and England, circulating in political Tory circles and writing satirical attacks such as his Bickerstaff Papers and "A Description of a City Shower." In 1713, Swift was made Dean of St. Patrick's Cathedral in Dublin. Although a prestigious appointment, Swift was disappointed because the position meant he would have to remain in Ireland. He went on to found the influential Scriblerus Club along with other literary giants such as Alexander Pope and William Congreve, but by 1714 George I was named king after the death of Queen Anne and the Tories were no longer in power in parliament. For Swift, any chance of leading the life he once imagined in England was no more. He is said to have returned to Ireland "... to die ... like a poisoned rat in a hole." He would write nothing until 1718 when he began to describe the plight of the Irish people in a series of pamphlets. He wrote his most famous works in the following years: *Gulliver's Travels* (1726), *The Drapier's Letters* (1724–1725), "A Modest Proposal" (1729), and between 1727 and 1736 five volumes of work with his friend and colleague Alexander Pope. By 1736, Swift's Ménière's disease became even more debilitating and he began to lose his memory. He suffered a paralytic stroke in 1738, and by 1742 he could no longer care for himself. Jonathan Swift died on October 19, 1745. His body rests in St. Patrick's Cathedral in Dublin, Ireland.

Although Swift was a man that did not seem to want to remain in Ireland, "A Modest Proposal" did highlight the brutal realities of life in that country, namely the inhumane treatment of the poverty-stricken and starving Irish Catholics by the wealthy English Protestants. At that time, 90 per cent of the wealth and property in Ireland was owned and controlled by landlords that were neither Irish nor living in Ireland. These English landlords would charge such high rents that the Irish tenants would not be able to pay them. Although "A Modest Proposal" is a satire aimed at many subjects—absentee landlords, the bleeding of the Irish people through the rent system, the theory of mercantilism, and even the grossly naive belief of many that the "problem of Ireland" could be solved with a simple proposal—Swift was also satirizing the stoic suffering of the Irish people themselves and what he saw as their bewildering refusal to rise up and protest their treatment at the hands of the English. However, it is important to remember that legislation was put in place by the English that would severely limit the rights of the Irish to get an education, purchase property, participate in government, and even speak their own language.

In His Own Words

"Satire is a sort of glass wherein beholders do generally discover everybody's face but their own; which is the chief reason for that kind reception it meets within the world, and that so very few are offended with it."

"Good manners is the art of making those people easy with whom we converse. Whoever makes the fewest people uneasy is the best bred in the room."

Before We Begin

1. Are there any present-day social or economic (local or global) problems that you feel aren't being addressed properly or adequately?
2. What are the differences between sarcasm and satire?
3. Can humour be used to deal with difficult or disturbing subjects? Can you think of any examples of its positive effects in dealing with such issues?

 **Now Read**

A Modest Proposal

for Preventing the Children of Poor People in Ireland from Being a Burden to Their Parents or Country, and for Making Them Beneficial to the Public

It is a melancholy object to those who walk through this great town or travel in the country, when they see the streets, the roads, and cabin doors, crowded with beggars of the female sex, followed by three, four, or six children, all in rags and importuning every passenger for an alms. These mothers, instead of being able to work for their honest livelihood, are forced to employ all their time in strolling to beg sustenance for their helpless infants, who, as they grow up, either turn thieves for want of work, or leave their dear native country to fight for the Pretender in Spain, or sell themselves to the Barbados.

I think it is agreed by all parties that this prodigious number of children in the arms, or on the backs, or at the heels of their mothers, and frequently of their fathers, is in the present deplorable state of the kingdom a very great additional grievance; and therefore whoever could find out a fair, cheap, and easy method of making these children sound, useful members of the commonwealth would deserve so well of the public as to have his statue set up for a preserver of the nation.

But my intention is very far from being confined to provide only for the children of professed beggars; it is of a much greater extent, and shall take in the whole number of infants at a certain age who are born of parents in effect as little able to support them as those who demand our charity in the streets.

As to my own part, having turned my thoughts for many years upon this important subject, and maturely weighed the several schemes of other projectors, I have always found them grossly mistaken in their computation. It is true, a child just dropped from its dam may be supported by her milk for a solar year, with little other nourishment; at most not above the value of two shillings, which the mother may certainly get, or the value in scraps, by her lawful occupation of begging; and it is exactly at one year old that I propose to provide for them in such a manner as instead of being a charge upon their parents or the parish, or wanting food and raiment for the rest of their lives, they shall on the contrary contribute to the feeding, and partly to the clothing, of many thousands.

There is likewise another great advantage in my scheme, that it will prevent those voluntary abortions, and that horrid practice of women murdering their bastard children, alas, too frequent among us, sacrificing the poor innocent babes, I doubt, more to avoid the expense than the shame, which would move tears and pity in the most savage and inhuman breast.

The number of souls in this kingdom being usually reckoned one million and a half, of these I calculate there may be about 200,000 couples whose wives are breeders; from which number I subtract 30,000 couples who are able to maintain their own children, although I apprehend there cannot be so many under the present distress of the kingdom; but this being granted, there will remain 170,000 breeders. I again subtract 50,000 for those women who miscarry, or whose children die by accident or disease within the year. There only remain 120,000 children of poor parents annually born. The question therefore is, how this number shall be reared and provided for, which, as I have already said, under the present situation of affairs, is utterly impossible by all the methods hitherto proposed. For we can neither employ them in handicraft or agriculture; we neither build houses (I mean in the country) nor cultivate land. They can very seldom pick up a livelihood by stealing till they arrive at six years old, except where they are of towardly parts; although I confess they learn the rudiments much earlier, during which time they can however be looked upon only as probationers, as I have been informed by a principal gentleman in the county of Cavan, who protested to me that he never knew above one or two instances under the age of six, even in a part of the kingdom so renowned for the quickest proficiency in that art.

I am assured by our merchants that a boy or a girl before 12 years old is no sale-able commodity; and even when they come to this age they will not yield above three pounds, or three pounds and half a crown at most on the Exchange; which cannot turn to account either to the parents or the kingdom, the charge of nutriment and rags having been at least four times that value.

I shall now therefore humbly propose my own thoughts, which I hope will not be liable to the least objection.

I have been assured by a very knowing American of my acquaintance in London, that a young healthy child well nursed is at a year old a most delicious, nourishing, and wholesome food, whether stewed, roasted, baked, or boiled; and I make no doubt that it will equally serve in a fricassee or a ragout.

I do therefore humbly offer it to public consideration that of the 120,000 children, already computed, 20,000 may be reserved for breed, whereof only one-fourth part to be males, which is more than we allow to sheep, black cattle, or swine; and my reason is that these children are seldom the fruits of marriage, a circumstance not much regarded by our savages, therefore one male will be sufficient to serve four females. That the remaining 100,000 may at a year old be offered in sale to the persons of quality and fortune through the kingdom, always advising the mother to let them suck plentifully in the last month, so as to render them plump and fat for a good table. A child will make two dishes at an entertainment for friends; and when the family dines alone, the fore or hind quarter will make a reasonable dish, and seasoned with a little pepper or salt will be very good boiled on the fourth day, especially in winter.

I have reckoned upon a medium that a child just born will weigh 12 pounds, and in a solar year if tolerably nursed increaseth to 28 pounds.

I grant this food will be somewhat dear, and therefore very proper for landlords, who, as they have already devoured most of the parents, seem to have the best title to the children.

Infant's flesh will be in season throughout the year, but more plentiful in March, and a little before and after. For we are told by a grave author, an eminent French physician, that fish being a prolific diet, there are more children born in Roman Catholic countries about nine months after Lent than at any other season; therefore, reckoning a year after Lent, the markets will be more glutted than usual, because the number of popish infants is at least three to one in this kingdom; and therefore it will have one other collateral advantage, by lessening the number of Papists among us.

I have already computed the charge of nursing a beggar's child (in which list I reckon all cottagers, labourers, and four-fifths of the farmers) to be about two shillings per annum, rags included; and I believe no gentleman would repine to give ten shillings for the carcass of a good fat child, which, as I have said, will make four dishes of excellent nutritive meat, when he hath only some particular friend or his own family to dine with him. Thus the squire will learn to be a good landlord, and grow popular among the tenants; the mother will have eight shillings net profit, and be fit for work till she produces another child.

Those who are more thrifty (as I must confess the times require) may flay the carcass; the skin of which artificially dressed will make admirable gloves for ladies, and summer boots for fine gentlemen.

As to our city of Dublin, shambles may be appointed for this purpose in the most convenient parts of it, and butchers we may be assured will not be wanting; although I rather recommend buying the children alive, and dressing them hot from the knife as we do roasting pigs.

A very worthy person, a true lover of his country, and whose virtues I highly esteem, was lately pleased in discoursing on this matter to offer a refinement upon my scheme. He said that many gentlemen of this kingdom, having of late destroyed their deer, he conceived that the want of venison might be well supplied by the bodies of young lads and maidens, not exceeding 14 years of age nor under 12, so great a number of both sexes in every county being now ready to starve for want of work and service; and these to be disposed of by their parents, if alive, or otherwise by their nearest relations. But with due deference to so excellent a friend and so deserving a patriot, I cannot be altogether in his sentiments; for as to the males, my American acquaintance assured me from frequent experience that their flesh was generally tough and lean, like that of our schoolboys, by continual exercise, and their taste disagreeable; and to fatten them would not answer the charge. Then as to the females, it would, I think with humble submission, be a loss to the public, because they soon would become breeders themselves: and besides, it is not improbable that some scrupulous people might be apt to censure such a practice (although indeed very unjustly) as a little bordering upon cruelty; which, I confess, hath always been with me the strongest objection against any project, howsoever well intended.

But in order to justify my friend, he confessed that this expedient was put into his head by the famous Psalmanazar, a native of the island Formosa, who came from thence to London above 20 years ago, and in conversation told my friend that in his country when any young person happened to be put to death, the executioner sold the carcass to persons of quality as a prime dainty; and that in his time the body of a plump girl of 15, who was crucified for an attempt to poison the emperor, was sold to his Imperial Majesty's prime minister of state, and other great mandarins of the court, in joints from the gibbet, at 400 crowns. Neither indeed can I deny that if the same use were made of several plump young girls in this town, who without a chair, and appear at the playhouse and assemblies in foreign fineries which they never will pay for, the kingdom would not be the worse.

Some persons of a desponding spirit are in great concern about that vast number of poor people who are aged, diseased, or maimed, and I have been desired to employ my thoughts what course may be taken to ease the nation of so grievous an encumbrance. But I am not in the least pain upon that matter, because it is very well known that they are every day dying and rotting by cold and famine, and filth and vermin, as fast as can be reasonably expected. And as to the younger labourers, they are now in almost as hopeful a condition. They cannot get work, and consequently pine away for want of nourishment to a degree that if at any time they are accidentally hired to common labour, they have not strength to perform it; and thus the country and themselves are happily delivered from the evils to come.

I have too long digressed, and therefore shall return to my subject. I think the advantages by the proposal which I have made are obvious and many, as well as of the highest importance.

For first, as I have already observed, it would greatly lessen the number of Papists, with whom we are yearly overrun, being the principal breeders of the nation as well as our most dangerous enemies; and who stay at home on purpose to deliver the kingdom to the Pretender, hoping to take their advantage by the absence of so many good Protestants, who have chosen rather to leave their country than stay at home and pay tithes against their conscience to an Episcopal curate.

Secondly, the poorer tenants will have something valuable of their own, which by law may be made liable to distress, and help to pay their landlord's rent, their corn and cattle being already seized and money a thing unknown.

Thirdly, whereas the maintenance of 100,000 children, from two years old and upwards, cannot be computed at less than ten shillings a piece per annum, the nation's stock will be thereby increased 50,000 pounds per annum, besides the profit of a new dish introduced to the tables of all gentlemen of fortune in the kingdom who have any refinement in taste. And the money will circulate among ourselves, the goods being entirely of our own growth and manufacture.

Fourthly, the constant breeders, besides the gain of eight shillings sterling per annum by the sale of their children, will be rid of the charge of maintaining them after the first year.

Fifthly, this food would likewise bring great custom to taverns, where the vintners will certainly be so prudent as to procure the best receipts for dressing it to perfection, and consequently have their houses frequented by all the fine gentlemen, who justly value themselves upon their knowledge in good eating; and a skilful cook, who understands how to oblige his guests, will contrive to make it as expensive as they please.

Sixthly, this would be a great inducement to marriage, which all wise nations have either encouraged by rewards or enforced by laws and penalties. It would increase the care and tenderness of mothers toward their children, when they were sure of a settlement for life to the poor babes, provided in some sort by the public, to their annual profit instead of expense. We should see an honest emulation among the married women, which of them could bring the fattest child to the market. Men would become as fond of their wives during the time of their pregnancy as they are now of their mares in foal, their cows in calf, or sows when they are ready to farrow; nor offer to beat or kick them (as is too frequent a practice) for fear of a miscarriage.

Many other advantages might be enumerated. For instance, the addition of some thousand carcasses in our exportation of barrelled beef, the propagation of swine's flesh, and improvement in the art of making good bacon, so much wanted among us by the great destruction of pigs, too frequent at our tables, which are no way comparable in taste or magnificence to a well-grown, fat, yearling child, which roasted whole will make a considerable figure at a lord mayor's feast or any other public entertainment. But this and many others I omit, being studious of brevity.

Supposing that 1000 families in this city would be constant customers for infants' flesh, besides others who might have it at merry meetings, particularly weddings and christenings, I compute that Dublin would take off annually about 20,000 carcasses, and the rest of the kingdom (where probably they will be sold somewhat cheaper) the remaining 80,000.

I can think of no one objection that will possibly be raised against this proposal, unless it should be urged that the number of people will be thereby much lessened in the kingdom. This I freely own, and it was indeed one principal design in offering it to the world. I desire the reader will observe that I calculate my remedy for this one individual kingdom of Ireland and for no other that ever was, is, or I think ever can be upon earth. Therefore let no man talk to me of other expedients: of taxing our absentees at five shillings a pound; of using neither clothes nor household furniture except what is of our own growth and manufacture; of utterly rejecting the materials and instruments that promote foreign luxury; of curing the expensiveness of pride, vanity, idleness, and gaming in our women; of introducing a vein of parsimony, prudence, and temperance; of learning to love our country, in the want of which we differ even from Laplanders and the inhabitants of Topinamboo; of quitting our animosities and factions, nor acting any longer like the Jews, who were murdering one another at the very moment their city was taken; of being a little cautious not to sell our country and conscience for nothing; of teaching landlords to have at least one degree of mercy toward their tenants; lastly, of putting a spirit of honesty, industry, and skill into our shopkeepers, who, if a resolution could now be taken to buy only our native goods, would immediately unite to cheat and exact upon us in the price, the measure, and the goodness, nor could ever yet be brought to make one fair proposal of just dealing, though often and earnestly invited to it.

Therefore I repeat, let no man talk to me of these and the like expedients, till he hath at least some glimpse of hope that there will ever be some hearty and sincere attempt to put them in practice.

But as to myself, having been wearied out for many years with offering vain, idle, visionary thoughts, and at length utterly despairing of success, I fortunately fell upon this proposal, which, as it is wholly new, so it hath something solid and real, of no expense and little trouble, full in our own power, and whereby we can incur no danger in disobliging England. For this kind of commodity will not bear exportation, the flesh being of too tender a consistence in salt, although perhaps I could name a country which would be glad to eat up our whole nation without it.

After all, I am not so violently bent upon my own opinion as to reject any offer proposed by wise men, which shall be found equally innocent, cheap, easy, and effectual. But before something of that kind shall be advanced in contradiction to my scheme, and offering a better, I desire the author or authors will be pleased maturely to consider two points. First, as things now stand, how they will be able to find food and raiment for 100,000 useless mouths and backs. And secondly, there being a round million of creatures in human figure throughout this kingdom, whose sole subsistence put into a common stock would leave them in debt 2 millions of pounds sterling, adding those who are beggars by profession to the bulk of farmers, cottagers, and labourers, with their wives and children who are beggars in effect; I desire those politicians who dislike my overture, and may perhaps be so bold to attempt an answer, that they will first ask the parents of these mortals whether they would not at this day think it a great happiness to have been sold for food at a year old in the manner I prescribe, and thereby have avoided such a perpetual scene of misfortunes as they have since gone through by the oppression of landlords, the common sustenance, with neither house nor clothes to cover them from the inclemencies of the weather, and the most inevitable prospect of entailing the like or greater miseries upon their breed forever.

I profess, in the sincerity of my heart, that I have not the least personal interest in endeavouring to promote this necessary work, having no other motive than the public good of my country, by giving some pleasure to the rich. I have no children by which I can propose to get a single penny; the youngest being nine years old, and my wife past childbearing.

F.Y.I.

Barbados: an island in the West Indies that was settled in 1627 by the British. Plantation owners on the island used slave labour to produce sugar for Europe.

Episcopal curate: a member of the Episcopal clergy engaged as assistant to a vicar, rector, or parish priest

Formosa: the Portuguese name for Taiwan

fricassee: a dish of stewed or fried pieces of meat served in a thick white sauce

gibbet: an upright post with an arm on which the bodies of executed criminals were left hanging as a warning or deterrent to others

Laplanders: a term used for people from a region of northern Europe that extends from the Norwegian Sea to the White Sea and lies mainly within the Arctic Circle. It consists of the northern parts of Norway, Sweden, and Finland, and the Kola Peninsula of Russia.

Lent: In the Christian Church, Lent is the period preceding Easter in which Christians commemorate Jesus Christ's time in the desert with 40 days of fasting, abstinence, and penitence.

Mandarins: a term for a high-ranking Chinese official

Papist: a Roman Catholic, often used in a derogatory manner

Popish: a derogatory term for Roman Catholic

pound: a British unit of currency

Pretender: James Francis Edward Stuart (1688–1766) was the son of King James II, who ruled England, Ireland, and Scotland from 1685 to 1688. James II and his wife, Mary of Modena, were both Catholic. When he became king, Protestant opposition continued to undermine him during his time on the throne. When Mary became pregnant with James Francis Edward Stuart, this same opposition feared that the child would continue a line of Catholic kings. During a battle with William of Orange, the man the Protestant opposition wanted to place on the throne, many of the Protestants in James II's army deserted to William's forces, and James II was forced to flee to France. After James II died in 1701, his son was proclaimed the rightful heir to the

English throne. However, the English Parliament had laws put in place that would make it impossible for another Catholic to become monarch. Despite this, James Francis Edward Stuart made repeated attempts to regain the throne. This is why the British gave him the nickname "The Old Pretender."

Psalmanazar: George Psalmanazar (1679?–1763) was an infamous French forger and impostor. He gained infamy after pretending to be from Formosa (Taiwan) and writing a book about the culture and customs of this country, about which very little was known in Europe. One of the more colourful sections of his book was on Formosan laws, particularly the law that allowed a husband to eat a wife if he caught her committing adultery. Psalmanazar made up the entire book; he had never been to Formosa. Unfortunately, many people in England actually believed the "findings" in the book.

ragout: pronounced "ragoo," a highly seasoned dish of small pieces of meat stewed with vegetables

shambles: a butcher's slaughterhouse

solar year: another term for the regular cycle of the seasons

tithes: one-tenth of annual produce or earnings, formerly taken as a tax for the support of the Church and clergy

Topinamboo: refers to a district of Brazil

Words to Build On

alms: money or food given to poor people

apt: having a tendency to do something

censure: to express severe disapproval of someone or something

dam: the female parent of an animal, especially a domestic mammal

dear: expensive

disobliging: deliberately unhelpful

dressing: cleaning and preparing meat or shellfish for cooking or eating

effectual: successful in producing a desired or intended result

expedients: convenient and practical actions that may also be improper or immoral

flay: to strip the skin off a corpse or carcass

groat: an English silver coin worth four old pence, issued between 1351 and 1662

medium: a means of doing something

parsimony: extreme unwillingness to spend money or use resources

probationers: people who are serving a probationary or trial period in a job or position to which they are newly appointed

raiment: an archaic term for clothing

repine: to feel or express discontent

rudiments: the first principles of a subject

scrupulous: very concerned about avoiding doing wrong

squire: a man of high social standing who owns and lives on an estate in a rural area, the chief landowner in the area

vintners: wine merchants

yearling: having lived for a year; a year old

Tricks of the Trade

Essay

Historical allusion

Irony

Satire

In Your Own Words: Comprehension

1. Although Swift is the author of "A Modest Proposal," his is not the voice in the essay. Who is the voice in the essay?

2. Describe how the essay begins.

3. What is the problem outlined in the essay and what is the "scheme" the speaker proposes?

4. Who do you think is "the very knowing American acquaintance" mentioned in paragraph 9?

5. Although this is a satire, Swift employs many rhetorical techniques used in argument essays. Identify these techniques.

6. What is the difference between argument and persuasion? Which one is "A Modest Proposal"?

7. This is a classic essay structure. Map out the major components.

8. Who is the essay addressed to?

In Your Own Words: Analysis

1. "A Modest Proposal" is a disturbing piece of writing. What parts do you find the most disturbing and why?

2. The speaker states in paragraph 12, "I grant this food will be somewhat dear, and therefore very proper for landlords, who, as they have already devoured most of the parents, seem to have the best title to the children." What does he mean?

3. Give examples of vocabulary that Swift uses to dehumanize the Irish people of this time. What is the effect of this?

4. Explain the title. Why did Swift give his essay this title?

5. Some scholars have claimed that Swift is laying some of the blame for the plight of the Irish in the 1700s on the Irish themselves. Do you see any evidence of this in the essay?

6. Slavery was in effect not only in England, but in Europe and the Americas at the time Swift wrote "A Modest Proposal," so many readers at this time would not have seen slavery as an inhumane practice. Why does the speaker not propose selling Irish children into slavery?

7. Fiction writers do not write as themselves; they create a persona to tell stories. Similarly, Swift does not write as himself. As a satirist, he creates a mask (a character) and it is from behind this mask that he presents his argument. However, there are moments in "A Modest Proposal" when Swift temporarily lets the mask "slip" to reveal the writer behind the work and his purpose. Identify these moments and explain why and how they sound different from the rest of the essay.

8. What is the startling realization made in the final paragraph of "A Modest Proposal"?

Now Write

1. Jonathan Swift was writing during turbulent political times. Research English/Irish relations during the 1700s. What aspects of Swift's "A Modest Proposal" are true?

2. Like Swift, Lawrence Solomon proposes solutions to deal with a social problem in his essay "Homeless in Paradise." Compare and/or contrast the two essays.

3. Irony involves statements in which one thing is stated but the opposite is implied. Eighteenth-century satire, like Swift's masterpiece, uses "doubleness" to make the reader see the familiar in unfamiliar ways. Write an essay in which you identify how this applies to "A Modest Proposal." In relation to Swift's essay, state what he hopes to achieve through the use of irony and whether, in your opinion, Swift achieves this.

Henry David Thoreau

Henry David Thoreau (1817–1862) was an American essayist, poet, naturalist, and translator. His father was a shopkeeper who later ran a successful pencil factory while his mother ran a boarding house. Thoreau was a serious boy, and he also inherited his mother's love of family, her sharp wit, and her frugality. It was also his mother, Maria Thoreau, who had a great love of nature. She would often take her four children outdoors, directing their attention to birds, flowers, and trees.

After Thoreau graduated from Harvard University he worked for a short time as a schoolteacher but quit his post because he refused to cane his students. He and his brother John opened their own school, but when John suddenly died the school was closed.

Thoreau met the philosopher and poet Ralph Waldo Emerson during his time at Harvard. He later worked on Emerson's farm and tutored Emerson's son Edward. Emerson became a kind of mentor and father-figure to Thoreau, encouraging him to write. In the spring of 1844, Thoreau accidently set fire to half a forest and several farms while he was trying to fry fish for dinner. Feeling little remorse, other than for his burnt fish dinner, Thoreau used the experience to find a place where he didn't have to live near humans. He was invited to live in a self-built hut (the size of a tool shed, 10 feet by 15 feet long) on Emerson's property, Walden Pond. Both Emerson and Thoreau were proponents of the transcendentalist philosophy, a nineteenth-century American movement composed of authors, artists, and thinkers living in New England. The movement grew out of a reaction to German and British philosophical traditions, and its father is known to be Emerson, who himself was heavily influenced by Buddhist and Hindu religious texts. Transcendental philosophy includes the belief that humans are essentially good, and when they are in a "natural" state this goodness will come out. Furthermore, transcendentalists believe that knowledge and truth can be sought beyond what is experienced by the human senses alone. Its proponents also held strong political views and were part of abolitionist, anti-war, and womens' rights movements. Thoreau sometimes took the philosophy to extremes; he even attended "funerals" for trees. Thoreau lived on the Walden property for two years, keeping a journal, but not living in isolation. He visited town for the supplies he needed and he ate with his family once a week. But it was here, at the age of 28, that he transformed his journal entries into what would become his first book, *Walden* (1854). Although it was ignored in its time, the book later became an American classic.

Thoreau never left North America, but his words travelled far. Many Americans, Canadians, and even some Europeans have created an incredible mythology around Thoreau; some have even gone as far as creating their own "New Waldens," a misinformed and romantic idealization of what they believe was propagated by Thoreau: living in rural areas, in isolation, and in some cases trying to live in what Thoreau called a "primitive way." But Thoreau did not set himself up as a prophet or leader. In his writing he encourages others to find their own path and answer to their own conscience, as opposed to following his.

The other seminal work Thoreau is known for is his essay "Civil Disobedience" (1849), which is based on a lecture he delivered to the townspeople explaining why he spent a night in jail. He believed if citizens refused to pay their taxes and were sent to jail, the US government would have no choice but to abolish slavery. In July 1846 Thoreau left his cabin on Walden to go into town to have his shoes mended. There he met the local constable who requested Thoreau pay his outstanding poll tax. Thoreau refused to pay out of principle: he was against slavery and the war the United States was waging with Mexico. The constable arrested him. After one night in jail, Thoreau's Aunt Maria, a known abolitionist, paid the tax for him. Yet even after the tax was paid, Thoreau refused to leave. The constable, Sam Staples, had to throw him out the following day.

In its printed form, Thoreau's speech became a kind of manual for social reformers around the world. In India, Mahatma Gandhi used it in his successful campaign to rid India of British Imperial rule; it was used by the Danish to fight Nazi invaders during World War II; Martin Luther King Jr. used it in his non-violent fight to end racial segregation in the United States.

After life in the cabin, Thoreau moved into Emerson's house. He worked at several odd jobs to pay off his debts, as he could not sustain an income from writing. He developed bronchitis and, because his health was declining, he moved back into his family home. Here he died of tuberculosis at age 44. His final words were "moose" and "Indian."

In His Own Words

"I hate the present modes of living and getting a living. Farming and shopkeeping and working at a trade or profession are all odious to me. I should relish getting my living in a simple, primitive fashion."

"Rather than love, than money, than fame, give me truth."

"Disobedience is the true foundation of liberty. The obedient must be slaves."

Before We Begin

1. Would you be willing to go to prison for your beliefs?
2. Have you ever publically protested against a government policy or decision? Do you believe in participatory democracy?
3. Can we depend on the goodness or generosity of others to help us in a time of need, or do we need safeguards in place, such as government programs and assistance?

✺ **Now Read**

Civil Disobedience

I heartily accept the motto, "That government is best which governs least;" and I should like to see it acted up to more rapidly and systematically. Carried out, it finally amounts to this, which also I believe, "That government is best which governs not at all;" and when men are prepared for it, that will be the kind of government which they will have. Government is at best but an expedient; but most governments are usually, and all governments are sometimes, inexpedient. The objections which have been brought against a standing army, and they are many and weighty, and deserve to prevail, may also at last be brought against a standing government. The standing army is only an arm of the standing government. The government itself, which is only the mode which the people have chosen to execute their will, is equally liable to be abused and perverted before the people can act through it. Witness the present Mexican war, the work of comparatively a few individuals using the standing government as their tool; for, in the outset, the people would not have consented to this measure.

This American government—what is it but a tradition, though a recent one, endeavouring to transmit itself unimpaired to posterity, but each instant losing some of its integrity? It has not the vitality and force of a single living man; for a single man can bend it to his will. It is a sort of wooden gun to the people themselves. But is it not the less necessary for this; for the people must have some complicated machinery or other, and hear its din, to satisfy that idea of government which they have. Governments show thus how successfully men can be imposed on, even impose on themselves, for their own advantage. It is excellent, we must all allow. Yet this government never of itself furthered any enterprise, but by the alacrity with which it got out of its way. *It* does not keep the country free. *It* does not settle the West. *It* does not educate. The character inherent in the American people has done all that has been accomplished; and it would have done somewhat more, if the government had not sometimes got in its way. For government is an expedient by which men would fain succeed in letting one another alone; and, as has been said, when it is most expedient, the governed are most let alone by it. Trade and commerce, if they were not made of India-rubber, would never manage to bounce over the obstacles which legislators are continually putting in their way; and, if one were to judge these men wholly by the effects of their actions and not partly by their intentions, they would deserve to be classed and punished with those mischievous persons who put obstructions on the railroads.

But, to speak practically and as a citizen, unlike those who call themselves no-government men, I ask for, not at once no government, but *at once* a better government. Let every man make known what kind of government would command his respect, and that will be one step toward obtaining it.

After all, the practical reason why, when the power is once in the hands of the people, a majority are permitted, and for a long period continue, to rule is not because they are most likely to be in the right, nor because this seems fairest to the minority, but because they are physically the strongest. But a government in which the majority rule in all cases cannot be based on justice, even as far as men understand it. Can there not be a government in which majorities do not virtually decide right and wrong, but conscience?—in which majorities decide only those questions to which the rule of expediency is applicable? Must the citizen ever for a moment, or in the least degree, resign his conscience to the legislator? Why has every man a conscience, then? I think that we should be men first, and subjects afterward. It is not desirable to cultivate a respect for the law, so much as for the right. The only obligation which I have a right to assume is to do at any time what I think right. It is truly enough said, that a corporation has no conscience; but a corporation of conscientious men is a corporation *with* a conscience. Law never made men a whit more just; and, by means of their respect for it, even the well-disposed are daily made the agents of injustice. A common and natural result of an undue respect for law is, that you may see a file of soldiers, colonel, captain, corporal, privates, powder-monkeys, and all, marching in admirable order over hill and dale to the wars, against their wills, ay, against their common sense and consciences, which makes it very steep marching indeed, and produces a palpitation of the heart. They have doubt that it is a damnable business in which they are concerned; are all peaceably inclined. Now, what are they? Men at all? or small movable forts and magazines, at the service of some unscrupulous man in power? Visit the Navy-Yard, and behold a marine, such a man as an American government can make, or such as it can make a man with its black arts—a mere shadow and reminiscence of humanity, a man laid out alive and standing, and already, as one may say, buried under arms with funeral accompaniments, though it may be—

> "Not a drum was heard, not a funeral note,
>   As his corse to the rampart we hurried;
> Not a soldier discharged his farewell shot
>   O'er the grave where our hero we buried."

The mass of men serve the state thus, not as men mainly, but as machines, with their bodies. They are the standing army, and the militia, jailers, constables, posse comitatus, etc. In most cases there is no free exercise whatever of the judgment or of the moral sense; but they put themselves on a level with wood and earth and stones; and wooden men can perhaps be manufactured that will serve the purpose as well. Such command no more respect than men of straw or a lump of dirt. They have the same sort of worth only as horses and dogs. Yet such as these even are commonly esteemed good citizens. Others—as most legislators, politicians, lawyers, ministers, and officeholders—serve the state chiefly with their heads; and, as they rarely make any moral distinctions, they are as likely to serve the Devil, without *intending* it, as God. A very few, as heroes, patriots, martyrs, reformers in the great sense, and *men,* serve the stat; with their consciences also, and so necessarily resist it for the most part; and they are commonly treated as enemies by it. A wise man will only be useful as a man, and will not submit to be "clay," and "stop a hole to keep the wind away," but leave that office to his dust at least:

> "I am too high-born to be propertied,
>   To be a secondary at control,
>   Or useful serving-man and instrument
>   To any sovereign state throughout the world."

He who gives himself entirely to his fellowmen appears to them useless and selfish; but he who gives himself partially to them is pronounced a benefactor and philanthropist.

How does it become a man to behave toward this American government today? I answer, that he cannot without disgrace be associated with it. I cannot for an instant recognize that political organization as *my* government which is the *slave's* government also.

All men recognize the right of revolution; that is, the right to refuse allegiance to, and to resist, the government, when its tyranny or its inefficiency are great and unendurable. But almost all say that such is not the case now. But such was the case, they think, in the Revolution of 1775. If one were to tell me that this was a bad government because it taxed certain foreign commodities brought to its ports, it is most probable that I should not make an ado about it, for I can do without them. All machines have their friction; and possibly this does enough good to counterbalance the evil. At any rate, it is a great evil to make a stir about it. But when the friction comes to have its machine, and oppression and robbery are organized, I say, let us not have such a machine any longer. In other words, when a sixth of the population of a nation which has undertaken to be the refuge of liberty are slaves, and a whole country is unjustly overrun and conquered by a foreign army, and subjected to military law I think that it is not too soon for honest men to rebel and revolutionize. What makes this duty the more urgent is the fact that the country so overrun is not our own, but ours is the invading army.

Paley, a common authority with many on moral questions, in his chapter on the "Duty of Submission to Civil Government," resolves all civil obligation into expediency; and he proceeds to say, "that so long as the interest of the whole society requires it, that is, so long as the established government cannot be resisted or changed without public inconveniency, it is the will of God that the established government be obeyed, and no longer...This principle being admitted, the justice of every particular case of resistance is reduced to a computation of the quantity of the danger and grievance on the one side, and of the probability and expense of redressing it on the other." Of this, he says, every man shall judge for himself. But Paley appears never to have contemplated those cases to which the rule of expediency does not apply, in which a people, as well as an individual, must do justice, cost what it may. If I have unjustly wrested a plank from a drowning man, I must restore it to him though I drown myself. This, according to Paley, would be inconvenient. But he that would save his life, in such a case, shall lose it. This people must cease to hold slaves, and to make war on Mexico, though it cost them their existence as a people.

In their practice, nations agree with Paley; but does anyone think that Massachusetts does exactly what is right at the present crisis?

> "A drab of state, a cloth-o'-silver slut,
> To have her train borne up, and her soul trail in the dirt."

Practically speaking, the opponents to a reform in Massachusetts are not a hundred thousand politicians at the South, but a hundred thousand merchants and farmers here, who are more interested in commerce and agriculture than they are in humanity, and are not prepared to do justice to the slave and to Mexico, *cost what it may*. I quarrel not with far-off foes, but with those who, near at home, co-operate with, and do the bidding of, those far away, and without whom the latter would be harmless. We are accustomed to say, that the mass of men are unprepared; but improvement is slow, because the few are not materially wiser or better than the many. It is not so important that many should be as good as you, as that there be some absolute goodness some-where; for that will leaven the whole lump. There are thousands who are *in opinion* opposed to slavery and to the war, who yet in effect do nothing to put an end to them; who, esteeming themselves children of Washington and Franklin, sit down with their hands in their pockets, and say that they know not what to do, and do nothing; who even postpone the question of freedom to the question of free trade, and quietly read the prices-current along with the latest advices from Mexico, after dinner, and, it may be, fall asleep over them both. What is the price-current of an honest man and patriot today? They hesitate, and they regret, and sometimes they petition; but they do noth-ing in earnest and with effect. They will wait, well disposed, for others to remedy the evil, that they may no longer have it to regret. At most, they give only a cheap vote, and a feeble countenance and Godspeed, to the right, as it goes by them. There are 999 patrons of virtue to one virtuous man. But it is easier to deal with the real possessor of a thing than with the temporary guardian of it.

All voting is a sort of gaming, like checkers or backgammon, with a slight moral tinge to it, a playing with right and wrong, with moral questions; and betting naturally accompanies it. The character of the voters is not staked. I cast my vote, perchance, as I think right; but I am not vitally concerned that that right should prevail. I am willing to leave it to the majority. Its obligation, therefore, never exceeds that of expediency. Even voting *for the right* is *doing* nothing for it. It is only expressing to men feebly your desire that it should prevail. A wise man will not leave the right to the mercy of chance, nor wish it to prevail through the power of the majority. There is but little virtue in the action of masses of men. When the majority shall at length vote for the abolition of slavery, it will be because they are indifferent to slavery, or because there is but little slavery left to be abolished by their vote. *They* will then be the only slaves. Only *his* vote can hasten the abolition of slavery who asserts his own freedom by his vote.

I hear of a convention to be held in Baltimore, or elsewhere, for the selection of a candidate for the presidency, made up chiefly of editors, and men who are politicians by profession; but I think, what is it to any independent, intelligent, and respectable man what decision they may come to? Shall we not have the advantage of his wisdom and honesty, nevertheless? Can we not count upon some independent votes? Are there not many individuals in the country who do not attend conventions? But no: I find that the respectable man, so called, has immediately drifted from his position, and despairs of his country, when his country has more reason to despair of him. He forth-with adopts one of the candidates thus selected as the only *available* one, thus proving that he is himself *available* for any purposes of the demagogue. His vote is of no more worth than that of any unprincipled foreigner or hireling native, who may have been bought. O for a man who is a *man,* and, as my neighbour says, has a bone in his back which you cannot pass your hand through! Our statistics are at fault: the population has been returned too large. How many *men* are there to a square thousand miles in this country? Hardly one. Does not America offer any inducement for men to settle here? The American has dwindled into an Odd Fellow—one who may be known by the development of his organ of gregariousness, and a manifest lack of intellect and cheerful self-reliance; whose first and chief concern, on coming into the world, is to see that the almshouses are in good repair; and, before yet he has lawfully donned the virile garb, to collect a fund for the support of the widows and orphans that may be; who, in short, ventures to live only by the aid of the Mutual Insurance company, which has promised to bury him decently.

It is not a man's duty, as a matter of course, to devote himself to the eradication of any, even the most enormous wrong; he may still properly have other concerns to engage him; but it is his duty, at least, to wash his hands of it, and, if he gives it no thought longer, not to give it practically his support. If I devote myself to other pursuits and contemplations, I must first see, at least, that I do not pursue them sitting upon another man's shoulders. I must get off him first, that he may pursue his contemplations too. See what gross inconsistency is tolerated. I have heard some of my townsmen say, "I should like to have them order me out to help put down an insurrection of the slaves, or to march to Mexico; see if I would go;" and yet these very men have each, directly by their allegiance, and so indirectly, at least, by their money, furnished a substitute. The soldier is applauded who refuses to serve in an unjust war by those who do not refuse to sustain the unjust government which makes the war; is applauded by those whose own act and authority he disregards and sets at naught; as if the state were penitent to that degree that it hired one to scourge it while it sinned, but not to that degree that it left off sinning for a moment. Thus, under the name of Order and Civil Government, we are all made at last to pay homage to and support our own meanness. After the first blush of sin comes its indifference; and from immoral it becomes, as it were, unmoral, and not quite unnecessary to that life which we have made.

The broadest and most prevalent error requires the most disinterested virtue to sustain it. The slight reproach to which the virtue of patriotism is commonly liable, the noble are most likely to incur. Those who, while they disapprove of the character and measures of a government, yield to it their allegiance and support are undoubtedly its most conscientious supporters, and so frequently the most serious obstacles to reform. Some are petitioning the state to dissolve the Union, to disregard the requisitions of the president. Why do they not dissolve it themselves—the union between themselves and the state—and refuse to pay their quota into its treasury? Do not they stand in the same relation to the state that the state does to the Union? And have not the same reasons prevented the state from resisting the Union which have prevented them from resisting the state?

How can a man be satisfied to entertain an opinion merely, and enjoy *it?* Is there any enjoyment in it, if his opinion is that he is aggrieved? If you are cheated out of a single dollar by your neighbour, you do not rest satisfied with knowing that you are cheated, or with saying that you are cheated, or even with petitioning him to pay you your due; but you take effectual steps at once to obtain the full amount, and see that you are never cheated again. Action from principle, the perception and the performance of right, changes things and relations; it is essentially revolutionary, and does not consist wholly with anything which was. It not only divides states and churches, it divides families; ay, it divides the *individual,* separating the diabolical in him from the divine.

Unjust laws exist: shall we be content to obey them, or shall we endeavour to amend them, and obey them until we have succeeded, or shall we transgress them at once?

Men generally, under such a government as this, think that they ought to wait until they have persuaded the majority to alter them. They think that, if they should resist, the remedy would be worse than the evil. But it is the fault of the government itself that the remedy *is* worse than the evil. *It* makes it worse. Why is it not more apt to anticipate and provide for reform? Why does it not cherish its wise minority? Why does it cry and resist before it is hurt? Why does it not encourage its citizens to be on the alert to point out its faults, and *do* better than it would have them? Why does it always crucify Christ, and excommunicate Copernicus and Luther, and pronounce Washington and Franklin rebels?

One would think, that a deliberate and practical denial of its authority was the only offence never contemplated by government; else, why has it not assigned its definite, its suitable and proportionate penalty? If a man who has no property refuses but once to earn nine shillings for the state, he is put in prison for a period unlimited by any law that I know, and determined only by the discretion of those who placed him there; but if he should steal 90 times nine shillings from the state, he is soon permitted to go at large again.

If the injustice is part of the necessary friction of the machine of government, let it go: perchance it will wear smooth—certainly the machine will wear out. If the injustice has a spring, or a pulley, or a rope, or a crank, exclusively for itself, then perhaps you may consider whether the remedy will not be worse than the evil; but if it is of such a nature that it requires you to be the agent of injustice to another, then, I say, break the law. Let your life be a counter friction to stop the machine. What I have to do is to see, at any rate, that I do not lend myself to the wrong which I condemn.

As for adopting the ways which the state has provided for remedying the evil, I know not of such ways. They take too much time, and a man's life will be gone. I have other affairs to attend to. I came into this world, not chiefly to make this a good place to live in, but to live in it, be it good or bad. A man has not everything to do, but something; and because he cannot do *everything,* it is not necessary that he should do *something* wrong. It is not my business to be petitioning the governor or the legislature any more than it is theirs to petition me; and if they should not hear my petition, what should I do then? But in this case the state has provided no way: its very Constitution is the evil. This may seem to be harsh and stubborn and unconciliatory; but it is to treat with the utmost kindness and consideration the only spirit that can appreciate or deserves it. So is all change for the better, like birth and death, which convulse the body.

I do not hesitate to say, that those who call themselves abolitionists should at once effectually withdraw their support, both in person and property, from the government of Massachusetts, and not wait till they constitute a majority of one, before they suffer the right to prevail through them. I think that it is enough if they have God on their side, without waiting for that other one. Moreover, any man more right than his neighbours constitutes a majority of one already.

I meet this American government, or its representative, the state government, directly, and face to face, once a year—no more—in the person of its tax-gatherer; this is the only mode in which a man situated as I am necessarily meets it; and it then says distinctly, Recognize me; and the simplest, the most effectual, and, in the present posture of affairs, the indispensablest mode of treating with it on this head, of expressing your little satisfaction with and love for it, is to deny it then. My civil neighbour, the tax-gatherer, is the very man I have to deal with—for it is, after all, with men and not with parchment that I quarrel—and he has voluntarily chosen to be an agent of the government. How shall he ever know well what he is and does as an officer of the government, or as a man, until he is obliged to consider whether he shall treat me, his neighbour, for whom he has respect, as a neighbour and well-disposed man, or as a maniac and disturber of the peace, and see if he can get over this obstruction to his neighbourliness without a ruder and more impetuous thought or speech corresponding with his action. I know this well, that if 1000, if 100, if 10 men whom I could name—if 10 *honest* men only—ay, if *one* HONEST man, in this State of Massachusetts, *ceasing to hold slaves,* were actually to withdraw from this co-partnership, and be locked up in the county jail therefor, it would be the abolition of slavery in America. For it matters not how small the beginning may seem to be: what is once well done is done forever. But we love better to talk about it: that we say is our mission. Reform keeps many scores of newspapers in its service, but not one man. If my esteemed neighbour, the state's ambassador, who will devote his days to the settlement of the question of human rights in the council chamber, instead of being threatened with the prisons of Carolina, were to sit down the prisoner of Massachusetts, that state which is so anxious to foist the sin of slavery upon her sister—though at present she can discover only an act of inhospitality to be the ground of a quarrel with her—the legislature would not wholly waive the subject the following winter.

Under a government which imprisons any unjustly, the true place for a just man is also a prison. The proper place today, the only place which Massachusetts has provided for her freer and less desponding spirits, is in her prisons, to be put out and locked out of the state by her own act, as they have already put themselves out by their principles. It is there that the fugitive slave, and the Mexican prisoner on parole, and Indian come to plead the wrongs of his race should find them; on that separate, but more free and honourable ground, where the state places those who are not *with* her, but *against* her—the only house in a slave state in which a free man can abide with honour. If any think that their influence would be lost there, and their voices no longer afflict the ear of the state, that they would not be as an enemy within its walls, they do not know by how much truth is stronger than error, nor how much more eloquently and effectively he can combat injustice who has experienced a little in his own person. Cast your whole vote, not a strip of paper merely, but your whole influence. A minority is powerless while it conforms to the majority; it is not even a minority then; but it is irresistible when it clogs by its whole weight. If the alternative is to keep all just men in prison, or give up war and slavery, the state will not hesitate which to choose. If a thousand men were not to pay their tax bills this year, that would not be a violent and bloody measure, as it would be to pay them, and enable the state to commit violence and shed innocent blood. This is in fact, the definition of a peaceable revolution, if any such is possible. If the tax-gatherer, or any other public officer, asks me, as one has done, "But what shall I do?" my answer is, "If you really wish to do anything, resign your office." When the subject has refused allegiance, and the officer has resigned his office, then the revolution is accomplished. But even suppose blood should flow. Is there not a sort of blood shed when the conscience is wounded? Through this wound a man's real manhood and immortality flow out, and he bleeds to an everlasting death. I see this blood flowing now.

F.Y.I.

abolitionists: people who formed a movement to bring an end to slavery

"but he that would save his life, in such a case, shall lose it": reference to the New Testament, Matthew 10:39

Copernicus: Renaissance astronomer Nicolaus Copernicus (1473–1543) was born in Poland and formulated the theory that the Earth was not the centre of the universe. Although in this essay Thoreau claims Copernicus was excommunicated, he was not.

hireling native: a person who works only for money or is hired to do distasteful things

India-rubber: latex from West Indian trees

Luther: Martin Luther (1483–1546) was a German monk and Protestant Reformation leader

Mexican War: an armed conflict between the United States and Mexico (1846–1848) as a result of the US annexation of Texas, which Mexico considered its territory.

odd fellow: Independent Order of Odd Fellows—a fraternal organization dating back to the mid-1700s. Thoreau speaks of its existence in America, though it originated in England.

Paley: William Paley (1743–1805) was a British Christian philosopher known for his teleological arguments that proved the existence of God.

posse comitatus: Latin for "power of the country" or a group empowered to uphold the law

powder-monkeys: boys who carried gun powder barrels for soldiers

Revolution of 1775: the American Revolution began in Lexington, Massachusetts in 1775.

tax-gatherer: a tax collector; here Thoreau refers to Sam Staples, the local constable, tax collector, and jailer for Concord. He arrested Thoreau for not having paid his poll tax for several years.

Words to Build on

alarity: speed or willingness

almshouses: a home for the poor maintained by charity

demagogue: a leader who tries to win support by inflaming people's emotions or prejudices

din: a loud and distracting noise

donned: to put on clothing

expedient: necessary for a purpose but not always fair or right

fain: ready or willing

foist: impose on

garb: dress in distinctive clothes

insurrection: an uprising against authority

leaven: a transforming influence

militia: a supplementary military force made up of civilians

penitent: regretting and wishing to atone for sins

philanthropist: a person who donates money to worthy causes

posterity: all succeeding generations

scourge: a person or thing that causes suffering

tinge: a touch or trace of something

whit: the least bit

Tricks of the Trade

Persuasive essay

Rhetorical strategies

Supporting evidence

Tone

In Your Own Words: Comprehension

1. What is Thoreau's ideal form of government?
2. How does Thoreau characterize a standing government in paragraph 1?
3. What does Thoreau think a government should use its powers for?
4. What are some of the obstacles to effective government?
5. Explain Thoreau's statement: "The mass of men serve the state thus, not as men, mainly, but as machines, with their bodies" (paragraph 5).
6. What does Thoreau think citizens should do to abolish practices such as slavery and war?
7. What are Thoreau's criticisms about the procedures that governments have in place to enable citizens to bring about reform?
8. According to Thoreau, where is the only place a just man can reside in a country with an unjust government?

In Your Own Words: Analysis

1. Many people today, especially in America, believe that voting is the most important thing a citizen can do. In fact, in some countries, citizens are fined if they do not vote. How do Thoreau's views on voting differ from this?
2. Why does Thoreau use variations of the word "expedient" in this essay?

3. Thoreau asks a series of questions in paragraphs 14 and 16. What is behind this stylistic device? Does he expect answers to these questions?

4. After reading "Civil Disobedience," what do you think Thoreau's views on the common man were?

5. In paragraphs 4 and 5, Thoreau creates lists of masses of men who serve the state. What is the effect of these lists? How do the lists reinforce Thoreau's belief that government turns men into mindless machines?

6. Give examples of sections in the essay where Thoreau switches from first person ("I") to second person ("you"). What effect does this have on how Thoreau sees himself in relation to his audience?

7. Why does Thoreau compare the government to a machine?

8. Find examples in the essay of moments when Thoreau alienates his audience and find examples of when he allies himself with his audience.

⁂ Now Write

1. What are the duties of a citizen according to Thoreau? At the time of writing "Civil Disobedience" Thoreau was a single man in his thirties. He had no serious health issues, no family, and no dependents. Is it possible to carry out the duties of a citizen, as Thoreau describes them in his essay, when one does not have a lifestyle like Thoreau's?

2. What would Thoreau have thought of Lawrence Solomon's solutions (see "Homeless in Paradise") to the homeless problem in North America? Write an essay in which you state why Thoreau would agree or disagree with Solomon's solutions.

3. Two of the most well-known peaceful revolutionaries, Martin Luther King Jr. and Mahatma Gandhi, were greatly influenced by Thoreau's "Civil Disobedience." Write an essay in which you explain the aspects of this essay that influenced the philosophies of King and Gandhi.

4. Thoreau proposes breaking the law as a way to fight unjust government laws and policies. Write an essay outlining alternative methods to eliminate a form of injustice you see today.

Oscar Wilde

Oscar Wilde (1854–1900) was born Oscar Fingal O'Flahertie Wills Wilde, and his life would be as remarkable as his name. Few authors and poets have had such a lasting impact on so many mediums—poetry, fiction, theatre, art, design, film, and even T-shirts—as Wilde. The son of the prominent poet and Irish nationalist, Jane Francesca Wilde, and Sir William Wilde, Ireland's leading eye and ear surgeon and a tireless philanthropist as well as an author of books on Irish archaeology and folk-tales, Wilde's childhood was spent at home where he was schooled in history, science, German, French, Greek, literature, and the classics. He excelled at Trinity College in Dublin and Magdalen College in Oxford, winning many prizes and awards for his poetry. It would be during his time at school that he began to create the flamboyant and stylized foundations for what would come to be known as the Aesthetic Movement and Decadent Movement.

Wilde went on to have great success after leaving school: a commercially lucrative lecture tour on aestheticism throughout America and Canada; a bright marriage to Constance Lloyd, a woman he genuinely loved and admired; the birth of two sons he adored; a string of literary accomplishments that included his novel *The Picture of Dorian Gray* and his comedies *Lady Windemere's Fan* and *The Importance of Being Earnest;* and the admiration and praise of such writers as George Bernard Shaw, Walt Whitman, and John Ruskin. It was his introduction to and subsequent relationship with the English poet Lord Alfred "Bosie" Douglas, however, that would bring about Wilde's downfall. Bosie's father was John Sholto Douglas, the ninth Marquess of Queensberry, a violent-tempered and opinionated man credited with inventing the rules of modern boxing. He was not happy with the relationship between his young son and Wilde. He demanded that Wilde end the affair, to which Wilde, unfortunately, countered by having the Marquess arrested on a charge of criminal libel. However, it was Wilde that would be prosecuted and sentenced to prison on the grounds of sodomy. It was during his time in prison that he wrote his 50,000 word letter, *De Profundis*, to Bosie, who distanced himself from Wilde during the entire trial and incarceration period. They would reunite briefly after Wilde was released from prison, but on November 30, 1900, Oscar Wilde died in a Paris hotel room with only his friend Robert Ross and a Catholic priest present.

De Profundis can be seen as a monologue of sorts in which Oscar Wilde asks the questions and anticipates the responses of the recipient. Since the author wrote it knowing he would eventually publish this letter publically, the recipient in question would be a much larger audience than just Bosie. It is a work filled with recrimination for Bosie, the Marquess, and Wilde himself, and it is a work that speaks of art and the artist as being beyond the sordid details of everyday life. It is also, at its heart, a love letter, and it is filled with the tears, longing, memories, love, and bitterness inherent in such writing.

In His Own Words

"I have said to you to speak the truth is a painful thing. To be forced to tell lies is much worse."

"A thing is, according to the mode in which one looks at it."

"Most people are other people. Their thoughts are someone else's opinions, their lives a mimicry, their passions a quotation."

"The supreme vice is shallowness."

Before We Begin

1. Have you ever felt so hurt or betrayed by someone you loved that all you wanted to do was tell the world what really happened?
2. Can a person ever really tell the whole truth when writing about him or herself?
3. Have you ever been surprised, disappointed, or shocked by something that you found out about a person who is generally recognized as being "extraordinary" in some way?

 Now Read

from *De Profundis*

Am I right in saying that hate blinds people? Do you see it now? If you don't, try to see it.

How clearly I saw it then, as now, I need not tell you. But I said to myself: "At all costs, I must keep love in my heart. If I go into prison without love what will become of my soul?" The letters I wrote to you at that time from Holloway were my effort to keep love as the dominant note of my own nature. I could if I had chosen have torn you to pieces with bitter reproaches. I could have rent you with maledictions. I could have held up a mirror to you, and shown you such an image of yourself that you would not have recognized it as your own till you found it mimicking back your gestures of horror, and then you would have known whose shape it was, and hated it and yourself forever. More than that indeed. The sins of another were being placed to my account. Had I so chosen, I could on either trial have saved myself at his expense, not from shame indeed, but from imprisonment. Had I cared to show that the Crown witnesses—the three most important—had been carefully coached by your father and his solicitors, not in reticences merely, but in assertions, in the absolute transference, deliberate, plotted, and rehearsed, of the actions and doings of someone else on to me, I could have had each one of them dismissed from the box by the judge, more summarily than even wretched perjured Atkins was. I could have walked out of Court with my tongue in my cheek, and my hands in my pockets, a free man. The strongest pressure was put upon me to do so. I was earnestly advised, begged, entreated to do so by people whose sole interest was my welfare, and the welfare of my house. But I refused. I did not choose to do so. I have never regretted my decision for a single moment, even in the most bitter periods of my imprisonment. Such a course of action would have been beneath me. Sins of the flesh are nothing. They are maladies for physicians to cure, if they should be cured. Sins of the soul alone are shameful. To have secured my acquittal by such means would have been a lifelong torture to me. But do you really think that you were worthy of the love I was showing you then, or that for a single moment I thought you were? Do you really think that at any period in our friendship you were worthy of the love I showed you, or that for a single moment I thought you were? I knew you were not. But love does not traffic in a market place, nor use a huckster's scales. Its joy, like the joy of the intellect, is to feel alive. The aim of love is to love: no more, and no less. You were my enemy: such an enemy as no man ever had. I had given you my life: and to gratify the lowest and most contemptible of all human passions, Hatred and Vanity and Greed, you had thrown it away. In less than three years you had entirely ruined me from every point of view. For my own sake there was nothing for me to do but to love you. I knew that if I allowed myself to hate you that in the dry desert of existence over which I had to travel, and am travelling still, every rock would lose its shadow, every palm tree be withered, every well of water prove poisoned at its source. Are you beginning now to understand a little? Is your imagination awakening from the long lethargy in which it has lain? You know already what hate is. Is it beginning to dawn on you what love is and what is the nature of love? It is not too late for you to learn, though to teach it to you I may have had to go to a convict's cell.

After my terrible sentence, when the prison dress was on me, and the prison house closed, I sat amidst the ruins of my wonderful life, crushed by anguish, bewildered with terror, dazed through pain. But I would not hate you. Every day I said to myself: "I must keep love in my heart today, else how shall I live through the day?" I reminded myself that you meant no evil, to me at any rate: I set myself to think that you had but drawn a bow at a venture, and that the arrow had pierced a king between the joints of his harness. To have weighed you against the smallest of my sorrows, the meanest of my losses, would have been, I felt, unfair. I determined I would regard you as one suffering too. I forced myself to believe that at last the scales had fallen from your long-blinded eyes. I used to fancy and with pain what your horror must have been when you contemplated your terrible handiwork. There were times, even in those dark days, the darkest of all my life, when I actually longed to console you, so sure was I that at last you had realized what you had done.

It did not occur to me then that you could have the supreme vice, shallowness. Indeed it was a real grief to me when I had to let you know that. I was obliged to reserve for my family business my first opportunity of receiving a letter: but my brother-in-law had written to me to say that if I would only write once to my wife she would, for my own sake and for our children's sake, take no action for divorce. I felt my duty was to do so. Setting aside other reasons, I could not bear the idea of being separated from Cyril, that beautiful, loving, lovable child of mine, my friend of all friends, my companion beyond all companions, one single hair of whose little golden head should have been dearer and more valuable to me than, I will not say you from top to toe, but the entire chrysolite of the whole world: was so indeed to me always, though I failed to understand it till too late.

Two weeks after your application, I get news of you. Robert Sherard, that bravest and most chivalrous of all brilliant beings, comes to see me, and among other things tells me that in that ridiculous *Mercure de France,* with its absurd affectation of being the true centre of literary corruption, you are about to publish an article on me with specimens of my letters. He asks me if it really was by my wish. I was greatly taken aback, and much annoyed, and gave orders that the thing was to be stopped at once. You had left my letters lying about for blackmailing companions to steal, for hotel servants to pilfer, for housemaids to sell. That was simply your careless want of appreciation of what I had written to you. But that you should seriously propose to publish selections from the balance was almost incredible to me. And which of my letters were they? I could get no information. That was my first news of you. It displeased me.

The second piece of news followed shortly afterwards. Your father's solicitors had appeared in prison, and served me with a bankruptcy notice for a paltry £700, the amount of their taxed costs. I was adjudged a public insolvent and ordered to be produced in Court. I felt most strongly, and feel still, and will revert to the subject again, that these costs should have been paid by your family. You had taken personally on yourself the responsibility of stating that your family would do so. It was that which had made the solicitor take up the case in the way he did. You were absolutely responsible. Even irrespective of your engagement on your family's behalf you should have felt that as you had brought the whole ruin on me, the least that could have been done was to spare me the additional ignominy of bankruptcy for an absolutely contemptible sum of money, less than half of what I spent on you in three brief summer months at Goring. Of that, however, no more here. I did, through the solicitor's clerk, I fully admit, receive a message from you on the subject, or at any rate in connection with the occasion. The day he came to receive my depositions and statements, he leant across the table—the prison warder being present—and, having consulted a piece of paper which he pulled from his pocket, said to me in a low voice: "Prince Fleur de Lys wishes to be remembered to you." I stared at him. He repeated the message again. I did not know what he meant. "The gentleman is abroad at present," he added mysteriously. It all flashed across me, and I remember that, for the first and last time in my entire prison life, I laughed. In that laugh was all the scorn of all the world. Prince Fleur de Lys! I saw—and subsequent events showed me that I rightly saw—that nothing that had happened had made you realize a single thing. You were in your own eyes still the graceful prince of a trivial comedy, not the sombre figure of a tragic show. All that had occurred was as but a feather for the cap that gilds a narrow head, a flower to pink the doublet that hides the heart that hate, and hate alone, can warm, that love, and love alone, finds cold. Prince Fleur de Lys! You were, no doubt, quite right to communicate with me under an assumed name. I myself, at that time, had no name at all. In the great prison where I was then incarcerated, I was merely the figure and letter of a little cell in a long gallery, one of a thousand lifeless numbers, as of a thousand lifeless lives. But surely there were many real names in real history which would have suited you much better, and by which I would have had no difficulty at all in recognizing you at once? I did not look for you behind the spangles of a tinsel vizard suitable only for an amusing masquerade. Ah! had your soul been, as for its own perfection even it should have been, wounded with sorrow, bowed with remorse, and humble with grief, such was not the disguise it would have chosen beneath whose shadow to seek entrance to the House of

Pain! The great things of life are what they seem to be, and for that reason, strange as it may sound to you, are often difficult to interpret. But the little things of life are symbols. We receive our bitter lessons most easily through them. Your seemingly casual choice of a feigned name was, and will remain, symbolic. It reveals you.

Six weeks later a third piece of news arrives. I am called out of the hospital ward, where I was lying wretchedly ill, to receive a special message from you through the Governor of the Prison. He reads me out a letter you had addressed to him in which you stated that you proposed to publish an article "on the case of Mr. Oscar Wilde" in the *Mercure de France* (a "magazine," you added for some extraordinary reason, "corresponding to the English *Fortnightly Review*") and were anxious to obtain my permission to publish extracts and selections from . . . what letters? The letters I had written you from Holloway Prison: the letters that should have been to you things sacred and secret beyond anything in the whole world! These actually were the letters you proposed to publish for the jaded *décadent* to wonder at, for the greedy *feuilletoniste* to chronicle, for the little lions of the *Quartier Latin* to gape and mouth at. Had there been nothing in your own heart to cry out against so vulgar a sacrilege you might at least have remembered the sonnet he wrote who saw with such sorrow and scorn the letters of John Keats sold by public auction in London and have understood at last the real meaning of my lines

> . . . I think they love not Art
> who break the crystal of a poet's heart
> That small and sickly eyes may glare and gloat.

For what was your article to show? That I had been too fond of you? The Paris *gamin* was quite aware of the fact. They all read the newspapers, and most of them write for them. That I was a man of genius? The French understood that, and the peculiar quality of my genius, much better than you did, or could have been expected to do. That along with genius goes often a curious perversity of passion and desire? Admirable: but the subject belongs to Lombroso rather than to you. Besides, the pathological phenomenon in question is found also amongst those who have not genius. That in your war of hate with your father I was at once shield and weapon to each of you? Nay more, that in that hideous hunt for my life, that took place when the war was over, he never could have reached me had not your nets been already about my feet? Quite true: but I am told that Henri Bauer had already done it extremely well. Besides, to corroborate his view, had such been your intention, you did not require to publish my letters: at any rate those written from Holloway Prison.

Will you say, in answer to my questions, that in one of my Holloway letters I had myself asked you to try, as far as you were able, to set me a little right with some small portion of the world? Certainly, I did so. Remember how and why I am here at this very moment. Do you think I am here on account of my relations with the witnesses on my trial? My relations, real or supposed, with people of that kind were matters of no interest either to the Government or to Society. They knew nothing of them and cared less. I am here for having tried to put your father into prison. My attempt failed, of course. My own Counsel threw up their briefs. Your father completely turned the tables on me, and had me in prison, has me there still. That is why there is contempt felt for me. That is why people despise me. That is why I have to serve out every day, every hour, every minute of my dreadful imprisonment. That is why my petitions have been refused.

You were the only person who, and without in any way exposing yourself to scorn or danger or blame, could have given another colour to the whole affair, have put the matter in a different light, have shown to a certain degree how things really stood. I would not, of course, have expected, nor indeed wished you to have stated how and for what purpose you had sought my assistance in your trouble at Oxford: or how, and for what purpose, if you had a purpose at all, you had practically never left my side for nearly three years. My incessant attempts to break off a friendship that was so ruinous to me as an artist, as a man of position, as a member of Society even, need not have been chronicled with the accuracy with which they have been set down here. Nor would I have desired you to have described the scenes you used to make with such almost monotonous recurrence: nor to have reprinted your wonderful series of telegrams to me with their strange mixture of romance and finance: nor to have quoted from letters the more revolting or heartless passages as I have been forced to do. Still, I thought it would have been good, as well for you as for me, if you had made some protest against your father's version of our friendship, one no less grotesque than venomous and as absurd in its inference to you as it was dishonouring in its reference to me. That version has now actually passed into serious history: it is quoted, believed, and chronicled: the preacher has taken it for his text, and the moralist for his barren theme: and I who appealed to all the ages have had to accept my verdict from one who is an ape and a buffoon. I have said, and with some bitterness, I admit, in this letter that such was the irony of things that your father would live to be the hero of a Sunday school tract: that you would rank with the infant Samuel: and that my place would be between Gilles de Retz and the Marquis de Sade. I dare say it is best so. I have no desire to complain. One of the many lessons that one learns in prison is, that things are what they are and will be what they will be. Nor have I any doubt that the leper of medievalism and the author of *Justine* will prove better company than *Sandford and Merton*.

But at the time I wrote to you I felt that for both our sakes it would be a good thing, a proper thing, a right thing, not to accept that account which your father had put forward through his Counsel for the edification of a Philistine world, and that is why I asked you to think out and write something that would be nearer the truth. It would at least have been better for you than scribbling to the French papers about the domestic life of your parents. What did the French care whether or not your parents had led a happy domestic life? One cannot conceive a subject more entirely uninteresting to them. What did interest them was how an artist of my distinction, one who by the school and movement of which he was the incarnation had exercised a marked influence on the direction of French thought, could, having led such a life, have brought such an action. Had you proposed for your article to publish the letters, endless I fear in number, in which I had spoken to you of the ruin you were bringing on my life, of the madness of moods of rage that you were allowing to master you to your own hurt as well as to mine, and of my desire, nay, my determination to end a friendship so fatal to me in every way, I could have understood it, though I would not have allowed such letters to be published: when your father's Counsel desiring to catch me in a contradiction suddenly produced in Court a letter of mine, written to you in March 1893, in which I stated that, rather than endure a repetition of the hideous scenes you seemed to take such a terrible pleasure in making, I would readily consent to be "blackmailed by every renter in London," it was a very real grief to me that that side of my friendship with you should inadvertently be revealed to the common gaze: but that you should have been so slow to see, so lacking in all sensitiveness, and so dull in apprehension of what is rare, delicate, and beautiful, as to propose yourself to publish the letters in which and through which I was trying to keep alive the very spirit and soul of love, that it might dwell in my body through the long years of that body's humiliation—this was, and still is to me a source of the very deepest pain, the most poignant disappointment. Why you did so, I fear I know but too well. If hate blinded your eyes, vanity sewed your eyelids together with threads of iron. The "faculty by which, and by which alone, one can understand others in their real as in their ideal relations" your narrow egotism had blunted, and long disuse had made of no avail. The imagination was as much in prison as I was. Vanity had barred up the windows, and the name of the warder was hate.

All this took place in the early part of November of the year before last. A great river of life flows between me and a date so distant. Hardly, if at all, can you see across so wide a waste. But to me it seems to have occurred, I will not say yesterday, but today. Suffering is one very long moment. We cannot divide it by seasons. We can only record its moods, and chronicle their return. With us time itself does not progress. It revolves. It seems to circle round one centre of pain. The paralyzing immobility of a life every circumstance of which is regulated after an unchangeable pattern, so that we eat and drink and lie down and pray, or kneel at least for prayer, according to the inflexible laws of an iron formula: this immobile quality, that makes each dreadful day in the very minutest detail like its brother, seems to communicate itself to those external forces, the very essence of whose existence is ceaseless change. Of seed-time or harvest, of the reapers bending over the corn, or the grape gatherers threading through the vines, of the grass in the orchard made white with broken blossoms or strewn with fallen fruit: of these we know nothing, and can know nothing.

For us there is only one season, the season of sorrow. The very sun and moon seem taken from us. Outside, the day may be blue and gold, but the light that creeps down through the thickly muffled glass of the small iron-barred window beneath which one sits is grey and niggard. It is always twilight in one's cell, as it is always twilight in one's heart. And in the sphere of thought, no less than in the sphere of time, motion is no more. The thing that you personally have long ago forgotten, or can easily forget, is happening to me now, and will happen to me again tomorrow. Remember this, and you will be able to understand a little of why I am writing, and in this manner writing . . .

A week later, I am transferred here. Three more months go over and my mother dies. No one knew better than you how deeply I loved and honoured her. Her death was terrible to me; but I, once a lord of language, have no words in which to express my anguish and my shame. Never even in the most perfect days of my development as an artist could I have found words fit to bear so august a burden; or to move with sufficient stateliness of music through the purple pageant of my incommunicable woe. She and my father had bequeathed me a name they had made noble and honoured, not merely in literature, art, archaeology, and science, but in the public history of my own country, in its evolution as a nation. I had disgraced that name eternally. I had made it a low byword among low people. I had dragged it through the very mire. I had given it to brutes that they might make it brutal, and to fools that they might turn it into a synonym for folly. What I suffered then, and still suffer, is not for pen to write or paper to record. My wife, always kind and gentle to me, rather than that I should hear the news from indifferent lips, travelled, ill as she was, all the way from Genoa to England to break to me herself the tidings of so irreparable, so irredeemable, a loss. Messages of sympathy reached me from all who had still affection for me. Even people who had not known me personally, hearing that a new sorrow had broken into my life, wrote to ask that some expression of their condolence should be conveyed to me

Three months go over. The calendar of my daily conduct and labour that hangs on the outside of my cell door, with my name and sentence written upon it, tells me that it is May.

My friends come to see me again. I enquire, as I always do, after you. I am told that you are in your villa at Naples, and are bringing out a volume of poems. At the close of the interview it is mentioned casually that you are dedicating them to me. The tidings seemed to give me a sort of nausea of life. I said nothing, but silently went back to my cell with contempt and scorn in my heart. How could you dream of dedicating a volume of poems to me without first asking my permission? Dream, do I say? How could you dare do such a thing? Will you give as your answer that in the days of my greatness and fame I had consented to receive the dedication of your early work? Certainly I did so: just as I would have accepted the homage of any other young men beginning the difficult and beautiful art of literature. All homage is delightful to an artist and doubly sweet when youth brings it. Laurel and bay leaf wither when aged hands pluck them. Only youth has a right to crown an artist. That is the real privilege of being young if youth only knew it. But the days of abasement and infamy are different from those of greatness and fame. You had yet to learn that.

Prosperity, pleasure, and success, may be rough of grain and common in fibre, but sorrow is the most sensitive of all created things. There is nothing that stirs in the whole world of thought to which sorrow does not vibrate in terrible and exquisite pulsation. The thin beaten-out leaf of tremulous gold that chronicles the direction of forces the eye cannot see is in comparison coarse. It is a wound that bleeds when any hand but that of love touches it, and even then must bleed again, though not in pain.

You could write to the Governor of Wandsworth Prison to ask my permission to publish my letters in the *Mercure de France*, *"corresponding to our English Fortnightly Review."* Why not have written to the Governor of the Prison at Reading to ask my permission to dedicate your poems to me, whatever fantastic description you may have chosen to give them? Was it because in the one case the magazine in question had been prohibited by me from publishing letters, the legal copyright of which, as you are, of course, perfectly well aware, was and is vested entirely in me, and in the other you thought that you could enjoy the wilfulness of your own way without my knowing anything about it till it was too late to interfere? The mere fact that I was a man disgraced, ruined and in prison should have made you, if you desired to write my name on the fore-page of your work, beg it of me as a favour, an honour, a privilege: that is the way in which one should approach those who are in distress and sit in shame.

Where there is sorrow there is holy ground. Some day people will realize what that means. They will know nothing of life till they do. Robbie and natures like his can realize it. When I was brought down from my prison to the Court of Bankruptcy, between two policemen, Robbie waited in the long dreary corridor that, before the whole crowd, whom an action so sweet and simple hushed into silence, he might gravely raise his hat to me, as, handcuffed and with bowed head, I passed him by. Men have gone to heaven for smaller things than that. It was in this spirit, and with this mode of love, that the saints knelt down to wash the feet of the poor, or stooped to kiss the leper on the cheek. I have never said one single word to him about what he did. I do not know to the present moment whether he is aware that I was even conscious of his action. It is not a thing for which one can render formal thanks in formal words. I store it in the treasure-house of my heart. I keep it there as a secret debt that I am glad to think I can never possibly repay. It is embalmed and kept sweet by the myrrh and cassia of many tears. When wisdom has been profitless to me, philosophy barren, and the proverbs and phrases of those who have sought to give me consolation as dust and ashes in my mouth, the memory of that little, lovely, silent act of love has unsealed for me all the wells of pity: made the desert blossom like a rose, and brought me out of the bitterness of lonely exile into harmony with the wounded, broken, and great heart of the world. When people are able to understand, not merely how beautiful Robbie's action was, but why it meant so much to me, and always will mean so much, then, perhaps, they will realize how and in what spirit they should approach me . . .

F.Y.I.

Atkins: refers to Fred Atkins, a man that Wilde had a casual sexual relationship with. He was called to testify as a witness for the prosecution at Wilde's trial.

the Crown: short for The Crown Prosecution Service, a department responsible for public prosecutions of people charged with criminal offences in England and Wales.

Cyril: refers to Wilde's oldest son

decadent: refers to a specific group of French and English writers of the late nineteenth century. Its literary style was extremely refined and most noted for its artificiality and strangeness.

feuilletoniste: from the French word *feuillet* meaning sheet of paper, this term refers to those involved in the writing of the sections in European newspapers that deal with light fiction and articles, reviews, and serials.

gamin: a French term for a young homeless boy who wanders the streets.

Gilles de Retz: (1404–1440) his name is connected with the famous story of "Bluebeard," the cruel chevalier who takes his young bride to his castle and gives her the keys to every room except one. He pretends to leave the castle, knowing his bride's curiosity will force her to disobey him. She enters the room only to discover the murdered remains of his six former wives. Gilles de Retz led a debauched and immoral life, becoming involved in alchemy and Satanism. He was hanged and burned after being found guilty of abducting and murdering more than 140 children.

Henri Bauer: a leading writer in France who was sympathetic and supportive of Wilde during his trial and incarceration.

Holloway: the prison Wilde was held in during his trial.

the infant Samuel: this could be a reference to the biblical passage Samuel 3:1–10 or to the famous painting by Sir Joshua Reynolds called *The Infant Samuel* in which a cherubic young boy kneels and prays to a divine light shining in the top left corner of the painting.

Lombroso: refers to Cesare Lombroso (1835–1909), an Italian criminologist and the founder of the Italian School of Positivist Criminology. In 1889, Lombroso wrote a book entitled *The Man of Genius,* which claimed that artistic genius was a form of hereditary insanity. This book was an elaboration on an earlier article that outlined 13 distinctive features of "the art of the insane."

Marquis de Sade: (1740–1814) the French aristocrat and writer famous for his libertine life and his philosophical/erotic novels such as *Juliette, Justine* (which Wilde mentions in his letter), and *The 120 Days of Sodom*. His work involves philosophical discussions about destroying morality, religion, and law to achieve true freedom, mixed in with intensely pornographic episodes. The term "sadism" is derived from de Sade's name.

Mercure de France: a famous French gazette and literary publication founded in 1672. It still exists today.

Quartier Latin: in English this means the Latin Quarter. This is an area of Paris located on the left bank of the River Seine near the famous Sorbonne University. It is considered the lively centre of the city's university life.

Robbie: refers to Robert Ross (1869–1918), a journalist and art critic, who was a very close friend of Oscar Wilde. There is speculation that he was Wilde's first male lover. Although Ross had to leave the country after Wilde's trial to keep his own sexual history from becoming public, he supported Wilde publicly, emotionally, and financially during his trial and after he was released from prison, and was with Wilde when he died. Robert Ross became the executor of Wilde's literary estate after the writer's death.

Robert Sherard: (1861–1943) a good friend of Wilde's and one of the few people to remain supportive during and after his trial and incarceration. Sherard wrote the first biographies of Wilde after his death.

Sandford and Merton: refers to a very popular children's book called *The History of Sandford and Merton: A Work Intended for the Use of Children*, published in three volumes between 1783 and 1789. The book became famous for the characters Tommy Merton, the spoiled and arrogant aristocratic boy, and Henry Sandford, the honest and virtuous farmer's son. The author, Thomas Day (1748–1789), meant for the book to be a way to impart the educational and philosophical tenets of Jean-Jacques Rousseau to British children. Tommy represents the evils of the decadence of modern life, and Henry represents the virtue and strengths of valuing labour.

Words to Build on

abasement: to lower, humiliate, or degrade

affectation: artificial behaviour

cassia: a type of tree that produces a spice called cassia bark as well as aromatic oils

chrysolite: a yellowish-green gem

edification: mental or moral instruction or improvement

gilds: to give a false brilliance

homage: acknowledgement of superiority or reverence

huckster: a person who sells items in the street

ignominy: dishonour or disgrace

incessant: continual, repeated

insolent: rude and disrespectful

lethargy: a state of extreme fatigue, sluggishness, or unconsciousness

maledictions: curses

mire: wet or soft mud

myrrh: dark fragrant sap taken from trees to make incense and an embalming agent

niggard: meagre, not elaborate

paltry: insignificant, lacking in importance

pathological: the study of the nature of a disease and its causes, processes, and development

philistine: a person who is hostile or indifferent to arts and culture

pilfer: to steal small amounts of something

reproaches: expressions of disapproval of or disappointment in someone

reticence: to be reluctant or unwilling

to pink the doublet: to cut a design, commonly a diamond shape, into a fitted buttoned jacket shape

tremulous: trembling or quivering

vizard: a kind of disguise in the form of a visor or mask

In Your Own Words: Comprehension

1. What is the one concept that Wilde repeats he must keep in his heart to survive his imprisonment?

2. Who are the people Wilde blames for his situation? How and why does he blame them?

3. What are some of the things that Wilde states caused him "real grief"?

4. What is the name that Lord Alfred Douglas gave himself that enraged Wilde?

5. Why does Wilde think he is really in prison?

6. According to Wilde, from what do we receive our most bitter lessons?

7. What are the names of the people that Wilde considered invaluable friends?

8. According to Wilde, what are the reasons Douglas should have asked his permission to publish some of their personal letters as well as dedicate new work to him?

In Your Own Words: Analysis

1. What is the effect of Wilde's opening?

2. Find the moments in the letter when Wilde moves from forgiving to condemning and the moments when he moves from poetic to business like. What is the pattern?

3. Oscar Wilde's famous novel, *The Picture of Dorian Gray*, is a story of a young man whose portrait reflects his aging process and the decay of his soul while his physical body remains young and beautiful. He will remain this way unless he gazes upon the portrait. What are the moments in the letter when Wilde alludes to this idea with regard to Lord Alfred Douglas? Provide examples.

4. This letter was published under the title *De Profundis*, which is Latin for "from the depths." Why do you think Wilde used this title?

5. There are moments when Wilde makes reference to his abilities and talents as an artist. Write a brief description of his personality based on these details.

6. Wilde writes, "What I have suffered then, and still suffer, is not for pen to write or paper to record." What is the suffering he is referring to? What does this line seem to say about suffering?

7. Most letters are written with the belief that only the recipient will read them; however, Oscar Wilde gave very detailed instructions to Robert Ross about how and when a copy of this letter should be published. Find moments in the letter when it seems as though Wilde is no longer writing to Lord Alfred Douglas directly. What is it about these moments that make you think that Wilde was writing for a larger audience?

❈ Now Write

1. In this section of *De Profundis*, Oscar Wilde often mentions the subject of regret. How would you define regret? With reference to the text, how would Wilde define regret, and what are the regrets he came to experience as a result of his behaviour and choices?

2. *De Profundis* has been referred to as an autobiography, but one that attempts to reinvent its subject, turning what is real into something fictional. How does Wilde try to "reinvent" himself within the letter? Does this reinvention take something that is non-fiction and turn it into fiction?

3. Oscar Wilde was a very big celebrity during his own time, and his life (and that of his family) was forever affected by the scandal surrounding his relationship with Lord Alfred Douglas and his subsequent trial and imprisonment. *De Profundis* was a way for Wilde to try and explain his behaviour both as a man and as an artist. Think of celebrity scandals today and how celebrities try to rationalize and justify their behaviour and subsequent treatment during these scandals. How does their behaviour and actions after the fact compare to Wilde's situation? Are celebrities who have run-ins with the law treated differently than Wilde was?

Emily Carr

Emily Carr (1871–1945) was a painter, writer, and nature-lover born to English parents in Victoria, British Columbia. Carr has been described as individualistic and adventuresome, qualities that were highly unusual for a woman raised in western Canada at the time. Orphaned at an early age, she managed to convince her guardians to allow her to study art in San Francisco. After trips to England and France, she returned home to create her unique painting style.

Her many trips to First Nations villages and remote areas in British Columbia were the inspiration for her powerful paintings and sketches. Though never officially a member of the Group of Seven, its members, especially Lawren Harris, recognized her talent and unique style as well as her influence on their work. The Group named her "The Mother of Modern Arts." Long before the Group headed outdoors to paint Canadian landscapes, Emily Carr packed up her easel and paints and went into the BC interior, often alone. Although Carr worked in multiple mediums and has been given high praise for her work, not all see her actions towards First Nations groups as being favourable. In her writing, Native women are often presented as passive and victimized; her work also reflects a popular colonialist notion in Carr's time: that First Nations people and cultures were "vanishing" and something had to be done, ironically, by non-Natives to preserve their traditions.

Success and recognition came in her final years, though due to illness Carr was not able to paint and she faced some economic hardship. Most of Carr's paintings are held in museums, galleries, and private collections. In 1990, one of Carr's paintings, *Wind in the Tree Tops*, sold for $2.16 million, becoming one of the most expensive Canadian paintings ever sold at auction.

Carr was also a writer, and she brought the same eye for detail to her stories and autobiographical works. At the age of 70 she suffered a heart attack and, since she was confined to bed, devoted her time to writing. Much like her painting, she drew inspiration from First Nations peoples, specifically the ancient cultures of the Haida and Tlingit. Her first book, *Klee Wyck* (1941), was a great success and even received the Governor General's Literary Award. *Growing Pains* (1946) is about her childhood and her life as a young artist in the United States and England. Due to the candid and revelatory nature of this work, Carr asked that this work be published after her death. She is buried in Victoria, where her gravestone reads "Artist and Author, Lover of Nature."

In Her Own Words

"I did not know book rules. I made two for myself. They were about the same as the principles I used in painting—get to the point as directly as you can; never use a big word if a little one will do."

"I think that one's art is a growth inside one. I do not think one can explain growth. It is silent and subtle. One does not keep digging up a plant to see how it grows."

Before We Begin

1. Is there favouritism in your family? Does (or did) one of your parents prefer one sibling over another? Why?
2. If a child displays a skill or ability early in life, should he or she be given special treatment by his or her parents or family? Does that talent always have to be nurtured to encourage the child's success later in life?
3. What makes an autobiography worth reading? Is it only famous people whose life story is worth reading, or can anyone's life be of interest to readers?

 Now Read

Mother

To show Mother I must picture Father, because Mother was Father's reflection—smooth, liquid reflecting of definite, steel-cold reality.

Our childhood was ruled by Father's unbendable iron will, the obeying of which would have been intolerable but for Mother's patient polishing of its dull metal so that it shone and reflected the beauty of orderliness that was in all Father's ways, a beauty you had to admire, for, in spite of Father's severity and his overbearing omnipotence, you had to admit the justice even in his dictatorial bluster. But somehow Mother's reflecting was stronger than Father's reality, for, after her death, it lived on in our memories and strengthened, while Father's tyrannical reality shrivelled up and was submerged under our own development.

Father looked taller than he really was because he was so straight. Mother was small-made and frail. Our oldest sister was like Father; she helped Mother raise us and finished our upbringing when Mother died.

I was 12 when Mother died—the raw, green Victoria age, 12 years old.

The routine of our childhood home ran with mechanical precision. Father was ultra-English, a straight, stern autocrat. No one ever dreamt of crossing his will. Mother loved him and obeyed because it was her loyal pleasure to do so. We children *had* to obey from both fear and reverence.

Nurse Randal has told me of my first birthday. I was born during a mid-December snow storm; the north wind howled and bit. Contrary from the start, I kept the family in suspense all day. A row of sparrows, puffed with cold, sat on the rail of the balcony outside Mother's window, bracing themselves against the danger of being blown into the drifted snow piled against the window. Icicles hung, wind moaned, I dallied. At three in the morning I sent Father plowing on foot through knee-deep snow to fetch Nurse Randal.

I never did feel that it was necessary to apologize to my father for being late. It made variety for him, seeing that he always got his way in everything—when Father commanded everybody ran.

Every evening at a quarter to six Mother would say, "Children, is every gate properly shut and fastened? Are no toys littering the garden, no dolls sitting on humans' chairs? Wash your faces, then, and put on clean pinafores; your father will soon be home."

If visiting children happened to be playing with us in our garden, or a neighbour calling on Mother, they scurried for the gate as fast as they could. Father would not have said anything if he had found them in his house—that was just it, he would not have said anything to them at all. He would have stalked in our front door, rushed through the house and out of the side door frowning terribly, hurrying to tend Isabella, the great, purple-fruited grapevine that crawled half over our house and entirely over Father's heart. Her grapes were most beautifully fogged with dusky bloom, behind which she pretended her fruit was luscious; but they were really tough-skinned, sour old grapes.

Father was burstingly proud of miserable old Isabella. He glassed her top so that her upstairs grapes ripened a whole month earlier than her downstairs ones. He tacked Isabella up, he pinched her back, petted, trained her, gave her everything a vine could possibly want, endured far more waywardness from her than all of us together would dare to show.

After Father had fussed over Isabella and eaten a good dinner, he went upstairs to see Mother who was far more often in bed ill than up. He was good to Mother in his own way, gave her every possible comfort, good help, good doctoring, best food, but I resented that he went to Isabella first and Mother after. He was grumpy too when he did go. He sat beside her bed for half an hour in almost complete silence, then he went downstairs to read his paper till bedtime.

I heard a lady say to Mother, "Isn't it difficult, Mrs. Carr, to discipline our babies when their fathers spoil them so?"

Mother replied, "My husband takes no notice of mine till they are old enough to run round after him. He then recognizes them as human beings and as his children, accepts their adoration. You know how little tots worship big, strong men!"

The other mother nodded and my mother continued, "Each of my children in turn my husband makes his special favourite when they come to this man-adoring age. When this child shows signs of having a will of its own he returns it to the nursery and raises the next youngest to favour. This one," she put her hand on me, "has overdrawn her share of favouritism because there was no little sister to step into her shoes. Our small son is much younger and very delicate. His father accuses me of coddling him, but he is the only boy I have left—I lost three."

Father kept sturdy me as his pet for a long time.

"Ah," he would say, "this one should have been the boy."

The very frailness of her little son made Mother love him harder. She did not mind the anxiety and trouble if only he lived.

Father insisted that I be at his heels every moment that he was at home. I helped him in the garden, popping the bulbs into holes that he dug, holding the strips of cloth and the tacks while he trained Isabella. I walked nearly all the way to town with him every morning. He let me snuggle under his arm and sleep during the long Presbyterian sermons. I held his hand during the walk to and from church. This all seemed to me fine until I began to think for myself—then I saw that I was being used as a soother for Father's tantrums; like a bone to a dog, I was being flung to quiet Father's temper. When he was extra cranky I was taken into town by my big sister and left at Father's wholesale warehouse to walk home with him because my chatter soothed him. I resented this and began to question why Father should act as if he was God. Why should people dance after him and let him think he was? I decided disciplining would be good for Father and I made up my mind to cross his will sometimes. At first he laughed, trying to coax the waywardness out of me, but when he saw I was serious his fury rose against me. He turned and was harder on me than on any of the others. His soul was so bitter that he was even sometimes cruel to me.

"Mother," I begged, "need I be sent to town any more to walk home with Father?"

Mother looked at me hard. "Child," she cried, "what ails you? You have always loved to be with your father. He adores you. What is the matter?"

"He is cross, he thinks he is as important as God."

Mother was supremely shocked; she had brought her family up under the English tradition that the men of a woman's family were created to be worshipped. My insurrection pained her. She was as troubled as a hen that has hatched a duck. She wanted to question me but her loyalty to Father forbade.

She said to me, "Shall you and I have a picnic?"—she knew that above all things I loved a picnic.

"All to ourselves?" I asked.

"Just you and I."

It was the most wonderful thing she could have suggested. I was so proud. Mother, who always shared herself equally among us, was giving to me a whole afternoon of herself.

It was wild lily time. We went through our garden, our cow-yard and pasture, and came to our wild lily field. Here we stood a little, quietly looking. Millions upon millions of white lilies were spangled over the green field. Every lily's brown eye looked down into the earth but her petals rolled back over her head and pointed at the pine tree tops and the sky. No one could make words to tell how fresh and sweet they smelled. The perfume was delicate yet had such power its memory clung through the rest of your life and could carry you back any time to the old lily field, even after the field had become city and there were no more lilies in it—just houses and houses. Yes, even then your nose could ride on the smell and come galloping back to the lily field.

Between our lily field and Beacon Hill Park there was nothing but a black, tarred fence. From the bag that carried Mother's sewing and our picnic, she took a big key and fitted it into the padlock. The binding-chain fell away from the pickets. I stepped with Mother beyond the confines of our very fenced childhood. Pickets and snake fences had always separated us from the tremendous world. Beacon Hill Park was just as it had always been from the beginning of time, not cleared, not trimmed. Mother and I squeezed through a crack in its greenery; bushes whacked against our push. Soon we came to a tiny, grassy opening, filled with sunshine and we sat down under a mock-orange bush, white with blossom and deliciously sweet.

I made a daisy chain and Mother sewed. All round the opening crowded spirea bushes loaded with droops of creamy blossom having a hot, fluffy smell. In these bees droned and butterflies fluttered, but our mock-orange bush was whiter and smelled stronger and sweeter. We talked very little as we sat there.

Mother was always a quiet woman—a little shy of her own children. I am glad she was not chatty, glad she did not perpetually "dear" us as so many English mothers that we knew did with their children. If she had been noisier or quieter, more demonstrative or less loving, she would not have been just right. She was a small, grey-eyed, dark-haired woman, had pink cheeks and struggled breathing. I do not remember to have ever heard her laugh out loud, yet she was always happy and contented. I was surprised once to hear her tell the Bishop, "My heart is always singing." How did hearts sing? I had never heard Mother's, I had just heard her difficult, gasping little breaths. Mother's moving was slow and weak, yet I always think of her as having Jenny-Wren-bird's quickness. I felt instinctively that was her nature. I became aware of this along with many other things about my mother, things that unfolded to me in my own development.

Our picnic that day was perfect. I was for once Mother's oldest, youngest, her companion-child. While her small, neat hands hurried the little stitches down the long, white seams of her sewing, and my daisy chains grew and grew, while the flowers of the bushes smelled and smelled and sunshine and silence were spread all round, it almost seemed rude to crunch the sweet biscuit which was our picnic—ordinary munching of biscuits did not seem right for such a splendid time.

When I had three daisy chains round my neck, when all Mother's seams were stitched, and when the glint of sunshine had gone quiet, then we went again through our gate, locked the world out, and went back to the others.

It was only a short while after our picnic that Mother died. Her death broke Father; we saw then how he had loved her, how alone he was without her—none of us could make up to him for her loss. He retired from business. His office desk and chair were brought home and put into the room below Mother's bedroom. Here Father sat, staring over his garden. His stare was as empty as a pulpit without a preacher and with no congregation in front of it. We saw him there when we came from school and went stupidly wandering over the house from room to room instead of rushing straight up to Mother's bedroom. By-and-by, when we couldn't bear it any longer, we'd creep up the stairs, turn the door handle, go into emptiness, get caught there and scolded for having red eyes and no bravery.

I was often troublesome in those miserable days after Mother died. I provoked my big sister and, when her patience was at an end, she would say, trying to shame me, "Poor Mother worried about leaving you. She was happy about her other children, knowing she could trust them to behave—good reasonable children—you are different!"

This cut me to the quick. For years I had spells of crying about it. Then by-and-by I had a sweetheart. He wanted me to love him and I couldn't, but one day I almost did—he found me crying and coaxed.

"Tell me."

I told him what my big sister had said. He came close and whispered in my ear, "Don't cry, little girl. If you were the naughtiest, you can bet your mother loved you a tiny bit the best—that's the way mothers are."

F.Y.I.

Jenny-Wren bird: a plain-looking light brown bird native to North America but whose call or song is highly melodic and pleasant

pinafore: an apron-like garment worn over a dress

Words to Build on

autocrat: an absolute ruler or dictator

bluster: to behave pompously and utter empty threats

insurrection: an open resistance to authority, a rebellion

omnipotence: having absolute power

spirea bushes: a shrub with clusters of small white and pink flowers

Tricks of the Trade

Autobiography

In Your Own Words: Comprehension

1. Carr's chapter is called "Mother," yet she begins with her father. Explain why.
2. How does Carr describe her father and mother?
3. How does Carr describe her parents' relationship?
4. To which parent is Carr closer? How and why does this change?
5. How does Carr describe her own personality?
6. Who is Isabella, and how does Carr feel about her?
7. What does the term "companion-child" mean? Have you heard it used before?

In Your Own Words: Analysis

1. Carr wrote her autobiography later in life. This section is about a time before her parents died, when Carr was not yet 12 years old. What evidence here indicates that Carr will be an artist?
2. Carr wanted her autobiography to be published after her death. What evidence do you see in her writing that would cause her to make this choice?
3. Consider Carr's comment on her style of writing (see "In Her Own Words"). What are some examples from Carr's writing that demonstrate she followed her own advice?
4. How is nature represented in Carr's writing?
5. Why does Carr's sweetheart tell her mothers usually love their "naughtiest" children best? Why do you think she ends the chapter with this detail?

 **Now Write**

1. Emily Carr was raised in the "English style" and at a time when parents believed in the adage that "children should be neither seen nor heard." How is this shown in her writing? How does she react to this belief about how children should be raised?

2. Is it possible for someone to write a true account of his or her own life? What details does Carr provide that make you feel there is truth in her account?

3. Research Carr's philosophy or attitudes on art. Write an essay in which you connect what she writes about her early life in "Mother" to her thoughts on painting.

George Orwell

George Orwell (1903–1950) is the pen name of Eric Arthur Blair, who was born in Bengal, India, to parents who served in the Indian Civil Service. He was educated at Eton College, a prestigious boys' school that dates back to the 1400s and still exists today, which he entered on a scholarship. He later claimed that his experiences in such schools formed his opinions of the class system in England. After completing his education, he followed in his father's footsteps in 1922 when he joined the Indian Imperial Police in Burma. Such beginnings create a sharp contrast in Orwell's life: his early experiences in British political and cultural imperialism to his later position as a political rebel and anti-elitist. He resigned his position in Burma after six years and returned home to pursue a career in writing. He submitted his first work, *Down and Out in London and Paris*, using the pseudonym George Orwell since at the time he was also working as a teacher, and the book was an autobiographical account of his life as he worked in a series of low-paying jobs.

By the 1930s his socialist views were well-established, and when the civil war broke out in Spain in 1936, he volunteered to fight for the Republican cause. Unlike some of the other famous writers and journalists who covered the war, like Ernest Hemingway, Orwell was actually directly involved in combat. After being shot through the throat by a sniper, he returned to England with his wife.

During World War II he joined the Home Guard and worked for the BBC as a reporter who composed and spread wartime propaganda. It is certain he drew on this experience when writing his well-known satirical work *Animal Farm* (1945) and his other masterpiece *Nineteen-Eighty Four* (1948), which is still culturally relevant since terms such as "Big Brother," "doublethink," and "thought crime" have become part of English vernacular.

His essay "Politics and the English Language" was originally published in the April 1946 issue of *Horizon* magazine. In it, Orwell presents his argument of how language can be manipulated by writers, politicians, and dictators to control people and create social injustice and oppression. He also explains how truth and language are intertwined and how clear thinking and a fair democratic government cannot exist without clarity in language.

In His Own Words

"In a time of deceit, telling the truth is a revolutionary act."

"Journalism is printing what someone else does not want printed: everything else is public relations."

"There are some ideas so absurd that only an intellectual could believe them."

Before We Begin

1. Do you ever use phrases and words in your own writing that are just fillers and mean nothing? What are some examples of these and why do you use them?
2. What have you noticed about the relationship between politicians and the way they use language? What are some examples?
3. What are some rules you were taught in high school about what makes good writing?

 **Now Read**

Politics and the English Language

Most people who bother with the matter at all would admit that the English language is in a bad way, but it is generally assumed that we cannot by conscious action do anything about it. Our civilization is decadent and our language—so the argument runs—must inevitably share in the general collapse. It follows that any struggle against the abuse of language is a sentimental archaism, like preferring candles to electric light or hansom cabs to aeroplanes. Underneath this lies the half-conscious belief that language is a natural growth and not an instrument which we shape for our own purposes.

Now, it is clear that the decline of a language must ultimately have political and economic causes: it is not due simply to the bad influence of this or that individual writer. But an effect can become a cause, reinforcing the original cause and producing the same effect in an intensified form, and so on indefinitely. A man may take to drink because he feels himself to be a failure, and then fail all the more completely because he drinks. It is rather the same thing that is happening to the English language. It becomes ugly and inaccurate because our thoughts are foolish, but the slovenliness of our language makes it easier for us to have foolish thoughts. The point is that the process is reversible. Modern English, especially written English, is full of bad habits which spread by imitation and which can be avoided if one is willing to take the necessary trouble. If one gets rid of these habits one can think more clearly, and to think clearly is a necessary first step towards political regeneration: so that the fight against bad English is not frivolous and is not the exclusive concern of professional writers. I will come back to this presently, and I hope that by that time the meaning of what I have said here will have become clearer. Meanwhile, here are five specimens of the English language as it is now habitually written.

These five passages have not been picked out because they are especially bad—I could have quoted far worse if I had chosen—but because they illustrate various of the mental vices from which we now suffer. They are a little below the average, but are fairly representative samples. I number them so that I can refer back to them when necessary:

"(1) I am not, indeed, sure whether it is not true to say that the Milton who once seemed not unlike a seventeenth-century Shelley had not become, out of an experience ever more bitter in each year, more alien [sic] to the founder of that Jesuit sect which nothing could induce him to tolerate."

Professor Harold Laski (Essay in *Freedom of Expression*).

"(2) Above all, we cannot play ducks and drakes with a native battery of idioms which prescribes such egregious collocations of vocables as the Basic *put up with* for *tolerate* or *put at a loss* for *bewilder*."

Professor Lancelot Hogben (*Interglossa*).

"(3) On the one side we have the free personality: by definition it is not neurotic, for it has neither conflict nor dream. Its desires, such as they are, are transparent, for they are just what institutional approval keeps in the forefront of consciousness; another institutional pattern would alter their number and intensity; there is little in them that is natural, irreducible, or culturally dangerous. But *on the other side*, the social bond itself is nothing but the mutual reflection of these self-secure integrities. Recall the definition of love. Is not this the very picture of a small academic? Where is there a place in this hall of mirrors for either personality or fraternity?"

Essay on psychology in *Politics* (New York).

"(4) All the 'best people' from the gentlemen's clubs, and all the frantic fascist captains, united in common hatred of Socialism and bestial horror of the rising tide of the mass revolutionary movement, have turned to acts of provocation, to foul incendiarism, to medieval legends of poisoned wells, to legalize their own destruction of proletarian organizations, and rouse the agitated petty-bourgeoisie to chauvinistic fervour on behalf of the fight against the revolutionary way out of the crisis."

Communist pamphlet.

"(5) If a new spirit *is* to be infused into this old country, there is one thorny and contentious reform which must be tackled, and that is the humanization and galvanization of the B.B.C. Timidity here will bespeak canker and atrophy of the soul. The heart of Britain may be sound and of strong beat, for instance, but the British lion's roar at present is like that of Bottom in Shakespeare's *Midsummer Night's Dream*—as gentle as any sucking dove. A virile new Britain cannot continue indefinitely to be traduced in the eyes or rather ears, of the world by the effete languors of Langham Place, brazenly masquerading as "standard English." When the Voice of Britain is heard at nine o'clock, better far and infinitely less ludicrous to hear aitches honestly dropped than the present priggish, inflated, inhibited, school-ma'amish arch braying of blameless bashful mewing maidens!"

Letter in *Tribune.*

Each of these passages has faults of its own, but, quite apart from avoidable ugliness, two qualities are common to all of them. The first is staleness of imagery: the other is lack of precision. The writer either has a meaning and cannot express it, or he inadvertently says something else, or he is almost indifferent as to whether his words mean anything or not. This mixture of vagueness and sheer incompetence is the most marked characteristic of modern English prose, and especially of any kind of political writing. As soon as certain topics are raised, the concrete melts into the abstract and no one seems able to think of turns of speech that are not hackneyed: prose consists less and less of *words* chosen for the sake of their meaning, and more and more of *phrases* tacked together like the sections of a prefabricated henhouse. I list below, with notes and examples, various of the tricks by means of which the work of prose-construction is habitually dodged:

Dying metaphors. A newly invented metaphor assists thought by evoking a visual image, while on the other hand a metaphor which is technically "dead" (e.g. *iron resolution*) has in effect reverted to being an ordinary word and can generally be used without loss of vividness. But in between these two classes there is a huge dump of worn-out metaphors which have lost all evocative power and are merely used because they save people the trouble of inventing phrases for themselves. Examples are: *Ring the changes on, take up the cudgels for, toe the line, ride roughshod over, stand shoulder to shoulder with, play into the hands of, no axe to grind, grist to the mill, fishing in troubled waters, on the order of the day, Achilles' heel, swan song, hotbed.* Many of these are used without knowledge of their meaning (what is a "rift," for instance?), and incompatible metaphors are frequently mixed, a sure sign that the writer is not interested in what he is saying. Some metaphors now current have been twisted out of their original meaning without those who use them even being aware of the fact. For example, *toe the line* is sometimes written *tow the line*. Another example is *the hammer and the anvil*, now always used with the implication that the anvil gets the worst of it. In real life it is always the anvil that breaks the hammer, never the other way about: a writer who stopped to think what he was saying would be aware of this, and would avoid perverting the original phrase.

Operators or *verbal false limbs.* These save the trouble of picking out appropriate verbs and nouns, and at the same time pad each sentence with extra syllables which give it an appearance of symmetry. Characteristic phrases are: *render inoperative, militate against, make contact with, be subjected to, give rise to, give grounds for, have the effect of, play a leading part (role) in, make itself felt, take effect, exhibit a tendency to, serve the purpose of,* etc., etc. The keynote is the elimination of simple verbs. Instead of being a single word, such as *break, stop, spoil, mend, kill,* a verb becomes a *phrase,* made up of a noun or adjective tacked on to some general-purposes verb such as *prove, serve, form, play, render.* In addition, the passive voice is wherever possible used in preference to the active, and noun constructions are used instead of gerunds *(by examination of* instead of *by examining).* The range of verbs is further cut down by means of the *-ize* and *de-* formations, and the banal statements are given an appearance of profundity by means of the *not un-* formation. Simple conjunctions and prepositions are replaced by such phrases as *with respect to, having regard to the fact that, by dint of, in view of, in the interests of, on the hypothesis that;* and the ends of sentences are saved from anti-climax by such resounding commonplaces as *greatly to be desired, cannot be left out of account, a development to be expected in the near future, deserving of serious considera-tion, brought to a satisfactory conclusion,* and so on and so forth.

Pretentious diction. Words like *phenomenon, element, individual* (as noun), *object-ive, categorical, effective, virtual, basic, primary, promote, constitute, exhibit, exploit, utilize, eliminate, liquidate,* are used to dress up simple statements and give an air of scientific impartiality to biased judgments. Adjectives like *epoch-making, epic, historic, unforgettable, triumphant, age-old, inevitable, inexorable, veritable,* are used to dignify the sordid processes of international politics, while writing that aims at glorifying war usually takes on an archaic colour, its characteristic words being: *realm, throne, chariot, mailed fist, trident, sword, shield, buckler, banner, jackboot, clarion.* Foreign words and expressions such as *cul de sac, ancien regime, deus ex machina, mutatis mutandis, status quo, gleichschaltung, weltanschauung,* are used to give an air of culture and elegance. Except for the useful abbreviations *i.e., e.g.,* and *etc.,* there is no real need for any of the hundreds of foreign phrases now current in English. Bad writers, and especially scientific, political, and sociological writers, are nearly always haunted by the notion that Latin or Greek words are grander than Saxon ones, and unnecessary words like *expedite, ameliorate, predict, extraneous, deracinated, clandestine, subaqueous* and hun-dreds of others constantly gain ground from their Anglo-Saxon opposite numbers. The jargon peculiar to Marxist writing *(hyena, hangman, cannibal, petty bourgeois, these gentry, lacquey, flunkey, mad dog, White Guard,* etc.) consists largely of words and phrases translated from Russian, German, or French; but the normal way of coining a new word is to use a Latin or Greek root with the appropriate affix and, where neces-sary, the *-ize* formation. It is often easier to make up words of this kind *(deregional-ize, impermissible, extramarital, non-fragmentatory,* and so forth) than to think up the English words that will cover one's meaning. The result, in general, is an increase in slovenliness and vagueness.

Meaningless words. In certain kinds of writing, particularly in art criticism and liter-ary criticism, it is normal to come across long passages which are almost completely lacking in meaning. Words like *romantic, plastic, values, human, dead, sentimental, nat-ural, vitality,* as used in art criticism, are strictly meaningless, in the sense that they not only do not point to any discoverable object, but are hardly ever expected to do so by the reader. When one critic writes, "The outstanding feature of Mr. X's work is its liv-ing quality," while another writes, "The immediately striking thing about Mr. X's work is its peculiar deadness," the reader accepts this as a simple difference of opinion. If words like *black* and *white* were involved, instead of the jargon words *dead* and *living*, he would see at once that language was being used in an improper way. Many political words are similarly abused. The word *Fascism* has now no meaning except in so far as it signifies "something not desirable." The words *democracy, socialism, freedom, patriotic, realistic, justice*, have each of them several different meanings which cannot be reconciled with one another. In the case of a word like *democracy*, not only is there no agreed definition, but the attempt to make one is resisted from all sides. It is almost universally felt that when we call a country democratic we are praising it: consequently the defenders of every kind of regime claim that it is a democracy, and fear that they might have to stop using the word if it were tied down to any one meaning. Words of this kind are often used in a consciously dishonest way. That is, the person who uses them has his own private definition, but allows his hearer to think he means something quite different. Statements like *Marshal Pétain was a true patriot, The Soviet Press is the freest in the world, The Catholic Church is opposed to persecution*, are almost always made with intent to deceive. Other words used in variable meanings, in most cases more or less dishonestly, are: *class, totalitarian, science, progressive, reactionary, bourgeois, equality.*

Now that I have made this catalogue of swindles and perversions, let me give another example of the kind of writing that they lead to. This time it must of its nature be an imaginary one. I am going to translate a passage of good English into modern English of the worst sort. Here is a well-known verse from *Ecclesiastes:*

"I returned and saw under the sun, that the race is not to the swift nor the battle to the strong, neither yet bread to the wise, nor yet riches to men of understanding, nor yet favour to men of skill; but time and chance happeneth to them all."

Here it is in modern English:

"Objective consideration of contemporary phenomena compels the conclusion that success or failure in competitive activities exhibits no tendency to be commensurate with innate capacity, but that a considerable element of the unpredictable must invariably be taken into account."

This is a parody, but not a very gross one. Exhibit (3), above, for instance, contains several patches of the same kind of English. It will be seen that I have not made a full translation. The beginning and ending of the sentence follow the original meaning fairly closely, but in the middle the concrete illustrations—race, battle, bread—dissolve into the vague phrase "success or failure in competitive activities." This had to be so, because no modern writer of the kind I am discussing—no one capable of using phrases like "objective consideration of contemporary phenomena"—would ever tabulate his thoughts in that precise and detailed way. The whole tendency of modern prose is away from concreteness. Now analyze these two sentences a little more closely. The first contains 49 words but only 60 syllables, and all its words are those of everyday life. The second contains 38 words of 90 syllables: 18 of its words are from Latin roots, and one from Greek. The first sentence contains six vivid images, and only one phrase ("time and chance") that could be called vague. The second contains not a single fresh, arresting phrase, and in spite of its 90 syllables it gives only a shortened version of the meaning contained in the first. Yet without a doubt it is the second kind of sentence that is gaining ground in modern English. I do not want to exaggerate. This kind of writing is not yet universal, and outcrops of simplicity will occur here and there in the worst-written page. Still, if you or I were told to write a few lines on the uncertainty of human fortunes, we should probably come much nearer to my imaginary sentence than to the one from *Ecclesiastes*.

As I have tried to show, modern writing at its worst does not consist in picking out words for the sake of their meaning and inventing images in order to make the meaning clearer. It consists in gumming together long strips of words which have already been set in order by someone else and making the results presentable by sheer humbug. The attraction of this way of writing is that it is easy. It is easier—even quicker, once you have the habit—to say *In my opinion it is a not unjustifiable assumption that* than to say *I think*. If you use ready-made phrases, you not only don't have to hunt about for words; you also don't have to bother with the rhythms of your sentences, since these phrases are generally so arranged as to be more or less euphonious. When you are composing in a hurry—when you are dictating to a stenographer, for instance, or making a public speech—it is natural to fall into a pretentious, Latinized style. Tags like *a consideration which we should do well to bear in mind* or *a conclusion to which all of us would readily assent* will save many a sentence from coming down with a bump. By using stale metaphors, similes, and idioms, you save much mental effort, at the cost of leaving your meaning vague, not only for your reader but for yourself. This is the significance of mixed metaphors. The sole aim of a metaphor is to call up a visual image. When these images clash—as in *The Fascist octopus has sung its swan song, the jackboot is thrown into the melting pot*—it can be taken as certain that the writer is not seeing a mental image of the objects he is naming; in other words he is not really thinking. Look again at the examples I gave at the beginning of this essay. Professor Laski (1) uses five negatives in 53 words. One of these is superfluous, making nonsense of the whole passage, and in addition there is the slip *alien* for akin, making further nonsense, and several avoidable pieces of clumsiness which increase the general vagueness. Professor Hogben (2) plays ducks and drakes with a battery which is able to write prescriptions, and, while disapproving of the everyday phrase *put up with*, is unwilling to look *egregious* up in the dictionary and see what it means. (3), if one takes an uncharitable attitude towards it, is simply meaningless: probably one could work out its intended meaning by reading the whole of the article in which it occurs. In (4), the writer knows more or less what he wants to say, but an accumulation of stale phrases chokes him like tea leaves blocking a sink. In (5), words and meaning have almost parted company. People who write in this manner usually have a general emotional meaning—they dislike one thing and want to express solidarity with another—but they are not interested in the detail of what they are saying. A scrupulous writer, in every sentence that he writes, will ask himself at least four questions, thus: What am I trying to say? What words will express it? What image or idiom will make it clearer? Is this image fresh enough to have an effect? And he will probably ask himself two more: Could I put it more shortly? Have I said anything that is avoidably ugly? But you are not obliged to go to all this trouble. You can shirk it by simply throwing your mind open and letting the ready-made phrases come crowding in. They will construct your sentences for you—even think your thoughts for you, to a certain extent—and at need they will perform the important service of partially concealing your meaning even from yourself. It is at this point that the special connection between politics and the debasement of language becomes clear.

In our time it is broadly true that political writing is bad writing. Where it is not true, it will generally be found that the writer is some kind of rebel, expressing his private opinions and not a "party line". Orthodoxy, of whatever colour, seems to demand a lifeless, imitative style. The political dialects to be found in pamphlets, leading articles, manifestos, White Papers, and the speeches of under-secretaries do, of course, vary from party to party, but they are all alike in that one almost never finds in them a fresh, vivid, homemade turn of speech. When one watches some tired hack on the platform mechanically repeating the familiar phrases—*bestial atrocities, iron heel, bloodstained tyranny, free peoples of the world, stand shoulder to shoulder*—one often has a curious feeling that one is not watching a live human being but some kind of dummy: a feeling which suddenly becomes stronger at moments when the light catches the speaker's spectacles and turns them into blank discs which seem to have no eyes behind them. And this is not altogether fanciful. A speaker who uses that kind of phraseology has gone some distance towards turning himself into a machine. The appropriate noises are coming out of his larynx, but his brain is not involved as it would be if he were choosing his words for himself. If the speech he is making is one that he is accustomed to make over and over again, he may be almost unconscious of what he is saying, as one is when one utters the responses in church. And this reduced state of consciousness, if not indispensable, is at any rate favourable to political conformity.

In our time, political speech and writing are largely the defence of the indefensible. Things like the continuance of British rule in India, the Russian purges and deportations, the dropping of the atom bombs on Japan, can indeed be defended, but only by arguments which are too brutal for most people to face, and which do not square with the professed aims of political parties. Thus political language has to consist largely of euphemism, question-begging, and sheer cloudy vagueness. Defenceless villages are bombarded from the air, the inhabitants driven out into the countryside, the cattle machine-gunned, the huts set on fire with incendiary bullets: this is called *pacification*. Millions of peasants are robbed of their farms and sent trudging along the roads with no more than they can carry: this is called *transfer of population* or *rectification of frontiers*. People are imprisoned for years without trial, or shot in the back of the neck, or sent to die of scurvy in Arctic lumber camps: this is called *elimination of unreliable elements*. Such phraseology is needed if one wants to name things without calling up mental pictures of them. Consider for instance some comfortable English professor defending Russian totalitarianism. He cannot say outright, "I believe in killing off your opponents when you can get good results by doing so." Probably, therefore, he will say something like this:

"While freely conceding that the Soviet regime exhibits certain features which the humanitarian may be inclined to deplore, we must, I think, agree that a certain curtailment of the right to political opposition is an unavoidable concomitant of transitional periods, and that the rigours which the Russian people have been called upon to undergo have been amply justified in the sphere of concrete achievement."

The inflated style is itself a kind of euphemism. A mass of Latin words falls upon the facts like soft snow, blurring the outlines and covering up all the details. The great enemy of clear language is insincerity. When there is a gap between one's real and one's declared aims, one turns as it were instinctively to long words and exhausted idioms, like a cuttlefish squirting out ink. In our age there is no such thing as "keeping out of politics." All issues are political issues, and politics itself is a mass of lies, evasions, folly, hatred, and schizophrenia. When the general atmosphere is bad, language must suffer. I should expect to find—this is a guess which I have not sufficient knowledge to verify—that the German, Russian, and Italian languages have all deteriorated in the last 10 or 15 years, as a result of dictatorship.

But if thought corrupts language, language can also corrupt thought. A bad usage can spread by tradition and imitation, even among people who should and do know better. The debased language that I have been discussing is in some ways very convenient. Phrases like *a not unjustifiable assumption, leave much to be desired, would serve no good purpose, a consideration which we should do well to bear in mind,* are a continuous temptation, a packet of aspirins always at one's elbow. Look back through this essay, and for certain you will find that I have again and again committed the very faults I am protesting against. By this morning's post I have received a pamphlet dealing with conditions in Germany. The author tells me that he "felt impelled" to write it. I open it at random, and here is almost the first sentence that I see: "(The allies) have an opportunity not only of achieving a radical transformation of Germany's social and political structure in such a way as to avoid a nationalistic reaction in Germany itself, but at the same time of laying the foundations of a co-operative and unified Europe." You see he "feels impelled" to write—feels, presumably, that he has something new to say—and yet his words, like cavalry horses answering the bugle, group themselves automatically into the familiar dreary pattern. This invasion of one's mind by ready-made phrases *(lay the foundations, achieve a radical transformation)* can only be prevented if one is constantly on guard against them, and every such phrase anaesthetizes a portion of one's brain.

I said earlier that the decadence of our language is probably curable. Those who deny this would argue, if they produced an argument at all, that language merely reflects existing social conditions and that we cannot influence its development by any direct tinkering with words and constructions. So far as the general tone or spirit of a language goes, this may be true, but it is not true in detail. Silly words and expressions have often disappeared, not through any evolutionary process but owing to the conscious action of a minority. Two recent examples were *explore every avenue* and *leave no stone unturned,* which were killed by the jeers of a few journalists. There is a long list of flyblown metaphors which could similarly be got rid of if enough people would interest themselves in the job; and it should also be possible to laugh the *not un-* formation out of existence, to reduce the amount of Latin and Greek in the average sentence, drive out foreign phrases and strayed scientific words, and, in general, to make pretentiousness unfashionable. But all these are minor points. The defence of the English language implies more than this, and perhaps it is best to start by saying what it does *not* imply.

To begin with it has nothing to do with archaism, with the salvaging of obsolete words and turns of speech, or with the setting up of a "standard English" which must never be departed from. On the contrary, it is especially concerned with the scrapping of every word or idiom which has outworn its usefulness. It has nothing to do with correct grammar and syntax, which are of no importance so long as one makes one's meaning clear, or with the avoidance of Americanisms, or with having what is called a "good prose style." On the other hand it is not concerned with fake simplicity and the attempt to make written English colloquial. Nor does it even imply in every case preferring the Saxon word to the Latin one, though it does imply using the fewest and shortest words that will cover one's meaning. What is above all needed is to let the meaning choose the word, and not the other way about. In prose, the worst thing one can do with words is to surrender to them. When you think of a concrete object, you think wordlessly, and then, if you want to describe the thing you have been visualizing you probably hunt about till you find the exact words that seem to fit it. When you think of something abstract you are more inclined to use words from the start, and unless you make a conscious effort to prevent it, the existing disconnect will come rushing in and do the job for you, at the expense of blurring or even changing your meaning. Probably it is better to put off using words as long as possible and get one's meaning as clear as one can through pictures or sensations. Afterwards one can choose—not simply *accept*—the phrases that will best cover the meaning, and then switch round and decide what impression one's words are likely to make on another person. This last effort of the mind cuts out all stale or mixed images, all prefabricated phrases, needless repetitions, and humbug and vagueness generally. But one can often be in doubt about the effect of a word or a phrase, and one needs rules that one can rely on when instinct fails. I think the following rules will cover most cases:

i.   Never use a metaphor, simile, or other figure of speech which you are used to seeing in print.
ii. Never use a long word where a short one will do.
iii. If it is possible to cut a word out, always cut it out.
iv. Never use the passive where you can use the active.
v.   Never use a foreign phrase, a scientific word, or a jargon word if you can think of an everyday English equivalent.
vi. Break any of these rules sooner than say anything barbarous.

These rules sound elementary, and so they are, but they demand a deep change of attitude in anyone who has grown used to writing in the style now fashionable. One could keep all of them and still write bad English, but one could not write the kind of stuff that I quoted in these five specimens at the beginning of this article.

I have not here been considering the literary use of language, but merely language as an instrument for expressing and not for concealing or preventing thought. Stuart Chase and others have come near to claiming that all abstract words are meaningless, and have used this as a pretext for advocating a kind of political quietism. Since you don't know what Fascism is, how can you struggle against Fascism? One need not swallow such absurdities as this, but one ought to recognize that the present political chaos is connected with the decay of language, and that one can probably bring about some improvement by starting at the verbal end. If you simplify your English, you are freed from the worst follies of orthodoxy. You cannot speak any of the necessary dialects, and when you make a stupid remark its stupidity will be obvious, even to yourself. Political language—and with variations this is true of all political parties, from Conservatives to Anarchists—is designed to make lies sound truthful and murder respectable and to give an appearance of solidity to pure wind. One cannot change this all in a moment, but one can at least change one's own habits, and from time to time one can even, if one jeers loudly enough, send some worn-out and useless phrase—some jackboot, Achilles' heel, hotbed, melting pot, acid test, veritable inferno, or other lump of verbal refuse— into the dustbin where it belongs.

F.Y.I.

Stuart Chase: (1888–1985) an American economist and engineer who wrote on the topic of semantics; he wrote the influential book *The Tyranny of Words* (1938).

Words to Build On

akin: of similar character

archaism: something that is very old or old-fashioned, especially an archaic word or style of language or art

conjunctions: words, such as *and, for, but, if,* used to connect clauses or sentences or to coordinate words in the same clause

cuttlefish: a swimming marine mollusc resembling a broad-bodied squid, having eight arms and two long tentacles used for grabbing prey

diction: the choice and use of words and phrases in speech or writing

euphemism: a mild or indirect word or expression substituted for one considered to be too harsh or blunt when referring to something unpleasant or embarrassing

gerunds: verb forms ending in *-ing* which function as a noun; for example, "*Writing* is difficult work."

hackneyed: an expression, phrase, or idea that is unoriginal and overused

hansom cab: a two-wheeled horse-drawn cab that could hold two passengers inside, with the driver seated behind

jargon: specialized words, terms, or expressions used by a profession or group that non-experts would not readily understand

metaphor: a figure of speech in which a word or phrase is applied to an object or action to which it is not literally applicable

passive voice: when the writer makes the object of an action into the subject of a sentence, which means whoever or whatever is performing the action is not the grammatical subject of the sentence; for example, "Why was the road crossed by the chicken?" The passive voice is not always clear and is often wordy, so it is not favoured by most professors and readers in general.

prepositions: words governing, and usually preceding, a noun or pronoun and expressing a connection to another word or element in the clause; for example, "the woman *in* the room," "the boy departed *during* the storm," and "what was it *for?*"

Tricks of the Trade

Argumentative essay

Closing technique

Metaphor

Rhetorical strategies

Supporting evidence

Tone

In Your Own Words: Comprehension

1. According to Orwell, what is the problem with English and writing?

2. Where does Orwell believe the problem lies with English being in a "bad way"?

3. What are the effects of bad English, and more specifically bad writing, according to Orwell?

4. How does Orwell view the relationship between language and politics, or the decline in language in relation to the existence of oppressive political regimes?

5. In Orwell's opinion, modern writing at its worst does what?

6. What does Orwell mean when he states "All issues are political issues, and politics itself is a mass of lies, evasions, folly, hatred, schizophrenia" (paragraph 15)?

7. Does he see a cure or hope for these ills when it comes to improving the language?

8. List Orwell's rules for improving written English. Does he break any of his own rules in this essay? Identify the rules he breaks.

In Your Own Words: Analysis

1. Do you agree with Orwell's belief in the need to purge Latin and Greek words from English? Is this realistic and will it improve the English language by making writing and thinking more clear and accessible?

2. What is the tone of Orwell's essay? Does it change throughout the essay?

3. What is Orwell's thesis or main argument? What evidence does he use to support his views?

4. Orwell's essay was written in 1946. What aspects of this essay are still relevant today?

5. In Orwell's opinion, bad writing is stale writing. What characterizes stale writing?

6. What is Orwell trying to demonstrate when he translates from *Ecclesiastes*?

7. How does "ugly and inaccurate" language contribute to "foolish" thinking?

8. What does Orwell state in the end of his essay? Is his conclusion effective?

Now Write

1. Examine the history of the language used either in advertising or war-time propaganda. Write an essay in which you explain how the examples you find reflect what Orwell discusses in his essay.
2. Write an essay in which you compare the advice that both Stephen King ("What Writing Is") and George Orwell give on writing. What is the major concern that each writer has about writing? Do they share anything in common in terms of these concerns or in the advice they give?
3. What would Orwell say about the state of the English language today? For example, what would he think of technological jargon and its inclusion in everyday language? Think of phrases such as "I'll just google it" and terms such as "unfriend" and "tweeted." Using Orwell's essay, explain how he would view the impact of computer technology and the Internet on language use.
4. Find an essay you have written in the past or any other piece you have written. In what three ways could you improve it by applying Orwell's rules for better writing?

Martin Luther King, Jr.

Dr. Martin Luther King, Jr. (1929–1968) was born into a family of Baptist ministers who served in Atlanta churches, starting with King Jr.'s grandfather. King Jr. attended segregated public schools and skipped two high school grades before starting college at the age of 15. At 19 he received his bachelor's degree from Morehouse College and spent three years studying theology at a seminary in Pennsylvania where he received his second degree.

In the 1950s he studied at Boston University, earning a PhD and continuing his civil rights work for which he would later become known around the world. King Jr. was also pastor of the Dexter Avenue Baptist Church in Montgomery, Alabama, and a member of the executive committee of the NAACP (National Association for the Advancement of Colored People). He led the first major American non-violent demonstration of the twentieth century in December 1955, a bus boycott that lasted over 300 days. During this time, he was arrested, subjected to physical and verbal abuse, and had his home bombed. A year later the US Supreme Court declared the laws requiring segregation on buses unconstitutional.

The ideals that guided King Jr. for most of his life came from his Christian faith and the works of various writers and philosophers. The operational techniques of civil disobedience he used were inspired by thinkers such as Ghandi and the American writer Henry David Thoreau. He never wavered in his commitment to non-violence, and King Jr. travelled and spoke extensively in his lifetime, wherever there was injustice and a need for action. He led a peaceful march of 250,000 people to whom he delivered his "I Have a Dream" speech. King Jr. was not just a brilliant orator, however; he was also a skilled writer who wrote five books and many articles. He is most famous for his "Letter from a Birmingham Jail," which is a kind of manifesto for the civil rights movement.

Martin Luther King Jr. was named "Man of the Year" by *Time* magazine in 1963. At the age of 35 he became the youngest man ever to be awarded the Nobel Peace Prize, donating all of the money from the prize to the civil rights movement. He was a tireless supporter not just of civil rights for African Americans, but also for the rights of the poor and of workers. He was assassinated in 1968 while he was in Memphis, Tennessee, organizing support for striking city workers.

King Jr. believed that a solid education was imperative in achieving understanding and, ultimately, social justice. In his article from the *Maroon Tiger* (Morehouse College's student-run newspaper), he asks what the purpose of education is. Is it to gain knowledge, facilitate social development, or to secure steady employment in the future? Written when he was just 18 years old, "The Purpose of Education" showcases his reflections on what it means to be educated.

In His Own Words

"A nation or civilization that continues to produce soft-minded men purchases its own spiritual death on the instalment plan."

"An individual has not started living until he can rise above the narrow confines of his individualistic concerns to the broader concerns of all humanity."

"Rarely do we find men who willingly engage in hard, solid thinking. There is an almost universal quest for easy answers and half-baked solutions. Nothing pains some people more than having to think."

Before We Begin

1. Why are you in college or university? What do you hope to gain?
2. What do you think the purpose of education is?
3. Do lessons on morality (teaching right from wrong) belong in the classroom at any level?

 **Now Read**

The Purpose of Education

Essay, January 1947

This essay, written sometime during King's junior year at Morehouse, may be an early draft of the article of the same name published in The Maroon Tiger. *He suggests that education should not only "teach man to think intensively" but also provide "worthy objectives upon which to concentrate."*

Last week we attempted to discuss the purpose of religion. This week our attention moves toward education. I will attempt to answer the question, what is the purpose of education?

To my mind, education has a two-fold function in society. On the one hand it should discipline the mind for sustained and persistent speculation. On the other hand it should integrate human life around central, focusing ideals. It is a tragedy that the latter is often neglected in our educational system.

Education should equip us with the power to think effectively and objectively. To think is one of the hardest things in the world, and to think objectively is still harder. Yet this is the job of education. Education should cause us to rise beyond the horizon of legions of half truth, prejudices, and propaganda. Education should enable us to "weigh and consider," to discern the true from the false, the relevant from the irrelevant, and the real from the unreal. The first function of education, therefore, is to teach man to think intensively. But this is not the whole of education. If education stops here it can be the most dangerous force in society. Some of the greatest criminals in society have been men [who] possessed the power of concentration and reason, but they had no morals. Perhaps the most dangerous periods in civilization have been those periods when there was no moral foundation in society.

Education without morals is like a ship without a compass, merely wandering nowhere. It is not enough to have the power of concentration, but we must have worthy objectives upon which to concentrate. It is not enough to know truth, but we must love truth and sacrifice for it.

Article, February 1947

Writing in the campus newspaper, The Maroon Tiger, *King argues that education has both a utilitarian and a moral function. Citing the example of Georgia's former governor Eugene Talmadge, he asserts that reasoning ability is not enough. He insists that character and moral development are necessary to give the critical intellect human purposes. King Sr. later recalled that his son told him, "Talmadge has a Phi Beta Kappa key, can you believe that? What did he use all that precious knowledge for? To accomplish what?"*

As I engage in the so-called "bull sessions" around and about the school, I too often find that most college men have a misconception of the purpose of education. Most of the "brethren" think that education should equip them with the proper instruments of exploitation so that they can forever trample over the masses. Still others think that education should furnish them with noble ends rather than means to an end.

It seems to me that education has a two-fold function to perform in the life of man and in society: the one is utility and the other is culture. Education must enable a man to become more efficient, to achieve with increasing facility the legitimate goals of his life.

Education must also train one for quick, resolute, and effective thinking. To think incisively and to think for one's self is very difficult. We are prone to let our mental life become invaded by legions of half truths, prejudices, and propaganda. At this point, I often wonder whether or not education is fulfilling its purpose. A great majority of the so-called educated people do not think logically and scientifically. Even the press, the classroom, the platform, and the pulpit in many instances do not give us objective and unbiased truths. To save man from the morass of propaganda, in my opinion, is one of the chief aims of education. Education must enable one to sift and weigh evidence, to discern the true from the false, the real from the unreal, and the facts from the fiction.

The function of education, therefore, is to teach one to think intensively and to think critically. But education which stops with efficiency may prove the greatest menace to society. The most dangerous criminal may be the man gifted with reason, but with no morals.

The late Eugene Talmadge, in my opinion, possessed one of the better minds of Georgia, or even America. Moreover, he wore the Phi Beta Kappa key. By all measuring rods, Mr. Talmadge could think critically and intensively; yet he contends that I am an inferior being. Are those the types of men we call educated?

We must remember that intelligence is not enough. Intelligence plus character—that is the goal of true education. The complete education gives one not only power of concentration, but worthy objectives upon which to concentrate. The broad education will, therefore, transmit to one not only the accumulated knowledge of the race but also the accumulated experience of social living.

If we are not careful, our colleges will produce a group of close-minded, unscientific, illogical propagandists, consumed with immoral acts. Be careful, "brethren!" Be careful, teachers!

F.Y.I.

bull session: although the term is defined as an informal discussion or conversation among a small group of people, the bull session King Jr. is referring to is one in which the participants discuss political, social, and moral issues.

Eugene Talmadge: (1884–1946) a lawyer, livestock trader, and a three-term governor for the state of Georgia. He was elected a fourth time but died before he could take office. Viewed as a dictator and a racist, Talmadge came under fire for firing the dean of the University of Georgia's College of Education and the president of Georgia's State Teachers College on the charge that they both favoured racial integration of education. As a result of his actions, the Southern Association of Colleges and Schools had the accreditation from numerous Georgia colleges and universities removed, making a degree from a Georgia university useless since it would not be recognized outside the state of Georgia.

Phi Beta Kappa key: the symbol of the Phi Beta Kappa Society, an academic honour society whose mission is to "celebrate and advocate excellence in the liberal arts and sciences." Its motto is "Love of learning is the guide of life." On the key are the Greek letters that make up the Society's name, three stars, and a pointing finger. It is said that the three stars represent the ambition of young scholars and the three principles on which the Society is founded: friendship, morality, and learning.

Words to Build on

brethren: although a plural of the word brother, it is mainly used in reference to fellow male members of a religion, society, or sect.

morass: something that impedes, takes over, and overwhelms

In Your Own Words: Comprehension

1. What is the two-fold function of education?
2. What does King Jr. fear education has become?
3. Why is having the ability to think critically so crucial to King Jr.?
4. According to the essay, where are some areas in life that we don't always get the truth?
5. What does King Jr. mean when he uses the term "mental life"?
6. According to King Jr., what makes a man a dangerous criminal?
7. Why is having only intelligence not enough?

In Your Own Words: Analysis

1. Martin Luther King Jr. wrote this essay in 1946. How old was he at the time? Is his thesis and writing style unusual for a person this age?
2. Do "bull-sessions" exist at colleges and universities today? Are the same types of topics that King Jr. would have discussed in his day found in current student discussions?
3. What does King Jr. mean when he writes, "...most of the brethren think that education should equip them with the proper instruments of exploitation so that they can forever trample over the masses." Are there specific college and university programs, such as advertising and business marketing, where his fears are realized?
4. Compare the first paragraph from the early draft and the first paragraph of the final draft of the essay. What are the differences? What do you think changed for King Jr. between the first draft and the final draft?

5. Consider the two versions of this essay in its entirety. What has changed from the first draft?

6. Martin Luther King Jr. is a well-respected and famous individual. How important is the writer's identity in determining a reader's interest in a piece? Would people be affected as much if this essay was written by an unknown author?

7. Are the ideas and positions in this essay naïve and out of date?

✳ Now Write

1. Write an essay in which you explain what King Jr. believes makes for an educated person compared to what you and/or colleges and universities today think makes for an educated person.

2. What types of issues and topics are written about and discussed in your college or university campus newspaper? Could King Jr.'s essay be included in a campus newspaper today? Provide reasons why an essay such as his could or could not appear in your present-day campus newspaper.

3. The Martin Luther King, Jr., Research and Education Institute has an online site that allows people to view its archives. Visit the site and read King's other essays. From your research, outline three other topics that King was passionate about. Why do you think these three topics were so important to him?

Maxine Hong Kingston

Maxine Hong Kingston (b. 1940) is an award-winning author, professor, and feminist who was born in Stockton, California, to Chinese immigrant parents. She demonstrated a love of writing at an early age, inspired by her mother's storytelling abilities. After relocating to Hawaii in the 1960s, she completed her first work, *The Woman Warrior: Memoirs of a Girlhood Among Ghosts* (1975), which won the National Book Critics Circle award. The book was a sensation worldwide and has become a modern classic: it is a staple of university literature courses in North America, was made into a stage play in 1994, and is also taught at a US military academy, something that has caused Kingston some discomfort since she is an outspoken pacifist. It was initially Kingston's American publisher who insisted on the use of the term "warrior" in the title of her most famous work since it was "catchier." She later wrote a novel, a book of poetry, and a companion memoir to *The Woman Warrior*, *China Men* (1980), a work that relays the lives of the male immigrants in her family. In 1997, President Bill Clinton awarded Kingston a National Humanities Medal. She was also named a Living Treasure of Hawaii by a Honolulu Buddhist sect, primarily for writing *The Woman Warrior*.

"No Name Woman" is the first of the five sections of *The Woman Warrior* and tells the story of Kingston's paternal aunt who is punished by the villagers in China for sexual transgressions. The narrator begins in the first person, but some stories in the book are told using other voices. For example, the first chapter uses direct narrative by Brave Orchid, the narrator's mother, with minimal framing by the daughter. Critics and booksellers differed on how to classify this work since it questions and even blurs the boundaries between memory, myth, legend, fantasy, and truth. Some see strong fictional elements in its use of narrative voice and characters, while others claim it is a memoir since it vividly retells incidents from the writer's childhood years in California. The narrative style is unusual because Kingston blends her parents' Chinese dialect with English syntactical forms and American slang, thus bridging cultures. The narrator/protagonist/daughter does not look directly to herself to begin her quest or search for an identity; she adopts or "tries on" the identities of five other women, some of whom are real and some mythical. In doing so, the narrator reveals how one's identity is ultimately composed of intersecting points between oneself, other people, and their stories. Thus, Kingston expands the notion of memory as collective and also how identity, like memory itself, is a process by which one can actively define or redefine oneself.

The Woman Warrior is a quest for meaning, and although Kingston draws on her cultural inheritance for guidance and strength, she exposes differences in growing up female and American. As with other memoirs and autobiographies, this work seeks answers to questions like "Who am I?" "What is home?" and "Where do I belong?"

Ever the innovator, Kingston wrote another memoir, this one in verse form, when she turned 65. *I Love a Broad Margin to My Life* (2011) takes its title from Henry David Thoreau's *Walden*. These same words hang over Kingston's writing desk and inspire her to continue to expand her view of life. In this memoir she writes, "I'm standing on top of a hill; / I can see everywhichway— / the long way that I came, and the few / places I have yet to go. Treat / my whole life as if it were a day."

In Her Own Words

"I wanted to be a writer since I was nine years old . . . [w]hen I was a child I was writing book-length things. Writing was like *breathing*, but I never thought about making a living from it."

"To me success means effectiveness in the world, that I am able to carry my ideas and values into the world—that I am able to change it in positive ways."

"In a time of destruction, create something."

"Before we can leave our parents, they stuff our heads like the suitcases which they jam-pack with homemade underwear."

Before We Begin

1. Every family has its secrets. Are secrets about family members best forgotten, or is it better to reveal family secrets?
2. Have you ever asked your parents about their lives before you were born? Did they tell you anything that surprised you or seemed uncharacteristic of your parent?
3. What are the differences between looking up to a famous role model and looking up to a person from your own family? Is there a member of your family whose personality or life has helped you understand yourself or your own life?
4. What are some of the difficulties the children of immigrants experience both at home and at school? What are the differences between those who are born American or Canadian (the first generation) and their parents who immigrated?

 Now Read

No Name Woman

"You must not tell anyone," my mother said, "what I am about to tell you. In China your father had a sister who killed herself. She jumped into the family well. We say that your father has all brothers because it is as if she had never been born.

"In 1924 just a few days after our village celebrated 17 hurry-up weddings—to make sure that every young man who went 'out on the road' would responsibly come home—your father and his brothers and your grandfather and his brothers and your aunt's new husband sailed for America, the Gold Mountain. It was your grandfather's last trip. Those lucky enough to get contracts waved goodbye from the decks. They fed and guarded the stowaways and helped them off in Cuba, New York, Bali, Hawaii. 'We'll meet in California next year,' they said. All of them sent money home.

"I remember looking at your aunt one day when she and I were dressing; I had not noticed before that she had such a protruding melon of a stomach. But I did not think, 'She's pregnant,' until she began to look like other pregnant women, her shirt pulling and the white tops of her black pants showing. She could not have been pregnant, you see, because her husband had been gone for years. No one said anything. We did not discuss it. In early summer she was ready to have the child, long after the time when it could have been possible.

"The village had also been counting. On the night the baby was to be born the villagers raided our house. Some were crying. Like a great saw, teeth strung with lights, files of people walked zigzag across our land, tearing the rice. Their lanterns doubled in the disturbed black water, which drained away through the broken bunds. As the villagers closed in, we could see that some of them, probably men and women we knew well, wore white masks. The people with long hair hung it over their faces. Women with short hair made it stand up on end. Some had tied white bands around their foreheads, arms, and legs.

"At first they threw mud and rocks at the house. Then they threw eggs and began slaughtering our stock. We could hear the animals scream their deaths—the roosters, the pigs, a last great roar from the ox. Familiar wild heads flared in our night windows; the villagers encircled us. Some of the faces stopped to peer at us, their eyes rushing like searchlights. The hands flattened against the panes, framed heads, and left red prints.

"The villagers broke in the front and the back doors at the same time, even though we had not locked the doors against them. Their knives dripped with the blood of our animals. They smeared blood on the doors and walls. One woman swung a chicken, whose throat she had slit, splattering blood in red arcs about her. We stood together in the middle of our house, in the family hall with the pictures and tables of the ancestors around us, and looked straight ahead.

"At that time the house had only two wings. When the men came back, we would build two more to enclose our courtyard and a third one to begin a second courtyard. The villagers pushed through both wings, even your grandparents' rooms, to find your aunt's, which was also mine until the men returned. From this room a new wing for one of the younger families would grow. They ripped up her clothes and shoes and broke her combs, grinding them underfoot. They tore her work from the loom. They scattered the cooking fire and rolled the new weaving in it. We could hear them in the kitchen breaking our bowls and banging the pots. They overturned the great waist-high earthenware jugs; duck eggs, pickled fruits, vegetables burst out and mixed in acrid torrents. The old woman from the next field swept a broom through the air and loosed the spirits-of-the-broom over our heads. 'Pig.' 'Ghost.' 'Pig,' they sobbed and scolded while they ruined our house.

"When they left, they took sugar and oranges to bless themselves. They cut pieces from the dead animals. Some of them took bowls that were not broken and clothes that were not torn. Afterward we swept up the rice and sewed it back up into sacks. But the smells from the spilled preserves lasted. Your aunt gave birth in the pigsty that night. The next morning when I went for the water, I found her and the baby plugging up the family well.

"Don't let your father know that I told you. He denies her. Now that you have started to menstruate, what happened to her could happen to you. Don't humiliate us. You wouldn't like to be forgotten as if you had never been born. The villagers are watchful."

Whenever she had to warn us about life, my mother told stories that ran like this one, a story to grow up on. She tested our strength to establish realities. Those in the emigrant generations who could not reassert brute survival died young and far from home. Those of us in the first American generations have had to figure out how the invisible world the emigrants built around our childhoods fits in solid America.

The emigrants confused the gods by diverting their curses, misleading them with crooked streets and false names. They must try to confuse their offspring as well, who, I suppose, threaten them in similar ways—always trying to get things straight, always trying to name the unspeakable. The Chinese I know hide their names; sojourners take new names when their lives change and guard their real names with silence.

Chinese Americans, when you try to understand what things in you are Chinese, how do you separate what is peculiar to childhood, to poverty, insanities, one family, your mother who marked your growing with stories, from what is Chinese? What is Chinese tradition and what is the movies?

If I want to learn what clothes my aunt wore, whether flashy or ordinary, I would have to begin, "Remember Father's drowned-in-the-well sister?" I cannot ask that. My mother has told me once and for all the useful parts. She will add nothing unless powered by Necessity, a riverbank that guides her life. She plants vegetable gardens rather than lawns; she carries the odd-shaped tomatoes home from the fields and eats food left for the gods.

Whenever we did frivolous things, we used up energy; we flew high kites. We children came up off the ground over the melting cones our parents brought home from work and the American movie on New Year's Day—*Oh, You Beautiful Doll* with Betty Grable one year, and *She Wore a Yellow Ribbon* with John Wayne another year. After the one carnival ride each, we paid in guilt; our tired father counted his change on the dark walk home.

Adultery is extravagance. Could people who hatch their own chicks and eat the embryos and the heads for delicacies and boil the feet in vinegar for party food, leaving only the gravel, eating even the gizzard lining—could such people engender a prodigal aunt? To be a woman, to have a daughter in starvation time was a waste enough. My aunt could not have been the lone romantic who gave up everything for sex. Women in the old China did not choose. Some man had commanded her to lie with him and be his secret evil. I wonder whether he masked himself when he joined the raid on her family.

Perhaps she had encountered him in the fields or on the mountain where the daughters-in-law collected fuel. Or perhaps he first noticed her in the market place. He was not a stranger because the village housed no strangers. She had to have dealings with him other than sex. Perhaps he worked an adjoining field, or he sold her the cloth for the dress she sewed and wore. His demand must have surprised, then terrified her. She obeyed him; she always did as she was told.

When the family found a young man in the next village to be her husband, she had stood tractably beside the best rooster, his proxy, and promised before they met that she would be his forever. She was lucky that he was her age and she would be the first wife, an advantage secure now. The night she first saw him, he had sex with her. Then he left for America. She had almost forgotten what he looked like. When she tried to envision him, she only saw the black and white face in the group photograph the men had had taken before leaving.

The other man was not, after all, much different from her husband. They both gave orders: she followed. "If you tell your family, I'll beat you. I'll kill you. Be here again next week." No one talked sex, ever. And she might have separated the rapes from the rest of living if only she did not have to buy her oil from him or gather wood in the same forest. I want her fear to have lasted just as long as rape lasted so that the fear could have been contained. No drawn-out fear. But women at sex hazarded birth and hence lifetimes. The fear did not stop but permeated everywhere. She told the man, "I think I'm pregnant." He organized the raid against her.

On nights when my mother and father talked about their life back home, sometimes they mentioned an "outcast table" whose business they still seemed to be settling, their voices tight. In a commensal tradition, where food is precious, the powerful older people made wrongdoers eat alone. Instead of letting them start separate new lives like the Japanese, who could become samurais and geishas, the Chinese family, faces averted but eyes glowering sideways, hung on to the offenders and fed them leftovers. My aunt must have lived in the same house as my parents and eaten at an outcast table. My mother spoke about the raid as if she had seen it, when she and my aunt, a daughter-in-law to a different household, should not have been living together at all. Daughters-in-law lived with their husbands' parents, not their own; a synonym for marriage in Chinese is "taking a daughter-in-law." Her husband's parents could have sold her, mortgaged her, stoned her. But they had sent her back to her own mother and father, a mysterious act hinting at disgraces not told me. Perhaps they had thrown her out to deflect the avengers.

She was the only daughter; her four brothers went with her father, husband, and uncles "out on the road" and for some years became western men. When the goods were divided among the family, three of the brothers took land, and the youngest, my father, chose an education. After my grandparents gave their daughter away to her husband's family, they had dispensed all the adventure and all the property. They expected her alone to keep the traditional ways, which her brothers, now among the barbarians, could fumble without detection. The heavy, deep-rooted women were to maintain the past against the flood, safe for returning. But the rare urge west had fixed upon our family, and so my aunt crossed boundaries not delineated in space.

The work of preservation demands that the feelings playing about in one's guts not be turned into action. Just watch their passing like cherry blossoms. But perhaps my aunt, my forerunner, caught in a slow life, let dreams grow and fade and after some months or years went toward what persisted. Fear at the enormities of the forbidden kept her desires delicate, wire and bone. She looked at a man because she liked the way the hair was tucked behind his ears, or she liked the question-mark line of a long torso curving at the shoulder and straight at the hip. For warm eyes or a soft voice or a slow walk—that's all—a few hairs, a line, a brightness, a sound, a pace, she gave up family. She offered us up for a charm that vanished with tiredness, a pigtail that didn't toss when the wind died. Why, the wrong lighting could erase the dearest thing about him.

It could very well have been, however, that my aunt did not take subtle enjoyment of her friend, but, a wild woman, kept rollicking company. Imagining her free with sex doesn't fit, though. I don't know any women like that, or men either. Unless I see her life branching into mine, she gives me no ancestral help.

To sustain her being in love, she often worked at herself in the mirror, guessing at the colours and shapes that would interest him, changing them frequently in order to hit on the right combination. She wanted him to look back.

On a farm near the sea, a woman who tended her appearance reaped a reputation for eccentricity. All the married women blunt-cut their hair in flaps about their ears or pulled it back in tight buns. No nonsense. Neither style blew easily into heart-catching tangles. And at their weddings they displayed themselves in their long hair for the last time. "It brushed the backs of my knees," my mother tells me. "It was braided, and even so, it brushed the backs of my knees."

At the mirror my aunt combed individuality into her bob. A bun could have been contrived to escape into black streamers blowing in the wind or in quiet wisps about her face, but only the older women in our picture album wear buns. She brushed her hair back from her forehead, tucking the flaps behind her ears. She looped a piece of thread, knotted into a circle between her index fingers and thumbs, and ran the double strand across her forehead. When she closed her fingers as if she were making a pair of shadow geese bite, the string twisted together catching the little hairs. Then she pulled the thread away from her skin, ripping the hairs out neatly, her eyes watering from the needles of pain. Opening her fingers, she cleaned the thread, then rolled it along her hairline and the tops of her eyebrows. My mother did the same to me and my sisters and herself. I used to believe that the expression "caught by the short hairs" meant a captive held with a depilatory string. It especially hurt at the temples, but my mother said we were lucky we didn't have to have our feet bound when we were seven. Sisters used to sit on their beds and cry together, she said, as their mothers or their slaves removed the bandages for a few minutes each night and let the blood gush back into their veins. I hope that the man my aunt loved appreciated a smooth brow, that he wasn't just a tits-and-ass man.

Once my aunt found a freckle on her chin, at a spot that the almanac said predestined her for unhappiness. She dug it out with a hot needle and washed the wound with peroxide.

More attention to her looks than these pullings of hairs and pickings at spots would have caused gossip among the villagers. They owned work clothes and good clothes, and they wore good clothes for feasting the new seasons. But since a woman combing her hair hexes beginnings, my aunt rarely found an occasion to look her best. Women looked like great sea snails—the corded wood, babies, and laundry they carried were the whorls on their backs. The Chinese did not admire a bent back; goddesses and warriors stood straight. Still there must have been a marvellous freeing of beauty when a worker laid down her burden and stretched and arched.

Such commonplace loveliness, however, was not enough for my aunt. She dreamed of a lover for the 15 days of New Year's, the time for families to exchange visits, money, and food. She plied her secret comb. And sure enough she cursed the year, the family, the village, and herself.

Even as her hair lured her imminent lover, many other men looked at her. Uncles, cousins, nephews, brothers would have looked, too, had they been home between journeys. Perhaps they had already been restraining their curiosity, and they left, fearful that their glances, like a field of nesting birds, might be startled and caught. Poverty hurt, and that was their first reason for leaving. But another, final reason for leaving the crowded house was the never-said.

She may have been unusually beloved, the precious only daughter, spoiled and mirror gazing because of the affection the family lavished on her. When her husband left, they welcomed the chance to take her back from the in-laws; she could live like the little daughter for just a while longer. There are stories that my grandfather was different from other people, "crazy ever since the little Jap bayoneted him in the head." He used to put his naked penis on the dinner table, laughing. And one day he brought home a baby girl, wrapped up inside his brown western-style greatcoat. He had traded one of his sons, probably my father, the youngest, for her. My grandmother made him trade back. When he finally got a daughter of his own, he doted on her. They must have all loved her, except perhaps my father, the only brother who never went back to China, having once been traded for a girl.

Brothers and sisters, newly men and women, had to efface their sexual colour and present plain miens. Disturbing hair and eyes, a smile like no other, threatened the ideal of five generations living under one roof. To focus blurs, people shouted face to face and yelled from room to room. The immigrants I know have loud voices, unmodulated to American tones even after years away from the village where they called their friendships out across the fields. I have not been able to stop my mother's screams in public libraries or over telephones. Walking erect (knees straight, toes pointed forward, not pigeon-toed, which is Chinese-feminine) and speaking in an inaudible voice, I have tried to turn myself American-feminine. Chinese communication was loud, public. Only sick people had to whisper. But at the dinner table, where the family members came nearest one another, no one could talk, not the outcasts nor any eaters. Every word that falls from the mouth is a coin lost. Silently they gave and accepted food with both hands. A preoccupied child who took his bowl with one hand got a sideways glare. A complete moment of total attention is due everyone alike. Children and lovers have no singularity here, but my aunt used a secret voice, a separate attentiveness.

She kept the man's name to herself throughout her labour and dying; she did not accuse him that he be punished with her. To save her inseminator's name she gave silent birth.

He may have been somebody in her own household, but intercourse with a man outside the family would have been no less abhorrent. All the village were kinsmen, and the titles shouted in loud country voices never let kinship be forgotten. Any man within visiting distance would have been neutralized as a lover—"brother," "younger brother," "older brother"—115 relationship titles. Parents researched birth charts probably not so much to assure good fortune as to circumvent incest in a population that has but 100 surnames. Everybody has 8 million relatives. How useless then sexual mannerisms, how dangerous.

As if it came from an atavism deeper than fear, I used to add "brother" silently to boys' names. It hexed the boys, who would or would not ask me to dance, and made them less scary and as familiar and deserving of benevolence as girls.

But, of course, I hexed myself also—no dates. I should have stood up, both arms waving, and shouted out across libraries, "Hey, you! Love me back." I had no idea, though, how to make attraction selective, how to control its direction and magnitude. If I made myself American-pretty so that the five or six Chinese boys in the class fell in love with me, everyone else—the Caucasian, Negro, and Japanese boys—would too. Sisterliness, dignified and honorable, made much more sense.

Attraction eludes control so stubbornly that whole societies designed to organize relationships among people cannot keep order, not even when they bind people to one another from childhood and raise them together. Among the very poor and the wealthy, brothers married their adopted sisters, like doves. Our family allowed some romance, paying adult brides' prices and providing dowries so that their sons and daughters could marry strangers. Marriage promises to turn strangers into friendly relatives—a nation of siblings.

In the village structure, spirits shimmered among the live creatures, balanced and held in equilibrium by time and land. But one human being flaring up into violence could open up a black hole, a maelstrom that pulled in the sky. The frightened villagers, who depended on one another to maintain the real, went to my aunt to show her a personal, physical representation of the break she had made in the "roundness." Misallying couples snapped off the future, which was to be embodied in true offspring.

The villagers punished her for acting as if she could have a private life, secret and apart from them.

If my aunt had betrayed the family at a time of large grain yields and peace, when many boys were born, and wings were being built on many houses, perhaps she might have escaped such severe punishment. But the men—hungry, greedy, tired of planting in dry soil—had been forced to leave the village in order to send food-money home. There were ghost plagues, bandit plagues, wars with the Japanese, floods. My Chinese brother and sister had died of an unknown sickness. Adultery, perhaps only a mistake during good times, became a crime when the village needed food.

The round moon cakes and round doorways, the round tables of graduated sizes that fit one roundness inside another, round windows and rice bowls—these talismans had lost their power to warn this family of the law: a family must be whole, faithfully keeping the descent line by having sons to feed the old and the dead, who in turn look after the family. The villagers came to show my aunt and her lover-in-hiding a broken house. The villagers were speeding up the circling of events because she was too short-sighted to see that her infidelity had already harmed the village, that waves of conse-quences would return unpredictably, sometimes in disguise, as now, to hurt her. This roundness had to be made coin-sized so that she would see its circumference: punish her at the birth of her baby. Awaken her to the inexorable. People who refused fatalism because they could invent small resources insisted on culpability. Deny accidents and wrest fault from the stars.

After the villagers left, their lanterns now scattering in various directions toward home, the family broke their silence and cursed her. "*Aiaa*, we're going to die. Death is coming. Death is coming. Look what you've done. You've killed us. Ghost! Dead ghost! Ghost! You've never been born." She ran out into the fields, far enough from the house so that she could no longer hear their voices, and pressed herself against the earth, her own land no more. When she felt the birth coming, she thought that she had been hurt. Her body seized together. "They've hurt me too much," she thought. "This is gall, and it will kill me." With forehead and knees against the earth, her body convulsed and then relaxed. She turned on her back, lay on the ground. The black well of sky and stars went out and out and out forever; her body and her complexity seemed to disappear. She was one of the stars, a bright dot in blackness, without home, without a companion, in eternal cold and silence. An agoraphobia rose in her, speed-ing higher and higher, bigger and bigger; she would not be able to contain it; there would no end to fear.

Flayed, unprotected against space, she felt pain return, focusing her body. This pain chilled her—a cold, steady kind of surface pain. Inside, spasmodically, the other pain, the pain of the child, heated her. For hours she lay on the ground, alternately body and space. Sometimes a vision of normal comfort obliterated reality: she saw the family in the evening gambling at the dinner table, the young people massaging their elders' backs. She saw them congratulating one another, high joy on the mornings the rice shoots came up. When these pictures burst, the stars drew yet further apart. Black space opened.

She got to her feet to fight better and remembered that old-fashioned women gave birth in their pigsties to fool the jealous, pain-dealing gods, who do not snatch piglets. Before the next spasms could stop her, she ran to the pigsty, each step a rushing out into emptiness. She climbed over the fence and knelt in the dirt. It was good to have a fence enclosing her, a tribal person alone.

Labouring, this woman who had carried her child as a foreign growth that sickened her every day, expelled it at last. She reached down to touch the hot, wet, moving mass, surely smaller than anything human, and could feel that it was human after all—fingers, toes, nails, nose. She pulled it up on to her belly, and it lay curled there, butt in the air, feet precisely tucked one under the other. She opened her loose shirt and buttoned the child inside. After resting, it squirmed and thrashed and she pushed it up to her breast. It turned its head this way and that until it found her nipple. There, it made little snuffling noises. She clenched her teeth at its preciousness, lovely as a young calf, a piglet, a little dog.

She may have gone to the pigsty as a last act of responsibility: she would protect this child as she had protected its father. It would look after her soul, leaving supplies on her grave. But how would this tiny child without family find her grave when there would be no marker for her anywhere, neither in the earth nor the family hall? No one would give her a family hall name. She had taken the child with her into the wastes. At its birth the two of them had felt the same raw pain of separation, a wound that only the family pressing tight could close. A child with no descent line would not soften her life but only trail after her, ghostlike, begging her to give it purpose. At dawn the villagers on their way to the fields would stand around the fence and look.

Full of milk, the little ghost slept. When it awoke, she hardened her breasts against the milk that crying loosens. Toward morning she picked up the baby and walked to the well.

Carrying the baby to the well shows loving. Otherwise abandon it. Turn its face into the mud. Mothers who love their children take them along. It was probably a girl; there is some hope of forgiveness for boys.

"Don't tell anyone you had an aunt. Your father does not want to hear her name. She has never been born." I have believed that sex was unspeakable and words so strong and fathers so frail that "aunt" would do my father mysterious harm. I have thought that my family, having settled among immigrants who had also been their neighbours in the ancestral land, needed to clean their name, and a wrong word would incite the kinspeople even here. But there is more to this silence: they want me to participate in her punishment. And I have.

In the 20 years since I heard this story I have not asked for details nor said my aunt's name; I do not know it. People who can comfort the dead can also chase after them to hurt them further—a reverse ancestor worship. The real punishment was not the raid swiftly inflicted by the villagers, but the family's deliberately forgetting her. Her betrayal so maddened them, they saw to it that she would suffer forever, even after death. Always hungry, always needing, she would have to beg food from other ghosts, snatch and steal it from those whose living descendants give them gifts. She would have to fight the ghosts massed at crossroads for the buns a few thoughtful citizens leave to decoy her away from village and home so that the ancestral spirits could feast unharassed. At peace, they could act like gods, not ghosts, their descent lines providing them with paper suits and dresses, spirit money, paper houses, paper automobiles, chicken, meat, and rice into eternity—essences delivered up in smoke and flames, steam and incense rising from each rice bowl. In an attempt to make the Chinese care for people outside the family, Chairman Mao encourages us now to give our paper replicas to the spirits of outstanding soldiers and workers, no matter whose ancestors they may be. My aunt remains forever hungry. Goods are not distributed evenly among the dead.

My aunt haunts me—her ghost drawn to me because now, after 50 years of neglect, I alone devote pages of paper to her, though not origamied into houses and clothes. I do not think she always means me well. I am telling on her, and she was a spite suicide, drowning herself in the drinking water. The Chinese are always very frightened of the drowned one, whose weeping ghost, wet hair hanging and skin bloated, waits silently by the water to pull down a substitute.

F.Y.I.

Aiaa: a transcription of a sound in Cantonese that indicates exclamation, surprise, disbelief, pain, or sorrow; pronounced *"ah-yeah"*

bride price: an offering of goods or a monetary amount that the groom and his family paid to the bride's family

Chairman Mao: formal title of Mao Zedong (1893–1976), Chinese chairman of the Communist Party of China from 1949–1976 and head of state from 1949–1959.

ghosts: not only used to indicate the spirits of those who have died, but also used to label human beings who are considered "insignificant"; the word is also used in reference to non-Chinese peoples

Gold Mountain: the name early Chinese immigrants gave to North America because of the belief that the continent possessed inconceivable riches or "gold"

loom: an apparatus used for weaving carpets, clothing, and other items and is traditionally associated with women in most cultures around the world

mooncakes: round cakes traditionally made in China as offerings or at celebrations for the Moon Festival held in autumn

paper suits and dresses, spirit money, paper automobiles: traditionally in Chinese culture, family and friends make offerings for the dead that often take the form of objects the deceased had used in his or her daily life. The items are replicated in paper form and burned as part of the funerary ritual

talisman: an object that is thought to protect the possessor and to bring good luck

Words to Build on

acrid: having an unpleasant or bitter taste or smell

agoraphobia: extreme fear of open or public places, which leads one to experience panic attacks and/or become reclusive

almanac: an annual calendar containing important dates, statistical information, and astronomical data

atavism: something that is ancient or ancestral

bunds: an embankment or causeway

commensal: a biological term referring to an association between two organisms in which one benefits and the other derives neither benefit nor harm

doted: to be extremely and uncritically fond of someone

eccentricity: exhibiting unconventional or strange behaviour

fatalism: the belief that situations are determined by fate or destiny and are thus inevitable

flayed: having had the skin peeled off (i.e. from a corpse or carcass)

forerunner: a person or thing that precedes or comes before someone or something

gall: to behave in a bold way

hexes: magic spells or curses

inexorable: impossible to stop or prevent

maelstrom: a state of confusion or violent movement

plain miens: the manner in which a person is conducting him or herself, in this case not "showy" but "plain"

prodigal: a person who wastes money or is extravagant

tractably: easy to control or influence

wrest: to forcibly pull away from someone's hands

Tricks of the Trade

Irony

Character

Narrative voice

Oral storytelling/Orature

In Your Own Words: Comprehension

1. Who tells the story of "No Name Woman"?
2. What are "hurry-up weddings"? How did they ensure men "would responsibly come home"?
3. Why did Chinese people immigrate to America?
4. What does the narrator's mother notice about the aunt?
5. What do the villagers do when they find out about the aunt's situation? Why do they react in this way?

6. What does the aunt's family do?

7. What eventually happens to the aunt?

8. Why does the narrator state her mother tells stories? And why does she tell her the story of her aunt?

9. How does the narrator describe her mother?

10. What conclusion does the narrator eventually come to about her aunt?

In Your Own Words: Analysis

1. How would you describe the opening paragraph of "No Name Woman"?

2. Why is this section of Kingston's work called "No Name Woman"?

3. Why do the villagers use the word "ghost" for the aunt?

4. What does "she tested our strength to establish realities" mean?

5. According to the narrator, what do those of the first American generation, in other words the children of immigrants, have to "figure out"?

6. Why does the narrator believe there is confusion (inconsistencies) in the stories of Chinese emigrants to America?

7. Why is understanding her aunt and her aunt's life important to the narrator?

8. Why does the narrator ask "could such people engender a prodigal aunt"? What does she mean?

9. Kingston's story is about the narrator's ancestors, or "forerunners" as she says, who display an individuality that characterizes them as outside the norm. Who are the eccentric characters in this piece, and why does the narrator find it important to identify them so that she can see their lives "branching" into her own life?

10. What is significant or symbolic about paper in this piece? Why does the narrator conclude the story of her aunt by stating, "I alone devote pages of paper to her though not origamied into houses or clothes"?

❋ Now Write

1. Maxine Hong Kingston has written two works about the men and women in her family, which document their stories and the process of their immigrating to America. She has stated that this separation was necessary because the two genders had distinctly different experiences, both in the culture and as immigrants. Using "No Name Woman," describe how and explain why the experiences of men and women who immigrate are different.

2. Research the topic of food and eating in Chinese culture. Using "No Name Woman," write an essay examining the narrator's descriptions of food.

3. What is the role of women in Chinese culture, in the family, and in village life, according to the narrator? Write an essay describing this life as the narrator relays it in "No Name Woman" and also explain the purpose of the stories the narrator's mother tells: could the stories complicate, confuse, or give courage to a daughter who is growing up in America?

Deborah Tannen

Deborah Tannen (b. 1945) is a linguistics specialist and professor at Georgetown University. She is also a best-selling author who has written almost 20 books, including *Talking from 9 to 5: Women and Men at Work* (1995) and *You Just Don't Understand: Women and Men in Conversation* (1991). Tannen has been active in her field for over 30 years, and academics and journalists still view even her early observations and theories as being highly relevant today. Although her main focus is the conversational styles of men and women, her research includes both spoken and written communication, cross-cultural communication, modern Greek discourse, and the relationship between conversational and literary discourse. In 1978, Tannen visited Greece while she was conducting research for a book about a well-known Greek female novelist whom she had known for many years. During her stay in Athens, she observed the way Greeks give advice and even their ways of disagreeing with one another. She published an article on her findings, comparing Greek grammatical constructions and expressions to North American English communication patterns.

"Sex, Lies, and Conversation" is adapted from *You Just Don't Understand*, a book that was on the *New York Times* best seller list for four years and has been translated into 30 languages. In it, Tannen explores the differences in men's and women's conversational styles and writes of how this inability to understand the two different communication styles often leads to misunderstandings and frustration in relationships, even contributing to higher divorce rates; however, Tannen believes that once their distinct styles are mutually understood, communication can come more naturally and many conflicts can be avoided.

More information about Tannen and her other works, such as those about mother–daughter relationships, how men and women communicate in the workplace, and how sisters communicate with one another, can be found on her website at www9. georgetown.edu/faculty/tannend/index.html.

In Her Own Words

"The biggest mistake is believing there is one right way to listen, to talk, to have a conversation—or a relationship."

"It's our tendency to approach every problem as if it were a fight between two sides. We see it in headlines that are always using metaphors for war. It's a general atmosphere of animosity and contention that has taken over our public discourse."

"Since women often think in terms of closeness and support, they struggle to preserve intimacy. Men, concerned with status, tend to focus more on independence. These traits can lead women and men to starkly different views of the same situation."

Before We Begin

1. Do you think men and women have different styles of communication? What kinds of differences have you noticed?
2. Have you ever found it difficult to communicate with someone of the opposite sex? Why was it so difficult?
3. What are some of the ways we can become better face-to-face conversationalists?

 Now Read

Sex, Lies, and Conversation: Why Is It So Hard for Men and Women to Talk to Each Other?

I was addressing a small gathering in a suburban Virginia living room—a women's group that had invited men to join them. Throughout the evening, one man had been particularly talkative, frequently offering ideas and anecdotes, while his wife sat silently beside him on the couch. Toward the end of the evening, I commented that women frequently complain that their husbands don't talk to them. This man quickly concurred. He gestured toward his wife and said, "She's the talker in our family." The room burst into laughter; the man looked puzzled and hurt. "It's true," he explained. "When I come home from work I have nothing to say. If she didn't keep the conversation going, we'd spend the whole evening in silence."

This episode crystallizes the irony that although American men tend to talk more than women in public situations, they often talk less at home. And this pattern is wreaking havoc with marriage.

The pattern was observed by political scientist Andrew Hacker in the late 1970s. Sociologist Catherine Kohler Riessman reports in her new book *Divorce Talk* that most of the women she interviewed—but only a few of the men—gave lack of communication as the reason for their divorces. Given the current divorce rate of nearly 50 per cent, that amounts to millions of cases in the United States every year—a virtual epidemic of failed conversation.

In my own research, complaints from women about their husbands most often focused not on tangible inequities such as having given up the chance for a career to accompany a husband to his, or doing far more than their share of daily life-support work like cleaning, cooking, social arrangements, and errands. Instead, they focused on communication: "He doesn't listen to me," "He doesn't talk to me." I found, as Hacker observed years before, that most wives want their husbands to be, first and foremost, conversational partners, but few husbands share this expectation of their wives.

In short, the image that best represents the current crisis is the stereotypical cartoon scene of a man sitting at the breakfast table with a newspaper held up in front of his face, while a woman glares at the back of it, wanting to talk.

Linguistic Battle of the Sexes

How can women and men have such different impressions of communication in marriage? Why the widespread imbalance in their interests and expectations?

In the April issue of *American Psychologist*, Stanford University's Eleanor Maccoby reports the results of her own and others' research showing that children's development is most influenced by the social structure of peer interactions. Boys and girls tend to play with children of their own gender, and their sex-separate groups have different organizational structures and interactive norms.

I believe these systematic differences in childhood socialization make talk between women and men like cross-cultural communication, heir to all the attraction and pitfalls of that enticing but difficult enterprise. My research on men's and women's conversations uncovered patterns similar to those described for children's groups.

For women, as for girls, intimacy is the fabric of relationships, and talk is the thread from which it is woven. Little girls create and maintain friendships by exchanging secrets; similarly, women regard conversation as the cornerstone of friendship. So a woman expects her husband to be a new and improved version of a best friend. What is important is not the individual subjects that are discussed but the sense of closeness, of a life shared, that emerges when people tell their thoughts, feelings, and impressions.

Bonds between boys can be as intense as girls', but they are based less on talking, more on doing things together. Since they don't assume talk is the cement that binds a relationship, men don't know what kind of talk women want, and they don't miss it when it isn't there.

Boys' groups are larger, more inclusive, and more hierarchical, so boys must struggle to avoid the subordinate position in the group. This may play a role in women's complaints that men don't listen to them. Some men really don't like to listen, because being the listener makes them feel one-down, like a child listening to adults or an employee to a boss.

But often when women tell men, "You aren't listening," and the men protest, "I am," the men are right. The impression of not listening results from misalignments in the mechanics of conversation. The misalignment begins as soon as a man and a woman take physical positions. This became clear when I studied videotapes made by psychologist Bruce Dorval of children and adults talking to their same-sex best friends. I found that at every age, the girls and women faced each other directly, their eyes anchored on each other's faces. At every age, the boys and men sat at angles to each other and looked elsewhere in the room, periodically glancing at each other. They were obviously attuned to each other, often mirroring each other's movements. But the tendency of men to face away can give women the impression they aren't listening even when they are. A young woman in college was frustrated: Whenever she told her boyfriend she wanted to talk to him, he would lie down on the floor, close his eyes, and put his arm over his face. This signalled to her, "He's taking a nap." But he insisted he was listening extra hard. Normally, he looks around the room, so he is easily distracted. Lying down and covering his eyes helped him concentrate on what she was saying.

Analogous to the physical alignment that women and men take in conversation is their topical alignment. The girls in my study tended to talk at length about one topic, but the boys tended to jump from topic to topic. The second-grade girls exchanged stories about people they knew. The second-grade boys teased, told jokes, noticed things in the room, and talked about finding games to play. The sixth-grade girls talked about problems with a mutual friend. The sixth-grade boys talked about 55 different topics, none of which extended over more than a few turns.

Listening to Body Language

Switching topics is another habit that gives women the impression men aren't listening, especially if they switch to a topic about themselves. But the evidence of the tenth-grade boys in my study indicates otherwise. The tenth-grade boys sprawled across their chairs with bodies parallel and eyes straight ahead, rarely looking at each other. They looked as if they were riding in a car, staring out the windshield. But they were talking about their feelings. One boy was upset because a girl had told him he had a drinking problem, and the other was feeling alienated from all his friends.

Now, when a girl told a friend about a problem, the friend responded by asking probing questions and expressing agreement and understanding. But the boys dismissed each other's problems. Todd assured Richard that his drinking was "no big problem" because "sometimes you're funny when you're off your butt." And when Todd said he felt left out, Richard responded, "Why should you? You know more people than me."

Women perceive such responses as belittling and unsupportive. But the boys seemed satisfied with them. Whereas women reassure each other by implying, "You shouldn't feel bad because I've had similar experiences," men do so by implying, "You shouldn't feel bad because your problems aren't so bad."

There are even simpler reasons for women's impression that men don't listen. Linguist Lynette Hirschman found that women make more listener noise, such as "mhm," "uhuh," and "yeah," to show "I'm with you." Men, she found, more often give silent attention. Women who expect a stream of listener noise interpret silent attention as no attention at all.

Women's conversational habits are as frustrating to men as men's are to women. Men who expect silent attention interpret a stream of listener noise as overreaction or impatience. Also, when women talk to each other in a close, comfortable setting, they often overlap, finish each other's sentences, and anticipate what the other is about to say. This practice, which I call "participatory listenership," is often perceived by men as interruption, intrusion, and lack of attention.

A parallel difference caused a man to complain about his wife, "She just wants to talk about her own point of view. If I show her another view, she gets mad at me." When most women talk to each other, they assume a conversationalist's job is to express agreement and support. But many men see their conversational duty as pointing out the other side of an argument. This is heard as disloyalty by women, and refusal to offer the requisite support. It is not that women don't want to see other points of view, but that they prefer them phrased as suggestions and inquiries rather than as direct challenges.

In his book *Fighting for Life*, Walter Ong points out that men use "agonistic" or warlike, oppositional formats to do almost anything; thus discussion becomes debate, and conversation a competitive sport. In contrast, women see conversation as a ritual means of establishing rapport. If Jane tells a problem and June says she has a similar one, they walk away feeling closer to each other. But this attempt at establishing rapport can backfire when used with men. Men take too literally women's ritual "troubles talk," just as women mistake men's ritual challenges for real attack.

The Sounds of Silence

These differences begin to clarify why women and men have such different expectations about communication in marriage. For women, talk creates intimacy. Marriage is an orgy of closeness: you can tell your feelings and thoughts, and still be loved. Their greatest fear is being pushed away. But men live in a hierarchical world, where talk maintains independence and status. They are on guard to protect themselves from being put down and pushed around.

This explains the paradox of the talkative man who said of his silent wife, "She's the talker." In the public setting of a guest lecture, he felt challenged to show his intelligence and display his understanding of the lecture. But at home, where he has nothing to prove and no one to defend against, he is free to remain silent. For his wife, being home means she is free from the worry that something she says might offend someone, or spark disagreement, or appear to be showing off; at home she is free to talk.

The communication problems that endanger marriage can't be fixed by mechanical engineering. They require a new conceptual framework about the role of talk in human relationships. Many of the psychological explanations that have become second nature may not be helpful, because they tend to blame either women (for not being assertive enough) or men (for not being in touch with their feelings). A sociolinguistic approach by which male–female conversation is seen as cross-cultural communication allows us to understand the problem and forge solutions without blaming either party.

Once the problem is understood, improvement comes naturally, as it did to the young woman and her boyfriend who seemed to go to sleep when she wanted to talk. Previously, she had accused him of not listening, and he had refused to change his behaviour, since that would be admitting fault. But then she learned about and explained to him the differences in women's and men's habitual ways of aligning themselves in conversation. The next time she told him she wanted to talk, he began, as usual, by lying down and covering his eyes. When the familiar negative reaction bubbled up, she reassured herself that he really was listening. But then he sat up and looked at her. Thrilled, she asked why. He said, "You like me to look at you when we talk, so I'll try to do it." Once he saw their differences as cross-cultural rather than right and wrong, he independently altered his behaviour.

Women who feel abandoned and deprived when their husbands won't listen to or report daily news may be happy to discover their husbands trying to adapt once they understand the place of small talk in women's relationships. But if their husbands don't adapt, the women may still be comforted that for men, this is not a failure of intimacy.

Accepting the difference, the wives may look to their friends or family for that kind of talk. And husbands who can't provide it shouldn't feel their wives have made unreasonable demands. Some couples will still decide to divorce, but at least their decisions will be based on realistic expectations.

In these times of resurgent ethnic conflicts, the world desperately needs cross-cultural understanding. Like charity, successful cross-cultural communication should begin at home.

F.Y.I.

sociolinguistic: a field related to language and its social aspects

Words to Build on

agonistic: combative or relating to a fight, from the Greek word meaning "contest"

analogous: similar or parallel

concurred: agree in opinion

crystallizes: to become definite

tangible: being perceivable by touch or having material form

Tricks of the Trade

Introductory essay techniques

Rhetorical strategies

Supporting evidence

Types of essays: Cause and effect

In Your Own Words: Comprehension

1. What do most women cite as the reason for their divorces?

2. What does Tannen cite as being the best visual representation of this "crisis" in communication between men and women?

3. According to Tannen's article, what are the differences in how girls and boys communicate?

4. According to Tannen, what are the differences between "report" and "rapport" talk? Explain which gender does which type of talk and why.

5. Using the article, explain the differences in how men and women communicate.

6. What evidence does Tannen use to support her article?

7. According to this article, is there a "right" way and a "wrong" way to communicate between men and women?

8. What advice does Tannen give to couples who experience frustration when communicating?

In Your Own Words: Analysis

1. How would you describe the technique Tannen uses to begin her article? Is it effective? Why?

2. Think of the evidence Tannen uses in this article. Is it convincing? Why?

3. There are people who formulate and process information in different ways. Consider those who have autism, who are blind, or who are hearing impaired. How does this impact their communication styles and needs?

4. Do you recognize your own conversational style or behaviours in Tannen's examples? Does your style match with what Tannen states is true of your gender?

5. Tannen's examples are based on North American and heterocentric views. Can any of Tannen's points apply to gay, lesbian, or transgendered people? Do the communication styles in these relationships differ? If so, how?

6. Consider Tannen's biography. Who is her audience for this article? How does her style and tone in the article suit her audience?

7. What is Tannen's thesis or main idea?

8. Professors often tell their students not to use the first-person pronoun "I" in essay writing because it weakens the writer's argument and makes the reader focus on the author's personality and probable biases as opposed to the strength of the author's points. Is this true of Tannen's use of the first-person pronoun? When does she change her pronoun use and why?

9. Does the type of behaviours that Tannen mentions between married couples also surface during the early dating stages? Do men and women behave differently when dating or when they are first falling in love? What happens in the early stages of courtship and why does this change?

Now Write

1. Do you agree with all of Tannen's points on gender and communication? Write an essay in which you explain which points you agree with and which you do not. Be sure to explain why. Remember, there is no need to use "I' in an essay, even when you are expressing your opinion.

2. What factors, other than gender, contribute to communication breaking down? Explain these factors and provide support.

3. Tannen's article focuses on gender differences in conversation. Are there distinct cultural differences in the ways people of different cultures and ethnicities communicate? Write an essay in which you take what Tannen says about gender and apply it to cultural differences in communication styles.

4. What makes someone a good conversationalist? What are the characteristics of an effective communicator? Read Catherine Blyth's *The Art of Conversation* (2008). Compare what Blyth concludes makes for a good communicator with what Tannen writes.

Margaret Visser

Margaret Visser (b. 1940) is a writer who was born in South Africa and educated in Zimbabwe, Zambia, and at the University of Toronto. She taught Greek and Latin at Toronto's York University for 18 years. An award-winning author, she writes on history and mythology and has been called the "anthropologist of everyday life" because her books examine our beliefs and customs involving food, clothing, and good manners. Two of her books are *The Gift of Thanks* (2008), which is about the concept and practice of gratitude, and *Much Depends on Dinner* (1999), which examines traditions and customs around sharing meals. She regularly appears on radio and television and has lectured both in North America and Europe. "High Heels" appears in her collection of essays titled *The Way We Are* (2000), in which Visser examines the origins and history of everyday items such as our fashion choices and the history of this "sexy" form of footwear that was originally worn by men.

In Her Own Words

"High heels can induce the desired contours, but for surfaces and outlines stockings are essential. Stockings make female legs different from men's. They also render flesh visible but untouchable—at least for the moment—thereby provoking the senses."

"Believing in fate has probably always arisen in part because of the delights and terrors of storytelling. We have to realize—to learn—that in life we are not the readers but the authors of our own narratives."

"It is the nature of human beings not to be able to leave nature alone."

Before We Begin

1. Do you have an uncomfortable outfit or article of clothing that you wear? Why do you continue to wear this item?
2. Podiatrists say high heels are not healthy and various websites display images of women's feet that have been "deformed" by high heels. Why do women continue to wear high heels in spite of this?
3. Are there any items of clothing we wear that were not worn by people 100 years ago? Is there clothing or accessory items worn in the past that we do not wear today?
4. What is sexy? Define it.

✸ **Now Read**

High Heels

In Alfred Hitchcock's movie *The Lady Vanishes,* a nun is shockingly revealed to be no nun. She is sitting sedately enough, but we suddenly notice, protruding from beneath her habit, a pair of high-heeled shoes. Footwear of that shape immediately signals to us that this is a woman playing the sexual game.

When clothing resembling nuns' habits was ordinary female apparel, there were no such things as heels of any sort. Heels appeared for the first time in France in the 1590s. They were quite high and worn first by men. It was soon realized that heels had their uses as stirrup-holders on riding boots. But their first purpose was to raise their owners, enable them to pose impressively, and stretch their legs so that their calf muscles bulged curvaceously out.

Women quickly took to wearing heels although their legs were hidden by voluminous skirts, and when they did hemlines rose to show off their shoes. High-heeled shoes are still meant predominantly for posing in, as Miss America does in her swimsuit. She keeps her legs together, one knee gently bent. Pictures of women in bathing suits with heeled legs astride make a more up-to-date, but not necessarily a more feminist, statement.

High heels have never been made for comfort or for ease of movement. Their first wearers spoke of themselves as "mounted" or "propped" upon them; they were strictly court wear, and constituted proof that one intended no physical exertion, and need make none.

The Chinese had long known footwear that had the same effect, with high wooden pillars under the arch of each shoe, so that wearers required one or even two servants to help them totter along. Women had their feet deformed, by binding, into tiny, almost useless fists, which were shod in embroidered bootees: men got out of the thought of these an unconscionable thrill.

The European versions of stilt-shoes were Venetian chopines, which grew in height to 20 inches and more. The shoes attached to these pedestals sloped slightly towards the toe, and this is believed to be one origin of the heel. The other was the thoroughly mundane and practical patten or wooden clog, which raised the whole foot and was slipped over shoes to protect them from mud and water in the street.

High heels seem to have derived from an attempt to lighten raised shoes, by first creating an arch, then letting the toe down to the ground. The metatarsi of the foot (the long bones that end in toes) would remain bent, and bear the weight of the downward thrust.

And immediately the comforts of left and right shoes ceased to exist. "Straights," or both shoes made exactly alike, arrived with heels; people had to swap their left and right shoes every day, to keep them in shape. Fitted lefts and rights returned only when fashion dispensed with heels—until the pantograph changed shoemaking technology in the nineteenth century and made heeled lefts and rights feasible.

High heels became distinctively female dress during the eighteenth century: men heartily approved. "Heels" cause a woman's bottom to undulate twice as much as flat shoes permit; they pleasingly hobble the female and give the male a protective function; they add curve to the leg by shortening the heel cords and raising calf muscles. Slingback shoes and curving heels help draw attention to the *back* of a woman: it is the ancient device of rewarding the turning of a male's head. Tall cones or "stiletto" heels are aggressive yet incapacitating, like long fingernails.

There has always been a preference for tiny feet in women: even prehistoric Venuses' legs tend to taper to a point. This might be because animals, especially streamlined ones like cats, dogs, and horses, have short feet or hooves. High heels and skimpy shoes reduce feet and lengthen legs; they emphasize the animal in woman. Also—and this is important sexually—stretched legs show that she is taut and *trying*.

Pointed toes redouble the discomfort factor, and cut feet smaller still. Points plus heels aim at lightness, emphasizing the "animal" message—but also stylizing it. They give women an ethereal aspect by raising them from the earth and from common sense.

After the French Revolution the idea of using high heels to advertise status became embarrassing, and women and men went immediately into flats (very insubstantial ones if you were upper class). Men soon regained a small heel to secure the straps under their feet that held their trouserlegs tight. It was at this very date that ballerinas, heelless in ordinary life, took to dancing on points.

Fashion historians tell us that women don strong shoes, low heels, and round toes whenever society feels threatened and politics uncertain. They are a sure sign that people—men as well as women—are worried, and gearing up for a fight.

F.Y.I.

Alfred Hitchcock: (1899–1980) an English film director who is known for his ingenuity in terms of filmmaking and his ability to create suspense. His most famous films include *Psycho* (1960) and *The Birds* (1963).

nun's habits: the distinctive dress of a particular religious order, often a loose garment that covers a nun from her head to her ankles

pantograph: an instrument for copying a plan or drawing

Words to Build on

ethereal: light and airy, originating from the Greek word for ether

hobble: walk or move with a limp

mundane: dull or routine

sedately: to be calm, dignified, or unhurried

shod: past participle of "shoe," as in having or wearing shoes or other footwear

taut: tight or not slack, in referring to muscles or rope

totter: to stand or walk in an unsteady manner

undulate: have a wavy or rippling appearance

Tricks of the Trade

Introductory essay techniques

In Your Own Words: Comprehension

1. What were the reasons men wore high heels?

2. What is Visser's thesis or main idea?

3. What physiological changes happen when women wear high heels?

4. What are women's feet in high heels meant to emulate?

5. Why does Visser believe high heels came out of raised shoes?

6. When did upper-class people stop wearing heels and start wearing flat shoes?

7. Why do some consider small feet preferable on a woman?

In Your Own Words: Analysis

1. Why does Visser use Hitchcock's film to introduce her essay? What effect do you think this has on readers?

2. Men and women wore heels for different reasons. What is the main difference between why men wore high heels and why women wore high heels?

3. Do world events affect fashion and style, or is fashion merely frivolous?

4. Who is Visser's intended audience, and what is her purpose in writing this essay?

5. What does Visser mean when she states "[p]oints plus heels aim at lightness, emphasizing the 'animal' message but also stylizing it"?

6. Why type of essay is Visser's and why?

7. Explain the final paragraph of this essay.

❊ Now Write

1. Clothing is more than just a means of covering the naked body or a form of fashion and frivolity: clothing has power. Describe how clothing impacts both the wearer and those who see the wearer.

2. What are some animal terms used to describe women and men? Are there similarities in how these genders are viewed and the animal qualities and characteristics they represent, or are they completely different?

3. Write an essay in which you examine why historians would study fashion. What is your opinion on Visser's closing statement that footwear changes "whenever society feels threatened and politics are uncertain"?

Drew Hayden Taylor

Drew Hayden Taylor (b. 1962) is a writer, journalist, comic, documentarian, play-wright, and novelist. He is an Ojibway from the Curve Lake Nation. He has written 20 books in addition to plays, short stories, and magazine articles. He has also worked as a stand-up comedian, held the position of artistic director of Native Earth Performing Arts, and he has worked on documentaries exploring First Nations experience.

His identity "crisis" began when he was in his mid-twenties and he moved from the reserve to "the big bad city of Toronto." Having to navigate between two worlds is not easy; this is especially challenging in one's youth and if the two cultures possess divergent beliefs and attitudes. However, writing and getting older helped him overcome his issues and be more accepting of himself. In his writing, he "plays with" the rich traditions of European and Native cultures by drawing from the beliefs, storytelling methods, myths, and legends of both.

Like many comedians and satirists, Taylor is known to hold nothing sacred. What has been called his first "adult" novel, *Motorcycles and Sweetgrass,* was a finalist for the Governor General's Literary Award. The work is described by its publisher as "a story of magic, family, a mysterious intruder . . . and a band of marauding racoons." Taylor uses humour as a way to examine First Nations politics, identity, and culture. This work also encompasses the premise of how one can create a bridge between First Nations beliefs and traditions of the past and a vision of the future.

Drew Hayden Taylor can be found roaming the globe, preaching what he calls "the gospel of Native literature." For more information on Taylor and his work, visit his website at www.drewhaydentaylor.com.

In His Own Words

"I really like cooking. And it's ironically very similar to being a writer...you work hard, you labour long over something that other people will enjoy."

"I think [humour] is very important. During my time in Toronto it became rather obvious to me both in our literature and the dominant culture's literature and just in the media's representation, Canada often viewed Native people as being oppressed, depressed, and suppressed...like we were the tragic Indian, the vanishing Indian, the sad Indian and that was not my reality. I've been very fortunate to have travelled to over 130 Native communities across Canada and the United States and I saw positive things and for me one of the best ways to relate that is through humour It's my belief that it is our sense of humour that has allowed us to survive 500 years of colonization."

"As Native humorists, we aren't reinventing the wheel. What makes me laugh, will probably make you laugh, and what makes you laugh, will make me laugh. I go home at night and watch the *Simpsons* and have a good time. Funny is funny. Many people think

Native humour is a lot different, but really it isn't that different. Humour is exceedingly cross-cultural. Ninety-five per cent of the people who come to my plays are non-Native. For my comedies to work, the humour has to be universal. Let me give you an example: you have tandoori chicken, chicken cacciatore, you have McChicken. It's all chicken, but it's the spices you use to cook that chicken that give it its cultural uniqueness."

"There are differences between tribes, or even reserve to reserve. Some cultures have a very aggressive, in-your-face type of humour. You don't know if you want to laugh or punch them. This would describe the Mohawk, Iroquois, and Haida. Other nations are more subtle and practise around-the-corner humour, such as the Cree or Ojibway. Sometimes you don't know it's a joke until they start to laugh."

Before We Begin

1. Have you been mistaken for someone of another culture? How did that make you feel?
2. Have you ever assigned specific physical attributes or character traits to a certain ethnicity? Where did you acquire these notions?
3. Can humour unite people of different backgrounds? What are some examples of humour bridging differences between groups?

 **Now Read**

Pretty Like a White Boy: The Adventures of a Blue-Eyed Ojibway

In this big, huge world, with all its billions and billions of people, it's safe to say that everybody will eventually come across personalities and individuals that will touch them in some peculiar yet poignant way. Individuals that in some way represent and help define who you are. I'm no different—mine was Kermit the Frog. Not just because Natives have a long tradition of savouring frogs' legs, but because of his music. You all may remember Kermit is quite famous for his rendition of *It's Not Easy Being Green*. I can relate. If I could sing, my song would be *It's Not Easy Having Blue Eyes in a Brown Eyed Village*.

Yes, I'm afraid it's true. The author happens to be a card carrying Indian. Once you get past the aforementioned eyes, the fair skin, light brown hair, and noticeable lack of cheekbones, there lies the heart and spirit of an Ojibway storyteller. Honest "Injun," or as the more politically correct term may be, "Honest Aboriginal."

You see, I'm the product of a white father I never knew, and an Ojibway woman who evidently couldn't run fast enough. As a kid I knew I looked a bit different but, then again, all kids are paranoid when it comes to their peers. I had a fairly happy childhood, frolicking through the bulrushes. But there were certain things that, even then, made me notice my unusual appearance. Whenever we played cowboys and Indians, guess who had to be the bad guy (the cowboy)?

It wasn't until I left the reserve for the big bad city that I became more aware of the role people expected me to play, and the fact that physically I didn't fit in. Everybody seemed to have this preconceived idea of how every Indian looked and acted. One guy, on my first day of college, asked me what kind of horse I preferred. I didn't have the heart to tell him "hobby."

I've often tried to be philosophical about the whole thing. I have both White and Red blood in me, I guess that makes me pink. I am a "Pink Man." Try to imagine this: I'm walking around on any typical reserve in Canada, my head held high, proudly announcing to everyone, "I am a Pink Man." It's a good thing I ran track in school.

My pinkness is constantly being pointed out to me over and over and over again. "You don't look Indian?" "You're not Indian, are you?" "Really?!?!" I got questions like that from both White and Native people, for a while I debated having my Status card tattooed on my forehead.

And like most insecure people and especially a blue-eyed Native writer, I went through a particularly severe identity crisis at one point. In fact, I admit it, one depressing spring evening I died my hair black. Pitch black.

The reason for such a dramatic act, you may ask? Show business. You see, for the last eight years or so, I've worked in various capacities in the performing arts, and as a result I often get calls to be an extra or even try out for an important role in some Native-oriented movie. This anonymous voice would phone, having been given my number, and ask if I would be interested in trying out for a movie. Being a naturally ambitious, curious, and greedy young man, I would always readily agree, stardom flashing in my eyes and hunger pains from my wallet.

A few days later I would show up for the audition, and that was always an experience. What kind of experience you may ask? Picture this: the movie calls for the casting of seventeenth-century Mohawk warriors living in a traditional longhouse. The casting director calls the name Drew Hayden Taylor, and I enter. The casting director, the producer, and the film's director look up from the table and see my face, blue eyes flashing in anticipation. I once was described as a slightly chubby beach boy. But even beach boys have tans. Anyway, there would be a quick flush of confusion, a recheck of the papers, a hesitant "Mr. Taylor?" Then they would ask if I was at the right audition. It was always the same. By the way, I never got any of the parts I tried for, except for a few anonymous crowd shots. Politics tells me it's because of the way I look, reality tells me it's probably because I can't act. I'm not sure which is better.

It's not just film people either. Recently I've become quite involved in theatre—Native theatre to be exact. And one cold October day I was happily attending the Toronto leg of a province-wide tour of my first play, *Toronto at Dreamers Rock*. The place was sold out, the audience very receptive, and the performance was wonderful. Ironically one of the actors was also half-White. The director later told me he had been talking with the actor's father, an older non-Native chap. Evidently he had asked a few questions about me, and how I did my research. This made the director curious and asked about his interest. He replied, "He's got an amazing grasp of the Native situation for a white person."

Not all these incidents are work-related either. One time a friend and I were coming out of a rather upscale bar (we were out Yuppie watching) and managed to catch a cab. We thanked the cab driver for being so comfortably close on such a cold night, he shrugged and nonchalantly talked about knowing what bars to drive around. "If you're not careful, all you'll get is drunk Indians." I hiccuped.

Another time, the cab driver droned on and on about the government. He started out by criticizing Mulroney, and eventually to his handling of the Oka crisis. This perked up my ears, until he said "If it were me, I'd have tear-gassed the place by the second day. No more problems." He got a dime tip. A few incidents like this and I'm convinced I'd make a great undercover agent for one of the Native political organizations.

But then again, even Native people have been known to look at me with a fair amount of suspicion. Many years ago when I was a young man, I was working on a documentary on Native culture up in the wilds of Northern Ontario. We were at an isolated cabin filming a trapper woman and her kids. This one particular nine-year-old girl seemed to take a shine to me. She followed me around for two days both annoying me and endearing herself to me. But she absolutely refused to believe that I was Indian. The whole film crew tried to tell her but to no avail. She was certain I was white. Then one day as I was loading up the car with film equipment, she asked me if I wanted some tea. Being in a hurry I declined the tea. She immediately smiled with victory, crying out, "See, you're not Indian. All Indians drink tea!"

Frustrated and a little hurt I whipped out my Status card and thrust it at her. Now there I was, standing in a Northern Ontario winter, showing my Status card to a nine-year-old non-status Indian girl who had no idea what one was. Looking back, this may not have been one of my brighter moves.

But I must admit, it was a Native woman that boiled everything down in one simple sentence. You may know that woman—Marianne Jones from *The Beachcombers* television series. We were working on a film together out west and we got to gossiping. Eventually we got around to talking about our respective villages. Her village is on the Queen Charlotte Islands, or Haida Gwaii as the Haida call them, and mine in central Ontario.

Eventually, childhood on the reserve was being discussed and I made a comment about the way I look. She studied me for a moment, smiled, and said "Do you know what the old women in my village would call you?" Hesitant but curious, I shook my head. "They'd say you were pretty like a white boy." To this day I'm still not sure if I like that.

Now some may argue that I am simply a Metis with a Status card. I disagree—I failed French in Grade 11. And the Metis, as everyone knows, have their own separate and honourable culture, particularly in western Canada. And, of course, I am well aware that I am not the only person with my physical characteristics.

I remember once looking at a video tape of a drum group, shot on a reserve up near Manitoulin Island. I noticed one of the drummers seemed quite fair-haired, almost blond. I mentioned this to my girlfriend of the time and she shrugged saying, "Well, that's to be expected. The highway runs right through the reserve." Perhaps I'm being too critical. There's a lot to be said for both cultures. For example, on the one hand, you have the Native respect for Elders. They understand the concept of wisdom and insight coming with age.

On the White hand, there's Italian food. I mean I really love my mother and family but seriously, does anything really beat good veal scallopine? Most of my Aboriginal friends share my fondness for this particular type of food. Wasn't there a warrior at Oka named Lasagna? I found it ironic, though curiously logical, that Columbus was Italian. A connection I wonder?

Also, Native people have this wonderful respect and love for the land. They believe they are part of it, a mere link in the cycle of existence. Now as many of you know, this conflicts with the accepted Judeo-Christian i.e., western view of land management. I even believe somewhere in the first chapters of the Bible it says something about God giving man dominion over nature. Check it out, Genesis 4 (?): Thou shalt clear cut. So I grew up understanding that everything around me is important and alive. My Native heritage gave me that.

And again, on the White hand, there's breast implants. Darn clever them White people. That's something Indians would never have invented, seriously. We're not ambitious enough. We just take what the Creator decides to give us, but no, not the White man. Just imagine it, some serious looking White (and let's face it people, we know it was a man who invented them) doctor sitting around in his laboratory muttering to himself, "Big tits, big tits, hmmm, how do I make big tits?" If it was an Indian, it would be "Big tits, big tits, white women sure got big tits," and leave it at that.

So where does that leave me on the big philosophical score board? What exactly are my choices again? Indian—respect for elders, love of the land. White people—food and big tits. In order to live in both cultures I guess I'd have to find an Indian woman with big tits who lives with her grandmother in a cabin out in the woods and can make fettuccini alfredo on a wood stove.

Now let me make this clear—I'm not writing this for sympathy, or out of anger, or even some need for self-glorification. I am just setting the facts straight. For as you read this, a new Nation is born. This is a declaration of independence, my declaration of independence.

I've spent too many years explaining who and what I am repeatedly, so as of this moment, I officially secede from both races. I plan to start my own separate nation. Because I am half Ojibway, and half Caucasian, we will be called the Occasions. And of course, since I'm founding the new nation, I will be a Special Occasion.

F.Y.I.

card carrying Indian: Taylor is referring to the identity card the Government of Canada issues to Aboriginal people, formally known as a Certificate of Indian Status, or Status card. The card includes a photo, name, birthdate, and the person's Nation.

Haida: a member of an Aboriginal people living on the west coast of Canada

Honest Injun: an American expression used to emphasize the truth of a statement, but considered offensive when used. "Injun" is a corruption of the word "Indian," and the expression was originally thought to be one of sarcastic derision. Children in the 1950s used to swear oaths or make promises using this expression.

longhouse: a dwelling of the Iroquois peoples that is shared by several families. Traditionally, the longhouse belonged to the women of the family and upon marriage the husband moved into the wife's longhouse.

Metis: The Metis are an Aboriginal group with a distinct history, language, culture, and territory that includes the waterways of Ontario, areas surrounding the Great Lakes, and the historic Northwest. The Metis are descended from Native women and European men. The children of these unions were of mixed ancestry and became a new group of Aboriginal people called the Metis.

Mohawk: one of the five original Nations of the Iroquois Federation. The territory of the Mohawks is eastern Ontario, southern Quebec, and northern New York. As original members of the Iroquois League, the Mohawk protected the Iroquois Confederation against invasion for hundreds of years.

Ojibway: name of an Algonquian people living around Lake Superior and certain adjacent areas. The term also can refer to the language spoken by these people.

Oka: The Oka Crisis was a land dispute between the Mohawk nation and the town of Oka, Quebec, in 1990. The town was developing plans to expand a golf course and residential development onto the land belonging to the Mohawk that included a burial ground of their ancestors. The Mohawk community erected a barricade blocking access to the area and the Canadian government eventually called in the military. The Oka Crisis lasted 78 days and one soldier was killed. The town finally cancelled the golf course expansion.

reserve: an area of land set aside for the use of a specific group of Aboriginal people

Yuppie: 'YUP' is an acronym coined in the 1980s that stands for "young urban professional."

Words to Build on

bulrushes: a tall water plant

hobby: refers to a hobby horse, which is a child's toy consisting of a long stick with a figure of a horse's head on one end

Tricks of the Trade

Rhetorical strategies

Tone

Types of essays: Definition

In Your Own Words: Comprehension

1. How does Taylor describe his childhood?

2. What happened when Taylor left the reserve for the city?

3. What does Taylor do during his identity crisis? Why does he do this?

4. Why does Taylor want to be in "show business," and why does he have trouble getting parts in films?

5. How does Taylor define white culture? How does he describe Native culture?

6. Explain what Taylor means by "I found it ironic, though curiously logical, that Columbus was Italian. A connection I wonder?"

7. Why would Taylor make a "great undercover agent for one of the Native political organizations"? What specific incidents make him think this?

In Your Own Words: Analysis

1. Explain the title of Taylor's essay.

2. What is Taylor's thesis?

3. What kinds of support does Taylor use for his essay? Are his examples effective?

4. What tone is used in this essay? Is it effective?

5. What is the difference between Taylor's use of the terms "Pink Man" and "Occasion"? Does he prefer one over the other as a way to define himself?

6. Do you find Taylor's use of humour in his essay funny? Give examples to show why or why not.

7. Does Taylor seem to identify more with his Native heritage or with his non-Native heritage? Be sure to support your answer with examples from the essay.

8. Are there any sections of Taylor's essay that you find disturbing or offensive? If so, why?

9. Did your ideas of what it is to be Native or biracial change after reading Taylor's essay?

Now Write

1. "Pretty Like a White Boy" is a definition essay. Write an essay in which you explain whether Taylor has successfully "defined" who he is for the reader and whether his definition involves objective or subjective details.

2. Both Drew Hayden Taylor and Pat Capponi focus on judging others by their appearances. How are their experiences similar and how are they different? Write an essay in which you compare these points and how each writer responds to being judged by his or her appearance.

3. Is humour really cross-cultural? Consider Taylor's quotes on humour in the "In His Own Words" section. Write an essay and use examples to argue whether humour can bridge cultural gaps and challenge racism and bigotry.

Pat Capponi

Pat Capponi (b. 1949) is a writer and well-known mental health advocate whose life and work reflect her strong beliefs in speaking out for those who have become marginalized in cities. A great deal of her adult life was spent in and out of hospitals and shabby rooming houses in downtown Toronto. She has since turned things around with her writing and has become a voice for the poor and those with mental health issues. An author of five works of non-fiction, most notably *Upstairs in the Crazy House* (1992) and *Dispatches from the Poverty Line* (1997), her current work is a series of mysteries set in Toronto's Parkdale neighbourhood based around characters who live in a boarding house. Her protagonist, Dana Leoni, the impoverished and unwitting sleuth of the series, is so much like Capponi that she often refers to Leoni as "me." Capponi says, "She's basically me, only she's young and straight and doesn't wear a cowboy hat." In this excerpt from *Dispatches from the Poverty Line*, the misunderstandings and miscommunications between those of different socioeconomic classes are examined when people come together on committees to solve serious issues in communities.

In Her Own Words

"As a leader, you have to show people that if you do something you're not going to get 'killed.' They watch. So I went first. At meetings with media, I learned a lot. I learned that you don't look at people's diagnosis before you know the person. It was a good lesson. I was lucky. I got to meet people, talk with people, and not know what was supposed to be wrong with them. Because then you see the whole person before you see the illness."

"I want to make people more human. It's not that we're all noble savages, because we're not. But in the main, all in all, we're pretty decent people."

Before We Begin

1. How do people form stereotypes? Have you ever been stereotyped?

2. In what types of situations do people of different classes typically get the opportunity to meet or socialize in our time?

3. Have you ever wanted to help in a situation but could not? What stopped you from taking a step towards action? Alternatively, when was there a time when you knew you had to take action and did so?

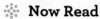 **Now Read**

from *Dispatches from the Poverty Line*

We live in a time when manipulation of public opinion has been elevated to a science, when stereotypes are accepted as true representatives of their segment of the population. And, as always, stereotypes cause a great deal of pain to those tarred with the same brush . . . .

I am not innocent as far as taking refuge in stereotypes goes. As much as I try to catch myself at it, on occasion I'm forced to admit to myself, and sometimes to others, that I've fallen prey to its comforting lure.

I've served on many committees, task forces, working groups, and boards in my 17 years of mental health advocacy. Before consumer involvement became more widely accepted, I was often the only ex-patient at the table, trying to deal with hospital administrators, bureaucrats, psychiatrists, nurses, and family groups. I didn't think any board could scare me again, or silence me through intimidation.

I was, however, being forced to admit that one hospital board in particular was giving me a great deal of angst. It left me feeling as though I'd been flung back through time . . . I used to tell audiences of consumers and mental health staff that one of our biggest problems was that there was no consensus in the system concerning the value of involving clients in the management and delivery of services. One day I'd be working with an agency that possessed the equivalent of New York sophistication around the issues, and the next I'd feel as though I were in Alabama before the civil rights movement got under way. It wasn't unusual for these opposites to be within a few city blocks of each other.

That was part of my problem with this board, that it was Alabama-like while believing itself to be cutting edge. But there was more. There were deep and obvious class distinctions, and even though I was, at the time, gainfully employed, a published author, someone who possessed the respect of my community, I felt intimidated, looked down on, stereotyped and all the rest. It got so that I had to force myself to attend.

The board was a status board, composed of high-powered bankers, lawyers, publishers, and consultants, as well as hospital executives. I was the only one in jeans, in a hat. I was the only one from my particular class and background. I was the only voice expressing criticism of the liberal establishment we were running.

It was dreadful. Meetings were corporate; when I would leave for a cigarette I felt I should be bowing and backing up to the door. Nobody laughed, it seemed, ever. Nobody talked out of turn.

Then, one afternoon when I had screwed up my courage to attend, I bumped into the "fat cat" lawyer in the hallway. He made a joke, and I made one back before I had time to think about it. We both laughed, and I thought we both stared at each other, surprised at the unlikely evidence of a sense of humour beneath the stereotype. Ice got broken. Then the banker who had offered me lifts home before, which I'd declined—what would I have to talk to him about in the car?—offered again, and I accepted. I even teased him about his brand new BMW and the pervasive smell of leather from the seats. He demonstrated how his car phone responded to voice orders to dial numbers, and I confess I got a kick out of the gimmickry . . . .

I remember another kind of breakthrough event at that board. I was trying once again to explain why I needed more people like me (from my class and experience) around the table. How easy it was to get intimidated in the setting we were in, if you didn't find the corporate air invigorating. How easy it was to dismiss the views I was putting forward because it was only me they were hearing them from. How our class differences, our life experiences, created gulfs between us.

My banker friend took umbrage. He was sure, he said, that he was quite capable of relating to me as a person, as another human being. He felt we were operating on a level playing field, and that I wasn't giving them enough credit.

My lawyer friend then made a remarkable statement.

"That's not true," he said. "Pat didn't start out on a level playing field with me. I took one look at her and summed her up. It wasn't until later that I started to see her differently."

"And I," I said, "did the same thing, summed up you guys at a glance, and what I felt was your attitude towards me. It got easier to walk around with a chip on my shoulder than to try and relate to you."

Even the publisher chimed in: "I understand what you mean about intimidation. I never saw myself as intimidating, I like to think I'm an easygoing, friendly guy. But some of my staff have been pointing out to me that people who work for me don't have that same picture, because I have power over them. It's not easy or comfortable to realize that you may scare people, but a lot of times it's true."

Only the banker held out for the level playing field precept, but of course the conversation was ruled out of order and we were on to the next item on the agenda.

A month or two later, I decided to transfer my bank account to a branch nearer my residence. To get an account in the first place had been a challenge. I don't have credit cards, or a driver's licence: therefore, I don't have a system-recognized identity.

This is a very common dilemma for those who make up the underclass, and it accounts for the prevalence and huge success of Money Mart cheque-cashing services in poor areas. As long as I've been an advocate, various groups of workers have tried to break through the banking system, to work out generally acceptable ways of identifying clients to tellers through letters of introduction, or special cards, with no real success . . . .

In order for me to get an account in the first place, my publisher, Cynthia Good, had to take me into her branch, where we met with her "personal banking representative," and on the basis of Cynthia's knowledge of me, I got an account in time to deposit the cheque I'd received for the movie rights to my book.

I confess I felt quite mainstream for a while, with my PIN number and cheques and account book, as though I'd arrived. It was enough to make me overconfident. I decided it was silly to travel 40 minutes to that branch when there was one a few blocks from me. I still had a balance of a little over $5000, so I didn't anticipate any problems.

I walked into my local branch and was soon seated across from yet another "personal banking representative."

"What can I do for you today?" she asked, pleasantly.

"I'd like to transfer my account to here, please," I responded, handing over my account book and bank card.

"I see, um, would you have some identification?"

I was puzzled.

"Nothing you guys seem to accept. But I only want to transfer, not open, an account."

She persists:

"A major credit card? A driver's licence?"

I have a birth certificate. I remember trying to rent a video using it, and the owner of the store turning the card over and saying, "Your signature's not on it."

I shake my head. I give her the card of the other personal banking representative, the one in whose presence I had been validated.

She phones. She shakes her head. That person is on vacation. She purses her lips, not liking to create difficulties for me, but there are rules.

"I'm sorry, we really do need identification."

I'm getting angry, and I suspect she feels it, which accounts for her visible nervousness. It won't help to get snippy with her. I could just pack it in and leave—it wouldn't be the end of the world, after all. But the battle for reason is under way. It would feel too much like defeat to withdraw now.

I try for a reasoned, measured tone.

"I don't want to withdraw anything. I have $5000 in my account. You have my card, my cheques, my account book."

I hear steps behind me, I'm sure the security guard is getting ready to pounce.

"It's a different branch of the same bank. C'mon, be reasonable."

"Don't you even have your Indian Status Card?"

"I'm not Indian!"

Ordinarily, I would take it as a compliment, being mistaken for one of the First People, but in this context, I know there's some heavy stereotyping, and quite possibly some heavy attitude, going on.

I get a flash. I'm terrible about names, remembering names. I can recall most minute details of conversations, mannerisms, backgrounds, and clothing but not names. But I do remember the division my BMW banker is president of. And I do remember it's this same corporation.

I ask her to look up the name of the guy in charge of ——.

"Why?" she asks, immediately suspicious.

"I know him, he can tell you I exist."

Perhaps to humour me, she flips open a book and recites some names.

"That's him," I cry, vindicated. "Give him a call, will you?"

I suppose it's like telling a private to ring up a general at the request of a possible lunatic, an Aboriginal impersonator: it's not done.

She excuses herself to consult with a superior. Long minutes pass. I feel myself examined from the glassed-in cubicles where the decision makers sit. I feel the breath of the security officer. I feel renewed determination.

She's back.

"I'm sorry about the delay. His secretary had some difficulty reaching him, he's in a meeting. But he is available now."

My understanding smile is as false and strained as her apology.

She picks up the phone and annoyingly turns her chair away from me while she speaks in low tones into the receiver. A few heartbeats, then she passes the phone to me.

Not waiting for his voice, I say:

"I told you there's no level playing field."

He laughs, loudly and honestly.

In under 10 minutes, I have my new account, my new card, cheques, and a small degree of satisfaction.

Chalk up one for the good guys.

I take refuge in a nearby park, liking and needing the sun and a place to enjoy it. I've checked out the four or five in my neighbourhood, and on days when I need to walk, I go up to the one opposite the Dufferin Mall. I love the solitude, the birds, the green—a perfect setting for reading and tanning. Picking an empty bench, away from small clumps of people dotting the large park, I open my paperback and disappear into it.

It doesn't seem very long (my watch died a few months ago) before an old fellow, tottering on his cane, shuffles towards me. I look up at his approach, smile briefly, and dive back into P.D. James. I am dismayed when he chooses to perch on the other end of my bench, and I try to ignore his presence while my conscience starts bothering me. Now, I only smiled at him because I am aware that some folks think I look a bit tough, and I didn't want him worrying, but he might have mistaken the gesture for a come-chat-with-me invitation. He's probably lonely, isolated, this is probably his big daily outing. Would it kill me to spend a couple of minutes talking to him? Damn.

I close my book, look over at him looking over at me expectantly.

"Beautiful day, isn't it?"

I can barely make out his reply, cloaked in a thick accent, but his head bobbing up and down is pretty clear. I'm stuck for the next sentence, he keeps going enthusiastic-ally. I make out his name, repeating it triumphantly: "Victor! Hi, I'm Pat."

One arthritic hand grasps mine briefly, then goes back to rest on his cane with the other one.

"I'm retired." He's getting better at speaking clearly, maybe it was just a lack of op-portunity that made him rusty. "I was an engineer."

"You live around here?"

He turns painfully, pointing vaguely over his shoulder.

"Right over there, a beautiful place. Very beautiful place."

"Good for you."

I offer him a cigarette, which he accepts, and we sit in companionable silence in the sun. I'm thinking after the smoke I will move on, find another park, maybe nearer my home.

He's talking again, and when I realize what he's saying my jaw drops open.

"If you come see my place, I will give you twenty dollars."

"Jesus Christ! Are you crazy?" I'm so annoyed, and shocked, and thrown off balance by his offer, that I'm blustering. I want to whack him, except he'd probably fall over, like the dirty-old-man character on *Laugh-In*.

"Listen to me," I lecture, as I shake a finger in his face. "First off, you're committing a crime. Secondly, it's stupid and dangerous for you. You can't go around offering money to people you don't know for things I don't want to think about. You've insulted me. I could have you arrested! Do you understand?"

Now I'm pretty sure what his daily tour of the park is about, and I worry about the school-age girls that hang out at lunch time.

"If I see you doing this to anyone else, I will report you, do you get that? I'll be watching you!"

He's stuttering out an apology, which I don't believe, and I refrain from kicking his cane, though I really want to.

On my way home, in between feeling outraged and feeling dirtied, I start to laugh at my own stereotyping of a lonely old man in need of conversation in juxtaposition with his own stereotyping of me.

People ought to wear summing-up signs sometimes, just so you'd know what to expect.

F.Y.I.

fat cat: colloquial expression used here to mean a person who is well-to-do or exceedingly successful and shows little concern about those who are not

Laugh-In: an American sketch comedy show that aired from 1968 to 1973

mental health advocacy: individuals or agencies that are working to improve the lives of people with some type of mental illness

Words to Build on

angst: anxiety

took umbrage: to become upset, insulted, or angered by something

Tricks of the Trade

Rhetorical strategies

Types of essays: Comparison and contrast

Types of essays: Illustration

In Your Own Words: Comprehension

1. What is Capponi's thesis statement?

2. How does she begin this piece? What would you call the introductory technique she uses?

3. What does the expression "tarred with the same brush" mean?

4. How does Capponi connect to the "'fat cat' lawyer"?

5. What makes a person intimidating according to the article?

6. What is the "level playing field precept" Capponi refers to?

7. Summarize Capponi's bank account situation.

8. Why can the banking representative not transfer Capponi's account?

9. How is the bank account situation resolved?

10. Do you think Capponi is happy about the way the bank account situation is resolved?

In Your Own Words: Analysis

1. Capponi compares the style of two different committees—one New York–like and the other Alabama-like. What are the characteristics of each, and why does she use these categories?

2. State what Capponi thinks is one of the "biggest problems" when it comes to mental health services. Why would this be such an important factor?

3. Based on the information given in the article, what does Capponi look like? Would you judge her based on her looks? Why or why not?

4. Capponi shows how the banker and the lawyer on this committee disagree. Whom do you side with and why? Do most of us "sum people up" with one look?

5. Capponi uses a great deal of dialogue in this article. Why would writers who write non-fiction pieces use dialogue to describe encounters and events like those who write fiction?

6. What does Capponi think the elderly man at the end of the article is looking for? Do you think she is right in her assumption of what he wants?

7. What resolution does Capponi come to about stereotypes?

Now Write

1. Capponi mentions at least three instances where she is stereotyped in this article. Explain each situation. Are they based on class, gender, or ethnicity?

2. There are many situations both in school and in the workplace when people of different experiences, talents, and abilities are required to work together to accomplish some type of task. Write an essay answering the following questions: what guidelines help a group work at its best? What can hinder a group's progress?

3. Stereotypes are used as staples in television and movies. What are some stereotypes that you can readily think of that you have seen in movies or on television? Write an essay identifying some of these stereotypes from movies and/or television. Why do people involved in these mediums continue to use stereotypes?

Kenneth J. Harvey

Kenneth J. Harvey (b. 1962) was born in St. John's, Newfoundland. An award-winning and internationally bestselling author, Harvey has been called "Canada's literary bad boy" because of his biting and no-holds-barred style. In addition to his well-received fiction (his award-winning novel *Blackstrap Hawco* was voted one of the best books of the decade 2000–2009 by Amazon.ca), Harvey has had numerous editorials and essays appear on CBC Radio and in Canadian newspapers and journals. In addition, he sits on the board of directors of the Ottawa International Writers Festival. The essay "Virtual Adultery" examines the idea that video and online pornography are not just detached and innocent forms of fantasy and escapism.

In His Own Words

"The media is the great watering hole where every pompous ego sidles up to lap up the glory of his or her own reflection. Every arrogant insecure self-righteous loudmouth also pisses in the same pool."

"I—for one—suspect that there is nothing as repressive, nothing as thwarting, nothing as abnormal and beastly as the pretence of perfection."

"The world of electronic entertainment has revolutionized our concepts of fantasy. Decades ago, motion pictures began entrancing us, filling our minds with preconceived images, edging personal imagination towards a dark, less-involved corner of the consciousness and replacing it with a communal cinematic imagination."

Before We Begin

1. Can men be anti-pornography advocates?
2. How do you define adultery? Are emotional affairs the same as physical affairs?
3. Is pornography a harmless recreational activity?

 **Now Read**

Virtual Adultery

How many women do you meet secretly every day? When your wife or girlfriend is out working, buying groceries, or running to the video store for a movie? You have these women hidden in your home. You have kept them out of sight, until you can be alone with them. When your wife is safely gone, you engage in sexual activity with these women, right in your living room or even—shamelessly—in your marriage bed. You meet with them wherever there is a television and a video machine, or a computer screen.

Adultery is defined in the *Scribner–Bantam English Dictionary* as "sexual relations between two persons either of whom is married to another."

"Sexual relations" are not necessarily *physical* encounters. One can have relations with another through verbal or electronic contact. Sex is largely in the mind, and a man utilizes all of his God-given talents of imagination to prompt the video or computer relationship into a "real life" involvement.

Most relationships are well over 90 per cent psychological or emotional (that is, mental) and 10 per cent physical. Simply add up the amount of time spent in the raptures of sex with your wife (or husband. This applies equally to women) and the percentage will drop well below 10 per cent. Even having physically reciprocated sex for one hour per day—every day of your life—means your relationship is comprised of only 4 per cent physical sex. The remaining 96 per cent is in the mind. And there are countless relationships that even devote the full 100 percentage points to the psychological and emotional. In other words, some couples just don't have sex.

A relationship is often difficult to define, to put one's finger on. It can be as subtle and intangible as a video transmission signal, or the pulse of images from a television screen.

For example, a man develops a psychological attachment to the female companion he is viewing in an X-rated video. If there was no psychological (emotional) trueness then there would be no point in carrying out the exercise. It would merely be a bland biological act, less elevating and exciting. And if it were merely a biological act of relief then no video woman would be required for the fruitless solitary act that lacks the possibility of procreation. There is an emotional relationship, as well as a sexual one, going on between the man and his virtual partner.

This is what compounds the mere biological state of excitation. It is this psychological actuality of having sexual relations with another woman, this sense of adventure, of illicitness, that fuels the man's compulsive urge to cheat with her (and countless others) again and again, behind his wife's back.

Because we are creatures who seek out the most convenient, labour-efficient ways of accomplishing any task, we have fashioned a handy expedient way to perform adultery. We have manufactured a grey area that reasons the guilt out of existence, that sanctions and satisfies our urge to bed other women, to discover and investigate the physiological differences of a multitude of bodies.

Video is accessible to all. There is no risk of disease, no day-to-day complications. But it is attachment all the same. A man becomes intimate with these women, holds them longingly in his mind, and returns to the ones he most admires innumerable times throughout his life. And they—in keeping with the nature of a relationship— openly welcome him into their passionate arms.

It could be argued that a video woman is not actually "real." But—if so—then wouldn't that argument then validate the point that pornography makes objects of women? If these video women are not considered "real" (solid living flesh and blood) then they must be objects, used merely for the gratification of men's sexual urges. Then again, why would a man wish to objectify a woman, to make her one-dimensional when the purpose is to have her appear as "real" as possible? The more "real" the image, the greater the thrill. Eyes glued to the screen, taking in every detail to simulate and thus boost reality.

Objectification is not the argument here. The key words are "sexual relations." Women in X-rated videos speak to the viewer, customize their actions to suit the viewer's wishes. And with the advent of virtual reality and *interactive* computer pornography the boudoir scene takes another step nearer reciprocation.

A man does—indeed—have sexual relations with the women at the receiving end of his mental advances. Why else would the tapes be kept secret, hidden away in a top drawer, the computer screen nestled away behind locked doors, unless there was the implication of contact and—succeeding contact—the withering afterglow of guilt?

The sale of video pornography is a multibillion dollar business. With figures as high as these, the real question is: who is *not* cheating on their wives? A man—with his private stock of video women—might think he is not committing adultery. He might even pride himself on the fact that he's remained faithful all these years. Yet he holds the most intimate and explicit actions of particular women in his mind. He recognizes the sounds of their voices. He knows the details of their faces and the contours of their naked bodies. He compares his secret companions with his wife: their looks, their differences in sexual technique.

How could a man possibly engage in such comparisons, unless privileged to the information gathered from his involvement in various adulterous relationships?

F.Y.I.

video store, video machine, and video tape: Harvey's essay was written before the invention of Blu-ray technology, downloading/streaming capabilities, or DVDs. Video refers to the VHS format once used for movies.

Words to Build on

afterglow: a pleasant effect or feeling that lingers after something enjoyable is done, experienced, or achieved

boudoir: a woman's private sitting room, dressing room, or bedroom

compounds: to intensify or make stronger

raptures: an expression of ecstatic feeling

reciprocation: the act of making or doing something in return

Tricks of the Trade

Rhetorical strategies

Types of essays: Argumentative

In Your Own Words: Comprehension

1. According to Harvey, where can one meet women every day?

2. What are the different ways a person can have "relations" with another person?

3. What has been created with online pornography?

4. According to the essay, what are some of the advantages of online "relations"?

5. What is the problem with the argument that online women are not "real"?

6. What are the writer's main ideas and thesis? Where do they appear?

7. Why does "a man—with his private stock of video women" commit adultery if he hasn't been physically intimate with another woman?

In Your Own Words: Analysis

1. How does the author begin this essay? Is it effective?

2. What makes this an argumentative essay?

3. What type of evidence does Harvey use? Is it all the same? Is it convincing?

4. Who is Harvey's target audience?

5. How does the writer end this essay? Is it an effective ending?

6. This article was written in 1998. Have things changed since then regarding pornography?

7. What are some of the problems associated with pornography?

Now Write

1. How do North Americans view adultery? What are these ideas based on? Do they relate to biology or are they cultural?

2. Write an essay responding to Harvey's argument. Do you agree or disagree with him?

3. According to the excerpt from Jean Vanier's book *Becoming Human*, many people deal with loneliness through various addictions. With reference to both Vanier and Harvey, examine how pornography can increase feelings of separation and loneliness in people.

Jean Vanier

Jean Vanier (b. 1928) has been called "a Canadian who inspires the world" and has dedicated his life to illuminating the idea that global change can happen when people gather and build community with others, such as the poor and those with developmental disabilities, whom society has marginalized. This philosopher and humanitarian is the founder of the international community, L'Arche, which has become a living example of Vanier's beliefs.

Vanier was born in Geneva, Switzerland, where his father, the nineteenth Governor General of Canada, Major-General Georges Vanier, was sent on a diplomatic assignment. His parents would set an early example of lives lived in service to others. He convinced his father to let him join England's Royal Naval Academy at the age of 13. While too young to serve in active duty, he worked with his mother for the Red Cross in aiding concentration camp survivors returning to Paris after its liberation. At the age of 17, Vanier was given an officer's commission, but he would resign the commission just five years later after realizing that he was being called to more than just a glamorous naval career. While studying theology and philosophy at the Institut Catholique in Paris, he met a Dominican priest and professor, Father Thomas Philippe, who later became a chaplain at an institution for men called Val Fleury in Trosly-Breuil, France. Leaving a professorship at the University of Toronto to join Father Thomas at Val Fleury, Vanier was greatly moved and saddened by the isolated and lonely existence of not only the residents of the institution but of the general treatment of people with developmental disabilities at the time. He felt "called" to purchase a small house that he named "L'Arche" and invite two men he had met at other institutions to come live and share their lives together. That was the beginning of the L'Arche communities, the Faith and Light/Faith and Sharing movements, and the International Federation of L'Arche, which are all committed to creating societies that are built on compassion and inclusivity.

"Loneliness" is taken from Vanier's book *Becoming Human* (1998), in which Vanier published his CBC Massey Lectures. It addresses not only the often tragic results of treating loneliness as though it were a disease, but also provides ways in which we can learn to embrace loneliness and use it to better understand ourselves and, more importantly, others, recognizing that this is the first step in creating community.

In His Own Words

"We have to remind ourselves constantly that we are not saviours. We are simply a tiny sign, among thousands of others, that love is possible, that the world is not condemned to a struggle between oppressors and oppressed, that class and racial warfare is not inevitable."

"This evolution towards a real responsibility for others is sometimes blocked by fear. It is easier to stay on the level of a pleasant way of life in which we keep our freedom and our distance. But that means that we stop growing and shut ourselves up in our own small concerns and pleasures."

"Individualistic material progress and the desire to gain prestige by coming out on top have taken over from the sense of fellowship, compassion, and community. Now people live more or less on their own in a small house, jealously guarding their goods and planning to acquire more, with a notice on the gate that says, 'Beware of the Dog'."

Before We Begin

1. Have you ever been struck with a feeling of loneliness while you were surrounded by other people? Is it possible to feel lonely while in a crowd?
2. Have you ever spent too much money, ate too much, or drank too much and afterwards wondered why you acted that way?
3. Are there any activities that you have never done or would never consider doing alone? What are they? Why do you feel this way?

 **Now Read**

from *Becoming Human*

Loneliness

This book is about the liberation of the human heart from the tentacles of chaos and loneliness, and from those fears that provoke us to exclude and reject others. It is a liberation that opens us up and leads us to the discovery of our common humanity. I want to show that this discovery is a journey from loneliness to a love that transforms, a love that grows in and through belonging, a belonging that can include as well as exclude. The discovery of our common humanity liberates us from self-centred compulsions and inner hurts; it is the discovery that ultimately finds its fulfillment in forgiveness and in loving those who are our enemies. It is the process of truly becoming human.

This book is not essentially about the formation and organization of society; it is not essentially political in scope. But since society is made up of individuals, as we open up to others and allow ourselves to be concerned with their condition, then the society in which we live must also change and become more open. We will begin to work together for the common good. On the other hand, if we commit ourselves to the making of a society in which we are concerned only with our own rights, then that society must become more and more closed in on itself. Where we do not feel any responsibility towards others, there is no reason for us to work harmoniously towards the common good.

Over the last 34 years, my experience has been primarily with men and women who have intellectual disabilities. In August 1964, I founded L'Arche: a network of small homes and communities where we live together, men and women with intellectual disabilities and those who feel called to share their lives with them. Today, there are over 100 L'Arche communities in the world. Living in L'Arche, I have discovered a lot about loneliness, belonging, and the inner pain that springs from a sense of rejection. Community life with men and women who have intellectual disabilities has taught me a great deal about what it means to be human. To some, it may sound strange for me to say that it is the weak, and those who have been excluded from society, who have been my teachers. I hope that I can reveal a bit of what I have learned—and am still learning—about being human, and about helping others to discover our common humanity.

It was only in L'Arche that I really discovered what loneliness is. There were probably many times before L'Arche when I had felt lonely but until then I had not seen loneliness as a painful reality, maybe because I had succeeded in keeping myself busy by doing things. Perhaps I had never named it or needed to give it a name.

When I started welcoming those with intellectual disabilities into L'Arche, men and women from institutions, psychiatric hospitals, dysfunctional families, I began to realize how lonely they were. I discovered the terrible feeling of chaos that comes from extreme loneliness.

A sense of loneliness can be covered up by the things we do as we seek recognition and success. This is surely what I did as a young adult. It is what we all do. We all have this drive to do things that will be seen by others as valuable, things that will make us feel good about ourselves and give us a sense of being alive. We only become aware of loneliness at times when we cannot perform or when imagination seems to fail us.

Loneliness can appear as a faint disease, an inner dissatisfaction, a restlessness in the heart.

Loneliness comes at any time. It comes in times of sickness or when friends are absent; it comes during sleepless nights when the heart is heavy, during times of failure at work or in relationships; it comes when we lose trust in ourselves and in others. In old age, loneliness can rise up and threaten to overwhelm us. At such times, life can lose its meaning. Loneliness can feel like death.

When people are physically well, performing creatively, successful in their lives, loneliness seems absent. But I believe that loneliness is something essential to human nature; it can only be covered over, it can never actually go away. Loneliness is part of being human because there is nothing in existence that can completely fulfill the needs of the human heart.

Loneliness in one form is, in fact, essential to our humanity. Loneliness can become a source of creative energy, the energy that drives us down new paths to create new things or to seek more truth and justice in the world. Artists, poets, mystics, prophets, those who do not seem to fit into the world or the ways of society, are frequently lonely. They feel themselves to be different, dissatisfied with the status quo and with mediocrity; dissatisfied with our competitive world where so much energy goes into ephemeral things. Frequently, it is the lonely man or woman who revolts against injustice and seeks new ways. It is as if a fire is burning within them, a fire fuelled by loneliness.

Loneliness is the fundamental force that urges mystics to a deeper union with God. For such people, loneliness has become intolerable, but, instead of slipping into apathy or anger, they use the energy of loneliness to seek God. It pushes them towards the absolute. An experience of God quenches this thirst for the absolute, but at the same time, paradoxically, whets it because this is an experience that can never be total; by necessity, the knowledge of God is always practical. So loneliness opens up mystics to a desire to love each and every human being as God loves them.

Loneliness, then, can be a force for good. More frequently, however, loneliness shows other, less positive faces. It can be a source of apathy and depression, and even of a desire to die. It can push us into escapes and addictions in the need to forget our inner pain and emptiness. This apathy is how loneliness most often shows itself in the elderly and in those with disabilities. It is the loneliness we find in those who fall into depression, who have lost the sense of meaning in their lives, who are asking the question born of despair: What is left?

I once visited a psychiatric hospital that was a kind of warehouse of human misery. Hundreds of children with severe disabilities were lying, neglected, on their cots. There was a deadly silence. Not one of them was crying. When they realize that nobody cares, that nobody will answer them, children no longer cry. It takes too much energy. We cry out only when there is hope that someone may hear us.

Such loneliness is born of the most complete and utter depression, from the bottom of the deepest pit in which the human soul can find itself. The loneliness that engenders depression manifests itself as chaos. There is confusion, and coming out of this confusion there can be a desire for self-destruction, for death. So, loneliness can become agony, a scream of pain. There is no light, no consolation, no touch of peace and of the joy life brings. Such loneliness reveals the true meaning of chaos.

Life no longer flows in recognizable patterns. For the person engulfed in this form of loneliness there is only emptiness, anguish, and inner agitation; there are no yearnings, no desires to be fulfilled, no desire to live. Such a person feels completely cut off from everyone and everything. It is a life turned in upon itself. All order is gone, and those in this chaos are unable to relate or listen to others. Their lives seem to have no meaning. They live in complete confusion, closed up in themselves.

Thus loneliness can become such uncontrolled anguish that one can easily slip into the chaos of madness.

Let me tell you some stories, from my own experience, of the damage loneliness can create. I met Eric for the first time in 1977. He was in the children's ward of the local psychiatric hospital, 40 kilometres from the L'Arche community in Trosly, France. He was blind and deaf, as well as severely intellectually disabled; he could neither walk nor eat by himself. He came to L'Arche at the age of 16, full of tremendous needs, anguish, and fears. He often sat on the ground, and whenever he felt someone close by, would stretch out his arms and try to clutch that person and to climb up on them. Once he had succeeded in getting someone to hold him, his actions would become wild: he would lose control, struggling to be held and, at the same time, jumping up and down. Holding Eric under these conditions became intolerable for anyone and, inevitably, it ended in a struggle, trying to get rid of him as he fought to remain held. He was someone who seemed to be living in immense anguish.

Anguish is inner agitation, a chaotic, unfocused energy. Anguish breaks sleep and other patterns and brings us to a place of confusion. To be lonely is to feel unwanted and unloved, and therefore unloveable. Loneliness is a taste of death. No wonder some people who are desperately lonely lose themselves in mental illness or violence to forget the inner pain.

Eric was a terribly lonely young man. He needed to be loved, but his needs were so great that no one person could fulfill them. It took a long time in L'Arche before he found some inner peace. Little by little, as he learned to trust those around him, he discovered he was loved.

By way of contrast, Pierre was the seventh child in a family of 13, a man who had spent seven years in prison. I met him in Montreal. He had run away from home when he was 12 years old because he felt unnoticed and unwanted by his family. So, for a long time he lived with gangs on the street. In his heart, Pierre was a lonely man who felt lost. He had nowhere to go, no meaning in his life. He needed a friend, a teacher, someone who could help him find himself and a sense of purpose.

When he was 16 Pierre committed a crime, which I believe was a cry for help. He went to jail for it. While he was there, he fell in love with a woman who regularly visited the prison. They got married, and his life took on new meaning; he finally had someone and something to live for. It was the beginning of his process of becoming human, and it happened because he felt loved.

In our L'Arche communities we experience that deep inner healing comes about mainly when people feel loved, when they have a sense of belonging. Our communities are essentially places where people can serve and create, and, most importantly, where they can love as well as be loved. This healing flows from relationships—it is not something automatic.

I have come to learn that embodied in this approach there is an important principle: the necessity of human commitment to the evolution of the new, the necessity of accepting constant movement as the key to our humanity and as the only road to becoming truly human.

In Eric and Pierre, there were chaos and disorder. Yet in the midst of the chaos, there was a way out. Are not all our lives a movement from order to disorder, which in turn evolves into a new order?

Order and Disorder

The passage of life itself suggests a constantly recurring pattern of movement from order to chaos, from chaos to order, again and again.

Birth, adolescence, and old age are all passages that are filled with anguish. Finally there is the ultimate corruption and disorder that death brings. Throughout our lives there is the disorder created by sickness, accidents, loss of work, loss of friends—all the crises that destroy our agendas, security, and carefully laid plans. Such disorder demands a gradual re-ordering of our lives and the period of transition such a crisis represents is not an easy one to live through. It is a time of loss, when we have yet to receive something new. It is a time of grief.

In human beings, there is a constant tension between order and disorder, connectedness and loneliness, evolution and revolution, security and insecurity. Our universe is constantly evolving; the old order gives way to a new order, and this in its turn crumbles when the next order appears. It is no different in our lives in the movement from birth to death.

Change of one sort or another is the essence of life, so there will always be the loneliness and insecurity that come with change. When we refuse to accept that loneliness and insecurity are part of life, when we refuse to accept that they are the price of change, we close the door on many possibilities for ourselves; our lives become lessened; we are less than fully human. If we try to prevent, or ignore, the movement of life, we run the risk of falling into the inevitable depression that must accompany an impossible goal. Life evolves; change is constant. When we try to prevent the forward movement of life, we may succeed for a while but, inevitably, there is an explosion; the groundswell of life's constant movement, constant change, is too great to resist.

And so empires of ideas, as well as empires of wealth and power, come and go. To live well is to observe in today's apparent order the tiny anomalies that are the seeds of change, the harbingers of the order of tomorrow. This means living in a state of a certain insecurity, in anguish and loneliness, which, at its best, can push us towards the new. Too much security and the refusal to evolve, to embrace change, leads to a kind of death. Too much insecurity, however, can also mean death. To be human is to create sufficient order so that we can move on into insecurity and seeming disorder. In this way, we discover the new.

Those who have the eyes to see this new order, as it arises, will often be considered too revolutionary, too modern, too liberal. Dictators everywhere have clamped down on movements for liberation; those who lead are always so certain that anarchy will arise if they do not govern with a firm hand. In reality, leaders are frightened of sharing or losing power. They too are frightened of change. They want to control everything. Those who see the coming new order will frequently be alone, persecuted.

But how do we learn to read the signs of evolution and to see where it is going? We can only help the new to evolve if we have certain clear principles. Here are five principles that have helped me.

First: all humans are sacred, whatever their culture, race, or religion, whatever their capacities or incapacities, and whatever their weaknesses or strengths may be. Each of us has an instrument to bring to the vast orchestra of humanity, and each of us needs help to become all that we might be.

Second: our world and our individual lives are in the process of evolving. Evolution is a part of life but it is not always easy to determine the good and the bad in something that is evolving. How to maintain the old and prepare the way for the new? It is not a question of rejecting the past but of letting the past flow into the present and letting this process guide us as to how to live in the future. It is a question of loving all the essential values of the past and reflecting on how they are to be lived in the new. These values include openness, love, wholeness, unity, peace, the human potential for healing and redemption, and, most important, the necessity of forgiveness. So, everything that permits and encourages the flow of life and growth is necessary.

Third: maturity comes through working with others, through dialogue, and through a sense of belonging and a searching together. In order to evolve towards greater maturity and wholeness, we humans need a certain security; only when we have attained this can we advance in insecurity with others towards the new.

Fourth: human beings need to be encouraged to make choices, and to become responsible for their own lives and for the lives of others. We need to be encouraged to evolve in order to become mature, and to break out of the shell of self-centredness and out of our defence mechanisms, which are as oppressive to others as they are to ourselves. In other words, we humans need to be rooted in good earth in order to produce good fruit. But for this we need to freely risk life in order to give of ourselves.

Fifth: in order to make such choices, we need to reflect and to seek truth and meaning. Reality is the first principle of truth. To be human means to remain connected to our humanness and to reality. It means to abandon the loneliness of being closed up in illusions, dreams, and ideologies, frightened of reality, and to choose to move towards connectedness. To be human is to accept ourselves just as we are, with our own history, and to accept others as they are. To be human means to accept history as it is and to work, without fear, towards greater openness, greater understanding, and a greater love of others. To be human is not to be crushed by reality, or to be angry about it or to try to hammer it into what we think it is or should be, but to commit ourselves as individuals, and as a species, to an evolution that will be for the good of all.

Each one of us needs to work at searching for truth, not be afraid of it. We need to strive to live in truth, because the truth sets us free, even if it means living in loneliness and anguish at certain moments. Perhaps this search for truth is a process of letting ourselves be enfolded in truth rather than possessing truth, as if it were an object that we could possess, that we could use against others.

The truth will set us free only if we let it penetrate our hearts and rend the veil that separates head from heart. It is important not only to join the head and the heart, but to love truth, also, and to let it inspire our lives, our attitudes, and our way of living. The truth of religion and morality shows itself when they liberate us and give us a deep respect and compassion for others.

This process of searching for truth demands an openness; it demands an evolution of thought, for individuals and entire societies, as the whole world changes and we discover new intimations of what *is*. There are unchanging principles, such as the call to be people of love and not of hate, which govern our lives. We need to integrate our experiences into these principles and let these principles enlighten our experience.

Such an evolution in thought can mean searching and groping in the dark, sometimes in anguish, thinking through old ideas, formulating them in new words and new ways. Philosophy, anthropology, theology, and those sciences that tell us what it means to be human can be dangerous if they become ideologies that dictate reality; instead, they need to be understood as the means by which we humbly listen to and marvel at reality.

We must not try to return to the past, but instead launch out into the future to understand each other and what it means to be human, to understand what is happening in the world—in order to become more fully human and to work for peace and unity. It is only as we begin to integrate such a sense of reality more fully into our being, as we thirst for that which gives meaning to our lives, that we discover the fundamental meaning of loneliness: a cry, often a painful cry of anguish, for more respect and love of others, to be even more enfolded in truth, held in God. Such a cry could bring a new wholeness to humanity.

F.Y.I.

L'Arche: French for "the ark" and a reference to the story in the Old Testament of Noah and the great flood; this is also the name Jean Vanier gave to the small house in Trosly-Breuil that was the start of his humanitarian vision of a society of compassion and inclusivity for those who are often marginalized. L'Arche is an international community of small homes and centres in which people with developmental disabilities come to live and build relationships with volunteers and caregivers from a wide range of backgrounds, experiences, and cultures. There are over 130 L'Arche communities in 34 countries spread over six continents.

Trosly: Trosly-Breuil is a village in the north of France and the location of the first L'Arche community.

Words to Build On

anomalies: something that is unusual or deviates from the regular pattern or condition

apathy: to be indifferent, to show little interest, concern, or emotion usually regarding matters of importance

engenders: to create or bring into existence

ephemeral: lasting for a very brief moment

groundswell: a strong gathering of force in public feeling or opinion

harbingers: someone or something that foreshadows events about to happen

liberal: not formed or ruled by tradition, authority, or establishment

mediocrity: the state of being ordinary or even inferior

mystics: individuals who believe in truths or realities that exist beyond that which can be explained scientifically or even humanly

status quo: Latin for "the state in which," it means the way things currently are or their normal condition

whet: to increase, stimulate, or enhance

yearning: an intense and sometimes painful longing, desire, or need

Tricks of the Trade

Rhetorical strategies

Types of essays: Cause and effect

In Your Own Words: Comprehension

1. According to Vanier, when do we feel lonely?

2. Can loneliness ever be cured? Why or why not?

3. Are there any positives attributed to loneliness? What are they?

4. What are the dangers of loneliness?

5. What is it we feel when we experience loneliness?

6. What does Vanier say is the "essence of life"?

7. What are the three things that Vanier feels everyone needs to do? Why are these necessary?

In Your Own Words: Analysis

1. Why does Vanier use the stories of Eric and Pierre in this piece? Is the use of these stories effective?

2. What type of support does Vanier use to illustrate his observation that the modern world sees loneliness as a type of disease?

3. What is Vanier trying to do by breaking "disease" into two words?

4. With reference to the text, expand on the idea that loneliness is something that we construct for ourselves.

5. Vanier writes, "Are not all our lives a movement from order to disorder, which in turn evolves into a new order?" What does he mean? What do you consider "a new order" to be?

6. Which one of Vanier's five principles seems to be the most challenging for many people? Which one seems to be the most frightening? Explain.

7. Why does Vanier break up his piece into sections with headings? Does it make it easier for the reader to follow along?

8. Flannery O'Connor wrote, "You shall know the truth, and the truth shall make you odd." How does this relate to Vanier's thoughts on loneliness?

❁ Now Write

1. We live in a culture that views loneliness as a disease—something to be overcome and eradicated. Making reference to Vanier's "Loneliness," write an essay outlining three reasons why people fear loneliness.

2. Jean Vanier writes that people who try to run from their loneliness often turn to distractions to "self-medicate." Some turn to alcohol, drugs, and violence. There are other seemingly less drastic measures that people use to run from "the hole that can never be filled—that can only be covered up temporarily." Write an essay outlining three modern cultural distractions, vices, fads, or industries that exploit and feed people's feelings of loneliness.

3. Write an essay in which you discuss Timothy Hornyak's excerpt from *Loving the Machine* (on robots as caregivers for seniors) and/or Kenneth J. Harvey's article about online adultery, taking into account Vanier's thoughts and beliefs on relationships, community, and loneliness.

Lawrence Solomon

Lawrence Solomon (b. 1948) is a writer and environmentalist. He is the founder and managing director of Energy Probe, an organization founded in 1969 that monitors and voices concern over the Canadian government's environmental policies. Energy Probe's site includes a blog where Solomon comments on environmental issues such as global warming, alternative forms of energy, and carbon taxes. He has written several books about environmental issues, including the most recent and controversial *The Deniers* (2008), which is about environment spokespeople like Al Gore and the mainstream media whom Solomon believes are "alarmist" for spreading misinformation and causing the public to panic over global warming. He believes that not all scientists are in agreement about the causes of what he refers to as "climate change." The book is based on his column in the *National Post*.

Although Solomon is viewed mainly as an environmentalist, he is also a journalist who has written for many publications, including *The Globe and Mail* and *The Wall Street Journal*. He was also the editor and publisher of the now defunct but award-winning magazine *Next City*. Because of his work in mainstream publications, he often writes on other current issues including globalization, the economy, poverty, and homelessness. In his article "Homeless in Paradise," Solomon not only pinpoints what he believes to be the sole cause for the rise in homelessness, but he also outlines the often disastrous effects of homelessness for those living on the streets as well as communities and cities as a whole. Finally, he offers a multilayered plan for effectively addressing and reversing this disturbing urban trend.

In His Own Words

"Scientists with integrity can hold unconventional and unpopular views."

Before We Begin

1. Homelessness is a serious issue in most major North American cities. Can we ever effectively address the issues of the homeless?
2. What thoughts and images come to mind when you think about those who are homeless?
3. What are the reasons that homelessness is a problem in most major cities in North America?
4. Solomon is an environmentalist who believes that being concerned about the environment also means being concerned about social issues such as poverty and homelessness. How do you see the two issues being connected?

✳ **Now Read**

Homeless in Paradise

In the 1960s and 1970s, homelessness was virtually unknown in North America, the term not even in public parlance. In 1964, Columbia University researchers scoured four Manhattan parks to count those sleeping there: they found one man. Likewise, in Chicago, Vancouver, Los Angeles, Montreal, and other major cities, homelessness was the exception and not the rule. In the 1960s, big city newspapers rarely ran stories on the homeless, unlike the last decade when they averaged one homeless story every two days. Until the 1980s, the homeless were not part of a widespread phenomenon; they were exceptional hard-luck cases.

Then these exceptions became the rule. Not because poverty suddenly increased—it didn't. Not because welfare was drastically reduced—generally welfare became more generous. Not much because mental institutions suddenly released their patients—the deinstitutionalization of mental patients that took place in the 1960s and early 1970s explains a small fraction, perhaps one-tenth or one-twentieth, of the torrent of home-lessness that engulfed our major cities in the 1980s.

One factor, and one factor alone—changes in housing policy—accounts for the im-mense rise of homelessness: governments outlawed much of what was then the bottom end of the housing market—the derelict apartment buildings, seedy hotels, and room-ing houses—while legalizing vagrancy. In this way, and with only the best of intentions, governments replaced a vast supply of substandard, but low-cost housing with a much vaster, much more substandard, and much lower-cost supply of housing in the form of our streets, back alleys, and parks.

Before the government inadvertently converted our public spaces into sleeping quarters, poor people—including alcoholics and the mentally ill—lived in low-rent districts, muddling along as best they could. Those poorer still doubled up with them, or sublet rooms in exchange for cash or household services, typically babysitting for women, odd jobs for men. There was nothing particularly noble about most of these arrangements: the poor who put up still needier relatives on their living room couches would have preferred the space for themselves; those put up often felt dependent and unwelcome, and, had they the wherewithal, many would have left their position of ser-vitude. Nevertheless they made do, keeping up appearances and maintaining relations, however poorly. Relatively few people relied on shelters.

Then came urban renewal, a euphemism for slum clearance that levelled much of the low-quality housing stock across the continent. Newark and New York City lost almost half of their low-rent housing between 1970 and 1990; New York City's Bowery, with 10,000 beds in 1965, had but 3000 in 1980. In the 1970s and 1980s, Chicago lost 20 per cent of its low-rent housing; of the 10,000 spaces in the Loop area's cubicle hotels, 600 remained. By the early 1980s, Toronto lost virtually all of its 500 flophouse beds; by the end of the decade, it had lost one-third of its rooming houses. Between the mid-1970s and the late 1980s, the number of unsubsidized low-cost units fell 54 per cent in the typical large US metropolitan area. Public housing—once a shining hope—failed utterly in housing the very poor.

While the stock of low-cost housing declined, the cost and difficulty of living on the cheap increased. Welfare recipients who doubled up with family members faced benefit reductions, giving them and their families reasons to drift apart. Rent control legislation, which stopped apartment building construction, backfired on the poor. While it kept rents low, a surplus of apartment seekers gave landlords the luxury of picking and choosing tenants: in competition with stable tenants able to pay rent on time and unlikely to damage property, the down-and-out had no chance. The housing shortage and rising land prices also spurred gentrification of old neighbourhoods that housed the destitute, leading to their eviction. Even tenant rights legislation backfired. Because it prevented landlords from evicting the prostitutes, drug dealers, and rowdy tenants who caused good tenants to leave, they stopped renting to anyone with the potential to be troublesome. When governments extended rent control and tenant rights to rooming houses and single-room occupancy hotels, and tightened housing regulations to force landlords to better maintain the dwindling stock of decaying housing, the landlords themselves vacated. Much of the low-income housing was lost to fires, often arson was suspected.

With so much low-rent housing demolished, and so much of the balance reserved for respectable tenants, the poorest of the poor had no place to go but the streets, newly freed up through the repeal of vagrancy laws. To those with addictions, this dark cloud had a silver lining: without accommodation costs, they could devote more of their meagre income to their habit.

Those we call homeless are not a homogeneous lot and, often, not even homeless. In many cities, the majority of panhandlers, squeegee kids, and other street people that we come across have fairly conventional abodes. Meanwhile, the majority of the truly homeless escape our view: in a 1989 study of Chicago's homeless, interviewers found most to be "neat and clean" and only 20 per cent to panhandle or take handouts. Most homeless do not make a career of it: they find themselves on the street following some unmanageable stress—the death or illness of a loved one, the breakup of a relationship, debt, and legal problems top the list—and then they pull out of it. Yet most remain deeply disturbed. According to a recent study of Toronto's homeless by the Clarke Institute of Psychiatry, two-thirds have a lifetime diagnosis of mental illness, and two-thirds suffer from alcohol and substance abuse. Only one homeless person in seven in this highly vulnerable population suffers from neither.

Although most are mentally ill, few are seriously so. Only about 10 per cent of the homeless population has suffered from some severe mental illness, most often not the schizophrenia we associate with the homeless but a dark depression. While most of the severely ill lack proper treatment, few belong in institutions. The vast majority of mentally ill people, today as before deinstitutionalization, live in the community. Only today we've made the pavement the only practical housing choice for all too many of them.

The more important characteristics of the homeless—whether or not they're mentally ill—are that they have fewer work skills, fewer social skills, and less resourcefulness than the housed population. They have difficulty maintaining relationships with friends and family. Almost half reported that they could rely on "no one" in their lives. Only 4 per cent were married or in common-law relationships. All this speaks to their lack of community and numbing sense of isolation—conditions that, above all, explain much of the social pathology that is homelessness. Being society's least valued members, they are the first to be fired, the last to be hired, those most shunned in civil society, modern lepers.

Those who live on the streets do not appear as a line item in government books, except for the odd outreach program. Neither do taxpayers take a direct hit. Some resent, others pity, the panhandlers; some fear the talkers and ravers that they encounter, but most see the homeless as an unsettling but cost-free fixture on the urban landscape.

Failing to deal with homelessness is a false economy, quite apart from the great moral costs of turning our backs on this defenceless population. The homeless cast a pall on our use of our cities, prompting parents and their children to abandon the public parks they frequent, pedestrians to avoid places they might be accosted, and merchants to relocate. The homeless show up big time in our penal system—30 per cent have spent time in police stations or jail in the previous year—and in our health care budget.

As shown in a study published in June in the *New England Journal of Medicine*—the first extensive documentation of the impact of homelessness on the health care system—the homeless have been exacting a silent toll on a society that ignores their plight. The homeless at New York City's public hospitals stayed an average of 4.1 days longer, and cost an average of $2414 more per admission, than low-income patients who had homes. One group of psychiatric patients, whom clinicians believed couldn't be discharged safely, averaged 70 days more than otherwise called for. At the city's flagship Bellevue Hospital, nearly half the admissions were homeless. "The homeless account for less than one-half of 1 per cent of the city's population, but they are having a huge impact on the health care system," said Sharon Salit, the report's lead author. "The extra costs for a single hospital admission are as much as the annual welfare rental allowance for a single individual in New York."

About half the homeless admissions required treatment for mental illness or substance abuse, and half for skin disorders, respiratory complaints, trauma, and parasites—problems generally regarded as preventable among other populations. "For want of a place to clean between their toes, change their shoes and socks, and elevate their feet when they get swollen, homeless patients get infections in their feet" that often become a chronic condition called cellulitis, said Dr. Lewis Goldfrank, Bellevue's director of emergency medicine. "We almost never see that among people who have homes." A 1996 study of Los Angeles's homeless warned that TB [tuberculosis] could reach epidemic proportions.

The homeless need medical care, especially psychiatric care. We must generously fund outpatient programs: just as nobody would release Alzheimer's patients onto the streets without adequate treatment and supervision, we cannot let these vulnerable people fend for themselves. We must also ensure that those few who are a danger to themselves or to the public receive compassionate care inside an institution. But most of all, the homeless need homes and an end to their alienation, without which their condition cannot improve. Most homeless advocates, while understanding the need for more housing, too often seek quick-fix solutions in government housing, forgetting that the last thing the homeless need is to be warehoused in anonymous public housing supervised by a faceless government bureaucracy. We must require the homeless to engage the rest of us.

The way out of homeless begins by backing out of the same path that created it. We must restore vagrancy laws, both to safeguard the public sphere for us all and to require housing for those unable to properly look after themselves. To shelter those evicted from the streets, welfare must provide the down-and-out with housing vouchers that can be used anywhere, not just in shelters but in exchange for that couch in a relative's living room. (To discourage a black market, each voucher should identify its recipient and be dated, and the landlords, rooming houses, and others who accept vouchers without housing the voucher recipient should be liable to fines.) Generous vouchers will minimize substandard housing.

To encourage friends and relatives to take the homeless in and other landlords to re-enter the business, we must throw out rules preventing easy evictions of tenants who disturb the peace or otherwise fail to meet their obligations to their neighbours and the landlord (even publicly funded hostels and shelters routinely evict or refuse to admit disorderly occupants). This accountability will prod some of today's homeless—whom the Clarke Institute found to be more aggressive, antisocial, moody, irritable, and less open to taking responsibility for change—to get along with those around them, as their counterparts once did.

While the government re-regulates the use of public spaces, it should deregulate the housing market to let the homeless find inexpensive housing niches for themselves. The largest sources of appropriate housing—ones that many municipalities wrongly ban—are basement apartments and other occupancies in residential districts.

Because most homeless individuals are neat, clean, and non-violent, many would find shelter in middle- and lower-class residences willing to set aside some space in exchange for the housing voucher. Such a relationship would especially appeal to homeowners on fixed incomes, who find themselves single and perhaps frail in a large home, and who themselves need a little income and an occasional helping hand with household chores.

We live in times of plenty, with the means and the obligation to humanely look after our most unfortunate members of society. In helping others, we will also help ourselves through more hospitable streets, a healthier society, and the personal gratification of doing our share to help people who have fallen on hard times, and not always from sins of their own making.

F.Y.I.

the Clarke Institute: presently known as the Centre for Addiction and Mental Health (CAMH), it is a psychiatric hospital on College Street in Toronto known for its work in the areas of forensic psychology, drug addiction, and sex addiction.

deinstitutionalization: the process or system of releasing mental health patients from a live-in care facility to outpatient status where they live in the community.

flophouse: an informal term used to describe a cheap boarding house, especially for transients and vagrants.

social pathology: the study of factors such as poverty, old age, and crime, and the social problems they produce.

Words to Build on

abode: one's dwelling or home

euphemism: a mild or vague expression used in the place of one that is thought to be too harsh or direct, such as "pass away" for "die"

gentrification: raising the value of a neighbourhood through its renovation or by the introduction of new housing and businesses

seedy: dilapidated or shabby-looking

vagrancy: the state of being vagrant, or having no permanent address or means of supporting oneself

voucher: a document or kind of "ticket" that can be exchanged for goods or services

Tricks of the Trade

Rhetorical strategies

Types of essays: Persuasive

Types of essays: Comparison and contrast

Types of essays: Cause and effect

In Your Own Words: Comprehension

1. Explain Solomon's plan to reduce homelessness.
2. According to Solomon, what factors caused the rise in homelessness?
3. Before the changes to housing policies, how does Solomon say the poor lived?
4. How does Solomon describe those who are homeless?
5. What effects does homelessness have on the health care system?
6. What does Solomon state about homelessness and mental illness?

In Your Own Words: Analysis

1. Explain the title of Solomon's essay.
2. What makes Solomon's essay a persuasive essay?
3. What is Solomon's technique for opening his essay? Is it effective? Why?
4. Where does Solomon's thesis appear? Why does he position his thesis here?
5. What types of evidence does Solomon use to support his thesis?

6.   Why does Solomon offer his plans to reduce homelessness in the last half of his essay? Why does he not present his plan near the beginning?

7.   Do you find his "solutions" viable? Are any of his solutions possible to implement in the city where you live? Why or why not?

⁑ Now Write

1.   What are some common views about the homeless (age, gender, reasons)? Does Solomon challenge the stereotypes people have of those who are homeless in his essay?

2.   A city needs good housing for its citizens. Research your city's housing situation and urban plan. What are some strengths of your city's urban plan? Is there quality housing for all? Why or why not?

3.   Research whether there are more men than women who are homeless in your province or city. Write an essay in which you examine the reasons for this.

Stephen King

Stephen King (b. 1947), the often-called "Master of Horror," was born in Portland, Maine. His writing career "officially" began when he was 12 years old and he and his older brother, David, started their own town newspaper, *Dave's Rag*. King continued to write all through high school and published his first short story, "I Was a Teenage Grave Robber," when he was 18. In high school he thought of himself as a "mediocre" student, but he did receive a scholarship to the University of Maine where he studied English.

After graduating from teacher's college he taught high school English in the early 1970s and wrote stories and novels in his free time. He began to write a story about Carietta White, a teenage girl who takes supernatural revenge on her high school classmates who ridicule and torture her. King did not think the story was worth anything, and he threw it into the trash bin. His wife, Tabitha, found the pages and encouraged her husband to finish the story. The story eventually became the novel *Carrie*, which was published in 1973. *Carrie's* publication earned King 30 times more than what he was making as a teacher. The book's success (and later the popularity of the film) meant King was able to leave teaching and concentrate on writing full time.

King is a prolific writer who has written numerous short stories and novels; his works have been translated into over 30 languages and have sold 300 million copies worldwide. In 1999 King began to write a book about writing called *On Writing: A Memoir of the Craft*. That same year he was severely injured and almost died as the result of an automobile accident: King was hit by an intoxicated driver while he was walking on a country road. His memoir, finally published in 2000 and now in its second printing, is considered one of the best books about the craft of writing. Funny and filled with good advice, it offers insights into King's own life as well as his writing process. For King, it was his writing that helped him recover after his accident. This work is part memoir, part "tool kit" for writers: it recounts significant events in his life that affected him and made him into a world-renowned author, and it contains invaluable advice for anyone who writes or wants to write. In 2000, King became one of the first best-selling authors to make one of his books available to fans online for $2.50. However, the number of worldwide hits was so overwhelming that the web server crashed.

King still has a home in Bangor, Maine, where he lives with his wife, novelist Tabitha King. His official website, www.stephenking.com, includes an FAQ (frequently asked questions) section where the author answers questions from fans.

In His Own Words

"I am the literary equivalent of a Big Mac and fries."

"Talent is cheaper than table salt. What separates the talented individual from the successful one is a lot of hard work."

"If you don't have the time to read, you don't have the time or the tools to write."

"People want to know why I do this, why I write such gross stuff. I like to tell them I have the heart of a small boy . . . and I keep it in a jar on my desk."

Before We Begin

1. Do you think people are born with the natural ability to be a good writer?
2. What do you know about Stephen King?
3. Why do some people dislike and/or even fear writing?
4. When you have to write, what is your process?

 **Now Read**

What Writing Is

Telepathy, of course. It's amusing when you stop to think about it—for years people have argued about whether or not such a thing exists, folks like J.B. Rhine have busted their brains trying to create a valid testing process to isolate it, and all the time it's been right there, lying out in the open like Mr. Poe's "Purloined Letter." All the arts depend upon telepathy to some degree, but I believe that writing offers the purest distillation. Perhaps I'm prejudiced, but even if I am we may as well stick with writing, since it's what we came here to think and talk about.

My name is Stephen King. I'm writing the first draft of this part at my desk (the one under the eave) on a snowy morning in December of 1997. There are things on my mind. Some are worries (bad eyes, Christmas shopping not even started, wife under the weather with a virus), some are good things (our younger son made a surprise visit home from college, I got to play Vince Taylor's "Brand New Cadillac" with The Wallflowers at a concert), but right now all that stuff is up top. I'm in another place, a basement place where there are lots of bright lights and clear images. This is a place I've built for myself over the years. It's a far-seeing place. I know it's a little strange, a little bit of a contradiction, that a far-seeing place should also be a basement place, but that's how it is with me. If you construct your own far-seeing place, you might put it in a treetop or on the roof of the World Trade Center or on the edge of the Grand Canyon. That's your little red wagon, as Robert McCammon says in one of his novels.

This book is scheduled to be published in the late summer or early fall of 2000. If that's how things work out, then you are somewhere downstream on the timeline from me . . . but you're quite likely in your own far-seeing place, the one where you go to receive telepathic messages. Not that you *have* to be there; books are a uniquely portable magic. I usually listen to one in the car (always unabridged; I think abridged audiobooks are the pits), and carry another wherever I go. You just never know when you'll want an escape hatch: mile-long lines at tollbooth plazas, the 15 minutes you have to spend in the hall of some boring college building waiting for your adviser (who's got some yank-off in there threatening to commit suicide because he/she is flunking Custom Kurmfurling 101) to come out so you can get his signature on a drop-card, airport boarding lounges, laundromats on rainy afternoons, and the absolute worst, which is the doctor's office when the guy is running late and you have to wait half an hour in order to have something sensitive mauled. At such times I find a book vital. If I have to spend time in purgatory before going to one place or the other, I guess I'll be all right as long as there's a lending library (if there is it's probably stocked with nothing but novels by Danielle Steel and *Chicken Soup* books, ha-ha, joke's on you, Steve).

So I read where I can, but I have a favourite place and probably you do, too—a place where the light is good and the vibe is usually strong. For me it's the blue chair in my study. For you it might be the couch on the sunporch, the rocker in the kitchen, or maybe it's propped up in your bed—reading in bed can be heaven, assuming you can get just the right amount of light on the page and aren't prone to spilling your coffee or cognac on the sheets.

So let's assume that you're in your favourite receiving place just as I am in the place where I do my best transmitting. We'll have to perform our mentalist routine not just over distance but over time as well, yet that presents no real problem; if we can still read Dickens, Shakespeare, and (with the help of a footnote or two) Herodotus, I think we can manage the gap between 1997 and 2000. And here we go—actual telepathy in action. You'll notice I have nothing up my sleeves and that my lips never move. Neither, most likely, do yours.

Look—here's a table covered with a cloth. On it is a cage the size of a small fish aquarium. In the cage is a white rabbit with a pink nose and pink-rimmed eyes. In its front paws is a carrot-stub upon which it is contentedly munching. On its back, clearly marked in blue ink, is the numeral 8.

Do we see the same thing? We'd have to get together and compare notes to make absolutely sure, but I think we do. There will be necessary variations, of course: some receivers will see a cloth which is turkey red, some will see one that's scarlet, while others may see still other shades. (To colourblind receivers, the red tablecloth is the dark gray of cigar ashes.) Some may see scalloped edges, some may see straight ones. Decorative souls may add a little lace, and welcome—my tablecloth is your tablecloth, knock yourself out.

Likewise, the matter of the cage leaves quite a lot of room for individual interpretation. For one thing, it is described in terms of *rough comparison,* which is useful only if you and I see the world and measure the things in it with similar eyes. It's easy to become careless when making rough comparisons, but the alternative is a prissy attention to detail that takes all the fun out of writing. What am I going to say, "on table is a cage three feet, six inches in length, two feet in width, and fourteen inches high"? That's not prose, that's an instruction manual. The paragraph also doesn't tell us what sort of material the cage is made of—wire mesh? steel rods? glass?—but does it really matter? We all understand the cage is a see-through medium; beyond that, we don't care. The most interesting thing here isn't even the carrot-munching rabbit in the cage, but the number on its back. Not a six, not a four, not nineteen-point-five. It's an eight. This is what we're looking at, and we all see it. I didn't tell you. You didn't ask *me.* I never opened my mouth and you never opened yours. We're not even in the same *year* together, let alone the same room ... except we *are* together. We're close.

We're having a meeting of the minds.

I sent you a table with a red cloth on it, a cage, a rabbit, and the number eight in blue ink. You got them all, especially that blue eight. We've engaged in an act of telepathy. No mythy-mountain shit; real telepathy. I'm not going to belabour the point, but before we go any further you have to understand that I'm not trying to be cute; there *is* a point to be made.

You can approach the act of writing with nervousness, excitement, hopefulness, or even despair—the sense that you can never completely put on the page what's in your mind and heart. You can come to the act with your fists clenched and your eyes narrowed, ready to kick ass and take down names. You can come to it because you want a girl to marry you or because you want to change the world. Come to it any way but lightly. Let me say it again: *you must not come lightly to the blank page.*

I'm not asking you to come reverently or unquestioningly; I'm not asking you to be politically correct or cast aside your sense of humour (please God you have one). This isn't a popularity contest, it's not the moral Olympics, and it's not church. But it's *writing,* damn it, not washing the car or putting on eyeliner. If you can take it seriously, we can do business. If you can't or won't, it's time for you to close the book and do something else.

Wash the car, maybe.

F.Y.I.

Herodotus: (ca. 484 BCE – ca. 425 BCE) an ancient Greek historian who is regarded as the "Father of History" in Western culture. He was the first historian known to collect his materials systematically, test their accuracy to a certain extent, and arrange them in a well-constructed and vivid narrative. He is most famous for writing *The Histories*.

J.B. Rhine: (1895–1980) originally a botanist, Rhine became involved in parapsychology and psychology. He founded the parapsychology lab at Duke University, the *Journal of Parapsychology*, and the Parapsychological Association. Rhine is also known for creating the term ESP.

moral Olympics: a competition regarding right and wrong

Mr. Poe's Purloined Letter: a reference to the author Edgar Allan Poe (1809–1849) and his short story, "The Purloined Letter"

Robert McCammon: (b. 1952) an American novelist from Birmingham, Alabama. The reference comes from his novel *Swan Song*.

telepathy: the communication of thoughts, feelings, desires, images, and information between people using mechanisms that cannot be understood by known scientific laws. Often called "mind reading," it is better referred to as thought transference.

Words to Build on

abridged: any text that is shortened by removing certain content

distillation: a process of purification through separation

eave: the edge of a roof that projects beyond the wall

unabridged: any text that is not condensed and retains all of the original content

In Your Own Words: Comprehension

1. According to King, all the arts depend upon telepathy to some degree. Explain what he means by this.

2. What does Stephen King call his other place?

3. What is the one thing that Stephen King always carries with him and why?

4. Where is his favourite place to read?

5. For King, can a writer pay too much attention to detail? What happens when he or she does?

6. Explain what King writes about how to "...approach the act of writing."

7. What does King state that writing isn't?

In Your Own Words: Analysis

1. Writing teachers often tell students not to use fragments. However, King begins many of his essays with fragments. Why does he do this? What is the effect? What are the fragments in this piece?

2. Explain what King means when he states that writing is telepathic.

3. Is this essay written for anyone or does it only address the needs of professional writers?

4. At one point in the essay, King engages in a telepathic experiment with the reader. Where does this experiment occur in the reading and is it effective?

5. Why does King go into detail regarding the date he is writing this essay, the date it will be published, and the date readers will be able to read this piece? What does this say about writing?

6. Most likely you have read one of Stephen King's novels or short stories. Is the voice in his fiction the same as the voice in this essay?

7. After reading this essay, which piece of advice on writing do you find to be the most useful?

⁂ Now Write

1. Using this essay and your own experience, explain how reading and writing are interconnected.

2. Stephen King has stated that he is "the literary equivalent of a Big Mac and fries." Explain what this statement means and how it compares to the sentiments he expresses about writing in this essay.

3. Outline the advice King gives to writers. Write an essay in which you explain how his advice about writing can be applied to an academic essay, a business letter, and an email.

David Sedaris

David Sedaris (b. 1956) is an American humorist and personal essayist who was born in New York but raised in Raleigh, North Carolina. Born in America and raised in the southern United States, he is half-Greek, and he and his five siblings were raised Greek Orthodox, a subject that sometimes appears in his writing. Much of his writing centres on his family, childhood, and any absurd aspects of his adult life. Sedaris refers to what he writes as the "comic essay." He finds humour in both serious moments as well as the mundane. Many of the ideas for his stories and essays are taken from a diary he keeps, a practice that dates back to his 20s.

His first collection of short stories, *Barrel Fever: Stories and Essays* (1994), contains both fiction and autobiographical essays, including the essay "SantaLand Diaries," which not only brought him his first taste of success in 1992 when he read it on National Public Radio but was later turned into a theatre production in 1996. It recounts the time he worked as a Christmas elf at Macy's department store. *Me Talk Pretty One Day* (2000), another collection of autobiographical essays, was to be made into a film by director Wayne Wang, but Sedaris later backed out due to worries about how his family might be portrayed on screen. Another of his books, *Squirrel Seeks Chipmunk: A Modest Bestiary* (2010), is an illustrated book of animal stories. Although a work of fiction, not all are fables since, as Sedaris says, "fables have morals," and many of these animal stories that feature animals falling in love, dealing with marital issues, and going to the hairdresser, do not.

Sedaris's essays have also been published in print and online by *Esquire* magazine, the *New York Times*, and his pieces appear regularly in *The New Yorker*, which also named him one of the funniest writers in America. In addition to his collections of fiction and essays, he is also a playwright. He has written five plays with his sister, the comedic actor and writer Amy Sedaris—the two collaborate under the moniker, "The Talent Family."

He has been compared to writers such as Mark Twain and Dorothy Parker, while he includes the Canadian writer Alice Munro among his influences. Sedaris often "tests" the quality of his material by reading it aloud on his tours where people pay hundreds of dollars to hear his unique dead-pan style of delivery. He has received three Grammy nominations for Best Spoken Word and Best Comedy Album and is a frequent and popular guest on television shows such as *Late Show with David Letterman* and *The Daily Show with Jon Stewart*.

Apart from the United States, Sedaris has lived in Britain and Japan but now currently resides in a small French village with his partner.

In His Own Words

"I'm a humorist. I'm not a reporter, I never pretended to be a reporter. I've always been very upfront about the way I write, and I've always used the tools humorists use, such as exaggeration."

"After a few months in my parents' basement, I took an apartment near the state university, where I discovered both crystal methamphetamine and conceptual art. Either one of these things are dangerous, but in combination they have the potential to destroy entire civilizations."

"I don't think my life is more interesting than anybody else's. I think the only difference between me and everyone else is this . . . I write things down. That's all."

Before We Begin

1.   Have you ever had to learn a new language as an adult? Describe your experience.
2.   Is it easier for children to learn a new language? Why?
3.   Does education always have to be "fun" for teaching and learning at all levels to be effective?

 **Now Read**

Me Talk Pretty One Day

At the age of 41, I am returning to school and have to think of myself as what my French textbook calls "a true debutant." After paying my tuition, I was issued a student ID, which allows me a discounted entry fee at movie theatres, puppet shows, and Festyland, a far-flung amusement park that advertises with billboards picturing a cartoon stegosaurus sitting in a canoe and eating what appears to be a ham sandwich.

I've moved to Paris with hopes of learning the language. My school is an easy 10-minute walk from my apartment, and on the first day of class I arrived early, watching as the returning students greeted one another in the school lobby. Vacations were recounted, and questions were raised concerning mutual friends with names like Kang and Vlatnya. Regardless of their nationalities, everyone spoke in what sounded to me like excellent French. Some accents were better than others, but the students exhibited an ease and confidence I found intimidating. As an added discomfort, they were all young, attractive, and well dressed, causing me to feel not unlike Pa Kettle trapped backstage after a fashion show.

The first day of class was nerve-racking because I knew I'd be expected to perform. That's the way they do it here—it's everybody into the language pool, sink or swim. The teacher marched in, deeply tanned from a recent vacation, and proceeded to rattle off a series of administrative announcements. I've spent quite a few summers in Normandy, and I took a month-long French class before leaving New York. I'm not completely in the dark, yet I understood only half of what this woman was saying.

"If you have not *meimslsxp* or *lgpdmurct* by this time, then you should not be in this room. Has everyone *apzkiubjxow*? Everyone? Good, we shall begin." She spread out her lesson plan and sighed, saying, "All right, then, who knows the alphabet?"

It was startling because (a) I hadn't been asked that question in a while and (b) I realized, while laughing, that I myself did *not* know the alphabet. They're the same letters, but in France they're pronounced differently. I know the shape of the alphabet but had no idea what it actually sounded like.

"Ahh." The teacher went to the board and sketched the letter *a*. "Do we have anyone in the room whose first name commences with an *ahh*?"

Two Polish Annas raised their hands, and the teacher instructed them to present themselves by stating their names, nationalities, occupations, and a brief list of things they liked and disliked in this world. The first Anna hailed from an industrial town outside of Warsaw and had front teeth the size of tombstones. She worked as a seamstress, enjoyed quiet times with friends, and hated the mosquito.

"Oh, really," the teacher said. "How very interesting. I thought that everyone loved the mosquito, but here, in front of all the world, you claim to detest him. How is it that we've been blessed with someone as unique and original as you? Tell us, please."

The seamstress did not understand what was being said but knew that this was an occasion for shame. Her rabbity mouth huffed for breath, and she stared down at her lap as though the appropriate comeback were stitched somewhere alongside the zipper of her slacks.

The second Anna learned from the first and claimed to love sunshine and detest lies. It sounded like a translation of one of those Playmate of the Month data sheets, the answers always written in the same loopy handwriting: "Turn-ons: Mom's famous five-alarm chili! Turn-offs: insecurity and guys who come on too strong!!!!"

The two Polish Annas surely had clear notions of what they loved and hated, but like the rest of us, they were limited in terms of vocabulary, and this made them appear less than sophisticated. The teacher forged on, and we learned that Carlos, the Argentine bandonion player, loved wine, music, and, in his words, "making sex with the womens of the world." Next came a beautiful young Yugoslav who identified herself as an optimist, saying that she loved everything that life had to offer.

The teacher licked her lips, revealing a hint of the saucebox we would later come to know. She crouched low for her attack, placed her hands on the young woman's desk, and leaned close, saying, "Oh yeah? And do you love your little war?"

While the optimist struggled to defend herself, I scrambled to think of an answer to what had obviously become a trick question. How often is one asked what he loves in this world? More to the point, how often is one asked and then publicly ridiculed for his answer? I recalled my mother, flushed with wine, pounding the tabletop late one night, saying, "Love? I love a good steak cooked rare. I love my cat, and I love . . . " My sisters and I leaned forward, waiting to hear our names. "Tums," our mother said. "I love Tums."

The teacher killed some time accusing the Yugoslavian girl of masterminding a program of genocide, and I jotted frantic notes in the margins of my pad. While I can honestly say that I love leafing through medical textbooks devoted to severe dermatological conditions, the hobby is beyond the reach of my French vocabulary, and acting it out would only have invited controversy.

When called upon, I delivered an effortless list of things that I detest: blood sausage, intestinal pates, brain pudding. I'd learned these words the hard way. Having given it some thought, I then declared my love for IBM typewriters, the French word for *bruise,* and my electric floor waxer. It was a short list, but still I managed to mispronounce *IBM* and assign the wrong gender to both the floor waxer and the typewriter. The teacher's reaction led me to believe that these mistakes were capital crimes in the country of France.

"Were you always this *palicmkrexis*?" she asked. "Even a *fiuscrzsa ticiwelmun* knows that a typewriter is feminine."

I absorbed as much of her abuse as I could understand, thinking—but not saying—that I find it ridiculous to assign a gender to an inanimate object incapable of disrobing and making an occasional fool of itself. Why refer to Lady Crack Pipe or Good Sir Dishrag when these things could never live up to all that their sex implied?

The teacher proceeded to belittle everyone from German Eva, who hated laziness, to Japanese Yukari, who loved paintbrushes and soap. Italian, Thai, Dutch, Korean, and Chinese—we all left class foolishly believing that the worst was over. She'd shaken us up a little, but surely that was just an act designed to weed out the deadweight. We didn't know it then, but the coming months would teach us what it was like to spend time in the presence of a wild animal, something completely unpredictable. Her temperament was not based on a series of good and bad days but, rather, good and bad moments. We soon learned to dodge chalk and protect our heads and stomachs whenever she approached us with a question. She hadn't yet punched anyone, but it seemed wise to protect ourselves against the inevitable.

Though we were forbidden to speak anything but French, the teacher would occasionally use us to practise any of her five fluent languages.

"I hate you," she said to me one afternoon. Her English was flawless. "I really, really hate you." Call me sensitive, but I couldn't help but take it personally.

After being singled out as a lazy *kfdtinvfm*, I took to spending four hours a night on my homework, putting in even more time whenever we were assigned an essay. I suppose I could have gotten by with less, but I was determined to create some sort of identity for myself: David the hard worker, David the cut-up. We'd have one of those "complete this sentence" exercises, and I'd fool with the thing for hours, invariably settling on something like "A quick run around the lake? I'd love to! Just give me a moment while I strap on my wooden leg." The teacher, through word and action, conveyed the message that if this was my idea of an identity, she wanted nothing to do with it.

My fear and discomfort crept beyond the borders of the classroom and accompanied me out onto the wide boulevards. Stopping for a coffee, asking directions, depositing money in my bank account: these things were out of the question, as they involved having to speak. Before beginning school, there'd been no shutting me up, but now I was convinced that everything I said was wrong. When the phone rang, I ignored it. If someone asked me a question, I pretended to be deaf. I knew my fear was getting the best of me when I started wondering why they don't sell cuts of meat in vending machines.

My only comfort was the knowledge that I was not alone. Huddled in the hallways and making the most of our pathetic French, my fellow students and I engaged in the sort of conversation commonly overheard in refugee camps.

"Sometime me cry alone at night."

"That be common for I, also, but be more strong, you. Much work and someday you talk pretty. People start love you soon. Maybe tomorrow, okay."

Unlike the French class I had taken in New York, here there was no sense of competition. When the teacher poked a shy Korean in the eyelid with a freshly sharpened pencil, we took no comfort in the fact that, unlike Hyeyoon Cho, we all knew the irregular past tense of the verb *to defeat*. In all fairness, the teacher hadn't meant to stab the girl, but neither did she spend much time apologizing, saying only, "Well, you should have been *vkkdyo* more *kdeynfulh*."

Over time it became impossible to believe that any of us would ever improve. Fall arrived and it rained every day, meaning we would now be scolded for the water dripping from our coats and umbrellas. It was mid-October when the teacher singled me out, saying, "Every day spent with you is like having a Caesarean section." And it struck me that, for the first time since arriving in France, I could understand every word that someone was saying.

Understanding doesn't mean that you can suddenly speak the language. Far from it. It's a small step, nothing more, yet its rewards are intoxicating and deceptive. The teacher continued her diatribe and I settled back, bathing in the subtle beauty of each new curse and insult.

"You exhaust me with your foolishness and reward my efforts with nothing but pain, do you understand me?"

The world opened up, and it was with great joy that I responded, "I know the thing that you speak exact now. Talk me more, you, plus, please, plus."

F.Y.I.

bandonion: a small accordion or concertina; a musical instrument that is played by pushing its ends together to force air into reeds to produce sound

Festyland: also called "Parc Festyland," a small theme park in Normandy, France. The park's main theme is a stereotyped version of the year 1066. Festyland's mascot is a smiling dragon wearing a Viking helmet, and its catchphrase is *"Defiez le!"* which means "Brave it!"

Pa Kettle: one-half of the popular comedic movie characters, Ma and Pa Kettle, made famous by actors Marjorie Main and Percy Kilbride from 1949 to 1957. Pa's character usually wore a plain white collarless button-down shirt, baggy plain black trousers, and his trademark black bowler hat.

saucebox: a term that dates back to sometime before 1706, referring to a person who is "saucy," rude , impertinent, bold, someone who "talks back" to others

Words to Build On

cut-up: to behave in a comical manner

debutant: usually used to mean a young and often wealthy young woman at the time of her debut into high society

diatribe: a strong verbal attack or criticism

Tricks of the Trade

Essay

Irony

Satire

In Your Own Words: Comprehension

1. Why is Sedaris taking these classes?

2. What is expected on the first day?

3. How does the teacher treat her students? Do not use the word "bad" or "mean" in your answer.

4. What is the trick question that is asked? Why is it hard to answer?

5. How does Sedaris feel about the teacher? How does he react to her behaviour towards the students?

6. Compare this class in France to the class Sedaris had taken in New York.

7. What is Sedaris doing in class while the teacher is questioning the other students?

8. How does Sedaris describe his own fluency in French? Does his fluency level change?

In Your Own Words: Analysis

1. Explain the title of the essay "Me Talk Pretty One Day." What does it mean?

2. Sedaris states, "The teacher continued her diatribe and I settled back, bathing in the subtle beauty of each new curse and insult." Explain this statement and why he feels this way.

3. Why does he use seemingly incomprehensible words and phrases such as "*fiuscrzsa ticiwelmun*"?

4. How did the treatment from the teacher inside the class affect Sedaris outside the class?

5. What is Sedaris's main point or thesis in this essay?

6. What is the difference between understanding and speaking a language?

7. Are there any moments in this essay when you said to yourself, "that can't be true!" If so, which moments are they and why?

8. How is this essay different from most academic essays you have read?

✳ Now Write

1. The famous Greek writer Alexandros Papadiamandis (1851–1911) read and translated works from English, French, Italian, and German. However, when he met writers who spoke these languages he did not have the fluency needed to engage in conversations with them. Why would this be? Write an essay in which you explain the reasons why it is often easier to read a language than it is to speak it.

2. Find three or four characteristics of satire. Explain how these are reflected in Sedaris's work.

3. It is sometimes said the best learning occurs when the student is made to feel "uncomfortable." Yet today we live in a time when educators are told they should make learning "fun" and "engaging." With reference to Sedaris's essay, write about how moments of discomfort in the classroom can motivate one to learn.

Vandana Shiva

Vandana Shiva (b. 1952) was born in the valley of Dehradun, an ancient city in the Himalayan Mountains of India. She studied science in India, philosophy at the University of Guelph, and received her PhD in quantum theory physics from the University of Western Ontario. Shiva is a scientist, a philosopher, and an environment-alist . She is also a world-renowned activist, known for her efforts to preserve forests, organize women involved in food production, and protect local biodiversity.

Her name first came to international attention in the 1970s when she participated in the non-violent Chipko movement of rural women who went out and embraced trees, acting as human chains to prevent logging and deforestation. Shiva, who has contributed over 300 articles to scientific, technical, and political journals, plays a major role in the global ecofeminist movement. She runs her own organic farm in India and has founded an Indian seed-saving organization, Navdanya, which translates as "Nine Crops"; it supports local farmers and conserves crops through the philosophy of saving and sharing seeds.

Shiva has received many honours and awards from around the world for her work, including the United Nations Earth Day International Award. She has written numerous books, including *Ecofeminsim* (1993) and *Soil Not Oil* (2008). Shiva, much like Mahatma Gandhi, who fought against British salt monopolies in pre-independence India, sees social justice issues as going hand-in-hand with environmental concerns.

In Her Own Words

"I believe Gandhi is the only person who knew about real democracy—not democracy as the right to go and buy what you want, but democracy as the responsibility to be accountable to everyone around you. Democracy begins with freedom from hunger, freedom from unemployment, freedom from fear, and freedom from hatred. To me, those are the real freedoms on the basis of which good human societies are based."

"Clearly, a wilderness movement started by Native Americans would not have had the same roots. So today the environmental movement has become opposed to issues of justice. You can see this in the way issues are framed. It's a permanent replay of jobs-versus-the-environment, in nature-versus-bread. These are extremely artificial dichotomies. I think we have reached a stage now where we need to find solutions to economic injustice in the same place and in the same ways that we find solutions to sustainability. Sustainability on environmental grounds and justice in terms of everyone having a place in the production and consumption system—these are two aspects of the same issue. They have been artificially separated and have to be put back again in the Western way of thinking."

Before We Begin

1. Many of today's celebrities have rallied around issues relating to poverty. Can they have a positive and significant impact on the poor and the problems they face?
2. Can global poverty ever be eradicated? Why or why not?
3. How do you define poverty? What is your definition of "being poor"?

 **Now Read**

Two Myths that Keep the World Poor

From rock singer Bob Geldof to UK politician Gordon Brown, the world suddenly seems to be full of high-profile people with their own plans to end poverty. Jeffrey Sachs, however, is not simply a do-gooder but one of the world's leading economists, head of the Earth Institute, and in charge of a UN panel set up to promote rapid development. So when he launched his book *The End of Poverty*, people everywhere took notice. *Time* magazine even made it into a cover story.

But, there is a problem with Sachs's how-to-end poverty prescriptions. He simply doesn't understand where poverty comes from. He seems to view it as the original sin. "A few generations ago, almost everybody was poor," he writes, then adding: "The Industrial Revolution led to new riches, but much of the world was left far behind."

This is a totally false history of poverty. The poor are not those who have been "left behind"; they are the ones who have been robbed. The wealth accumulated by Europe and North America are largely based on riches taken from Asia, Africa, and Latin America. Without the destruction of India's rich textile industry, without the takeover of the spice trade, without the genocide of the Native American tribes, without African slavery, the Industrial Revolution would not have resulted in new riches for Europe or North America. It was this violent takeover of Third World resources and markets that created wealth in the North and poverty in the South.

Two of the great economic myths of our time allow people to deny this intimate link and spread misconceptions about what poverty is.

First, the destruction of nature and of people's ability to look after themselves are blamed not on industrial growth and economic colonialism, but on poor people themselves. Poverty, it is stated, causes environmental destruction. The disease is then offered as a cure: further economic growth is supposed to solve the very problems of poverty and ecological decline that it gave rise to in the first place. This is the message at the heart of Sachs's analysis.

The second myth is an assumption that if you consume what you produce, you do not really produce, at least not economically speaking. If I grow my own food, and do not sell it, then it doesn't contribute to GDP, and therefore does not contribute towards "growth."

People are perceived as "poor" if they eat food they have grown rather than commercially distributed junk foods sold by global agri-business. They are seen as poor if they live in self-built housing made from ecologically well-adapted materials like bamboo and mud rather than in cinder block or cement houses. They are seen as poor if they wear garments manufactured from handmade natural fibres rather than synthetics.

Yet sustenance living, which the wealthy West perceives as poverty, does not necessarily mean a low quality of life. On the contrary, by their very nature economies based on sustenance ensure a high quality of life—when measured in terms of access to good food and water, opportunities for sustainable livelihoods, robust social and cultural identity, and a sense of meaning in people's lives. Because these poor don't share in the perceived benefits of economic growth, however, they are portrayed as those "left behind."

This false distinction between the factors that create affluence and those that create poverty is at the core of Sachs's analysis. And because of this, his prescriptions will aggravate and deepen poverty instead of ending it. Modern concepts of economic development, which Sachs sees as the "cure" for poverty, have been in place for only a tiny portion of human history. For centuries, the principles of sustenance allowed societies all over the planet to survive and even thrive. Limits in nature were respected in these societies and guided the limits of human consumption. When society's relationship with nature is based on sustenance, nature exists as a form of common wealth. It is redefined as a "resource" only when profit becomes the organizing principle of society and sets off a financial imperative for the development and destruction of these resources for the market.

However much we choose to forget or deny it, all people in all societies still depend on nature. Without clean water, fertile soils, and genetic diversity, human survival is not possible. Today, economic development is destroying these onetime commons, resulting in the creation of a new contradiction: development deprives the very people it professes to help of their traditional land and means of sustenance, forcing them to survive in an increasingly eroded natural world.

A system like the economic growth model we know today creates trillions of dollars of super profits for corporations while condemning billions of people to poverty. Poverty is not, as Sachs suggests, an initial state of human progress from which to escape. It is a final state people fall into when one-sided development destroys the ecological and social systems that have maintained the life, health, and sustenance of people and the planet for ages. The reality is that people do not die for lack of income. They die for lack of access to the wealth of the commons. Here, too, Sachs is wrong when he says: "In a world of plenty, 1 billion people are so poor their lives are in danger." The indigenous people in the Amazon, the mountain communities in the Himalayas, peasants anywhere whose land has not been appropriated and whose water and biodiversity have not been destroyed by debt-creating industrial agriculture are ecologically rich, even though they earn less than a dollar a day.

On the other hand, people are poor if they have to purchase their basic needs at high prices no matter how much income they make. Take the case of India. Because of cheap food and fibre being dumped by developed nations and lessened trade protections enacted by the government, farm prices in India are tumbling, which means that the country's peasants are losing US$26 billion each year. Unable to survive under these new economic conditions, many peasants are now poverty-stricken and thousands commit suicide each year. Elsewhere in the world, drinking water is privatized so that corporations can now profit to the tune of US$1 trillion a year by selling an essential resource to the poor that was once free. And the US$50 billion of "aid" trickling North to South is but a tenth of the $500 billion being sucked in the other direction due to interest payments and other unjust mechanisms in the global economy imposed by the World Bank and the IMF.

If we are serious about ending poverty, we have to be serious about ending the systems that create poverty by robbing the poor of their common wealth, livelihoods, and incomes. Before we can make poverty history, we need to get the history of poverty right. It's not about how much wealthy nations can give so much as how much less they can take.

F.Y.I.

agri-business: farming in the form of a large-scale business operation or commercial farming that is mainly focused on producing so-called "cash crops."

Bob Geldof: (b. 1951) an Irish musician, songwriter, singer, and author who is also a political activist, especially known for his efforts to alleviate poverty in Africa. He was one of the organizers of the Live 8 concerts.

Gordon Brown: (b. 1951) British Labour Party politician who was Prime Minister from 2007–2010.

IMF: International Monetary Fund

Industrial Revolution: a historical term for the social and economic transformation that occurred during the eighteenth and nineteenth centuries in Britain, northern Europe, and America that brought about the shift from a home-based, handmade manufacturing economy to large-scale factory production.

Jeffrey Sachs: (b. 1954) is an American economist and director of the Earth Institute at Columbia University. Sachs is known for being an economic adviser and aiding countries in their transition from communism to market economies.

North and South: current references to the rich and poor countries of the northern and southern hemispheres of the world—previously referred to as "First World" and "Third World" countries.

Third World: used to refer to the developing countries of Asia, Africa, and Latin America. The term originated during the Cold War and was used to refer to countries that were not aligned with either the "West" or the "East." Today the term is used for nations with the smallest UN Human Development Index. Development workers now refer to these countries as "the South" and not "Third World," a term that is considered outdated and offensive.

UN: the United Nations—an international organization of countries set up in 1945 to promote international peace, co-operation, and security among member nations.

Words to Build on

sustenance living/sustainable livelihoods: ways of living that have minimal impact on the environment or Earth's resources

Tricks of the Trade

Types of essays: Comparison and contrast

Types of essays: Exemplification

In Your Own Words: Comprehension

1. Why does Shiva disagree with Jeffrey Sachs's views on poverty?

2. What does Shiva mean by the statement "the poor are not those who have been 'left behind'"?

3. According to Shiva, what is the first myth that keeps people poor?

4. What is the second myth that keeps people poor?

5. How does Shiva view the role of "nature" or the natural world in human society?

6. What is the "economic growth model" and why does Shiva view it as a threat to the poor?

7. Why does Shiva view certain indigenous groups as being "rich"?

8. What is Shiva's thesis? Where does it appear in this article?

In Your Own Words: Analysis

1. Shiva states that "people are perceived as 'poor' if they eat food they have grown rather than commercially distributed junk foods sold by global agri-business. They are seen as poor if they live in self-built housing made from ecologically well-adapted materials like bamboo and mud rather than cinder block or cement houses." Do you agree with Shiva's description? Why or why not?

2. What is Shiva's definition of sustenance living? Is this realistically possible for most populations around the world? Why or why not?

3. Why does Shiva believe Jeffrey Sachs's methods of ending poverty will aggravate and increase poverty as opposed to ending it?

4. If the poor are "ecologically rich" why do they become poor?

❈ Now Write

1. Do you agree or disagree with the two myths that Shiva presents in this article? Write an essay supporting your views with reference to Shiva's article.

2. Consider the connection Shiva sees between environmental concerns and social justice issues. Do all citizens have rights to their country's natural resources? What are these resources and why or why not should the inhabitants of any land have "access to the wealth of the commons," as Shiva calls it?

3. Shiva makes the point that the strength of Europe and North America's economies are based on colonization and slavery. If this is the case, are groups such as African Americans and African Canadians and First Nations peoples, whose ancestors have contributed their labour and lost rights to their lands, right to request compensation? What are the ways in which historical injustice can be compensated or repaid?

4. Research the work and life of Vandana Shiva and Lawrence Solomon. Write an essay in which you explain how environmental and agricultural sciences are connected to issues such as homelessness and poverty.

Timothy Hornyak

Timothy N. Hornyak (b. 1972) is a freelance journalist who was born and raised in Montreal and later graduated from McGill and Carleton universities. He writes about technology, science, and travel. His book *Loving the Machine: The Art and Science of Japanese Robots* (2006) is about the history and development of Japanese robots. His interest in Japanese culture can be traced back to his childhood, as he claims he watched "too many" Akiro Kirosawa films. After moving to Tokyo, he co-authored the *Lonely Planet* guidebooks to Tokyo and Japan. He became interested in robotics after meeting Sony's robot dog AIBO and Honda's humanoid robot. Currently he writes for US technology websites CNET and IEEE Spectrum, as well as *Lonely Planet*, *National Geographic News*, *Travel + Leisure*, among other media. He is based in Montreal and Tokyo.

In His Own Words

"What exactly is a robot? The word is difficult to define. The *Oxford English Dictionary* says a robot is 'a machine (sometimes resembling a human being in appearance) designed to function in place of a living agent, especially one which carries out a variety of tasks automatically or with a minimum of external impulse.' Japan's authoritative *Kojien* dictionary describes a robot thus: 'a person or cyborg; in general, a machine or apparatus for work or control that can be made to perform automatically.'"

"Japan's first modern robot, built in 1928, was a direct descendant of the medieval *karakuri* dolls, created to awe and entertain. Rather than a robot doll, however, it was more a robot Buddha—a giant golden man that could move its upper body . . . [t]his unique marvel may have been years ahead of its time technologically."

Before We Begin

1. Do you believe there will come a time when robots take over most of humankind's mundane and routine tasks?
2. List the kinds of jobs that robots will undertake.
3. Can the use of robots bring any harmful or negative effects to humankind? What are these?
4. Recently, Japanese scientists unsuccessfully tried to make a "kissing" robot. Is there anything a robot cannot do that only a person can do?
5. Where does the word "robot" come from? Use a dictionary to locate the origin of this word. Is it a Japanese word?

❖❖ **Now Read**

from *Loving the Machine: The Art and Science of Japanese Robots*

For the Elderly, Ageless Companions

In today's Japan, robots for use in the home are also being deployed in a surprising proving ground: the elderly. Japan's rapidly aging society is facing a major crisis. The low birthrate, unsurpassed longevity, and deep-seated aversion to immigration mean the population is expected to shrink by 20 per cent by 2050; about a third will consist of people over 65. The impact on the health care system will be staggering, made worse by the shortage of younger workers to support and care for their elders.

To meet the demand for caregivers, people in government, welfare services, and robot industries have developed elaborate visions of nursing robots; the Japan Robot Association sees eldercare robots inflating the personal robot industry to $40 billion in 2025 from the current $4 billion. While the idea of a robot nurse may hold out little comfort for some, more and more are being sold to help with basic daily activities like bathing.

Sanyo Electric's Hirb wheelchair bathtub is a kind of robotic washing machine for humans that is already in use in nursing homes, saving labour and time. To give weakened old muscles a boost, University of Tsukuba professor Yoshiyuki Sankai developed the Hybrid Assistive Limb (HAL) robot suit, a strap-on white exoskeleton that detects motor nerve signals from the brain and effectively doubles an average person's physical strength. In one demonstration, a graduate student wearing HAL holds three large 20-pound bags of rice out in front of his chest without any visible effort. It's an impressive sight, though it's hard to picture aged Japanese dressing up in a machine every day before going out.

Of course, purely physical robots, while efficient, can do little to provide for therapeutic needs—which is where Paro, a robot baby harp seal, comes in. One of Japan's most irresistibly adorable robotic creations, Paro is an example of how difficult it can be to regard a machine as simply a collection of components coursing with electricity when our eyes say differently.

Paro looks like a stuffed animal, down to its snow-white antibacterial pelt. It can't do much except wriggle, moving its head, tail, and flippers, and whine in disarming fashion, but it does respond to its environment. Pick up Paro for a hug and its big black eyes close as if it's sleeping. Stroke it and it will try to repeat whatever action triggered the stroke. Ignore it and Paro gets upset. It can also be given a new name and respond to it as well as simple expressions of greeting or praise.

Under its soft fur are a 32-bit processor, numerous sensors, and very quiet actuators. Takanori Shibata of the National Institute of Advanced Industrial Science and Technology specifically developed Paro as an object of emotional attachment and calls it a "Mental Commitment Robot." Shibata, who has studied under Rodney Brooks at

MIT's AI Lab, chose a seal form because he believed people would be less likely to notice dissimilarities with the real thing than more familiar animals like dogs and cats.

Paro's main purpose is to provide robot therapy in old folks' homes, where stress and boredom are major problems. The benefits of pet therapy have been proven, but many institutions bar animals for hygiene reasons. Shibata's research has shown that when seniors caress Paro and interact with it, stress levels drop and interaction with others increases. Time spent with Paro has proven to be as effective as real animal therapy; furthermore, caregiver burnout was reduced. Deployed in 50 nursing homes across the country, Paro has been tremendously well received, garnering a number of awards. It has been sold on the general market since spring 2005 at ¥350,000 a head. "To users, Paro is like a real pet, something cute and alive," says Hisayoshi Ishii, a Paro sales official with maker Intelligent System Co., a Toyama venture firm where the 22-inch-long seals are made by hand, each with a unique face.

More anthropomorphic robots for seniors are also on the Japanese market. The plight of the lonely elderly of rural areas, separated from their children who have left to live in large cities like Tokyo, is very familiar in Japan. For these people, Nagoya's Business Design Laboratory Co. promotes its human-shaped communication robot yorisoi ifbot with a quaint illustration: an older couple is merrily enjoying tea in their country garden, while sitting next to them is a little spacesuit-like robot, clearly a substitute for the child that has long gone.

With its transparent bubble head, it looks much like any other talking toy spaceman (its maker says it comes from Planet ifbot Star), but is advertised as a new member of the family. It can't move about that well on its wheels, but compensates with sophisticated communication. It has tens of thousands of speech patterns and 40 kinds of feelings expressed through its mouth, eyes, and eyelids, and can communicate at the level of a five-year-old child, according to the firm. Its AI functions include voice recognition, and perhaps most useful for elderly users, verbal diversions, including riddles, memory and word games. "Ifbot's game functions are intended to make seniors use their brains a lot," says the company's Masashi Igarashi, "and thus prevent or delay the onset of dementia."

With its blinking lights and friendly chatterbox manner, ifbot can also provide something that has become prized in Japan's highly stressed society: *iyashi*, a healing and relaxing effect. When the company loaned the toy to seniors for one-month trials, they could barely get the old folks to return them. Owners have even composed humorous haiku about them.

Since sales began in 2004, Business Design Laboratory has been marketing its quizmaster-cum-buddy to nursing homes. It takes about a week for residents to get used to ifbot, but then they are smitten, according to Igarashi. He recalls a comment from one 79-year-old ifbot user: "It cares about me, tells jokes, and is a partner that I can't part from. I'd like to keep up the relationship for a long time."

Home Humanoids at Your Service

Robots have become companions, but the fact that they were also physical mechanisms that can be built, tinkered with, customized, and then enjoyed is fuelling a do-it-yourself boom among Japanese hobbyists of all ages. One of the hottest products in the consumer robot market today is the robot kit, a set of components that, once assembled, becomes anything from a small radio-controlled robot insect to a bipedal humanoid.

Robot enthusiasts have been building their own robots from scratch for years. But the hobby robot market exploded in 2004 with the launch of Kondo Kagaku Co.'s KHR-1, billed as the first kit in the world from which a complete humanoid could be built. The pre-assembled version is a top seller and a huge hit at ¥126,000 apiece. The un-assembled version includes more than 200 pieces and takes about five hours to put together. The complete KHR-1 is a mechanical-looking, blocky little figure that can walk, do backward rolls, and dozens of other cool custom moves. KHR-1 has no sensors or intelligence, but a bundled software package allows for sophisticated movement sequences to be easily programmed in minutes on a cable-linked PC.

"Even if you know nothing about programming, you can simply create new moves by posing the robot," says Yukiko Nakagawa of RT Corp. "It's like stop-motion animation, and so simple that kids can do it." RT is an online retailer that hosts monthly "robot school" seminars in Tokyo's Akihabara electronics mecca; similar classes are held at Osaka's new Robo Cafe, where one can play with robots ranging from vintage 1950s tin men to the latest autonomous toys while sipping latte. Many KHR-1 buyers are men in their 30s or retirees, but during one RT class at an Akihabara Robot Culture Festival, the room was not only crammed with masses of wires, PCs, and robots in various states of completion, but parents and children. In fact, the walls of nearby Tsukumo Robotto Okoku, a shop exclusively selling robots, robot parts, and DIY robot literature, are decorated with photos of Japanese families, proudly posing with RC humanoids they have built together. (The wall also includes a photo of actor Will Smith, who dropped by during a promotion junket for his movie *I, Robot*.)

But building your own robot isn't for everyone. The store also sells Nuvo, a high-end, ready-made little biped that was billed as the world's first humanoid robot for home use when it was launched by Tokyo robot venture firm ZMP Inc. in April 2005. Compared to the DIY kits, the ¥588,000 Nuvo is the sport coupe of small bipeds. It has a similar 15-inch frame, but is a sophisticated robot, loaded with interactive features like speech recognition and Internet cellphone access. Its single, unblinking camera eye is perhaps its most practical asset, allowing it to serve as a home monitor for owners on the go.

Companionship is Nuvo's forte, and the robot is nothing if not likeable. When it boots up on the floor and stands from a prone posture, its 15 servomotors brew up a minor storm of mechanical whining. It is then ready to obey about 50 basic commands. Say "Hello" and it responds with a bow. Request some tunes and Nuvo announces in a boy's voice, "Music start!" before launching into some Beethoven; users can upload their own music files as with an iPod. "Let's dance" produces a flurry of choreographed whines and waving of spherical hands. With 15 degrees of freedom, it can waddle about, pick itself up with ease after a fall, or perform acrobatic stunts.

Over a hundred people, from engineers to choreographers and musicians, collaborated in Nuvo's development with ZMP. For Nuvo's appearance, the start-up recruited industrial designer Ken Okuyama, whose works include the Ferrari Rossa. Okuyama gave Nuvo its sleek, brightly coloured look.

Art director Shinichi Hara also fashioned a luxury "Nuvo Japanism" edition with a finish featuring traditional Japanese motifs and executed in gold, black, and red *urushi* lacquer; it comes in a wooden box lined with red, like a gorgeously wrought work of art. But the high price of even the standard Nuvo has been an obstacle to sales. ZMP acknowledges it has to bring the cost down to around the level of laptop computers to give Nuvo a chance of becoming the television set or refrigerator of the twenty-first century.

The race to produce the first useful and affordable home humanoid has already begun. Only a few months after Nuvo's launch, Mitsubishi Heavy Industries Ltd.—a massive industrial concern that manufactures everything from supertankers to Patriot missile systems—commercialized the lemon-coloured Wakamaru. (The name is derived from Ushiwakamaru, the childhood name of the legendary twelfth-century general Minamoto no Yoshitsune, one of the greatest, most tragic samurai in Japanese history.) At 39 inches, it is a good height for a robot helper, though it moves about on a wheeled base tucked beneath its skirt rather than legs.

Despite its heroic, masculine name, the machine cuts a rather maternal figure that goes well with a domestic setting—it was specifically designed to help out with chores around the home. Wakamaru has few bells and whistles. It cannot do somersaults or pick itself up, and trundles around the room slowly and deliberately, waving its arms with an undersea grace now and again. "Please summon me at any time," it says, to no one in particular.

Like Nuvo, its practicality lies in its interactive functions. It can rouse itself automatically at its recharging station, scoot into the bedroom, and wake its owner. It can read out email via its wireless, 24-hour Internet link, and let remote users view their homes through its eyes, or alert them when it detects motion. Wakamaru's agenda function can remind its owner of what's on for the day.

Its face recognition and tracking abilities allow it to distinguish up to 10 people. A vocabulary of 10,000 words and four microphones provide for rudimentary, though by no means smooth, conversation (it often misunderstands requests). Wakamaru can call up and read out in a nasal, synthesized voice news or a weather forecast from the Net. It can entertain with astrology readings and a calisthenics routine. Tiny cameras on its face and the top of its head, coupled with obstacle sensors, room maps, and external wall-mounted markers, help it understand its surroundings, so it is aware of its location and can automatically return to its recharging station when its battery power ebbs.

One of Wakamaru's most redeeming features, though, is its ability to make eye contact with users and track their movements with its 360-degree head cam. By staring into a user's eyes, it mimics a basic technique of human communication. It is not so shocking when an animal robot companion like Paro does this, but the effect is all the more startling coupled with Wakamaru's patently artificial, machinelike appearance,

The Wakamaru project was a significant departure from Mitsubishi's mainline heavy industry operations. The company had been developing robots for hazardous work like nuclear reactor servicing. Engineers, however, did not view it as a particularly adventurous undertaking. "We thought, 'What new thing can we produce? A home robot,'" says Toshiaki Murata, a manager at the company's machinery headquarters.

"We thought we'd give it a go. The humanoid form was a natural choice and makes it easier for people to feel close to the robot."

If robot helpmates are to succeed anywhere, the best place is the Japanese living space—and once again the reasons lie in the history of Japanese humanoids. "Japanese love robots due to the influence of manga robots like Mighty Atom and Ironman No. 28," says Murata. "I think Wakamaru is the first step toward realizing the dream of a robot that can help out at home."

Love and Labour

As robots become everyday household appliances, playthings, and companions in Japan, the psychological dynamics of interaction with humans is an area that must be developed. Robots that are increasingly humanlike in appearance and behaviour beg the questions: how far will Japanese—and the rest of us, of course—be willing to take their relationships with artificial partners? Will there be robot addicts, like cellphone junkies?

Already, Japan is home to vast numbers of people who spend more time with machines than human beings. Hitoshi Matsubara, a professor of AI at Future University Hakodate in Hokkaido and author of a book entitled *Tetsuwan Atomu jitsugen dekiruka?* (Can We Make Mighty Atom?), admits there is some cause for concern. "There's a tendency for people to just sit there and become absorbed passively in video games, television, and other devices," says Matsubara. "But robots are physical things that require active participation. That's a positive aspect."

"Maybe people won't work if every home has a robot," muses Junko Nishikawa, a Tokyo office worker in her 20s. "We learn that it's valuable to labour by ourselves. People who understand that are qualified to live with a robot." Sentiments like these are easy to express when robots are slow and clumsy, but as they become more dexterous and intelligent, it becomes ever more tempting to imagine them helping out around the house. The next big step in commercial humanoids will be when some of the most sophisticated robots in the world, which now showcase the high-tech prowess of the companies that created them, step off the stage and into the home.

F.Y.I.

AI: abbreviation for Artificial Intelligence, which is the theory and development of computer systems designed to perform tasks that normally require human intelligence, such as speech, visual perception, decision making, and translation between languages

Haiku: a Japanese poem whose name means "light verse"; traditionally about nature and written in 17 syllables, in three lines of five, seven, and five syllables each

MIT: abbreviation for the Massachusetts Institute of Technology, a world-renowned education institute located in Cambridge, Massachusetts, created in 1865 and dedicated to teaching, research, and the advancement of science and technology

Words to Build on

actuators: components that cause a machine or device to operate

anthropomorphic: when one attributes human characteristics to non-human or non-living things, objects or, concepts

venture firm: an investment company that invests its shareholders' money in risky but potentially profitable ventures

Tricks of the Trade

Supporting evidence

In Your Own Words: Comprehension

1. According to Hornyak, what are the uses of robots?
2. What are the reasons the Japanese favour the use of robots?
3. According to Hornyak, why does the aging population need extra help in Japan?
4. What makes the robot Paro useful? What is its main purpose?
5. What are the advantages of pet therapy for seniors?
6. Why not use real animals for pet therapy? Why use a fake baby seal?
7. What are some of the harmful effects of stress? Can interacting with non-living things be effective in reducing stress?

In Your Own Words: Analysis

1. Timothy Hornyak uses various statistics to support his points. Do you find these convincing? Why or why not? Which statistic do you find particularly strong?
2. What is the tone used in this article? Does he show any bias in this piece? If so, provide an example.
3. Why aren't North Americans as open to embracing robotic technology as the Japanese?
4. Think about how robots are presented in popular culture (like in American movies) and compare this to how Hornyak presents them in his work.
5. Based on what Hornyak writes about robots, are there any types of human personalities that wouldn't or couldn't interact with a robot? Are there people not suited to living with robots?
6. What areas of your life could be improved if you had access to robotic technology?
7. Judging by what Hornyak writes, what can we expect to see in the future in terms of robotic technology?

❖ Now Write

1. Considering the needs of human beings today and what they may need in the future, what are the best jobs or tasks for robots? Include your own examples and explanations, not just those that Hornyak includes in his article.

2. Today's technology is often seen as a kind of "cure-all." What are we losing as a society when we put so much faith in technology?

3. No matter how sophisticated robotic technology becomes, what are at least three major attributes specific to humans that robots will never be able to possess, replicate, or replace?

4. Japan is often praised for being a culture of high life expectancy. However, recent data shows that though people are living longer, many seniors are living in remote areas and suffering from loneliness, neglect, and poverty, especially since their adult children have moved to cities. Research statistics on Japan's life expectancy rates. Is robotic technology the best solution to help alleviate the problems Japan's seniors face?

Karim Rashid

Karim Rashid (b. 1960) was born in Egypt to an Egyptian father and English mother. He was raised and educated in England and Canada. Rashid earned an arts degree from the Ontario College of Art and Design and a bachelor degree in industrial design from Carleton University in Ottawa. His career and fame began as a designer, but he is also a DJ, hotelier, and self-proclaimed "world changer." He has 3000 designs in production, hundreds of which, such as the Garbo trash can and the Oh! stackable chair made for Umbra, have proved commercially lucrative as well as becoming design icons. Rashid has designed for companies around the world, including Tommy Hilfiger, Audi, Samsung, and Swarovski. A multiple award-winning designer, his work appears in famous galleries such as the Museum of Modern Art in New York and Centre Pompidou in Paris, and he also lectures at colleges and universities internationally. Though he does have many supporters and fans among clients, the public, and other designers, he has also been criticized for not having much of an environmental conscience because of his support for constantly and rapidly upgrading and replacing products. To view some of Rashid's designs and his famous, "Karimanifesto," go to his website www.karimrashid.com.

In His Own Words

"People project meaning onto objects. If an object allows you to interact with it, then it becomes part of your being, and over time you see things in it that first you might not have seen."

"The tendency is to think that when the world shrinks, we're going to lose some sort of essence of our culture, our identity, but I have a theory that for every thing, tradition, or ritual that we lose, we gain a new one."

"The thing that inspires me is people, because at the end of the day, all this is about us. None of this needs to exist if it's not about the human experience."

Before We Begin

1. In his book, Rashid writes, "We are not here to please everyone else; we are here to do great things for ourselves…" What does Rashid mean by this? How do you feel about this idea?
2. Is technology the great leveller of social class? In other words, are today's and tomorrow's technological devices available to everyone?
3. Do you consider yourself a self-reliant person? What makes you see yourself this way?
4. Go online and view some of Rashid's designs. What do you think of them and how would you describe them?

 **Now Read**

from *design your self*

The future is here and it is beautiful.

Not that many years ago, calculators were the size of a thick paperback book. Now we carry endless gigabytes of information on a computer half that size. More to the point, most of the technological breakthroughs we enjoy today we could not have imagined a decade ago. The world is changing, and everything that surrounds us is steadily becoming more user friendly, more designed, and more contemporary.

Within my lifetime, I will wake up in the morning to soothing sounds. The smart polarizing glass will go from black to clear. I will make my way to the bathroom on a floor that's just the right temperature. The bathroom will be fully automated; it will take my vital signs as I go about my business.

When I walk into the kitchen, the best possible cup of coffee will be waiting for me in the most comfortable mug ever designed, and it will be precisely the way I like it. The refrigerator will tell me what's fresh, and if I reach for something, it will provide recipes based on what's available.

The computer wallpaper tells me the time and what my day looks like. It tells me who I'm meeting and when, what the meeting is about, and who will be in attendance.

If I ask for music, I get music; news, I get news.

The lights will follow me back to the bedroom. The closet will open as I get ready to dress, and it will make suggestions about what I might wear. It will even remember who I'm meeting and what I was wearing the last time I met with those people, and what I might consider today—according to the weather, of course.

As I make my way back into the living room, I notice that the vase has changed colours. That lets me know the water needs changing.

Before I leave, I put on a pair of high-performance shoes I ordered online.

When I leave, closing the door behind me, the house gets to work, cleaning itself.

I get into a car, and the electric seat is customized to my anatomy. Even the steering wheel is completely ergonomic—from just the touch of my hand it knows it's me and the engine starts and we're ready to roll.

The car asks me where I'm going and what I'd like to listen to.

When I get to the office, the doors sense my approach and open to let me through. My office chair is a dream, anthropomorphically attuned to my entire body.

If it's cold, the microfibres in my clothes warm up slightly so that I'm at exactly the temperature I find most comfortable.

When I go to lunch, I need nothing but an appetite. I don't carry a wallet. I don't have anything in my pockets. No keys, no cellphone, nothing. There's a microchip in my index finger that contains my credit card information, one in my earlobe that is a phone, and another in my iris for visual communication. When I want to dial, I simply ask the chip to dial and I'm connected. Internet access is built into my anatomy.

If I have to travel, I will be picked up by a small electric car that checks me in en route to the airport. All I travel with is a small computer and a single change of clothes. The computer has everything I need on it: movies, books, design plans, calendars, music, and so on.

I arrive in a new city, hang up my self-cleaning clothes, change into my fresh outfit, and go to work, dinner, or play.

When I return to the hotel, the windows turn opaque and become video screens. Sleep no longer exists, there is only dream time.

When I wake up in the morning, the world is there to serve me so that I can be the best version of me I can be.

My desire is to see people living in our time, participating in our contemporary world, and delivered from nostalgia and antiquated notions. My hope is that we become conscious and sensorially attuned with this world, in this moment. If it is human nature to live in the past, we have to change it. To look back is to impede our forward momentum. There is nothing to be afraid of; we should embrace technology, allow progress to run its course, and *believe* how much better our lives can be. That is what I have set out to do. I want to change the world.

Words to Build on

ergonomics: a field of study that deals with the relations between people and their work environment, especially as it affects efficiency and safety

impede: to delay or prevent someone or something by obstructing them

In Your Own Words: Comprehension

1. Circle every personal pronoun (I, me, my) Rashid uses in this chapter. How many times does he use a personal pronoun?

2. Describe a typical day in Rashid's view of the future.

3. Explain what Rashid means by "Sleep no longer exists, there is only dream time."

4. Define "anthropomorphically." What does it mean in the context of this sentence?

5. Define "sensorially." What does it mean in the context of this sentence?

6. What is Rashid's greatest desire?

7. According to Rashid, what type of technology will be associated with one's body?

8. What does Rashid mean when he states, "The future is here and it is beautiful."

In Your Own Words: Analysis

1. Reflect on the number of times Rashid uses the pronouns "I," "me," and "my." What effect does this have in relation to the subject of this article?

2. In his description of the future, Rashid uses the pronoun "we" only once. What is it in reference to? What are your thoughts on this?

3. In terms of Rashid's description of a typical day in the future, what are the benefits of these technological advancements and what are the drawbacks?

4. According to Rashid, "there is nothing to be afraid of" in the future. Do you agree with him? If not, what is there to fear?

5. How would you define "technology"? Look up the word and make a note of how it is officially defined. What is different about your definition and the one you found in the dictionary?

6. What are some ideas or inventions for the future that Rashid describes that you would like to see? Are there any that you find disturbing?

7. Do any of Rashid's ideas or inventions already exist? Which ones?

8. Rashid states, "If it is human nature to live in the past, we have to change it." Do you agree? What are the implications of such a statement? What would historians think about Rashid's statement?

❊ Now Write

1. What is the difference between what humans need and what we desire or want? In the context of Rashid's chapter, he speaks of what he "needs," but are these needs or wants?

2. Compare and contrast the life and work of Karim Rashid with those of the nineteenth-century writer and textile artist William Morris, who was like the Karim Rashid of his time in terms of his work and success in diverse fields of design. What do these two men have in common and how do they differ?

3. Technology brings us many benefits but there are also drawbacks. Write an essay in which you compare and contrast what human beings gain from using various forms of technology versus what they lose. You may want to examine any of the following areas: language and thought, human relationships, conversation, self-expression, and manners. Write your essay with reference to Rashid's *design your self*.

4. When you think of Rashid's description of the future, who will be comfortable in it and who will be left out? Write an essay in which you explain whether everyone will have a place in Rashid's vision of the future or whether there will be any particular group for whom this world presents challenges.

Rex Murphy

Rex Murphy (b. 1947) is one of Canada's most controversial and respected authors and commentators on global, political, and social events. Born in Carbonear, Newfoundland, Murphy would inherit his love of learning from his mother and his love of language from his father, even though his father possessed no greater than a Grade 4 education. Well known for having an extraordinarily large and rich vocabulary, Murphy is also a charismatic orator who is able to greatly entertain audiences at his public speaking engagements.

Although quite shy as a child, Murphy was an excellent student, skipping two grades and entering Memorial University at the age of just 15. To rid himself of his shyness, he signed up for debates. In a now famous debate at the student union conference in Lennoxville, Quebec, Murphy spoke out against then-premier of Newfoundland Joey Smallwood's free university tuition program for provincial students as being nothing but a fraud. Back in St. John's, Premier Smallwood was so enraged that he went on provincial television and forbade Murphy from returning to Newfoundland. Murphy would return to the province, and Smallwood would finally make good on his promise of free tuition for all Newfoundland students. Murphy graduated three years later with a Rhodes scholarship to Oxford University but returned to Newfoundland to further his studies and establish himself as a talented broadcaster, teacher, and writer.

Murphy can be seen on CBC's *The National*, heard on his weekly CBC radio show *Cross Country Checkup*, and read in his column in the *National Post*. In the following articles, "A Saint Sorely Taxed," "Ego Warriors," and "There's Something About Cassandra," he takes on the subject of celebrities as social and global "saviours" in typical Murphy fashion: no-holds-barred and no fool suffered lightly. His ability to examine any topic from politics to pop culture in an engaging, insightful, humorous, and often scathing manner has made Murphy a national treasure as well as a target. Either way, as a former executive producer of *The National* once pointed out, "Very few Canadians turn off the set when Rex Murphy is on."

In His Own Words

"Celebrity is rocket fuel—it is very high-octane stuff—but for all but the most skillful or lucky it's only good for a short, fast rise."

"Each new apocalypse averted by rock stars should have its own wristband. Hand-me-downs are for losers."

"About the celebrity machine...it is powered only by the need to feed itself. And it will be equally content and very likely more gleeful, should his [Barack Obama] fortunes turn, in excoriating what and whom it once exalted."

Before We Begin

1. Who do you know more about: world leaders or actors and athletes? Why do you think this is?
2. Do you watch celebrity entertainment shows or read celebrity entertainment magazines? What interests you about them?
3. How do you feel when celebrities get involved in political or social events? Does their involvement inspire or repulse you?

 **Now Read**

from *Canada and Other Matters of Opinion*

A SAINT SORELY TAXED | October 17, 2006

It's nice to see that Madonna has come down from her neon cross—a Las Vegas–looking crucifixion of the emphatically Material Girl was part of the safe shock of her recent tour. After all, if you can't blaspheme Christianity these days, what can you blaspheme?

Now she's descended on Africa, following the trendy, spangled footsteps of Brad and Angelina and other monstrously rich celebrities who have turned Africa and its misery into their own publicity-fat conscience theme park. They should start a foundation: good deeds that make it to *Entertainment Tonight,* adoptions that land you the cover of *People* magazine.

Madonna, her entourage, her private jet, and Guy Ritchie have plucked one African baby from an orphanage, and the world is all a-twitter at another celebrity good deed. The story is almost big enough to drown out the news that U2, the rock band, has moved some of its assets from its native Ireland to the Netherlands. The Netherlands has a very favourable tax rate, even better than Ireland, which for artists is already a tax haven of unimaginable indulgence.

U2 is, of course, Bono's band, Bono, the greatest scold of rich governments on the face of the earth. Bono was the man who nagged Paul Martin in public for Canada's not giving enough for African debt relief, but then, Bono—friend of Bill Clinton, consort of the princes of the world, World Economic Forum attendee, gazillionaire—nags everyone about Africa. He even read the riot act of liberal outrage to his own government because the Irish government, like Canada, was slack on debt relief for Africa. Uriah Heep with groupies.

Bono and his multimillionaire bandmates have hauled their songwriting business out of Ireland because Ireland has modestly upped the tax levy on artists making over half a million a year. So he wants Ireland to give more of its taxes to help poor Africa, but he, Bono, wants to pay less in taxes to Ireland. I'd call him a whited sepulchre, except that's a biblical reference, and Madonna would probably claim copyright.

Bono did not hesitate, at a concert here last year around election time, to tag Paul Martin, his friend, for not living up to his pledge to increase Canada's foreign aid. Bono said he was crushed. Well, I guess the "Make Poverty History" front-man has less trouble with inconsistency and hypocrisy when it's his bank account and those of his bandmates that actually take the hit. Yet Bono's been shining his rock-star celebrity halo so assiduously in public that you'd think he was a cross between Mother Theresa and Cardinal Léger.

This guy has been lecturing whole continents for decades—he's the self-declared pope of poverty—about Africa, but now hauls part of his empire from his home country to Amsterdam. Lecture us no more, Mr. Bono. A tax haven is not a pulpit. Amsterdam is not an African village. However, all is not lost. Maybe Bono will adopt someone. Let us pray—let us *all* pray—it's Madonna. They deserve each other.

EGO WARRIORS | July 14, 2007

The reviews are in concerning last weekend's eco-sanctimony staged by global warming's Nostradamus, Al Gore, and most of them aren't pretty. It was, according to the advance hype—and the hype for this event matched anything Hollywood revs up for Johnny Depp in a bandana or a new Jessica Simpson big-screen onslaught—going to command an audience in excess of 2 billion.

There is nothing original in rounding up a beaker full of rock stars and movie celebrities, faded songsters, and a rapper or two to variously strum, gyrate, and posture for a *cause du jour.* We have had "We Are the World" and Live Aid, Willie Nelson doing his minstrel bit for the American farmer, and last year's care-a-palooza, the Make Poverty History jamboree, which didn't.

NBC devoted three hours of prime time to last Saturday's effort, which trawled a measly 2.7 million viewers, a number that would be embarrassing for a home-cooking show or a rerun of *Three's Company.* Not even such A-list, world-dominating entertainers as Madonna and Shakira, assisted by those cleavage climatologists the Pussycat Dolls, could lure the torpid and the unaware, in any numbers, to the home screen. Nor could Snoop Dogg (the bard of "Nuthin' but a 'G' Thang"), appearing on stage in Hamburg (Hamburg? Who knew?) jolt the sing-a-long into a zone of even mild, credible buzz.

What happened?

I suppose the spectacle of the world's most wasteful people, rock-star plutocrats with their cribs and bling, caravans of trailer trucks and 100 000-watt amplifiers, taking a day out of their wealth-stuffed lives to preach to the less well off of the world on the moral importance of consuming less "to save the planet" set the hypocrisy bar so high that it put too great a strain on the digestion of ordinary people. In the wicked words of one rock star who declined to climb aboard the bandwagon, "Private jets for climate change."

Unless outfitted with a cast-iron stomach—and I mean a real one—how could anybody endure Madonna of the Nine Mansions wrapping herself in the ascetics of the eco-movement? Hyper-indulgent, super-pampered, colossally wealthy, manically consumerist entertainment celebrities preaching restraint to others: Live Earth was a weird and monstrous journey to a whole new dimension of live irony. Come back, Uriah Heep. All is forgiven.

Not even the professional environmentalists could stay their gorge at Madonna's participation. They gave the world the news that the Material Girl owns shares in the most politically incorrect enterprises, such as Alcoa, the American aluminum giant, the Ford Motor Company, and Weyerhaeuser, which—gasp!—chops trees for money.

Then there was the sheer, deep folly of it all. What has Shakira, or her hips, got to offer on the question of the world's weather over the next hundred years? But Shakira is Robert Oppenheimer on steroids compared with Geri Halliwell of the long-forgotten fluff band the Spice Girls—"Yo, I'll tell you what I want, what I really, really want, etc., etc., etc., etc."

Geri Halliwell, Snoop Dogg, Shakira, Madonna, and the Pussycat arborists are an unlikely think tank (maybe a think tank top?) on global warming or anything else. They are career publicists of themselves, artists in the merchandising of fluff and ego.

But beyond the obvious hypocrisy; beyond the saccharine, Mickey Rooneyesque "let's put on a show" conceit of the Live Earth dud-spectacular, I think something rather deeper and, perhaps grimly encouraging, accounts for its failure.

The public has just gotten tired of "stars." These luminescent bodies are now in much the same leaky boat as most politicians because, by trying to wed themselves to some aspects of politics to strengthen or underwrite their highly capitalist careers, they are seen as manipulative in precisely the same cynical way politicians are. Entertainers are, primarily, politicians of their own careers.

They don't have the "cred" they used to have. They have been exposed as shills for themselves before anything else. And so it's not the elephantine "carbon footprint" of Madonna or the big bands that turned people away from Live Earth. It's the growing perception that all the strutting icons up there on all those stages are playing a game, just as the politicians play a game, and for very much the same self-serving, egoistic reasons.

It's an *Animal Farm* moment for our time: "The creatures outside looked from pig to man, and from man to pig, and from pig to man again; but already it was impossible to say which was which."

Now it's impossible to say which are the stars and which are the politicians. Madonna and Gore—can you spot the difference?

> Al Gore is still talking, but I think his moment too—as politician who morphed into the less demanding though more remunerative role of celebrity—is either passing or passed. Al doesn't generate the "vibe" anymore. Celebrity is rocket fuel—it is very high-octane stuff—but for all but the most skilful or lucky it's only good for a short, fast rise. Al will still trot—or private jet—the world, and play John the Baptist for the coming global warming Armageddon. He's still good for a walk-on at an awards show—Snoop Dogg presents, Lindsay Lohan is in the wings—and a headliner at some conference of the perpetually and professionally worrying class. The Nobel Prize was his apogee, and even that moment didn't have the feel of real, class-A achievement. Is it because the Nobel itself is a decaying gold star? Or is it because there was something just a little too neat, maybe compensatory, about awarding the world's bluest blue ribbon to the man who lost—dare we write the name—to the "witless" George W. Bush?

THERE'S SOMETHING ABOUT CASSANDRA | November 1, 2008

Where is Cameron Diaz? Haven't seen—and, worse, haven't heard from—her in so long a while. Has she been disappeared? Is she in Guantanamo, the Bush–Cheney gulag for dissident celebrities?

A little more than four years ago, on a panel boasting the finest minds the world has known since the days of ancient Athens, when Socrates was tutoring Plato, Ms. Diaz was offering advice on the coming election between George Bush and John Kerry.

The setting was the daily edification we all know and love as *The Oprah Winfrey Show*. The grand empath, her Oprahness, had designed a program to stir the youth of America to vote, and crowded onto the couch (besides Ms. Diaz) an almost frightening constellation of intelligence and prestige.

There was Sean Combs, a putty artist of nomenclature, whom you may know as Puff Daddy, P. Diddy, Puffy, Diddy, Daddy Piff, or Diddy Puff. The backup intellects for the occasion, doo-woppers for Mr. Diddy's famous Vote or Die campaign, were Christina Aguilera and Drew Barrymore.

Think of it as a symphony of mind.

It was the sylphlike Ms. Diaz who most lucidly framed the choice between George (Neanderthal, Halliburton, frat boy, Karl Rove puppet, tool of Big Oil, IQ of a lug wrench) Bush and John (elegant) Kerry. She issued a warning to the timid and vacant minds of young America, especially to the female half of that monstrous demographic: "If you think rape should be legal, then don't vote!"

And lest that wouldn't hold their attention—the young of America are notoriously detached—the delectable Cassandra who had transfixed the world in *There's Something About Mary* further cautioned that they "could lose the right to their bodies." Which would be inconvenient.

America didn't listen that day—at least, young America didn't. George (amoeba, cretin, theocrat, warmonger) Bush defeated John (sweet) Kerry, rape has been legal in that despoiled country for four years, and millions of young women have had to get government permission to use their bodies for anything—getting out of bed, going to a global warming protest, dropping by Starbucks, or attending the MTV Awards (where a body is an absolute must—although there's a cover charge on the brain).

We haven't heard from Ms. Diaz this cycle, which is such a shame. Maybe she's just tired. Or taken up macramé. Speaking Bluetooth to power can drain the old soul. But America is nothing if not the country of renewal. If one oracle vanishes, another leaps from the self-help rack at Barnes and Noble, or from the back pages of the better fashion magazines.

The Cameron Diaz of the 2008 election—and, need I say, supporter of Barack (cool, mesmeric, "thrill up my leg," hope, change, new dawn, better dawn, dawn all day) Obama—is Erica Jong. Ms. Jong wrote a book called *Fear of Flying*, which is to literature what *Charlie's Angels* is to theology.

But Ms. Jong is, make no mistake about it, a seer and guru of Diaz-like dimensions. She hangs about with an almost equally illustrious crowd, numbering such geopolitical high foreheads as Jane (Hanoi, exercise videos, Ted Turner) Fonda and Naomi (Al Gore's "earth tones" clothing consultant, author of *The Treehouse)* Wolf as among her fellow thinkers.

Ms. Jong, and God bless her courage, issued a warning this week—via the Italian press, where the Apocalypse (not surprisingly) has its own feature page—that should Barack Obama lose the election on Tuesday, "blood will run in the streets." Fearful that that was a tad ambiguous, she—this was the novelist in her breaking out—referenced America's founding trauma.

"If Obama loses, it will spark the second American Civil War." There you have it. Vote for Barack Obama, or Gettysburg will have a sequel, and poor Ken Burns will have to do that damn series all over again. The stakes are high. You betcha. (And, oh yes, Jane Fonda's having "back pains" just thinking about this. Which probably means she should stop thinking with her back, but I digress.)

Well, we all know what happened when America ignored Cameron Diaz four years ago. Global warming, Katrina, stock-market meltdown, and, of course, that rape thing. The question is, will Americans similarly ignore the prescience of the artist who gave the world the concept of a "zipless fuck"?

I cannot think it will. America will not a second time be heedless. There will not be blood on the streets. No second Civil War. And America, and Barack Obama, will have no one to thank for it but Erica Jong, and the immortal slogan: Save Jane's Back—Vote Obama. Intellect will out: John McCain and Sarah Palin are toast.

In my books, this is right up there with Cameron Diaz. Sigh.

Among the many blessings, uncounted till this very moment, of the election of Barack Obama to the American presidency, are the reduction in Jane Fonda's "back pains" and the averting of the second American Civil War. I do not know which of this two history will choose to merit the superior wreath in Obama's civil crown. For, insomuch as he has stayed a scene of civil slaughter—at least according to Erica Jong and the illuminati of *The View*—he must be regarded as a true American hero. But to have assuaged the ravages wrought by years of producing exercise videos (Jane Fonda was the spandex queen of losing weight by televised exhibition) in which she so aerobically starred, to have reduced Jane Fonda's back pain, is an accomplishment from which Clio may stagger back in bewildered amazement. The goddess of History probably has no scale in which to enter achievement of this magnitude.

And good news for Cameron Diaz—Bush is gone and rape is, once more, illegal. Making statements of pathetic ignorance is, however, as legal as ever.

F.Y.I.

"amoeba, cretin, theocrat, warmonger": each word used on its own can have negative connotations, but having them linked together in this manner is meant to illustrate the strength of the insult.

Cardinal Léger: (1904–1991) a Canadian Cardinal of the Roman Catholic Church. He is known for his humanitarian work around the globe. He received the first Pearson Medal of Peace, and he was made a Companion of the Order of Canada and a Grand Officer of the National Order of Quebec for his humanitarian efforts.

Cassandra: in Greek this name means "she who traps men." Cassandra is a figure in Greek mythology that was granted the gift of prophesy by the god Apollo for being tremendously beautiful. When she spurned his advances, Apollo cursed her so that from that moment on, no one would ever believe her predictions. Cassandra has come to be seen as a tragic figure because of her ability to see and understand the future but her powerlessness to use these gifts effectively.

Gettysburg: this one word makes reference to the famous three-day battle in Gettysburg, Pennsylvania, fought during the American Civil War. The Battle of Gettysburg not only had the largest number of casualties, but is often seen as the major turning point in the war because it was a decisive victory for the northern troops as Major General Meade ended Confederate General Lee's invasion of the north.

high foreheads: a term used to refer to exceedingly intelligent people or deep thinkers. As in this article, it is not often meant to be a compliment.

Ken Burns: (b. 1953) an American director and producer. He is known for his style of using archival footage and photographs in his documentaries on American subjects such as jazz, baseball, the Brooklyn Bridge, and American national parks. He won numerous awards for his acclaimed nine-part documentary *The Civil War*, on which he served as director, producer, co-writer, chief cinematographer, music director, and executive producer.

macramé: a technique used to make textiles by forming tight threads or yarn into tight knots instead of weaving or knitting them.

Paul Martin: (b. 1938) the twenty-first Prime Minister of Canada and the former leader of the Liberal Party of Canada.

Robert Oppenheimer: (1904–1967) the brilliant American theoretical physicist who is known primarily for his role as the scientific director of the special World War II military project called the Manhattan Project, which created the first nuclear weapons.

Uriah Heep: one of the most famous literary villains, Uriah Heep is a character in Charles Dickens's classic novel, *David Copperfield*. A character known for his insincerity, false humility, dishonesty, and hypocrisy, his name is used to describe a person or behaviour that is "sucking up" or "kissing ass."

Words to Build on

arborist: a person who specializes in the care of trees

ascetics: people who deny themselves material comforts and pleasures and live a life of self-denial and strict discipline of the body

assiduously: to do something with constant attention

bard: a lyric poet; the term is often applied to William Shakespeare

consort: a spouse or companion of royal personages or deities; a consort is usually slightly inferior in status and function

dissident: a person who disagrees with accepted beliefs or standards

edification: intellectual, moral, or spiritual improvement

empath: a person who is extremely sensitive to the feelings of others and is said to actually be able to feel the pain of others and ease it

gulag: a system of forced labour camps in the former Soviet Union

luminescent: describing something that looks as though it is emitting a gentle light

minstrel: a lyrical poet or musician that travels from place to place to perform

nomenclature: a system of words used to name things in a particular field of study, such as science or law

oracle: a person that can foresee the future and advise on how to proceed

plutocrats: people whose wealth is the source of their control or influence

prescience: to have knowledge of actions or events that have not happened yet

scold: a person who never stops criticizing or nagging others

sepulchre: a vault, grave, or tomb used to bury the dead

spangled: to have adorned something, such as an item of clothing or fabric, by sewing small sparkling pieces of metal or plastic on it

sylphlike: having the qualities of a slim and graceful girl

torpid: to be sluggish, apathetic, and numb or to be unable to move or feel

In Your Own Words: Comprehension

1. In "A Saint Sorely Taxed," what does Bono "nag" countries such as Canada and Ireland about?

2. Why does Murphy think Bono is not in a position to lecture countries on matters concerning money?

3. In "Ego Warriors," what does Murphy think about celebrity-driven charity concerts such as Live Earth and Make Poverty History?

4. What does Murphy see as the link between celebrities and politicians?

5. In "There's Something about Cassandra," how did Cameron Diaz try to encourage young people to vote?

6. What did Erica Jong try to do to make sure that Barack Obama would be elected president?

7. In the three articles, which celebrity does Murphy seem to target the most?

In Your Own Words: Analysis

1. Explain each of the titles for the articles.

2. What is the thesis for each of Murphy's articles?

3. What evidence does Murphy provide to support his position in each article?

4. How would you define hypocrisy? What does Murphy consider hypocritical about the behaviour of Madonna and Bono?

5. Why do celebrities think that they are qualified to be spokespeople for social causes? Where does this belief come from?

6. Other than the celebrities Murphy mentions in the articles, can you name any other celebrities whose behaviour, actions, or comments have confused or offended you?

7. Judging by the evidence Murphy provides in the articles, were any of the mentioned celebrities effective in garnering support for these causes? Do you agree or disagree with Murphy?

✳ Now Write

1. From the very beginning, celebrities have always been involved in social causes. Research the topic of Hollywood entertainers and their efforts during World War II. Compare and contrast the actions of celebrities today with the actions of celebrities during the 1940s. Are they similar or different?

2. In "There's Something about Cassandra," Murphy outlines some of the ways celebrities tried to get people, especially young people, to vote. Why were these strategies ineffective? Did they really address the reasons why people don't vote? What are some more effective ways to get voters, especially young voters, to get involved in the process of elections?

3. Can celebrities be effective in helping social causes such as global debt relief and the environment, or can they actually harm such causes? Argue whether celebrities are effective or ineffective in helping with serious concerns.

Fiction

Leo Tolstoy

Leo Tolstoy (1828–1910) was born into an aristocratic family on a country estate just south of Moscow, Russia. The title of Count was conferred to his ancestor by Peter the Great. Tolstoy studied languages and law in university and was a prolific writer: he wrote stories, novels, essays, diaries, and letters. Biographers have often viewed Tolstoy's life in phases: in the first he was a "sinner" (drinking and visiting brothels) and in the latter half of his life a "prophet" and moral thinker (becoming vegetarian and being celibate). When Tolstoy was 33, he married Sofya Andreyevna Behrs, a woman 16 years younger than himself; their marriage was a long one and produced 13 children, but it was fraught with difficulties. It was Sofya who transcribed and edited Tolstoy's work. He is most well-known as the writer of one of the most famous works of literature in the Western canon, the epic novel *War and Peace* (1869), which he later declared was "verbose rubbish."

His story "God Sees the Truth but Waits" (1872) is a fleshed-out version of a fable that appears at the end of *War and Peace* as told by the character Platon Karatayev, a peasant named for the Greek philosopher Plato who tells a story that Tolstoy uses to relay the belief that one cannot expect justice from human institutions. The "expanded" story first appeared in a children's primer (a textbook intended to teach children to read) and then later in a publication for adults. Of his works, Tolstoy stated "I consign my own artistic production to the category of 'bad art,' excepting the story 'God Sees the Truth but Waits,' which seeks a place in the first class (religious art) . . . "

In 1891, Tolstoy was convinced that any money he gained from writing was a sin and despite others' objections, he renounced all royalties on anything written 10 years before this date and anything he wrote afterwards. Nine years before his death he was declared a heretic and excommunicated by the Russian Orthodox Church for writing works that were "repugnant to Christ and the Church." It was Tolstoy's belief that the Church distorted the teachings of Christ. Further, during his life he experienced great inner turmoil over his aristocratic inheritance and the reality that while some were obscenely rich, others had to live in extreme poverty. He dedicated himself to various philanthropic pursuits, including funding education for the children of peasants and continuously raising funds for famine relief.

In His Own Words

"When ignorance does not know something, it says that what it does not know is stupid."

"At the approach of danger there are always two voices that speak with equal force in the heart of man: one very reasonably tells the man to consider the nature of the danger and the means of avoiding it; the other even more reasonably says that it is too painful and harassing to think of the danger, since it is not a man's power to provide for everything and escape from the general march of events; and that it is therefore better to turn aside from the painful subject till it has come, and to think of what is pleasant. In solitude a man generally yields to the first voice; in society to the second."

Before We Begin

1. Most religions express the importance of forgiveness. In the New Testament, Peter asks Jesus "'Lord, how many times shall I forgive my brother when he sins against me? Up to seven times?' And Jesus answered, 'I tell you, not seven, but seventy times seven.'" Are there any acts that cannot be forgiven? What can be gained from the act of forgiveness?

2. Tolstoy once wrote, "The one thing that is necessary, in life as in art, is to tell the truth." What do you think Tolstoy means by this statement? Do you agree?

3. Is materialism a sin? Does our attachment to people and things such as our homes, cars, and phones keep us from being truly free?

 **Now Read**

God Sees the Truth but Waits

(A Fable)

In the town of Vladimir there lived a young merchant by the name of Aksyonov. He owned two shops and a house.

Aksyonov was handsome, with light-brown curly hair, very jovial, and a singer without equal. Ever since he was a young man he drank a great deal and when he was tipsy he would go on the rampage. But after he married he gave up drinking and there were only occasional lapses.

One summer Aksyonov went off to the fair at Nizhny. As he was saying goodbye to his family his wife told him: "Please don't go now, Ivan Dmitriyevich, I've had a bad dream about you."

Aksyonov laughed and retorted: "You're really scared I might start drinking at the fair, aren't you?"

His wife replied: "I can't say *what* I'm scared of, but it was such a nasty dream: you came back from town and took your cap off—and then I saw you'd gone completely grey!"

Aksyonov laughed again. "Don't worry, I'll do some good business there, make a nice little profit, and then I can bring you back some expensive presents!"

And he said goodbye to his family and set off.

Halfway there he met a merchant friend and stayed overnight with him at an inn. After having tea together they went to bed, in adjoining rooms. Aksyonov was an early riser. He woke up in the middle of the night and, since it was easier travelling when it was cool, he roused his driver and told him to harness the horse. Then he went round to the office at the back of the inn, settled up with the innkeeper, and drove off. After about 20 miles he stopped again to feed the horse, rested for a while in the inn vestibule, after which he went outside and ordered dinner and a samovar. Then he took his guitar and started playing. Suddenly a troika with bells ringing drove up to the yard and out of the carriage stepped an official with two soldiers. He went up to Aksyonov and asked him who he was and where he was from. Aksyonov told him everything down to the last detail and asked if he'd care to have some tea with him. But the official only kept badgering him with questions: Where had he slept the previous night? Had he been alone with the merchant? Had he seen the merchant the morning before he left? Why had he started out so early? Aksyonov was amazed at this cross-examination: he had told them everything, exactly as it had happened.

"Why are you questioning me?" he asked. "I'm no thief, I'm not some kind of highwayman. I'm going honestly about my business and you've no reason to question me."

Then the official summoned the soldiers and said: "I'm the district police inspector and I'm asking you these questions because the merchant who was with you last night has had his throat cut. Now, show me your belongings—and you (he turned to the soldiers)—search him!"

They went into the office, seized his trunk and bag, opened them, and began their search. Suddenly the police inspector took a knife from the bag and shouted:

"Whose knife is this?"

Aksyonov looked and saw that the knife they had found in the bag was bloodstained and he was scared out of his wits.

"How does there come to be blood on the knife?" asked the police inspector.

Aksyonov tried to answer, but he was dumbstruck.

"I . . . I . . . d-don't know . . . I . . . that knife . . . I mean . . . it's n-not mine," he stammered.

"This morning the merchant was found in bed with his throat cut. No one else but you could have done it. The hut was locked on the inside and no one else was there. And now we find this bloodstained knife in your bag. I can see you're guilty from your face. Come on, tell me how you murdered him and how much money you stole."

Aksyonov swore to God that he was not the murderer, that he hadn't set eyes on the merchant after they'd had tea together, that the 8000 roubles he had on him were his own and that the knife wasn't his. But his voice kept breaking, his face was ashen, and he was quaking all over with fear, just like a guilty man.

The police inspector ordered the soldiers to tie him up and take him to the cart. As he was bundled into it, his legs bound with rope, Aksyonov crossed himself and burst into tears. All his baggage and money were confiscated and he was sent off to the jail in the neighbouring town. Inquiries were made in Vladimir as to his character and all the townspeople testified that, ever since he was young, Aksyonov liked to have a few drinks and enjoy himself but he was a good man. He was accused of murdering the merchant from Ryazan and of stealing 20,000 rubles.

His wife was grief-stricken and simply did not know what to think. Although her children were still young and one of them was at the breast, she took them off with her to the town where her husband was imprisoned. At first they refused to let her see him but she prevailed upon the authorities and was taken to him. After one look at him in his prison clothes, in fetters, with criminals for company, she collapsed and it was some time before she came to her senses. Then she gathered her children around her, sat down next to him, and began telling him about all that had been happening at home, after which she asked what had happened to him. He told her everything.

"What are we going to do now?" she asked.

"We must petition the Tsar," he replied. "They can't let an innocent man perish."

His wife told him that she had already sent a petition to the Tsar, but it had been rejected. Aksyonov did not reply and looked down at the floor. "You see," continued his wife, "it wasn't for nothing that I dreamt your hair had gone grey. And now all your troubles have well and truly turned it grey. It was a great mistake going to the fair when you did."

As she ran her fingers through his hair she added: "Darling Vanya, tell me, your wife, the truth! Did you do it?"

Aksyonov replied: "How can you possibly think that I did it?" And he buried his face in his hands and sobbed. Then a soldier came to announce that it was time for his wife and children to leave. And Aksyonov bade his family farewell for the last time.

After his wife had left Aksyonov thought about what they had said and when he recalled that she too had thought him guilty, and had in fact asked him point-blank if he had killed the merchant, he told himself: "Obviously, no one except God can know the truth...only from Him should I ask for help, from Him alone can I expect mercy."

And from that time onwards Aksyonov stopped sending in petitions, stopped hoping, and simply prayed to God.

Aksyonov was sentenced to a flogging and then to be sent to hard labour in Siberia. The sentence was carried out.

He was duly flogged and later, when his wounds had healed, he was packed off with other convicts to Siberia.

Aksyonov lived 26 years in the Siberian penal settlement. His hair turned as white as snow and his beard grew long, straggly, and grey. All his old gaiety simply vanished. He developed a stoop, went around quietly, said little, never smiled, and prayed frequently.

In prison Aksyonov learnt how to make boots and with the money he earned he bought a *Saints' Calendar* and read it whenever he had enough light. On church holidays he would go to the prison chapel, read the Gospels and sing in the choir—he still had a good voice. The authorities liked Aksyonov for being so meek and mild, while his prison comrades respected him and called him "Grandpa" and "Man of God." Whenever they wanted to make a petition his fellow convicts invariably asked Aksyonov to submit it to the authorities; whenever quarrels broke out among the convicts they always came to Aksyonov to settle them. No one ever wrote to Aksyonov from home, therefore he had no idea whether his wife and children were alive.

One day a batch of new convicts arrived. In the evening all the regular convicts gathered around the new arrivals and proceeded to fire questions at them, asking what town or village they hailed from and of what they had been convicted.

Aksyonov too sat on a bunk near the new convicts, looked down at the floor and listened to their various narratives. Among the new arrivals was a tall, handsome man of 60, with a grey, close-cropped beard. He was telling them why he had been arrested.

"Well, lads," he was saying. "I've been sent here for nothing at all. All I did was un-hitch a horse from a sledge. I was arrested and accused of stealing it. But I told them that all I wanted was to get somewhere double-quick and then I would let the horse go. And the driver was a friend of mine! So, what was wrong with that?

"'No,' they insisted. 'You *stole* it!' But they didn't even know if anything had in fact been stolen and where. There's things for which I could easily have been sent here long ago, but they couldn't find enough evidence to convict me. And now they go and send me against the law! But I'm leading you on . . . I've been to Siberia before, though it was a short stay!"

"And where might you be from?" asked one of the convicts.

"From Vladimir, we're small tradesmen there. My Christian name's Makar and my surname's Semyonych."

At this Aksyonov pricked up his ears and asked: "Semyonych, did you ever hear of some merchants in Vladimir by the name of Aksyonov? Are they still alive?"

"Of course I've heard of them! Well-to-do people, although the father happens to be in Siberia. He's in the same position as us, I'm sorry to say. And what did they send you here for, Grandpa?"

Aksyonov hated talking about his own misfortunes and all he did was sigh and say: "To pay for my sins I've done 26 years penal servitude."

Makar Semyonov asked: "*What* sins?"

"Well, sins that got me what I deserved," he replied. He was reluctant to say more, but his fellow convicts told Makar how Aksyonov came to be in Siberia. They told him the story of the merchant who was murdered while travelling, about the knife that had been planted on Aksyonov, and how he had been wrongly convicted.

When Makar heard this he stared at Aksyonov, clapped his hands on his knees and said: "That's amazing. Really amazing! But how you've changed, Grandpa!"

The others asked him why he was so amazed and where he'd seen Aksyonov before, but Makar would not answer their questions and merely replied: "It's amazing! You never know when you might bump into someone!"

When he heard this it struck Aksyonov that this man might well know who had murdered the merchant.

"You either heard about it before, Semyonych," he said, "or you've seen me before."

"How could I *not* hear about it? The world's full of stories like that. But it was all such a long time ago. Whatever I heard then I've forgotten by now."

"Did you ever hear who murdered the merchant, by any chance?" asked Aksyonov. Makar Semyonov laughed and replied: "It's obvious the murderer was the one in whose bag the knife was found. If someone planted a knife on you he hasn't been caught—no man is a thief until he's caught! And how could anyone have slipped a knife into your bag? He'd have had to be standing right at the head of your bed—and then you'd have heard him."

The moment Aksyonov heard these words he suspected that *this* was the man who had murdered the merchant. He got up and went away. All that night Aksyonov could not sleep. He was utterly depressed and first he visualized his wife as she had looked when she saw him off for the last time, when he went to the fair. And he could see her just as if she were standing there right before him. He could see her face and her eyes, and he could hear her laughing and talking to him. Then he pictured his children as they had been then, so tiny, one of them in his little fur jacket, the other at his mother's breast. And then he imagined himself as he had been at the time—so cheerful, so young. He recalled how he had sat in the porch of the inn where he had been arrested playing the guitar. How light-hearted he had been then! And he recalled the place of execution where he had been flogged, the executioner, the crowd all around, the fetters and the other convicts, all his 26 years of prison life, his old age. All this he recalled and he became so dejected he felt like putting an end to his life there and then.

"All because of that villain!" Aksyonov thought.

And he became so furious with Makar Semyonov that he could have attacked him on the spot, and taken his revenge. All night long he recited prayers, but it did not calm him down. During the day he did not go near Makar Semyonov, nor did he so much as look at him.

And so two weeks passed. Aksyonov could not sleep at night and he sank into such a deep depression that he just did not know what to do with himself.

One night, when he was wandering around the prison, he saw someone throwing earth out from under one of the bunks. He stopped to take a closer look. Suddenly Makar Semyonov leapt out from under the bunk and looked at Aksyonov in terror. Aksyonov wanted to move on and make as if he had not seen what the other was doing, but Makar grabbed his arm and told him how he was digging a tunnel under the wall, how every day he would carry some earth in the tops of his boots and get rid of it by scattering it in the road when they were being marched to work.

"If you keep your mouth shut I'll take you with me, Grandpa," he said. "But if you inform on me I'll be flogged—and then you won't get away with it. I'll kill you!"

When Aksyonov looked at the villain who had done him so much harm his whole body was convulsed with rage and he tore his arm away.

"There's no point in my escaping from here," he said. "And you can't kill me now— you did that long ago. As to whether I shall inform on you or not, God will show me in my heart what to do."

Next day, when the convicts were being marched to work, the soldiers caught Makar scattering earth over the ground. They searched the prison and discovered the hole. The governor arrived and started questioning everyone as to who had dug the hole. All of them denied it. Those who knew the culprit did not betray Makar Semyonov, as they knew he would be flogged to within an inch of his life. Then the governor turned to Aksyonov. Knowing him to be a truthful man he asked: "*You* always tell the truth. Now, tell me before God, who did this?"

Makar stood there as if butter wouldn't melt in his mouth and looked only at the governor, ignoring Aksyonov. Aksyonov's hands and lips were trembling and it was a long time before he could utter a word. "I *could* cover up for him, but why should I forgive the man who ruined me?" he thought. "Let him pay the price for all my suffering. On the other hand, they're bound to flog him if I testify against him. And what if my suspicions are wrong? Would it make me feel any easier?"

The governor repeated the question: "Tell me the truth, old man. Who was trying to dig a tunnel?"

Aksyonov glanced at Makar Semyonov and said: "I saw nothing and I know nothing."

And so they did not find out who had been digging the tunnel. The following night, when Aksyonov had lain down in his bunk and had almost dozed off, he heard someone come over to him and sit at the foot of the bunk. He peered through the darkness and recognized Makar.

Aksyonov asked: "What more do you want from me? What are you doing here?"

Makar Semyonov did not reply. Aksyonov sat up and repeated: "What else do you want? Get away from me or I'll call one of the guards."

At this Makar Semyonov leant towards Aksyonov and whispered: "Ivan Dmitriyevich! Forgive me!"

Aksyonov replied: "Forgive you for what?"

"*I* murdered the merchant. I planted the knife on you. I wanted to murder you, too, but someone made a noise in the yard, so I slipped the knife into your bag and escaped through the window."

Aksyonov was silent, not knowing what to say. Makar Semyonov climbed down from the bunk, prostrated himself, and said: "Ivan Dmitriyevich, forgive me. For God's sake forgive me! I'll confess to the murder and they'll grant you a pardon. Then you'll be able to go home."

Aksyonov retorted: "It's easy enough for you to go and tell them, but just think what *I'll* have to endure! Where shall I go? My wife's dead, my children will have forgotten me. I've *nowhere* to go "

Makar Semyonov remained crouching and beat his head on the floor. "Ivan Dmitriyevich! Forgive me!" he repeated. "The flogging they gave me was easier to bear than looking at you now! When I think how you took pity on me and didn't inform. Oh, forgive me for Christ's sake! Forgive me—I'm such a rotten bastard!"

And he burst into loud sobbing.

When Aksyonov heard Makar Semyonov weeping he too wept.

"God will forgive you," he said. "Perhaps I'm a hundred times worse!"

And suddenly his heart became lighter. No longer did he pine for home, no longer did he even want to leave prison. All he thought of was his last hour . . .

Makar Semyonov ignored what Aksyonov had said and he confessed. When official permission finally came for Aksyonov to return home he had passed away.

F.Y.I.

fair at Nizhny: founded in 1523, this annual working fair was the largest in the country and made Nizhny Russia's commercial centre. The fair was eventually closed in 1930.

rouble(s): the chief monetary unit in Russia

Ryazan: a town south-east of Moscow located on the River Oka

Saints' Calendar: Until the reign of Peter the Great, this set of religious writings was once the official calendar of the Russian Church. Also called *Minei Cheti* (Monthly Readings), a selection from this collection is chosen to be read on saints' feast-days for every month of the year.

samovar: literally means "self-boiler" since it is an ornate Russian container used for preparing tea, with an internal heating tube to keep water at boiling point. The pot is heated with charcoal or coal. The samovar can be traced back 3000 years.

Siberia: a vast region in the northeastern part of Russia. In the past, it was an area that criminals and political dissidents were sent to as a form of punishment or exile.

troika: a Russian carriage or sleigh drawn by a team of three horses; "tri" is Russian for a group of three

Tsar: variation of "Czar," or the title used for the supreme rulers or emperors who ruled Russia until 1917

Vanya: Aksyonov's wife calls him "Vanya," which is the diminutive form of "Ivan"

Vladimir: founded in 1108, Vladimir was once the capital of Russia. It is located east of Moscow and is home to the famous St. Dmitry and Assumption cathedrals.

Words to Build on

bade: form of the verb "bid," used here to mean "utter farewell"

gaiety: the state of being light-hearted or merry

highwayman: the name given to a robber on horseback who was armed with guns and attacked travellers on public roads

in fetters: a chain or shackle attached to the hands or feet

Tricks of the Trade

Climax

Irony

Realism

In Your Own Words: Comprehension

1. What is Aksyonov like at the start of the story? How does he change?
2. Who is telling this story? Does the narrator foreshadow any of the events that are to come?
3. Name and describe the main conflicts in this story.
4. The title of this story is a Russian proverb. A proverb is a short saying in popular use that is believed to embody a general truth. Explain the meaning of the proverb "God sees the truth but waits" and how it relates to the story.
5. Who suspects and/or accuses Aksyonov, and how does he react to these accusations?
6. How does Aksyonov come to find out who framed him for the crime?
7. Who kills the merchant and why?

In Your Own Words: Analysis

1. What are the sins that Aksyonov refers to when he says, "To pay for my sins I've done 26 years penal servitude"? And what does he mean when at the end of the story he states "[p]erhaps I'm a hundred times worse"?

2. Does this story have more than one climax? What are the two main events in the protagonist's life? Could these be considered climaxes of the story? Why or why not?

3. Critics have commented on the narrative flaws of Tolstoy's story. What are some unrealistic aspects of this story?

4. How is it that Aksyonov is accused and found guilty of a heinous crime and yet he is seen as a pious and truthful man in prison?

5. Explain Semyonov's statement "no man is a thief until he's caught."

6. Why doesn't Aksyonov tell the governor what he saw?

7. Why does the narrator state "[a]nd suddenly his heart became lighter"? What does this mean?

Now Write

1. Tolstoy wrote, "The concern of art consists precisely in making comprehensible and accessible that which might be incomprehensible and inaccessible in the form of reasoned explanation." Using "God Sees the Truth but Waits" and one other story from this text, show how this is reflected in these stories.

2. We live in an age of self-help guides and quick fixes, where people don't recognize that true transformation can be a lengthy and often painful process. In fiction, writers create round or dynamic characters that have to undergo some type of change. Select one other story in addition to "God Sees the Truth but Waits" and examine the stages, elements, and end results of the protagonists' process of transformation.

3. Find Tolstoy's story "A Prisoner of the Caucasus" and compare it to "God Sees the Truth but Waits." Tolstoy declares the former an example of "universal art" and the latter a perfect example of "religious art." Define what he means by these terms and compare the writing style and themes of the two stories.

4. In some cultures, even today, "an eye for an eye" is still viewed as an acceptable form of justice. What is justice and what is the difference between justice and revenge? Is the perpetrator of the crime in this story punished? Why doesn't Aksyonov seek justice?

Guy de Maupassant

Guy de Maupassant (1850–1893), thought to be one of the fathers of the modern short story, is known for his impeccably tight and clever plotting as well as his ability to illuminate the emotional lives of ordinary people through his use of both naturalism and realism. He has inspired writers as diverse as Leo Tolstoy, H.P. Lovecraft, Kate Chopin, and Ernest Hemingway.

He was born Henri-Rene-Albert-Guy de Maupassant near Dieppe, France. Although he was born into a well-to-do bourgeois family, when he was 11 years old his mother obtained a legal separation from his father, something that was virtually unheard of at the time. He and his younger brother went to live with her, and as she was fond of the classics, especially Shakespeare, she was a great influence on him. His early education began at a seminary that he purposely got himself expelled from; it would also leave him with an intense dislike for religion. However, he did very well in college, especially in poetry and theatre.

In 1870, the Franco-Prussian War began. Maupassant, just out of college, enlisted and saw active duty. It was this experience that gave him material for many of his stories. After the war, he moved to Paris and spent nearly 10 years as a clerk in the Navy Department. However, during this time, he continuously wrote short stories, poetry, and novels, all the while being guided by his friend, the great French writer Gustave Flaubert (1821–1880). Flaubert would introduce Maupassant to Émile Zola (1840–1902) and Ivan Turgenev (1818–1883), who were both writers of the naturalist and realist literary style and were an influence on him. In 1880, Maupassant published "Boule de Suif" ("Butterball"). It was an instant and great success both critically and commercially. It would make Maupassant a celebrity, which meant that he could concentrate on his writing. He would write nothing but successful novels and short stories for the next 10 years.

Gustave Flaubert labelled "Butterball" as "a masterpiece that will endure," and he was correct. It is considered a masterpiece of naturalism and the short story. In it, Maupassant reflects not only on France's retreat during the Franco-Prussian War, but also explores questions of morality and ethics in a class-driven society.

In His Own Words

"Conversation. What is it? A Mystery! It's the art of never seeming bored, of touching everything with interest, of pleasing with trifles, of being fascinating with nothing at all. How do we define this lively darting about with words, of hitting them back and forth, this sort of brief smile of ideas which should be conversation?"

"It is the lives we encounter that make life worth living."

"I have coveted everything and taken pleasure in nothing."

Before We Begin

1. When do people of different socioeconomic classes get a chance to mix or social-ize together?
2. What comes to mind when you see the title "Butterball"?
3. What kinds of professions does society consider morally unacceptable? Can a person who makes a living doing a morally unacceptable job also have a code of ethics?

 **Now Read**

Butterball

For several days in succession, tattered remnants of the defeated army had been pass-ing through the town. They were no longer troops, but rampaging hordes. The men had long, filthy beards, their uniforms were in shreds, and they advanced slackly, without a flag, without a regiment. All of them seemed crushed, broken, incapable of thought or resolve, marching merely out of habit, and dropping with fatigue the minute they stopped. The greater number were reservists, pacific characters and quiet well-to-do men, bent beneath the weight of their rifles; or alert little militiamen, quick to panic and easily roused to enthusiasm, as ready for attack as for flight; then, in their midst, a few red-trousered soldiers, the debris of a division that had been given a good thrash-ing in some great battle; sombre artillerymen marching in line with these various foot soldiers; and, at times, the shining helmet of a dragoon, dragging his feet along and barely keeping up with the lighter step of the infantry.

Legions of irregular combatants bearing heroic names: the "Avengers of Defeat"—the "Citizens of the Tomb"—the "Companions of Death"—went by in turn, looking like bandits.

Their leaders, formerly cloth and seed merchants, or dealers in tallow and soap, were occasional warriors, who had been appointed officers because of their wealth or the length of their moustaches. Loaded with weapons, flannel and gold braid, they spoke with booming voices, discussed plans of campaign, and declared that they could, all by themselves, support France in its death-agony on their boastful shoulders; but they were sometimes frightened of their own soldiers, men fit only for the gallows, often excessively brave, always indulging in pillage and debauchery.

The Prussians were about to enter Rouen, people said.

The National Guard, which had, for the last two months, been carrying out very cautious reconnoitring in the nearby woods, sometimes shooting their own sentries, and ready to leap into action every time a little rabbit stirred in the undergrowth, had returned to hearth and home. Their weapons, their uniforms, all the murderous para-phernalia with which they had been striking fear along all the milestones of the high-ways for three leagues around had suddenly disappeared.

The last French soldiers had finally crossed the Seine to reach Pont-Audemer via Saint-Sever and Bourg-Achard; and, walking behind them, the general, in despair, unable to try anything with this ragged assortment, himself swallowed up in the over-whelming rout of a people used to victory and now disastrously beaten despite its legendary bravery, made his way along on foot between two aides-de-camp.

Then a profound calm, a terrified and silent sense of foreboding had come to hover above the city. Many pot-bellied men from the middle class, emasculated by com-merce, awaited the victors anxiously, trembling at the idea that their roasting spits or their big kitchen knives might be viewed as weapons.

Life seemed to have come to a standstill; the shops were closed, the streets mute. Sometimes an inhabitant, intimidated by this silence, would quickly slip along the walls.

The anguish of expectation made them desire the enemy's arrival.

On the afternoon of the day following the departure of the French troops, a few uhlans, emerging from God knows where, swept through the city. Then, a little later, a dark mass came down from the slopes of the Sainte-Catherine district, while two other streams of invaders appeared coming along the Darnétal and Bois-Guillaume roads. The vanguards of the three bodies, at exactly the same moment, joined forces on the square in front of the town hall; and, along all the neighbouring roads, the German army started to arrive, battalion after battalion, making the cobbles echo to their harsh, rhythmic steps.

Commands, shouted out in an unknown guttural tongue, rose along the houses which seemed dead and deserted, while from behind the closed shutters, eyes peeped out at these victorious men, masters of the city, of the fortunes and lives in it, by "right of conquest." The inhabitants in their darkened rooms were struck by the panic in-duced by natural cataclysms, by those great murderous upheavals of the earth, against which all wisdom and all strength are useless. For the same sensation reappears each time that the established order of things is overturned, when security no longer exists and all that was protected by the laws of men or those of nature finds itself at the mercy of a fierce and mindless brutality. The earthquake that crushes an entire populace be-neath their collapsing houses; the overflowing river which rolls along in its torrent drowned peasants with the carcasses of cattle and the beams torn from rooftops; or the glorious army massacring those who put up any resistance, leading the others away as prisoners, pillaging in the name of the sabre and giving thanks to a God with the sound of the cannon—all are so many terrible scourges which confound any belief in eternal justice, any trust that we have learnt to place in Heaven's protection and man's reason.

But at every door, small detachments were starting to knock, before disappearing into the houses. After invasion came occupation. The vanquished now had to fulfill their duty of showing themselves gracious towards the victors.

After a while, once the first terror had evaporated, a new calm set in. In many house-holds, the Prussian officer ate at table with the family. He was sometimes well brought-up, and out of politeness would express his sympathy for France and his repugnance at having to take part in this war. People felt grateful to him for these sentiments; then, after all, maybe they might need his protection one day or another. By dealing tactfully with him, they might get away with a few men less to feed. And why hurt the feelings of someone on whom they were entirely dependent? To behave like that would be an act less of bravery than of rashness—and rashness is no longer a failing of the Rouen middle classes, as it had been at the time of the heroic defences in which their city once distinguished itself. Furthermore, drawing on the supreme reason of French urbanity, people told themselves that, after all, it was perfectly permissible to be polite at home so long as they did not show themselves familiar with the foreign soldier in public. Once outside the house, they no longer wanted to know him, but indoors they were quite prepared to have a chat, and the German would stay on a little longer each evening, warming himself at the communal hearth.

The city itself started, little by little, to regain its ordinary appearance. The French still emerged only rarely, but the streets were crawling with Prussian soldiers. In any case, the officers of the Blue Hussars, arrogantly scraping their great tools of death along the cobbles, did not seem to have for the ordinary citizens much more contempt than had the light infantrymen who, the year before, had been drinking in the same cafés.

Nonetheless, there was something in the air, something subtle and unfamiliar, a strange and intolerable atmosphere, like a spreading odour, the odour of invasion. It filled the houses and the public places, changed the way food tasted, gave people the impression they were travelling far from home among dangerous barbarian tribes.

The victors were demanding money, a lot of money. The inhabitants always paid; in any case, they were rich. But the more a Norman merchant is rolling in money, the more he suffers from having to make any sacrifice, or see any scrap of his fortune passing into the hands of someone else.

However, two or three leagues downriver from the city, towards Croisset, Dieppedalle, or Biessart, the bargemen and fishers would often dredge up from the depths the corpse of some German, all swollen in his uniform, killed with a thrust of the knife or a well-aimed kick, his head crushed by a stone—or sometimes he had been pushed into the water from a bridge. The muddy river buried these obscure acts of vengeance, savage and legitimate, anonymous deeds of heroism, silent assaults, more perilous than battles fought out in the open, and without any of their resounding glory.

For hatred towards the foreigner always causes a few intrepid characters to take up arms, ready as they are to die for an idea.

Finally, as the invaders, although admittedly imposing their inflexible discipline on the city, perpetrated none of the horrors that rumour had ascribed to them all along their triumphal march, people grew emboldened, and the need to do business again started to weigh on the hearts of the local merchants. Some of them had major business interests in Le Havre, which was still occupied by the French army, and they wanted to try and reach this port by travelling overland to Dieppe, where they would take a boat.

They used the influence of the German officers they had got to know, and authorization for them to leave the city was obtained from the general-in-chief.

So it was that a big four-horse coach was reserved for the trip, and 10 persons registered with the coachman; and they resolved to leave one Tuesday morning, before daybreak, so as to avoid attracting a crowd of onlookers.

A frost had frozen the earth solid for days now, and on Monday, around three o'clock, big black clouds coming from the north brought snow, which fell uninterruptedly all evening and all night.

At half-past four in the morning, the travellers gathered in the yard of the Hotel de Normandie, where they were to board the stagecoach.

They were still very sleepy, and shivered with cold under their wraps. They could barely see each other in the darkness; and the heavy winter clothes they had put on

made them all look like overweight priests with their long cassocks. But two men recognized one another, a third came up to them, and they started chatting.

"I'm taking my wife along," said one.

"So am I."

"Me too."

The first added, "We're not coming back to Rouen, and if the Prussians move towards Le Havre, we'll go to England."

They all had the same plans, being of similar mind.

But the coach was still not being harnessed. A little lamp, carried by a stable-boy,
emerged from time to time from one dark doorway, only to disappear immediately into
another. Horses' hooves stamped on the ground, the noise muffled by the stable-litter,
and a man's voice talking to the animals and swearing could be heard from the depths
of the building. A low jangle of bells announced the fact that the harnesses were being positioned; this jangle soon became a clear and continuous ringing, following the
rhythm of the horses' movements, sometimes stopping, then starting up again with a
sudden shake accompanied by the dull thud of an iron-shod clog clomping across the
ground.

The door suddenly closed. All noise ceased. The frozen citizens had fallen silent;
they stood there, motionless and stiff.

An uninterrupted curtain of white snowflakes glimmered ceaselessly as it fell to the
earth; it effaced shapes and covered everything with a foamy, icy powder; and in the
great silence of the city, calm and buried under the winter weather, all that could be
heard was this indescribable, vague, floating whisper, the noise of falling snow, more of
a sensation than a noise, the intermingling of light atoms that seemed to be filling the
whole of space and blanketing the world.

The man reappeared with his lamp, pulling along at the end of a rope an unwilling
and refractory horse. He set him to the shafts, attached the traces, and spent a long time
going round making sure that the harness was secure, for he had only one hand free, as
the other was carrying his lamp. As he was going to fetch the second horse, he noticed
all these motionless travellers, already white with snow, and said to them, "Why don't
you get into the coach? At least you'll be sheltered there."

They had not thought of this, no doubt, and they leapt at the chance. The three men
installed their wives in the back of the coach, and got up after them; then the other
shapeless and hidden figures in turn took the last seats without exchanging a word.

The floor was covered with straw and their feet snuggled into it. The ladies at the
back, who had brought along little copper footwarmers heated by chemical fuel, lit
these apparatuses and spent some time enumerating their advantages in low voices,
repeating to each other things that they had already known for a long time.

Finally, once the coach had been harnessed with six horses instead of four because it
was harder to pull, a voice outside asked, "Has everyone got in?" A voice inside replied,
"Yes." And off they went.

The coach rolled on ever so slowly, at the most laboured pace. The wheels sank into
the snow; the whole vehicle emitted groans and muffled creaks; the horses slipped,
panted, steamed; and the coachman's giant whip continually cracked, flew out on this
side and that, curling and uncurling like a slender snake, and suddenly lashing a firm
round crupper that then tautened in a more violent effort.

But the day was imperceptibly dawning. Those light snowflakes that one traveller, a pure-blooded Rouennais, had compared to a shower of cotton, were no longer falling. A murky light was filtering through heavy dark clouds that brought out even more the dazzling whiteness of the countryside where there sometimes appeared a line of tall trees decked with hoar frost, and sometimes a hovel wearing a hood of snow.

In the coach, they looked at each other curiously, in the wan light of dawn.

Right at the back, in the best seats, M. and Mme Loiseau, wholesale wine merchants from the rue Grand-Pont, were sitting opposite each other dozing.

The former clerk of a boss who had been ruined in business, Loiseau had bought up his stock and made his fortune. He sold very poor wine very cheaply to the small countryside retailers and enjoyed the reputation among his friends and acquaintances of being a sly old fox, a real Norman, full of cunning and joviality.

His reputation as a swindler was so well established that one evening, in the *préfecture,* M. Tournel, the author of fables and songs, a man of biting and subtle wit, a local celebrity, had proposed to the ladies who he could see were starting to drowse, that they play a game of "*Loiseau vole*"; the witticism itself *flew* through the prefect's drawing-rooms; then, having reached those in the rest of the town, made everyone in the province laugh for a whole month until their jaws ached!

Loiseau was, besides that, famous for his practical jokes of every kind, the tricks he played both pleasant and unpleasant; and nobody could mention him without immediately adding, "He's priceless, is old Loiseau."

Diminutive in stature, he presented a prominent paunch, topped with a red face, framed by two sets of greying side whiskers.

His wife, tall, sturdy, resolute, with a loud voice and a mind soon made up, brought order and good bookkeeping to the firm, while he enlivened it with his merry activities.

Next to them, more dignified, belonging to a higher caste, sat M. Carré-Lamadon, a considerable personage, well established in the cotton business, proprietor of three spinning mills, officer of the Legion of Honour, and member of the General Council. He had remained, throughout the Empire period, at the head of the most loyal opposition solely in order to ensure that he would be paid more to give his support to the same cause that he combated "with courteous weapons," as he himself put it. Mme Carré-Lamadon, much younger than her husband, continued to be a comforting presence to officers from good families stationed in Rouen.

She was sitting opposite her husband, all small and dainty, a pretty little thing, bundled up in her furs, and gazing with a woebegone expression at the dismal interior of the coach.

The people next to her, the Count and Countess Hubert de Bréville, bore one of the oldest and noblest names in Normandy. The Count, an old gentleman of distinguished demeanour, attempted to bring out, by affecting similar dress, his natural resemblance to good King Henri IV who, following a legend that redounded to the family's glory, had made a lady of Bréville pregnant; her husband, by virtue of this deed, had become a count and the governor of a province.

Having M. Carré-Lamadon as a colleague on the General Council, Count Hubert represented the Orleanist party in the *département.* The story of his marriage to the daughter of a small shipowner from Nantes had always been shrouded in mystery. But as the Countess bore herself like a lady, received her guests better than anyone else, and was even said to have been the lover of one of the sons of Louis-Philippe, the whole nobility fêted her, and her salon remained the premier salon in the region, the only one in which old habits of gallantry were preserved, and to which it was difficult to gain access.

The fortune of the de Bréville couple, all in real estate, amounted, it was said, to 500,000 pounds in revenue.

These six persons formed the solid ballast of the coach, the section that represented well-to-do society of independent means, serene and strong: decent people, pillars of the establishment, imbued with Religion and High Principles.

By a strange quirk of fate all the women found themselves sitting on the same side, and the Countess had two other women next to her: two nuns who were telling their beads over and over, mumbling "Our Fathers" and "Hail Marys." One was old, with a face pitted by smallpox, as if she had received a point-blank barrage of grapeshot full in the face. The other, very frail, had a pretty, sickly face and the chest of a consumptive, ravaged by that all-devouring faith which makes martyrs and mystics.

Opposite the two nuns, a man and a woman drew everyone's eyes to them.

The man, a well-known character, was Cornudet the "democrat," the terror of re-spectable folk. For 20 years, he had been dipping his great red beard in the beer glasses of all the democratic cafes. He had, with his brothers and friends, swallowed up quite a large fortune inherited from his father, a former confectioner, and he had impatiently waited for the Republic to arrive, so he could at last gain the place merited by so many revolutionary acts of consumption. On September 4, as a consequence of some prac-tical joke perhaps, he had been led to believe that he had been appointed prefect, but when he tried to assume his functions, the lads in the office, who had remained in sole charge of the building, refused to recognize him, and he was forced to beat a retreat. Anyhow he was a good sort, inoffensive and ready to give his services, and he had busied himself with incomparable ardour in organizing the defence. He had ensured that holes were dug in the plains, all the young trees in the nearby forests were cut down, ambushes were set on all the roads, and at the approach of the enemy, satis-fied with his preparations, he had fallen back with all due haste onto the city. Now he thought he could make himself more useful in Le Havre, where new retrenchments were going to be necessary.

The woman, one of the so-called "women of easy virtue," was famous for her pre-cocious corpulence, which had earned her the nickname of Butterball. She was small, round all over, as fat as lard, with puffed-up fingers congested at the joints so they looked like strings of short sausages; with a glossy, taut skin, and a huge and prominent bosom straining out from beneath her dress, she nonetheless remained an appetiz-ing and much sought-after prospect, so fresh that she was a pleasure to see. Her face was a russet apple, a peony bud about to flower; above, two magnificent black eyes opened wide, shaded by great thick eyelashes that cast a shadow all around; and below, a charming mouth, with pursed lips all moist for kissing, well furnished with gleaming microscopic baby teeth.

Furthermore she was said to be full of the most inestimable talents.

As soon as she was recognized, a low murmur ran from one respectable woman to the next, and the words "prostitute" and "a public scandal" were whispered so loud that she looked up. Then she let her eyes travel across her fellow-travellers with such a bold and provocative gaze that a great silence immediately fell, and all present lowered their eyes, with the exception of Loiseau, who ogled her with a leer.

But conversation soon resumed between the three ladies whom the presence of this hussy had suddenly made friendly, almost intimate with each other. It seemed to them that it was their duty to barricade themselves behind their wifely dignity in the face of this shameless whore; for law-abiding love always looks down its nose at its free-and-easy colleague.

The three men too, drawn together by the shared sense of being on the conservative side opposite Cornudet, talked money, referring to the poor with a certain tone of disdain. Count Hubert described the damage that the Prussians had inflicted on him, the losses that would result from the stolen livestock and the lost harvests, with the self-assurance of a grand seigneur, a millionaire 10 times over, who would be adversely affected by these ravages for perhaps a year, if that. M. Carré-Lamadon, facing many trials and tribulations in the cotton industry, had taken the precaution of sending 600,000 francs to England, a little something put by for a rainy day. As for Loiseau, he had taken pains to sell to the French Commissariat all the ordinary wine he still had in his cellars, so that the State owed him a huge sum that he was expecting to get his hands on once he reached Le Havre.

And all three of them darted friendly glances at each other. Although coming from different milieux, they felt that they were part of the brotherhood of money, the great freemasonry of the haves, who, every time they put their hands in their trouser pockets, let you hear the clink of gold coins.

The coach was making such slow progress that at 10 in the morning they had travelled less than four leagues. The men got out three times to climb the hillsides on foot. They were starting to become anxious, for they were supposed to be having lunch at Tostes and now they were starting to think they would not get there before nightfall. They were all looking out for a wayside inn, when the coach foundered in a deep snowdrift and they took two hours to dig it out.

Their appetite was growing, making them feel light-headed; and not a single cheap restaurant or tavern was visible, for the approach of the Prussians and the passage of the starving French troops had scared off all commerce.

The men went to try and find provisions in the wayside farms, but they could not even find any bread, for the mistrustful peasants concealed their reserves for fear of being pillaged by the soldiers who, without a bite to eat, would forcibly make off with anything they discovered.

Around one o'clock in the afternoon, Loiseau announced that he really was starting to feel a damned great hole in his stomach. Everyone else, too, had been suffering for a long time, and as the violent need to eat continued to increase, it ended up killing off all conversation.

From time to time someone would yawn; someone else almost immediately did likewise; and each of them in turn, depending on their character, their knowledge of the proprieties, and their social position, would open their mouths noisily or modestly, hurriedly holding their hands in front of the gaping holes from which clouds of steam emerged.

Butterball, on several occasions, leant down as if she were looking for something beneath her skirts. She hesitated for a second, looked round at her neighbours, then tranquilly sat up again. They all had pale, drawn faces. Loiseau asserted that he would pay a thousand francs for a knuckle of ham. His wife made a gesture as if to protest, then she calmed down. She always suffered when she heard people discussing money being wasted, and she could not even understand why anyone might joke about such a subject. "The fact is, I'm not feeling very well," said the Count. "Why didn't I think to bring some food?" Everyone else likewise reproached themselves.

However, Cornudet had a flask full of rum; he offered it round; it was coldly refused. Loiseau alone took a couple of sips, and when he returned the flask, he thanked him: "It's nice, you know; it warms you up and it takes your mind off your appetite." The alcohol put him in a good mood and he suggested that they do as on the little ship in the song, and eat the plumpest of the travellers. This indirect allusion to Butterball shocked the better brought-up people. They made no reply; Cornudet alone smiled. The two nuns had stopped mumbling their rosary, and sat upright and motionless, their hands folded deep into their great sleeves, obstinately lowering their eyes, offering up to heaven, no doubt, the sufferings it was inflicting on them.

Finally, at three o'clock, as they were crossing an interminable plain, without a single village in sight, Butterball quickly bent down and took out from under the coach seat a wide basket covered with a white cloth.

She took out of it first a little china plate, a slender silver cup, then a huge earthenware vessel in which two whole chickens, already sliced, had been preserved in their jelly; and many other things could be seen wrapped up in the basket: pâtés, fruits, titbits—she had packed enough provisions for a three-day journey so that she would not have to rely on the kitchens of the inns. The necks of four bottles peeped out from between the parcels of food. She picked up a chicken wing and, delicately, started to eat it, with one of those small light loaves called "Regence" in Normandy.

All eyes were on her. Then the odour spread, causing nostrils to flare, bringing to everyone's mouth a flood of saliva accompanied by a painful contraction of the jaw under the ears. The contempt of the ladies for this whore grew fierce, like a longing to kill her, or to throw her out of the coach into the snow—her, her little cup, her basket, and her provisions.

But Loiseau was devouring with his eyes the earthenware dish containing the chicken. He said, "Madame has taken wise precautions, unlike us—good for her! There are some people who always manage to think of everything."

She looked up at him.

"Would you like some, Monsieur? It's hard when you haven't had anything to eat all morning."

He bowed.

"Good heavens, quite frankly I won't say no; I can't hold out any longer. All's fair in love and war, don't you think, Madame?"

And casting a look around, he added, "At times like this, it's a real pleasure to find people who'll help you out."

He had a newspaper, which he spread out so as not to stain his trousers, and using the point of a knife he always kept tucked into his pocket, he picked out a thigh nicely coated with jelly, tore it apart with his teeth, then chewed it with such evident satisfaction that a heavy sigh of distress spread through the coach.

But Butterball, with a humble, gentle voice, suggested to the nuns that they share her light meal. They both accepted like a shot, and, without lifting their eyes, started to eat as fast as they could, after stammering out their thanks. Cornudet too did not turn down his neighbour's offer, and they formed with the nuns a sort of table by spreading out newspapers across their knees.

Their mouths opened and closed without cease, swallowing, chomping, gobbling it all down ferociously. Loiseau, in his corner, was going at his food hammer and tongs, and in low tones he encouraged his wife to imitate him. For a long time she resisted the temptation, but, after a tense quiver in the pit of her stomach, she finally gave in. Then her husband, suddenly waxing eloquent, asked their "charming companion" whether she would allow him to offer a little morsel to Mme Loiseau. She said, "But of course, Monsieur," with a friendly smile, and held out the earthenware dish.

An embarrassing moment occurred when they had uncorked the first bottle of Bordeaux; there was only one small cup. They passed it round, each one wiping the rim in turn. Cornudet alone, out of gallantry no doubt, set his lips to the place that was still moist from the mouth of the woman next to him.

Then, surrounded on all sides by people eating, and suffocated by the odours emanating from the food, the Count and Countess de Bréville, as well as M. and Mme Carré-Lamadon, started to suffer that hateful torment which still bears the name of Tantalus. All at once the factory owner's young wife emitted a sigh which made everyone look round; she was as white as the snow outside; her eyes closed, her head fell forward: she had fainted. Her husband, in a panic, implored everyone to help. They were all losing their heads, when the older of the two nuns, holding up the sick woman's head, slipped between her lips Butterball's little cup and made her swallow a few drops of wine. The pretty young lady stirred, opened her eyes, smiled and declared with a dying voice that she now felt perfectly well. But so that the same thing did not happen all over again, the nun forced her to drink a whole glass of Bordeaux, and added, "It's just hunger, that's all."

Then Butterball, blushing with embarrassment, looked at the four travellers who had still not broken their fast, and said with a stammer, "Good Lord, if I might make so bold as to offer these ladies and gentlemen . . . " She fell silent, afraid of provoking scandal. Loiseau broke in, "Oh for goodness' sake, in cases like this all men are brothers and must help each other out. Come on, ladies, don't stand on ceremony; accept, devil take it! Do we even know if we'll find a house to spend the night in? At the rate we're going, we won't reach Tostes before noon tomorrow." They hesitated, nobody daring to take responsibility for saying yes.

But the Count resolved the matter. He turned round to the fat girl sitting there all intimidated, and putting on his gentlemanly airs, said to her, "We are grateful to accept, Madame."

The ice had been broken, and from now on it was all so much easier. Once the Rubicon had been crossed, they all tucked in. The basket was emptied. It still contained a pâté de foie gras, a lark pâté, a piece of smoked tongue, some Crassane pears, a slab of Pont-l'Evêque cheese, some petits fours, and a big jar full of gherkins and onions in vinegar, for Butterball, like all women, loved crudités.

They could hardly eat the young hussy's provisions without talking to her. So they started to make conversation, reservedly at first, then, as she kept her end up very well, they let themselves go a bit more. Mmes de Bréville and Carré-Lamadon, who were women of tact and refinement, put on a delicate and gracious air. The Countess in particular showed that amiable condescension of very noble ladies who can rub shoulders with anyone and still emerge unsullied, and she was charming. But sturdy Mme Loiseau, who had the soul of a gendarme, remained sour-faced, speaking little and eating a great deal.

Naturally they discussed the war. They recounted the horrible deeds done by the Prussians, and the brave exploits of the French; and all these people who were busy taking flight paid homage to the courage of other people. Soon personal anecdotes started to flow, and Butterball told them, with real feeling and that warmth of expression that women of the street sometimes have when conveying their natural upsurges of emotion, how she had left Rouen.

"I thought at first I'd be able to stay," she said. "I had a house full of things to eat, and I preferred to feed a few soldiers rather than go into exile heaven knows where. But when I saw those Prussians, I was quite simply knocked over! They made my heart swell with rage, and I spent the whole day weeping for shame. Oh, if only I were a man! I watched them from my window, those big fat pigs with their pointed helmets, and my maid had to hold my hands tight to stop me throwing my furniture down on them. Then some of them came to lodge in my house, so I jumped at the throat of the first one. They're no more difficult to strangle than anyone else! And I'd really have finished him off, if they hadn't dragged me away by the hair. I had to go into hiding after that. Anyway, as soon as I had a chance, I left, and here I am."

They congratulated her warmly. She was growing in the esteem of her companions, who had not shown such boldness; and Cornudet, as he listened to her, continued to wear an approving and benevolent smile like that of an apostle; it was much as a priest might hear a devout parishioner praising God, for long-bearded democrats have a monopoly on patriotism just as men of the cloth have a monopoly on religion. He in turn spoke in doctrinaire tones, with the pompous weightiness he had learnt from the proclamations that were stuck up on the walls each day, and he ended up with a display of eloquence in which he magisterially laid into "that scoundrelly Badinguet."

But this immediately made Butterball angry for she was a Bonapartist. She went more red in the face than a ripe cherry and, stuttering with indignation, exclaimed, "I'd like to have seen the rest of you in his place! Now that *would* have been a pretty pickle! *You're* the ones who betrayed him! There'd be nothing left but to leave France if we were governed by good-for-nothings like you!"

Cornudet, impassive, kept his disdainful, superior smile, but everyone sensed that coarse insults were about to start flying, when the Count stepped in and managed, not without difficulty, to calm down the exasperated girl, proclaiming in authoritative tones that all sincerely held opinions were worthy of respect. However, the Countess and the wife of the factory owner, who harboured in their souls the irrational fear all decent people harboured towards the idea of a republic, and that instinctive affection that all women nurse towards flashy, despotic governments, felt drawn in spite of themselves to this prostitute full of dignity, whose feelings so closely resembled theirs.

The basket was empty. The ten of them had got to the bottom of it without difficulty, regretting that it was not any bigger. The conversation continued for some time, somewhat more frigidly now that they had finished eating.

Night was falling, the darkness gradually deepened, and the cold, which they felt more now that they were digesting, made Butterball shiver, despite her fat. Then Mme de Bréville offered her her footwarmer, the fuel of which had been topped up several times, and Butterball immediately accepted, for her feet felt completely frozen. Mmes Carré-Lamadon and Loiseau gave theirs to the nuns.

The coach driver had lit his lamps. They cast a bright light onto the cloud of steam rising from the sweating cruppers of the wheel-horses, and on either side of the road they lit up the snow which seemed to unwind under their flickering gleam.

It was impossible to make out anything inside the coach, but all at once there was a slight scuffle between Butterball and Cornudet, and Loiseau, whose eye pierced through the darkness, thought he saw the bushy-bearded man suddenly pull away, as if he had been dealt a well-aimed, soundless punch.

Tiny flickers of flame appeared ahead on the road. It was Tostes. They had been on the move for 11 hours, which, with the four lots of two hours' rest allotted to the horses to draw breath and have their oats, made 14. They entered the town, and stopped outside the Hôtel du Commerce.

The coach door opened! A well-known noise sent a shudder down the spines of all the passengers; the rattle of a sabre sheath bumping along the ground. Straight away, the voice of a German shouted something.

Although the coach had halted, nobody got out, as if they thought they would be massacred as they emerged. Then the driver appeared holding one of his lamps, which suddenly cast its rays right into the back of the coach where the two rows of frightened faces were gazing open-mouthed and wide-eyed with surprise and terror.

Next to the coach driver was standing, fully visible in the lamplight, a tall, extremely slim blond young man, strapped tightly into his uniform like a girl into her corset, and wearing askew his flat, waxed cap, which gave him the appearance of the lackey in an English hotel. His enormous moustache, with its long straight sweep, tapering down to a point on both sides until it formed a single blond strand, so slender that it was impossible to tell where it ended, seemed to weigh on the corners of his mouth and, pulling on his cheek, gave his lips a downward turn.

Speaking in French with an Alsatian accent, he requested the travellers to get out, saying stiffly, "Vill you please to get out, Ladies und Chentlemen?"

The two nuns were the first to obey, with the docility of saintly girls used to doing as they were told. The Count and Countess were the next to appear, followed by the factory owner and his wife, then by Loiseau pushing his sturdy better half in front of him. As he set foot on the ground, he said to the officer, "Good evening, Monsieur," more out of prudence than politeness. The other, insolent like all men who are in complete control, stared at him without a reply.

Butterball and Cornudet, although they had been sitting next to the door, were the last to climb out, solemn and haughty in the face of the enemy. The big fat girl tried to master her feelings and keep calm; the "democrat" kept coiling his long reddish beard with a tragic and slightly trembling hand. They were keen to preserve their dignity, realizing that in this sort of encounter, everyone is to some extent a representative of their country; they were both equally revolted by the spinelessness of their companions—she tried to show she had more pride than the other, respectable women, while he, fully aware that it was up to him to set an example, preserved in his entire attitude the mission of resistance that he had embarked upon when he undertook to break up the roads.

They went into the vast kitchen of the inn, and the German, having asked to see the authorization for departure signed by the general-in-chief, on which were written the names, particulars, and professions of each traveller, looked the entire group over at length, comparing each of them to the written description.

Then he said brusquely, "Zat vill be all," and disappeared.

They started to breathe again. They were still hungry; supper was ordered. It took half an hour to prepare it, and while two servant women made a show of getting it ready, the group went to look at their rooms. They were all in a long corridor which ended with a glazed door with a meaningful number.

Finally they were about to sit down at table when the innkeeper himself appeared. He had been a horse vendor, and was a big asthmatic man, who still had fits of wheezing and hoarseness, and whose larynx emitted a phlegmy cough. His father had bequeathed to him the name of Follenvie.

He asked, "Mademoiselle Elisabeth Rousset?"

Butterball shuddered and turned round.

"That's me."

"Mademoiselle, the Prussian officer wishes to speak to you immediately."

"To me?"

"Yes, if you are indeed Mademoiselle Elisabeth Rousset."

She looked disconcerted, reflected for a moment, than said bluntly, "Maybe he does, but I won't go."

There was a stir around her; everyone started arguing, trying to guess the cause behind this order. The Count came up and said, "You are wrong, Madame; your refusal may bring considerable difficulties in its wake, not just for you, but for all your companions too. One should never resist those who are stronger. If you go, it will surely not mean you running into any danger; it's doubtless to do with some formality that has been neglected."

Everyone joined their voices to his, they begged her, they urged her, they expostulated with her, and finally they convinced her; for they all feared the complications which might result from her stubborn refusal. At last she said, "All right, but it's only for you that I'll do it!"

The Countess took her hand. "And we are grateful to you for it."

She went out. They waited for her to come back before sitting down to eat.

Everyone said how sorry they were that they had not been summoned instead of that violent and irascible girl, and they mentally prepared various platitudes to trot out in case they were called in turn.

But after 10 minutes she reappeared, breathing heavily, red and flustered, exasperated. She was stuttering, "Oh, the villain! The villain!"

They all crowded round to ask what had happened, but she said nothing; and as the Count persisted, she replied with great dignity, "No, it's none of your business, I can't say a thing."

They thereupon sat down to a tall soup tureen from which rose the appetizing odour of cabbage. Despite the preceding alarm, the supper was a merry occasion. The cider was good, and the Loiseau couple as well as the nuns had some, as it was cheaper. The others asked for wine; Cornudet demanded beer. He had a particular way of uncorking the bottle, making the liquid foam, and contemplating it as he tilted his glass, which he then held up between the lamp and his eye so he could appreciate its colour. When he drank, his bushy beard, which had kept the traces of his favourite brew, seemed to bristle with affection; he would gaze down from the corner of his eyes so as not to lose sight of his beer mug, and he seemed to be fulfilling the sole function for which he had been born. He looked exactly as if he were drawing up in his mind a comparison and, as it were, an affinity between the two great passions which occupied his entire life: Pale Ale and Revolution; and it was quite true that he could not sample the one without thinking about the other.

M. and Mme Follenvie were dining at the far end of the table. The man, puffing and blowing like a locomotive with a leak, had too much congestion in his chest to be able to speak while he ate, but his wife never stopped talking. She recounted all the impressions she had felt at the arrival of the Prussians, what they did, what they said—cursing them first and foremost because they were costing her money, and secondly because she had two sons in the army. She addressed her remarks especially to the Countess, flattered to be talking with a lady of quality.

Then she lowered her voice to make some more delicate comments, and her husband interrupted her from time to time, saying, "You'd do better to keep quiet, Madame Follenvie." But she took no notice, and continued:

"Yes, Madame, those men do nothing but eat potatoes and pork, and then pork and potatoes. And you can't say they're clean. Oh no! They do their business everywhere, saving your presence. And if only you could see them drilling for hours and days on end: they're all out there, in a field, and it's forward march, and about turn, and right turn, and left turn. At least if they were cultivating the land, or working on the roads of their own country! . . . But far from it, Madame, those military types are no use to anyone! And the poor ordinary folk have to feed them and they're out there learning how to slaughter people! I'm just an old woman without any education, it's true, but when I see them knocking their constitutions into a cocked hat, stamping up and down, morning, noon and night, I say to myself, 'When there are people making so many useful discoveries, why should others go out of their way to make a nuisance of themselves? Honestly, isn't it perfectly dreadful to kill people, whether they're Prussian, or English, or Polish, or French?' If you get your own back on someone who's done something against you, it's bad, 'cause you're caught and punished; *but* when they exterminate our lads as if they were game, with rifles, then *that's* all right, since they give medals to the one that wipes out the most—isn't that so? No, believe you me, *that* I'll never understand!"

Cornudet raised his voice:

"War is barbarous when a peaceful neighbour is attacked; it's a sacred duty when it's a matter of defending your fatherland."

The old woman lowered her head.

"Yes, when you defend yourself it's another matter; but shouldn't we really be killing all the kings who do it all just for fun?"

Cornudet's eye lit up.

"Bravo, citizen!" he said.

M. Carré-Lamadon was deep in thought. Although he was a great admirer of the illustrious captains in the army, this peasant woman's common sense made him dream of the opulent wealth that would be brought into the country by so many idle and thus wasteful bodies, so many forces that were being sustained unproductively, when they could be set to work on the great industrial labours that it will take centuries to complete.

Mme Loiseau, leaving her seat, went to speak in low tones to the innkeeper. The big man was laughing, coughing, spitting; his enormous belly was quivering with joy at his neighbour's jokes, and he bought six half hogsheads of Bordeaux from him, for the spring, once the Prussians had gone.

Hardly was supper over when, as they were all dropping with exhaustion, they went to bed.

However, Loiseau, who had been observing things attentively, put his wife to bed, then glued his ear and his eye in succession to the keyhole, in an attempt to discover what he called "the mysteries of the corridor."

After about an hour, he heard a rustling noise, quickly looked, and saw Butterball appearing even more podgy than before in a dressing gown of blue cashmere, edged with white lace. She was holding a lighted candle and heading to the room with the jokey label at the far end of the corridor. But a door to the side half-opened and, when she returned after a few minutes, Cornudet, in braces, was following her. They spoke in low tones, then stopped. Butterball seemed to be vigorously barring entry to her room. Loiseau, unfortunately, could not hear the words, but eventually, as they started to raise their voices, he was able to catch something of what they were saying. Cornudet was energetically persisting. He was saying, "Come on, you're being silly, what difference does it make to you?"

She seemed indignant and replied, "No, my friend, there are times when that sort of thing just isn't done; and then, here, it would be shameful."

He refused to understand, no doubt, and asked why. Then she flew into a rage, raising her voice even more:

"*Why?* You don't understand *why?* When there are Prussians in the house, maybe in the next room?"

He was silent. This patriotic sense of shame coming from a whore who refused to accept a man's caresses when the enemy was nearby must have awoken the faltering dignity in his heart, for, after merely embracing her, he padded stealthily back to his room.

Loiseau, quite aroused, left the keyhole, cut a caper in his room, tied on his knotted headscarf, lifted up the sheet under which lay the heavy carcass of his lady wife, and awoke her with a kiss, murmuring, "D'you love me, sweetheart?"

Then the whole house became silent. But there soon rose, from an indeterminate direction which could be the cellar just as much as the attic, a powerful, monotonous, regular snoring, a muffled and prolonged noise, with rumblings like those of a boiler under pressure. M. Follenvie was asleep.

As they had decided they would leave at eight o'clock the next morning, everyone gathered in the kitchen; but the coach, its roofed tilt with snow, was standing alone in the middle of the yard, without horses and without a driver. They looked for him in the stables, in the forage, in the coach-houses. Then all the men resolved to scour the countryside, and they set off. They found themselves on the square, with the church in the background and, on either side, low-roofed houses in which Prussian soldiers were visible. The first they saw was peeling potatoes. The second, further on, was washing the barber's shop. Another, with a beard up to his eyes, was cuddling a small child in tears, dandling him on his knees and trying to quieten him down; and the strapping peasant women, whose men were with the "army at war," were indicating in sign language to their obedient victors the work that had to be done: cutting wood, ladling the soup onto the bread, grinding the coffee; one of them was even washing the linen of his hostess, a completely lame old grandma.

The Count, in astonishment, questioned the beadle who was coming out of the presbytery. The old churchman replied:

"Oh, those ones are no trouble; they're not even Prussians, by the sound of it. They come from further away, I don't really know where; and they've all left a wife and children behind; war's no fun for them, you can be sure! I bet the women weep for their menfolk over there just as much as here; and they're in for as much of a hard time of it as our people are. Here, in any case, we're not too badly off for the time being, since they're not being a nuisance and they work as if they were in their own homes. You see, Monsieur, poor folks have to help each other out . . . It's the high and mighty that make war."

Cornudet, indignant at the cordial mutual understanding that had been established between victors and vanquished, withdrew, preferring to closet himself in the inn. Loiseau made a joke: "They're repopulating the place." M. Carré-Lamadon made a solemn remark: "They are making reparations." But nobody could find the coachman. Eventually they came across him in the village cafe, sitting quietly at a table with the officer's adjutant. The Count accosted him.

"Hadn't we given you orders to harness the horses for eight o'clock?"

"Well, yes, but I've since been given other orders."

"What orders?"

"Not to harness at all."

"Who gave you these orders?"

"The Prussian commander, hang it all!"

"Why?"

"I haven't the slightest idea. Go and ask him. I'm forbidden to harness the horses, so I won't harness them. And that's that."

"Did he tell you this himself?"

"No, Monsieur, it was the innkeeper who gave me the orders on his behalf."

"When was that?"

"Yesterday evening, as I was going to bed."

The three men returned, full of disquiet.

They asked to see M. Follenvie, but the servant-woman replied that Monsieur, because of his asthma, never got up before 10 o'clock. He had even given strict instructions that he was not to be woken any earlier, except in case of fire.

They wanted to see the officer, but this was absolutely impossible, although he was lodging at the inn. M. Follenvie alone was authorized to speak to him on civilian matters. So they waited. The women went back up to their rooms, and kept themselves busy with this and that.

Cornudet settled down right next to the tall fireplace in the kitchen where there was a blazing fire. He asked for one of the little tables from the cafe to be brought to him, and a bottle of beer, and he drew on his pipe—which enjoyed among the democrats a prestige almost equal to his own, as if it had served the fatherland by serving Cornudet. It was a superb meerschaum, admirably seasoned, as black as its master's teeth, but sweet-smelling, nicely curved, gleaming, fitting snugly in his hand, and adding the final touch to his physiognomy. And he sat there motionless, his eyes sometimes staring into the flames of the hearth, sometimes gazing at the fine head of foam in his beer mug; and each time he had pulled on his beer, he drew his long slender fingers through his long greasy hair with a satisfied look on his face, as he sniffed at his moustache with its fringe of foam.

Loiseau, claiming he wanted to stretch his legs, went to sell off some of his wine to the local retailers. The Count and the factory owner started to talk politics. They set about prophesying the future of France. The one believed in the house of Orleans, the other in some unknown saviour, a hero who would reveal himself when things were in desperate straits: a du Guesclin, a Joan of Arc perhaps? Or another Napoleon I? Ah, if only the Prince Imperial weren't so young! Cornudet, as he listened to them, smiled like a man who knows what destiny is planning. His pipe filled the kitchen with its aroma.

As 10 o'clock was striking, M. Follenvie appeared. They quickly questioned him, but he could merely repeat, two or three times over, without variant, these words:

"What the officer told me was: 'Monsieur Follenvie, you will forbid the coach to be harnessed tomorrow for these travellers. I do not wish them to leave without my orders. You understand. That is all.'"

Then they wanted to see the officer. The Count sent him his card, to which M. Carré-Lamadon added his name and all his titles. The Prussian sent back word that he would allow these two men to speak to him when he had had his lunch, at about one o'clock.

The ladies reappeared and everyone had a bite to eat, in spite of their anxiety. Butterball seemed ill and deeply troubled.

They were finishing the coffee when the adjutant came to fetch the gentlemen.

Loiseau accompanied the two of them, but as they tried to take Cornudet along with them so as to give greater solemnity to the proceedings, he declared with pride that he intended never to have anything to do with Germans; and he settled back down in front of the fireplace, asking for another bottle of beer.

The three men went up and were led into the finest room in the inn, where the officer received them, stretched out in an armchair, his feet on the mantelpiece, smoking a long porcelain pipe, and wrapped up in a flamboyant dressing gown, no doubt stolen from the abandoned dwelling of some middle-class man with bad taste. He did not stand up, did not greet them, did not look at them. He was a magnificent specimen of the loutishness that comes naturally to the victorious soldier.

After a few moments he finally said, "Vat do you vant?"

The Count spoke up. "We want to leave, Monsieur."

"No."

"May I make so bold as to ask you for the cause of this refusal?"

"Becoss I do not vant it."

"I will respectfully point out to you, Monsieur, that your general-in-chief has grant-ed us permission to leave for Dieppe; and I do not think that we have done anything to deserve this harsh treatment from you."

"I do not vant it . . . zat is all . . . You can leef me."

Having bowed, the three of them withdrew.

The afternoon was awful. They could not in the least understand this German capri-ciousness; and the strangest ideas went round and round in their heads. They were all gathered in the kitchen, endlessly discussing the matter, imagining the most unlikely things. Perhaps there was a plan to keep them as hostages—but with what aim? Or else take them off as prisoners? Or, perhaps, demand a huge ransom from them? At this thought, they were seized by an intense panic. The richest of them were the most horror-stricken, seeing themselves already constrained, if they were going to save their own skins, to pour sackfuls of gold into the hands of this insolent soldier. They racked their brains to concoct plausible lies, conceal the extent of their wealth, and pass them-selves off as poor, very poor men. Loiseau removed his watch chain and hid it in his pocket. The falling night increased their apprehensions. The lamp was lit and, as there were still hours to go before dinner, Mme Loiseau suggested a game of *trente-et-un*. It would take their minds off things. They accepted. Cornudet himself, having extin-guished his pipe out of politeness, took part.

The Count shuffled the cards—dealt . . . Butterball got 31 straight away; and soon the interest they took in the game laid to rest the fear that was haunting every mind. But Cornudet noticed that the Loiseau couple were in cahoots, and cheating.

As they were about to sit down at table, M. Follenvie reappeared; and in his hoarse voice, he uttered these words: "The Prussian officer asks whether Mademoiselle Elisabeth Rousset has changed her mind yet."

Butterball remained erect and pale; then suddenly turning crimson, she was so suf-focated with rage that she could no longer speak. Finally she exploded: "You can go and tell that slob, that bastard, that swine of a Prussian that I will never consent; you hear me? Never, never, never."

The hefty innkeeper went out. Then Butterball was surrounded, questioned, urged by everyone to disclose the mystery behind her visit. At first she resisted: but soon her exasperation got the better of her. "What does he want, you ask? . . . What does he want? He wants to sleep with me!" she cried. Nobody was shocked by the expression, so great was their indignation. Cornudet smashed his beer mug as he banged it violently down onto the table. There was a clamour of loud protest against that vile trooper, and anger swept through them; all were united in resistance, as if each of them had been asked to share in the sacrifice demanded of her. The Count declared in disgust that those people behaved like the barbarians of olden times. The women especially showed Butterball a lively and caressing commiseration. The nuns, who only appeared at meal-times, had lowered their heads and said nothing.

Still, they had dinner as soon as their first outburst of indignation had calmed down; but they said little; they were thinking.

The ladies retired early, and the men, as they smoked, organized a game of *écarté* to which they summoned M. Follenvie, as they intended to question him by stealth so as to discover ways of overcoming the officer's resistance. But he was completely absorbed in his card game, listened to nobody, and did not answer; he just kept repeating, "On with the game, gentlemen, on with the game!" His concentration was so intense that he forgot to hawk and spit, which sometimes meant his chest emitted blasts as from an organ pipe. His wheezing lungs went up and down the scales of asthma, from the deep, solemn notes up to the shrill squeaky hoarseness of young cockerels trying to crow.

He even refused to go up to bed when his wife, who was dropping with sleep, came to fetch him. So she went off by herself, for she was "a lark," always up with the sun, whereas her husband was "a night owl," always ready to spend the night with friends. He shouted out to her, "You can put my egg-nog in front of the fire," and turned back to his game. When they saw they would never get a word more from him, they declared it was time to turn in, and they all went off to bed.

They again rose quite early the following morning, with a tremulous hope and a greater desire to be off and away, stricken with terror at the idea of the day they would have to spend in this horrid little inn.

Alas! The horses stayed in the stable, the coach driver was nowhere to be seen. Having nothing better to do, they went to take a stroll round the coach. Breakfast was a gloomy affair; and a certain chilliness had set in towards Butterball, for they had all slept on it and were starting to change their minds. Now they were almost resentful at this girl for not slipping off in secret to see the Prussian and thus create a nice surprise for her companions when they woke up. What could have been simpler? And in any case, who'd have known it? She could have saved appearances by getting the officer to say that she had taken pity on their distress. For her, it was all of so little importance!

But no one was yet prepared to admit to these thoughts.

In the afternoon, as they were all dying of boredom, the Count suggested that they go for a walk around the village. Everyone wrapped up warm, and the little group set off, apart from Cornudet, who preferred to stay by the fireside, and the nuns, who spent their days in church or at the priest's home.

The cold, which was growing daily more intense, stung their noses and ears cruelly; their feet hurt so much that each step was painful; and when the countryside opened up before them, it appeared so dreadfully gloomy to them under that limitless whiteness that they all immediately turned back, their souls frozen and their hearts bitter.

The four women walked ahead, the three men followed on, a few steps behind.

Loiseau, who understood the situation, suddenly asked if "that hussy" was going to make them stay much longer in a place like this. The Count, courteous as ever, said that they could not ask a woman to make such a painful sacrifice, and that the decision would have to come from her. M. Carré-Lamadon remarked that if the French were to make an offensive return via Dieppe, as they were said to be planning, the armies might join battle at Tostes. This reflection made the two other men anxious. "What if we escaped on foot?" said Loiseau. The Count shrugged. "You can't be serious. In this snow? With the women? In any case, they'd immediately come after us and catch us up in 10 minutes, and we'd be brought back as prisoners at the mercy of the soldiers." This was true; they fell silent.

The ladies started talking fashion; but a certain constraint seemed to have come between them.

Suddenly, at the end of the street, the officer appeared. Against the snow that blocked the horizon, he stood out distinctly like a giant wasp in uniform, walking with his knees apart in that gait particular to military men who are trying their utmost not to stain their immaculately waxed boots.

He bowed as he passed in front of the ladies, and stared disdainfully at the men who, in any case, standing on their dignity, refused to raise their hats, although Loiseau made a gesture as if he were about to touch his forelock.

Butterball had blushed to the ears; and the three married women were overwhelmed by feelings of deep humiliation at being encountered by this soldier in the company of this whore he had treated in so cavalier a fashion.

Then they talked about him, his bearing, his face. Mme Carré-Lamadon, who had known many officers and judged them from the point of view of a connoisseur, found him not bad at all; she even expressed the regret that he was not French, as he would have made a handsome hussar and all the women would certainly have doted on him.

Once they were back, they had no idea what to do next. A few sharp words were even exchanged, and on quite trivial matters. The dinner was silent, and soon over; then everyone went up to bed, hoping to sleep so as to kill time.

They came down the following day with tired faces and exasperation in their hearts. The women hardly spoke to Butterball.

A bell rang. It was for a baptism. The fat young woman had a child being brought up by peasants in Yvetot. She did not see him even once a year, and never spared him a thought; but the idea of the child about to be baptized filled her heart with a sudden violent affection for her own youngster, and she absolutely insisted on attending the ceremony.

As soon as she had gone, everyone exchanged glances, and then drew up the chairs together, sensing that it was high time to take a decision. Loiseau had an inspiration: in his opinion, they should suggest to the officer that he just keep Butterball, and let the others go.

M. Follenvie agreed to perform the errand, but he came back down almost immediately. The German, who knew human nature, had shown him the door. He intended to keep everyone there until his desires were satisfied.

Then the vulgar temperament of Mme Loiseau exploded. "But we're not going to stay here until we die of old age! Since it's that slut's job to do what she does with any man who wants, I don't see she's got any right to turn down one rather than another. I ask you—she picked up everyone she could find in Rouen, even the coach drivers! Yes, Madame, the coach driver of the *préfecture!* I know all about it; he buys his wine from us. And today, when she could be getting us out of a tight corner, the snotty-nosed little hussy decides to put on airs and graces! . . . Well in my opinion, the officer's behaving very well about it. Perhaps he hasn't had any for quite a while; and there were three of us ladies here that he'd certainly have preferred. But instead, he's quite happy to take the woman that belongs to everyone. He respects married women. Just remember this: he's in charge. All he needed was to say, 'I want,' and he could have got his soldiers to take us by force."

The two women shuddered slightly. The eyes of little Mme Carré-Lamadon were shining, and she was rather pale, as if she imagined that the officer was already taking her by force.

The men, who were standing apart talking things over, came up. Loiseau was enraged: he wanted to deliver "that wretched girl," bound hand and foot, to the enemy. But the Count, the scion of three generations of ambassadors, and with all the bearing of a diplomat, urged cunning. "We need to force her to make up her mind," he said.

So they started to plot.

The women came together in a huddle, they lowered their voices, and the discussion became general, as everyone gave their opinion. In fact, it was all handled decorously. The ladies in particular invented the most delicate turns of phrase and charming subtleties of expression to say the most indecent things. A stranger would not have understood a word, so carefully did they observe the linguistic proprieties. But the thin glaze of modesty in which every woman of the world is coated merely covers the surface, and they came into their own in this risqué adventure, and enjoyed themselves to the full when it came to it, feeling altogether in their element, and pawing at love with the sensuality of a greedy chef preparing someone else's dinner.

Their cheerfulness started spontaneously to return, as they finally started to see the funny side of the story. The Count made some rather off-colour jokes, but he told them so well that they raised a smile. Loiseau in turn came out with some smuttier stories which offended nobody; and the thought brutally expressed by his wife was at the forefront of everyone's mind: "Since it's that whore's job, why should she turn down *him* rather than anyone else?" Pretty little Mme Carré-Lamadon even seemed to think that if it was her, she would turn down anyone else rather than *him*.

They prepared the blockade at length, as if they were about to lay siege to a fortress. Everyone agreed on the role they were to play, the arguments they would rely on, the manoeuvres they would need to execute. They settled the plan of attack, the ruses they would employ, and the surprise assaults they would launch, to force that living citadel to receive the enemy into her walls.

Cornudet however stayed apart, refusing to have anything to do with the whole business.

They were all so deeply intent on their plans that they did not hear Butterball return. But the Count whispered "Shhh," and they all looked up. There she was. They suddenly fell silent and a certain embarrassment at first prevented them from speaking to her. The Countess, who had learnt more than the others how to be duplicitously agreeable from her experience in the salons, asked her, "Did you have a good time at the baptism?"

The fat young woman, still filled with emotion, told them all about it: how people had looked, the way they had stood, and even what the church had been like. She added, "It's nice to pray sometimes."

Nonetheless, until lunch, the ladies contented themselves with being friendly towards her, to gain her trust and make her more docile to their advice.

Once they had sat down to table, they started to make their approaches. They began to talk vaguely about self-sacrifice. They cited ancient examples: Judith and Holofernes, and then, without any real reason, Lucretia with Sextus, and Cleopatra forcing all her enemy generals to sleep with her and reducing them to serve her as if they were slaves. Whereupon they spun out a completely fantastic history, concocted in the imaginations of those ignorant millionaires, in which the female citizens of Rome went to Capua to lull Hannibal to sleep in their arms, and his lieutenants with him, and whole phalanxes of mercenaries to boot. They cited all the women who have brought conquerors to a halt, made of their own bodies a battlefield, a means of dominating, a weapon; all who have vanquished with their heroic caresses hideous or hated men, and surrendered their chastity to vengeance, all in a spirit of self-sacrifice.

They even spoke in veiled terms of that Englishwoman of noble family who had allowed herself to be inoculated with a horrible contagious illness so as to infect Bonaparte, who was miraculously saved, by a sudden moment of weakness, just as the hour of the fateful rendezvous was striking.

And all this was narrated in a decent, moderate way, sometimes made livelier by a tone of enthusiasm designed to arouse emulation.

Anyone might have thought, in the end, that the only role of a woman in this world was a perpetual sacrifice of her person, a continual self-abandonment to the whims of the soldiery.

The two nuns seemed not to hear, being absorbed in deep meditation. Butterball said nothing.

For the whole afternoon they allowed her to think things over. But instead of calling her "Madame" as they had until then, they simply addressed her as "Mademoiselle," without anyone knowing quite why, as if they had wanted to take her down a peg or two from the esteem she had managed to earn, and make her feel how shameful her position was.

Just as the soup was being served, M. Follenvie reappeared, repeating the words he had said the day before. "The Prussian officer asks whether Mademoiselle Elisabeth Rousset has changed her mind yet."

Butterball retorted sharply, "No, Monsieur."

But at dinner the coalition weakened. Loiseau came out with three unfortunate turns of phrase. Everyone was racking their brains to think of new examples, but they could not find any. Then the Countess, without premeditation perhaps, but feeling a vague need to pay homage to Religion, questioned the older of the nuns about the great deeds in the lives of the saints. Now, many of them had committed acts which would in our eyes be crimes; but the Church doubtless absolves such misdeeds when they are performed for the greater glory of God, or for the good of one's neighbour. This was a powerful argument: the Countess turned it to her account. Then, either through one of those tacit understandings, those veiled complicities in which anyone who wears ecclesiastical habits excels, or simply through a happy lack of intelligence, a useful stupidity, the old nun added her formidable support to the conspiracy. They had thought she was timid, but she showed herself to be bold, verbose, violent. *She* was not troubled by the tentative gropings of casuistry; her doctrine seemed a rod of iron; her faith never hesitated; her conscience had not a single scruple. She found Abraham's sacrifice perfectly simple, for she would have killed mother and father straight away if given orders from on high; and nothing, in her view, could fail to be pleasing to the Lord when the intention behind it was praiseworthy. The Countess, making the most of the sacred authority of her unexpected accomplice, made her produce what amounted to an edifying paraphrase on that moral axiom: "The end justifies the means."

She continued to question her.

"And so, Sister, you think that God accepts all our good intentions, and forgives the deed when the motive is pure?"

"Who could doubt it, Madame? An action that is blameworthy in itself often becomes meritorious thanks to the thought that inspires it."

And so they went on, unravelling God's designs, foreseeing his decisions, making out that he took an interest in things which, to tell the truth, barely concerned him.

All this was veiled, cunning, discreet. But every word uttered by the holy sister in her wimple made another breach in the courtesan's indignant resistance. Then, as the conversation went off at something of a tangent, the woman with the rosary talked about the houses of her order, about her mother superior, about herself, and her charming little neighbour, dear Sister Saint-Nicéphore. They had been asked to go to Le Havre to work in the hospitals looking after the hundreds of soldiers affected by smallpox. And she depicted those poor sick men, describing their illness in detail. And here they were, stopped en route by the whims of this Prussian; a great number of Frenchmen might be dying, when they could have saved them perhaps! It was her speciality, saving soldiers; she had been in the Crimea, in Italy, in Austria; and as she recounted her campaigns, she suddenly revealed herself to be one of those trumpet-and-drum nuns, seemingly made to be camp-followers and to pick up the wounded from the hurly-burly of battles and, more effectively than any commanding officer, to bring to heel strapping but undisciplined soldiers with a single word; a real "Tantarara!" nun, whose ravaged face, pitted with countless pockmarks, seemed an image of the devastations of war.

Nobody uttered a word after she had finished; they thought she had created an excellent effect.

As soon as the meal was over, they quickly went up to their rooms, and came down the next morning quite late.

Breakfast was a tranquil affair. They were giving the seed sown the night before time to germinate and bear fruit.

The Countess suggested going for a walk in the afternoon; then the Count, as had been agreed, took the arm of Butterball, and remained behind the others, with her.

He talked to her in that familiar, paternal, somewhat disdainful tone which staid men use with women of the street, calling her "my dear child," addressing her from the heights of his social position, his incontrovertible honour. He went straight away to the heart of the matter.

"So you prefer to leave us here, exposed like yourself to all the acts of violence that would follow a defeat of the Prussian troops, rather than to consent to one of those little deeds of kindness that you have so often performed in your life?"

Butterball did not reply.

He came at her with gentleness, with reason, with an appeal to sentiment. He managed to remain "Monsieur le Comte," while at the same time stooping to flirtatious banter when necessary, full of compliments, amiable, in fact. He spoke in the highest terms of the service she would be doing them, spoke of their gratitude; then suddenly, addressing her cheerfully and familiarly, he exclaimed, "You know what, my dear, he'd be able to boast of having enjoyed a pretty girl of a kind he won't often find in *his* country."

Butterball did not reply and went to catch up with the others.

Once back at the inn, she went up to her room and did not reappear. Their anxiety was extreme. What was she going to do? If she resisted, what a pickle they'd be in!

The hour struck for dinner; they waited for her in vain. M. Follenvie came in and announced that Mlle Rousset was feeling unwell, and that they could start their meal. They all pricked up their ears. The Count went up to the innkeeper and said, in a low voice, "All fixed?"

"Yes."

Observing the proprieties, he said nothing to his companions, but simply gave them a quick nod. Immediately a great sigh of relief was heaved from every chest, and their faces brightened up considerably. Loiseau cried, "Good heavens! The champagne is on me, if there's any to be found in this establishment;" and Mme Loiseau was disquieted when the proprietor returned with four bottles in his hands. Everyone had suddenly become communicative and noisy; a ribald merriment filled every heart. The Count seemed to notice that Mme Carré-Lamadon was charming, the factory owner paid compliments to the Countess. The conversation was lively, playful, full of witticisms.

Suddenly, Loiseau, his face anxious and lifting his arms up, bellowed, "Quiet!" Everyone immediately fell silent, surprised and almost panic stricken. Then he strained his ears to listen, motioned with his hands to say "Shhh!" raised his eyes to the ceiling, listened again, and then resumed, in his natural voice, "Don't worry, everything's all right."

They struggled to understand, but soon a smile crossed every face.

After a quarter of an hour he started the same joke all over, repeating it several times in the course of the evening; and he kept pretending to be shouting up to someone in the storey above, giving him bits of advice full of double entendres, drawing on all the wit of a travelling salesman. At times he would strike a sad and solemn pose to sigh, "Poor lass"; or else he would murmur between clenched teeth, with an expression of rage, "Go on, you beggarly Prussian!" Sometimes, when they were least expecting it, he would repeatedly cry in vibrant tones, "Enough! Enough!" adding, as if talking to himself, "So long as we get to see her again; I hope he doesn't kill her, wretched man!"

Although these jokes were in deplorable taste, they amused everyone and offended no one, for indignation is dependent on social milieu as much as everything else, and the atmosphere that had little by little developed around them was thick with licentious ideas.

At dessert, the women themselves made witty and discreet allusions. Every eye gleamed; they'd had a lot to drink. The Count, who even when he let himself go a little maintained an appearance of great gravity, came up with a highly enjoyable comparison between the end of the winter season at the pole and the joy of shipwrecked men who see a route to the south opening up before them.

Loiseau, his tongue set wagging, stood up with a glass of champagne in his hand. "I drink to our deliverance!" Everyone was on their feet; they acclaimed him. The two nuns themselves, urged on by the ladies, consented to take a tiny sip of this sparkling wine they had never tasted. They declared it was like fizzy lemonade, although more refined.

Loiseau summed up the situation.

"It's a great shame we don't have a piano because we could strike up a quadrille!"

Cornudet had not said a word, not made a move; he even seemed to be absorbed in the most serious thoughts, and sometimes, with a furious gesture, he would draw on his great beard as if he wanted to pull it out even longer. Finally, around midnight, as the party was about to break up, Loiseau, swaying on his feet, suddenly gave him a light punch in the stomach and jabbered to him, "You're not exactly a barrel of laughs this evening; got nothing to say, citizen?" But Cornudet looked up suddenly, and stared round at the group with eyes bright with anger.

"Let me tell the whole lot of you that what you've just done is absolutely vile!"

He stood up, went to the door, repeated, "Absolutely vile!" and vanished.

This at first cast a pall on the proceedings. Loiseau, completely taken aback, stood there dumbstruck; but he soon regained his composure and suddenly, creased with laughter, started to repeat, "Sour grapes! Talk about sour grapes!" As no one understood, he told them about the "mysteries of the corridor." Then there was a formidable outburst of renewed gaiety. The ladies were overcome by hilarity. The Count and M. Carré-Lamadon laughed till they cried. They couldn't believe it.

"What? You're sure? He wanted to . . . "

"I saw it, I tell you."

"And she turned him down . . . "

"Because the Prussian was in the room next door."

"You've got to be joking."

"I swear it."

The Count was choking with laughter. The factory owner was holding his hands to his belly. Loiseau continued:

"And now you can see why this evening he didn't find the joke funny at all, no, not in the slightest."

And all three went off again, aching and breathless.

Thereupon they separated. But Mme Loiseau, who was easily nettled, remarked to her husband as they were getting into bed, that little Mme Carré-Lamadon, that "old bag," had been forcing herself to smile all evening. "You know, when women get the hots for a uniform, whether it's French or Prussian, good heavens, they don't mind in the slightest! . . . My God, but it's sad!"

And all night long, in the darkness of the corridor, there could be heard a continual to and fro of rustles, faint and barely audible noises like that of light breathing, the scampering of bare feet, imperceptible creakings. And of course it was quite a while before they got to sleep, for streaks of light shone for a long time beneath their doors. Champagne has that effect; it disturbs your sleep, so they say.

The next day, a clear winter sun made the snow gleam dazzlingly. The coach, finally harnessed, was waiting in front of the door, while an army of white pigeons, strutting around in their thick feathers, their pink eyes with a black dot in the middle agleam, were gravely promenading between the legs of the six horses, and pecking for food in the steaming dung that they scattered.

The coachman, enveloped in his sheepskin coat, was smoking a pipe on his seat, and all the travellers, radiant with relief, were rapidly having provisions wrapped up for the rest of the journey.

The only one they were still waiting for was Butterball. She appeared.

She seemed a little troubled and ashamed; and she advanced timidly towards her companions who all, with one movement, turned away as if they had not seen her. The Count took his wife's arm with a dignified air and led her away from this impure contact.

The fat young woman stopped in stupefaction; then, summoning up all her courage, she went up to the factory owner's wife, humbly murmuring "Good day, Madame." The other merely nodded curtly and impertinently, accompanying her gesture with a stare of outraged virtue. Everyone seemed tremendously busy, and they kept their distance from her as if she had been transporting an infectious disease in her skirts. Then they hurried over to the coach where she was the last to arrive, all alone, taking in silence the seat she had occupied during the first half of the route.

They seemed not to see her, not to know her; but Mme Loiseau, considering her distantly, said in indignant half-tones to her husband, "A good thing I don't have to sit next to her."

The heavy carriage shook, and the journey recommenced.

At first nobody spoke. Butterball did not dare to lift her eyes. She felt at one and the same time indignant at all her fellow travellers, and humiliated at having yielded, soiled by the kisses of that Prussian into whose arms they had hypocritically flung her.

But the Countess, turning to Mme Carré-Lamadon, soon broke this painful silence. "I believe you know Mme d'Etrelles?"

"Yes indeed, she's a friend of mine."

"She's a charming woman!"

"Delightful! A really high-class person, very well educated too, and an artist to her fingertips; she sings delightfully well, and draws to perfection."

The factory owner was chatting to the Count, and in the midst of the clatter of the windows a word sometimes became audible: "Coupon . . . falls due . . . premium . . . settlement . . . "

Loiseau, who had swiped the old pack of cards from the inn, greasy as it was from five years' contact with the dirty unwiped tables, launched into a game of bezique with his wife.

The nuns took from their belts the long rosaries hanging there, and together made the sign of the cross; and all at once their lips began to move quickly, getting faster and faster, forcing the pace of their indistinct murmur as if competing to see who could recite the *Oremus* most often; and from time to time they would kiss a medal, make the sign of the cross again, and then recommence their rapid and continual mumblings.

Cornudet was reflecting, motionless.

After three hours on the road, Loiseau gathered up his cards. "I'm hungry," he said.

Then his wife took out a parcel tied up with string from which she brought out a piece of cold veal. She cut it neatly into thin, firm slices, and both of them set to.

"What about doing the same?" said the Countess. They agreed, and she unwrapped the provisions prepared for the two married couples. There was, in one of those long jars with a china hare on the lid to indicate that *lièvre en pâté* is contained within, a succulent selection of meats in which white rivers of fat trickled through the brown flesh of the game, mixed together with other finely minced meat. A nice slab of Gruyère, wrapped in a newspaper, still had the words "News in Brief" imprinted on its smooth sticky surface.

The two nuns took out a slice of sausage smelling of garlic; and Cornudet, digging deep into both of the vast pockets of his short sackcloth coat, pulled out one of four hard-boiled eggs and from another the heel of a loaf. He detached the shell, tossed it into the straw at his feet, and started to bite into the eggs, letting bright yellow specks fan onto his big bushy beard, where they seemed to shine like stars.

Butterball, in the haste and turmoil of getting up, had not had time to think of anything; and she stared, exasperated and choking with anger, at all those people placidly eating. At first, a tumultuous rage made her tense up, and she opened her mouth as if to pour out the stream of insults rising to her lips at their disgraceful behaviour; but she was unable to speak, choked as she was by frustration.

Nobody spared her a glance or a thought. She felt drowned in the contempt of those oh-so-respectable rascals who had first sacrificed her and then cast her aside like some unclean, useless object. Then she thought of her basket, crammed with all the good things they had greedily devoured: her two chickens glistening with jelly, her pâtés, her pears, her four bottles of Bordeaux; and her fury suddenly subsided, like a cord pulled too taut and suddenly snapping, and she felt on the verge of tears. She made a terrific effort, stiffening and swallowing her sobs as children do, but her tears rose, shining on the rim of her eyes, and soon two big fat drops fell from her eyes and trickled slowly down her cheeks. Others followed them more rapidly, running down like drops of water filtering through a rock, and falling regularly on the plump curve of her bosom. She remained bolt upright, staring in front of her, her face pale and rigid, hoping no one would see her.

But the Countess noticed and alerted her husband with a gesture. He shrugged, as if to say, "Well? It's not my fault." Mme Loiseau uttered a mute laugh of triumph and murmured, "She's crying for shame."

The two nuns had resumed their prayers, having rolled the remnants of their sausage up in a piece of paper.

Then Cornudet, busy digesting his eggs, stretched his long legs out on the seat opposite, threw himself back, folded his arms, smiled like a man who has just thought of a good trick to play, and started to whistle the Marseillaise.

Everyone's face darkened. The people's song, it was obvious, was not to the liking of his fellow travellers. They turned edgy and irritable, and seemed ready to start howling, like dogs when they hear a hurdy-gurdy. He noticed this; now there was no stopping him. Sometimes he even hummed the words:

> *"Oh sacred love of fatherland,*
> *Our vengeful arms lead and sustain!*
> *Beloved freedom, join your strength.*
> *To your defenders, might and main!"*

They sped along more quickly, as the snow had hardened: and all the way to Dieppe, during the long grey and gloomy hours of the journey, as the coach bounced along, and night fell, and then in the pitch darkness of the coach, he kept up, with a ferocious obstinacy, his vengeful and monotonous whistling, forcing his weary and exasperated fellow travellers to listen to the song from beginning to end, and to remember each word and fit it to the right note.

And Butterball carried on crying; and sometimes a sob that she had been unable to hold back escaped, in the pause between two verses, into the dark.

F.Y.I.

Alsatian: a person from Alsace, a place in the eastern part of France between the Rhine River and the Vosges Mountains. Alsace and its neighbour, Lorraine, were ruled by Germany in 1871 after the Franco-Prussian War and were returned to France by the Treaty of Versailles (1919).

Bonapartist: a name given to citizens of France who considered themselves followers or supporters of Napoleon I (1769–1821), the Bonaparte family, its policies and dynastic claims.

commissariat: a commissariat is the department of an army in charge of seeing to the provision of food supplies for the troops and the animals, such as the horses used by cavalry.

Hannibal: (247–183/182 BCE) often called "the father of strategy" because even his enemies would come to adopt many of his military tactics, this general from Carthage is regarded by many as the greatest military tactician and strategist in history. Hannibal is also thought to be one of the greatest generals of antiquity, together with Alexander the Great and Julius Caesar. Some believe he was the one to say the famous words, "We will either find a way, or make one."

hurdy-gurdy: a pear-shaped wooden string instrument long associated with street musicians; it is still used as a European folk instrument today. This instrument uses a hand crank to rotate a barrel inside its case on which multiple tunes are set, causing a small pipe organ to play.

Judith and Holofernes: principal characters in the Old Testament story of the murder of the general Holofernes by the Hebrew widow Judith. Upon orders to lay siege to the town of Bethulia, Holofernes is almost victorious in taking the town, when one night Judith enters his camp, gets him drunk, and seduces him. While he is drunk, she beheads him and takes the head back to Bethulia. The Hebrews defeat Holofernes's army. To view one of the most famous depictions of the beheading of Holofernes, see Artemisia Gentileschi's "Judith Beheading Holofernes" at http://www.artbible.info/art/large/680.html.

La Marseillaise: written by Claude-Joseph Rouget de Lisle in 1792, the Marseillaise was adopted as the national anthem of France in 1795. Originally titled "Chant de guerre pour l 'Armée du Rhin" ("War Song for the Army of the Rhine"), the title was changed after the song became a call to arms by Marseille war volunteers upon their arrival in Paris during the revolution (1789). Its lyrics reflect the invasion of France by Prussian and Austrian armies. Napoleon I had it banned during his reign, as did Louis XVIII and Napoleon III. In 1879, the song was reinstated as France's national anthem and has remained so ever since. To see the lyrics for this anthem, go to http://www. marseillaise.org/english/english.html.

Lucretia and Sextus: their story was made famous by the Roman historian Livy and the Greek historian Dionysius of Halicarnassus. Lucretia's rape by Sextus Tarquinius, the son of a king, and her consequent suicide were believed to be the cause for the revolution in Rome that abolished the monarchy and established the Roman Republic. The rape and suicide of Lucretia has been a major theme in European art and literature, most notably in William Shakespeare's *The Rape of Lucrece* (1594).

Norman: a name given to the Vikings, or Norsemen, and their descendants who settled in the north of France. They founded Normandy, France. Normans were pagan pirates from Denmark, Norway, and Iceland who later converted to Christianity and adopted the French language. They continued their Viking ancestors' penchant for conquest.

prefecture: a district under the government of a prefect

Prussians: people from the Kingdom of Prussia. Prussia was a German kingdom from 1701 to 1918. Prussian troops played a great role in helping defeat Napoleon Bonaparte at the Battle of Waterloo in 1815.

quadrille: an intricate dance made up of four couples in square formation

Rouen: the historic capital city of Normandy in northern France on the River Seine. It was once the largest and most prosperous cities of medieval Europe.

Seine: a famous and extensive river in France. It starts in a lake in La Seine and ends in an estuary, or a partially enclosed coastal body of water in which river water is mixed with seawater, in Le Havre.

stagecoach: a public, four-wheeled coach pulled by horses formerly used to transport mail or passengers over a regular route that had scheduled stops at stations or stages.

Tantalus: in Greek mythology, Tantalus was a king who was sent to Hades for his crimes against the gods. As punishment, he was made to stand in water that receded whenever he tried to bend down to drink. He was also given a tree in which the fruit would pull away from his hand whenever he reached for a piece to eat, thereby suffering from everlasting thirst and hunger. The word *tantalizing* is derived from Tantalus; something that is tantalizing is usually desirable but unattainable.

uhlan: one of a body of horse cavalry armed with lances, pistols, and sabres that formed part of the Polish, German, Austrian, and Russian armies.

Words to Build on

capriciousness: the quality of being prone to sudden and inexplicable changes in mood or behaviour

caste: a strict system of social distinction often determined by social standing, wealth, hereditary rank, or position

expostulated: to express strong disapproval or disagreement

feted: to celebrate or honour someone or something with a festival, feast, or an elaborate entertainment, such as a masque or ball

grapeshot: because of its resemblance to a bunch of grapes, the name grapeshot was given to the cluster of small iron balls once used as cannon charge. Maupassant uses this word to describe the cluster of pits or pock marks in the nun's face.

irascible: to be bad-tempered or easily irritated

urbanity: refers to the characteristics, preferences, traits, and points of view associated with urban areas. Another term that is used for people who possess urbanity is "citified." Urbanity is often associated with refinement, elegance, and class.

Tricks of the Trade

Climax

Naturalism

Turning point

In Your Own Words: Comprehension

1. Who is telling this story?
2. Make a list of all the characters in the carriage. What profession and to which socioeconomic background does each belong?
3. Why are all these characters in the same carriage?
4. How do the passengers in the coach treat Butterball? Is their treatment consistent throughout the story?
5. Describe Butterball (the character) in your own words.
6. Do Butterball's actions in the story reflect her own moral code or her political leanings? What's the difference?
7. How do the other characters convince her to go against her beliefs?
8. Are the characters in the carriage ever in any imminent danger? Are they poorly treated by anyone? Is this why they give up Butterball to the Prussians?
9. Are there any characters without proper names in the story?
10. What is the story's turning point and climax?

In Your Own Words: Analysis

1. Butterball is referred to as a "woman of easy virtue." Does this mean she is a prostitute? Consider these terms: prostitute, call girl, sex worker, escort, and courtesan. Are these words just labels that mean the same thing, or is there a real difference between any of these terms?

2. The original French title "Boule de Suif" means "ball of suet," raw beef or fat. Why is this used to describe Butterball the character? The narrator states that Butterball was "a pleasure to see." Does the new title of the English translation have other connotations for North American readers?

3. Butterball is not judged harshly because of her weight; in fact, she is considered desirable by the men of her time because of it. How does this compare to the way we view overweight or obese women today? When people today consider an overweight person attractive or desirable solely because of his or her physical appearance is it because fat is fetishized?

4. Many stories by Maupassant have been successfully adapted to film. Maupassant's writing inspired Stephen King to write *The Shining*, which was also turned into a successful film. Would "Butterball" make a good film? What elements of this story and characters would translate well into film?

Now Write

1. This story was written in France in 1880. Research some of the attitudes towards prostitutes and prostitution today. Are any of the ideas our society has today similar to those shown by the characters in "Butterball"? Write an essay comparing these views.

2. The French writer Gustave Flaubert, one of the greatest western novelists, considered "Butterball" a masterpiece. It was a massive hit when it was published in France and it made Maupassant very wealthy. The story won both popular and critical acclaim and is considered to be the perfect example of the short story form. In your own opinion, what makes this story so great? Write an essay outlining three or four basic elements of a short story and explain how "Butterball" exemplifies these elements.

3. A churchman in the story states, ". . . poor folks have to help each other out . . . It's the high and mighty that make war." Write an essay showing how this statement applies to the story. Is military war the only war being fought in "Butterball"?

4. Analyze the character of Butterball. Is she a victim of circumstance or a figure of pathos? Is she a hero or an anti-hero? Explain your reasoning for the answer in your essay.

Kate Chopin

Kate Chopin (1851–1904) was born Catherine O'Flaherty in St. Louis, Missouri. Her father, Thomas O'Flaherty, immigrated to the United States from County Galway, Ireland, and married her mother, Eliza Faris, who was a native of St. Louis. Chopin was described as being short, quiet, but possessing a "quick Irish wit" along with a personality that loved people and conversation.

Chopin met and married Oscar Chopin, the son of a wealthy cotton-growing family, who was raised in France and did not impose many of the customary restrictions of the time on his wife. Being raised in the South, Kate Chopin believed in the Confederate cause during the American Civil War and supported an economy based on slave labour. When Oscar Chopin died of malaria, Chopin became a widow at the age of 32 and was left with the responsibility of raising six children. She never remarried; instead she used her time to write, producing two novels and about 100 short stories.

Most of her fiction is set in Louisiana and focuses on the lives of women. Her stories were popular in her own time, but her reputation grew with her most famous work, *The Awakening* (1899). Although it was banned and labelled "shocking" and "sex fiction" at the time, it became an American classic. It is the story of a woman's sexual awakening, and as such it was removed from many libraries due to its content.

Chopin greatly admired the writings of Guy de Maupassant, learning from him how to be an accurate observer of life and how to relay this onto paper. She did something in her works that few other nineteenth-century writers did: she put female characters front and centre in stories, thereby reinforcing the importance of their lives.

"The Story of an Hour" (1894) is about an hour-long time span in the life of Mrs. Louise Mallard. Considered to be one of Chopin's most famous stories, it also includes some of the themes that Chopin explores in later works: women's control (or lack thereof) over their own fate, and their desires in life and their roles in marriage, in the community, and in society at large. Fans of Chopin's work have formed The Kate Chopin Society, which offers more information on her life and work at www.katechopin.org.

In Her Own Words

"And moreover, to succeed, the artist must possess the courageous soul . . . the brave soul. The soul that dares and defies."

"There are some people who leave impressions not so lasting as the imprint of an oar upon the water."

Before We Begin

1. The famous American writer Kate Chopin was also a southerner who owned slaves. Should this affect how one reads her work? Has a public figure (actor, musician, athlete) you once idolized ever disappointed you? Should we care to know all the details of the personal lives of celebrities? How should this affect the way we view their works?

2. Do you believe that significant, life-altering events can occur in a short span of time? What are some examples of such events or occurrences?

3. Has technology affected the way we receive news in emergency situations?

 **Now Read**

The Story of an Hour

Knowing that Mrs. Mallard was afflicted with a heart trouble, great care was taken to break to her as gently as possible the news of her husband's death.

It was her sister Josephine who told her, in broken sentences; veiled hints that revealed in half concealing. Her husband's friend Richards was there, too, near her. It was he who had been in the newspaper office when intelligence of the railroad disaster was received, with Brently Mallard's name leading the list of "killed." He had only taken the time to assure himself of its truth by a second telegram, and had hastened to forestall any less careful, less tender friend in bearing the sad message.

She did not hear the story as many women have heard the same, with a paralyzed inability to accept its significance. She wept at once, with sudden, wild abandonment, in her sister's arms. When the storm of grief had spent itself she went away to her room alone. She would have no one follow her.

There stood, facing the open window, a comfortable, roomy armchair. Into this she sank, pressed down by a physical exhaustion that haunted her body and seemed to reach into her soul.

She could see in the open square before her house the tops of trees that were all aquiver with the new spring life. The delicious breath of rain was in the air. In the street below a peddler was crying his wares. The notes of a distant song which someone was singing reached her faintly, and countless sparrows were twittering in the eaves.

There were patches of blue sky showing here and there through the clouds that had met and piled one above the other in the west facing her window.

She sat with her head thrown back upon the cushion of the chair, quite motionless, except when a sob came up into her throat and shook her, as a child who has cried itself to sleep continues to sob in its dreams.

She was young, with a fair, calm face, whose lines bespoke repression and even a certain strength. But now there was a dull stare in her eyes, whose gaze was fixed away off yonder on one of those patches of blue sky. It was not a glance of reflection, but rather indicated a suspension of intelligent thought.

There was something coming to her and she was waiting for it, fearfully. What was it? She did not know; it was too subtle and elusive to name. But she felt it, creeping out of the sky, reaching toward her through the sounds, the scents, the colour that filled the air.

Now her bosom rose and fell tumultuously. She was beginning to recognize this thing that was approaching to possess her, and she was striving to beat it back with her will—as powerless as her two white slender hands would have been.

When she abandoned herself a little whispered word escaped her slightly parted lips. She said it over and over under her breath: "free, free, free!" The vacant stare and the look of terror that had followed it went from her eyes. They stayed keen and bright. Her pulses beat fast, and the coursing blood warmed and relaxed every inch of her body.

She did not stop to ask if it were or were not a monstrous joy that held her. A clear and exalted perception enabled her to dismiss the suggestion as trivial.

She knew that she would weep again when she saw the kind, tender hands folded in death; the face that had never looked save with love upon her, fixed and grey and dead. But she saw beyond that bitter moment a long procession of years to come that would belong to her absolutely. And she opened and spread her arms out to them in welcome.

There would be no one to live for her during those coming years; she would live for herself. There would be no powerful will bending hers in that blind persistence with which men and women believe they have a right to impose a private will upon a fellow-creature. A kind intention or a cruel intention made the act seem no less a crime as she looked upon it in that brief moment of illumination.

And yet she had loved him—sometimes. Often she had not. What did it matter! What could love, the unsolved mystery, count for in face of this possession of self-assertion which she suddenly recognized as the strongest impulse of her being!

"Free! Body and soul free!" she kept whispering.

Josephine was kneeling before the closed door with her lips to the keyhole, imploring for admission. "Louise, open the door! I beg; open the door—you will make yourself ill. What are you doing, Louise? For heaven's sake open the door."

"Go away. I am not making myself ill." No; she was drinking in a very elixir of life through that open window.

Her fancy was running riot along those days ahead of her. Spring days, and summer days, and all sorts of days that would be her own. She breathed a quick prayer that life might be long. It was only yesterday she had thought with a shudder that life might be long.

She arose at length and opened the door to her sister's importunities. There was a feverish triumph in her eyes, and carried herself unwittingly like a goddess of Victory. She clasped her sister's waist, and together they descended the stairs. Richards stood waiting for them at the bottom.

Someone was opening the front door with a latchkey. It was Brently Mallard who entered, a little travel stained, composedly carrying his grip-sack and umbrella. He had been far from the scene of accident, and did not even know there had been one. He stood amazed at Josephine's piercing cry; Richards's quick motion to screen him from the view of his wife.

But Richards was too late.

When the doctors came they said she had died of heart disease—of joy that kills.

F.Y.I.

telegram: a brief printed message composed on a telegraph machine and delivered by hand

Words to Build on

eaves: overhanging edges of a roof

elixir: a drink with restorative properties

elusive: difficult to catch hold of

intelligence: information

Tricks of the Trade

American realism

Climax

Imagery

Irony

Narrative point of view

In Your Own Words: Comprehension

1. What is the setting for this story?
2. What is the season this story takes place in, and how is it relevant to the story?
3. Why does Mrs. Mallard wish "no one follow her" after she hears the news of her husband's death?
4. Once Mrs. Mallard is alone, what kinds of thoughts come into her head?
5. Why does Mrs. Mallard lock the door and not allow her sister in the room?
6. Is there anything strange about Richards running to inform Mrs. Mallard about her husband's death?
7. Consider the words that the narrator associates with the word "joy." What is unusual about these word associations?

In Your Own Words: Analysis

1. Who is telling this story? Is there any indication that it is a male or female voice speaking?

2. Why would the narrator mention Mrs. Mallard's "heart trouble" in the very first sentence of the story?

3. At what point in the story does the narrator refer to the main character as Mrs. Mallard? At what point does this change to the more familiar "Louise"? Is there a reason this change occurs?

4. What is unusual about Mrs. Mallard's reaction to the news of her husband's death? In what ways is her reaction different from that of a typical Victorian wife?

5. The narrator states that "something was coming to her," but she fears it. What is coming and what does Mrs. Mallard fear and why?

6. What kind of marriage do the Mallard's have? Is Mr. Mallard a good husband? Provide examples from the text to support your answer.

7. Does Mrs. Mallard love her husband? Provide examples from the text to support your answer.

8. Why is this story called "The Story of an Hour"?

9. This story is about a marriage in 1894. Could such a relationship exist today?

10. Could the events of this story take place today?

11. In terms of plot plausibility, is anything in this story unbelievable or unrealistic?

Now Write

1. There is not much in terms of physical setting to this story, and yet Chopin does a great deal with common household rooms and structures. Analyze the setting to show how it relates to the themes of the story.

2. Kate Chopin was a great admirer of Guy de Maupassant's writing, even translating some of his stories from French into English. In a diary entry about his works, Chopin wrote "Here was life, not fiction. Here was a man who escaped from tradition and authority, who had entered into himself and looked out upon life through his own being and with his own eyes; and who, in a direct and simple way, told us what he saw." Write an essay in which you compare the writing style of "The Story of an Hour" with Maupassant's "Butterball."

3. The climax of this story occurs in the very last line, when Mrs. Mallard experiences a "joy that kills." Select one other story from this text and compare its climax to the one in Chopin's story. Are both equally effective climaxes? Why?

Leonid Andreyev

Leonid Nikolayevich Andreyev (1871–1919) was a prolific Russian novelist, short story writer, photographer, and influential playwright. Born in the Oryol province of Russia, Andreyev was, as his mother referred to him, "a very serious child" who had radical mood swings. As a teenager, he once lay beneath a passing train to "test Providence's will." Although he was handsome, intelligent, and humorous, he suffered from severe bouts of melancholy and depression; he made repeated suicide attempts throughout his life. Some believe that he actually had bipolar disorder (manic depression). This darkness and pessimism would be constants in all of his literary work.

Although it is said that Andreyev read an enormous number of novels and stories as a child, when he grew up he went to Moscow and St. Petersburg to study law. However, once again his depression was so severe that he tried to kill himself. He left his law studies and took a position on a Moscow newspaper as a police–court reporter. Besides writing for the paper, Andreyev wrote poems that did not garner much attention. It was his first short story, "Bargamot and Garaska" (1898), that drew the attention of the author and social activist Maxim Gorky (the two would later be imprisoned together for "political crimes"). Gorky encouraged Andreyev to devote himself to writing. He did, and between the years 1905 and 1917 Leonid Andreyev would become Russia's premiere author. His first book of short novels and stories sold a quarter-million copies in a matter of months. His plays would go on to be produced throughout Europe and America; two of them were historically staged by Constantin Stanislavski and Vsevolod Meyerhold, giants in the Russian theatre. His most famous work, *He Who Gets Slapped*, was made into a critically acclaimed and successful motion picture by MGM studios in 1924.

Although he continued to write political pieces, Andreyev's work tapered off after 1915. After his involvement in the February Revolution, a political uprising that forced the abdication of Czar Nicholas II and the end of both the Romanov dynasty and the Russian Empire, Andreyev moved to Finland in 1917 and continuously wrote impassioned warnings addressed to the world regarding the crimes, decadence, and dangers of the Bolsheviks. Once a star and staple in Russian theatre and literature, he would live out his life in relative exile and poverty. Leonid Andreyev died of heart failure on September 12, 1919, at the age of 48.

Andreyev's work covered many topics and subjects: politics, provincial life, medical settings, court and prison tales, psychology, and psychiatry. His work is seen as symbolic and romantic, dark and anarchistic. Many of his contemporaries characterized his work as "impenetrable" because it is so difficult to find anything redeeming amidst the gloom. Leo Tolstoy was reported as saying, "Leonid Andreyev tries to frighten me, but I am not afraid." In his short story, "The Little Angel," Andreyev once again places an abstract idea at the heart of the tale, and both the characters and the action play out their parts around it. It is the abstract idea, in this case "hope," that, according to the introduction to a translation of Andreyev's work, "redeems the gloom or horror of the actual tale."

In His Own Words

"Bread without love is like grass without salt—the stomach may be filled, but it leaves a bad taste in the mouth."

"Only the footsteps of the blind are short, but their thoughts are long."

"If the lot of the Man be to become a God, his throne will be the Book."

Before We Begin

1. Have you ever wondered what creates a bully?
2. Can a child bully his or her parents? How?
3. Have you ever been forced to socialize with or be nice to people you resented or who angered you? For what reason?

 **Now Read**

The Little Angel

At times Sashka wished to give up what is called living: to cease to wash every morning in cold water, on which thin sheets of ice floated about; to go no more to the grammar school, and there to have to listen to everyone scolding him; no more to experience the pain in the small of his back and indeed over his whole body when his mother made him kneel in the corner all the evening. But, since he was only 13 years of age, and did not know all the means by which people abandon life at will, he continued to go to the grammar school and to kneel in the corner, and it seemed to him as if life would never end. A year would go by, and another, and yet another, and still he would be going to school, and be made to kneel in the corner. And since Sashka possessed an indomitable and bold spirit, he could not supinely tolerate evil, and so found means to avenge himself on life. With this object in view he would thrash his companions, be rude to the Head, impertinent to the masters, and tell lies all day long to his teachers and to his mother—but to his father he never lied. If in a fight he got his nose broken, he would purposely make the damage worse, and howl, without shedding a single tear, but so loudly that all who heard him were fain to stop their ears to keep out the disagreeable sound. When he had howled as long as he thought advisable, he would suddenly cease, and, putting out his tongue, draw in his copybook a caricature of himself howling at an usher who pressed his fingers to his ears, while the victor stood trembling with fear. The whole copybook was filled with caricatures, the one which most frequently occurred being that of a short stout woman beating a boy as thin as a lucifer-match with a rolling pin. Below in a large scrawling hand would be written the legend: "Beg my pardon, puppy!" and the reply, "Won't! blow'd if I do!"

Before Christmas Sashka was expelled from school, and when his mother attempted to thrash him, he bit her finger. This action gave him his liberty. He left off washing in the morning, ran about all day bullying the other boys, and had but one fear, and that was hunger, for his mother entirely left off providing for him, so that he came to depend upon the pieces of bread and potatoes which his father secreted for him. On these conditions Sashka found existence tolerable.

One Friday (it was Christmas Eve) he had been playing with the other boys, until they had dispersed to their homes, followed by the squeak of the rusty frozen wicket gate as it closed behind the last of them. It was already growing dark, and a grey snowy mist was travelling up from the country, along a dark alley; in a low black building, which stood fronting the end of the alley, a lamp was burning with a reddish, unblinking light. The frost had become more intense, and when Sashka reached the circle of light cast by the lamp, he saw that fine dry flakes of snow were floating slowly on the air. It was high time to be getting home.

"Where have you been knocking about all night, puppy?" exclaimed his mother, doubling her fist, without, however, striking. Her sleeves were turned up, exposing her fat white arms, and on her forehead, almost devoid of eyebrows, stood beads of perspiration. As Sashka passed by her he recognized the familiar smell of vodka. His mother scratched her head with the short dirty nail of her thick forefinger, and since it was no good scolding, she merely spat, and cried: "Statisticians! that's what they are!"

Sashka shuffled contemptuously, and went behind the partition, from whence might be heard the heavy breathing of his father, Ivan Savvich, who was in a chronic state of shivering, and was now trying to warm himself by sitting on the heated bench of the stove with his hands under him, palms downwards.

"Sashka! the Svetchnikovs have invited you to the Christmas tree. The housemaid came," he whispered.

"Get along with you!" said Sashka with incredulity.

"Fact! The old woman there has purposely not told you, but she has mended your jacket all the same."

"Nonsense," Sashka replied, still more surprised.

The Svetchnikovs were rich people, who had put him to the grammar school, and after his expulsion had forbidden him their house.

His father once more took his oath to the truth of his statement, and Sashka became meditative.

"Well then, move, shift a bit," he said to his father, as he leapt upon the short bench, adding:

"I won't go to those devils. I should prove jolly well too much for them, if I were to turn up. *Depraved boy*," drawled Sashka in imitation of his patrons. "They are none too good themselves, the smug-faced prigs!"

"Oh! Sashka, Sashka," his father complained, sitting hunched up with cold, "you'll come to a bad end."

"What about yourself, then?" was Sashka's rude rejoinder. "Better shut up. Afraid of the old woman. Ba! old muff!"

His father sat on in silence and shivered. A faint light found its way through a broad clink at the top, where the partition failed to meet the ceiling by a quarter of an inch, and lay in bright patches upon his high forehead, beneath which the deep cavities of his eyes showed black.

In times gone by Ivan Savvich had been used to drink heavily, and then his wife had feared and hated him. But when he had begun to develop unmistakable signs of consumption, and could drink no longer, she took to drink in her turn, and gradually accustomed herself to vodka. Then she avenged herself for all she had suffered at the hands of that tall narrow-chested man, who used incomprehensible words, had lost his place through disobedience and drunkenness, and who brought home with him just such longhaired, debauched, and conceited fellows as himself.

In contradistinction to her husband, the more Feoktista Petrovna drank the healthier she became, and the heavier became her fists. Now she said what she pleased, brought men and women to the house just as she chose, and sang with them noisy songs, while he lay silent behind the partition huddled together with perpetual cold, and meditating on the injustice and sorrow of human life. To everyone with whom she talked, she complained that she had no such enemies in the world as her husband and son, they were stuck-up statisticians!

For the space of an hour his mother kept drumming into Sashka's ears: "But I say you shall go," punctuating each word with a heavy blow on the table, which made the tumblers, placed on it after washing, jump and rattle again.

"But I say I won't!" Sashka coolly replied, dragging down the corners of his mouth with the will to show his teeth—a habit which had earned for him at school the nickname of Wolfkin.

"I'll thrash you, won't I just!" cried his mother.

"All right! thrash away!"

But Feoktista Petrovna knew that she could no longer strike her son now that he had begun to retaliate by biting, and that if she drove him into the street he would go off larking, and sooner get frostbitten than go to the Svetchnikovs, therefore she appealed to her husband's authority.

"Calls himself a father, and can't protect the mother from insult!"

"Really, Sashka, go. Why are you so obstinate?" he jerked out from the bench. "They will perhaps take you up again. They are kind people." Sashka only laughed in an insulting manner.

His father, long ago, before Sashka was born, had been tutor at the Svetchnikovs's, and had ever since looked on them as the best people in the world. At that time he had also held an appointment in the statistical office of the Zemstvo, and had not yet taken to drink. Eventually he was compelled through his own fault to marry his landlady's daughter. From that time he severed his connection with the Svetchnikovs and took to drink. Indeed, he let himself go to such an extent that he was several times picked up drunk in the streets and taken to the police station. But the Svetchnikovs did not cease to assist him with money, and Feoktista Petrovna, although she hated them, together with books and everything connected with her husband's past, still valued their acquaintance, and was in the habit of boasting of it.

"Perhaps you might bring something for me too from the Christmas tree," continued his father. He was using craft to induce his son to go, and Sashka knew it, and despised his father for his weakness and want of straightforwardness; though he really did wish to bring back something for the poor sickly old man, who had for a long time been without even good tobacco.

"All right!" he blurted out; "give me my jacket. Have you put the buttons on? No fear! I know you too well!"

The children had not yet been admitted to the drawing room, where the Christmas tree stood, but remained chattering in the nursery. Sashka, with lofty superciliousness, stood listening to their naive talk, and fingering in his breeches pocket the broken cigarettes which he had managed to abstract from his host's study. At this moment there came up to him the youngest of the Svetchnikovs, Kolya, and stood motionless before him, a look of surprise on his face, his toes turned in, and a finger stuck in the corner of his pouting mouth. Six months ago, at the insistence of his relatives, he had given up this bad habit of putting his finger in his mouth, but he could not quite break himself of it. He had blond locks cut in a fringe on his forehead and falling in ringlets on his shoulders, and blue, wondering eyes; in fact, he was just such a boy in appearance as Sashka particularly loved to bully.

"Are 'oo weally a naughty boy?" he inquired of Sashka. "Miss said 'oo was. I'm a dood boy."

"That you are!" replied Sashka, considering the other's short velvet trousers and great turndown collars.

"Would 'oo like to have a dun? There!" and he pointed at him a little pop-gun with a cork tied to it. The Wolfkin took the gun, pressed down the spring, and, aiming at the nose of the unsuspecting Kolya, pulled the trigger. The cork struck his nose, and rebounding, hung by the string. Kolya's blue eyes opened wider than ever, and filled with tears. Transferring his finger from his mouth to his reddening nose he blinked his long eyelashes and whispered:

"Bad—bad boy!"

A young lady of striking appearance, with her hair dressed in the simplest and the most becoming fashion, now entered the nursery. She was sister to the lady of the house, the very one indeed to whom Sashka's father had formerly given lessons.

"Here's the boy," said she, pointing out Sashka to the bald-headed man who accompanied her. "Bow, Sashka, you should not be so rude!"

But Sashka would bow neither to her nor to her companion of the bald head. She little suspected how much he knew. But, as a fact, Sashka did know that his miserable father had loved her, and that she had married another; and, though this had taken place subsequent to his father's marriage, Sashka could not bring himself to forgive what seemed to him like treachery.

"Takes after his father!" sighed Sofia Dmitrievna. "Could not you, Plutov Michailovich, do something for him? My husband says that a commercial school would suit him better than the grammar school. Sashka, would you like to go to a technical school?"

"No!" curtly replied Sashka, who had caught the offensive word "husband."

"Do you want to be a shepherd then?" asked the gentleman.

"Not likely!" said Sashka, in an offended tone.

"What then?"

Now Sashka did not know what he would like to be, but upon reflection replied: "Well, it's all the same to me, even a shepherd, if you like."

The bald-headed gentleman regarded the strange boy with a look of perplexity. When his eyes had travelled up from his patched boots to his face, Sashka put out his tongue and quickly drew it back again, so that Sofia Dmitrievna did not notice anything, but the old gentleman showed an amount of irascibility that she could not understand.

"I should not mind going to a commercial school," bashfully suggested Sashka.

The lady was overjoyed at Sashka's decision, and meditated with a sigh on the beneficial influence exercised by an old love.

"I don't know whether there will be a vacancy," dryly remarked the old man avoiding looking at Sashka, and smoothing down the ridge of hair which stuck up on the back of his head. "However, we shall see."

Meanwhile the children were becoming noisy, and in a great state of excitement were waiting impatiently for the Christmas tree.

The excellent practice with the pop-gun made in the hands of a boy, who commanded respect both for his stature and for his reputation for naughtiness, found imitators, and many a little button of a nose was made red. The tiny maids, holding their sides, bent almost double with laughter, as their little cavaliers with manly contempt of fear and pain, but all the same wrinkling up their faces in suspense, received the impact of the cork.

At length the doors were opened, and a voice said: "Come in, children; gently, not so fast!" Opening their little eyes wide, and holding their breath in anticipation, the children filed into the brightly illumined drawing room in orderly pairs, and quietly walked round the glittering tree. It cast a strong, shadowless light on their eager faces, with rounded eyes and mouths. For a minute there reigned the silence of profound enchantment, which all at once broke out into a chorus of delighted exclamation. One of the little girls, unable to restrain her delight, kept dancing up and down in the same place, her little tress braided with blue ribbon beating meanwhile rhythmically against her shoulders. Sashka remained morose and gloomy—something evil was working in his little wounded breast. The tree blinded him with its red, shriekingly insolent glitter of countless candles. It was foreign, hostile to him, even as the crowd of smart, pretty children which surrounded it. He would have liked to give it a shove and topple it over on their shining heads. It seemed as though some iron hand were gripping his heart and wringing out of it every drop of blood. He crept behind the piano and sat down there in a corner unconsciously crumpling to pieces in his pocket the last of the cigarettes and thinking that though he had a father and mother and a home, it came to the same thing as if he had none, and nowhere to go to. He tried to recall to his imagination his little penknife, which he had acquired by a swap not long ago, and was very fond of; but his knife all at once seemed to him a very poor affair with its ground-down blade and only half of a yellow haft. Tomorrow he would smash it up, and then he would have nothing left at all!

But suddenly Sashka's narrow eyes gleamed with astonishment, and his face in a moment resumed its ordinary expression of audacity and self-confidence. On the side of the tree turned towards him—which was the back of it, and less brightly illumined than the other side—he discovered something such as had never come within the circle of his existence, and without which all his surroundings appeared as empty as though peopled by persons without life. It was a little angel in wax carelessly hung in the thickest of the dark boughs, and looking as if it were floating in the air. His transparent dragonfly wings trembled in the light, and he seemed altogether alive and ready to fly away. The rosy fingers of his exquisitely formed hands were stretched upwards, and from his head there floated just such locks as Kolya's. But there was something here that was wanting in Kolya's face, and in all other faces and things. The face of the little angel did not shine with joy, nor was it clouded by grief; but there lay on it the impress of another feeling, not to be explained in words, nor defined by thought, but to be attained only by the sympathy of a kindred feeling. Sashka was not conscious of the force of the mysterious influence which attracted him towards the little angel, but he felt that he had known him all his life, and had always loved him, loved him more than his penknife, more than his father, more than anything else. Filled with doubt, alarm, and a delight which he could not comprehend, Sashka clasped his hands to his bosom and whispered:

"Dear—dear little angel!"

The more intently he looked the more fraught with significance the expression of the little angel's face became. He was so infinitely far off, so unlike everything which surrounded him there. The other toys seemed to take a pride in hanging there pretty and decked out upon the glittering tree, but he was pensive, and fearing the intrusive light purposely hid himself in the dark greenery, so that none might see him. It would be a mad cruelty to touch his dainty little wings.

"Dear—dear!" whispered Sashka.

His head became feverish. He clasped his hands behind his back, and in full readiness to fight to the death to win the little angel, he walked to and fro with cautious, stealthy steps. He avoided looking at the little angel, lest he should direct the attention of others towards him, but he felt that he was still there, and had not flown away.

Now the hostess appeared in the doorway, a tall, stately lady with a bright aureole of grey hair dressed high upon her head. The children trooped round her with expressions of delight, and the little girl—the same that had danced about in her place—hung wearily on her hand, blinking heavily with sleepy eyes.

As Sashka approached her he seemed almost choking with emotion.

"Auntie—auntie!" said he, trying to speak caressingly, but his voice sounded harsher than ever. "Auntie, dear!"

She did not hear him, so he tugged impatiently at her dress.

"What's the matter with you? Why are you pulling my dress?" said the grey-haired lady in surprise. "It's rude."

"Auntie—auntie, do give me one thing from the tree; give me the little angel."

"Impossible," replied the lady in a tone of indifference. "We are going to keep the tree decorated till the New Year. But you are no longer a child; you should call me by name—Maria Dmitrievna."

Sashka, feeling as if he were falling down a precipice, grasped the last means of saving himself.

"I am sorry I have been naughty. I'll be more industrious for the future," he blurted out. But this formula, which had always paid with his masters, made no impression upon the lady of the grey hair.

"A good thing, too, my friend," she said, as unconcernedly as before.

"Give me the little angel," demanded Sashka, gruffly.

"But it's impossible. Can't you understand that?"

But Sashka did not understand, and when the lady turned to go out of the room he followed her, his gaze fixed without conscious thought upon her black silk dress. In his surging brain there glimmered a recollection of how one of the boys in his class had asked the master to mark him 3, and when the master refused he had knelt down before him, and putting his hands together as in prayer, had begun to cry. The master was angry, but gave him 3 all the same. At the time Sashka had immortalized this episode in a caricature, but now his only means left was to follow the boy's example. Accordingly he plucked at the lady's dress again, and when she turned round, dropped with a bang onto his knees, and folded his hands as described above. But he could not squeeze out a single tear!

"Are you out of your mind?" exclaimed the grey-haired lady, casting a searching look round the room; but luckily no one was present.

"What is the matter with you?"

Kneeling there with clasped hands, Sashka looked at her with dislike, and rudely repeated:

"Give me the little angel."

His eyes, fixed intently on the lady to catch the first word she should utter, were anything but good to look at, and the hostess answered hurriedly:

"Well, then, I'll give it to you. Ah! what a stupid you are! I will give you what you want, but why could you not wait till the New Year?"

"Stand up! And never," she added in a didactic tone, "never kneel to anyone: it is humiliating. Kneel before God alone."

"Talk away!" thought Sashka, trying to get in front of her, and merely succeeding in treading on her dress.

When she had taken the toy from the tree, Sashka devoured her with his eyes, but stretched out his hands for it with a painful pucker of the nose. It seemed to him that the tall lady would break the little angel.

"Beautiful thing!" said the lady, who was sorry to part with such a dainty and presumably expensive toy. "Who can have hung it there? Well, what do you want with such a thing? Are you not too big to know what to do with it? Look, there are some picture books. But this I promised to give to Kolya; he begged so earnestly for it." But this was not the truth.

Sashka's agony became unbearable. He clenched his teeth convulsively, and seemed almost to grind them. The lady of the grey hair feared nothing so much as a scene, so she slowly held out the little angel to Sashka.

"There now, take it!" she said in a displeased tone; "what a persistent boy you are!"

Sashka's hands as they seized the little angel seemed like tentacles, and were tense as steel springs, but withal so soft and careful that the little angel might have imagined himself to be flying in the air.

"A-h-h!" escaped in a long diminuendo sigh from Sashka's breast, while in his eyes glistened two little teardrops, which stood still there as though unused to the light. Slowly drawing the little angel to his bosom, he kept his shining eyes on the hostess, with a quiet, tender smile which died away in a feeling of unearthly bliss. It seemed, when the dainty wings of the little angel touched Sashka's sunken breast, as if he experienced something so blissful, so bright, the like of which had never before been experienced in this sorrowful, sinful, suffering world.

"A-h-h !" sighed he once more as the little angel's wings touched him. And at the shining of his face the absurdly decorated and insolently glowing tree seemed to be extinguished, and the grey-haired, portly dame smiled with gladness, and the parchment-like face of the bald-headed gentleman twitched, and the children fell into a vivid silence as though touched by a breath of human happiness.

For one short moment all observed a mysterious likeness between the awkward boy who had outgrown his clothes and the lineaments of the little angel, which had been spiritualized by the hand of an unknown artist.

But the next moment the picture was entirely changed. Crouching like a panther preparing to spring, Sashka surveyed the surrounding company, on the lookout for someone who should dare wrest his little angel from him.

"I'm going home," he said in a dull voice, having in view a way of escape through the crowd, "home to Father."

His mother was asleep, worn out with a whole day's work and vodka-drinking. In the little room behind the partition there stood a small cooking lamp burning on the table. Its feeble yellow light, with difficulty penetrating the sooty glass, threw a strange shadow over the faces of Sashka and his father.

"Is it not pretty?" asked Sashka in a whisper, holding the little angel at a distance from his father, so as not to allow him to touch it.

"Yes, there's something most remarkable about him," whispered the father, gazing thoughtfully at the toy. And his face expressed the same concentrated attention and delight as did Sashka's.

"Look, he is going to fly."

"I see it too," replied Sashka in an ecstasy. "Think I'm blind? But look at his little wings! Ah! don't touch!"

The father withdrew his hand, and with troubled eyes studied the details of the little angel, while Sashka whispered with the air of a pedagogue:

"Father, what a bad habit you have of touching everything! You might break it."

There fell upon the wall the shadows of two grotesque, motionless heads bending towards one another, one big and shaggy, the other small and round.

Within the big head strange torturing thoughts, though at the same time full of delight, were seething. His eyes unblinkingly regarded the little angel, and under his steadfast gaze it seemed to grow larger and brighter, and its wings to tremble with a noiseless trepidation, and all the surroundings—the timber-built, soot-stained wall, the dirty table, Sashka—everything became fused into one level grey mass without light or shade. It seemed to the broken man that he heard a pitying voice from the world of wonders, wherein once he had dwelt, and whence he had been cast out forever. There they knew nothing of dirt, of weary quarrelling, of the blindly cruel strife of egotism, there they knew nothing of the tortures of a man arrested in the streets with callous laughter, and beaten by the rough hand of the night watchman. There everything is pure, joyful, bright. And all this purity found an asylum in the soul of her whom he loved more than life, and had lost—when he had kept his hold upon his own useless life. With the smell of wax, which emanated from the toy, was mingled a subtle aroma, and it seemed to the broken man that her dear fingers touched the angel, those fingers which he would fain have caressed in one long kiss, till death should close his lips forever. This was why the little toy was so beautiful, this was why there was in it something specially attractive, which defied description. The little angel had descended from that heaven which her soul was to him, and had brought a ray of light into the damp room, steeped in sulphurous fumes, and to the dark soul of the man from whom had been taken all: love, and happiness, and life.

On a level with the eyes of the man, who had lived his life, sparkled the eyes of the boy, who was beginning his life, and embraced the little angel in their caress. For them present and future had disappeared: the ever-sorrowful, piteous father, the rough, unendurable mother, the black darkness of insults, of cruelty, of humiliations, and of spiteful grief. The thoughts of Sashka were formless, nebulous, but all the more deeply for that did they move his agitated soul. Everything that is good and bright in the world, all profound grief, and the hope of a soul that sighs for God—the little angel absorbed them all into himself, and that was why he glowed with such a soft divine radiance, that was why his little dragonfly wings trembled with a noiseless trepidation.

The father and son did not look at one another: their sick hearts grieved, wept, and rejoiced apart. But there was something in their thoughts which fused their hearts in one, and annihilated that bottomless abyss which separates man from man and makes him so lonely, unhappy, and weak. The father with an unconscious motion put his arm round the neck of his son, and the son's head rested equally without conscious volition upon his father's consumptive chest.

"*She* it was who gave it to thee, was it not?" whispered the father, without taking his eyes off the little angel.

At another time Sashka would have replied with a rude negation, but now the only reply possible resounded of itself within his soul, and he calmly pronounced the pious fraud: "Who else? of course she did."

The father made no reply, and Sashka relapsed into silence.

Something grated in the adjoining room, then clicked, and then was silent for a moment, and then noisily and hurriedly the clock struck, "One, two, three."

"Sashka, do you ever dream?" asked the father in a meditative tone.

"No! Oh, yes," he admitted, "once I had one, in which I fell down from the roof. We were climbing after the pigeons, and I fell down."

"But I dream always. Strange things are dreams. One sees the whole past, one loves and suffers as though it were reality."

Again he was silent, and Sashka felt his arm tremble as it lay upon his neck. The trembling and pressure of his father's arm became stronger and stronger, and the sensitive silence of the night was all at once broken by the pitiful sobbing sound of suppressed weeping. Sashka sternly puckered his brow, and cautiously—so as not to disturb the heavy trembling arm—wiped away a tear from his eyes. So strange was it to see a big old man crying.

"Ah! Sashka, Sashka," sobbed the father, "what is the meaning of everything?"

"Why, what's the matter?" sternly whispered Sashka. "You're crying just like a little boy."

"Well, I won't, then," said the father with a piteous smile of excuse. "What's the good?"

Feoktista Petrovna turned on her bed. She sighed, cleared her throat, and mumbled incoherent sounds in a loud and strangely persistent manner.

It was time to go to bed. But before doing so the little angel must be disposed of for the night. He could not be left on the floor so he was hung up by his string, which was fastened to the flue of the stove. There it stood out accurately delineated against the white Dutch tiles. And so they could both see him, Sashka and his father.

Hurriedly throwing into a corner the various rags on which he was in the habit of sleeping, Sashka lay down on his back, in order as quickly as possible to look again at the little angel.

"Why don't you undress?" asked his father as he shivered and wrapped himself up in his tattered blanket, and arranged his clothes, which he had thrown over his feet.

"What's the good? I shall soon be up again."

Sashka wished to add that he did not care to go to sleep at all, but he had no time to do so, since he fell to sleep as suddenly as though he had sunk to the bottom of a deep swift river.

His father presently fell asleep also. And gentle sleep and restfulness lay upon the weary face of the man who had lived his life, and upon the brave face of the little man who was just beginning his life.

But the little angel hanging by the hot stove began to melt. The lamp, which had been left burning at the entreaty of Sashka, filled the room with the smell of kerosene, and through its smoked glass threw a melancholy light upon a scene of gradual dissolution. The little angel seemed to stir. Over his rosy fingers there rolled thick drops which fell upon the bench. To the smell of kerosene was added the stifling scent of melting wax. The little angel gave a tremble as though on the point of flight, and—fell with a soft thud upon the hot flags.

An inquisitive cockroach singed its wings as it ran round the formless lump of melted wax, climbed up the dragonfly wings, and twitching its feelers went on its way.

Through the curtained window the grey-blue light of coming day crept in, and the frozen water carrier was already making a noise in the courtyard with his iron scoop.

F.Y.I

auntie: this is traditionally used only by young children as a way of addressing an elder

cavaliers: gallant or fashionable men

consumption: a contagious bacterial infection brought on by tuberculosis. This condition causes the body and its tissues to waste away, making it seem like the disease is "consuming" the patient.

flue: the pipe or passage in a chimney for smoke or waste gases to escape from

"to mark him 3": in Russian schools at the time 5 was the maximum mark

Words to Build On

contradistinction: a difference made apparent by contrast

diminuendo: a decrease in loudness or sound

fain: required or forced to

"Get along with you!": get lost

indomitable: impossible to subdue or defeat

irascibility: easily provoked to anger, or irritable

larking: to behave in a playful or mischievous way

nebulous: hazy or vague

pedagogue: a school teacher or one who instructs

prig: a self-righteous or moralistic person

superciliousness: assuming an air of contemptuous superiority

supinely: to tolerate or be indifferent to

trepidation: feeling fear of what may happen

Tricks of the Trade

Irony

Naturalism

Realism

Symbol

In Your Own Words: Comprehension

1. Who are the main characters in the story? Describe them.
2. Describe the relationship Sashka has with his parents.
3. Describe the relationship Sashka's parents have with each other.
4. What action gave Sashka "his liberty"?
5. Why did Sashka get expelled from school?
6. Why does he not want to go to the Svetchnikovs for Christmas?
7. How did Sashka get his nickname "Wolfkin"?
8. Why does Sashka start to behave like a "good" boy at the party?
9. How does Sashka feel about the angel? What happens to the angel?

In Your Own Words: Analysis

1. Why does Sashka, a 13-year-old boy who bullies others, have such an attraction to the angel on the Christmas tree?

2. Who gives Sashka the angel, and why does she do it?

3. What does it mean when Sashka's father breaks down and cries and asks his son, "What is the meaning of everything?" Is this odd for an adult to ask a child?

4. In terms of his mother and father, who is Sashka closer to? What is the reason for this?

5. Do you see a way that Sashka may be able to escape his surroundings of poverty and violence?

6. How do you explain the ending of the story? Were you expecting the story to end in another way?

7. How would you characterize the tone of the story?

8. What do you think the little angel represents?

❖ Now Write

1. Compare the childhood of Sashka in "The Little Angel" with the childhood of Piquette Tonnerre in Margaret Laurence's "The Loons." Write an essay in which you explore the similarities and differences in their family lives. Is it society that holds back these characters, or is it something internal?

2. One theme of "The Little Angel" is the temporary and illusory nature of hope. Write an essay in which you demonstrate how this is the theme of the story.

3. When children bully other children at school, school officials and psychologists often state that it is because the child is being bullied at home and replicating this behaviour when he or she leaves the home. This is not the case with Sashka in "The Little Angel." Write an essay in which you explore the reasons for Sashka's personality, beliefs, and behaviours.

Dorothy Parker

orothy Parker (1893–1967) was born Dorothy Rothschild at her parents' summer cottage in New Jersey, but she always insisted she was a "true New Yorker." She wrote poetry as a child and soon developed an obsession with trying to find just the right word, a quality that would last her entire life. Her mother's death and father's poor health meant she was not able to finish her education. On this she said: "because of circumstances, I didn't finish high school. But, by God, I read."

At a relatively young age, Parker became a short story writer, critic, and famous American humorist. She was 22 when she first mailed a poem to *Vanity Fair*. The magazine ended up hiring her to write feature stories and poems. She also wrote advertisements for *Vogue* and poetry and reviews for *The New Yorker*. In fact, it is Parker who is credited with inventing the "form" of the short story that still appears in the magazine today. At the height of her career in the 1920s, Americans were quoting her verse and sending her numerous fan letters.

Parker was supremely skilled at writing "light verse" characterized as being humorous and playful with her use of puns, alliteration, and surprise "twists." Many say her work reflected the colourful age in which she lived and the untraditional women of the time who were called "flappers": women who cut their hair short, wore trousers, smoked, drank, and went to "petting parties." Tame by today's standards but seen as scandalous in the 1920s, these parties were social events devoted to group kissing and touching and were essentially mass sexual foreplay.

From reading much of her work, one might get the impression that she personifies some of the more frivolous aspects of her time. In reality, however, Dorothy Parker felt so strongly about civil rights that she bequeathed her entire estate and copyrights to Reverend Martin Luther King Jr. and his organization. The NAACP (National Association for the Advancement of Colored People) has her ashes at their headquarters and has erected a plaque in a memorial garden in Baltimore that reads, "Here lie the ashes of Dorothy Parker. Humorist, writer, critic, Defender of human and civil rights . . . " For her own epitaph, however, Parker suggested "Excuse my dust."

In Her Own Words

"Wit has truth in it; wisecracking is simple calisthenics with words."

"I know that there are things that never have been funny, and never will be. And I know that ridicule may be a shield, but it is not a weapon."

"I hate writing. I love having written."

Before We Begin

1. What are some of the things that people have waited anxiously for? Once you come up with a list, what do these things have in common?
2. What are people typically obsessed with when they are in a relationship?
3. Is it only women who wait by the phone for calls, or do men behave in a similar fashion?

 **Now Read**

A Telephone Call

Please, God, let him telephone me now. Dear God, let him call me now. I won't ask anything else of You, truly I won't. It isn't very much to ask. It would be so little to You, God, such a little, little thing. Only let him telephone now. Please, God. Please, please, please.

If I didn't think about it, maybe the telephone might ring. Sometimes it does that. If I could think of something else. If I could think of something else. Maybe if I counted 500 by fives, it might ring by that time. I'll count slowly. I won't cheat. And if it rings when I get to 300, I won't stop; I won't answer it until I get to 500. Five, 10, 15, 20, 25, 30, 35, 40, 45, 50 . . . Oh, please ring. Please.

This is the last time I'll look at the clock. I will not look at it again. It's 10 minutes past seven. He said he would telephone at five o'clock. "I'll call you at five, darling." I think that's where he said "darling." I'm almost sure he said it there. I know he called me "darling" twice, and the other time was when he said goodbye. "Goodbye, darling." He was busy, and he can't say much in the office, but he called me "darling" twice. He couldn't have minded my calling him up. I know you shouldn't keep telephoning them—I know they don't like that. When you do that, they know you are thinking about them and wanting them, and that makes them hate you. But I hadn't talked to him in three days—not in three days. And all I did was ask him how he was; it was just the way anybody might have called him up. He couldn't have minded that. He couldn't have thought I was bothering him. "No, of course you're not," he said. And he said he'd telephone me. He didn't have to say that. I didn't ask him to, truly I didn't. I'm sure I didn't. I don't think he would say he'd telephone me, and then just never do it. Please don't let him do that, God. Please don't.

"I'll call you at five, darling." "Goodbye, darling." He was busy, and he was in a hurry, and there were people around him, but he called me "darling" twice. That's mine, that's mine. I have that, even if I never see him again. Oh, but that's so little. That isn't enough. Nothing's enough, if I never see him again. Please let me see him again, God. Please, I want him so much. I want him so much. I'll be good, God. I will try to be better, I will, if You will let me see him again. If You will let him telephone me. Oh, let him telephone me now.

Ah, don't let my prayer seem too little to You, God. You sit up there, so white and old, with all the angels about You and the stars slipping by. And I come to You with a prayer about a telephone call. Ah, don't laugh, God. You see, You don't know how it feels. You're so safe, there on Your throne, with the blue swirling under You. Nothing can touch You; no one can twist Your heart in his hands. This is suffering, God, this is bad, bad suffering. Won't You help me? For Your Son's sake, help me. You said You would do whatever was asked of You in His name. Oh, God, in the name of Thine only beloved Son, Jesus Christ, our Lord, let him telephone me now.

I must stop this. I mustn't be this way. Look. Suppose a young man says he'll call a girl up, and then something happens, and he doesn't. That isn't so terrible, is it? Why, it's going on all over the world, right this minute. Oh, what do I care what's going on all over the world? Why can't that telephone ring? Why can't it, why can't it? Couldn't you ring? Ah, please, couldn't you? You damned, ugly, shiny thing. It would hurt you to ring, wouldn't it? Oh, that would hurt you. Damn you, I'll pull your filthy roots out of the wall, I'll smash your smug black face in little bits. Damn you to hell.

No, no, no. I must stop. I must think about something else. This is what I'll do. I'll put the clock in the other room. Then I can't look at it. If I do have to look at it, then I'll have to walk into the bedroom, and that will be something to do. Maybe, before I look at it again, he will call me. I'll be so sweet to him, if he calls me. If he says he can't see me tonight, I'll say, "Why, that's all right, dear. Why, of course it's all right." I'll be the way I was when I first met him. Then maybe he'll like me again. I was always sweet, at first. Oh, it's so easy to be sweet to people before you love them.

I think he must still like me a little. He couldn't have called me "darling" twice today, if he didn't still like me a little. It isn't all gone, if he still likes me a little; even if it's only a little, little bit. You see, God, if You would just let him telephone me, I wouldn't have to ask You anything more. I would be sweet to him, I would be gay, I would be just the way I used to be, and then he would love me again. And then I would never have to ask You for anything more. Don't You see, God? So won't You please let him telephone me? Won't You please, please, please?

Are You punishing me, God, because I've been bad? Are You angry with me because I did that? Oh, but, God, there are so many bad people—You could not be hard only to me. And it wasn't very bad; it couldn't have been bad. We didn't hurt anybody, God. Things are only bad when they hurt people. We didn't hurt one single soul; You know that. You know it wasn't bad, don't You, God? So won't You let him telephone me now?

If he doesn't telephone me, I'll know God is angry with me. I'll count 500 by fives, and if he hasn't called me then, I will know God isn't going to help me, ever again. That will be the sign. Five, 10, 15, 20, 25, 30, 35, 40, 45, 50, 55 . . . It was bad. I knew it was bad. All right, God, send me to hell. You think You're frightening me with Your hell, don't You? You think Your hell is worse than mine.

I mustn't. I mustn't do this. Suppose he's a little late calling me up—that's nothing to get hysterical about. Maybe he isn't going to call—maybe he's coming straight up here without telephoning. He'll be cross if he sees I have been crying. They don't like you to cry. He doesn't cry. I wish to God I could make him cry. I wish I could make him cry and tread the floor and feel his heart heavy and big and festering in him. I wish I could hurt him like hell.

He doesn't wish that about me. I don't think he even knows how he makes me feel. I wish he could know, without my telling him. They don't like you to tell them they've made you cry. They don't like you to tell them you're unhappy because of them. If you do, they think you're possessive and exacting. And then they hate you. They hate you whenever you say anything you really think. You always have to keep playing little games. Oh, I thought we didn't have to; I thought this was so big I could say whatever I meant. I guess you can't, ever. I guess there isn't ever anything big enough for that. Oh, if he would just telephone, I wouldn't tell him I had been sad about him. They hate sad people. I would be so sweet and so gay, he couldn't help but like me. If he would only telephone. If he would only telephone.

Maybe that's what he is doing. Maybe he is coming up here without calling me up. Maybe he's on his way now. Something might have happened to him. No, nothing could ever happen to him. I can't picture anything happening to him. I never picture him run over. I never see him lying still and long and dead. I wish he were dead. That's a terrible wish. That's a lovely wish. If he were dead, he would be mine. If he were dead, I would never think of now and the last few weeks. I would remember only the lovely times. It would be all beautiful. I wish he were dead. I wish he were dead, dead, dead.

This is silly. It's silly to go wishing people were dead just because they don't call you up the very minute they said they would. Maybe the clock's fast; I don't know whether it's right. Maybe he's hardly late at all. Anything could have made him a little late. Maybe he had to stay at his office. Maybe he went home, to call me up from there, and somebody came in. He doesn't like to telephone me in front of people. Maybe he's worried, just a little, little bit, about keeping me waiting. He might even hope that I would call him up. I could do that. I could telephone him.

I mustn't. I mustn't, I mustn't. Oh, God, please don't let me telephone him. Please keep me from doing that. I know, God, just as well as You do, that if he were worried about me, he'd telephone no matter where he was or how many people there were around him. Please make me know that, God. I don't ask You to make it easy for me— You can't do that, for all that You could make a world. Only let me know it, God. Don't let me go on hoping. Don't let me say comforting things to myself. Please don't let me hope, dear God. Please don't.

I won't telephone him. I'll never telephone him again as long as I live. He'll rot in hell, before I'll call him up. You don't have to give me strength, God; I have it myself. If he wanted me, he could get me. He knows where I am. He knows I'm waiting here. He's so sure of me, so sure. I wonder why they hate you, as soon as they are sure of you. I should think it would be so sweet to be sure.

It would be so easy to telephone him. Then I'd know. Maybe it wouldn't be a foolish thing to do. Maybe he wouldn't mind. Maybe he'd like it. Maybe he has been trying to get me. Sometimes people try and try to get you on the telephone, and they say the number doesn't answer. I'm not just saying that to help myself; that really happens. You know that really happens, God. Oh, God, keep me away from that telephone. Keep me away. Let me still have just a little bit of pride. I think I'm going to need it, God. I think it will be all I'll have.

Oh, what does pride matter, when I can't stand it if I don't talk to him? Pride like that is such a silly, shabby little thing. The real pride, the big pride, is in having no pride.

I'm not saying that just because I want to call him. I am not. That's true, I know that's true. I will be big. I will be beyond little prides.

Please, God, keep me from telephoning him. Please, God.

I don't see what pride has to do with it. This is such a little thing, for me to be bringing in pride, for me to be making such a fuss about. I may have misunderstood him. Maybe he said for me to call him up, at five. "Call me at five, darling." He could have said that, perfectly well. It's so possible that I didn't hear him right. "Call me at five, darling." I'm almost sure that's what he said. God, don't let me talk this way to myself. Make me know, please make me know.

I'll think about something else. I'll just sit quietly. If I could sit still. If I could sit still. Maybe I could read. Oh, all the books are about people who love each other, truly and sweetly. What do they want to write about that for? Don't they know it isn't true? Don't they know it's a lie, it's a God damned lie? What do they have to tell about that for, when they know how it hurts? Damn them, damn them, damn them.

I won't. I'll be quiet. This is nothing to get excited about. Look. Suppose he were someone I didn't know very well. Suppose he were another girl. Then I'd just telephone and say, "Well, for goodness' sake, what happened to you?" That's what I'd do, and I'd never even think about it. Why can't I be casual and natural, just because I love him? I can be. Honestly, I can be. I'll call him up, and be so easy and pleasant. You see if I won't, God. Oh, don't let me call him. Don't, don't, don't.

God, aren't You really going to let him call me? Are You sure, God? Couldn't You please relent? Couldn't You? I don't even ask You to let him telephone me now, God; only let him do it in a little while. I'll count 500 by fives. I'll do it so slowly and so fairly. If he hasn't telephoned then, I'll call him. I will. Oh, please, dear God, dear kind God, my blessed Father in Heaven, let him call before then. Please, God. Please.

Five, 10, 15, 20, 25, 30, 35 . . .

F. Y. I.

black face: the colour of the telephone's casing

"You said You would do whatever was asked of You in His name": Parker is making reference to John 14:13–14, a well-known verse from the Bible. However, she is only using the last section of the entire verse. The entire verse reads, "Because I go to the Father: and whatsoever you shall ask the Father in my name, that will I do: that the Father may be glorified in the Son. If you shall ask me anything in my name, that I will do." This passage is often misinterpreted and taken to mean that during the Last Supper, Jesus was telling the apostles that God would grant them anything they asked for as long as it was asked for "in the name of Jesus." This would mean that Jesus's name would become a password used to get a job, pass a test, win a contest, or even get a phone call from someone.

Words to Build on

cross: extremely irritated and annoyed

gay: light-hearted and carefree

exacting: making great demands on one's skill, attention, or other resources

relent: to abandon or mitigate a harsh attitude, especially by finally yielding to a request

tread the floor: to walk the floor in a specific manner, such as pacing

Tricks of the Trade

Narrative point of view

In Your Own Words: Comprehension

1. Who is telling the story?

2. How does the narrator feel about the man whose call she waits for?

3. What is the setting of this story?

4. Why doesn't the narrator just call the man?

5. When the narrator states "I mustn't, I mustn't, I mustn't," is she referring to more than just making a telephone call?

6. What role does God play in this story?

7. Is this story a monologue or is it a prayer? What is the difference?

8. What are some of the narrator's doubts? What is she confused about in this story?

In Your Own Words: Analysis

1. If the narrator feels something for the man in the story, why does she say "I wish he were dead"?

2. At what stage of a relationship do you think the narrator and the man she thinks about are in (i.e., early dating stages or have they known each other for a while)? What clues can you provide from the story?

3. Throughout the story the narrator makes statements about what she thinks men believe, such as "they don't like you to tell them you're unhappy because of them." Do you think any of these statements about men are true? How does the narrator come to this information?

4. What does the narrator compare her "suffering" to in waiting for a call? What do you think of this comparison?

5. Is there a climax in this story? Elaborate on your answer.

6. Explain what the narrator means when she states: "Are You punishing me, God, because I've been bad? Are You angry with me because I did that?...And it wasn't very bad; it couldn't have been bad, We didn't hurt anybody, God. Things are only bad when they hurt people."

7. What does the narrator mean when she states: "the real pride, the big pride, is in having no pride"?

8. This story was first published in 1928. Could this scenario take place today, in an age of cellphones and BlackBerrys where people do not have to wait at home for a call?

9. Why does Parker use repetitive phrases throughout the story? Give two examples and explain.

10. Parker writes, "I wish I could make him . . . feel his heart heavy and big and festering in him." The word "festering" has multiple meanings. Look up the word in the dictionary and choose the meaning that best suits the context of the passage.

✿ Now Write

1. Does what Deborah Tannen states about gender and communication in her essay "Sex, Lies, and Conversation" apply to Parker's story? Write an essay that shows whether her theories do or do not apply.

2. With technological advances that allow us to communicate anywhere and anyhow, have we overcome the dilemma the narrator faces in Parker's story? Write an essay explaining why the situation the narrator finds herself in could or could not still happen today.

3. This story incorporates themes of obsession, self-doubt, and the relationship between love and hate. For example, some people believe the last two are not mutually exclusive. Choose one of these themes and write an essay in which you examine how the theme is presented in the story and what the writer is saying to the reader.

Jorge Luis Borges

Jorge Luis Borges (1899–1986) was born into a middle-class family in Argentina and was raised in Palermo, a suburb of Buenos Aires with a reputation for being home to many sordid and knife-wielding hoodlums called *compadritos*. It is believed the stories Borges had heard about this colourful neighbourhood in the nineteenth century, with its working-class immigrants, brothels, lust-filled couples dancing the tango, and violent men seeking vengeance, inspired his early work, which contains elements of violence and danger. Fatal knife fights are often featured in Borges's fiction.

Borges's maternal grandfather, Colonel Franciso Borges, married Francis Haslam, an Englishwoman from Staffordshire, from whom Borges inherited not only a love of stories but also a love of the English language. Much like Gabriel Garcia Marquez, who credited his narrative style to his grandmother, it was Borges's grandmother's "dry English wit" that led him to create his own concise writing style.

By the 1960s, Borges was completely blind, so he had others read to him. One of his readers was the Canadian Argentine-born writer Alberto Manguel, who was a teenager at the time. Manguel's experience with Borges can be read in his memoir, *With Borges*, in which Manguel describes Borges's life, personality, and reputation as a writer.

Although Borges admired many English writers, he was particularly fond of Oscar Wilde and at the age of nine translated Wilde's story "The Happy Prince." His translation was so good that it was published in a local newspaper and was believed to have been written by his father. Borges had even hoped to die in the same Paris hotel where Wilde's own life ended (the hotel manager was so disturbed by this, however, that he asked Borges to leave). In 1986, Borges died at age 86 in Switzerland.

NOTE: Read "Streetcorner Man" carefully—each sentence builds upon one another to create a surprising and suspenseful work from the writer who has been called the true father of magic realism.

In His Own Words

"Writing is nothing more than a guided dream."

"I cannot sleep unless I am surrounded by books."

"Art always opts for the individual, the concrete. Art is not Platonic"

"I have known uncertainty: a state unknown to the Greeks."

Before We Begin

1. Dance, specifically the tango, plays an important role in this story. Judging from how it is danced, what are your thoughts on the tango?
2. What is the relationship between sex and violence?
3. Do we naturally trust the tellers of tales or stories? What makes a storyteller trustworthy?
4. Can eye witnesses always be trusted? What could interfere with a person's ability to act as a witness and relay the truth about an event?

 **Now Read**

Streetcorner Man

Fancy your coming out and asking me, of all people, about the late Francisco Real. Sure, I knew him, even though he wasn't from around here. He was a big shot on the Northside—that whole stretch from the Guadalupe pond to the old Artillery Barracks. I never laid eyes on the guy above three times and these three times were all the same night. But nights like that you don't forget. It was when La Lujanera got it in her head to come around to my shack and bed down with me, and Rosendo Juarez took off from the Maldonado for good. Of course, you're not the kind that name would mean much to. But around Villa Santa Rita, Rosendo Juarez—the Slasher we called him—had a reputation for being pretty tough. He was one of don Nicolas Paredes's boys, the same as Paredes was one of Morel's gang, and he'd earned respect for the way he handled a knife. Sharp dresser too. Always rode up to the whorehouse on a dark horse, his riding gear decked out with silver. There wasn't a man or dog around didn't hold him in regard—and that goes for the women as well. Everybody knew he had at least a couple of killings to his name. He'd have on one of those soft hats with a narrow brim and tall crown, and it would sit there kind of cocky on his long thick hair he wore slicked straight back. Lady luck smiled on him, like they say, and around Villa all us younger guys used to ape him even to the way he spit. But then one night we got a good look at what this Rosendo was made of.

All this might seem made up, but the story of what happened that particular night starts when this flashy red-wheeled buggy—jamful of men—comes barrelling its way down those hard-packed dirt roads out between the brick kilns and the empty lots. Two guys in black were making a big racket twanging away on guitars, and the driver kept cracking his whip at the stray dogs snapping at the legs of the horse. Sitting all quiet in the middle was one guy wrapped in a poncho. This was the famous Butcher— he'd picked that name up working in the stockyards—and he was out for a good fight and maybe a killing. The night was cool and welcome. A couple of them sat up on the folded hood just like they were parading along some downtown avenue in Carnival. A lot more things happened that night, but it was only later on we got wind of this first part. Our gang was there at Julia's pretty early. This dance hall of hers, between the Gauna road and the river, was really just a big shed made out of sheets of corrugated iron. You could spot the place from two or three blocks off either by the red lamp hanging out front or by the rumpus. Julia, even though she was a darkie, took trouble to run things right—there was always plenty of fiddlers and good booze and dancing partners ready to go all night. But La Lujanera—she was Rosendo's woman—had the others all beat by a mile. She's dead now, and I can tell you years go by when I don't give her a thought anymore. But in her day you ought to have seen her—what eyes she had! One look at her was enough to make a man lose sleep.

The rum, the music, the women, Rosendo with that rough talk pouring out of his mouth and a slap on the back for each of us that I tried to take for a sign of real friendship—the thing is, I was happy as they come. I was lucky too. I had me a partner who could follow my steps just like she knew ahead of time which way I was going to turn. The tango took hold of us, driving us along and then splitting us up and then bringing us back together again. There we were in the middle of all this fun, like in some kind of dream, when all of a sudden I feel the music kind of getting louder. Turns out it was those two guitar pickers riding in the buggy, coming closer and closer, their music getting mixed up with ours. Then the breeze shifted, you couldn't hear them anymore, and my mind went back to my own steps and my partner's, and to the ins and outs of the dance. A good half hour later there was this pounding on the door and a big voice calling out like it could have been the cops. Everything went silent. Then somebody out there starts shouldering the door and the next thing we know a guy busts in. Funny thing is he looked exactly like his voice.

To us he wasn't Francisco Real—not yet—but just some big hefty guy. He was all in black from head to toe, except for this reddish-brown scarf draped over one shoulder. I remember his face. There was something Indian and kind of angular about it.

When the door come flying in it smacked right into me. Before I even knew what I was doing I was on top of the guy, throwing him a left square in the teeth while my right goes inside my vest for my knife. But I never got a chance. Steadying himself, he puts his arms out and shoves me aside like he's brushing something out of the way. There I was down on my ass—back of him now—my hand still inside the jacket grabbing for the knife. And him wading forward like nothing happened. Just wading forward, a whole head taller than all these guys he's pushing his way through—and acting like he never even saw them. The first of our guys—bunch of gaping wops—just back out of his way, scared as hell. But only the first. In the next bunch the Redhead was waiting for him, and before the newcomer could lay a hand on his shoulder, Red's knife was out and he let him have one across the face with the flat of the blade. Soon as they saw that they all jumped the guy. The hall was pretty long, maybe more than nine or ten yards, and they drove him from one end almost to the other—like Christ in one of the Stations—roughing him up, hooting at him, spitting all over him. First they let him have it with their fists, then, seeing he didn't bother shielding the blows, they started slapping him openhanded and flicking the fringes of their scarves at him, mocking him. At the same time they were saving him for Rosendo, who all this time was standing with his back against the far wall and not moving a muscle, not saying a word. All he did was puff on his cigarette, a little worried-looking, like he already knew what came clear to the rest of us only later on. The Butcher, who was hanging on but was beginning to bleed here and there—that whole hooting pack behind him—got pushed closer and closer to Rosendo. Laughed at, lashed at, spit on, he only started talking when the two of them came face to face. Then he looked at Rosendo and, wiping his face on his sleeve, said something like this:

"I'm Francisco Real and I come from the Northside. People call me the Butcher. I let all these punks lay their hands on me just now because what I'm looking for is a man. Word's going around there's someone out in these lousy mudflats supposed to be pretty good with a knife. They call him the Slasher and they say he's pretty tough. I'd like to meet up with the guy. Maybe he can teach a nobody like me how a man with guts handles himself."

He had his say looking straight at Rosendo, and all at once this big knife he must have had up his sleeve was flashing in his hand. Instead of pressing in, now everyone starts opening up space for a fight—at the same time staring at the two of them in dead silence. Even the thick lips of the blind nigger playing the fiddle were turned that way.

Right then I hear this commotion behind me and in the frame of the door I get me a glimpse of six or seven men who must have been the Butcher's gang. The oldest, a leathery-faced guy with a big grey moustache, who looked like a hick, comes in a few steps and, going all goggle-eyed at the women and the lights, takes off his hat, respectful. The rest of them kept their eyes peeled, ready to swing into action if anything underhanded went on.

What was the matter with Rosendo all this time, not bouncing that loudmouth the hell out? He was still keeping quiet, not even raising his eyes. I don't know if he spit his cigarette out or if it fell from his mouth. Finally he manages to come up with a couple of words, but so low the rest of us at the other end of the dance floor didn't get what he said. Francisco Real challenged him again, and again Rosendo refused. At this point, the youngest of the newcomers lets out a whistle. La Lujanera gave the guy a look that went right through him. Then, her hair swinging down over her shoulders, she wedged her way through the crowd and, going up to her man, slips his knife out and hands it to him.

"Rosendo," she says to him, "I think you're going to need this."

Way up under the roof was this kind of long window that opened out over the river. Rosendo took the knife in his two hands and turned it over like he never laid eyes on it before. Then all of a sudden he raises his arms up over his head and flips the knife behind him out the window into the Maldonado. I felt a chill go through me.

"The only reason I don't carve you up is cause you sicken me," the Butcher says then, making to let Rosendo have it. That split second La Lujanera threw her arms around the Butcher's neck, giving him one of those looks of hers, and says to him, mad as hell, "Let the bastard alone—making us think he was a man."

For a minute Francisco Real couldn't figure it out. Then wrapping his arms around her like it was forever, he calls to the musicians to play loud and strong and orders the rest of us to dance. The music went Eke wildfire from one end of the hall to the other. Real danced sort of stiff but held his partner up tight, and in nothing flat he had her charmed. When they got near the door he shouted, "Make way, boys, she's all mine now!" and out they went, cheek to cheek, like the tango was floating them off.

I must have turned a little red with shame. I took a couple of turns with some woman, then dropped her cold. On account of the heat and the jam, I told her, then edged my way around the room toward the door. It was a nice night out—but for who? There was their buggy at the corner of the alley with two guitars standing straight up on the seat like men. Boy, it galled me seeing that—it was as much as saying we weren't even good enough to clip a lousy guitar. The thought that we were a bunch of nobodys really had me burned up, and I snatched the carnation from behind my ear and threw it in a puddle. I stood there a while staring at it, trying to take my mind off things. I wished it was already tomorrow—I wished that night were over. Then the next thing I knew there's this elbow shoving me aside and it almost came like a relief. It was Rosendo—all by himself, slinking off.

"You're always getting in the way, kid," he says to me half snarling. I couldn't tell if he was just getting something off his chest or what. He disappeared in the dark toward the Maldonado. I never laid eyes on him again.

I stood there looking at the things I'd seen all my life—the big wide sky, the river going on down there in its own blind way, a horse drowsing, the dirt roads, the kilns—and it came to me that in the middle of this ragweed and all these dump heaps and this whole stinking place, I'd grown up just another weed myself. What else was going to come out of this crap but us—lots of lip but soft inside, all talk but no standing up to anyone? Then I thought no, the worse the neighborhood the tougher it had to be. Crap? Back toward the dance hall the music was still going strong, and on the breeze came a smell of honeysuckle. Nice night, but so what? There were so many stars, some right on top of others, it made you dizzy just looking at them. I tried hard to tell myself that what happened meant nothing to me, but I just couldn't get over Rosendo's yellow streak and the newcomer's plain guts. Real even managed to get hold of a woman for the night—for that night and a lot of nights and maybe forever, I thought, because La Lujanera was really something. God knows which way they headed. They couldn't have wandered very far. By then the two of them were probably going at it in some ditch.

When I got back, the dance was in full swing. I slipped into the crowd, quiet as I could, noticing that some of our boys had taken off and that the Northside bunch were dancing along with everyone else. There was no shoving, no rough stuff. Everybody was watching out and on good behaviour. The music sounded sleepy, and the girls tangoing away with the outsiders didn't have much to say.

I was on the lookout for something, but not for what happened. Outside there were sounds of a woman crying and then that voice we all knew by then—but real low, almost too low, like somehow it didn't belong to anyone anymore.

"Go on in, you slut," it was telling her—then more tears. After that the voice sounded desperate.

"Open the door, you understand me? Open it, you lousy tramp. Open it, bitch."

At that point the shaky door opens and in comes La Lujanera, all alone. Just like someone's herding her.

"Must be a ghost out there behind her," said the Redhead.

"A dead man, friend." It was the Butcher, and he staggers in, his face like a drunk's, and in the space we opened up for him he takes a couple of reeling steps—tall, hardly seeing—then all at once goes down like a log. One of his friends rolled him over and fixed him a pillow with his scarf, but all this fussing only got him smeared with blood. We could see there was a big gash in his chest. The blood was welling up and blackening a bright red neckerchief I hadn't noticed before because his scarf covered it. For first aid one of the women brought rum and some scorched rags. The man was in no shape to explain. La Lujanera looked at him in a daze, her arms hanging by her sides. There was one question on everyone's face and finally she got out an answer. She said after leaving with the Butcher they went to a little field and at that point someone she didn't know turned up and challenged him to fight and then gave him this stab. She swore she didn't know who it was, but that it wasn't Rosendo. Was anyone going to believe that?

The man at our feet was dying. It looked to me like the hand that done the job done it well. Just the same, the man hung on. When he knocked that second time Julia was brewing some mates. The cup went clear around the circle and back to me before he died. When the end came, he said in a low voice, "Cover my face." All he had left was pride and he didn't want us gaping at him while his face went through its agony. Someone put his hat over him and that's how he died—without a sound—under that high black crown. It was only when his chest stopped heaving they dared uncover him. He had that worn-out look dead men have. In his day, from the Artillery Barracks all the way to the Southside, he was one of the scrappiest men around. When I knew he was dead and couldn't talk, I stopped hating him.

"All it takes to die is being alive," says one of the girls in the crowd. And in the same way another one says, "A man's so full of pride and now look—all he's good for is gathering flies."

Right then the Northside gang starts talking to each other in low voices. Then two of them come out together saying, "The woman killed him." After that, in a real loud voice, one of them threw the accusation in her face, and they all swarmed in around her. Forgetting I had to be careful, I was on them like a light. I don't know what kept me from reaching for my knife. There were a lot of eyes watching—maybe everybody's—and I said, putting them down, "Look at this woman's hands. How could she get the strength or the nerve to knife a man?"

Then, kind of offhand, I added, "Whoever would have dreamed the deceased, who—like they say—was a pretty tough guy in his own neck of the woods, would end up this way? And in a place sleepy as this, where nothing ever happens till some outsider comes around trying to show us a little fun and for all his pains only gets himself spit on?"

Nobody offered his hide for a whipping.

Right then, in the dead silence, you could make out the approach of riders. It was the law. Everybody—some more, some less—had his own good reason for staying clear of the police. The best thing was to dump the body in the Maldonado. You remember that long window the knife went flying out of? Well, that's where the man in black went. A bunch of guys lifted him up. There were hands stripping him of every cent and trinket he had, and someone even hacked off one of his fingers to steal his ring. They helped themselves, all right—real daring bunch with a poor defenseless stiff once a better guy already straightened him out. One good heave and the current did the rest. To keep him from floating, they maybe even tore out his guts. I don't know—I didn't want to look. The old-timer with the grey moustache never took his eyes off me. Making the best of all the commotion, La Lujanera slipped away.

When the lawmen came in for a look, the dance was going good again. That blind fiddler could really scrape some lively numbers on that violin of his—the kind of thing you never hear anymore. It was beginning to get light outside. The fence posts on a nearby slope seemed to stand alone, the strands of wire still invisible in the early dawn.

Nice and easy, I walked the two or three blocks back to my shack. A candle was burning in the window, then all at once went out. Let me tell you, I hurried when I saw that. Then, Borges, I put my hand inside my vest—here by the left armpit where I always carry it—and took my knife out again. I turned the blade over, real slow. It was as good as new, innocent-looking, and you couldn't see the slightest trace of blood on it.

F.Y.I.

Artillery Barracks: a storage place for military weapons

Christ in one of the Stations: the "Stations" refers to the Stations of the Cross that mark the significant moments leading up to Christ's crucifixion.

gaping wops: the word "wop" is a derogatory and racist term for Italians—an acronym which means "without official papers"

the Maldonado: at the time of this story, a creek marking the northern boundary of the city of Buenos Aires; the neighbourhood itself was called Palermo as well as Maldonado

maté: a type of tea native to Argentina that acts as a stimulant and has levels of caffeine similar to coffee. The last cup or two of maté is usually the most bitter and often preferred as it has the strongest taste.

Streetcorner Man: the title refers to both an actual street corner and a neighbour-hood store or bar located on a corner, a hangout for local hoods and those living in the *barrio*

tango: a highly sexual dance done by couples and believed to have been born in the slums and brothels of Argentina. This dance was considered so erotic and scandalous that women in the 1920s would not dance the tango with men in public places.

Villa Santa Rita: Spanish for village of St. Rita

Words to Build on

brick kiln: an oven used to bake bricks

mudflats: a stretch of muddy land left uncovered at low tide

rumpus: a disturbance or brawl

Tricks of the Trade

Character

Climax

Modernism

Magic realism

Narrative point of view

Setting

Symbol

In Your Own Words: Comprehension

1. Who is telling the story? What details do we learn about him?

2. Describe the setting of this story.

3. How would you describe the tone of the opening lines?

4. Do you get the sense that the narrator is relating a story from his recent past or his distant past? Explain your answer.

5. Make a list of all the characters. Provide a brief description for each.

6. Who is the protagonist or main character of the story? Is that made clear from the beginning?

7. At what point in the story does the narrator anticipate that there will be a fight?

8. How is Real's arrival foreshadowed?

9. How does the narrator feel about Real?

10. What is the climax of this story?

11. Who murders Real in the story and at what point in the story do we find out?

In Your Own Words: Analysis

1. How is Borges successful in luring us as readers into this violent underworld?

2. What does it mean when the narrator says in the first line of the story, "Fancy your coming out and asking me, of all people, about the late Francisco Real. Sure, I knew him even though he wasn't from around here." To whom is he speaking? What relationship does he have with that person?

3. Are we as readers naturally trusting of the voice telling the story? What does Borges do to build trust between the narrator and the readers?

4. There are numerous references to dance and music in "Streetcorner Man." How are these elements significant? What do they add to the story?

5. How does the murderer feel about what he has done? Does he show any guilt or remorse for his act?

6. At the end of the story the narrator states, "A candle was burning in the window, then all at once went out. Let me tell you, I hurried when I saw that." Why does he hurry?

7. Why does the narrator want to tell this story? Is his intent to "show off" his prowess, or is it to offer some kind of confession?

8. What motivates the murderer to kill Real?

9. Borges rarely depicts women in his fiction. Who are the women in the story, and what are their roles? Are they depicted solely on the basis of their sexuality, or is there more to their characters?

❖ Now Write

1. The interrelation of the seemingly opposite concepts of Eros and Thanatos (or sex and death) are themes of this story. Write an essay exploring the contradiction and the relation of the sexual drive and violent energy in "Streetcorner Man."

2. As a writer, Borges was fascinated by the types of characters that make up the "underworld" of Buenos Aires. Consider the definition of a hero or of heroic action. Can any character in this story be seen as heroic? Write an essay in which you argue that a character (or characters) in this story is heroic or that the story is actually an ironic statement on the heroic ideal.

3. Borges's story has been called an exercise in narrative sleight of hand. Compare the narrative style of "Streetcorner Man" with that of "Story of an Hour" by Kate Chopin.

4. What makes a narrator trustworthy? Can the narrator of "Streetcorner Man" be trusted, or is he blatantly deceitful? Compare the narrator in "Streetcorner Man" with another narrator from a story in this text that is also told in the first-person point of view.

Flannery O'Connor

Mary Flannery O'Connor (1925–1964) was born in Savannah, Georgia, on March 25, 1925, the only child of a devout Roman Catholic family. When she was 15, her father died of lupus. O'Connor was devastated and decided to remain at home and enrol in Georgia State College for women as a day student in an accelerated program. It was during her time at this college that she became known amongst her peers as a gifted writer and cartoonist with a talent for satire and comedy. Although painfully shy, she was also known for "her sly humour, her disdain for mediocrity, and her often merciless attacks on affectation and triviality."

In 1945 she received a journalism scholarship from State University of Iowa. However, she realized that journalism was not for her and soon connected with Paul Engle, who was head of what is now the world-renowned Writer's Workshop. Engle would go on to state that O'Connor was "one of the most gifted writers he had ever taught." After graduating in 1947, she was accepted at Yaddo, an artist's retreat in New York. It was here that she worked on completing her first novel, *Wise Blood*, and would become friends with the poet Robert Lowell.

In 1950, just as her father had, O'Connor developed lupus, a disease that could only be treated at the time with a heavy regimen of steroid drugs. Despite her ill health and the debilitating effects of the drugs, O'Connor wrote some of her greatest works, including her short story collection *A Good Man Is Hard to Find* (1955), a novel *The Violent Bear It Away* (1960), and a second collection of short stories *Everything That Rises Must Converge*, which was published in 1965 after her death. An operation early in 1964 reactivated her lupus, and O'Connor's health deteriorated rapidly. After several days in a coma, she died on August 3, 1964.

Although her body of work is not considered large—31 short stories, two novels, a handful of essays, a few speeches, and numerous letters—Flannery O'Connor is considered a master of the short story genre, a giant of the Southern Gothic tradition, and one of the foremost authors in American literature. In describing the devout, shy, and unassuming author's short story collection *A Good Man Is Hard to Find*, Lowell wrote, "Much savagery, compassion, farce, art, and truth have gone into these stories. O'Connor's characters are wholeheartedly horrible, and almost better than life. I find it hard to think of a funnier or more frightening writer."

In Her Own Words

"All my stories are about the action of grace on a character who is not very willing to support it, but most people think of these stories as hard, hopeless, and brutal."

"Everywhere I go, I'm asked if I think the universities stifle writers. My opinion is that they don't stifle enough of them. There's many a best seller that could have been prevented by a good teacher."

"I am a writer because writing is the thing that I do best."

"I'm not afraid that the book will be controversial; I'm afraid it will not be controversial."

Before We Begin

1. Do you believe in fate or coincidence? What is the difference?
2. Can anything good ever come from a terrible event? Why or why not?
3. There is a saying that people make their own luck. What does this mean? Do you agree?
4. Have you ever heard the terms "good blood" and "bad blood"? What do they mean?
5. Have you ever used the "It's not my fault; I couldn't help it!" excuse? Do you truly believe it when you are saying it? How do you feel when you hear other people use it?
6. What is dread? What is the difference between "fear" and "dread"?

 **Now Read**

A Good Man Is Hard to Find

The grandmother didn't want to go to Florida. She wanted to visit some of her connections in east Tennessee and she was seizing at every chance to change Bailey's mind. Bailey was the son she lived with, her only boy. He was sitting on the edge of his chair at the table, bent over the orange sports section of the Journal. "Now look here, Bailey," she said, "see here, read this," and she stood with one hand on her thin hip and the other rattling the newspaper at his bald head. "Here this fellow that calls himself The Misfit is aloose from the Federal Pen and headed toward Florida and you read here what it says he did to these people. Just you read it. I wouldn't take my children in any direction with a criminal like that aloose in it. I couldn't answer to my conscience if I did."

Bailey didn't look up from his reading so she wheeled around then and faced the children's mother, a young woman in slacks, whose face was as broad and innocent as a cabbage and was tied around with a green headkerchief that had two points on the top like rabbit's ears. She was sitting on the sofa, feeding the baby his apricots out of a jar. "The children have been to Florida before," the old lady said. "You all ought to take them somewhere else for a change so they would see different parts of the world and be broad. They never have been to east Tennessee."

The children's mother didn't seem to hear her but the eight-year-old boy, John Wesley, a stocky child with glasses, said, "If you don't want to go to Florida, why dontcha stay at home?" He and the little girl, June Star, were reading the funny papers on the floor.

"She wouldn't stay at home to be queen for a day," June Star said without raising her yellow head.

"Yes and what would you do if this fellow, The Misfit, caught you?" the grandmother asked.

"I'd smack his face," John Wesley said.

"She wouldn't stay at home for a million bucks," June Star said. "Afraid she'd miss something. She has to go everywhere we go."

"All right, Miss," the grandmother said. "Just remember that the next time you want me to curl your hair."

June Star said her hair was naturally curly.

The next morning the grandmother was the first one in the car, ready to go. She had her big black valise that looked like the head of a hippopotamus in one corner, and underneath it she was hiding a basket with Pitty Sing, the cat, in it. She didn't intend for the cat to be left alone in the house for three days because he would miss her too much and she was afraid he might brush against one of the gas burners and accidentally asphyxiate himself. Her son, Bailey, didn't like to arrive at a motel with a cat.

She sat in the middle of the back seat with John Wesley and June Star on either side of her. Bailey and the children's mother and the baby sat in front and they left Atlanta at 8:45 with the mileage on the car at 55,890. The grandmother wrote this down because she thought it would be interesting to say how many miles they had been when they got back. It took them 20 minutes to reach the outskirts of the city.

The old lady settled herself comfortably, removing her white cotton gloves and putting them up with her purse on the shelf in front of the back window. The children's mother still had on slacks and still had her head tied up in a green kerchief, but the grandmother had on a navy blue straw sailor hat with a bunch of white violets on the brim and a navy blue dress with a small white dot in the print. Her collars and cuffs were white organdy trimmed with lace and at her neckline she had pinned a purple spray of cloth violets containing a sachet. In case of an accident, anyone seeing her dead on the highway would know at once that she was a lady.

She said she thought it was going to be a good day for driving, neither too hot nor too cold, and she cautioned Bailey that the speed limit was 55 miles an hour and that the patrolmen hid themselves behind billboards and small dumps of trees and sped out after you before you had a chance to slow down. She pointed out interesting details of the scenery: Stone Mountain; the blue granite that in some places came up to both sides of the highway; the brilliant red day banks slightly streaked with purple; and the various crops that made rows of green lacework on the ground. The trees were full of silver-white sunlight and the meanest of them sparkled. The children were reading comic magazines and their mother had gone back to sleep.

"Let's go through Georgia fast so we won't have to look at it much," John Wesley said.

"If I were a little boy," said the grandmother, "I wouldn't talk about my native state that way. Tennessee has the mountains and Georgia has the hills."

"Tennessee is just a hillbilly dumping ground," John Wesley said, "and Georgia is a lousy state too."

"You said it," June Star said.

"In my time," said the grandmother, folding her thin veined fingers, "children were more respectful of their native states and their parents and everything else. People did right then. Oh look at the cute little pickaninny!" she said and pointed to a Negro child standing in the door of a shack. "Wouldn't that make a picture, now?" she asked and they all turned and looked at the little Negro out of the back window. He waved.

"He didn't have any britches on," June Star said.

"He probably didn't have any," the grandmother explained. "Little niggers in the country don't have things like we do. If I could paint, I'd paint that picture," she said.

The children exchanged comic books.

The grandmother offered to hold the baby and the children's mother passed him over the front seat to her. She set him on her knee and bounced him and told him about the things they were passing. She rolled her eyes and screwed up her mouth and stuck her leathery thin face into his smooth bland one. Occasionally he gave her a faraway smile. They passed a large cotton field with five or six graves fenced in the middle of it, like a small island. "Look at the graveyard!" the grandmother said, pointing it out. "That was the old family burying ground. That belonged to the plantation."

"Where's the plantation?" John Wesley asked.

"Gone with the Wind," said the grandmother. "Ha. Ha." When the children finished all the comic books they had brought, they opened the lunch and ate it. The grandmother ate a peanut butter sandwich and an olive and would not let the children throw the box and the paper napkins out the window. When there was nothing else to do they played a game by choosing a cloud and making the other two guess what shape it suggested. John Wesley took one the shape of a cow and June Star guessed a cow and John Wesley said, no, an automobile, and June Star said he didn't play fair, and they began to slap each other over the grandmother.

The grandmother said she would tell them a story if they would keep quiet. When she told a story, she rolled her eyes and waved her head and was very dramatic. She said once when she was a maiden lady she had been courted by a Mr. Edgar Atkins Teagarden from Jasper, Georgia. She said he was a very good-looking man and a gentleman and that he brought her a watermelon every Saturday afternoon with his initials cut in it, E.A.T. Well, one Saturday, she said, Mr. Teagarden brought the watermelon and there was nobody at home and he left it on the front porch and returned in his buggy to Jasper, but she never got the watermelon, she said, because a nigger boy ate it when he saw the initials, E.A.T.! This story tickled John Wesley's funny bone and he giggled and giggled but June Star didn't think it was any good. She said she wouldn't marry a man that just brought her a watermelon on Saturday. The grandmother said she would have done well to marry Mr. Teagarden because he was a gentleman and had bought Coca-Cola stock when it first came out and that he had died only a few years ago, a very wealthy man.

They stopped at The Tower for barbecued sandwiches. The Tower was a part stucco and part wood filling station and dance hall set in a clearing outside of Timothy. A fat man named Red Sammy Butts ran it and there were signs stuck here and there on the building and for miles up and down the highway saying, TRY RED SAMMY'S FAMOUS BARBECUE. NONE LIKE FAMOUS RED SAMMY'S! RED SAM! THE FAT BOY WITH THE HAPPY LAUGH. A VETERAN! RED SAMMY'S YOUR MAN!

Red Sammy was lying on the bare ground outside The Tower with his head under a truck while a grey monkey about a foot high, chained to a small chinaberry tree, chattered nearby. The monkey sprang back into the tree and got on the highest limb as soon as he saw the children jump out of the car and run toward him.

Inside, The Tower was a long dark room with a counter at one end and tables at the other and dancing space in the middle. They all sat down at a board table next to the nickelodeon and Red Sam's wife, a tall burnt-brown woman with hair and eyes lighter than her skin, came and took their order. The children's mother put a dime in the machine and played "The Tennessee Waltz," and the grandmother said that tune always made her want to dance. She asked Bailey if he would like to dance but he only glared at her. He didn't have a naturally sunny disposition like she did and trips made him nervous. The grandmother's brown eyes were very bright. She swayed her head from side to side and pretended she was dancing in her chair. June Star said play something she could tap to so the children's mother put in another dime and played a fast number and June Star stepped out onto the dance floor and did her tap routine.

"Ain't she cute?" Red Sam's wife said, leaning over the counter. "Would you like to come be my little girl?"

"No I certainly wouldn't," June Star said. "I wouldn't live in a broken-down place like this for a million bucks!" and she ran back to the table.

"Ain't she cute?" the woman repeated, stretching her mouth politely.

"Aren't you ashamed?" hissed the grandmother.

Red Sam came in and told his wife to quit lounging on the counter and hurry up with these people's order. His khaki trousers reached just to his hip bones and his stomach hung over them like a sack of meal swaying under his shirt. He came over and sat down at a table nearby and let out a combination sigh and yodel. "You can't win," he said. "You can't win," and he wiped his sweating red face off with a grey handkerchief. "These days you don't know who to trust," he said. "Ain't that the truth?"

"People are certainly not nice like they used to be," said the grandmother.

"Two fellers come in here last week," Red Sammy said, "driving a Chrysler. It was a old beat-up car but it was a good one and these boys looked all right to me. Said they worked at the mill and you know I let them fellers charge the gas they bought? Now why did I do that?"

"Because you're a good man!" the grandmother said at once.

"Yes'm, I suppose so," Red Sam said as if he were struck with this answer.

His wife brought the orders, carrying the five plates all at once without a tray, two in each hand and one balanced on her arm. "It isn't a soul in this green world of God's that you can trust," she said. "And I don't count nobody out of that, not nobody," she repeated, looking at Red Sammy.

"Did you read about that criminal, The Misfit, that's escaped?" asked the grandmother.

"I wouldn't be a bit surprised if he didn't attact this place right here," said the woman. "If he hears about it being here, I wouldn't be none surprised to see him. If he hears it's two cent in the cash register, I wouldn't be a tall surprised if he . . ."

"That'll do," Red Sam said. "Go bring these people their Co'-Colas," and the woman went off to get the rest of the order.

"A good man is hard to find," Red Sammy said. "Everything is getting terrible. I remember the day you could go off and leave your screen door unlatched. Not no more."

He and the grandmother discussed better times. The old lady said that in her opinion Europe was entirely to blame for the way things were now. She said the way Europe acted you would think we were made of money and Red Sam said it was no use talking about it, she was exactly right. The children ran outside into the white sunlight and looked at the monkey in the lacy chinaberry tree. He was busy catching fleas on himself and biting each one carefully between his teeth as if it were a delicacy.

They drove off again into the hot afternoon. The grandmother took cat naps and woke up every few minutes with her own snoring. Outside of Toombsboro she woke up and recalled an old plantation that she had visited in this neighbourhood once when she was a young lady. She said the house had six white columns across the front and that there was an avenue of oaks leading up to it and two little wooden trellis arbours on either side in front where you sat down with your suitor after a stroll in the garden. She recalled exactly which road to turn off to get to it. She knew that Bailey would not be willing to lose any time looking at an old house, but the more she talked about it, the more she wanted to see it once again and find out if the little twin arbors were still standing. "There was a secret panel in this house," she said craftily, not telling the truth but wishing that she were, "and the story went that all the family silver was hidden in it when Sherman came through but it was never found . . ."

"Hey!" John Wesley said. "Let's go see it! We'll find it! We'll poke all the woodwork and find it! Who lives there? Where do you turn off at? Hey Pop, can't we turn off there?"

"We never have seen a house with a secret panel!" June Star shrieked. "Let's go to the house with the secret panel! Hey Pop, can't we go see the house with the secret panel!"

"It's not far from here, I know," the grandmother said. "It wouldn't take over 20 minutes."

Bailey was looking straight ahead. His jaw was as rigid as a horseshoe. "No," he said.

The children began to yell and scream that they wanted to see the house with the secret panel. John Wesley kicked the back of the front seat and June Star hung over her mother's shoulder and whined desperately into her ear that they never had any fun even on their vacation, that they could never do what THEY wanted to do. The baby began to scream and John Wesley kicked the back of the seat so hard that his father could feel the blows in his kidney.

"All right!" he shouted and drew the car to a stop at the side of the road. "Will you all shut up? Will you all just shut up for one second? If you don't shut up, we won't go anywhere."

"It would be very educational for them," the grandmother murmured.

"All right," Bailey said, "but get this: this is the only time we're going to stop for anything like this. This is the one and only time."

"The dirt road that you have to turn down is about a mile back," the grandmother directed. "I marked it when we passed."

"A dirt road," Bailey groaned.

After they had turned around and were headed toward the dirt road, the grandmother recalled other points about the house, the beautiful glass over the front doorway and the candle-lamp in the hall. John Wesley said that the secret panel was probably in the fireplace.

"You can't go inside this house," Bailey said. "You don't know who lives there."

"While you all talk to the people in front, I'll run around behind and get in a window," John Wesley suggested.

"We'll all stay in the car," his mother said.

They turned onto the dirt road and the car raced roughly along in a swirl of pink dust. The grandmother recalled the times when there were no paved roads and 30 miles was a day's journey. The dirt road was hilly and there were sudden washes in it and sharp curves on dangerous embankments. All at once they would be on a hill, looking down over the blue tops of trees for miles around, then the next minute, they would be in a red depression with the dust-coated trees looking down on them.

"This place had better turn up in a minute," Bailey said, "or I'm going to turn around."

The road looked as if no one had travelled on it in months.

"It's not much farther," the grandmother said and just as she said it, a horrible thought came to her. The thought was so embarrassing that she turned red in the face and her eyes dilated and her feet jumped up, upsetting her valise in the corner. The instant the valise moved, the newspaper top she had over the basket under it rose with a snarl and Pitty Sing, the cat, sprang onto Bailey's shoulder.

The children were thrown to the floor and their mother, clutching the baby, was thrown out the door onto the ground; the old lady was thrown into the front seat. The car turned over once and landed right-side-up in a gulch off the side of the road. Bailey remained in the driver's seat with the cat—grey-striped with a broad white face and an orange nose—clinging to his neck like a caterpillar.

As soon as the children saw they could move their arms and legs, they scrambled out of the car, shouting, "We've had an ACCIDENT!" The grandmother was curled up under the dashboard, hoping she was injured so that Bailey's wrath would not come down on her all at once. The horrible thought she had had before the accident was that the house she had remembered so vividly was not in Georgia but in Tennessee.

Bailey removed the cat from his neck with both hands and flung it out the window against the side of a pine tree. Then he got out of the car and started looking for the children's mother. She was sitting against the side of the red gutted ditch, holding the screaming baby, but she only had a cut down her face and a broken shoulder. "We've had an ACCIDENT!" the children screamed in a frenzy of delight.

"But nobody's killed," June Star said with disappointment as the grandmother limped out of the car, her hat still pinned to her head but the broken front brim standing up at a jaunty angle and the violet spray hanging off the side. They all sat down in the ditch, except the children, to recover from the shock. They were all shaking.

"Maybe a car will come along," said the children's mother hoarsely.

"I believe I have injured an organ," said the grandmother, pressing her side, but no one answered her. Bailey's teeth were clattering. He had on a yellow sport shirt with bright blue parrots designed in it and his face was as yellow as the shirt. The grandmother decided that she would not mention that the house was in Tennessee.

The road was about 10 feet above and they could see only the tops of the trees on the other side of it. Behind the ditch they were sitting in there were more woods, tall and dark and deep. In a few minutes they saw a car some distance away on top of a hill, corning slowly as if the occupants were watching them. The grandmother stood up and waved both arms dramatically to attract their attention. The car continued to come on slowly, disappeared around a bend and appeared again, moving even slower, on top of the hill they had gone over. It was a big black battered hearse-like automobile. There were three men in it.

It came to a stop just over them and for some minutes, the driver looked down with a steady expressionless gaze to where they were sitting, and didn't speak. Then he turned his head and muttered something to the other two and they got out. One was a fat boy in black trousers and a red sweatshirt with a silver stallion embossed on the front of it. He moved around on the right side of them and stood staring, his mouth partly open in a kind of loose grin. The other had on khaki pants and a blue striped coat and a grey hat pulled down very low, hiding most of his face. He came around slowly on the left side. Neither spoke.

The driver got out of the car and stood by the side of it, looking down at them. He was an older man than the other two. His hair was just beginning to grey and he wore silver-rimmed spectacles that gave him a scholarly look. He had a long creased face and didn't have on any shirt or undershirt. He had on blue jeans that were too tight for him and was holding a black hat and a gun. The two boys also had guns.

"We've had an ACCIDENT!" the children screamed.

The grandmother had the peculiar feeling that the bespectacled man was someone she knew. His face was as familiar to her as if she had known him all her life but she could not recall who he was. He moved away from the car and began to come down the embankment, placing his feet carefully so that he wouldn't slip. He had on tan and white shoes and no socks, and his ankles were red and thin. "Good afternoon," he said. "I see you all had you a little spill."

"We turned over twice!" said the grandmother.

"Oncet," he corrected. "We seen it happen. Try their car and see will it run, Hiram," he said quietly to the boy with the grey hat.

"What you got that gun for?" John Wesley asked. "Whatcha gonna do with that gun?"

"Lady," the man said to the children's mother, "would you mind, calling them children to sit down by you? Children make me nervous. I want all you all to sit down right together there where you're at."

"What are you telling US what to do for?" June Star asked.

Behind them the line of woods gaped like a dark open mouth. "Come here," said their mother.

"Look here now," Bailey began suddenly, "we're in a predicament! We're in . . ."

The grandmother shrieked. She scrambled to her feet and stood staring. "You're The Misfit!" she said. "I recognized you at once!"

"Yes'm," the man said, smiling slightly as if he were pleased in spite of himself to be known, "but it would have been better for all of you, lady, if you hadn't of reckernized me."

Bailey turned his head sharply and said something to his mother that shocked even the children. The old lady began to cry and The Misfit reddened.

"Lady," he said, "don't you get upset. Sometimes a man says things he don't mean. I don't reckon he meant to talk to you thataway."

"You wouldn't shoot a lady, would you?" the grandmother said and removed a clean handkerchief from her cuff and began to slap at her eyes with it.

The Misfit pointed the toe of his shoe into the ground and made a little hole and then covered it up again. "I would hate to have to," he said.

"Listen," the grandmother almost screamed, "I know you're a good man. You don't look a bit like you have common blood. I know you must come from nice people!"

"Yes mam," he said, "finest people in the world." When he smiled he showed a row of strong white teeth. "God never made a finer woman than my mother and my daddy's heart was pure gold," he said. The boy with the red sweatshirt had come around behind them and was standing with his gun at his hip. The Misfit squatted down on the ground. "Watch them children, Bobby Lee," he said. "You know they make me nervous." He looked at the six of them huddled together in front of him and he seemed to be embarrassed as if he couldn't think of anything to say. "Ain't a cloud in the sky," he remarked, looking up at it. "Don't see no sun but don't see no cloud neither."

"Yes, it's a beautiful day," said the grandmother. "Listen," she said, "you shouldn't call yourself The Misfit because I know you're a good man at heart. I can just look at you and tell."

"Hush!" Bailey yelled. "Hush! Everybody shut up and let me handle this!" He was squatting in the position of a runner about to sprint forward but he didn't move.

"I pre-chate that, lady," The Misfit said and drew a little circle in the ground with the butt of his gun.

"It'll take a half a hour to fix this here car," Hiram called, looking over the raised hood of it.

"Well, first you and Bobby Lee get him and that little boy to step over yonder with you," The Misfit said, pointing to Bailey and John Wesley. "The boys want to ast you something," he said to Bailey. "Would you mind stepping back in them woods there with them?"

"Listen," Bailey began, "we're in a terrible predicament! Nobody realizes what this is," and his voice cracked. His eyes were as blue and intense as the parrots in his shirt and he remained perfectly still.

The grandmother reached up to adjust her hat brim as if she were going to the woods with him but it came off in her hand. She stood staring at it and after a second she let it fall on the ground. Hiram pulled Bailey up by the arm as if he were assisting an old man. John Wesley caught hold of his father's hand and Bobby Lee followed. They went off toward the woods and just as they reached the dark edge, Bailey turned and supporting himself against a grey naked pine trunk, he shouted, "I'll be back in a minute, Mamma, wait on me!"

"Come back this instant!" his mother shrilled but they all disappeared into the woods.

"Bailey Boy!" the grandmother called in a tragic voice but she found she was looking at The Misfit squatting on the ground in front of her. "I just know you're a good man," she said desperately. "You're not a bit common!"

"Nome, I ain't a good man," The Misfit said after a second as if he had considered her statement carefully, "but I ain't the worst in the world neither. My daddy said I was a different breed of dog from my brothers and sisters. 'You know,' Daddy said, 'it's some that can live their whole life out without asking about it and it's others has to know why it is, and this boy is one of the latters. He's going to be into everything!'" He put on his black hat and looked up suddenly and then away deep into the woods as if he were embarrassed again. "I'm sorry I don't have on a shirt before you ladies," he said, hunching his shoulders slightly. "We buried our clothes that we had on when we escaped and we're just making do until we can get better. We borrowed these from some folks we met," he explained.

"That's perfectly all right," the grandmother said. "Maybe Bailey has an extra shirt in his suitcase."

"I'll look and see terrectly," The Misfit said.

"Where are they taking him?" the children's mother screamed.

"Daddy was a card himself," The Misfit said. "You couldn't put anything over on him. He never got in trouble with the Authorities though. Just had the knack of handling them."

"You could be honest too if you'd only try," said the grandmother. "Think how wonderful it would be to settle down and live a comfortable life and not have to think about somebody chasing you all the time."

The Misfit kept scratching in the ground with the butt of his gun as if he were thinking about it. "Yes'm, somebody is always after you," he murmured.

The grandmother noticed how thin his shoulder blades were just behind his hat because she was standing up looking down on him. "Do you ever pray?" she asked.

He shook his head. All she saw was the black hat wiggle between his shoulder blades. "Nome," he said.

There was a pistol shot from the woods, followed closely by another. Then silence. The old lady's head jerked around. She could hear the wind move through the tree tops like a long satisfied insuck of breath. "Bailey Boy!" she called.

"I was a gospel singer for a while," The Misfit said. "I been most everything. Been in the arm service, both land and sea, at home and abroad, been twict married, been an undertaker, been with the railroads, plowed Mother Earth, been in a tornado, seen a man burnt alive oncet," and he looked up at the children's mother and the little girl who were sitting close together, their faces white and their eyes glassy; "I even seen a woman flogged," he said.

"Pray, pray," the grandmother began, "pray, pray . . ."

"I never was a bad boy that I remember of," The Misfit said in an almost dreamy voice, "but somewheres along the line I done something wrong and got sent to the penitentiary. I was buried alive," and he looked up and held her attention to him by a steady stare.

"That's when you should have started to pray," she said. "What did you do to get sent to the penitentiary that first time?"

"Turn to the right, it was a wall," The Misfit said, looking up again at the cloudless sky. "Turn to the left, it was a wall. Look up it was a ceiling, look down it was a floor. I forget what I done, lady. I set there and set there, trying to remember what it was I done and I ain't recalled it to this day. Oncet in a while, I would think it was coming to me, but it never come."

"Maybe they put you in by mistake," the old lady said vaguely.

"Nome," he said. "It wasn't no mistake. They had the papers on me."

"You must have stolen something," she said.

The Misfit sneered slightly. "Nobody had nothing I wanted," he said. "It was a head-doctor at the penitentiary said what I had done was kill my daddy but I known that for a lie. My daddy died in nineteen ought nineteen of the epidemic flu and I never had a thing to do with it. He was buried in the Mount Hopewell Baptist churchyard and you can go there and see for yourself."

"If you would pray," the old lady said, "Jesus would help you."

"That's right," The Misfit said.

"Well then, why don't you pray?" she asked trembling with delight suddenly.

"I don't want no hep," he said. "I'm doing all right by myself."

Bobby Lee and Hiram came ambling back from the woods. Bobby Lee was dragging a yellow shirt with bright blue parrots in it.

"Thow me that shirt, Bobby Lee," The Misfit said. The shirt came flying at him and landed on his shoulder and he put it on. The grandmother couldn't name what the shirt reminded her of. "No, lady," The Misfit said while he was buttoning it up, "I found out the crime don't matter. You can do one thing or you can do another, kill a man or take a tire off his car, because sooner or later you're going to forget what it was you done and just be punished for it."

The children's mother had begun to make heaving noises as if she couldn't get her breath. "Lady," he asked, "would you and that little girl like to step off yonder with Bobby Lee and Hiram and join your husband?"

"Yes, thank you," the mother said faintly. Her left arm dangled helplessly and she was holding the baby, who had gone to sleep, in the other. "Hep that lady up, Hiram," The Misfit said as she struggled to climb out of the ditch, "and Bobby Lee, you hold onto that little girl's hand."

"I don't want to hold hands with him," June Star said. "He reminds me of a pig."

The fat boy blushed and laughed and caught her by the arm and pulled her off into the woods after Hiram and her mother.

Alone with The Misfit, the grandmother found that she had lost her voice. There was not a cloud in the sky nor any sun. There was nothing around her but woods. She wanted to tell him that he must pray. She opened and closed her mouth several times before anything came out. Finally she found herself saying, "Jesus. Jesus," meaning, Jesus will help you, but the way she was saying it, it sounded as if she might be cursing.

"Yes'm," The Misfit said as if he agreed. "Jesus thown everything off balance. It was the same case with Him as with me except He hadn't committed any crime and they could prove I had committed one because they had the papers on me. Of course," he said, "they never shown me my papers. That's why I sign myself now. I said long ago, you get you a signature and sign everything you do and keep a copy of it. Then you'll know what you done and you can hold up the crime to the punishment and see do they match and in the end you'll have something to prove you ain't been treated right. I call myself The Misfit," he said, "because I can't make what all I done wrong fit what all I gone through in punishment."

There was a piercing scream from the woods, followed closely by a pistol report. "Does it seem right to you, lady, that one is punished a heap and another ain't punished at all?"

"Jesus!" the old lady cried. "You've got good blood! I know you wouldn't shoot a lady! I know you come from nice people! Pray! Jesus, you ought not to shoot a lady. I'll give you all the money I've got!"

"Lady," The Misfit said, looking beyond her far into the woods, "there never was a body that give the undertaker a tip."

There were two more pistol reports and the grandmother raised her head like a parched old turkey hen crying for water and called, "Bailey Boy, Bailey Boy!" as if her heart would break.

"Jesus was the only One that ever raised the dead," The Misfit continued, "and He shouldn't have done it. He thown everything off balance. If He did what He said, then it's nothing for you to do but thow away everything and follow Him, and if He didn't, then it's nothing for you to do but enjoy the few minutes you got left the best way you can—by killing somebody or burning down his house or doing some other meanness to him. No pleasure but meanness," he said and his voice had become almost a snarl.

"Maybe He didn't raise the dead," the old lady mumbled, not knowing what she was saying and feeling so dizzy that she sank down in the ditch with her legs twisted under her.

"I wasn't there so I can't say He didn't," The Misfit said. "I wisht I had of been there," he said, hitting the ground with his fist. "It ain't right I wasn't there because if I had of been there I would of known. Listen lady," he said in a high voice, "if I had of been there I would of known and I wouldn't be like I am now." His voice seemed about to crack and the grandmother's head cleared for an instant. She saw the man's face twisted close to her own as if he were going to cry and she murmured, "Why you're one of my babies. You're one of my own children!" She reached out and touched him on the shoulder. The Misfit sprang back as if a snake had bitten him and shot her three times through the chest. Then he put his gun down on the ground and took off his glasses and began to clean them.

Hiram and Bobby Lee returned from the woods and stood over the ditch, looking down at the grandmother who half sat and half lay in a puddle of blood with her legs crossed under her like a child's and her face smiling up at the cloudless sky.

Without his glasses, The Misfit's eyes were red-rimmed and pale and defenceless looking. "Take her off and thow her where you thown the others," he said, picking up the cat that was rubbing itself against his leg.

"She was a talker, wasn't she?" Bobby Lee said, sliding down the ditch with a yodel.

"She would of been a good woman," The Misfit said, "if it had been somebody there to shoot her every minute of her life."

"Some fun!" Bobby Lee said.

"Shut up, Bobby Lee," The Misfit said. "It's no real pleasure in life."

F.Y.I.

barbecued sandwiches: a popular type of sandwich in the southern United States. Although recipes vary, this sandwich is usually made with a type of pulled or shredded pork tossed in barbecue sauce and served on a bun.

Gone With the Wind: a romantic novel written by Margaret Mitchell and published in 1936. The story takes place in Clayton County and Atlanta, Georgia, during the American Civil War and the reconstruction afterwards. It deals with the lives of privileged plantation owners and how they were affected by the war. It was made into a wildly popular movie in 1939. The book and film have two of literature and cinema's most famous icons: Scarlett O'Hara, the spoiled and manipulative hero of the story, and Tara, the glorious plantation on which many of the story's major scenes and intrigues take place. In "A Good Man Is Hard to Find," Flannery O'Connor makes use of the old joke created around the title of this popular book and even more popular movie.

pickaninny: once thought to be a slang word used to denote an item of small size or insignificance, it became a term used in the southern United States to refer to the children of African slaves and, later on, of African American citizens. It is documented that the term was used as early as 1831 in an anti-slavery pamphlet published in Scotland entitled "The History of Mary Prince, a West Indian Slave, related by herself." However, the term became widely used after the publication of the book *Uncle Tom's Cabin* in 1852. Although the term was still used in the United States as late as the 1960s, it is now considered highly offensive and has fallen out of use.

Sherman: William Tecumseh Sherman (1820–1891) was a general in the Union Army during the American Civil War (1861–1865). Although he was lauded for his military strategy, he was also criticized for his use of "total war" tactics against the Confederate States in which non-combatants (civilians) did not escape military force. When the grandmother in "A Good Man Is Hard to Find" tells the story about silverware hidden in a secret panel on the plantation never being found even "when Sherman came through," this is a reference to the military tactic of troops looting and destroying homesteads as they crossed through states.

"Tennessee Waltz": a well-known country and popular song now considered a "standard." It was written in 1947 but did not become a hit until 1950; it was made an official song of the state of Tennessee in 1965. It has been covered and recorded numerous times over the years and by all types of performers from around the world; it is even one of the best-selling records of all time in Japan.

Words to Build on

asphyxiate: to deprive of oxygen

card: a slang term used to describe someone who is funny and amusing

courting: to seek the affections of a woman with the hope of eventually marrying her

hearse: a large, long, black vehicle used to take a coffin to a cemetery

nickelodeon: an early movie theatre that charged only a nickel for admission

a sack of meal: a large and heavy burlap bag filled with crushed dried corn

slacks: trousers or pants that are not part of a suit

suitor: what a man is called when he is courting a woman

valise: a small piece of hand luggage used for a short trip

Tricks of the Trade

Caricature

Climax

Dialect

Foreshadowing

Grotesque

Imagery

Irony

Southern Gothic

Symbol

In Your Own Words: Comprehension

1. How many characters don't have names? Who are they and how are they referred to?

2. What is the real reason the grandmother doesn't want to go to Florida? What reason does she give her son?

3. What does the grandmother wear on the trip? Does this seem unusual? Why does she wear this?

4. How do John Wesley and June Star treat adults in this story? What is the adults' reaction to their behaviour?

5. When does it seem like the children show any excitement on the trip?

6. How would you describe The Misfit?

7. What words and phrases does the grandmother keep using to try and get through to The Misfit? Do they have any affect on him?

8. What are some of the reasons The Misfit gives to explain why he is the way he is?

9. What causes The Misfit to shoot the grandmother?

In Your Own Words: Analysis

1. Does the grandmother seem like a genuine person? With reference to the story, provide details to show why she is or isn't a person that means what she says.

2. Did this family have any chance in averting its fate? List the moments in the story that foreshadow the deadly ending of the story.

3. When his family wants to stop to see the plantation, the grandmother tells her son, Bailey, that "It would be very educational for them." Bailey, in turn, tells his family, "All right . . . but get this: this is the only time we are going to stop for anything like this. This is the one and only time." Is there a hidden meaning behind both these innocent and commonplace statements?

4. What is the reason for the car crash? What is the significance behind it?

5. Explain in your own words what The Misfit means when he tells the grandmother, "Lady . . . there never was a body that give the undertaker a tip."

6. Flannery O'Connor is known for using religious themes and symbols in her work. O'Connor herself described "A Good Man Is Hard to Find" as "a tale of redemptive grace in a fallen world." Where in the story do you see any moments or images of redemption?

7. Bobby Lee tells The Misfit, "She was a talker, wasn't she?" to which The Misfit replies, "She would have been a good woman . . . if it had been somebody there to shoot her every minute of her life." What does he mean by this?

8. Just before he shoots her, The Misfit tells the grandmother that if Jesus really didn't raise the dead, " . . . then it's nothing for you to do but enjoy the few minutes you got left the best way you can—by killing somebody or burning down his house or doing some other meanness. No pleasure but meanness." However, later when Bobby Lee refers to the grandmother being shot as "Some fun!" The Misfit ends the story by saying, "Shut up, Bobby Lee . . . It's no real pleasure in life." What does he mean by this? What brings about this sudden change of heart?

❄ Now Write

1. The grandmother is a very important character in "A Good Man Is Hard to Find." She is a character that is out of time and place, a character that seems as though she has been dropped into a scene that she has no idea how to play. It is her actions that bring her and her family to meet The Misfit, the other important character in the story. He, too, is a character that struggles with time and place. Write an essay comparing the two "misfits" and how their struggles with time and place affect them and those around them.

2. When this story was published, many were shocked by the extreme violence. Flannery O'Connor thought that it was acceptable to use terror to shock modern readers, who she thought were spiritually complacent. She said, "To the hard of hearing . . . [you] shout, and for the almost blind, [you] draw large and startling figures." Do the violence and other disturbing elements of this story help the author tell her story, or do they risk alienating and ultimately losing her reader?

3. O'Connor is often said to have written stories filled with the grotesque, especially in terms of her characters. When you think of the word "grotesque" what do you think of? Do any of the characters in this story seem grotesque?

James Baldwin

James Baldwin (1924–1987) was born in Harlem to Emma Berdis, who was not married at the time. She later married David Baldwin, a labourer and minister, who adopted her son when he was three and by whom she had eight children.

In his essay "Race and the African American Writer," Baldwin writes about helping his mother raise his siblings: "[a]s they were born, I took them over with one hand and held a book with the other . . . in this way I read *Uncle Tom's Cabin* and *A Tale of Two Cities* over and over and over again; in this way, in fact, I read just about everything I could get my hands on—except the Bible, probably because it was the only book I was encouraged to read." Eventually he would become so well-versed in the Bible that at 14 he was a Pentecostal street preacher. However, by 17 he left his family home and moved to Greenwich Village to work odd jobs and pursue his writing.

By 1948 he had become disillusioned by the treatment of African Americans in the United States and the slow progress towards equality, so he left for France. The other reason he left his native country was in the hopes that his work would be read as any other writer's work, beyond the limitations and associations with his ethnic identity.

Baldwin travelled extensively throughout Europe, yet it is his early childhood years in Harlem that formed a well-spring for his work. He is known for his short stories, novels, plays, essays, and a children's story book. His essays focus on civil rights since he felt passionately about issues of racial justice, and he returned to the United States to participate in the civil rights movement. In his novels, however, he also writes openly about homosexuality, an issue he felt strongly about since it related to his own life, which is reflected in *Giovanni's Room*, his most well-known novel.

"Sonny's Blues" (1965) takes place in the mid-twentieth century and deals with issues relating to identity and culture as it explores the relationship between two brothers. The nameless brother who narrates this story is on his way to work when he reads that Sonny was arrested in a heroin bust. The story highlights the differences in the brothers' personalities and the process by which one brother comes to form some compassion and understanding for the life of the other.

In His Own Words

"But I still believe that the unexamined life is not worth living: and I know that self-delusion, in the service of no matter what small or lofty cause, is a price no writer can afford. His subject is himself and the world and it requires every ounce of stamina he can summon to attempt to look on himself and the world as they are."

"Anyone who has ever struggled with poverty knows how extremely expensive it is to be poor."

"I imagine one of the reasons people cling to their hates so stubbornly is because they sense, once hate is gone, they will be forced to deal with pain."

"The power of the white world is threatened whenever a black man refuses to accept the white world's definitions."

"The paradox of education is precisely this—that as one begins to become conscious one begins to examine the society in which he is being educated."

Before We Begin

1. Music, specifically jazz, plays an important role in this story. How would you describe jazz music? Can you name any famous jazz artists?

2. What is meant by the phrase the "American Dream"? Is there a similar "Canadian Dream"? Do you believe it is possible for people to attain this dream?

3. Do artists need to take drugs to be creative or improve self-expression? Does taking drugs mask pain or help artists feel more free to create?

4. What are the reasons people become addicted to drugs? What effects does an addict's drug use have on those around him or her?

5. Do you think a sibling can be trusted to tell the story of another sibling's life? Why or why not?

 **Now Read**

Sonny's Blues

I read about it in the paper, in the subway, on my way to work. I read it, and I couldn't believe it, and I read it again. Then perhaps I just stared at it, at the newsprint spelling out his name, spelling out the story. I stared at it in the swinging lights of the subway car, and in the faces and bodies of the people, and in my own face, trapped in the darkness which roared outside.

It was not to be believed, and I kept telling myself that as I walked from the subway station to the high school. And at the same time I couldn't doubt it. I was scared, scared for Sonny. He became real to me again. A great block of ice got settled in my belly and kept melting there slowly all day long, while I taught my classes algebra. It was a special kind of ice. It kept melting, sending trickles of ice water all up and down my veins, but it never got less. Sometimes it hardened and seemed to expand until I felt my guts were going to come spilling out or that I was going to choke or scream. This would always be at a moment when I was remembering some specific thing Sonny had once said or done.

When he was about as old as the boys in my classes, his face had been bright and open, there was a lot of copper in it; and he'd had wonderfully direct brown eyes, and great gentleness and privacy. I wondered what he looked like now. He had been picked up, the evening before, in a raid on an apartment downtown, for peddling and using heroin.

I couldn't believe it: but what I mean by that is that I couldn't find any room for it anywhere inside me. I had kept it outside me for a long time. I hadn't wanted to know. I had had suspicions, but I didn't name them, I kept putting them away. I told myself Sonny was wild, but he wasn't crazy. And he'd always been a good boy, he hadn't ever turned hard or evil or disrespectful, the way kids can, so quick, so quick, especially in Harlem. I didn't want to believe that I'd ever see my brother going down, coming to nothing, all that light in his face gone out, in the condition I'd already seen so many others. Yet it had happened and here I was, talking about algebra to a lot of boys who might, every one of them for all I knew, be popping off needles every time they went to the head. Maybe it did more for them than algebra could.

I was sure that the first time Sonny had ever had horse, he couldn't have been much older than these boys were now. These boys, now, were living as we'd been living then, they were growing up with a rush and their heads bumped abruptly against the low ceiling of their actual possibilities. They were filled with rage. All they really knew were two darknesses, the darkness of their lives, which was now closing in on them, and the darkness of the movies, which had blinded them to that other darkness, and in which they now, vindictively, dreamed, at once more together than they were at any other time, and more alone.

When the last bell rang, the last class ended, I let out my breath. It seemed I'd been holding it for all that time. My clothes were set—I may have looked as though I'd been sitting in a steam bath, all dressed up, all afternoon. I sat alone in the classroom a long time. I listened to the boys outside, downstairs, shouting and cursing and laughing. Their laughter struck me for perhaps the first time. It was not the joyous laughter which—God knows why—one associates with children. It was mocking and insular, its intent was to denigrate. It was disenchanted, and in this, also, lay the authority of their curses. Perhaps I was listening to them because I was thinking about my brother and in them I heard my brother. And myself.

One boy was whistling a tune, at once very complicated and very simple, it seemed to be pouring out of him as though he were a bird, and it sounded very cool and moving through all that harsh, bright air, only just holding its own through all those other sounds.

I stood and walked over to the window and looked down into the courtyard. It was the beginning of the spring, and the sap was rising in the boys. A teacher passed through them every now and again, quickly, as though he or she couldn't wait to get out of that courtyard, to get those boys out of their sight and off their minds. I started collecting my stuff. I thought I'd better get home and talk to Isabel.

The courtyard was almost deserted by the time I got downstairs. I saw this boy standing in the shadow of the doorway, looking just like Sonny. I almost called his name. Then I saw it wasn't Sonny, but somebody we used to know, a boy from around our block. He'd been Sonny's friend. He'd never been mine, having been too young for me, and, anyway, I'd never liked him. And now, even though he was a grown-up man, he still hung around the block, still spent hours on the street corner, was always high and raggy. I used to run into him from time to time, and he'd often work around to asking me for a quarter or 50 cents. He always had some real good excuse, too, and I always gave it to him, I don't know why.

But now, abruptly, I hated him. I couldn't stand the way he looked at me, partly like a dog, partly like a cunning child. I wanted to ask him what the hell he was doing in the school courtyard.

He sort of shuffled over to me, and he said, "I see you got the papers. So you already know about it."

"You mean about Sonny? Yes, I already know about it. How come they didn't get you?"

He grinned. It made him repulsive and it also brought to mind what he'd looked like as a kid. "I wasn't there. I stay away from them people."

"Good for you." I offered him a cigarette and I watched him through the smoke. "You come all the way down here just to tell me about Sonny?"

"That's right." He was sort of shaking his head and his eyes looked strange, as though they were about to cross. The bright sun deadened his damp dark brown skin and it made his eyes look yellow and showed up the dirt in his conked hair. He smelled funky. I moved a little away from him and I said, "Well, thanks. But I already know about it and I got to get home."

"I'll walk you a little ways," he said. We started walking. There were a couple of kids still loitering in the courtyard and one of them said good night to me and looked strangely at the boy beside me.

"What're you going to do?" he asked me. "I mean, about Sonny?"

"Look. I haven't seen Sonny for over a year, I'm not sure I'm going to do anything. Anyway, what the hell *can* I do?"

"That's right," he said quickly, "ain't nothing you can do. Can't much help old Sonny no more, I guess."

It was what I was thinking and so it seemed to me he had no right to say it.

"I'm surprised at Sonny, though," he went on—he had a funny way of talking, he looked straight ahead as though he were talking to himself—"I thought Sonny was a smart boy, I thought he was too smart to get hung."

"I guess he thought so, too," I said sharply, "and that's how he got hung. And how about you? You're pretty goddamn smart, I bet."

Then he looked directly at me, just for a minute. "I ain't smart," he said. "If I was smart, I'd have reached for a pistol a long time ago."

"Look. Don't tell *me* your sad story, if it was up to me, I'd give you one." Then I felt guilty—guilty probably, for never having supposed that the poor bastard *had* a story of his own, much less a sad one, and I asked, quickly, "What's going to happen to him now?"

He didn't answer this. He was off by himself someplace. "Funny thing," he said, and from his tone he might have been discussing the quickest way to get to Brooklyn, "when I saw the papers this morning, the first thing I asked myself was if I had anything to do with it. I felt sort of responsible."

I began to listen more carefully. The subway station was on the corner, just before us, and I stopped. He stopped, too. We were in front of a bar and he ducked slightly, peering in, but whoever he was looking for didn't seem to be there. The juke box was blasting away with something black and bouncy, and I half watched the barmaid as she danced her way from the juke box to her place behind the bar. And I watched her face as she laughingly responded to something someone said to her, still keeping time to the music. When she smiled one saw the little girl, one sensed the doomed, still-struggling woman beneath the battered face of the semi-whore.

"I never *give* Sonny nothing," the boy said finally, "but a long time ago I come to school high and Sonny asked me how it felt." He paused, I couldn't bear to watch him, I watched the barmaid, and I listened to the music which seemed to be causing the pavement to shake. "I told him it felt great." The music stopped, the barmaid paused and watched the juke box until the music began again. "It did."

All this was carrying me someplace I didn't want to go. I certainly didn't want to know how it felt. It filled everything, the people, the houses, the music, the dark, quick-silver barmaid, with menace; and this menace was their reality.

"What's going to happen to him now?" I asked again.

"They'll send him away someplace and they'll try to cure him." He shook his head. "Maybe he'll even think he's kicked the habit. Then they'll let him loose"—he gestured, throwing his cigarette into the gutter. "That's all."

"What do you mean, that's *all*?"

But I knew what he meant.

"I *mean*, that's *all*." He turned his head and looked at me, pulling down the corners of his mouth. "Don't you know what I mean?" he asked, softly.

"How the hell *would* I know what you mean?" I almost whispered it, I don't know why.

"That's right," he said to the air, "how would *he* know what I mean?" He turned toward me again, patient and calm, and yet I somehow felt him shaking, shaking as though he were going to fall apart. I felt that ice in my guts again, the dread I'd felt all afternoon; and again I watched the barmaid, moving about the bar, washing glasses, and singing. "Listen. They'll let him out and then it'll just start over again. That's what I mean."

"You mean—they'll let him out. And then he'll just start working his way back in again. You mean he'll never kick the habit. Is that what you mean?"

"That's right," he said, cheerfully. "*You* see what I mean."

"Tell me," I said at last, "why does he want to die? He must want to die, he's killing himself, why does he want to die?"

He looked at me in surprise. He licked his lips. "He don't want to die. He want to live. Don't nobody want to die, ever."

Then I wanted to ask him—too many things. He could not have answered, or if he had, I could not have borne the answers. I started walking. "Well, I guess it's none of my business."

"It's going to be rough on old Sonny," he said. We reached the subway station. "This is your station?" he asked. I nodded. I took one step down. "Damn!" he said, suddenly. I looked up at him. He grinned again. "Damn if I didn't leave my money home. You ain't got a dollar on you, have you? Just for a couple days, is all."

All at once something inside gave and threatened to come pouring out of me. I didn't hate him anymore. I felt that in another moment I'd start crying like a child.

"Sure," I said. "Don't sweat." I looked in my wallet and didn't have a dollar, I only had a five. "Here," I said. "That hold you?"

He didn't look at it—he didn't want to look at it. A terrible, closed look came over his face, as though he were keeping the number on the bill a secret from him and me. "Thanks," he said, and now he was dying to see me go. "Don't worry about Sonny. Maybe I'll write him or something."

"Sure," I said. "You do that. So long."

"Be seeing you," he said. I went on down the steps.

And I didn't write Sonny or send him anything for a long time. When I finally did, it was just after my little girl died, he wrote me back a letter which made me feel like a bastard. Here's what he said:

Dear brother,

You don't know how much I needed to hear from you. I wanted to write you many a time but I dug how much I must have hurt you and so I didn't write. But now I feel like a man who's been trying to climb up out of some deep, real deep and funky hole and just saw the sun up there, outside. I got to get outside.

I can't tell you much about how I got here. I mean I don't know how to tell you. I guess I was afraid of something or I was trying to escape from something and you know I have never been very strong in the head (smile). I'm glad Mama and Daddy are dead and can't see what's happened to their son and I swear if I'd known what I was doing I would never have hurt you so, you and a lot of other fine people who were nice to me and who believed in me.

I don't want you to think it had anything to do with me being a musician. It's more than that. Or maybe less than that. I can't get anything straight in my head down here and I try not to think about what's going to happen to me when I get outside again. Sometimes I think I'm going to flip and *never* get outside and some-time I think I'll come straight back. I tell you one thing, though. I'd rather blow my brains out than go through this again. But that's what they all say, so they tell me. If I tell you when I'm coming to New York and if you could meet me, I sure would appreciate it. Give my love to Isabel and the kids and I was sure sorry to hear about little Gracie. I wish I could be like Mama and say the Lord's will be done, but I don't know it seems to me that trouble is the one thing that never does get stopped and I don't know what good it does to blame it on the Lord. But maybe it does some good if you believe it.

Your brother,
Sonny

Then I kept in constant touch with him and I sent him whatever I could and I went to meet him when he came back to New York. When I saw him, many things I thought I had forgotten came flooding back to me. This was because I had begun, finally, to wonder about Sonny, about the life that Sonny lived inside. This life, whatever it was, had made him older and thinner and it had deepened the distant stillness in which he had always moved. He looked very unlike my baby brother. Yet, when he smiled, when we shook hands, the baby brother I'd never known looked out from the depths of his private life, like an animal waiting to be coaxed into the light.

"How you been keeping?" he asked me.

"All right. And you?"

"Just fine." He was smiling all over his face. "It's good to see you again."

"It's good to see you."

The seven years' difference in our ages lay between us like a chasm: I wondered if these years would ever operate between us as a bridge. I was remembering, and it made it hard to catch my breath, that I had been there when he was born; and I had heard the first words he had ever spoken. When he started to walk, he walked from our mother straight to me. I caught him just before he fell when he took the first steps he ever took in this world.

"How's Isabel?"

"Just fine. She's dying to see you."

"And the boys?"

"They're fine, too. They're anxious to see their uncle."

"Oh, come on. You know they don't remember me."

"Are you kidding? Of course they remember you."

He grinned again. We got into a taxi. We had a lot to say to each other, far too much to know how to begin.

As the taxi began to move, I asked, "You still want to go to India?"

He laughed. "You still remember that. Hell, no. This place is Indian enough for me."

"It used to belong to them," I said.

And he laughed again. "They damn sure knew what they were doing when they got rid of it."

Years ago, when he was around 14, he'd been all hipped on the idea of going to India. He read books about people sitting on rocks, naked, in all kinds of weather, but mostly bad, naturally, and walking barefoot through hot coals and arriving at wisdom. I used to say that it sounded to me as though they were getting away from wisdom as fast as they could. I think he sort of looked down on me for that.

"Do you mind," he asked, "if we have the driver drive alongside the park? On the west side—I haven't seen the city in so long."

"Of course not," I said. I was afraid that I might sound as though I were humouring him, but I hoped he wouldn't take it that way.

So we drove along, between the green of the park and the stony, lifeless elegance of hotels and apartment buildings, toward the vivid, killing streets of our childhood. These streets hadn't changed, though housing projects jutted up out of them now like rocks in the middle of a boiling sea. Most of the houses in which we had grown up had vanished, as had the stores from which we had stolen, the basements in which we had first tried sex, the rooftops from which we had hurled tin cans and bricks. But houses exactly like the houses of our past yet dominated the landscape, boys exactly like the boys we once had been found themselves smothering in these houses, came down into the streets for light and air and found themselves encircled by disaster. Some escaped the trap, most didn't. Those who got out always left something of themselves behind, as some animals amputate a leg and leave it in the trap. It might be said, perhaps, that I had escaped, after all, I was a schoolteacher; or that Sonny had, he hadn't lived in Harlem for years. Yet, as the cab moved uptown through streets which seemed, with a rush, to darken with dark people, and as I covertly studied Sonny's face, it came to me that what we both were seeking through our separate cab windows was that part of ourselves which had been left behind. It's always at the hour of trouble and confrontation that the missing member aches.

We hit 110th Street and started rolling up Lenox Avenue. And I'd known this avenue all my life, but it seemed to me again, as it had seemed on the day I'd first heard about Sonny's trouble, filled with a hidden menace which was its very breath of life.

"We almost there," said Sonny.

"Almost." We were both too nervous to say anything more.

We live in a housing project. It hasn't been up long. A few days after it was up it seemed uninhabitably new, now, of course, it's already rundown. It looked like a parody of the good, clean, faceless life—God knows the people who live in it do their best to make it a parody. The beat-looking grass lying around isn't enough to make their lives green, the hedges will never hold out the streets, and they know it. The big windows fool no one, they aren't big enough to make space out of no space. They don't bother with the windows, they watch the TV screen instead. The playground is most popular with the children who don't play at jacks, or skip rope, or roller skate, or swing, and they can be found in it after dark. We moved in partly because it's not too far from where I teach, and partly for the kids; but it's really just like the houses in which Sonny and I grew up. The same things happen, they'll have the same things to remember. The moment Sonny and I started into the house I had the feeling that I was simply bringing him back into the danger he had almost died trying to escape.

Sonny has never been talkative. So I don't know why I was sure he'd be dying to talk to me when supper was over the first night. Everything went fine, the oldest boy remembered him, and the youngest boy liked him, and Sonny had remembered to bring something for each of them; and Isabel, who is really much nicer than I am, more open and giving, had gone to a lot of trouble about dinner and was genuinely glad to see him. And she'd always been able to tease Sonny in a way that I haven't. It was nice to see her face so vivid again and to hear her laugh and watch her make Sonny laugh. She wasn't, or, anyway, she didn't seem to be, at all uneasy or embarrassed. She chatted as though there were no subjects which had to be avoided and she got Sonny past his first, faint stiffness. And thank God she was there, for I was filled with that icy dread again. Everything I did seemed awkward to me, and everything I said sounded freighted with hidden meaning. I was trying to remember everything I'd heard about dope addiction and I couldn't help watching Sonny for signs. I wasn't doing it out of malice. I was trying to find out something about my brother. I was dying to hear him tell me he was safe.

"Safe?" my father grunted, whenever Mama suggested trying to move to a neighbourhood which might be safer for children. "Safe, hell! Ain't no place safe for kids, nor nobody."

He always went on like this, but he wasn't, ever, really as bad as he sounded, not even on weekends, when he got drunk. As a matter of fact, he was always on the lookout for "something a little better," but he died before he found it. He died suddenly, during a drunken weekend in the middle of the war, when Sonny was 15. He and Sonny hadn't ever got on too well. And this was partly because Sonny was the apple of his father's eye. It was because he loved Sonny so much and was frightened for him, that he was always fighting with him. It doesn't do any good to fight with Sonny. Sonny just moves back, inside himself, where he can't be reached. But the principal reason that they never hit it off is that they were so much alike. Daddy was big and rough and loud-talking, just the opposite of Sonny, but they both had—that same privacy.

Mama tried to tell me something about this, just after Daddy died. I was home on leave from the army.

This was the last time I ever saw my mother alive. Just the same, this picture gets all mixed up in my mind with pictures I had of her when she was younger. The way I always see her is the way she used to be on a Sunday afternoon, say, when the old folks were talking after the big Sunday dinner. I always see her wearing pale blue. She'd be sitting on the sofa. And my father would be sitting in his easy chair, not far from her. And the living room would be full of church folks and relatives. There they sit, in chairs all around the living room, and the night is creeping up outside, but nobody knows it yet. You can see the darkness growing against the windowpanes and you hear the street noises every now and again, or maybe the jangling beat of a tambourine from one of the churches close by, but it's real quiet in the room. For a moment nobody's talking, but every face looks darkening, like the sky outside. And my mother rocks a little from the waist, and my father's eyes are closed. Everyone is looking at something a child can't see. For a minute they've forgotten the children. Maybe a kid is lying on the rug, half asleep. Maybe somebody's got a kid in his lap and is absent-mindedly stroking the kid's head. Maybe there's a kid, quiet and big-eyed, curled up in a big chair in the corner. The silence, the darkness coming, and the darkness in the faces frighten the child obscurely. He hopes that the hand which strokes his forehead will never stop—will never die. He hopes that there will never come a time when the old folks won't be sitting around the living room, talking about where they've come from, and what they've seen, and what's happened to them and their kinfolk.

But something deep and watchful in the child knows that this is bound to end, is already ending. In a moment someone will get up and turn on the light. Then the old folks will remember the children and they won't talk any more that day. And when the light fills the room, the child is filled with darkness. He knows that every time this happens he's moved just a little closer to that darkness outside. The darkness outside is what the old folks have been talking about. It's what they've come from. It's what they endure. The child knows that they won't talk any more because if he knows too much about what's happened to *them*, he'll know too much too soon, about what's going to happen to *him*.

The last time I talked to my mother, I remember I was restless. I wanted to get out and see Isabel. We weren't married then and we had a lot to straighten out between us.

There Mama sat, in black, by the window. She was humming an old church song, *Lord, you brought me from a long ways off.* Sonny was out somewhere. Mama kept watching the streets.

"I don't know," she said, "if I'll ever see you again, after you go off from here. But I hope you'll remember the things I tried to teach you."

"Don't talk like that," I said, and smiled. "You'll be here a long time yet."

She smiled, too, but she said nothing. She was quiet for a long time. And I said, "Mama, don't you worry about nothing. I'll be writing all the time, and you be getting the cheques . . ."

"I want to talk to you about your brother," she said, suddenly. "If anything happens to me, he ain't going to have nobody to look out for him."

"Mama," I said, "ain't nothing going to happen to you *or* Sonny. Sonny's all right. He's a good boy and he's got good sense."

"It ain't a question of his being a good boy," Mama said, "nor of his having good sense. It ain't only the bad ones, nor yet the dumb ones that gets sucked under." She stopped, looking at me. "Your Daddy once had a brother," she said, and she smiled in a way that made me feel she was in pain. "You didn't never know that, did you?"

"No," I said. "I never knew that," and I watched her face.

"Oh, yes," she said, "your Daddy had a brother." She looked out of the window again. "I know you never saw your Daddy cry. But *I* did—many a time, through all these years."

I asked her, "What happened to his brother? How come nobody's ever talked about him?"

This was the first time I ever saw my mother look old.

"His brother got killed," she said, "when he was just a little younger than you are now. I knew him. He was a fine boy. He was maybe a little full of the devil, but he didn't mean nobody no harm."

Then she stopped, and the room was silent, exactly as it had sometimes been on those Sunday afternoons. Mama kept looking out into the streets.

"He used to have a job in the mill," she said, "and, like all young folks, he just liked to perform on Saturday nights. Saturday nights, him and your father would drift around to different places, go to dances and things like that, or just sit around with people they knew, and your father's brother would sing, he had a fine voice, and play along with himself on his guitar. Well, this particular Saturday night, him and your father was coming home from some place, and they were both a little drunk and there was a moon that night, it was bright like day. Your father's brother was feeling kind of good, and he was whistling to himself, and he had his guitar over his shoulder. They was coming down a hill, and beneath them was a road that turned off from the highway. Well, your father's brother, being always kind of frisky, decided to run down this hill, and he did, with that guitar banging and clanging behind him, and he ran across the road, and he was making water behind a tree. And your father was sort of amused at him and he was still coming down the hill, kind of slow. Then he heard a car motor and that same minute his brother stepped from behind the tree, into the road, in the moonlight. And he started to cross the road. And your father started to run down the hill, he says he don't know why. This car was full of white men. They was all drunk, and when they seen your father's brother they let out a great whoop and holler and they aimed the car straight at him. They was having fun, they just wanted to scare him, the way they do sometimes, you know. But they was drunk. And I guess the boy, being drunk, too, and scared, kind of lost his head. By the time he jumped it was too late. Your father says he heard his brother scream when the car rolled over him, and he heard the wood of that guitar when it give, and he heard them strings go flying, and he heard them white men shouting, and the car kept on a-going and it ain't stopped till this day. And, time your father got down the hill, his brother weren't nothing but blood and pulp."

Tears were gleaming on my mother's face. There wasn't anything I could say.

"He never mentioned it," she said, "because I never let him mention it before you children. Your Daddy was like a crazy man that night and for many a night thereafter. He says he never in his life seen anything as dark as that road after the lights of that car had gone away. Weren't nothing, weren't nobody on that road, just your Daddy and his brother and that busted guitar. Oh, yes. Your Daddy never did really get right again. Till the day he died he weren't sure but that every white man he saw was the man that killed his brother."

She stopped and took out her handkerchief and dried her eyes and looked at me.

"I ain't telling you all this," she said, "to make you scared or bitter or to make you hate nobody. I'm telling you this because you got a brother. And the world ain't changed."

I guess I didn't want to believe this. I guess she saw this in my face. She turned away from me, toward the window again, searching those streets.

"But I praise my Redeemer," she said at last, "that he called your Daddy home before me. I ain't saying it to throw no flowers at myself, but, I declare, it keeps me from feeling too cast down to know I helped your father get safely through this world. Your father always acted like he was the roughest, strongest man on earth. And everybody took him to be like that. But if he hadn't had *me* there—to see his tears!"

She was crying again. Still, I couldn't move. I said, "Lord, Lord, Mama, I didn't know it was like that."

"Oh, honey," she said, "there's a lot that you don't know. But you are going to find out." She stood up from the window and came over to me. "You got to hold on to your brother," she said, "and don't let him fall, no matter what it looks like is happening to him and no matter how evil you gets with him. You going to be evil with him many a time. But don't you forget what I told you, you hear?"

"I won't forget," I said. "Don't you worry, I won't forget. I won't let nothing happen to Sonny."

My mother smiled as though she were amused at something she saw in my face. Then, "You may not be able to stop nothing from happening. But you got to let him know you's *there*."

Two days later I was married, and then I was gone. And I had a lot of things on my mind and I pretty well forgot my promise to Mama until I got shipped home on a special furlough for her funeral.

And, after the funeral, with just Sonny and me alone in the empty kitchen, I tried to find out something about him.

"What do you want to do?" I asked him.

"I'm going to be a musician," he said.

For he had graduated, in the time I had been away, from dancing to the juke box to finding out who was playing what, and what they were doing with it, and he had bought himself a set of drums.

"You mean, you want to be a drummer?" I somehow had the feeling that being a drummer might be all right for other people but not for my brother Sonny.

"I don't think," he said, looking at me gravely, "that I'll ever be a good drummer. But I think I can play a piano."

I frowned. I'd never played the role of the older brother quite so seriously before, had scarcely ever, in fact, *asked* Sonny a damn thing. I sensed myself in the presence of something I didn't really know how to handle, didn't understand. So I made my frown a little deeper as I asked: "What kind of musician do you want to be?"

He grinned. "How many kinds do you think there are?"

"Be *serious*," I said.

He laughed, throwing his head back, and then looked at me. "I *am* serious."

"Well, then, for Christ's sake, stop kidding around and answer a serious question. I mean, do you want to be a concert pianist, you want to play classical music and all that, or—or, what?" Long before I finished he was laughing again. "For Christ's *sake*, Sonny!"

He sobered, but with difficulty. "I'm sorry. But you sound so—*scared*!" And he was off again.

"Well, you may think it's funny now, baby, but it's not going to be so funny when you have to make your living at it, let me tell you *that*." I was furious because I knew he was laughing at me and I didn't know why.

"No," he said, very sober now, and afraid, perhaps, that he'd hurt me, "I don't want to be a classical pianist. That isn't what interests me. I mean"—he paused, looking hard at me, as though his eyes would help me to understand, and then gestured helplessly, as though perhaps his hand would help—"I mean, I'll have a lot of studying to do, and I'll have to study *everything*, but I mean, I want to play *with*—jazz musicians." He stopped. "I want to play jazz," he said.

Well, the word had never before sounded as heavy, as real, as it sounded that afternoon in Sonny's mouth. I just looked at him and I was probably frowning a real frown by this time. I simply couldn't see why on earth he'd want to spend his time hanging around night clubs, clowning around on bandstands, while people pushed each other around a dance floor. It seemed—beneath him, somehow. I had never thought about it before, had never been forced to, but I suppose I had always put jazz musicians in a class with what Daddy called "good-time people."

"Are you *serious*?"

"Hell, *yes*, I'm serious."

He looked more helpless than ever, and annoyed, and deeply hurt.

I suggested, helpfully: "You mean—like Louis Armstrong?"

His face closed as though I'd struck him. "No. I'm not talking about none of that old-time down home crap."

"Well, look, Sonny, I'm sorry, don't get mad. I just don't altogether get it, that's all. Name somebody—you know, a jazz musician you admire."

"Bird."

"Who?"

"Bird! Charlie Parker! Don't they teach you nothing in the goddamn army?"

I lit a cigarette. I was surprised and then a little amused to discover that I was trembling. "I've been out of touch," I said. "You'll have to be patient with me. Now. Who's this Parker character?"

"He's just one of the greatest jazz musicians alive," said Sonny sullenly, his hands in his pockets, his back to me. "Maybe *the* greatest," he added, bitterly, "that's probably why *you* never heard of him."

"All right," I said, "I'm ignorant. I'm sorry. I'll go out and buy all the cat's records right away, all right?"

"It don't," said Sonny, with dignity, "make any difference to me. I don't care what you listen to. Don't do me no favours."

I was beginning to realize that I'd never seen him so upset before. With another part of my mind I was thinking that this would probably turn out to be one of those things kids go through and that I shouldn't make it seem important by pushing it too hard. Still, I didn't think it would do any harm to ask: "Doesn't all this take a lot of time? Can you make a living at it?"

He turned back to me and half leaned, half sat, on the kitchen table. "Everything takes time," he said, "and—well, yes, sure, I can make a living at it. But what I don't seem to be able to make you understand is that it's the only thing I want to do."

"Well, Sonny," I said gently, "you know people can't always do exactly what they want to do—"

"*No*, I don't know that," said Sonny, surprising me. "I think people *ought* to do what they want to do, what else are they alive for?"

"You getting to be a big boy," I said desperately, "it's time you started thinking about your future."

"I'm thinking about my future," said Sonny, grimly. "I think about it all the time."

I gave up. I decided, if he didn't change his mind, that we could always talk about it later. "In the meantime," I said, "you got to finish school." We had already decided that he'd have to move in with Isabel and her folks. I knew this wasn't the ideal arrangement because Isabel's folks are inclined to be dicty and they hadn't especially wanted Isabel to marry me. But I didn't know what else to do. "And we have to get you fixed up at Isabel's."

There was a long silence. He moved from the kitchen table to the window. "That's a terrible idea. You know it yourself."

"Do you have a *better* idea?"

He just walked up and down the kitchen for a minute. He was as tall as I was. He had started to shave. I suddenly had the feeling that I didn't know him at all.

He stopped at the kitchen table and picked up my cigarettes. Looking at me with a kind of mocking, amused defiance, he put one between his lips. "You mind?"

"You smoking already?"

He lit the cigarette and nodded, watching me through the smoke. "I just wanted to see if I'd have the courage to smoke in front of you." He grinned and blew a great cloud of smoke to the ceiling. "It was easy." He looked at my face. "Come on, now. I bet you was smoking at my age, tell the truth."

I didn't say anything but the truth was on my face, and he laughed. But now there was something very strained in his laugh. "Sure. And I bet that ain't all you was doing."

He was frightening me a little. "Cut the crap," I said. "We already decided that you was going to go and live at Isabel's. Now what's got into you all of a sudden?"

"*You* decided it," he pointed out. "*I* didn't decide nothing." He stopped in front of me, leaning against the stove, arms loosely folded. "Look, brother. I don't want to stay in Harlem no more, I really don't." He was very earnest. He looked at me, then over toward the kitchen window. There was something in his eyes I'd never seen before, some thoughtfulness, some worry all his own. He rubbed the muscle of one arm. "It's time I was getting out of here."

"Where do you want to *go*, Sonny?"

"I want to join the army. Or the navy, I don't care. If I say I'm old enough, they'll believe me."

Then I got mad. It was because I was so scared. "You must be crazy. You goddamn fool, what the hell do you want to go and join the *army* for?"

"I just told you. To get out of Harlem."

"Sonny, you haven't even finished *school*. And if you really want to be a musician, how do you expect to study if you're in the *army*?"

He looked at me, trapped, and in anguish. "There's ways. I might be able to work out some kind of deal. Anyway, I'll have the G.I. Bill when I come out."

"*If* you come out." We stared at each other. "Sonny, please. Be reasonable. I know the setup is far from perfect. But we got to do the best we can."

"I ain't learning nothing in school," he said. "Even when I go." He turned away from me and opened the window and threw his cigarette out into the narrow alley. I watched his back. "At least, I ain't learning nothing you'd want me to learn." He slammed the window so hard I though the glass would fly out, and turned back to me. "And I'm sick of the stink of these garbage cans!"

"Sonny," I said, "I know how you feel. But if you don't finish school now, you're going to be sorry later that you didn't." I grabbed him by the shoulders. "And you only got another year. It ain't so bad. And I'll come back and I swear I'll help you do *whatever* you want to do. Just try to put up with it till I come back. Will you please do that? For me?"

He didn't answer and he wouldn't look at me.

"Sonny. You hear me?"

He pulled away. "I hear you. But you never hear anything *I* say."

I didn't know what to say to that. He looked out of the window and then back at me. "OK," he said, and sighed. "I'll try."

Then I said, trying to cheer him up a little, "They got a piano at Isabel's. You can practise on it."

And as a matter of fact, it did cheer him up for a minute. "That's right," he said to himself. "I forgot that." His face relaxed a little. But the worry, the thoughtfulness, played on it still, the way shadows play on a face which is staring into the fire.

But I thought I'd never hear the end of that piano. At first, Isabel would write me, saying how nice it was that Sonny was so serious about his music and how, as soon as he came in from school, or wherever he had been when he was supposed to be at school, he went straight to that piano and stayed there until suppertime. And, after supper, he went back to that piano and stayed there until everybody went to bed. He was at that piano all day Saturday and all day Sunday. Then he bought a record player and started playing records. He'd play one record over and over again, all day long sometimes, and he'd improvise along with it on the piano. Or he'd play one section of the record, one chord, one change, one progression, then he'd do it on the piano. Then back to the record. Then back to the piano.

Well, I really don't know how they stood it. Isabel finally confessed that it wasn't like living with a person at all, it was like living with sound. And the sound didn't make any sense to her, didn't make any sense to any of them—naturally. They began, in a way, to be afflicted by this presence that was living in their home. It was as though Sonny were some sort of god, or monster. He moved in an atmosphere which wasn't like theirs at all. They fed him and he ate, he washed himself, he walked in and out of their door; he certainly wasn't nasty or unpleasant or rude, Sonny isn't any of those things; but it was as though he were all wrapped up in some cloud, some fire, some vision all of his own; and there wasn't any way to reach him.

At the same time, he wasn't really a man yet, he was still a child, and they had to watch out for him in all kinds of ways. They certainly couldn't throw him out. Neither did they dare to make a great scene about that piano because even they dimly sensed, as I sensed, from so many thousands of miles away, that Sonny was at that piano playing for his life.

But he hadn't been going to school. One day a letter came from the school board, and Isabel's mother got it—there had, apparently, been other letters but Sonny had torn them up. This day, when Sonny came in, Isabel's mother showed him the letter and asked where he'd been spending his time. And she finally got it out of him that he'd been down in Greenwich Village, with musicians and other characters, in a white girl's apartment. And this scared her and she started to scream at him, and what came up, once she began—though she denies it to this day—was what sacrifices they were making to give Sonny a decent home and how little he appreciated it.

Sonny didn't play the piano that day. By evening, Isabel's mother had calmed down but then there was the old man to deal with, and Isabel herself. Isabel says she did her best to be calm but she broke down and started crying. She says she just watched Sonny's face. She could tell, by watching him, what was happening with him. And what was happening was that they penetrated his cloud, they had reached him. Even if their fingers had been a thousand times more gentle than human fingers ever are, he could hardly help feeling that they had stripped him naked and were spitting on that nakedness. For he also had to see that his presence, that music, which was life or death to him, had been torture for them and that they had endured it, not at all for his sake, but only for mine. And Sonny couldn't take that. He can take it a little better today than he could then but he's still not very good at it and, frankly, I don't know anybody who is.

The silence of the next few days must have been louder than the sound of all the music ever played since time began. One morning, before she went to work, Isabel was in his room for something and she suddenly realized that all of his records were gone. And she knew for certain that he was gone. And he was. He went as far as the navy would carry him. He finally sent me a postcard from someplace in Greece, and that was the first I knew that Sonny was still alive. I didn't see him any more until we were both back in New York and the war had long been over.

He was a man then, of course, but I wasn't willing to see it. He came by the house from time to time, but we fought almost every time we met. I didn't like the way he carried himself, loose and dreamlike all the time, and I didn't like his friends, and his music seemed to be merely an excuse for the life he led. It sounded just that weird and disordered.

Then we had a fight, a pretty awful fight, and I didn't see him for months. By and by I looked him up, where he was living, in a furnished room in the Village, and I tried to make it up. But there were lots of other people in the room, and Sonny just lay on his bed, and he wouldn't come downstairs with me, and he treated these other people as though they were his family and I weren't. So I got mad and then he got mad, and then I told him that he might just as well be dead as live the way he was living. Then he stood up and he told me not to worry about him any more in life, that he *was* dead as far as I was concerned. Then he pushed me to the door, and the other people looked on as though nothing were happening, and he slammed the door behind me. I stood in the hallway, staring at the door. I heard somebody laugh in the room and then the tears came to my eyes. I started down the steps, whistling to keep from crying, I kept whistling to myself, *You going to need me, baby, one of these cold, rainy days.*

I read about Sonny's trouble in the spring. Little Grace died in the fall. She was a beautiful little girl. But she only lived a little over two years. She died of polio and she suffered. She had a slight fever for a couple of days, but it didn't seem like anything and we just kept her in bed. And we would certainly have called the doctor, but the fever dropped, she seemed to be all right. So we thought it had just been a cold. Then, one day, she was up, playing, Isabel was in the kitchen fixing lunch for the two boys when they'd come in from school, and she heard Grace fall down in the living room. When you have a lot of children you don't always start running when one of them falls, unless they start screaming or something. And, this time, Grace was quiet. Yet, Isabel says that when she heard that *thump* and then that silence, something happened in her to make her afraid. And she ran to the living room and there was little Grace on the floor, all twisted up, and the reason she hadn't screamed was that she couldn't get her breath. And when she did scream, it was the worst sound, Isabel says, that she's ever heard in all her life, and she still hears it sometimes in her dreams. Isabel will sometimes wake me up with a low, moaning, strangled sound, and I have to be quick to awaken her and hold her to me and where Isabel is weeping against me seems a mortal wound.

I think I may have written Sonny the very day that little Grace was buried. I was sitting in the living room in the dark, by myself, and I suddenly thought of Sonny. My trouble made his real.

One Saturday afternoon, when Sonny had been living with us, or, anyway, been in our house, for nearly two weeks, I found myself wandering aimlessly about the living room, drinking from a can of beer, and trying to work up the courage to search Sonny's room. He was out, he was usually out whenever I was home, and Isabel had taken the children to see their grandparents. Suddenly I was standing still in front of the living room window, watching Seventh Avenue. The idea of searching Sonny's room made me still. I scarcely dared to admit to myself what I'd be searching for. I didn't know what I'd do if I found it. Or if I didn't.

On the sidewalk across from me, near the entrance to a barbecue joint, some people were holding an old-fashioned revival meeting. The barbecue cook, wearing a dirty white apron, his conked hair reddish and metallic in the pale sun, and a cigarette between his lips, stood in the doorway, watching them. Kids and older people paused in their errands and stood there, along with some older men and a couple of very tough-looking women who watched everything that happened on the avenue, as though they owned it, or were maybe owned by it. Well, they were watching this, too. The revival was being carried on by three sisters in black, and a brother. All they had were their voices and their Bibles and a tambourine. The brother was testifying and while he testified two of the sisters stood together, seeming to say, Amen, and the third sister walked around with the tambourine outstretched and a couple of people dropped coins into it. Then the brother's testimony ended, and the sister who had been taking up the collection dumped the coins into her palm and transferred them to the pocket of her long black robe. Then she raised both hands, striking the tambourine against the air, and then against one hand, and she started to sing. And the two sisters and the brother joined in.

It was strange, suddenly to watch, though I had been seeing these street meetings all my life. So, of course, had everybody else down there. Yet, they paused and watched and listened and I stood still at the window. *'Tis the old ship of Zion,'* they sang, and the sister with the tambourine kept a steady, jangling beat, *'it has rescued many a thousand!'* Not a soul under the sound of their voices was hearing this song for the first time, not one of them had been rescued. Nor had they seen much in the way of rescue work being done around them. Neither did they especially believe in the holiness of the three sisters and the brother, they knew too much about them, knew where they lived, and how. The woman with the tambourine, whose voice dominated the air, whose face was bright with joy, was divided by very little from the woman who stood watching her, a cigarette between her heavy, chapped lips, her hair a cuckoo's nest, her face scarred and swollen from many beatings, and her black eyes glittering like coal. Perhaps they both knew this, which was why, when as rarely, they addressed each other, they addressed each other as Sister. As the singing filled the air, the watching, listening faces underwent a change, the eyes focusing on something within; the music seemed to soothe a poison out of them; and time seemed, nearly, to fall away from the sullen, belligerent, battered faces, as though they were fleeing back to their first condition, while dreaming of their last. The barbecue cook half shook his head and smiled, and dropped his cigarette and disappeared into his joint. A man fumbled in his pockets for change and stood holding it in his hand impatiently, as though he had just remembered a pressing appointment further up the avenue. He looked furious. Then I saw Sonny, standing on the edge of the crowd. He was carrying a wide, flat notebook with a green cover, and it made him look, from where I was standing, almost like a schoolboy. The coppery sun brought out the copper in his skin, he was very faintly smiling, standing very still. Then the singing stopped, the tambourine turned into a collection plate again. The furious man dropped in his coins and vanished, so did a couple of the women, and Sonny dropped some change in the plate, looking directly at the woman with a little smile. He started across the avenue, toward the house. He has a slow, loping walk, something like the way Harlem hipsters walk, only he's imposed on this his own half-beat. I had never really noticed it before.

I stayed at the window, both relieved and apprehensive. As Sonny disappeared from my sight, they began singing again. And they were still singing when his key turned in the lock.

"Hey," he said.

"Hey, yourself. You want some beer?"

"No. Well, maybe." But he came up to the window and stood beside me, looking out. "What a warm voice," he said.

They were singing *If I could only hear my mother pray again!*

"Yes," I said, "and she can sure beat that tambourine."

"But what a terrible song," he said, and laughed. He dropped his notebook on the sofa and disappeared into the kitchen. "Where's Isabel and the kids?"

"I think they went to see their grandparents. You hungry?"

"No." He came back into the living room with his can of beer. "You want to come someplace with me tonight?"

I sensed, I don't know how, that I couldn't possibly say no. "Sure. Where?"

He sat down on the sofa and picked up his notebook and started leafing through it. "I'm going to sit in with some fellows in a joint in the Village."

"You mean, you're going to play, tonight?"

"That's right." He took a swallow of his beer and moved back to the window. He gave me a sidelong look. "If you can stand it."

"I'll try," I said.

He smiled to himself, and we both watched as the meeting across the way broke up. The three sisters and the brother, heads bowed, were singing *God be with you till we meet again*. The faces around them were very quiet. Then the song ended. The small crowd dispersed. We watched the three women and the one man walk slowly up the avenue.

"When she was singing before," said Sonny, abruptly, "her voice reminded me for a minute of what heroin feels like sometimes—when it's in your veins. It makes you feel sort of warm and cool at the same time. And distant. And—and sure." He sipped his beer, very deliberately not looking at me. I watched his face. "It makes you feel—in control. Sometimes you've got to have that feeling."

"Do you?" I sat down slowly in the easy chair.

"Sometimes." He went to the sofa and picked up his notebook again. "Some people do."

"In order," I asked, "to play?" And my voice was very ugly, full of contempt and anger.

"Well"—he looked at me with great, troubled eyes, as though, in fact, he hoped his eyes would tell me things he could never otherwise say—"they *think* so. And *if* they think so—!"

"And what do *you* think?" I asked.

He sat on the sofa and put his can of beer on the floor. "I don't know," he said, and I couldn't be sure if he were answering my question or pursuing his thoughts. His face didn't tell me. "It's not so much to *play*. It's to *stand* it, to be able to make it at all. On any level." He frowned and smiled: "In order to keep from shaking to pieces."

"But these friends of yours," I said, "they seem to shake themselves to pieces pretty goddamn fast."

"Maybe." He played with the notebook. And something told me that I should curb my tongue, that Sonny was doing his best to talk, and I should listen. "But of course you only know the ones that've gone to pieces. Some don't—or at least they haven't *yet* and that's just about all *any* of us can say." He paused. "And then there are some who just live, really, in hell, and they know it and they see what's happening and they go right on. I don't know." He sighed, dropped the notebook, folded his arms. "Some guys, you can tell from the way they play, they on something *all* the time. And you can see that, well, it makes something real for them. But of course," he picked up his beer from the floor and sipped it and put it back down again, "they *want* to, too, you've got to see that. Even some of them that say they don't—*some*, not all."

"And what about you?" I asked—I couldn't help it. "What about you? Do *you* want to?"

He stood up and walked to the window and remained silent for a long time. Then he sighed. "Me," he said. Then: "While I was downstairs before, on my way here, listening to that woman sing, it struck me all of a sudden how much suffering she must have had to go through—to sing like that. It's *repulsive* to think you have to suffer that much."

I said: "But there's no way not to suffer—is there, Sonny?"

"I believe not," he said, and smiled, "but that's never stopped anyone from trying." He looked at me. "Has it?" I realized, with this mocking look, that there stood between us, forever, beyond the power of time or forgiveness, the fact that I had held silence—so long!—when he had needed human speech to help him. He turned back to the window. "No, there's no way not to suffer. But you try all kinds of ways to keep from drowning in it, to keep on top of it, and to make it seem—well, like *you*. Like you did something, all right, and now you're suffering for it. You know?" I said nothing. "Well you know," he said, impatiently, "why *do* people suffer? Maybe it's better to do something to give it a reason, *any* reason."

"But we just agreed," I said, "that there's no way not to suffer. Isn't it better, then, just to—take it?"

"But nobody just takes it," Sonny cried, "that's what I'm telling you! *Everybody* tries not to. You're just hung up on the *way* some people try—it's not *your* way!"

The hair on my face began to itch, my face felt wet. "That's not true," I said, "that's not true. I don't give a damn what other people do, I don't even care how they suffer. I just care how *you* suffer." And he looked at me. "Please believe me," I said, "I don't want to see you—die—trying not to suffer."

"I won't," he said, flatly, "die trying not to suffer. At least, not any faster than anybody else."

"But there's no need," I said, trying to laugh, "is there, in killing yourself?"

I wanted to say more, but I couldn't. I wanted to talk about willpower and how life could be—well, beautiful. I wanted to say that it was all within; but was it? Or, rather, wasn't that exactly the trouble? And I wanted to promise that I would never fail him again. But it would all have sounded—empty words and lies.

So I made the promise to myself and prayed that I would keep it.

"It's terrible sometimes, inside," he said, "that's what's the trouble. You walk these streets, black and funky and cold, and there's not really a living ass to talk to, and there's nothing shaking, and there's no way of getting it out—that storm inside. You can't talk it and you can't make love with it, and when you finally try to get with it and play it, you realize *nobody's* listening. So *you've* got to listen. You got to find a way to listen."

And then he walked away from the window and sat on the sofa again, as though all the wind had suddenly been knocked out of him. "Sometimes you'll do *anything* to play, even cut your mother's throat." He laughed and looked at me. "Or your brother's." Then he sobered. "Or your own." Then: "Don't worry. I'm all right now and I think I'll *be* all right. But I can't forget—where I've been. I don't mean just the physical place I've been, I mean where I've *been*. And *what* I've been."

"What have you been, Sonny?" I asked.

He smiled—but sat sideways on the sofa, his elbow resting on the back, his fingers playing with his mouth and chin, not looking at me. "I've been something I didn't realize, didn't know I could be. Didn't know anybody could be." He stopped, looking inward, looking helplessly young, looking old. "I'm not talking about it now because

I feel *guilty* or anything like that—maybe it would be better if I did. I don't know. Anyway, I can't really talk about it. Not to you, not to anybody." And now he turned to face me. "Sometimes, you know, and it was actually when I was most out of the world, I felt that I was in it, that I was *with* it, really, and I could play or I didn't really have to *play*, it just came out of me, it was there. And I don't know how I played, think-ing about it now, but I know I did awful things, those times, sometimes, to people. Or it wasn't that I *did* anything to them—it was that they weren't real." He picked up the beer can; it was empty; he rolled it between his palms: "And other times—well, I needed a fix, I needed to find a place to lean, I needed to clear a space to *listen*—and I couldn't find it, and I—went crazy, I did terrible things to *me*, I was terrible *for* me." He began pressing the beer can between his hands, I watched the metal begin to give. It glittered, as he played with it, like a knife, and I was afraid he would cut himself, but I said nothing. "Oh well. I can never tell you. I was all by myself at the bottom of something, stinking and sweating and crying and shaking, and I smelled it, you know? *My* stink, and I thought I'd die if I couldn't get away from it and yet, all the same, I knew that everything I was doing was just locking me in with it. And I didn't know," he paused, still flattening the beer can, "I didn't know, I still *don't* know, something kept telling me that maybe it was good to smell your own stink, but I didn't think that *that* was what I'd been trying to do—and—who can stand it?" And he abruptly dropped the ruined beer can, looking at me with a small, still smile, and then rose, walking to the window as though it were the lodestone rock. I watched his face, he watched the avenue. "I couldn't tell you when Mama died—but the reason I wanted to leave Harlem so bad was to get away from drugs. And then, when I ran away, that's what I was running from—really. When I came back, nothing had changed, *I* hadn't changed, I was just—older." And he stopped, drumming with his fingers on the win-dowpane. The sun had vanished, soon darkness would fall. I watched his face. "It can come again," he said, almost as though speaking to himself. Then he turned to me. "It can come again," he repeated. "I just want you to know that."

"All right," I said at last. "So it can come again. All right."

He smiled, but the smile was sorrowful. "I had to try to tell you," he said.

"Yes," I said. "I understand that."

"You're my brother," he said, looking straight at me, and not smiling at all.

"Yes," I repeated, "yes, I understand that."

He turned back to the window, looking out. "All that hatred down there," he said, "all that hatred and misery and love. It's a wonder it doesn't blow the avenue apart."

We went to the only night club on a short, dark street, downtown. We squeezed through the narrow, chattering, jam-packed bar to the entrance of the big room, where the bandstand was. And we stood there for a moment, for the lights were very dim, in this room and we couldn't see. Then, "Hello, boy," said a voice, and an enormous black man, much older than Sonny or myself, erupted out of all that atmospheric lighting and put an arm around Sonny's shoulder. "I been sitting right here," he said, "waiting for you."

He had a big voice, too, and heads in the darkness turned toward us.

Sonny grinned and pulled a little away, and said, "Creole, this is my brother. I told you about him."

Creole shook my hand. "I'm glad to meet you, son." he said, and it was clear that he was glad to meet me *there*, for Sonny's sake. And he smiled. "You got a real musician in *your* family," and he took his arm from Sonny's shoulder and slapped him, lightly, affectionately, with the back of his hand.

"Well. Now I've heard fit all," said a voice behind us. This was another musician, and a friend of Sonny's, a coal-black, cheerful-looking man, built close to the ground. He immediately began confiding to me, at the top of his lungs, the most terrible things about Sonny, his teeth gleaming like a lighthouse and his laugh coming up out of him like the beginning of an earthquake. And it turned out that everyone at the bar knew Sonny, or almost everyone; some were musicians, working there, or nearby, or not working, some were simply hangers-on, and some were there to hear Sonny play. I was introduced to all of them and they were all very polite to me. Yet, it was clear that, for them, I was only Sonny's brother. Here, I was in Sonny's world. Or, rather: his kingdom. Here, it was not even a question that his veins bore royal blood.

They were going to play soon, and Creole installed me, by myself, at a table in a dark corner. Then I watched them, Creole, and the little black man, and Sonny, and the others, while they horsed around, standing just below the bandstand. The light from the bandstand spilled just a little short of them and, watching them laughing and gesturing and moving about, I had the feeling that they, nevertheless, were being most careful not to step into that circle of light too suddenly: that if they moved into the light too suddenly, without thinking, they would perish in flame. Then, while I watched, one of them, the small, black man, moved into the light and crossed the bandstand and started fooling around with his drums. Then—being funny and being, also, extremely ceremonious—Creole took Sonny by the arm and led him to the piano. A woman's voice called Sonny's name, and a few hands started clapping. And Sonny, also being funny and being ceremonious, and so touched, I think, that he could have cried, but neither hiding it nor showing it, riding it like a man, grinned, and put both hands to his heart and bowed from the waist.

Creole then went to the bass fiddle and a lean, very bright-skinned brown man jumped up on the bandstand and picked up his horn. So there they were, and the atmosphere on the bandstand and in the room began to change and tighten. Someone stepped up to the microphone and announced them. Then there were all kinds of murmurs. Some people at the bar shushed others. The waitress ran around, frantically getting in the last orders, guys and chicks got closer to each other, and the lights on the bandstand, on the quartet, turned to a kind of indigo. Then they all looked different there. Creole looked about him for the last time, as though he were making certain that all his chickens were in the coop, and then he—jumped and struck the fiddle. And there they were.

All I know about music is that not many people ever really hear it. And even then, on the rare occasions when something opens within, and the music enters, what we mainly hear, or hear corroborated, are personal, private, vanishing evocations. But the man who creates the music is hearing something else, is dealing with the roar rising from the void and imposing order on it as it hits the air. What is evoked in him, then, is of another order, more terrible because it has no words, and triumphant, too, for that same reason. And his triumph, when he triumphs, is ours. I just watched Sonny's face. His face was troubled, he was working hard, but he wasn't with it. And I had the feeling that, in a way, everyone on the bandstand was waiting for him, both waiting for him for him and pushing him along. But as I began to watch Creole, I realized that it was Creole who held them all back. He had them on a short rein. Up there, keeping the beat with his whole body, wailing on the fiddle, with his eyes half closed, he was listening to everything, but he was listening to Sonny. He was having a dialogue with Sonny. He wanted Sonny to leave the shore line and strike out for the deep water. He was Sonny's witness that deep water and drowning were not the same thing—he had been there, and he knew. And he wanted Sonny to know. He was waiting for Sonny to do the things on the keys which would let Creole know that Sonny was in the water.

And, while Creole listened, Sonny moved, deep within, exactly like someone in torment. I had never before thought of how awful the relationship must be between the musician and his instrument. He has to fill it, this instrument, with the breath of life, his own. He has to make it do what he wants it to do. And a piano is just a piano. It's made out of so much wood and wires and little hammers and big ones, and ivory. While there's only so much you can do with it, the only way to find this out is to try and make it do everything.

And Sonny hadn't been near a piano for over a year. And he wasn't on much better terms with his life, not the life that stretched before him now. He and the piano stammered, started one way, got scared, stopped; started another way, panicked, marked time, started again; then seemed to have found a direction, panicked again, got stuck. And the face I saw on Sonny I'd never seen before. Everything had been burned out of it, and, at the same time, things usually hidden were being burned in, by the fire and fury of the battle which was occurring in him up there.

Yet, watching Creole's face as they neared the end of the first set, I had the feeling that something had happened, something I hadn't heard. Then they finished, there was scattered applause, and then, without an instant's warning, Creole started into something else, it was almost sardonic, it was *Am I Blue*. And, as though he commanded, Sonny began to play. Something began to happen. And Creole let out the reins. The dry, low, black man said something awful on the drums, Creole answered, and the drums talked back. Then the horn insisted sweet and high, slightly detached perhaps, and Creole listened, commenting now and then, dry, and driving, beautiful and calm and old. Then they all came together again, and Sonny was part of the family again. I could tell this from his face. He seemed to have found, right there beneath his fingers, a damn brand-new piano. It seemed that he couldn't get over it. Then, for a while, just being happy with Sonny, they seemed to be agreeing with him that brand-new pianos certainly were a gas.

Then Creole stepped forward to remind them that what they were playing was the blues. He hit something in all of them, he hit something in me, myself, and the music tightening and deepened, apprehension began to beat the air. Creole began to tell us what the blues were all about. They were not about anything very new. He and his boys up there were keeping it new, at the risk of ruin, destruction, madness, and death, in order to find new ways to make us listen. For, while the tale of how we suffer, and how we are delighted, and how we may triumph is never new, it always must be heard. There isn't any other tale to tell, it's the only light we've got in all this darkness.

And this tale, according to that face, that body, those strong hands on those strings, has another aspect in every country, land a new depth in every generation. Listen, Creole seemed to be saying, listen. Now these are Sonny's blues. He made the little black man on the drums know it, and the bright, brown man on the horn. Creole wasn't trying any longer to get Sonny in the water. He was wishing him Godspeed. Then he stepped back, very slowly, filling the air with the immense suggestion that Sonny speak for himself.

Then they all gathered around Sonny, and Sonny played. Every now and again one of them seemed to say, Amen. Sonny's fingers filled the air with life, his life. But that life contained so many others. And Sonny went all the way back, he really began with the spare, flat statement of the opening phrase of the song. Then he began to make it his. It was very beautiful because it wasn't hurried and it was no longer a lament. I seemed to hear with what burning he had made it his, with what burning we had yet to make it ours, how we could cease lamenting. Freedom lurked around us and I understood, at last, that he could help us to be free if we would listen, that he would never be free until we did. Yet, there was no battle in his face now. I heard what he had gone through, and would continue to go through until he came to rest in earth. He had made it his: that long line, of which we knew only Mama and Daddy. And he was giving it back, as everything must be given back, so that, passing through death, it can live forever. I saw my mother's face again, and felt, for the first time, how the stone of the road she had walked on must have bruised her feet. I saw the moonlit road where my father's brother died. And it brought something else back to me, and carried me past it. I saw my little girl again and felt Isabel's tears again, and I felt my own tears begin to rise. And I was yet aware that this was only a moment, that the world waited outside, as hungry as a tiger, and that trouble stretched above us, longer than the sky.

Then it was over. Creole and Sonny let out their breath, both soaking wet, and grinning. There was a lot of applause and some of it was real. In the dark, the girl came by and I asked her to take drinks to the bandstand. There was a long pause, while they talked up there in the indigo light and after a while I saw the girl put a Scotch and milk on top of the piano for Sonny. He didn't seem to notice it, but just before they started playing again, he sipped from it and looked toward me, and nodded. Then he put it back on top of the piano. For me, then, as they began to play again, it glowed and shook above my brother's head like the very cup of trembling.

F.Y.I.

Charlie "Bird" Parker: (1920–1955) an American jazz saxophonist who pioneered a jazz style known as "bebop." Bebop was an experimental form of music that challenged traditional musical forms. Parker died of a heroin overdose at the age of 35.

dicty: slang for dictatorial or bossy

dope: informal term for cannabis (marijuana)

Greenwich Village: a neighbourhood in downtown Manhattan (New York City) where many artists, musicians, and writers lived

horse: slang for heroin

Louis Armstrong: (1901–1971) an American jazz artist, vocalist, and trumpet player who was born in New Orleans and whose music would have been seen as old fashioned by jazz fans in the 1950s

polio: an infectious viral disease that affects the central nervous system and causes paralysis

revival meeting: a Christian meeting, specifically evangelical

Words to Build on

belligerent: hostile and aggressive

furlough: leave of absence

malice: the intention or desire to cause evil

menace: a person or thing that could cause harm

parody: an imitation of a style with exaggeration for comic effect

quicksilver: moving or changing quickly

raggy: informal word for ragged, meaning old, torn, or rough

sullen: moody and/or bad tempered

Tricks of the Trade

Character

Climax

Imagery

Symbol

In Your Own Words: Comprehension

1. What do you know about the narrator?

2. What does the narrator mean when he states in paragraph two "He became real to me again"?

3. How is Sonny described by the narrator?

4. What does the narrator read about Sonny in the newspaper?

5. How does the narrator describe life for young people in Harlem at this time?

6. After the father dies, the narrator arranges for Sonny to live in his fiancée's (Isabel's) family home. Describe Sonny's life with this family.

7. What word evoking a certain image is repeated in the first five paragraphs of this story? Why is the writer using this particular word?

8. How does Sonny describe what heroin feels like?

9. What drinks does the girl bring to Sonny when he is performing at the end of the story? Is this combination unusual?

10. Comment on the significance of Baldwin's choice of names for the characters of Sonny and Grace.

In Your Own Words: Analysis

1. How does the narrator treat Sonny's friends? Would you say his behaviour is typical of an older sibling towards a younger sibling's friends? Is he judgmental or is he fair in his assessments of the friends?

2. This is a story of two sets of siblings: the narrator and Sonny, and the father and his brother. In what ways are the relationships similar and how are they different?

3. Why do the parents decide not to tell Sonny and the narrator the story of the uncle when they are young? Is it right to keep this secret? Does it cause any harm?

4. Most of the characters in this story (the narrator, Sonny, their parents, Isabel) face deep emotional pain, either through some type of loss or sensitivity to life's struggles. How does each character deal with his or her pain?

5. Explain this quote from the story in your own words: "Creole began to tell us what the blues were all about. They were not about anything very new . . . For, while the tale of how we suffer, and how we are delighted, and how we may triumph is never new, it always must be heard. There isn't any other tale to tell, it's the only light we've got in all this darkness. And this tale, according to that face, that body, those strong hands on those strings, has another aspect in every country, and a new depth in every generation . . . Now these are Sonny's blues." What is the "tale" the narrator refers to? Do you agree with the narrator, that this tale must be heard? Why or why not?

6. Does the narrator ever come to understand Sonny, his music, and his addiction? Are the last two related in some way?

7. Does the narrator himself change in some way by the end of the story?

8. How does Baldwin depict Sonny as an artist in this story?

❊ Now Write

1. What should be the role of an artist in society? Does the artist have a social function? Write an essay in which you answer these questions using "Sonny's Blues." Does Sonny fit the role of an artist in society according to your definition? Why or why not? Must an artist also make sacrifices for his or her art?

2. What role does religion play in this story? Does it alleviate suffering, offer guidance, or hinder a character's development? Consider names of characters and any biblical allusions.

3. The narrator of this story does not approve of his brother's drug use, but is Baldwin's story really about misusing drugs? Consider the references to drugs and addiction in this story and write an essay examining what Baldwin is trying to convey about drugs and addiction.

4. Can art and culture, specifically music, help a person transcend his or her own pain and suffering? Write an essay making reference to "Sonny's Blues" to show how music is for more than just entertainment.

Margaret Laurence

Margaret Laurence (1926–1987) was born and raised in the Canadian prairie town of Neepawa, Manitoba. Both her parents died when she was a young girl, so she was raised by her grandfather and her aunt, who was a librarian and teacher. When Laurence was a girl it was her aunt who encouraged her love of reading literature and writing. Laurence decided early on that she wanted to write. She received her degree in English and began working as a journalist while also writing short stories. After marrying her husband, a civil engineer, Laurence lived in many countries around the world: England, Somalia, Ghana, Greece, Palestine, India, Egypt, and Spain. It was in Africa that Laurence would give serious attention to the craft of writing fiction: she wrote a number of stories and a novel, *This Side Jordan* (1960), which focuses on African subjects. Although she lived in many places, the Canadian prairies feature prominently in her work, and she is regarded as a Canadian literary icon. Her first novel with Canadian subject matter, *The Stone Angel* (1964), and others that would follow made her one of the greatest novelists of the twentieth century.

Her stories often feature strong women and their struggles for understanding and acceptance. In "The Loons," taken from her short story collection *A Bird in the House* (1970), Laurence explores the tension between the Metis community and white culture as it is reflected through the relationship of two young girls.

Laurence won many major awards, including the First Novel Award and the Governor General's Award, for her fiction. She died of cancer in Lakefield, Ontario, at the age of 61.

In Her Own Words

"When I say 'work' I only mean writing. Everything else is just odd jobs."

"When I was 18, I couldn't wait to get out of [my hometown], away from the prairies. I did not know then that I would carry the land and town all my life within my skull, that they would form the mainspring and source of writing I was to do, wherever and however far away I might live."

Before We Begin

1. Do young girls relate to each other in the same way that boys do? Do girls get along because they share the same experiences?

2. Have you experienced first-hand any of Canada's natural landscapes and environments? Which ones, and how did they affect you?

3. Have you ever visited a natural environment from your youth that has since been altered by urbanization?

4.   Is there such a thing as being born unlucky?
5.   What are the ways that people demonstrate their cultural/ethnic identity through personal style?

 **Now Read**

The Loons

Just below Manawaka, where the Wachakwa River ran brown and noisy over the pebbles, the scrub oak and grey-green willow and chokecherry bushes grew in a dense thicket. In a clearing at the centre of the thicket stood the Tonnerre family's shack. The basis of this dwelling was a small square cabin made of poplar poles and chinked with mud, which had been built by Jules Tonnerre some 50 years before, when he came back from Batoche with a bullet in his thigh the year that Riel was hung and the voices of the Metis entered their long silence. Jules had only intended to stay the winter in the Wachakwa Valley, but the family was still there in the 30s, when I was a child. As the Tonnerres had increased, their settlement had been added to, until the clearing at the foot of the town hill was a chaos of lean-tos, wooden packing cases, warped lumber, discarded car tires, ramshackle chicken coops, tangled strands of barbed wire, and rusty tin cans.

The Tonnerres were French half-breeds, and among themselves they spoke a *patois* that was neither Cree nor French. Their English was broken and full of obscenities. They did not belong among the Cree of the Galloping Mountain reservation, further north, and they did not belong among the Scots-Irish and Ukrainians of Manawaka, either. They were, as my Grandmother MacLeod would have put it, neither flesh, fowl, good salt herring. When their men were not working at odd jobs or as section hands on the CPR, they lived on relief. In the summers, one of the Tonnerre youngsters, with a face that seemed totally unfamiliar with laughter, would knock at the doors of the town's brick houses and offer for sale a lard-pail full of bruised wild strawberries, and if he got as much as a quarter he would grab the coin and run before the customer had time to change her mind. Sometimes old Jules, or his son Lazarus, would get mixed up in a Saturday night brawl, and would hit out at whoever was nearest, or howl drunkenly among the offended shoppers on Main Street; and then the Mountie would put them for the night in the barred cell underneath the court house, and the next morning they would be quiet again.

Piquette Tonnerre, the daughter of Lazarus, was in my class at school. She was older than I, but she had failed several grades, perhaps because her attendance had always been sporadic and her interest in schoolwork negligible. Part of the reason she had missed a lot of school was that she had had tuberculosis of the bone, and had once spent months in hospital. I knew this because my father was the doctor who had looked after her. Her sickness was almost the only thing I knew about her, however. Otherwise, she existed for me only as a vaguely embarrassing presence, with her hoarse voice and her clumsy limping walk and her grimy cotton dresses that were always miles too long.

I was neither friendly nor unfriendly towards her. She dwelt and moved somewhere within my scope of vision, but I did not actually notice her very much until that peculiar summer when I was 11.

"I don't know what to do about that kid," my father said at dinner one evening. "Piquette Tonnerre, I mean. The damn bone's flared up again. I've had her in hospital for quite a while now, and it's under control all right, but I hate like the dickens to send her home again."

"Couldn't you explain to her mother that she has to rest a lot?" my mother said.

"The mother's not there," my father replied. "She took off a few years back. Can't say I blame her. Piquette cooks for them, and she says Lazarus never do anything for himself as long as she's there. Anyway, I don't think she'd take much care of herself, once she got back. She's only 13, after all. Beth, I was thinking—what about taking her up to Diamond Lake with us this summer? A couple of months rest would give that bone a much better chance."

My mother looked stunned.

"But Ewen—what about Roddie and Vanessa?"

"She's not contagious," my father said. "And it would be company for Vanessa."

"Oh dear," my mother said in distress, "I'll bet anything she has nits in her hair."

"For Pete's sake," my father said crossly, "do you think Matron would let her stay in the hospital for all this time like that? Don't be silly, Beth."

Grandmother MacLeod, her delicately featured face as rigid as a cameo, now brought her mauve-veined hands together as though she were about to begin a prayer.

"Ewen, if that half-breed youngster comes along to Diamond Lake, I'm not going," she announced. "I'll go to Morag's for the summer."

I had trouble in stifling my urge to laugh, for my mother brightened visibly and quickly tried to hide it. If it came to a choice between Grandmother MacLeod and Piquette, Piquette would win hands down, nits or not.

"It might be quite nice for you, at that," she mused. "You haven't seen Morag for over a year, and you might enjoy being in the city for a while. Well, Ewen dear, you do what you think best. If you think it would do Piquette some good, then we'll be glad to have her, as long as she behaves herself."

So it happened that several weeks later, when we all piled into my father's old Nash, surrounded by suitcases and boxes of provisions and toys for my 10-month-old brother, Piquette was with us and Grandmother MacLeod, miraculously, was not. My father would only be staying at the cottage for a couple of weeks, for he had to get back to his practice, but the rest of us would stay at Diamond Lake until the end of August.

Our cottage was not named, as many were, "Dew Drop Inn" or "Bide-a-Wee," or "Bonnie Doon." The sign on the roadway bore in austere letters only our name, MacLeod. It was not a large cottage, but it was on the lakefront. You could look out the windows and see, through the filigree of the spruce trees, the water glistening greenly as the sun caught it. All around the cottage were ferns, and sharp-branched raspberry bushes, and moss that had grown over fallen tree trunks. If you looked carefully among the weeds and grass, you could find wild strawberry plants which were in white flower now and in another month would bear fruit, the fragrant globes hanging like miniature scarlet lanterns on the thin hairy stems. The two grey squirrels were still there, gossiping at us from the tall spruce beside the cottage, and by the end of the summer they would again be tame enough to take pieces of crust from my hands. The broad moose antlers that hung above the back door were a little more bleached and fissured after the winter, but otherwise everything was the same. I raced joyfully around my kingdom, greeting all the places I had not seen for a year. My brother, Roderick, who had not been born when we were here last summer, sat on the car rug in the sunshine and examined a brown spruce cone, meticulously turning it round and round in his small and curious hands. My mother and father toted the luggage from car to cottage, exclaiming over how well the place had wintered, no broken windows, thank goodness, no apparent damage from storm-felled branches or snow.

Only after I had finished looking around did I notice Piquette. She was sitting on the swing, her lame leg held stiffly out, and her other foot scuffing the ground as she swung slowly back and forth. Her long hair hung black and straight around her shoulders, and her broad coarse-featured face bore no expression—it was blank, as though she no longer dwelt within her own skull, as though she had gone elsewhere. I approached her very hesitantly.

"Want to come and play?"

Piquette looked at me with a sudden flash of scorn.

"I ain't a kid," she said.

Wounded, I stamped angrily away, swearing I would not speak to her for the rest of the summer. In the days that followed, however, Piquette began to interest me, and I began to want to interest her. My reasons did not appear bizarre to me. Unlikely as it may seem, I had only just realized that the Tonnerre family, whom I had always heard called half-breeds, were actually Indians, or as near as made no difference. My acquaintance with Indians was not extensive. I did not remember ever having seen a real Indian, and my new awareness that Piquette sprang from the people of Big Bear and Poundmaker, of Tecumseh, of the Iroquois who had eaten Father Brebeuf's heart— all this gave her an instant attraction in my eyes. I was a devoted reader of Pauline Johnson at this age, and sometimes would orate aloud and in an exalted voice, *West Wind, blow from your prairie nest; Blow from the mountains, blow from the west*—and so on. It seemed to me that Piquette must be in some way a daughter of the forest, a kind of junior prophetess of the wilds, who might impart to me, if I took the right approach, some of the secrets which she undoubtedly knew—where the whippoorwill made her nest, how the coyote reared her young, or whatever it was that it said in Hiawatha.

I set about gaining Piquette's trust. She was not allowed to go swimming, with her bad leg, but I managed to lure her down to the beach—or rather, she came because there was nothing else to do. The water was always icy, for the lake was fed by springs, but I swam like a dog, thrashing my arms and legs around at such speed and with such an output of energy that I never grew cold. Finally, when I had had enough, I came out and sat beside Piquette on the sand. When she saw me approaching, her hand squashed flat the sand castle she had been building, and she looked at me sullenly, without speaking.

"Do you like this place?" I asked, after a while, intending to lead on from there into the question of forest lore.

Piquette shrugged. "It's okay. Good as anywhere."

"I love it," I said. "We come here every summer."

"So what?" Her voice was distant, and I glanced at her uncertainly, wondering what I could have said wrong.

"Do you want to come for a walk?" I asked her. "We wouldn't need to go far. If you walk just around the point there, you come to a bay where great big reeds grow in the water, and all kinds of fish hang around there. Want to? Come on."

She shook her head.

"Your dad said I ain't supposed to do no more walking than I got to."

I tried another line.

"I bet you know a lot about the woods and all that, eh?" I began respectfully.

Piquette looked at me from her large dark unsmiling eyes.

"I don't know what in hell you're talkin' about," she replied. "You nuts or somethin'? If you mean where my old man, and me, and all them live, you better shut up, by Jesus, you hear?"

I was startled and my feelings were hurt, but I had a kind of dogged perseverance. I ignored her rebuff.

"You know something, Piquette? There's loons here, on this lake. You can see their nests just up the shore there, behind those logs. At night, you can hear them even from the cottage, but it's better to listen from the beach. My dad says we should listen and try to remember how they sound, because in a few years when more cottages are built at Diamond Lake and more people come in, the loons will go away."

Piquette was picking up stones and snail shells and then dropping them again.

"Who gives a good goddamn?" she said.

It became increasingly obvious that, as an Indian, Piquette was a dead loss. That evening I went out by myself, scrambling through the bushes that overhung the steep path, my feet slipping on the fallen spruce needles that covered the ground. When I reached the shore, I walked along the firm damp sand to the small pier that my father had built, and sat down there. I heard someone else crashing through the undergrowth and the bracken, and for a moment I thought Piquette had changed her mind, but it turned out to be my father. He sat beside me on the pier and we waited, without speaking.

At night the lake was like black glass with a streak of amber which was the path of the moon. All around, the spruce trees grew tall and close-set, branches blackly sharp against the sky, which was lightened by a cold flickering of stars. Then the loons began their calling. They rose like phantom birds from the nests on the shore, and flew out onto the dark still surface of the water.

No one can ever describe that ululating sound, the crying of the loons, and no one who has heard it can ever forget it. Plaintive, and yet with a quality of chilling mockery, those voices belonged to a world separated by eons from our neat world of summer cottages and the lighted lamps of home.

"They must have sounded just like that," my father remarked, "before any person ever set foot here."

Then he laughed. "You could say the same, of course, of sparrows, or chipmunks, but somehow it only strikes you that way with the loons."

"I know," I said.

Neither of us suspected that this would be the last time we would ever sit here together on the shore, listening. We stayed for perhaps half an hour, and then we went back to the cottage. My mother was reading beside the fireplace. Piquette was looking at the burning birch log, and not doing anything.

"You should have come along," I said, although in fact I was glad she had not.

"Not me," Piquette said. "You wouldn' catch me walkin' way down there jus' for a bunch of squawkin' birds."

Piquette and I remained ill at ease with one another. I felt I had somehow failed my father, but I did not know what was the matter, nor why she would not or could not respond when I suggested exploring the woods or playing house. I thought it was probably her slow and difficult walking that held her back. She stayed most of the time in the cottage with my mother, helping her with the dishes or with Roddie, but hardly ever talking. Then the Duncans arrived at their cottage, and I spent my days with Mavis, who was my best friend. I could not reach Piquette at all, and I soon lost interest in trying. But all that summer she remained as both a reproach and a mystery to me.

That winter my father died of pneumonia, after less than a week's illness. For some time I saw nothing around me, being completely immersed in my own pain and my mother's. When I looked outward once more, I scarcely noticed that Piquette Tonnerre was no longer at school. I do not remember seeing her at all until four years later, one Saturday night when Mavis and I were having Cokes in the Regal Cafe. The jukebox was booming like tuneful thunder, and beside it, leaning lightly on its chrome and its rainbow glass, was a girl.

Piquette must have been 17 then, although she looked about 20. I stared at her, astounded that anyone could have changed so much. Her face, so stolid and expressionless before, was animated now with a gaiety that was almost violent. She laughed and talked very loudly with the boys around her. Her lipstick was bright carmine, and her hair was cut short and frizzily permed. She had not been pretty as a child, and she was not pretty now, for her features were still heavy and blunt. But her dark and slightly slanted eyes were beautiful, and her skin-tight skirt and orange sweater displayed to enviable advantage a soft and slender body.

She saw me, and walked over. She teetered a little, but it was not due to her once-tubercular leg, for her limp was almost gone.

"Hi, Vanessa." Her voice still had the same hoarseness. "Long time no see, eh?"

"Hi," I said. "Where've you been keeping yourself, Piquette?"

"Oh, I been around," she said. "I been away almost two years now. Been all over the place—Winnipeg, Regina, Saskatoon. Jesus, what I could tell you! I come back this summer, but I ain't stayin'. You kids goin' to the dance?"

"No," I said abruptly, for this was a sore point with me. I was 15, and thought I was old enough to go to the Saturday night dances at the Flamingo. My mother, however, thought otherwise.

"Y'oughta come," Piquette said. "I never miss one. It's just about the on'y thing in this jerkwater town that's any fun. Boy, you couldn' catch me stayin' here. I don' give a shit about this place. It stinks."

She sat down beside me, and I caught the harsh oversweetness of her perfume.

"Listen, you wanna know something, Vanessa?" she confided, her voice only slightly blurred. "Your dad was the only person in Manawaka that ever done anything good to me."

I nodded speechlessly. I was certain she was speaking the truth. I knew a little more than I had that summer at Diamond Lake, but I could not reach her now any more than I had then. I was ashamed, ashamed of my own timidity, the frightened tendency to look the other way. Yet I felt no real warmth towards her—I only felt that I ought to, because of that distant summer and because my father had hoped she would be company for me, or perhaps that I would be for her, but it had not happened that way. At this moment, meeting her again, I had to admit that she repelled and embarrassed me, and I could not help despising the self-pity in her voice. I wished she would go away. I did not want to see her. I did not know what to say to her. It seemed that we had nothing to say to one another.

"I'll tell you something else," Piquette went on. "All the old bitches an' biddies in this town will sure be surprised. I'm gettin' married this fall—my boyfriend, he's an English fella, works in the stockyards in the city there, a very tall guy, got blond wavy hair. Gee, is he ever handsome. Got this real classy name. Alvin Gerald Cummings—some handle, eh? They call him Al."

For the merest instant, then, I saw her. I really did see her, for the first and only time in all the years we had both lived in the same town. Her defiant face, momentarily, became unguarded and unmasked, and in her eyes there was a terrifying hope.

"Gee, Piquette—" I burst out awkwardly, "that's swell. That's really wonderful. Congratulations—good luck—I hope you'll be happy—"

As I mouthed the conventional phrases, I could only guess how great her need must have been, that she had been forced to seek the very things she so bitterly rejected.

When I was 18, I left Manawaka and went away to college. At the end of my first year, I came back home for the summer. I spent the first few days in talking non-stop with my mother, as we exchanged all the news that somehow had not found its way into letters—what had happened in my life and what had happened here in Manawaka while I was away. My mother searched her memory for events that concerned people I knew.

"Did I ever write you about Piquette Tonnerre, Vanessa?" she asked one morning.

"No, I don't think so," I replied. "Last I heard of her, she was going to marry some guy in the city. Is she still there?"

My mother looked perturbed, and it was a moment before she spoke, as though she did not know how to express what she had to tell and wished she did not need to try.

"She's dead," she said at last. Then, as I stared at her, "Oh, Vanessa, when it happened, I couldn't help thinking of her as she was that summer—so sullen and gauche and badly dressed. I couldn't help wondering if we could have done something more at that time—but what could we do? She used to be around in the cottage there with me all day, and honestly, it was all I could do to get a word out of her. She didn't even talk to your father very much, although I think she liked him, in her way."

"What happened?" I asked.

"Either her husband left her, or she left him," my mother said. "I don't know which. Anyway, she came back here with two youngsters, both only babies—they must have been born very close together. She kept house, I guess, for Lazarus and her brothers, down in the valley there, in the old Tonnerre place. I used to see her on the street sometimes, but she never spoke to me. She'd put on an awful lot of weight, and she looked a mess, to tell you the truth, a real slattern, dressed any old how. She was up in court a couple of times—drunk and disorderly, of course. One Saturday night last winter, during the coldest weather, Piquette was alone in the shack with the children. The Tonnerres made home brew all the time, so I've heard, and Lazarus said later she'd been drinking most of the day when he and boys went out that evening. They had an old woodstove there—you know the kind, with exposed pipes. The shack caught fire. Piquette didn't get out, neither did the children."

I did not say anything. As so often with Piquette, there did not seem to be anything to say. There was a kind of silence around the image in my mind of the fire and the snow, and I wished I could put from my memory the look that I had seen once in Piquette's eyes.

I went up to Diamond Lake for a few days that summer, with Mavis and her family. The MacLeod cottage had been sold after my father's death, and I did not even go to look at it, not wanting to witness my long-ago kingdom possessed now by strangers. But one evening I went down to the shore by myself.

The small pier which my father had built was gone, and in its place there was a large and solid pier built by the government, for Galloping Mountain was now a national park, and Diamond Lake had been renamed Lake Wapakata, for it was felt that an Indian name would have a greater appeal to tourists. The one store had become several dozen, and the settlement had all the attributes of a flourishing resort—hotels, a dancehall, cafes with neon signs, the penetrating odours of potato chips and hot dogs.

I sat on the government pier and looked out across the water. At night the lake at least was the same as it had always been, darkly shining and bearing within its black glass the streak of amber that was the path of the moon. There was no wind that evening, and everything was quiet all around me. It seemed too quiet, and then I realized that the loons were no longer here. I listened for some time, to make sure, but never once did I hear that long-drawn call, half mocking and half plaintive, spearing through the stillness across the lake.

I did not know what had happened to the birds. Perhaps they had gone away to some far place of belonging. Perhaps they had been unable to find such a place, and had simply died out, having ceased to care any longer whether they lived or not.

I remember how Piquette had scorned to come along when my father and I sat there and listened to the lake birds. It seemed to me now that in some unconscious and totally unrecognized way, Piquette might have been the only one, after all, who had heard the crying of the loons.

F.Y.I.

Batoche: a municipality in central Saskatchewan, northeast of Saskatoon, and also an historic site of the Riel Rebellion of 1885

Big Bear: (Mistahimaskwa, c. 1825–1888) Plains Cree leader and chief during what was called the Northwest Rebellion. Despite his calls for moderation, he was convicted of treason-felony in 1885 and sentenced to three years imprisonment.

Brebeuf: St. Jean de Brebeuf (1593–1649) French-born Jesuit missionary who lived among the Hurons in New France and produced a Huron grammar book and dictionary. He was captured by the invading Iroquois and was tortured and killed.

CPR: Canadian Pacific Railway

Hiawatha: (ca. 1450) legendary chief of the Onondaga people of the northwestern United States. Follower of the prophet The Great Peacemaker, Hiawatha was a skilled politician and orator who put Peacemaker's philosophies into practice and is credited with the formation of the Iroquois Confederacy. He is also the inspiration for Henry Wadsworth Longfellow's most recognizable work *The Song of Hiawatha* (1855).

Manawaka, Wachakwa River, Diamond Lake: fictional place names based on places in Manitoba familiar to Laurence

Metis: a person of mixed descent; the Metis people emerged out of relations between Aboriginal women and European (French, Scottish) men. For more on the Metis, go to www.metisnation.ca.

Patois: a French dialect

Pauline Johnson: (Tekahionwake 1861–1913) was a Canadian writer and entertainer popular in the late nineteenth century. Today she is also respected as one of the first Aboriginal voices in Canadian literature. She was the daughter of George Johnson, a Mohawk and a chief of the Six Nations Reserve, and Emily Howells, a non-Native woman from Ohio. Pauline Johnson wrote and gave popular recitals of her poetry and performed comedy routines and plays all over Canada, the United States, and England. For more on Johnson, go to www.humanities.mcmaster.ca/~pjohnson/home.html.

Poundmaker: (Pitikwahanapiwiyin ca. 1842–1886) chief of the Plains Cree born to a Stoney shaman father and a Metis mother. Although present in many battles, his reputation grew from his skills as a proficient hunter, gifted orator, peacemaker, and diplomat.

relief: Employment Insurance

Riel: Louis Riel (1844–1885), Canadian politician and leader of the Metis, through whose work the Manitoba Act was passed, which established the province. Riel was subsequently executed by the government for his part in the Red River incident (1869–1870). Riel is regarded as a folk hero for his defence of Metis rights and culture. For more on Riel, go to www.gov.mb.ca/february_holiday/biography.html.

Tecumseh: (1768–1813) chief of the Shawnnee and native to Ohio. He formed a large tribal confederacy and he played a key role in battle when he allied his forces with the British and Canadians against the United States during the War of 1812.

Words to Build on

austere: severely simple

bracken: a large branching fern or mass of such ferns

carmine: of a vivid crimson or dark red

chinked: to fill a crack or opening with sealant

dogged: tenacious or overly persistent

filigree: anything delicate resembling fine ornamental work of silver, gold, or copper

fissured: an opening, usually long and narrow, made by cracking, splitting, or separation

gauche: lacking in ease or grace

homebrew: an alcoholic beverage, especially beer, that is made at home

plaintive: expressing sorrow

rebuff: a rejection of one who makes advances or offers help or sympathy

slattern: a promiscuous woman; a slut

ululating: to howl or make a hooting cry

Tricks of the Trade

Conflict	Realism
Imagery	Setting
Literary allusion/Historical allusion	Symbol
Metaphor	Turning point

In Your Own Words: Comprehension

1. What is Piquette Tonnerre's life like when she is a girl?

2. What does Grandmother MacLeod say when the father wants to take Piquette Tonnerre up to their cottage?

3. Why does Mr. MacLeod treat Piquette? What do you know about her condition?

4. How does Piquette react to Vanessa's offer of friendship?

5. Why is Diamond Lake re-named Lake Wapakata?

6. What happens to the loons at the end of the story?

7. What is the turning point in Vanessa's life? What is the turning point in Piquette's life?

In Your Own Words: Analysis

1. What time period does "The Loons" take place in?

2. What does Vanessa first believe Piquette possesses? How is Vanessa disappointed by what Piquette tells her?

3. What are the three ways in which Piquette tries to fit into white Anglo-Saxon society?

4. Who uses the term "half-breed" in this story, and what are the implications of this label?

5. What does Vanessa learn about her mother from the way she talks about Piquette?

6. What makes Piquette a stereotype? What makes her an individual and unique?

7. What does the last line of the story mean?

Now Write

1. Who is ultimately responsible for what happens to Piquette? Write an essay in which you explain whether Piquette is to blame for what happens to her or whether it is the society/time in which she lives that also plays a role in the circumstances of her life.

2. Compare the characters of Piquette and Vanessa to show that both girls are trapped in their circumstances.

3. Discuss how the loons function as a symbol for Piquette and her people. Be aware that some critics and writers have accused Laurence of being racist since she uses a bird (a loon) to represent a nation of people while others say Laurence was not culturally insensitive. What do you think?

4. Compare the characters of Piquette Tonnerre in Laurence's "The Loons" with Joe Cheechoo in Joseph Boyden's "Legless Joe versus Black Robe." Do these two characters have any qualities in common besides their ethnic background? How do their experiences differ?

Austin Clarke

Austin Clarke (b. 1934) was born in St. James, Barbados. He immigrated to Montreal in the 1950s and then relocated to Toronto. He is a graduate of both McGill University and the University of Toronto's Trinity College. He has been an educator, diplomat, and journalist. In 1963 he travelled to New York to interview leaders of the black civil rights movement and to make a documentary about the Muslim leader Malcolm X before X was assassinated. Clarke has received numerous awards for his writing, including the Giller Prize for his novel *The Polished Hoe* in 2002 and the Commonwealth Writers' Prize in 2003. In 1998 he was also made a Member of the

Order of Canada. Clarke's story "A Wedding in Toronto" is taken from his second short story collection, *When He Was Free and Young and He Used to Wear Silks* (1971). He lives in Toronto.

In His Own Words

"My second meeting with Malcolm was in my house on Asquith Avenue in Toronto . . . it was a more relaxed conversation—a rap session, if you will—in which we drank tea and talked about jazz—he liked Coltrane and Billie Holiday, as I did . . . and we discussed the contribution of 'black arts' and 'black culture' to the political and social environment of the civil rights movement. Malcolm told me that the explosion of these 'black arts' and 'black culture' contributed more to the success of civil rights than any other single social force."

"Being a writer restricts you into a room and that can be very depressing—it usually is depressing—and you need some release from that environment. And what better release than to come out of your cocoon and see real people. And then, of course, in the act of seeing these real people, and interacting with these real people, is the determination to go back into your little corner and create."

Before We Begin

1. What are the different ways people get married today? Where do people celebrate such an important social occasion?
2. Toronto is home to many different cultures. When do people's cultural traditions clash? What happens when they do?
3. Have you ever been in charge of a party or social gathering where things got out of control? How did you handle this situation?

 **Now Read**

A Wedding in Toronto

"A police coming in a man's house, and at a wedding reception to boot! and breaking up a party? Merely because some old can't-sleep bitch next door or down below can't find a man or something? What kind o' place, what sort o' country is this? It never happened in Barbados and it never could. Imagine a police in Barbados coming into a man's house, during a party, and a wedding party at that, to tell that man he is making too much noise! Man, that policeman's arse would be so stiff with lashes he would never do that again! A police coming into a man's apartment, and breaking up a wedding reception because some old bitch who can't sleep, complained?" Boysie never got over the shock of seeing the policeman at the door, standing like a monument to something, with an untranslatable expression on his face, with one hand resting perhaps absent-mindedly on the holster of his gun, and the other raised and caught in the slow-motion paralysis of knocking on the apartment door again. It was a loud, firm knock of authority. The wedding guests were, at that time, in the middle of speeches; and Boysie, who was the master of ceremonies, had been saying some amusing things about marriage. It was at the point when he was saying, *Ecce Homo,* over and over again (using his best stentorian, oratorical Barbadian dialect), exhorting them, as: "La-dies and gentlemen! ladies and gentlemen too! greetings and salutations, because on this most auspicious of evenings, on the aurora of long and felicitous matrimony, I say to you, to you, ladies and gentlemen, I say, *Ecce Homo,* behold the man! *Ecce Homo,* here I stand!" (Freeness, dressed to kill in a three-piece suit; Matthew Woods, spic and span; Estelle, beautiful as a virgin, as a star; and many other West Indians crammed into the happy apartment, screamed for joy when Boysie began this speech, his fifth for the afternoon's festivities. Each wedding guest, including Agatha the bride, and Henry the bridegroom, had made a speech. Some had made two speeches. Boysie had made his first about an hour after the wedding party returned to the apartment. It was five o'clock then. Now, after many toasts and speeches and eats and drinks, Boysie was captivating his audience again. The time was midnight. The guests liked it, and they bawled and told Boysie they liked it. Henry, sober and married; Agatha turning red, and flushed, and happy, and drunk as Dots, Boysie's wife, held her head back and exposed the silver cavities filled with silver, and said, "I could have another wedding reception like this tomorrow! One like this every month!") "I say to you, ladies and gentlemen, I say, *Ecce Homo,* behold the man! *Ecce Homo,* here I stand! Here I stand, ladies and gentlemen, with a glass of drink in my hand, wherewithal for to mitigate the aridity of my thirst. And as I have arisen from my esteemed seat this fifth time, and as I have quoth to you, *bon swarr* my dear Agaffa, goodevening Henry, you lucky old Bajan bastard!" And it was here, in the roar of acceptance by each person in the room when they held their glasses up, and Boysie's glass was held right there, at the correct angle, that the knock brutalized the apartment. Its suddenness made them notice it. But they had no suspicions. Boysie said, with his glass still raised, "Perhaps, ladies and gentlemen, it is some poor suppliant wanting warmth of this nocturnal congregation." And he moved away towards the door, his drink still in his hand, to invite the person inside to partake of the hospitality. Bernice went over to Agatha to fix the veil on her dress and therefore, fortunately, blocked her view of the police officer at the door standing with his hand on his holster. Boysie didn't lose his aplomb. The police officer was very polite to him. "Break it up soon, buddy. It's past midnight. The neighbours're complaining about the noise."

Boysie was going to offer the officer a drink, but he changed his mind.

"Don't let me get another report that you're making noise, eh? Break it up soon, buddy."

Boysie did not move from the door until the officer of the law walked back to the elevator; and he did not move until he saw him get into it; and Dots, who had put a record on the machine the moment she heard the officer's voice, was now standing beside Boysie, like a real wife, supportingly.

"And the poor girl's enjoying herself so much! And on her wedding day? Jesus Christ, these people is savages, man. They're damn uncivilized! You mean to tell me, on the girl's wedding day?" Boysie put his arm round Dots's new, shiny, almost bare shoulder, and he squeezed her a little bit, and said, "We going party till that son-of-a-bitch

come back!" Boysie left her, and went to Bernice and whispered in her ear, "The police!" Bernice suddenly got tense. "But only me and Dots, and now you, know 'bout It.
So keep it dark. Keep it dark." Bernice relaxed because of this confidence. "We got to go
on. How the hell could we ask the people to leave? How would Agaffa feel? How would
Henry feel, on his wedding night to boot?"

So Boysie and Dots and Bernice made certain not to let Agatha and Henry feel the
tension that had begun to creep into the party. It was impossible to recapture the gaiety
and the enjoyment that was in the room before the policeman knocked on the door.
Dots would have had the guests leave immediately after one more respectable drink;
she would have insisted upon it, because she had just moved into the apartment building and she wanted to live quietly, and also because Agatha and Henry had to go on
their honeymoon, to Niagara Falls. But Boysie said no, "This is a wedding. Not any old
damn party with beatniks." And he left Dots standing there arguing the wisdom of his
suggestion with Bernice, and he went to the record player, and looked through the pile
of calypso records. (This record player had arrived from Eaton's department store two
hours before the wedding reception began, delivered on a hire-purchase, the monthly
payments of which were 55 dollars and 25 cents and which Dots did not know how she
would meet; but the sound was high and loud and high-fidelity and stereophonic too,
and the beauty and the loudness of the sound allayed their fears of having the machine
repossessed. "Man, let we play the thing for today then, and enjoy it, and then see
what happen, man!" And Boysie agreed to that, although before Dots said so, he had
already agreed in his mind to keep the record player.) Boysie now selected a calypso
by the Mighty Sparrow, *Shanty Town People,* in which Sparrow was complaining of
having to move out of his comfortable apartment, in Trinidad, because people from
the slums had encroached on his location on the hill. The music raged, as the spirits in
the guests and in the drinks raged. Estelle was beautiful in her wedding-party dress.
She was thinking of how very close she herself had come to marriage. And more than
once, during the hectic afternoon and night, she wondered where the hell her man,
Sam Burrmann, was at this happy time. But she soon put him out of her mind; and
she devoted all her body and energy to Matthew Woods, who shook his body in time
in dance as if he was in some mad trance. *Sunday morning, they fighting, they drinking, they beating pan . . . send for the police, still the bacchanal won't cease.* It was a royal
time. It was an ironic time to have a calypso reproduce the exact conditions of a party at
which the police had come. And judging by the hour hand, it was Sunday morning too!
But no one cared for Toronto, or the police, or the neighbours: this was a wedding, and
as Dots said, "A person can only get married one time. Even if he divorce and marry
a second time, the second time don't seem to be like the first time! So the first time is
the time!" Boysie was dancing with her. Brigitte, a German immigrant working as a
domestic, had held on to Freeness the whole day, probably by design; probably by the
suggestion of Boysie (whose woman she was; Boysie who now in the castle of skin and
pride, in his briar patch of host and wedding-giver, had no time for outside women);
and Bernice was dancing with a man who nobody knew, who nobody invited, but
who was treated with the same courtesy and hospitality as the bridegroom, or as if he
was the bride's father. Agatha's father hadn't arrived yet. Agatha's mother hadn't arrived
yet. Agatha's friends, Agatha's many friends from the university, and her lawyer-friend
(all of whom had been sent invitations—that was Boysie's personal gift to the couple)

hadn't arrived yet. It had been a sorrowful sight at the church, when it was found out that no one was sitting on the bride's side as witness and evidence. Dots quickly saw the situation developing, and quickly saw the embarrassment it would cause Agatha when she arrived sweet and young, virginal and white in her long dress, to glance over the wide expanse of the desert of her friends. And Dots ushered and re-ushered half of the church over to Agatha's side. When the organ roared and snorted through the *Wedding March,* everybody was laughing, even Agatha. Reverend Markham was happy. It was his first interracial wedding ceremony. The choir was in good voice, loud when it was supposed to be loud, soft when the organist breathed with the organ and whispered that the choir should be like a piano, pianissimo. But when they were in the office signing away their lives and their promises to one another, Dots stood like a mother-hen on the top steps of the church, directing the people (those who didn't have cars) to cars and warning the photographer who had arrived late, "Look here! don't take the whole day, hear? We have things waiting at the wedding reception." And after that she whispered in Bernice's ears, "It's a shame, a great burning shame that that bastard, Agatha's father, thinks he is too great and too proud to come and witness his own daughter on her wedding day. A person does only have one wedding day in her life and that bastard didn't even come. He did not come."

"And the mother ain't turned up yet, neither."

"Bernice, gal, you are seeing and witnessing the ways o' white people. They would kill their own flesh and blood just to prove a blasted point."

"It is sad, though."

Estelle had overheard, and she said, "They love one another, though. Henry and Agatha. And they won't be living at the parents."

"Still's a blasted shame!"

And now, at the reception, nobody apparently tired after so many hours of eating and drinking and dancing with the problems of *Shanty Town People* being reproduced for them by the visit of the policeman and by the record itself, these West Indians and two white women, Brigitte and Agatha ("She's a Wessindian now, gal! We adopt Agatha now that her own people and her parents let her down. Godblummuh, we is one people who don't reject nobody through colour prejudice.") . . . *I tired and I disgust . . . big Sunday evening, they cussing, they fighting, they gambling, they beating pan and bup-bup!-iron bolt, and stone pelting, send for the police, still the bacchanal won't cease* . . . There were 50 persons invited to the reception. There were 50 persons in the two-bedroom apartment from five o'clock. There are 51 persons (with the uninvited man) in the apartment now, at 1:30 Sunday morning. Boysie has his arms in the air and is dancing as if his body has been seized by some voodoo, or St. Vitus dance mood; Dots has thrown one brocaded expensive slipper somewhere in a corner, and she is jumping up. The record, a favourite with everybody in the room, is put on again. It is put on three times, four times, five times, six times; and Boysie says on the seventh time, "Man, play that thing one more time, do, man!" And it is put on the eighth time . . . *and big Sunday morning, they cussing they fighting they gambling; they beating pan and bup-bup!-iron bolt and stone pelting, send for the police, still the bacchanal won't cease, so they violent so they fast, they better go back to their mansion on the Labasse* . . . A smudge of fatigue and sweat walked imperceptibly from under Estelle's hairy armpits. Bernice noticed it; and she took Estelle into Dots's bedroom and rubbed some of Dots's underarm deodorant, "Ban," on the storytelling odour. Estelle smiles, and dashes back out to dance. Agatha, with the first signs of marriedhood and possessiveness, sits and watches Henry dance with a very thin, tight, tense, and at the same time, sexy black woman, holding him like a leech in heat; and Agatha continues to watch as if she is comparing her body with the black woman's body in the bedroom of her mind; she watches the woman's hips as they do things with the rhythm of the calypso which she herself, legal and wedded to Henry for better and for worse, knows she cannot do; cannot ever learn to do in this way. Some men are in the kitchen, eating, as they have been doing since five o'clock. ("Boysie!" one of them said, about six o'clock, "we intend to eat every fucking thing in your apartment, boy! So, relax.") There is a big argument going on about cricket. None of these men has seen a cricket Test match in five years, not since they left their homes in the islands. But they are now arguing about Sir Frank Worrell, and the cover drive he made off Alec Bedser at Lords in 1950, many many years ago. One man says, "Be-Christ, them English people think they could play cricket! Be-Jesuschrist, they can't play no cricket in truth! They *playing* they great. But godblummuh! when Sir Frank leaned into that out-swinger from Bedser, and Sir Frank make a little thing, *so!* be-Christ, it went to the fucking boundary like lightning for four! Right offa Worrell wrist!" And another man smiled, took a sip of his whiskey and said, "And all o' wunnuh in here know that Worrell have more wrist-work in his strokes than Boysie in there have stones in his underwears!" And like a contagion, everybody in the kitchen bawled and poured himself another, larger drink. The record is changed. Sparrow is talking about his boyhood. The men dropped their glasses and ran for the women sitting around the room. They reached out their hands and lifted the dripping, shining, shiningly-dressed, rouged-and-perfume-smelling tired ladies off their chairs. Boysie is dancing with Dots, as if they are lovers: close. His brilliantined head, which had sweated for hours, four hours under his stocking-top, is sleeked down and shining; and Dots's hairdo, done amidst pain and time, talk and gossip in Azan's Beauty World the previous Thursday, when the shop was noisy and filled with domestics and talk about "I hear Enid sleeping with a Jew-man. You hear so, too?" and the waiting was long for those without an appointment, and for those with an appointment. "The girl we meet one day in the subway, that girl wearing the mini, the midi maxi whatever the hell you calls it! anyhow, she I talking about. She gone and get sheself in trouble. *Pregnunt!*" Dots had listened and had held her peace; and then someone said, Dots had never seen this woman in the parlour before, "This rich-rich Jewish girl I hear is marrieding some Bajan man or other, and somebody tell me his name is Henrysomething, or the other, but Christ! to imagine that I been here so blasted long and nobody, not even a Jew-man hasn't asked me a question. I must be getting old, and looking it, too!" And then they all laughed. Except Dots. *Now, I am a rebel, I seeking my revenge any kind o' way, I'm a devil. I don't laugh, I don't smile I don't play* . . . Boysie is not smiling. He doesn't smile when he is dancing. He is holding Dots so close that he can feel something stiffening in his trousers legs: but she is his wife and he her husband . . . *Anytime we meet, man-to-man, it's blood and sand!* (Estelle thinks back to the time not long ago when Bernice and Dots, Boysie and Henry visited her in the small room she lived in on Bedford Road, when they found her hungry and depressed, delirious with fever and thoughts about Sam Burrmann, a Jewish lawyer who left her after she told him she was pregnant for him; and she thinks about it now, dancing with the man nobody invited, the man who told her he is some kind of agent selling some product which Estelle does not understand, thinking of this man dancing with her so close, touching the child in her womb put there by another man. And she thinks of Bernice. "What a life, what a hard life these West Indians live in this place!" And she thinks of what her life might be. There is a man standing beside her, watching her face, but not caring for her thoughts because he wants her to have one thought on her mind, tonight after the reception. He is the man nobody invited. He is standing in front of her now like a threat, like a challenge. ("Henry married, Boysie married, every other bitch in here have a husband . . . I wonder if . . . ") The man wants to dance with this "prettiest lady in this place." The compliment is sincere, and Estelle makes herself prettier by doing something to her face and her lips, saliva on them now, and she stands up just as Sparrow says, *They treat me like a savage, of me they take advantage; when I young and growing up in town, all o' them bad-johns used to knock me down* . . . A tear is crawling like perspiration down Estelle's face. The man does not notice. He has his mind on other parts of her body.)

It was then that the second knocking was heard on the apartment door. Boysie went to the door. The same policeman, plus another one, were standing there. "I told ya," the first policeman said. There was no anger in his voice. He seemed rather peeved that someone had called to report noise in the apartment; he seemed as if he had been taken away from something he was doing, something he enjoyed doing; as a man who had been roused from a poker game would look; as if he had been disturbed from the pants of some woman, somewhere down in the jungle of apartments nearby. Boysie knew what to do.

The guests began leaving right away. Everybody except those who were staying for the night, those who lived there: Boysie and Dots, Bernice and Estelle. Henry looked at the policemen and said things in his heart which if they were audible would have given him a beating and then a long jail term. Agatha began to cry. She was still wearing her wedding gown; Henry was in his formal morning suit; he and she still in the clothes that began their new life together. The policemen waited until every one of the guests left. As Agatha walked beside Henry along the long corridor, as if she was still walking that interminable aisle up the mile to face the altar and the cross and the Maker stretched out on a cross and Reverend Markham, women with curlers in their hair peeped through open doors; and just as the policemen passed them and went down into the half-awake apartment building, in the elevator going out, one of the white ladies, in a torn pink nightgown which showed the blackness between her thighs vaguely, hissed, "Bitch! Trash!" and slammed her apartment door. The others, among the onlooking guard of honour and dishonour, shook their heads and did not slam their doors: but nobody knew what they were saying in their hearts behind their closed doors. In the confusion, in all the disappointment and crying (Dots and Bernice and Estelle remained sitting on the large new couch, crying for Agatha's sake; and Agatha herself had left in tears, and had touched each of their cheeks with the tears of her kisses as she tried to smile goodbye), the record player was still commenting: *They treat me like a savage they treat me like a savage . . . they treat me like a savage . . . they treat me like a savage . . . they treat me like a savage . . .* and before Estelle got up to take it off, she thought again of the strange man who nobody invited who had asked her to dance just at that point; and it seemed very long ago that her happiness happened. Now, Boysie was walking back along the quiet corridor, alone.

F.Y.I.

beatniks: a word coined by Herb Caen in an article he wrote for the *San Francisco Chronicle* in 1958. It was a combination of poet Jack Kerouac's term "Beat Generation" and the Russian suffix "nik." It meant a person that embodied the attitudes and styling of the Beat culture, albeit in the most superficial manner: goatees, black berets and turtlenecks, bongos, sunglasses, coffee houses, poetry readings, and marijuana cigarettes. This was a stereotype and generally seen as an insult by many famous Beat poets and artists.

brilliantined head: refers to a head that has been treated with a product called Brillantine. Invented by a French perfumer named Edouard Pinaud at the turn of the twentieth century, Brillantine is a hair-grooming product created to make men's hair softer, smoother, and more manageable. Coming in the form of a perfumed and oily liquid, it gave the hair a high-gloss shine and lustre.

calypso: a style of Afro-Caribbean music that originated in Trinidad and Tobago. The roots of this genre are found in African slavery. The songs formed a sense of community among the slaves, as they weren't allowed to speak to one another. The first official calypso recordings were made in 1912, but it wasn't until the 1930s when major calypso stars such as Lord Kitchener, Roaring Lion, and Lord Invader started to reach audiences worldwide. Although there are subgenres in which the lyrical content differs, these songs are often about anything from sociopolitical commentary to overtly sexual romps. Many times the authorities tried to censor or even outlaw certain songs due to their content.

Eaton's: refers to Eaton's department stores. In 1869, Timothy Eaton, originally from Ireland, opened a small retail store of "sound goods, good styles, and good value" that would eventually expand to become a household name for many Canadians. Built on a 100 per cent satisfaction or money back guarantee—no questions asked—Eaton's grew to be Canada's largest department store chain. In 1911, *Saturday Night* magazine declared: "Never before in the history of the world has it been possible for a store to be run on this humanitarian basis of beauty, use, and efficiency. All of Canada is proud of Eaton's; and Canada should be, for here we find a store that has set the world a pace in modern merchandising." In the same year, the *Illustrated London News* stated: "The T. Eaton Co. of Toronto can claim their stores are the greatest in the British Empire." Although the Eaton Centre in Toronto remains a popular tourist attraction, Eaton's went bankrupt in 1999.

Ecce Homo: Latin for "behold the man." These are the words Pontius Pilate said to the crowds as he presented the bound, beaten, and crowned with thorns Jesus Christ to them. *Ecce Homo* is also the title of many works of art depicting the Passion of Christ. The images range from his whipping, his crowning of thorns, and his mocking by the crowds to a solitary Jesus, beaten and wearing a purple robe. Modern interpretations of the *Ecce Homo* motif have come to include the depiction of human suffering and degradation through violence and war. For more on this term and its artistic interpretation, go to www.nationalgallery.org.uk/paintings/rembrandt-ecce-homo

the Maker stretched out on a cross: this phrase refers to the image of Jesus Christ crucified on a wooden cross.

Mighty Sparrow: the stage name for calypso singer, songwriter, and guitarist Slinger Francisco. Born July 9, 1935, in Grand Roy, Grenada, Mighty Sparrow, or Birdie, is known as the "Calypso King of the World." He is one of the most successful and renowned artists of the calypso style, having won Trinidad's famous Carnival Road March competition eight times and being named Calypso Monarch eleven times. While Sparrow's lyrics are often funny, clever, ironic, and ribald, he also includes social and political commentary in his songs. If you'd like to see some of Mighty Sparrow's live performances, there are many posted on YouTube.

St. Vitus: a Christian saint from Sicily martyred by the Roman Empire in 303 CE and counted as one of the Fourteen Holy Helpers of the Roman Catholic Church. During the Middle Ages, Germans celebrated the saint's feast day by dancing in front of his statue. The term "Saint Vitus' Dance" was also given to a neurological disease called chorea because the rapid movements of the feet or hands resemble dancing or piano playing. St. Vitus came to be known as the patron saint of dancers, actors, comedians, and epileptics.

Words to Build on

allayed: to lessen, relieve, reduce, or quiet

aplomb: self-confidence or assurance

aridity: dry, uninteresting, unsatisfying

bacchanal: a wild and drunken party or celebration

in his briar patch: briar refers to any prickly bush

interminable: endless

pianissimo: Italian for "softest," a music term meaning to play a piece or section softly/quietly

stentorian: loud and powerful

supplicant: a person who makes a humble and earnest request

Tricks of the Trade

Irony

Motif

Narrative structure

Narrative voice

Symbol

In Your Own Words: Comprehension

1. Explain the setting of this story. What year does the story take place?

2. Make a list of all the male and female characters in this story. Give a brief description of each character's role in the story.

3. Create a timeline of events in the story and identify the climax.

4. Who is the "un-invited man" in the apartment?

5. How is Agatha treated by the bridegroom's group of friends? Give evidence of this treatment.

6. How do the hosts, Boysie and Dots, and the wedding guests react when the police come to the apartment?

In Your Own Words: Analysis

1. A common theme of Austin Clarke's writing is "urban alienation." What does this phrase mean? Explain how this is shown in the story.

2. Look through the story and examine the lyrics of Mighty Sparrow's song "Shanty Town People." How do the lyrics act as a commentary on the events of the story?

3. The terms "savage" and "civilized" are used in the story. Who identifies or is labelled with these terms and why?

4. Explain how the phrase *Ecce Homo* is used to humorous and ironic effect.

5. Is it an act of racism when the police officer tells Boysie to "break it up soon"? Give evidence to support your answer.

6. Why does this story not have a traditional chronological narrative structure?

Now Write

1. This is a story in which there are often differences between surface appearances and reality. Discuss which characters embody contradiction and explain whether this makes them more believable or realistic characters.

2. Could the situations depicted in "A Wedding in Toronto" take place today? Explain which events could still take place today and which could not. Give evidence in your writing.

3. This story is about Barbadian immigrants living in Toronto. However, is it possible that these events could be about any other ethnic group? What are the elements in story that make it universal?

4. "A Wedding in Toronto" is a story that includes many beginnings and endings. Comment on these beginnings and endings: select specific events and relationships in this story and explain how they begin and how they end.

Gabriel Garcia Marquez

Gabriel Garcia Marquez (b. 1928) was born in Aracataca, a town in northern Colombia, where he was raised by his maternal grandparents. His early inspiration for storytelling came from his grandparents. His grandfather, a retired colonel, told him stories of the brutality of war, while his grandmother told him folktales filled with ghosts and various superstitions. This mix may have contributed to the development of his style, often called "magic realism."

He began his career as a journalist and editor and has lived in Mexico, Europe, and the United States. His works include short stories and novels, the most popular of which is the novel *One Hundred Years of Solitude*, which has sold over 10 million copies worldwide and is considered his masterpiece. Garcia Marquez also wrote *Love in the Time of Cholera*, which is loosely based on the courtship of his parents. Many of his works allow him to create stories that blend the realities of daily life with history, myth, and fantasy. His works feature themes related to memory, family history, community, and solitude. In addition to writing, he is also a political activist and is known for his liberal views: he is friends with the former Cuban leader Fidel Castro and has expressed sympathy for various Central American revolutionary groups. In 1982 he was awarded the Nobel Prize in Literature. He is such a cultural icon in Central America that people often write or paint lines from his books and stories on the sides of their cars. His story "The Handsomest Drowned Man in the World: A Tale for Children" was first published in English in *Playboy Magazine* (November 1971).

In His Own Words

"What matters in life is not what happens to you but what you remember and how you remember it."

"The tone that I eventually used in *One Hundred Years of Solitude* was based on the way my grandmother used to tell stories. She told things that sounded supernatural and fantastic, but she told them with complete naturalness....What was most important was the expression she had on her face. She did not change her expression at all when telling her stories and everyone was surprised. In previous attempts to write, I tried to tell the story without believing in it. I discovered that what I had to do was believe in them myself and write them with the same expression with which my grandmother told them: with a brick face."

"There's no doubt nostalgia is one of the important ingredients of my books and life. I make decisions out of sheer nostalgia. Nostalgia gives my books the distance they bear from reality."

Before We Begin

1. How would you react if you came across a dead body?

2. Have you ever invented a history or story about someone you didn't really know? What was it that helped you build or invent ideas about this person? For example, think about a "crush" from afar you might have had for someone in high school.

3. Are there are any stories you read as a child and then re-read years later as an adult? How did the story change for you when you re-read it?

 **Now Read**

The Handsomest Drowned Man in the World

A Tale for Children

The first children who saw the dark and slinky bulge approaching through the sea let themselves think it was an enemy ship. Then they saw it had no flags or masts and they thought it was a whale. But when it washed up on the beach, they removed the clumps of seaweed, the jellyfish tentacles, and the remains of fish and flotsam, and only then did they see that it was a drowned man.

They had been playing with him all afternoon, burying him the sand and digging him up again, when someone chanced to see them and spread the alarm in the village. The men who carried him to the nearest house noticed that he weighed more than any dead man they had ever known, almost as much as a horse, and they said to each other that maybe he'd been floating too long and the water had got into his bones. When they laid him on the floor they said he'd been taller than all other men because there was barely room for him in the house, but they thought that maybe the ability to keep on growing after death was part of the nature of certain drowned men. He had the smell of the sea about him and only his shape gave one to suppose that it was the corpse of a human being, because the skin was covered with a crust of mud and scales.

They did not even have to clean off his face to know that the dead man was a stranger. The village was made up of only 20-odd wooden houses that had stone courtyards with no flowers and which were spread about on the end of a desertlike cape. There was so little land that mothers always went about with the fear that the wind would carry off their children and the few dead that the years had caused among them had to be thrown off the cliffs. But the sea was calm and bountiful and all the men fit into seven boats. So when they found the drowned man they simply had to look at one another to see that they were all there.

That night they did not go out to work at sea. While the men went to find out if anyone was missing in neighbouring villages, the women stayed behind to care for the drowned man. They took the mud off with grass swabs, they removed the underwater stones entangled in his hair, and they scraped the crust off with tools used for scaling fish. As they were doing that they noticed that the vegetation on him came from faraway oceans and deep water and that his clothes were in tatters, as if he had sailed through labyrinths of coral. They noticed too that he bore his death with pride, for he did not have the lonely look of other drowned men who came out of the sea or that haggard, needy look of men who drowned in rivers. But only when they finished cleaning him off did they become aware of the kind of man he was and it left them breathless. Not only was he the tallest, strongest, most virile, and best built man they had ever seen, but even though they were looking at him there was no room for him in their imagination.

They could not find a bed in the village large enough to lay him on nor was there a table solid enough to use for his wake. The tallest men's holiday pants would not fit him, not the fattest ones Sunday shirts, nor the shoes of the one with the biggest feet. Fascinated by his huge size and his beauty, the women then decided to make him some pants from a large piece of sail and a shirt from some bridal brabant linen so that he could continue through his death with dignity. As they sewed, sitting in a circle and gazing at the corpse between stitches, it seemed to them that the wind had never been so steady nor the sea so restless as on that night and they supposed that the change had something to do with the dead man. They thought that if that magnificent man had lived in the village, his house would have had the widest doors, the highest ceiling, and the strongest floor, his bedstead would have been made from a midship frame held together by iron bolts, and his wife would have been the happiest woman. They thought that he would have had so much authority that he could have drawn fish out of the sea by calling their names and that he would have put so much work into his land that springs would have burst forth from among the rocks so that he would have been able to plant flowers on the cliffs. They secretly compared him to their own men, thinking that for all their lives theirs were incapable of doing what he could do in one night, and they ended up dismissing them deep in their hearts as the weakest, meanest, and most useless creatures on earth. They were wandering through that maze of fantasy when the oldest woman, who as the oldest had looked upon the drowned man with more compassion than passion, sighed:

"He has the face of someone called Esteban."

It was true. Most of them had only to take another look at him to see that he could not have any other name. The more stubborn among them, who were the youngest, still lived for a few hours with the illusion that when they put his clothes on and he lay among the flowers in patent leather shoes his name might be Lautaro. But it was a vain illusion. There had not been enough canvas, the poorly cut and worse sewn pants were too tight, and the hidden strength of his heart popped the buttons on his shirt. After midnight the whistling of the wind died down and the sea fell into its Wednesday drowsiness. The silence put an end to any last doubts: he was Esteban. The women who had dressed him, who had combed his hair, had cut his nails and shaved him were unable to hold back a shudder of pity when they had to resign themselves to his being dragged along the ground. It was then that they understood how unhappy he must have been with that huge body since it bothered him even after death. They could see him in life, condemned to going through doors sideways, cracking his head on crossbeams, remaining on his feet during visits, not knowing what to do with his soft, pink, sea lion hands while the lady of the house looked for her most resistant chair and begged him, frightened to death, sit here, Esteban, please, and he, leaning against the wall, smiling, don't bother, ma'am, I'm fine where I am, his heels raw and his back roasted from having done the same thing so many times whenever he paid a visit, don't bother, ma'am, I'm fine where I am, just to avoid the embarrassment of breaking up the chair, and never knowing perhaps that the ones who said don't go, Esteban, at least wait till the coffee's ready, were the ones who later on would whisper the big boob finally left, how nice, the handsome fool has gone. That was what the women were thinking beside the body a little before dawn. Later, when they covered his face with a handkerchief so that the light would not bother him, he looked so forever dead, so defenceless, so much like their men that the first furrows of tears opened in their hearts. It was one of the younger ones who began weeping. The others, coming to, went from sighs to wails, and the more they sobbed the more they felt like weeping, because the drowned man was becoming all the more Esteban for them, and so they wept so much, for he was the most destitute, most peaceful, and most obliging man on earth, poor Esteban. So when the men returned with the news that the drowned man was not from the neighboring villages either, the women felt an opening of jubilation in the midst of their tears.

"Praise the Lord," they sighed, "he's ours!"

The men thought the fuss was only womanish frivolity. Fatigued because of the difficult nighttime inquiries, all they wanted was to get rid of the bother of the newcomer once and for all before the sun grew strong on that arid, windless day. They improvised a litter with the remains of foremasts and gaffs, tying it together with rigging so that it would bear the weight of the body until they reached the cliffs. They wanted to tie the anchor from a cargo ship to him so that he would sink easily into the deepest waves, where fish are blind and divers die of nostalgia, and bad currents would not bring him back to shore, as had happened with other bodies. But the more they hurried, the more the women thought of ways to waste time. They walked about like startled hens, pecking with the sea charms on their breasts, some interfering on one side to put a scapular of the good wind on the drowned man, some on the other side to put a wrist compass on him, and after a great deal of *get away from there, woman, stay out of the way, look, you almost made me fall on top of the dead man*, the men began to feel mistrust in their livers and started grumbling about why so many main-altar decorations for a stranger, because no matter how many nails and holy-water jars he had on him, the sharks would chew him all the same, but the women kept piling on their junk relics, running back and forth, stumbling, while they released in sighs what they did not in tears, so that the men finally exploded with *since when has there ever been such a fuss over a drifting corpse, a drowned nobody, a piece of cold Wednesday meat*. One of the women, mortified by so much lack of care, then removed the handkerchief from the dead man's face and the men were left breathless too.

He was Esteban. It was not necessary to repeat it for them to recognize him. If they had been told Sir Walter Raleigh, even they might have been impressed with his gringo accent, the macaw on his shoulder, his cannibal-killing blunderbuss, but there could be only one Esteban in the world and there he was, stretched out like a sperm whale, shoeless, wearing the pants of an undersized child, and with those stony nails that had to be cut with a knife. They only had to take the handkerchief off his face to see that he was ashamed, that it was not his fault that he was so big or so heavy or so handsome, and if he had known that this was going to happen, he would have looked for a more discreet place to drown in, seriously, I even would have tied the anchor off a galleon around my neck and staggered off a cliff like someone who doesn't like things in order not to be upsetting people now with this Wednesday dead body, as you people say, in order not to be bothering anyone with this filthy piece of cold meat that doesn't have anything to do with me. There was so much truth in his manner that even the most mistrustful men, the ones who felt the bitterness of endless nights at sea fearing that their women would tire of dreaming about them and begin to dream of drowned men, even they and others who were harder still shuddered in the marrow of their bones at Esteban's sincerity.

That was how they came to hold the most splendid funeral they could conceive of for an abandoned drowned man. Some women who had gone to get flowers in the neighboring villages returned with other women who could not believe what they had been told, and those women went back for more flowers when they saw the dead man, and they brought more and more until there were so many flowers and so many people that it was hard to walk about. At the final moment it pained them to return him to the waters as an orphan and they chose a father and mother from among the best people, and aunts and uncles and cousins, so that through him all the inhabitants of the village became kinsmen. Some sailors who heard the weeping from a distance went off course and people heard of one who had himself tied to the mainmast, remembering ancient fables about sirens. While they fought for the privilege of carrying him on their shoulders along the steep escarpment by the cliffs, men and women became aware for the first time of the desolation of their streets, the dryness of their courtyards, the narrowness of their dreams as they faced the splendor and beauty of their drowned man. They let him go without an anchor so that he could come back if he wished and whenever he wished, and they all held their breath for the fraction of centuries the body took to fall into the abyss. They did not need to look at one another to realize that they were no longer all present, that they would never be. But they also knew that everything would be different from then on, that their houses would have wider doors, higher ceilings, and stronger floors so that Esteban's memory could go everywhere without bumping into beams and so that no one in the future would dare whisper the big boob finally died, too bad, the handsome fool has finally died, because they were going to paint their house fronts gay colours to make Esteban's memory eternal and they were going to break their backs digging for springs among the stones and planting flowers on the cliffs so that in future years at dawn the passengers on great liners would awaken, suffocated by the smell of gardens on the high seas, and the captain would have to come down from the bridge in his dress uniform, with his astrolabe, his pole star, and his row of war medals and, pointing to the promontory of roses on the horizon, he would say in 14 languages, look there, where the wind is so peaceful now that it's gone to sleep beneath the beds, over there, where the sun's so bright that the sunflowers don't know which way to turn, yes, over there, that's Esteban's village.

F.Y.I.

gringo: a derogatory term for a white foreigner, especially a North American or British person, in a Central American country

Sir Walter Raleigh: (1552–1618) an English aristocrat, pirate, poet, soldier, and explorer. He was a favourite of Queen Elizabeth I and was known to have sailed to South America.

Words to Build on

astrolabe: astronomical instrument

blunderbuss: an old-style firearm with a wide muzzle

boob: a foolish person

destitute: completely impoverished

flotsam: wreckage of a ship or its cargo

foremasts and gaffs: parts of a sailing vessel or ship

furrows: deep wrinkles

galleon: large multi-decked sailing ship

haggard: looking exhausted or distraught

marrow: the centre of a bone

nostalgia: a sentimental desire for the past, often in an idealized form

pole star: a highly visible star that is aligned with the Earth's axis

promontory: a prominent mass of land that overlooks a lower-lying mass of land or water; also called a peninsula

scapular: two small pieces of wool cloth connected by a string

sirens: sea nymphs who lured sailors to their death by using their beauty and alluring voices

slinky: moving in a seductive manner

Tricks of the Trade

Atmosphere

Climax

Magic realism

Narrative voice

Oral storytelling/Orature

Setting

In Your Own Words: Comprehension

1. Who is telling this story? What is unique about the narrative style?

2. Why aren't the villagers repulsed by the corpse?

3. Who are the first ones to accept the dead man and to incorporate him into their lives?

4. Describe the physical environment of the village before and at the time of the dead man's arrival?

5. Why do the women name the drowned man Esteban? After naming him, what do the women do?

6. Compare and contrast the attitudes of the women and the men towards Esteban.

7. What is the significance of the drowned man's funeral and the nature of the transformation that occurs in the village as a result of his presence?

In Your Own Words: Analysis

1. What are some examples of magic realism in this story?

2. How is the drowned man treated at the beginning of the story and how does this treatment change as the story progresses? Use quotes from the story to support your answer.

3. The subtitle for this story is "A Tale for Children." Why did Garcia Marquez choose this subtitle? Consider what C.S. Lewis, the author of *The Chronicles of Narnia*, told his godchild: "someday you will be old enough to start reading fairy tales again." What did Lewis mean by this? How does this quote relate to "The Handsomest Drowned Man in the World"?

4. The setting for this story involves an island and the sea. What elements or qualities are associated with islands and the sea? How are these shown or depicted in "The Handsomest Drowned Man in the World"?

5. Most readers and audiences equate climax with the most exciting part of the story. Is this true of the climax in "The Handsomest Drowned Man in the World"? Identify where the climax in the story occurs and compare this to the climax of another short story in this text.

Now Write

1. Compare and contrast the use of magic realism in Garcia Marquez's "The Handsomest Drowned Man in the World" and Angela Carter's "The Company of Wolves."

2. What are the ways in which a writer uses humour in his or her work? Compare how it is used, its purpose and effect, in the works of any of these writers: Gabriel Garcia Marquez, Joseph Boyden, Austin Clarke, and Katherine Govier.

3. How does Garcia Marquez create atmosphere in a story in which villagers and an island are not named and a time period is not specified? Without any of these specifics, how does Garcia Marquez make the reader believe in this place?

4. There is a well-known saying that we come into this world alone and we exit it alone. How is death treated in "The Handsomest Drowned Man in the World"?

5. What is nostalgia? (see the quote from the *In His Own Words* section). How is nostalgia treated in "The Handsomest Drowned Man in the World"?

Angela Carter

Angela Carter (1940–1992) was born in Sussex, England, and is considered to be one of the most important and widely read English writers of the late twentieth century. At 19 she graduated from school and went to work for a newspaper, following in the footsteps of her father who was also a journalist. She later returned to school to study English literature at the University of Bristol. She left England in 1969 to live in Japan where she continued writing while she worked as a bartender in Tokyo. She wrote about her experiences in Japan in a series of short stories and articles and then left to travel to Europe and the United States. She wrote short stories, novels, and screenplays, and her work is often described as sharp, edgy, and witty. Her popular novel *Nights at the Circus* (1984), about a sensational female acrobatic performer, showcases the unique way in which Carter can play with traditional story structure forms.

"The Company of Wolves" is from Carter's short story collection *The Bloody Chamber* (1979). All of the stories in this collection are based on traditional European fairytales or folktales, but they are more than just "adult versions" of these tales: through the stories, Carter challenges the way women are represented in the folktale form, re-examining what these stories say about women's identity, their relationships, marriage, and sexuality. Critics called her story collection "remarkable." Carter was at work on another novel, a "sequel" to Charlotte Bronte's *Jane Eyre*, when she died of cancer in 1992. After her death, a friend told a London newspaper that Carter's stories "teach us how to live sanely in a world we share with horrors." Carter is still so beloved that fans continue to post discussions about her work online.

In Her Own Words

"My intention was not to do 'versions,' or . . . 'adult' fairy tales, but to extract the latent content from the traditional stories."

"Reading a book is like rewriting it for yourself. You bring to a novel anything you read, all your experience of the world. You bring your history and you read it in your own terms."

"I was reading 'The Company of Wolves' the other day, and there are a whole lot of verbal games in that that I really enjoy doing, 'the deer departed,' for example. People very rarely notice these when I'm reading them, but I think if you read it on the page. There was one thing in the movie 'The Company of Wolves,' when the werewolf-husband says he's just going out to answer a call of nature, and one of the critics wrote to me and said, 'I didn't even notice this the first time.' That's the sort of thing I like doing. These are sort of private jokes with myself and with whoever notices, and I used to enjoy doing that very much. There are lots of them in 'Nights at the Circus,' which was intended as a comic novel."

Before We Begin

1. "The Company of Wolves" contains elements of the folktale "Little Red Riding Hood." Are you familiar with this tale? What are the main elements of the traditional story?

2. What is the appeal behind folktales and fairytales? Can children and adults both take pleasure in hearing or reading these types of stories?

3. The image of Little Red Riding Hood has been used in advertisements, cartoons, and pop songs. How did a story that was originally a highly sexual and violent cautionary tale of promiscuity for young women turn into a cute story for children?

 **Now Read**

The Company of Wolves

One beast and only one howls in the woods by night.

The wolf is carnivore incarnate and he's as cunning as he is ferocious; once he's had a taste of flesh then nothing else will do.

At night, the eyes of wolves shine like candle flames, yellowish, reddish, but that is because the pupils of their eyes fatten on darkness and catch the light from your lantern to flash it back to you—red for danger; if a wolf's eyes reflect only moonlight, then they gleam a cold and unnatural green, a mineral, a piercing colour. If the benighted traveller spies those luminous, terrible sequins stitched suddenly on the black thickets, then he knows he must run, if fear has not struck him stock-still.

But those eyes are all you will be able to glimpse of the forest assassins as they cluster invisibly round your smell of meat as you go through the wood unwisely late. They will be like shadows, they will be like wraiths, grey members of a congregation of nightmare; hark! his long, wavering howl . . . an aria of fear made audible.

The wolfsong is the sound of the rending you will suffer, in itself a murdering.

It is winter and cold weather. In this region of mountain and forest, there is now nothing for the wolves to eat. Goats and sheep are locked up in the byre, the deer departed for the remaining pasturage on the southern slopes—wolves grow lean and famished. There is so little flesh on them that you could count the starveling ribs through their pelts, if they gave you time before they pounced. Those slavering jaws; the lolling tongue; the rime of saliva on the grizzled chops—of all the teeming perils of the night and the forest, ghosts, hobgoblins, ogres that grill babies upon gridirons, witches that fatten their captives in cages for cannibal tables, the wolf is worst for he cannot listen to reason.

You are always in danger in the forest, where no people are. Step between the portals of the great pines where the shaggy branches tangle about you, trapping the unwary traveller in nets as if the vegetation itself were in a plot with the wolves who live there, as though the wicked trees go fishing on behalf of their friends—step between the gateposts of the forest with the greatest trepidation and infinite precautions, for if you stray from the path for one instant, the wolves will eat you. They are grey as famine, they are as unkind as plague.

The grave-eyed children of the sparse villages always carry knives with them when they go to tend the little flocks of goats that provide the homesteads with acrid milk and rank, maggoty cheese. Their knives are half as big as they are, the blades are sharpened daily.

But the wolves have ways of arriving at your own hearthside. We try and try but sometimes we cannot keep them out. There is no winter's night the cottager does not fear to see a lean, grey, famished snout questing under the door, and there was a woman once bitten in her own kitchen as she was straining the macaroni.

Fear and flee the wolf; for, worst of all, the wolf may be more than he seems.

There was a hunter once, near here, that trapped a wolf in a pit. This wolf had massacred the sheep and goats; eaten up a mad old man who used to live by himself in a hut halfway up the mountain and sing to Jesus all day; pounced on a girl looking after the sheep, but she made such a commotion that men came with rifles and scared him away and tried to track him to the forest but he was cunning and easily gave them the slip. So this hunter dug a pit and put a duck in it, for bait, all alive-oh; and he covered the pit with straw smeared with wolf dung. Quack, quack! went the duck and a wolf came slinking out of the forest, a big one, a heavy one, he weighed as much as a grown man and the straw gave way beneath him—into the pit he tumbled. The hunter jumped down after him, slit his throat, cut off all his paws for a trophy.

And then no wolf at all lay in front of the hunter but the bloody trunk of a man, headless, footless, dying, dead.

A witch from up the valley once turned an entire wedding party into wolves because the groom had settled on another girl. She used to order them to visit her, at night, from spite, and they would sit and howl around her cottage for her, serenading her with their misery.

Not so very long ago, a young woman in our village married a man who vanished clean away on her wedding night. The bed was made with new sheets and the bride lay down in it; the groom said, he was going out to relieve himself, insisted on it, for the sake of decency, and she drew the coverlet up to her chin and lay there. And she waited and she waited and then she waited again—surely he's been gone a long time? Until she jumps up in bed and shrieks to hear a howling, coming on the wind from the forest.

That long-drawn, wavering howl has, for all its fearful resonance, some inherent sadness in it, as if the beasts would love to be less beastly if only they knew how and never cease to mourn their own condition. There is a vast melancholy in the canticles of the wolves, melancholy infinite as the forest, endless as these long nights of winter and yet that ghastly sadness, that mourning for their own, irremediable appetites, can never move the heart for not one phrase in it hints at the possibility of redemption; grace could not come to the wolf from its own despair, only through some external mediator, so that, sometimes, the beast will look as if he half welcomes the knife that dispatches him.

The young woman's brothers searched the outhouses and the haystacks but never found any remains so the sensible girl dried her eyes and found herself another husband not too shy to piss into a pot who spent the nights indoors. She gave him a pair of bonny babies and all went right as a trivet until, one freezing night, the night of the solstice, the hinge of the year when things do not fit together as well as they should, the longest night, her first good man came home again.

A great thump on the door announced him as she was stirring the soup for the father of her children and she knew him the moment she lifted the latch to him although it was years since she'd worn black for him and now he was in rags and his hair hung down his back and never saw a comb, alive with lice.

"Here I am again, missus," he said. "Get me my bowl of cabbage and be quick about it."

Then her second husband came in with wood for the fire and when the first one saw she'd slept with another man and, worse, clapped his red eyes on her little children who'd crept into the kitchen to see what all the din was about, he shouted: "I wish I were a wolf again, to teach this whore a lesson!" So a wolf he instantly became and tore off the eldest boy's left foot before he was chopped by the hatchet they used for chopping logs. But when the wolf lay bleeding and gasping its last, the pelt peeled off again and he was just as he had been, years ago, when he ran away from his marriage bed, so that she wept and her second husband beat her.

They say there's an ointment the Devil gives you that turns you into a wolf the minute you rub it on. Or, that he was born feet first and had a wolf for his father and his torso is a man's but his legs and genitals are a wolf's. And he has a wolf's heart.

Seven years is a werewolf's natural span but if you burn his human clothes you condemn him to wolfishness for the rest of his life, so old wives hereabouts think it some protection to throw a hat or an apron at the werewolf, as if clothes made the man. Yet by the eyes, those phosphorescent eyes, you know him in all his shapes; the eyes alone unchanged by metamorphosis.

Before he can become a wolf, the lycanthrope strips stark naked. If you spy a naked man among the pines, you must run as if the Devil were after you.

∴

It is midwinter and the robin, the friend of man, sits on the handle of the gardener's spade and sings. It is the worst time in all the year for wolves but this strong-minded child insists she will go off through the wood. She is quite sure the wild beasts cannot harm her although, well-warned, she lays a carving knife in the basket her mother has packed with cheeses. There is a bottle of harsh liquor distilled from brambles; a batch of flat oatcakes baked on the heathstone; a pot or two of jam. The girl will take these delicious gifts to a reclusive grandmother so old the burden of her years is crushing her to death. Granny lives two hours' trudge through the winter woods; the child wraps herself up in her thick shawl, draws it over her head. She steps into her stout wooden shoes; she is dressed and ready and it is Christmas Eve. The malign door of the solstice still swings upon its hinges but she has been too much loved ever to feel scared.

Children do not stay young for long in this savage country. There are no toys for them to play with so they work hard and grow wise but this one, so pretty and the youngest of her family, a little late-comer, had been indulged by her mother and the grandmother who'd knitted her the red shawl that, today, has the ominous if brilliant look of blood on snow. Her breasts have just begun to swell; her hair is like lint, so fair it hardly makes a shadow on her pale forehead; her cheeks are an emblematic scarlet and white and she has just started her woman's bleeding, the clock inside her that will strike, henceforward, once a month.

She stands and moves within the invisible pentacle of her own virginity. She is an unbroken egg; she is a sealed vessel; she has inside her a magic space the entrance to which is shut tight with a plug of membrane; she is a closed system; she does not know how to shiver. She has her knife and she is afraid of nothing.

Her father might forbid her, if he were home, but he is away in the forest, gathering wood, and her mother cannot deny her.

The forest closed upon her like a pair of jaws.

There is always something to look at in the forest, even in the middle of winter—the huddled mounds of birds, succumbed to the lethargy of the season, heaped on the creaking boughs and too forlorn to sing; the bright frills of the winter fungi on the blotched trunks of the trees; the cuneiform slots of rabbits and deer, the herringbone tracks of the birds, a hare as lean as a rasher of bacon streaking across the path where the thin sunlight dapples the russet brakes of last year's bracken.

When she heard the freezing howl of a distant wolf, her practised hand sprang to the handle of her knife, but she saw no sign of a wolf at all, nor of a naked man, neither, but then she heard a clattering among the brushwood and there sprang on to the path a fully clothed one, a very handsome young one, in the green coat and wideawake hat of a hunter, laden with carcasses of game birds. She had her hand on her knife at the first rustle of twigs but he laughed with a flash of white teeth when he saw her and made her a comic yet flattering little bow; she'd never seen such a fine fellow before, not among the rustic clowns of her native village. So on they went, through the thickening light of the afternoon.

Soon they were laughing and joking like old friends. When he offered to carry her basket, she gave it to him although her knife was in it because he told her his rifle would protect them. As the day darkened, it began to snow again; she felt the first flakes settle on her eyelashes but now there was only half a mile to go and there would be a fire, and hot tea, and a welcome, a warm one surely, for the dashing huntsman as well as for herself.

This young man had a remarkable object in his pocket. It was a compass. She looked at the little round glass face in the palm of his hand and watched the wavering needle with a vague wonder. He assured her this compass had taken him safely through the wood on his hunting trip because the needle always told him with perfect accuracy where the north was. She did not believe it; she knew she should never leave the path on the way through the wood or else she would be lost instantly. He laughed at her again; gleaming trails of spittle clung to his teeth. He said, if he plunged off the path into the forest that surrounded them, he would guarantee to arrive at her grandmother's house a good quarter of an hour before she did, plotting his way through the undergrowth with his compass, while she trudged the long way, along the winding path.

I don't believe you. Besides, aren't you afraid of the wolves?

He only tapped the gleaming butt of his rifle and grinned.

Is it a bet? he asked her. Shall we make a game of it? What will you give me if I get to your grandmother's house before you?

What would you like? she asked disingenuously.

A kiss.

Commonplaces of a rustic seduction; she lowered her eyes and blushed.

He went through the undergrowth and took her basket with him but she forgot to be afraid of the beasts, although now the moon was rising, for she wanted to dawdle on her way to make sure the handsome gentleman would win his wager.

Grandmother's house stood by itself a little way out of the village. The freshly falling snow blew in eddies about the kitchen garden and the young man stepped delicately up the snowy path to the door as if he were reluctant to get his feet wet, swinging his bundle of game and the girl's basket and humming a little tune to himself.

There is a faint trace of blood on his chin; he has been snacking on his catch.

He rapped upon the panels with his knuckles.

Aged and frail, granny is three-quarters succumbed to the mortality the ache in her bones promises her and almost ready to give in entirely. A boy came out from the village to build up her hearth for the night an hour ago and the kitchen crackles with busy firelight. She has her Bible for company, she is a pious old woman. She is propped up on several pillows in the bed set into the wall peasant-fashion, wrapped up in the patchwork quilt she made before she was married, more years ago than she cares to remember. Two china spaniels with liver-coloured blotches on their coats and black noses sit on either side of the fireplace. There is a bright rug of woven rags on the pantiles. The grandfather clock ticks away her eroding time.

We keep the wolves outside by living well.

He rapped upon the panels with his hairy knuckles.

It is your granddaughter, he mimicked in a high soprano.

Lift up the latch and walk in, my darling.

You can tell them by their eyes, eyes of a beast of prey, nocturnal, devastating eyes as red as a wound; you can hurl your Bible at him and your apron after, granny, you thought that was a sure prophylactic against these infernal vermin ... now call on

Christ and his mother and all the angels in heaven to protect you but it won't do you any good.

His feral muzzle is sharp as a knife; he drops his golden burden of gnawed pheasant on the table and puts down your dear girl's basket, too. Oh, my God, what have you done with her?

Off with his disguise, that coat of forest-coloured cloth, the hat with the feather tucked into the ribbon; his matted hair streams down his white shirt and she can see the lice moving in it. The sticks in the hearth shift and hiss; night and the forest has come into the kitchen with darkness tangled in its hair.

He strips off his shirt. His skin is the colour and texture of vellum. A crisp stripe of hair runs down his belly, his nipples are ripe and dark as poison fruit but he's so thin you could count the ribs under his skin if only he gave you the time. He strips off his trousers and she can see how hairy his legs are. His genitals, huge. Ah! huge.

The last thing the old lady saw in all this world was a young man, eyes like cinders, naked as a stone, approaching her bed.

The wolf is carnivore incarnate.

When he had finished with her, he licked his chops and quickly dressed himself again, until he was just as he had been when he came through her door. He burned the inedible hair in the fireplace and wrapped the bones up in a napkin that he hid away under the bed in the wooden chest in which he found a clean pair of sheets. These he carefully put on the bed instead of the telltale stained ones he stowed away in the laundry basket. He plumped up the pillows and shook out the patchwork quilt, he picked up the Bible from the floor, closed it and laid it on the table. All was as it had been before except that grandmother was gone. The sticks twitched in the grate, the clock ticked and the young man sat patiently, deceitfully beside the bed in granny's nightcap.

Rat-a-tap-tap.

Who's there, he quavers in granny's antique falsetto.

Only your granddaughter.

So she came in, bringing with her a flurry of snow that melted in tears on the tiles, and perhaps she was a little disappointed to see only her grandmother sitting beside the fire. But then he flung off the blanket and sprang to the door, pressing his back against it so that she could not get out again.

The girl looked round the room and saw there was not even the indentation of a head on the smooth cheek of the pillow and how, for the first time she'd seen it so, the Bible lay closed on the table. The tick of the clock cracked like a whip. She wanted her knife from her basket but she did not dare to reach for it because his eyes were fixed upon her—huge eyes that now seemed to shine with a unique, interior light, eyes the size of saucers, saucers full of Greek fire, diabolic phosphorescence.

What big eyes you have.

All the better to see you with.

No trace at all of the old woman except for a tuft of white hair that had caught in the bark of an unburned log. When the girl saw that, she knew she was in danger of death.

Where is my grandmother?

There's nobody here but we two, my darling.

Now a great howling rose up all around them, near, very near as close as the kitchen garden, the howling of a multitude of wolves; she knew the worst wolves are hairy on the inside and she shivered, in spite of the scarlet shawl she pulled more closely round herself as if it could protect her although it was as red as the blood she must spill.

Who has come to sing us carols, she said.

Those are the voices of my brothers, darling; I love the company of wolves. Look out of the window and you'll see them.

Snow half-caked the lattice and she opened it to look into the garden. It was a white night of moon and snow; the blizzard whirled round the gaunt, grey beasts who squatted on their haunches among the rows of winter cabbage, pointing their sharp snouts to the moon and howling as if their hearts would break. Ten wolves; 20 wolves—so many wolves she could not count them, howling in concert as if demented or deranged. Their eyes reflected the light from the kitchen and shone like a hundred candles.

It is very cold, poor things, she said; no wonder they howl so.

She closed the window on the wolves' threnody and took off her scarlet shawl, the colour of poppies, the colour of sacrifices, the colour of her menses, and, since her fear did her no good, she ceased to be afraid.

What shall I do with my shawl?

Throw it on the fire, dear one. You won't need it again.

She bundled up her shawl and threw it on the blaze, which instantly consumed it. Then she drew her blouse over her head; her small breasts gleamed as if the snow had invaded the room.

What shall I do with my blouse?

Into the fire with it, too, my pet.

The thin muslin went flaring up the chimney like a magic bird and now off came her skirt, her woollen stockings, her shoes, and on to the fire they went, too, and were gone for good. The firelight shone through the edges of her skin; now she was clothed only in her untouched integument of flesh. This dazzling, naked she combed out her hair with her fingers; her hair looked white as the snow outside. Then went directly to the man with red eyes in whose unkempt mane the lice moved; she stood up on tiptoe and unbuttoned the collar of his shirt.

What big arms you have.

All the better to hug you with.

Every wolf in the world now howled a prothalamion outside the window as she freely gave him the kiss she owed him.

What big teeth you have!

She saw how his jaw began to slaver and the room was full of the clamour of the forest's *Liebestod* but the wise child never flinched, even as he answered: All the better to eat you with.

The girl burst out laughing; she knew she was nobody's meat. She laughed at him full in the face, she ripped off his shirt for him and flung it into the fire, in the fiery wake of her own discarded clothing. The flames danced like dead souls on Walpurgisnacht and the old bones under the bed set up a terrible clattering but she did not pay them any heed.

Carnivore incarnate, only immaculate flesh appeases him.

She will lay his fearful head on her lap and she will pick out the lice from his pelt and perhaps she will put the lice into her mouth and eat them, as he will bid her, as she would do in a savage marriage ceremony.

The blizzard will die down.

The blizzard died down, leaving the mountains as randomly covered with snow as if a blind woman had thrown a sheet over them, the upper branches of the forest pines limed, creaking, swollen with the fall.

Snowlight, moonlight, a confusion of paw prints.

All silent, all silent.

Midnight; and the clock strikes. It is Christmas day, the werewolves' birthday, the door of the solstice stands wide open; let them all sink through.

See! sweet and sound she sleeps in granny's bed, between the paws of the tender wolf.

F.Y.I.

Greek fire: an incendiary weapon used by Christians during the Byzantine Empire for the purpose of igniting enemy ships; used here by Carter to describe the hunter's eyes

hobgoblins: figures from fairytales and folktales that are often described as small hairy men; they are considered troublesome but friendly

Liebestod: literally means "love-death"; a term used in relation to art (poetry, opera) when two lovers consummate their love in death or when they find fulfillment only after death

lycanthrope: the original Greek term for werewolf (half human–half wolf) referring to the transformation of a person into a wolf

ogres: figures from fairytales and folktales that come in male and female (ogress) forms; they are considered large, cruel, and violent, often killing and consuming humans

solstice: an astronomical event that happens twice a year when the sun is at its highest point, marked by the longest and shortest days; linked in many cultures to various rites and celebrations connected to the summer and winter seasons

Walpursignacht: a religious holiday of pre-Christian origin celebrated in central and northern Europe on May 1; alleged to be the night that witches meet and await the arrival of spring

Words to Build on

benighted: overtaken by night or darkness

bonny: physically attractive and healthy looking

canticles: a song or chant with a Biblical text

flaxen-haired: hair coloured blonde or pale yellow

hearthside: the area in front or near a hearth or fireplace

incarnate: when a quality or spirit becomes "flesh" or takes human form, such as the expression "the devil incarnate" which is used when someone embodies evil qualities; here the wolf is "carnivore incarnate"

malign: malevolent, wicked, or harmful

muslin: cotton or cotton-blend fabric of a plain weave

pentacle: a figure used as a symbol, especially in magic (a pentagram)

phosphorescent: the emission of light without combustion or perceptible heat

prothalamion: a song or poem to celebrate a forthcoming wedding

rending: to tear forcibly

resonance: the reinforcement or prolongation of sound by reflection or synchronous vibration

threnody: a song or lamentation, especially for the dead

trivet: cast iron, three-legged stand to keep a pot raised while cooking, heating, and roasting food over a fire

wraiths: a ghost or apparition

Tricks of the Trade

Atmosphere

Eroticism/Erotic literature

Foreshadowing

Magic realism

Oral storytelling/Orature

Revisionist literature

Symbol

In Your Own Words: Comprehension

1. Who is telling this story? What is unique about the narrative style? Does the voice belong to a male or female narrator? How can you tell?

2. "The Company of Wolves" is not just a retelling of "Little Red Riding Hood": Carter's story interweaves many other legends and folktales involving the were-wolf. Identify the stories Carter includes in this text.

3. How is the female protagonist, the girl, described by the narrator?

4. What does the reader learn about werewolves from this story?

5. What is the climax of Carter's story? Compare this to the climax of the original version of "Little Red Riding Hood," when the girl says, "Grandmother, what big teeth you have!"

6. Why is this story called "The Company of Wolves"?

7. Although this story is written, Carter has infused it with some elements of a much older oral storytelling tradition. With specific reference to the story, identify some of these elements. Think of storytelling techniques and styles that appear in most folktales and fairytales since these have their roots in an older oral tradition.

In Your Own Words: Analysis

1. Carter's story is related to the story of Little Red Riding Hood. Compare Carter's version to what you know about the original tale. How is Carter's version similar and how is it different?

2. The narrator states, "We keep the wolves outside by living well." What does this statement mean?

3. How are wolves depicted in this story? Does this story show any empathy for wolves?

4. The hunter's compass needle, the forest setting, the girl's shawl, and fire are all symbolic. How does the narrator describe each of these elements and what does each represent and contribute to the story's broader themes?

5. Does Carter's girl in the "scarlet shawl" have a happy ending?

6. What are some elements of magic realism in "The Company of Wolves"?

❄ Now Write

1. In one of the original versions of "Little Red Riding Hood," the woodsman or hunter rescues the girl. In "The Company of Wolves" the narrator states "since her fear did her no good, she ceased to be afraid." Write an essay examining the girl's actions in the story and explain what makes her so fearless. Can she be seen as heroic?

2. In modern culture, childhood is always idealized. However, in many traditional fairytales and other stories childhood is far from ideal. Examine and compare how the state of childhood is treated in the following stories: "The Company of Wolves," "The Loons," and "Legless Joe versus Black Robe." Pay special attention to social class and setting.

3. In 1984, Angela Carter co-wrote the script for the feature film of this story by director Neil Jordan (*Crying Game*). Find and view Jordan's *The Company of Wolves*. Write an essay comparing the film to the written work.

4. Think about how the forest and nature in general are presented in "The Company of Wolves." The natural world is often idealized as something that must be protected. However, nature has another side that's destructive and changeable; the only moral code it has is survival. Write an essay that examines how Carter presents nature in this story. What place do humans have in Carter's version of the natural world?

5. In the original telling of "Little Red Riding Hood" the wolf is the "seducer" or "sexual predator." How does Carter revise this original view by making the female protagonist the aggressor? Write an essay that examines how this "updated" version is a story of female empowerment.

Michael Ondaatje

Michael Ondaatje (b. 1943) was born in Colombo, Sri Lanka, and is of Colombo Chetty and Burgher ancestry. He immigrated to Canada from England in 1962. In addition to writing fiction and poetry, he has taught at various universities and has been involved in films, plays, and photography. He is best known for his work *The English Patient* (1992), which was adapted into an Academy Award–winning film. Ondaatje's work is often called "cinematic" because it incorporates montage techniques and "shot-worthy" images. He also bases many of his stories on real people with unorthodox lives, and he will mix documentary with fiction in the telling of their tales. This can be seen in the following excerpt from his first novel, *In the Skin of a Lion* (1987), which won the City of Toronto Book Award. The novel has been called an exposé of the lives of early twentieth century immigrant workers. In order to write the work, Ondaatje consulted historical archives, but he also interviewed members of the Macedonian community for his research on the daredevil bridge worker, Nicholas Temelcoff. Ondaatje has won the Governor General's Literary Award four times, in addition to the Man Booker Prize and the Giller Prize. In 1988 he was named to the Order of Canada. Ondaatje lives in Toronto.

In His Own Words

"Reclaiming untold stories is an essential role for the writer. Especially in this country where one can no longer trust media."

"[I see myself as belonging to a generation of writers that] was the first of the real migrant tradition . . . of writers of our time—Rushdie, Ishiguro, Ben Okri, Rohinton Mistry—writers leaving and not going back, but taking their country with them into a new place."

Before We Begin

1. Have you ever looked at your city or town's monuments or structures and considered whose hands built them?
2. Can history or historical truths only be found in textbooks? Is the history found in books always reliable and complete? When would one have to turn to other sources, such as community members or eyewitnesses, to find the truth?
3. Today an academic education, or "book smarts," is often considered to be more valuable than skills acquired through trades. This change is evident in the programs offered by Canadian colleges. Skilled tradespeople were once highly valued. Why has this changed?

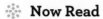 **Now Read**

from *In the Skin of a Lion*

A truck carries fire at five a.m. through central Toronto, along Dundas Street and up Parliament Street, moving north. Aboard the flatbed three men stare into passing darkness—their muscles relaxed in this last half-hour before work—as if they don't own the legs or the arms jostling against their bodies and the backboard of the Ford.

Written in yellow over the green door is DOMINION BRIDGE COMPANY. But for now all that is visible is the fire on the flatbed burning over the three-foot by three-foot metal dish, cooking the tar in a cauldron, leaving this odour on the streets for anyone who would step out into the early morning and swallow the air.

The truck rolls burly under the arching trees, pauses at certain intersections where more workers jump onto the flatbed, and soon there are eight men, the fire crackling, hot tar now and then spitting onto the back of a neck or an ear. Soon there are 20, crowded and silent.

The light begins to come out of the earth. They see their hands, the textures on a coat, the trees they had known were there. At the top of Parliament Street the truck turns east, passes the Rosedale fill, and moves towards the half-built viaduct.

The men jump off. The unfinished road is full of ruts and the fire and the lights of the truck bounce, the suspension wheezing. The truck travels so slowly the men are walking faster, in the cold dawn air, even though it is summer.

Later they will remove coats and sweaters, then by 11 their shirts, bending over the black rivers of tar in just their trousers, boots, and caps. But now the thin layer of frost is everywhere, coating the machines and cables, brittle on the rain puddles they step through. The fast evaporation of darkness. As light emerges they see their breath, the clarity of the air being breathed out of them. The truck finally stops at the edge of the viaduct, and its lights are turned off.

The bridge goes up in a dream. It will link the east end with the centre of the city. It will carry traffic, water, and electricity across the Don Valley. It will carry trains that have not even been invented yet.

Night and day. Fall light. Snow light. They are always working—horses and wagons and men arriving for work on the Danforth side at the far end of the valley.

There are over 4000 photographs from various angles of the bridge in its time-lapse evolution. The piers sink into bedrock 50 feet below the surface through clay and shale and quicksand—45,000 cubic yards of earth are excavated. The network of scaffolding stretches up.

Men in a maze of wooden planks climb deep into the shattered light of blond wood. A man is an extension of hammer, drill, flame. Drill smoke in his hair. A cap falls into the valley, gloves are buried in stone dust.

Then the new men arrive, the "electricals," laying grids of wire across the five arches, carrying the exotic three-bowl lights, and on October 18, 1918, it is completed. Lounging in mid-air.

The bridge. The bridge. Christened "Prince Edward." The Bloor Street Viaduct.

The last thing Rowland Harris, Commissioner of Public Works, would do in the evenings during its construction was have himself driven to the edge of the viaduct, to sit for a while. At midnight the half-built bridge over the valley seemed deserted—just lanterns tracing its outlines. But there was always a night shift of 30 or 40 men. After a while Harris removed himself from the car, lit a cigar, and walked onto the bridge. He loved this viaduct. It was his first child as head of Public Works much of it planned before he took over but he had bullied it through. It was Harris who envisioned that it could carry not just cars but trains on a lower trestle. It could also transport water from the east-end plants to the centre of the city. Water was Harris's great passion. He wanted giant water mains travelling across the valley as part of the viaduct.

He slipped past the barrier and walked towards the working men. Few of them spoke English but they knew who he was. Sometimes he was accompanied by Pomphrey, an architect, the strange one from England who was later to design for Commissioner Harris one of the city's grandest buildings—the water filtration plant in the east end. . . .

An April night in 1917. Harris and Pomphrey were on the bridge, in the dark wind. Pomphrey had turned west and was suddenly stilled. His hand reached out to touch Harris on the shoulder, a gesture he had never made before.

—*Look!*

Walking on the bridge were five nuns.

Past the Dominion Steel castings wind attacked the body directly. The nuns were walking past the first group of workers at the fire. The bus, Harris thought, must have dropped them off near Castle Frank and the nuns had, with some confusion at that hour, walked the wrong way in the darkness.

They had passed the black car under the trees and talking cheerfully stepped past the barrier into a landscape they did not know existed—onto a tentative carpet over the piers, among the night labourers. They saw the fire and the men. A few tried to wave them back. There was a mule attached to a wagon. The hiss and jump of machines made the ground under them lurch. A smell of creosote. One man was washing his face in a barrel of water.

The nuns were moving towards a 30-yard point on the bridge when the wind began to scatter them. They were thrown against cement mixers and steam shovels, careering from side to side, in danger of going over the edge.

Some of the men grabbed and enclosed them, pulling leather straps over their shoulders, but two were still loose. Harris and Pomphrey at the far end looked on helplessly as one nun was lifted up and flung against the compressors. She stood up shakily and then the wind jerked her sideways, scraping her along the concrete and right off the edge of the bridge. She disappeared into the night by the third abutment, into the long depth of air which held nothing, only sometimes a rivet or a dropped hammer during the day.

Then there was no longer any fear on the bridge. The worst, the incredible had happened. A nun had fallen off the Prince Edward Viaduct before it was even finished. The men covered in wood shavings or granite dust held the women against them. And Commissioner Harris at the far end stared along the mad pathway. This was his first child and it had already become a murderer.

The man in mid-air under the central arch saw the shape fall towards him, in that second knowing his rope would not hold them both. He reached to catch the figure while his other hand grabbed the metal pipe edge above him to lessen the sudden jerk on the rope. The new weight ripped the arm that held the pipe out of its socket and he screamed, so whoever might have heard him up there would have thought the scream was from the falling figure. The halter thulked, jerking his chest up to his throat. The right arm was all agony now—but his hand's timing had been immaculate, the grace of the habit, and he found himself a moment later holding the figure against him dearly.

He saw it was a black-garbed bird, a girl's white face. He saw this in the light that sprayed down inconstantly from a flare 15 yards above them. They hung in the halter, pivoting over the valley, his broken arm loose on one side of him, holding the woman with the other. Her body was in shock, her huge eyes staring into the face of Nicholas Temelcoff.

Scream, please, Lady, he whispered, the pain terrible. He asked her to hold him by the shoulders, to take the weight off his one good arm. A sway in the wind. She could not speak though her eyes glared at him bright, just staring at him. *Scream, please.* But she could not.

During the night, the long chutes through which wet concrete slid were unused and hung loose so the open spouts wavered a few feet from the valley floor. The tops of these were about 10 feet from him now. He knew this without seeing them, even though they fell outside the scope of light. If they attempted to slide the chute their weight would make it vertical and dangerous. They would have to go further—to reach the lower-deck level of the bridge where there were structures built for possible water mains.

We have to swing. She had her hands around his shoulders now, the wind assaulting them. The two strangers were in each other's arms, beginning to swing wilder, once more, past the lip of the chute which had tempted them, till they were almost at the lower level of the rafters. He had his one good arm free. Saving her now would be her responsibility.

Nicholas Temelcoff is famous on the bridge, a daredevil. He is given all the difficult jobs and he takes them. He descends into the air with no fear. He is a solitary. He assembles ropes, brushes the tackle and pulley at his waist, and falls off the bridge like a diver over the edge of a boat. The rope roars alongside him, slowing with the pressure of his half-gloved hands. He is burly on the ground and then falls with terrific speed, grace, using the wind to push himself into corners of abutments so he can check driven rivets, sheering valves, the drying of the concrete under bearing plates and padstones. He stands in the air banging the crown pin into the upper cord and then shepherds the lower cord's slip-joint into position. Even in archive photographs it is difficult to find him. Again and again you see vista before you and the eye must search along the wall of sky to the speck of burned paper across the valley that is him, an exclamation mark, somewhere in the distance between bridge and river. He floats at the three hinges of the crescent-shaped steel arches. These knit the bridge together. The moment of cubism.

He is happiest at daily chores—ferrying tools from pier down to trestle, or lumber that he pushes in the air before him as if swimming in a river. He is a spinner. He links everyone. He meets them as they cling—braced by wind against the metal they are riveting or the wood sheeting they hammer into—but he has none of their fear. Always he carries his own tackle, hunched under his ropes and dragging the shining pitons behind him. He sits on a coiled seat of rope while he eats his lunch on the bridge. If he finishes early he cycles down Parliament Street to the Ohrida Lake Restaurant and sits in the darkness of the room as if he has had enough of light. Enough of space.

His work is so exceptional and time-saving he earns one dollar an hour while the other bridge workers receive 40 cents. There is no jealousy towards him. No one dreams of doing half the things he does. For night work he is paid $1.25, swinging up into the rafters of a trestle holding a flare, free-falling like a dead star. He does not really need to see things, he has charted all that space, knows the pier footings, the width of the crosswalks in terms of seconds of movement—281 feet and 6 inches make up the central span of the bridge. Two flanking spans of 240 feet, two end spans of 158 feet. He slips into openings on the lower deck, tackles himself up to bridge level. He knows the precise height he is over the river, how long his ropes are, how many seconds he can free-fall to the pulley. It does not matter if it is day or night, he could be blindfolded. Black space is time. After swinging for three seconds he puts his feet up to link with the concrete edge of the next pier. He knows his position in the air as if he is mercury slipping across a map.

F.Y.I.

Bloor Street Viaduct: originally named the Prince Edward Viaduct for the Prince of Wales, Edward VIII, it is a truss arch bridge system in Toronto that connects Bloor Street East on the west side of the system with Danforth Avenue on the east. The construction project was finished in 1919 and has had a major impact on the development of Toronto. This bridge is of great historical significance since in essence it united the two halves of the city of Toronto.

Nicholas Temelcoff: the name of a Macedonian Canadian worker/bridge builder that Ondaatje discovered through research at the Toronto Multicultural Society. On April 23, 2009, at the ceremony for Project Bookmark Canada, a plaque containing a passage from the book was placed in honour of Temelcoff and the workers who built the bridge. Ondaatje stated: "I would love to have this bridge named after him, rather than calling it 'The Prince Edward Viaduct' . . . because this is where the real Nicholas Temelcoff worked, and this is where the fictional Nicholas Temelcoff worked." (http://projectbookmarkcanada.ca)

Pomphrey: Thomas Canfield Pomphrey (1882–1966) was born in Scotland, where he studied architecture, but later immigrated to Canada and was involved in various design and building projects in Toronto throughout the 1920s and into the 1930s.

Rowland Harris: based on the real-life Commissioner of Works for the City of Toronto, Rowland Caldwell Harris (1875–1945), who worked for the city from 1912 until his death in 1945. Under his leadership, Toronto built both the Bloor Street Viaduct and the R.C. Harris Water Treatment Plant, which was named after him.

Words to Build on

abutments: lateral supporting structures of a bridge or arch

burly: of stout, sturdy build

careering: to move or swerve about wildly

cubism: an art style in which objects are represented as an assemblage of geometrical forms

habit (nun's): the dress of the Catholic women's orders

ruts: any type of groove or deep tracks made by the passage of wheels

shale: soft, finely stratified rock that splits easily

trestle: an open, braced framework to support a bridge

vista: a scenic wide view or panorama

Tricks of the Trade

Character

Historical allusion

Imagery

Motif

In Your Own Words: Comprehension

1. What reasons are stated in the story for the bridge being built?

2. This story is rooted in a specific time and place. Where and when does this story take place? Provide evidence from the story.

3. Who are the characters in this story? List them and beside each name explain the identity of each character and his or her role in the events of this story.

4. Describe the working conditions of the bridge workers.

5. Why does the nun never speak? Why does Temelcoff ask her to scream?

6. Ondaatje describes Temelcoff's movement as "mercury slipping across a map." Explain what this means.

In Your Own Words: Analysis

1. How would you describe Ondaatje's writing style?

2. Can an inanimate object be a character? Consider the depiction of the bridge in this story.

3. What makes Temelcoff able to do the work he does?

4. Working-class characters (or labourers) are not often portrayed as key characters in fiction. How are they portrayed here? What kinds of words does Ondaatje use to describe the men and the work they do? Do you view Temelcoff as a heroic figure?

5. How does Ondaatje present the individual versus the collective or community?

6. In an omitted part of this excerpt, the nun is described as "always unlucky" as she is the one with "the small scar against her nose...she was always falling into windows, against chairs." Is "unlucky" an accurate descriptor for her judging by the passage in this text? Explain why or why not.

7. Ondaatje's narrator does not follow a chronological structure (past to present) in the telling of the bridge's construction. Explain why.

❊ Now Write

1. Write an essay in which you explain how Ondaatje portrays different social classes and the work they do.

2. Ondaatje's novel is about the valuable work all tradespeople do on building projects. How is the builder or construction worker's work similar to that of an artist such as a painter or sculptor? Make reference to the story and any other buildings or projects you know about.

3. Ondaatje's writing has been called highly "filmable" since his storytelling style is very visual. In this excerpt, the narrative voice describes setting and situations in terms of day and night, light and dark. How do different characters perceive day and night in this story and why are their attitudes different?

4. Write an essay explaining what the bridge in this excerpt means to the different characters.

5. Many people say they don't read fiction because they want to read the "truth" and not what an author invents. Much of Ondaatje's novel is based on historical truth (i.e. documented facts, real people and actual events). Can an artist/author convey aspects of history in his/her work that a historian cannot? Write an essay using this excerpt from Ondaatje's novel and explain the ways in which art, specifically fiction, relays certain truths and fills in what is lacking in historical accounts.

Katherine Alexander

Katherine Alexander (b. 1935) was born in Winnipeg, Manitoba, to Greek immigrant parents. After graduating from the University of Manitoba she lived in Greece but then returned to Canada to further her studies and teach. In 1987 she published *Children of Byzantium*, a novel of interconnected stories that describe the life of Eleni, a Greek immigrant who begins her life in a Greek village full of hope and promise and later moves to Canada with her husband where she finds hardship and isolation. "A Bit of Magic" is taken from her novel and is set in Winnipeg during the 1930s. At this time the effects of the Depression could be sharply felt: many husbands were left without work, and wives drew on various ingenious methods to try and feed their families. The story of Eleni explores not only traditional expectations of gender, but also how the mainstream Anglo-Canadian culture of the time viewed "foreigners" as exotic.

In Her Own Words

"Immigrants search for paradise in the new world, much the way poets sought perfection in the world of Byzantium. Yet neither poet nor immigrant can leave the old world behind."

"I suppose I would like the book to stand on its own—as the story of a woman, because that's really what I was writing about. I was writing about a woman who lives in silence, and what it does to her. I guess in my mind I play down the ethnic connection, and play up the role of the church, the patriarchal world, being a stranger in a strange land, both the male world and a different country—not necessarily that this is a Greek story. Of course, I wrote out of my background."

Before We Begin

1. Can artists (writers, filmmakers, musicians) outside a group or community accurately and authentically portray another group's or person's experiences?
2. Where and when do people pretend to be something or someone they are not?
3. What is the strangest thing you have ever done to earn some extra money?

❋ **Now Read**

A Bit of Magic

"I told Alekos I could look for a job," Matina said. "You can imagine how he reacted to that."

Eleni lay down her sewing. "Even if he allowed it," she said thoughtfully, "what would you do?"

"I don't know!" Matina sank back on the couch, bit at the edge of a fingernail. "Maybe Anna has the answer in those cups of hers." She turned to her sister-in-law who was coming into the living room with a tray of Turkish coffee.

Eleni pushed aside a pile of English magazines and children's books to make room on the coffee table.

"I offered to help out," Anna said. She set down the tray and handed around the coffee. "Pavlo refused to discuss it."

"He's right," Eleni said. "You have small children to worry about."

Matina put down her coffee. "Whereas you and I, Elenáki, with ours at school all day, have plenty of time." She twisted a strand of hair around her finger. "There must be something we're good for," she said, "something we can do. Even without Anna's education."

"Costa says things will get better soon," Eleni said.

"How long have they all been saying that!" Matina cried.

At the beginning, the Depression had been just a word to explain why they couldn't have the little extras they'd become used to over the years, but lately it had started to touch them in places they understood. Darning underwear and socks that were almost threadbare, layering newspaper inside shoes that were worn thin at the soles, frequent meals of *fasoláda,* the bean soup they all knew from earlier years in Greece, were daily reminders of the poverty they'd thought was behind them.

"Alekos complains every day about the rich customers at the store, with their maids and big cars, who won't pay their bills," Matina said. "When I ask him why he keeps selling to them, he says they owe so much he has to or they'll never pay up."

"I don't understand," Eleni said. She put down her coffee, picked up her sewing again.

"Do you think I do? We fight about it all the time. That and everything else."

Matina couldn't sit still, fidgeting with her coffee cup, turning it round and round in her fingers, watching Eleni calmly darning one of her son's undershirts for the dozenth time, Anna quietly sipping her coffee. Their complacency exasperated her. She was angry with Alekos much of the time as well, the way he'd criticize her whenever she tried to talk to him about money or the possibility of her taking a job; what could she do, he'd say sarcastically, except to go out and clean houses; or else he'd turn pompous and announce that he would never allow his wife to work.

"Turn over your cup," Anna said to Matina. "I'll have time to read at least one before Mike wakes up."

"All right. All right." She finished up the coffee, put the cup upside down on the saucer, turned it three times, made a wish, shook the cup to make sure the grounds were well drained, and handed it over.

Anna placed the cup on the palm of one hand and rotated it slowly with the fingers of the other, all the while staring down at the blackened shapes formed by the coffee. For all her scoffing, Matina couldn't help but get caught up in the aura of mystery created by her sister-in-law as she gazed solemnly into the turning cup. It was all nonsense, of course. Matina knew exactly what was coming next. Anna would stop the turning and point dramatically at the cup, as if, all at once, it was magically made clear to her and she could actually gaze beyond the coffee and into the future.

"Enough theatrics," Matina said. "Get on with it."

"Wait," Anna said sharply. "I have to be sure."

Matina let out a sigh, waited as long as she could. "Do you see a job or money in there?" she asked finally.

Anna pointed. "There, at the side. Do you see the bird? It's almost at the rim."

"All I see," Marina said staring in at the tiny cup, "is the big clump of grounds at the bottom. Doesn't that mean worry?"

"Yes, but see how the worry disappears? The bird is taking it away."

"Tell me more nice things," Matina said, settling in.

"I tell you only what the cup says."

Anna found letters and good omens, prophesied much activity, and said Matina's wish would come true. "I see you all dressed up," she said at one point. "A masquerade."

"Oh, good, a party."

Anna shook her head very slowly. "You'll be the only one in costume."

Mike's cries broke into their mood. Anna put down the cup, smiled normally once again, and went to get her son.

Matina was too restless to go straight home after she and Eleni left Anna's. She went walking instead, down one residential street and up another until she was practically lost. She realized where she was when she reached a cluster of small shops. In the days when they'd had their car, they'd sometimes driven through the area. She paused to admire an exquisite white crepe evening gown at Belle's French Fashions and an enormous bouquet of deep red roses that filled the window of McClary's Flower Shop, but walked quickly by the display of imported foods at Smith and Son. A group of ladies in fur capes and feather hats walking out of Morgan's Restaurant and Tea Room across the street caught her attention. When they disappeared, laughing, around the corner, she crossed over. She was curious to see inside, but heavy curtains covered the windows. A sign by the door read: *Tea-Cup Reading by Madame Rosa: Monday, Wednesday, Friday: 2–4.*

All the way home, Matina thought about what she'd stumbled across, and told herself that if she were superstitious she'd take it as an omen. Still, she hardly slept that night, and the next morning, as soon as Alekos had gone to work and Irini to school, she left for Eleni's. On the way, she stopped at the grocery store and bought a small packet of tea.

"English tea," she explained to Eleni.

"How do you make it?"

"Like *camomíli,* I imagine."

Eleni put a heaping spoonful of the tea into a saucepan, added cold water and put it on the stove. When it came to a boil, she turned the heat down, added some honey, and let the mixture simmer.

"Don't use that," Matina said as Eleni took the strainer out of the cutlery drawer.

"What's gotten into you?" Eleni asked.

"Make sure lots of leaves get into the cups," Matina said. Eleni poured as instructed and they watched the leaves settle at the bottom of each cup.

"Are you going to tell me what you're up to?" Eleni asked as they waited for the tea to cool down enough to drink.

"We're going to tell fortunes," Matina said.

"We need coffee grounds for that."

"The *englézi* read tea leaves. They even have shops where you can go to drink tea and then have a Madame somebody or other tell your fortune." She looked impatiently at Eleni. "You've seen them in passing."

"You didn't go inside one!"

"Oh, don't look so worried."

"I am worried. You've been acting very strangely lately. I wouldn't put it past you to go into one of those places just to make Alekos angry." They both knew how their husbands felt about women going into restaurants or tea rooms unaccompanied—it was something only *xénes,* foreigners, did.

"Drink," Matina said, handing her the cup.

"Fine. We won't talk about it. I'd just like to know what you're up to." Eleni sipped the tea, made a face, and pushed her cup away. "The *englézi* have no taste," she said.

"Don't be fussy." Matina drank and winced. They tried adding more honey but in the end had to throw out the bitter stuff in order to get at the leaves.

They clumped together in Matina's cup, but spread themselves around in Eleni's. "There, you see, they make different patterns," Matina cried happily. "Let's find letters and trips and birds and things now."

"You've gone crazy, Matina," Eleni said finally.

"No, listen, I have a wonderful idea, and you're going to help me." It seemed reasonable, she explained to Eleni, that if telling fortunes was as easy as Anna seemed to make it, and if the *englézi* offered tea cup reading in their stores, why not dress up in costume, read tea cups in a restaurant, and get paid for it?

"You intend to turn yourself into a *gyftisa,* a gypsy, and go out among strangers!" Eleni cried. "What will Alekos say?"

"You don't think I'd tell him!"

For every sensible argument Eleni could think of against the wild scheme, Matina had an answer: no one would ever find out; the children needed new clothes; Christmas was coming; but most important of all, they needed the money.

Eleni gave up trying to talk sense to Matina, peered at the leaves stuck to the bottom of her cup and handed it over. "All right, Madam *Gyftisa,* what do you see?"

Matina laughed and hugged Eleni. "I see a secret admirer, a mysterious stranger, sudden wealth, good luck in the form of, ah, let's see now, what is it, ah, it's getting clearer, yes, that's it . . . the letter M!" She paused dramatically, looked up. "The letter M," she went on most solemnly, "will be important to you. A person whose name begins with that initial will bring you great wealth." She put down the cup. "How's that?"

"How will you say all those things in English?"

"I'll be the mysterious lady from the mysterious east, like in the moving pictures. They all speak funny English, too"

"You'll need a special outfit then, mysterious lady."

"That's where you come in, *Elenáki*" Matina smiled sweetly. "You're so good at sewing."

After a week of practising her fortune telling on Anna and standing still for Eleni who sewed and fitted the costume for the mysterious lady of the east, Madame Zolta was ready to make her appearance.

"What does it mean?" Eleni asked.

"Zolta? I don't know. Nothing. It sounds oriental. Better than Madame Rosa. Very dull."

"You won't be dull in that outfit." Eleni surveyed her handiwork. Bits and pieces of materials from worn-out dresses and panels from curtains that had strangely lost some of their fullness had been worked into an ensemble that resembled nothing less than the most spectacular Hollywood Arabian Nights outfit.

Matina twirled around Eleni's living room bedecked in a pair of emerald-green Turkish-like balloon pants and a jewel-encrusted black velvet vest with flouncing red sleeves. A long scarf of black chiffon turbaned her head then draped around the lower part of her face.

"We need to make up the eyes," Eleni said, scanning her creation. "And we forgot shoes."

They rummaged in closets and trunks until Eleni found a pair of purple Chinese slippers embroidered with black and silver thread.

"Perfect," Matina cried.

They made up the eyes, lining them heavily in black, then Eleni held out the dark red velvet cloak that had once been Matina's hall curtains, and Matina stepped inside.

Once Madame Zolta was outfitted to their satisfaction, Matina decided an all-black turbaned outfit would be perfect for Madame's servant.

"Oh, no! Not me!"

"*Elenáki*?"

"Don't *Elenáki* me. I said I'd help with the sewing, that's all!"

"No one will recognize us."

"I can't go into a strange place full of foreigners."

"We'll be together. I'll do the talking."

"What if Costa finds out?"

"How could he find out? Our own mothers wouldn't recognize us in such outfits!"

Eleni crossed herself. "May the Virgin forgive me."

Matina jumped up and kissed her.

Madame Zolta, swathed in her red velvet cloak and heavily veiled, walked into Morgan's Restaurant and Tea Room the following Thursday afternoon at two o'clock sharp. She was accompanied by her maid, cloaked and turbaned in black. The maid carried a small black satchel.

Madame asked to speak to Mr. Morgan. He seemed a bit taken aback when he saw the pair, but he sat them down at a table in the rear of the dimly lit restaurant.

"I already got a dame who tells fortunes," he said.

Matina shrugged out of her cloak the way she'd been practising and lowered her eyelids. "I am coming two days only," she said in her best Greta Garbo voice. "Tuesday. Thursday."

Morgan pulled a cigar out of his inside coat pocket and twirled it in his fingers. "Tea cup reading every day," he said thoughtfully. Matina held her breath. Eleni stared at the table top. He snipped off the end of the cigar, put it to his lips, licked it around then took it out again.

"Yeah, well, I guess it wouldn't hurt. Tell ya what, ladies, we'll give it a try. Two cents a cup." Matina nodded. Eleni sat as though frozen. "What's your names?"

"Madame Zolta," Matina answered grandly, then gestured toward Eleni. "My maidservant."

"I only pay for one."

"My servant attends me."

"Sure, okay ladies, whatever you like." He shoved his cigar back in his pocket. "You can start today," he said and left them at the table.

Matina nudged Eleni, who was clasping the satchel. "Take out the cloths," she whispered. Eleni opened the bag and took out a piece of green embroidered material fringed in black. She spread it over the table top. Then she took out a small square of pale rose silk and covered the table lamp with that. She closed the satchel, put it at her feet, and the two women waited in silence.

In a matter of minutes, Morgan was back at their side. "What the . . . what's this?"

"I will tell the fortunes now," Madame Zolta said. "I have prepared."

"Not here lady. You gotta go table to table. And get rid of those." He pointed at the pieces of material covering his lamp and his table.

"Madame Zolta cannot be without special cloths," Matina said, "carried in special bag by maidservant." She tried to assume the look she'd seen on Anna's face whenever she was getting into the mood to read cups.

Morgan walked away muttering. They saw him go and speak to the three waitresses clustered at the front, shrug, and settle himself behind the counter.

Matina waited nervously, fingering the fringes of the tablecloth, afraid someone would recognize her, worried that she'd get confused during a reading. Eleni sat in silence. The two women watched for customers, but all they saw coming in from the autumn cold were *zevgarákia,* couples, who slid into the dark, high-backed booths lining the side walls of the restaurant. The round centre tables with petal-like lamps seemed to be reserved for the few ladies who came in.

The afternoon was almost over before two elderly ladies, one in a green jersey and matching hat, the other in a mauve print with a black hat, walked up to Madame Zolta's table, overturned tea cups in hand. Eleni jumped up and took her place behind Matina as they had practised, and Matina gave each what she hoped was a good afternoon's worth of heavily accented fortunes.

With their four pennies between them, they trudged home later that afternoon.

"It'll be better next time, you'll see," Matina said.

"I was so nervous. I'm glad the place is dark."

"Don't worry. We don't know any of those people. They're mostly rich ladies anyway."

"What about the *zevgarákia?*"

"They're too busy with each other to notice us."

The following Tuesday, the sign outside the Tea Room included a note about Madame Zolta, and that day the two women went home with a pair of nickels between them.

"You see, it's working!" Matina cried.

Eleni was still nervous.

In only a few weeks ladies were lining up awaiting their turns to have the fascinating Madame Zolta look into their futures. Soon Morgan began advertising her as *Clairevoyante Extraordinaire.* He suggested she begin reading daily.

"Madame Rosa?" Matina asked.

"There's plenty for two," Morgan said, fingering his unlit cigar.

"We will share?" Matina asked. Morgan nodded. "Not the two cents," she added.

"Don't sorry lady. You'll get your full cut."

"Madame Rosa, she go to tables?"

"Yeah."

"I go to tables." Matina was feeling more comfortable now as Madame Zolta; each day it became easier to make up pretty stories for the well-dressed ladies who sat across from her in the soft lights of the Tea Room.

On the way home, she explained Morgan's offer to Eleni, who'd only understood a few of his English words. "You don't have to come and play servant any more," Matina said.

"I don't mind," she said, but she did mind and they both knew it. Matina was her dearest friend, and the extra money made a difference, but as much as she tried she couldn't stop worrying about Costa, certain that he'd come home one night with an accusation she would be unable to deny.

"I know you hate it, *Elenáki.*" Matina linked their arms. "It's all right."

"I don't want to leave you alone."

"Servant must obey," Matina said in her Madame Zolta voice, and refused to discuss it further.

By the time winter set in, Madame Zolta had been at Morgan's Restaurant and Tea Room long enough so that all the children, Matina's, Eleni's and Anna's, had new woollen vests, underwear, and socks. Their husbands didn't notice; nor did they realize that fresh yarn rather than old was being knit into sweaters, mitts, and scarves. It was amazing, they were told, how one little soup bone could make such a meaty soup.

Husbands, Matina claimed, were easily fooled. It was a Sunday evening and they were in Anna's kitchen finishing up the dinner dishes. Eleni wondered if it might not be a good idea to tell them the truth.

"You can't mean that," Matina said. She stopped wiping a glass and stared at Eleni.

"They might find it amusing, you turning yourself into a gypsy and telling fortunes," Eleni said. "They know how you like to dress up."

Often, at parties, Matina would disappear, only to come back outfitted in some outlandish costume and start to perform. Sometimes she'd dance, other times she'd mimic what she'd seen in the moving pictures. Alekos was one of the first to laugh at her antics.

"You talk as though it's the same thing!" Matina snapped. "You know they have no sense of humour when it comes to their wives doing anything other than being their wives."

"She's right," Anna said.

"Not Pavlo," Eleni said. "He's always been so, I don't know, modern, I think."

"He is when we're alone, at home, and with the children. But Pavlo won't go against his brother."

"And we all know how stubborn my dear Alekos is."

"That's why I admire you, Matina," Anna said.

"You admire me?" Matina sank onto a chair. "You, with all your schooling?"

Anna threw her washcloth into the sink. "You're the one who had the courage to go out and do something that had to be done," she said. "You're never afraid, Matina. That's a wonderful trait"

In all the years they'd known her, Anna had never spoken so passionately. Eleni was silent as she put the dishes away in the cupboard. Even Matina, rarely at a loss for words, didn't know what to say. Her only refuge was her role. "I'm not afraid to make a fool of myself," she said with a laugh, "if that's something to be proud of."

Money was slowly piling up at home, well-hidden among the linens where no one but Matina probed. Every time she'd add a few coins or bills to her collection she'd think about how good the holidays would be this year. She'd find a way to explain the extra money to Alekos. The few dollars she made were nothing compared to the huge bills he had to contend with, but she found comfort in the fact that she was helping in some small way by not having to ask for everyday things. It was even getting easier with him now; he was still preoccupied with business, but there were fewer fights.

In the meantime, it gave her pleasure to appear at the Tea Room in her Arabian Nights costume, being sought out by well-dressed ladies. Her early fears of stumbling over her English, or of making the same speech more than once to the *englézes,* who all looked alike, never happened. In time it even became easier for her to vary the stories. It was as though, from the time she'd begun donning her strange apparel, her imagination had been given free rein, and tales of mysterious strangers, of adoring lovers and jealous dark-haired women, were easily woven out of the patterns she saw in the cups.

It amazed Matina, who hated the cold and went out in winter only when it was absolutely necessary, that so many ladies would brave the blustery weather merely to have their fortunes told. The couples who favoured the darkened booths didn't seem daunted by the cold either. Each time she glanced over at them, huddling together, oblivious to everything but each other, a wave of nostalgia for the early days with Alekos overcame her, but she quickly dismissed the past and returned to the important business of spinning tales.

On one especially bitter and windy day not one lady was waiting for Madame Zolta when she walked in, something that hadn't happened since the first few times. Matina sat at her back table telling herself it had finally turned cold enough to keep even her most loyal customers away, while arguing back that they may well have tired of her and her silly stories, until she realized that what was really bothering her was that she didn't want to stop appearing as Madame Zolta. It was no longer just the money they sorely needed that drew her to the Tea Room, or even the excitement of being someone else for a few hours every day, it was being admired and sought out by these *englézes* who, with all their riches, still needed someone like her to weave a bit of magic into their lives.

To get her mind off these confusing thoughts, she concentrated on the couples. They were mostly young, but an older man with a youngish girlfriend caught her eye. The man had his back to her and a hat covered his head, but she could tell he was old from the way he hunched his back. The girl was pretty in a modern sort of way with her short, sleek hairdo, and a hat perched on the side of her head. She held a cigarette casually between enamelled fingernails. Matina wondered about the man's wife; he surely had a wife; she was probably at home tending to the children, if she wasn't in another Tea Room hearing about a mythical secret admirer.

A few ladies mercifully appeared, shaking the snow off their fur collars as they came in, and soon the room was filled with the aroma of brewing tea. Matina quickly dismissed both her fears of being forgotten and the casual love affairs around her, concentrating instead on her paying clients. She flowed from table to table collecting her tickets, offering dreams of romance to warm up the day.

She was at a table with three ladies, tea cup in hand, when laughter intruded from behind. She turned at the infectious sound. It was the modern girl with the older man. He stood up then and turned, and for a moment, for a brief moment, even in her shock, she saw clearly how youthful the girl's laughter made him.

Then in an instant he was an old man again, an ugly old man, and she wanted to rush up and strike out at his gloating, leering, disgusting face, and tear at the girl, at her grinning young face, and at his, his stupid, stubborn, hateful old man's face, that was hers, hers for over 30 years, since they were children, lovers, poor together and happy, that pitiful aging man, no different from other aging men, yet she'd thought he was, more fool she, aging woman spinning dreams for other foolish women.

Matina never went back to the Tea Room. She burned the costume and refused to talk about any of it with Anna or Eleni. At Christmas the house was filled with the fragrance of roasting birds and honey-soaked delicacies, and at New Year's St. Basil left many presents for the children. When Alekos asked how she managed it all, she told him she'd been saving up and went on to talk of other things.

F.Y.I.

camomíli: chamomile tea comes from two Greek words: *chamo*, which means "ground," and *milon*, which means "apple," since chamomile was thought to smell like apples. In Greece this daisy-like flower grows in fields and rural areas and is usually consumed for medicinal purposes.

Elenáki: diminutive form of the name Eleni. In Greek, the suffix *"aki"* is added to names to denote affection.

englézi: Greek for English people

Greta Garbo: a Swedish actress (1905–1990) regarded as one of the greatest movie stars ever. She appeared in many American films during Hollywood's so-called Golden Age of the 1920s and 1930s.

gyftisa: a Greek word meaning "gypsy woman." The word "gypsy" originates from the Greek word for "Egyptian" and has been used to refer to nomadic peoples from places as diverse as India, Ireland, Eastern Europe, and Central Asia. Today the word is seen as derogatory because of the stereotypes and negative qualities associated with "gypsy" through the centuries in Europe, so the term "Roma" is now preferred.

Hollywood Arabian Nights outfit: *Arabian Nights,* as it is known in English, is a collection of stories whose roots can be traced back to medieval Arabic, Persian, Indian, Egyptian, and early Mesopotamian literature. The work is originally known as *One Thousand and One Nights* and contains characters, symbols, images, and plot devices that influenced generations of writers and poets worldwide, including Edgar Allan Poe, Gustave Flaubert, W.B. Yeats, Leo Tolstoy, C.P. Cavafy, Jorge Luis Borges, Salman Rushdie, and Angela Carter. Elements of this work have also been absorbed into popular culture in the form of films, comic books, and video games. These elements include magic carpets and lamps, genies, and characters such as Aladdin, Sinbad, and Ali Baba. In Alexander's story, the protagonist creates an outfit for her fortune-teller persona based on Hollywood versions, the first films appearing as early as the 1920s with Rudolph Valentino's silent film *The Sheik*. The story lines of such films were based on the traditional work but present some of western culture's racial stereotypes of the "East" as monolithic, mysterious, and inscrutable.

St. Basil: also known as St. Basil the Great was Bishop of Caesarea in Cappadocia, Asia Minor in the fourth century. He was well-known as a Christian theologian and is highly respected as a saint and one of the fathers of the early Eastern Christian Church. In Greek tradition, he is considered the original Santa Claus, a man born into a wealthy family who gave away all his possessions to help those in need. Today it is supposed he visits children to give presents every January 1 on St. Basil's Day.

Turkish coffee: coffee that is prepared according to the Turkish Ottoman method, by boiling finely powdered roast coffee beans in a pot and sometimes adding sugar, but always serving the coffee with a glass of water. Once the dregs settle, the coffee can be consumed. The coffee itself is rich in taste and consistency and has high levels of caffeine. In Greece, after the Turkish invasion of Cyprus in 1974, coffee companies changed the coffee's name: today it is referred to as *ελληνικός καφές,* or Greek coffee.

Once the drinker has finished his or her coffee, the cup is turned upside down and the coffee grounds can be read (in a way similar to tea leaves) to reveal the drinker's fortune. To view instructions on how this coffee is prepared, go to http://www.wonder-howto.com/how-to-arabic-or-turkish-coffee-277798.

the Virgin: reference to the Virgin Mary, mother of Jesus Christ

Words to Build on

chiffon: a light, diaphanous fabric usually of silk or nylon

complacency: a feeling of smug self-satisfaction

crepe: a woven or knitted fabric with a wrinkled surface

dame: North American slang word for woman

darning: to mend a hole in fabric by interweaving yarn across the hole with a needle

donning: to put on clothing

enamelled: a glasslike opaque or semi-transparent coating on surfaces for ornament or as a preservative lining

flouncing: to go or move in an exaggerated or agitated manner, usually in impatience and anger

infectious: the process of "infecting" others when not related to illness or disease and used here for spreading emotion or feeling

leering: to look slyly or lasciviously (a look expressing lust)

pompous: pretentious, self-important, or affectedly grand

Tricks of the Trade

Character

Climax

Imagery

Irony

Narrative point of view

Setting

In Your Own Words: Comprehension

1. What are some of the things the characters in this story have to do to survive the Depression?
2. List the female characters in this story. How are they similar, and how are they different?
3. List the husbands. What do we learn about these characters?

4. What is the difference between coffee cup reading and tea cup reading?

5. What do the women use to make the fortune-teller's outfit?

6. Why does Matina decide to use the name Madame Zolta?

7. What types of people go to the tea room? Who are Madame Zolta's customers?

8. How much money does Matina make for her first reading?

9. Why does Anna admire Matina?

10. Where do the women hide their money?

In Your Own Words: Analysis

1. How old are the women and their husbands in this story?

2. Why do the women have to earn money behind their husbands' backs?

3. What would the husbands do if they found out what the women were up to?

4. Why does Matina have to teach herself how to read tea leaves?

5. How is Matina transformed by her costume?

6. Explain what Matina means when she says, "I am not afraid to make a fool of myself...if that's something to be proud of" and when the narrator states, "her only refuge was her role."

7. How are the women transformed by the end of the story?

8. Explain why Matina wants to "rush up and strike out at his gloating, leering, disgusting face, and tear at the girl, at her grinning young face, and at his, his stupid, stubborn, hateful old man's face, that was hers, hers for over 30 years . . . "

9. Why does Matina burn her costume and refuse to talk to her friends about what happened on her last visit to the tea room?

❖ Now Write

1. Compare the types of deception that characters engage in in Govier's "The Immaculate Conception Photography Gallery" and Alexander's "A Bit of Magic." What is the outcome of their deception in these stories?

2. Why does one have to transform him or herself to accomplish some form of deception? Compare Alexander's "A Bit of Magic" with Carter's "The Company of Wolves" to show the connections between transformation and deception.

3. Do some research and find out what the word "gypsy" means. Is the use of this word still acceptable today? What elements of Matina's transformation involve stereotypes of "gypsies"? Considering the setting (time and place) of the story, why does she feel she needs to dress like a *gyftisa*, which itself is a derogatory term in Greek?

Katherine Govier

Katherine Govier (b. 1948) is an award-winning writer who was born in Edmonton and raised in Calgary, Alberta. She has written nine novels and three short story collections; her work has been translated in Italy, Holland, Slovenia, and Turkey. She is a co-founder of a national online writing program that connects Canadian writers in their homes to high school students in classrooms and is part of a program at Sheridan College for immigrant, refugee, or exiled writers. The short story "The Immaculate Conception Photography Gallery" (1994) is taken from a collection of the same name. This story also won a CBC Radio Literary Award. Govier is not a native Torontonian and through her writing, such as this story, one can see how she navigates places and views the people of the city she now calls home. It is the story of an Italian immigrant with a special skill for altering his customers' photographs and his unease at playing a part in the "eradication" of "unwanted" human reminders. Govier's website, www.govier. com, lists further author information, including upcoming publications.

In Her Own Words

"Most of my books have a very strong geography."

"Toronto was a bit of a mystery to me when I came here."

Before We Begin

1. Have you ever done anything against your better judgment or values? Why?
2. What types of things do we do to preserve memories?
3. Have you ever used Photoshop to alter images of yourself or another person? What were your reasons for doing this?

 Now Read

The Immaculate Conception Photography Gallery

Sandro named the little photography shop on St. Clair Avenue West, between Lord's Shoes and Bargain Jimmies, after the parish church in the village where he was born. He had hankered after wider horizons, the rippled brown prairies, the hard-edged mountains. But when he reached Toronto he met necessity in the form of a wife and babies, and, never having seen a western sunset, he settled down in Little Italy. He photographed the brides in their fat lacquered curls and imported lace, and their quick babies in christening gowns brought over from home. Blown up to near life size on cardboard cutouts, their pictures filled the windows of his little shop.

Sandro had been there 10 years already when he first really saw his sign, and the window. He stood still in front of it and looked. A particularly buxom bride with a lace bodice and cap sleeves cut in little scallops shimmered in a haze of concupiscence under the sign reading Immaculate Conception Photography Gallery. Sandro was not like his neighbours any more, he was modern, a Canadian. He no longer went to church. As he stared, one of the street drunks shuffled into place beside him. Sandro knew them all, they came into the shop in winter. (No one ought to have to stay outside in that cold, Sandro believed.) But he especially knew Becker. Becker was a smart man; he used to be a philosopher at a university.

"Immaculate conception," said Sandro to Becker. "What do you think?"

Becker lifted his eyes to the window. He made a squeezing gesture at the breasts. "I never could buy that story," he said.

Sandro laughed, but he didn't change the sign that year or the next and he got to be 45 and then 50 and it didn't seem worth it. The Immaculate Conception Photography Gallery had a reputation. Business came in from as far away as Rosedale and North Toronto, because Sandro was a magician with a camera. He also had skill with brushes and lights and paint, he reshot his negatives, he lined them with silver, he had tricks even new graduates of photography school couldn't (or wouldn't) copy.

Sandro was not proud of his tricks. They began in a gradual way, fixing stray hairs and taking wrinkles out of dresses. He did it once, then twice, then people came in asking for it. Perhaps he'd have gone on this way, with small lies, but he met with a situation that was larger than most; it would have started a feud in the old country. During a very large and very expensive wedding party Tony the bridegroom seduced Alicia the bridesmaid in the basketball storage room under the floor of the parish hall. Six months later Tony confessed, hoping perhaps to be released from his vows. But the parents judged it was too late to dissolve the union: Diora was used, she was no longer a virgin, there was a child coming. Tony was reprimanded, Diora consoled, the mothers became enemies, the newlyweds made up. Only Alicia remained to be dealt with. The offence became hers.

In Italy, community ostracism would have been the punishment of choice. But this was Canada, and if no one acknowledged Alicia on the street, if no one visited her mother, who was heavy on her feet and forced to sit on the sofa protesting her daughter's innocence, if no one invited her father out behind to drink homemade wine, Alicia didn't care. She went off to her job behind the till in a drugstore with her chin thrust out much as before. The in-laws perceived that the young woman could not be subdued by the old methods. This being the case, it was better she not exist at all.

Which was why Diora's mother turned up at Sandro's counter with the wedding photos. The pain Alicia had caused! she began. Diora's mother's very own miserable wages, saved these 18 years, had paid for these photographs! She wept. The money was spent, but the joy was spoiled. When she and Diora's father looked at the row of faces flanking bride and groom there she was—Alicia, the whore! She wiped her tears and made her pitch.

"You can solve our problem, Sandro. I will get a new cake, we will all come to the parish hall. You will take the photographs again. Of course," she added, "we can't pay you again."

Sandro smiled, it was so preposterous. "Even if I could afford to do all that work for nothing, I hate to say it, but Diora's out to here."

"Don't argue with me."

"I wouldn't be so bold," said Sandro. "But I will not take the photographs over."

The woman slapped the photographs where they lay on the counter. "You will! I don't care how you do it!" And she left.

Sandro went to the back and put his negatives on the light box. He brought out his magic solution and his razor blades and his brushes. He circled Alicia's head and shoulders in the first row and went to work. He felt a little badly, watching the bright circle of her face fade and swim, darken down to nothing. But how easily she vanished! He filled in the white spot with a bit of velvet curtain trimmed from the side.

"I'm like a plastic surgeon," he told his wife. "Take that patch of skin from the inner thigh and put it over the scar on the face. Then sand the edges. Isn't that what they do? Only it isn't a face I'm fixing, it's a memory."

His wife stood on two flat feet beside the sink. She shook the carrot she was peeling. "I don't care about Alicia," she said, "but Diora's mother is making a mistake. She is starting them off with a lie in their marriage. And why is she doing it? For her pride! I don't like this, Sandro."

"You're missing the point," said Sandro.

The next day he had another look at his work. Alicia's shoulders and the bodice of her dress were still there, in front of the chest of the uncle of the bride. He couldn't remove them; it would leave a hole in Uncle. Sandro had nothing to fill the hole, no spare male torsos in black tie. He considered putting a head on top, but whose head? There was no such thing as a free face. A stranger would be questioned, a friend would have an alibi. Perhaps Diora's mother would not notice the black velvet space, as where a tooth had been knocked out, between the smiling faces.

Indeed she didn't but kissed his hand fervently and thanked him with tears in her eyes. "Twenty-five thousand that wedding cost me. Twenty-five thousand to get this photograph and you have rescued it."

"Surely you got dinner and a dance too?" said Sandro.

"The wedding was one day. This is forever," said Diora's mother.

"I won't do that again," said Sandro, putting the cloth over his head and looking into his camera lens to do a passport photo. In the community the doctored photograph had been examined and re-examined. Alicia's detractors enjoyed the headless shoulders as evidence of a violent punishment.

"No, I won't do that again at all," said Sandro to himself, turning aside compliments with a shake of his head. But there was another wedding. After the prosciutto e melone, the veal picata, the many-tiered cake topped with swans, the father of the bride drew Sandro aside and asked for a set of prints with the groom's parent's removed.

"My God, why?" said Sandro.

"He's a bastard. A bad man."

"Shouldn't have let her marry his son, then," said Sandro, pulling a cigarette out of the pack in his pocket. These conversations made him nervous.

The father's weathered face was dark, his dinner jacket did not button around his chest. He moaned and ground his lower teeth against his uppers. "You know how they are, these girls in Canada. I am ashamed to say it, but I couldn't stop her."

Sandro said nothing.

"Look, I sat here all night long, said nothing, did nothing. I don't wanna look at him for the next 20 years."

Sandro drew in a long tube of smoke.

"I paid a bundle for this night. I wanna remember it nice-like."

The smoke made Sandro nauseous. He dropped his cigarette and ground it into the floor with his toe, damning his own weakness. "So what am I going to do with the table?" The father put out a hand like a tool, narrowed his eyes, and began to saw, where the other man sat.

"And leave it dangling, no legs?"

"So make new legs."

"I'm a photographer, not a carpenter," said Sandro. "I don't make table legs."

"Where you get legs is your problem," said the father. "I'm doing well here. I've got 10 guys working for me. You look like you could use some new equipment."

And what harm was it after all, it was only a photograph, said Sandro to himself, Then too there was the technical challenge. Waiting until they all got up to get their bonbonniere, he took a shot of the head table empty. Working neatly with his scalpel, he cut the table from this second negative, removed the in-laws and their chairs from the first one, stuck the empty table-end onto the table in the first picture, blended over the join neatly, and printed it. Presto! Only one set of in-laws.

"I don't mind telling you, it gives me a sick feeling," said Sandro to his wife. "I was there. I saw them. We had a conversation. They smiled for me. Now…" he shrugged. "An empty table. Lucky I don't go to church any more."

"Let the man who paid good money to have you do it confess, not you," she said. "A photograph is a photograph."

"That's what I thought too," said Sandro.

The next morning Sandro went to the Donut House, got himself a take-out coffee and stood on the street beside his window.

"Why do people care about photographs so much?" he asked Becker. Becker had newspaper stuffed in the soles of his shoes. He had on a pair of stained brown pants tied up at the waist with a paisley necktie. His bottle was clutched in a paper bag gathered around the neck.

"You can put them on your mantle," said Becker. "They don't talk back."

"Don't people prefer life?" said Sandro.

"People prefer things," said Becker.

"Don't they want their memories to be true?"

"No," said Becker.

"Another thing. Are we here just to get our photograph taken? Do we have a higher purpose?"

Becker pulled one of the newspapers out of his shoe. There were Brian and Mila Mulroney having a gloaty kiss. They were smeared by muddy water and depressed by the joint in the ball of Becker's foot.

"I mean real people," said Sandro. "Have we no loyalty to the natural?"

"These are existential questions, Sandro," said Becker. "Too many more of them and you'll be out here on the street with the rest of us."

Sandro drained the coffee from his cup, pitched it in the bin painted "Keep Toronto Clean" and went back into his gallery. The existential questions nagged. But he did go out and get the motor drive for the camera. In the next few months he eradicated a pregnancy from a wedding photo, added a daughter-in-law who complained of being left out of the Christmas shots, and made a groom taller. Working in the darkroom, he was hit by vertigo. He was on a slide, beginning a descent. He wanted to know what the bottom felt like.

After a year of such operations a man from the Beaches came in with a tiny black and white photo of a long-lost brother. He wanted it coloured and fitted into a family shot around a picnic table on Centre Island.

"Is this some kind of joke?" said Sandro. It was the only discretion he practised now: he wanted to talk about it before he did it.

"No. I'm going to send it to Mother. She thinks Christopher wrote us all off."

"Did he?" said Sandro.

"Better she should not know."

Sandro neglected to ask if Christopher was fat or thin. He ended up taking a medium-sized pair of shoulders from his own cousin and propping them up behind a bush, with Christopher's head on top. Afterward, Sandro lay sleepless in his bed. Suppose that in the next few months Christopher should turn up dead, say murdered. Then Mother would produce the photograph stamped Immaculate Conception Photography Gallery, 1816 St. Clair Avenue West. Sandro would be implicated. The police might come.

"I believe adding people is worse than taking them away," he said to his wife.

"You say yes to do it, then you do it. You think it's wrong, you say no."

"Let me try this on you, Becker," said Sandro the next morning. "To take a person out is only half a lie. It proves nothing except that he was not in that shot. To add a person is a whole lie: it proves that he was there, when he was not."

"You haven't proven a thing, you're just fooling around with celluloid. Have you got a buck?" said Becker.

"It is better to be a murderer than a creator. I am playing God, outplaying God at His own game." He was smarter than Becker now. He knew it was the photographs that lasted, not the people. In the end the proof was in the proof. Though he hadn't prayed in 30 years, Sandro began to pray. It was like riding a bicycle: he got the hang of it again instantly. "Make me strong," he prayed, "strong enough to resist the new equipment that I might buy, strong enough to resist the temptation to expand the gallery, to buy a house in the suburbs. Make me say no to people who want alterations."

But Sandro's prayers were not answered. When people offered him money to dissolve an errant relative, he said yes. He said yes out of curiosity. He said yes out of a desire to test his skills. He said yes out of greed. He said yes out of compassion. "What is the cost of a little happiness?" he said. "Perhaps God doesn't count photographs. After all, they're not one of a kind."

Sandro began to be haunted, in slow moments behind the counter in the Immaculate Conception, by the faces of those whose presence he had tampered with. He kept a file—Alicia the lusty bridesmaid, Antonia and Marco, the undesired in-laws. Their heads, their shoes and their hands, removed from the scene with surgical precision, he saved for the moment when, God willing, a forgiving relative would ask him to replace them. But the day did not come. Sandro was not happy.

"Becker," he said, for he had a habit now of buying Becker a coffee first thing in the morning and standing out if it was warm, or in if it was cold, for a chat. "Becker, let's say it's a good service I'm doing. It makes people happy, even if it tells lies."

"Sandro," said Becker, who enjoyed his coffee, "these photographs, doctored by request of the subjects, reflect back the lives they wish to have. The unpleasant bits are removed, the wishes are added. If you didn't do it, someone else would. Memory would. It's a service".

"It's also money," said Sandro. He found Becker too eager to make excuses now. He liked him better before.

"You're like Tintoretto, painting in his patron, softening his greedy profile, lifting the chin of his fat wife. It pays for the part that's true art.

"Which part is that?" said Sandro, but Becker didn't answer. He was still standing there when Diora came in. She'd matured, she'd gained weight, and her twins, now six years old, were handsome and strong. Sandro's heart flew up in his breast. Perhaps she had made friends with Alicia, perhaps Diora had come to have her bridesmaid reinstated.

"The long nightmare is over," said Diora. "I've left him."

The boys were running from shelf to shelf lifting up the photographs with their glass frames and putting them down again. Sandro watched them with one eye. He knew what she was going to say.

"I want you to take him out of those pictures," she said.

"You'd look very foolish as a bride with no groom," he said severely.

"No, no, not those," she said. "I mean the kids' birthday shots."

They had been particularly fine, those shots, taken only two weeks ago, Tony tall and dark, Diora and the children radiant and blonde.

"Be reasonable, Diora," he said. "I never liked him myself. But he balances the portrait. Besides, he was there."

"He was not there!" cried Diora. Her sons went on turning all the pictures to face the walls. "He was never there. He was running around, in his heart he was not with me. I was alone with my children."

"I'll take another one," said Sandro. "Of you and the boys. Whenever you like. This one stays like it is."

"We won't pay."

"But Diora," said Sandro, "everyone knows he's their father."

"They have no father," said Diora flatly.

"It's immaculate conception," said Becker gleefully.

But Diora did not hear. "It's our photograph, and we want him out. You do your job. The rest of it's none of your business." She put one hand on the back of the head of each of her twins and marched them out the door.

Sandro leaned on his counter idly flipping the pages of a wedding album. He had a vision of a great decorated room, with a cake on the table. Everyone had had his way, the husband had removed the wife, the wife the husband, the bridesmaid her parents, and so forth. There was no one there.

"We make up our lives out of the people around us," he said to Becker. "When they don't live up to standard, we can't just wipe them out."

"Don't ask me," said Becker. "I just lit out for the streets. Couldn't live up to a damn thing." Then he too went out the door.

"Lucky bugger," said Sandro.

Alone, he went to his darkroom. He opened his drawer of bits and pieces. His disappeared ones, the inconvenient people. His body parts, his halves of torsos, tips of shiny black shoes. Each face, each item of clothing punctured him a little. He looked at his negatives stored in drawers. They were scarred, pathetic things. I haven't the stomach for it, not any more, thought Sandro.

As he walked home, St. Clair Avenue seemed very fine. The best part was, he thought, there were no relationships. Neither this leaning drunk nor that window-shopper was so connected to any other as to endanger his, or her, existence. The tolerance of indifference, said Sandro to himself, trying to remember it so that he could tell Becker.

But Sandro felt ill at ease in his own home, by its very definition a dangerous and unreliable setting. His wife was stirring something, with her lips tight together. His children, almost grown up now, bred secrets as they looked at the television. He himself only posed in the doorway, looking for hidden seams and the faint hairlines of an airbrush.

That night he stood exhausted by his bed. His wife lay on her side with one round shoulder above the sheet. Behind her on the wall was the photo he'd taken of their village before he left Italy. He ought to reshoot it, take out that gas station and clean up the square a little. His pillow had an indentation, as if a head had been erased. He slept in a chair.

In the morning he went down to the shop. He got his best camera and set up a tripod on the sidewalk directly across the street. He took several shots in the solid bright morning light. He locked the door and placed the CLOSED sign in the window. In the darkroom he developed the film, floating the negatives in the pungent fluid until the row of shop fronts came through clearly, the flat brick faces, the curving concrete trim, the two balls on the crowns. Deftly he dissolved each brick of his store, the window and the sign. Deftly he reattached each brick of the store on the west side to the bricks of the store to the east.

I have been many things in my life, thought Sandro, a presser of shutters, a confessor, a false prophet. Now I am a bricklayer, and a good one. He taped the negatives together and developed them. He touched up the join and then photographed it again. He developed this second negative and it was perfect. Number 1812, Lord's Shoes, joined directly to 1820, Bargain Jimmies: the Immaculate Conception Photography Gallery at 1816 no longer existed. Working quickly, because he wanted to finish before the day was over, he blew it up to two feet by three feet. He cleared out his window display of brides and babies and stood up this new photograph—one of the finest he'd ever taken, he thought. Then he took a couple of cameras and a bag with the tripod and some lenses. He turned out the light, pulling the door shut behind him, and began to walk west.

F.Y.I.

bonbonniere: a gift or favour given to wedding guests at the reception hall at Italian and Greek weddings.

Immaculate Conception: the Immaculate Conception of Mary is Roman Catholic dogma that states the Virgin Mary, mother of Jesus Christ, was conceived without the stain of Original Sin. In Latin, the word for "stain" is *macula*, and Mary is often referred to in the Catholic Church as Immaculate Mary, or *Immaculata*, which is the Latin word for the Immaculate One. In the story, "The Immaculate Conception Photography Gallery," the character Becker voices the common misconception that the Immaculate Conception refers to the birth of her son, Jesus Christ. Not all branches of Christianity believe in the Immaculate Conception. In Islam, however, the Quran also mentions the Immaculate Conception of Mary.

prosciutto e melone: cured Italian ham with melon

Tintoretto: a Venetian Renaissance painter (1518–1594)

Words to Build on

bugger: a despicable or disreputable person

concupiscence: a strong sensuous longing or sexual desire; in Christian theology it is a selfish human desire for an object, person, or experience

confessor: a person who makes a confession or a priest authorized to hear confessions

detractors: those who hurt another's reputation or social standing

eradicate: to completely remove or destroy

existential: pertaining to existence

gloaty: to act in a manner that resembles gloating; looking upon or thinking upon someone with intensely smug or mean-spirited satisfaction

lit out: to depart or descend

ostracism: refers to exclusion, by general consent, from social acceptance, privileges, friendship, and other social benefits

patron: a paying customer or client, anyone who supports or endorses an artist, writer, gallery, museum, or foundation

preposterous: absurd and without sense

pungent: a very sharp taste or smell

vertigo: a dizzy feeling of tilting or spinning even though one is in stable surroundings

Tricks of the Trade

Foil

Foreshadowing

Irony

Symbol

In Your Own Words: Comprehension

1. What details reveal when and where the story takes place?

2. Why didn't Sandro go to western Canada?

3. Approximately how old is Sandro at the time the story takes place?

4. How many photographs does Sandro "doctor" in this story?

5. Who is telling the story?

In Your Own Words: Analysis

1. Is Sandro a well-rounded main character? Be sure to give specific examples from the story.

2. In history many kings have had jesters in their courts. In literature, however, jesters, fools, and clowns are often for more than just comic relief. Shakespeare portrayed this relationship in *King Lear* with Lear and the Fool. Is there such a character in this story? What does he or she do?

3. Govier draws particular attention to the name of Sandro's photography studio by using it as the title of her story. Explain the symbolic meaning of the name of Sandro's studio.

4. In a literary review of Govier's short story collection, Zaheera Jiwaji writes "Govier's characters bare their human failings and foibles, leaving readers smiling at their own imperfection." What kinds of "failings" or "foibles" is Govier exposing in this story?

5. Becker tells Sandro that people don't "want their memories to be true." Explain what Becker means by this. What role does memory play in people's lives?

6. Who are the women characters in this story? Are they realistic? Are they sympathetic? Why or why not?

7. Explain the story's ending. Where is Sandro heading when he leaves his shop? Why does Sandro take the action he does? How does the ending relate to the beginning of the story?

⁂ Now Write

1. Many people dislike having their picture taken. What are the reasons for this? Do you think men and women are equally uncomfortable with this act?

2. Today most Canadians live in large cities. People can live life anonymously without really knowing their neighbours. If this is the case, is community ostracism still possible? Write an essay in which you explain whether being ostracized today is, or is not, possible.

3. This story is about the Italian Canadian community in Toronto, but it is written by a non-Italian writer from Alberta. Can artists (writers, filmmakers, musicians) outside a group or community accurately and authentically portray another group's or person's experiences? Write an essay in which you state the reasons for this and provide examples from the text.

4. Does a photograph accurately capture real life? Can all photographs be manipulated, and thus never really reflect any reality or truth? Compare this to more authentic ways of capturing reality.

Diane Schoemperlen

Diane Schoemperlen (b. 1954) was born in Thunder Bay, Ontario, and educated at Lakehead University. She is a short story writer, a novelist, an editor, and a teacher. Schoemperlen has received much critical praise for her works, both in Canada and overseas. Critics have stated that no matter how "heavy" and serious a topic, her writing has elements that highlight the humourous side of life. She experiments with different forms in her writing: placing her characters in everyday situations and having them deal with common problems such as depression, loneliness, poverty, and unfulfilling personal relationships.

"Tell It to the Walls" is one of Schoemperlen's lesser known stories and is a retelling of an original Tamil folktale that she rewrote for the collection *The Monkey King & Other Stories* (1995). In this collection, Canadian and Sri Lankan writers have either followed the original story closely or updated the time and setting to the present. However, all were required to maintain the themes and storylines present in the original tales, so while Schoemperlen's retelling crosses cultural boundaries, it carries the same timeless message. In this story, a mature woman whose husband suddenly dies must deal with the aftermath: he leaves her penniless and she is forced to move in with her two married sons.

Schoemperlen currently lives in Kingston, Ontario

In Her Own Words

"While actually writing, the only question I am trying to answer with my work is: How can I best tell this story?"

"I love writing, the physical act of writing. Theories are not important to me. All I want to do is write. So for me, the current question is always: Why do I have to do all these other things (shopping, cleaning, eating, mowing the lawn, vacuuming, laundry, etc.) when all I want to do is write?"

Before We Begin

1. In many cultures, children are taught to respect their elders, especially their parents. However, this often isn't the case in families and communities, as can be seen in the numerous cases of elder abuse and neglect that occur around the world. Did you know that except for Alberta, all Canadian provinces give citizens the legal right to sue their children for the basic necessities of life? What do you think about this?

2. Have you ever thought about what your life will be like when you are 70 or 80 years old? Where will you be?

3. Is there a fairytale or folktale that you read or were told as a child that had a message or moral that has stayed with you?

 Now Read

Tell It to the Walls

After her husband died suddenly of a heart attack at the age of 59, Mabel Patterson's whole life changed. Although they had lived a happy and comfortable life together on the farm for over 30 years, Victor Patterson's unexpected passing left his wife in dire straits. He was a good but forgetful man who had made many bad investments and often neglected to pay the bills. He had always meant to buy life insurance but, sadly, he never got around to it. Victor, like most mortals, thought he had all the time in the world. After his death, Mabel found herself so poor that she had to move in with her two sons and their wives.

Neither of her sons, Charlie or Steve, had ever shown any inclination to become farmers. Some years before their father's death they had moved to the city a hundred miles away. After both had found good jobs and got married, they pooled their resources and bought a big duplex in the city. They all lived there together, Charlie and his wife Rose on the main floor, Steve and his wife Kathy upstairs. Both Rose and Kathy were now expecting their first children. They said Mabel could live in the basement. They said she would have her own bedroom down there, her own bathroom, and her very own TV. They said she would make lots of new friends in the city. And, they said, after the babies were born in the spring, Mabel would be able to see her grandchildren every day. Wouldn't it be wonderful? She would never be lonely again.

At first it *was* wonderful. But soon everything began to change. One day both Rose and Kathy were not feeling well. Rose asked Mabel if she wouldn't mind just washing the kitchen floor and putting in a few loads of laundry. Kathy upstairs wondered if

Mabel wouldn't mind just vacuuming the stairs and cleaning the oven. She had some ironing that needed doing too. Mabel was happy to help.

When Charlie came home from work that night, he was very hungry and tired. Rose was still resting so Mabel made her older son a big supper. Charlie complained that the salad was wilted and the meat was not spicy enough but he ate it anyway. He also said the kitchen floor was still dirty even though Mabel had washed it that very morning. When Mabel took a tray to Rose in the bedroom, Rose said she couldn't eat because she was so upset by the fact that Mabel had shrunk her favourite sweater in the wash. After supper Charlie asked Mabel to do the dishes because he was too tired.

When Steve upstairs came home late from work, he complained loudly because there was no supper waiting for him. Kathy was still resting so Mabel went upstairs and made her younger son a big supper. Steve complained that the rice was sticky and the meat was too spicy but he ate it anyway. He also said the stairs were still dirty even though Mabel had vacuumed them that very afternoon. When Mabel took a tray to Kathy in the bedroom, Kathy said she couldn't eat because she was so upset by the fact that Mabel had scorched her favourite blouse with the iron. After supper Mabel did the dishes because Steve wanted to watch TV.

The next day both Rose and Kathy were feeling a bit better. They were well enough to lie on their living room couches all day watching soap operas and phoning their friends. So Mabel spent all morning running up and down between the two households doing all the chores. Then she spent all afternoon running back and forth to the grocery store to satisfy the cravings of the two pregnant women. Rose wanted sweet pickles. Kathy wanted butterscotch ripple ice cream. Then Rose wanted orange sherbet. Then Kathy wanted a pineapple upside-down cake. This went on all afternoon until finally Mabel had been to the grocery store 12 times.

Although Rose and Kathy were well enough to eat, they were not well enough to cook. So once again Mabel prepared a big supper both upstairs and down. Once again her sons and their wives complained bitterly while stuffing themselves. They criticized her cooking and everything else she had done for them that day. After supper, Mabel once again did the dishes for both households because they all said they had better things to do.

By the time Mabel got back to her room in the basement, she was too tired and unhappy to watch her very own TV. It didn't work right half the time anyway. So she lay down on her bed and cried herself to sleep.

The next day was the same. And the next and the next and the next. Mabel did everything for her sons and their wives and then listened to them complain that everything she had done was wrong. They took turns telling her how stupid she was. Then she would go down to her basement room and cry.

It went on and on the same. Mabel could not understand how her sons who had once been happy, loving children on the farm had turned into such mean and nasty men in the city. She did not understand why they had both married such mean and lazy women. Mabel had no one to tell her troubles to. She'd had no time to make new friends in the city. She didn't want to make trouble in the households. After all, her sons and their wives had taken her in when she had nowhere else to go. Besides, she was afraid that if she complained about how they treated her, they would throw her out onto the street.

So day after day Mabel swallowed her hurt and her anger. She kept it all inside and gradually her body began to swell. The more she swallowed, the fatter she got. Soon she was so fat that she could barely get up and down the stairs between the two households. She could no longer fit into the bathtub in her very own bathroom. She could no longer roll over in the little bed in her very own bedroom. She was so fat that sometimes she could hardly even breathe.

Now when her sons and their wives had finished criticizing her for her bad cooking, her inept housekeeping, and her general stupidity, they would go on to ridicule her ever-increasing size. They said she was always eating like a pig. Apparently they hadn't noticed that she was so busy looking after them that she never had time to eat much herself. They said she was as big as a cow, a moose, an elephant, as big as the Goodyear blimp. They shuddered, they said, to think what their dear departed father would say if he could see her now. Steve said Victor must be rolling over in his grave.

One Saturday afternoon, Charlie and Rose and Steve and Kathy decided to go to a concert in the park. Mabel, who seldom got to go anywhere except the grocery store, said she would like to go too. But Charlie said they were too ashamed to be seen with her in public. People would point and stare, Rose said. Little children would think she was a monster made of blubber, Kathy said. They would run away screaming with fright. Besides, Steve said, she was too fat to fit in the car. Charlie said they'd have to tie her to the roof rack to get her to the park. The four of them set off for the concert laughing.

Mabel, left behind, could not bear to spend the afternoon alone in her basement room. She grabbed her purse and her coat (even though it didn't fit her any more) and walked to the bus stop at the corner of the street. She got on the first bus that came along. She was so fat that the driver charged her double because she took up two seats all by herself. The bus took her to the northern edge of the city.

She got off and she walked. Because of her massive size, she could not move very fast. Puffing and sweating, she kept stopping to catch her breath. Gradually she left the city behind. The road curled through countryside that reminded her of the farm she had shared with Victor for so long. This made her feel even sadder and lonelier than usual.

Just as Mabel thought she might collapse from the effort of walking so far, she spotted a deserted farmhouse just off the road to the left. She laboured up the laneway towards the old brick building. The windows were all broken and the roof was gone. She went inside.

Standing in the middle of the broken-down house, Mabel was finally overwhelmed by misery and despair. She couldn't keep her troubles inside for a minute longer. She had to talk to someone even though there was no one there.

So Mabel told the wall in front of her all about her older son Charlie. Charlie who said she was as big as a cow, Charlie who complained because the floor was dirty and the supper was not spicy enough, Charlie who said they'd have to tie her to the roof rack, Charlie who was ashamed to be seen with her in public. When she was finished, the first wall gave way beneath the weight of her woes. The bricks crashed down in a heap and lay on the ground in a cloud of dust. Mabel's body grew a little lighter.

Then she turned to the second wall and told it all about her daughter-in-law Rose. Rose who said she was as big as a moose, Rose who yelled at her for shrinking her favourite clothes in the wash, Rose who said people would point and stare, Rose who told her everyday that she was fat and stupid. Down came the second wall into another dusty heap of bricks. Mabel's body grew lighter still.

To the third wall she told the tales of her younger son, Steve. Steve who said she was as big as an elephant, Steve who complained because the stairs were dirty and the supper was too spicy, Steve who said she was too fat to fit in the car, Steve who said Victor would die of shame to see her now if he weren't already dead. The third wall collapsed too.

Then, feeling even lighter, Mabel turned to the remaining wall and told it all about her daughter-in-law Kathy. Kathy who said she was as big as the Goodyear blimp, Kathy who swore at her for scorching her favourite blouse with an iron, Kathy who said little children would run away screaming at the sight of her, Kathy who said she was probably the fattest, stupidest woman in the world. The fourth wall went tumbling to the ground.

Standing in the ruins of the old farmhouse with rubble and dust all around her, Mabel felt better than she had since Victor died. She looked down at herself and was surprised to discover that her body had shrunk back to its original size. All the hurt and anger she had swallowed had finally been released and all her fat had disappeared.

Mabel put on her coat and began the long journey home. When she got to the edge of the city, she once again took the first bus that came along. It was the same driver but he didn't recognize her. He told her she was looking lovely and he let her ride for free. She got off the bus downtown and went into a huge department store. She went upstairs to the cafeteria and had a cup of tea. She struck up a conversation with the lonely looking overweight woman at the next table. They parted with a promise to meet again next Saturday, same place, same time, for another cup of tea.

Then Mabel went down to the third floor and bought two dozen balls of wool and some knitting needles. In the electronics department on the second floor she bought a cassette player with little headphones and a whole box of tapes. Back on the busy street Mabel found the right bus and went home.

When her sons and their wives arrived home from the concert an hour later, all four of them started right away yelling because the house was a mess and there was nothing to eat. They thundered down the basement stairs and threw open the door of Mabel's very own bedroom. Their faces were red and their four mean mouths fell open at the sight of Mabel with her headphones on, humming and smiling and knitting bonnets and booties for the babies who would be born soon. She looked up at them and grinned. Then, with one thin arm, she waved them away.

F.Y.I.

Tamil folktale: Tamils are members of a Dravidian people who inhabit the southern Indian subcontinent and parts of Sri Lanka. "Tamil" indicates both their ethnicity and language and is a Dutch/Portuguese variation of the original word, "Damila." Schoemperlen's story is taken from a collection edited by Griffin Ondaatje. In the introduction he states: "the stories in this book have been dear to people in Sri Lanka for many years. Some of them began on the island and some began elsewhere and were welcomed, adopted, retold by Sri Lankans" (p. ix). Sri Lanka has a history of violent disputes between two groups: the Singhalese majority and the Tamil minority. The retelling of stories like "Tell It to the Walls" is an effort to move towards healing and to underscore aspects of life all humans share.

Words to Build on

dire straits: a state of extreme distress

inclination: an interest in or liking for something

Tricks of the Trade

Irony

Magic realism

In Your Own Words: Comprehension

1. What is the setting of the story?

2. Why is the protagonist, Mabel Patterson, alone?

3. Who is narrating this story? What is the narrative point of view?

4. How do Mabel's adult children treat her? Try to find more fitting descriptive words than "bad" or "poorly."

5. What does Mabel do while she's living there?

6. Why does Mabel start "to swell"?

7. Why doesn't Mabel just leave or confront her adult children about their behaviour?

8. What makes Mabel feel "even sadder and lonelier than usual"?

In Your Own Words: Analysis

1. Would this story have been the same if one of the other characters told the events? Did Schoemperlen choose the most effective narrative point of view?

2. What features or characteristics of this story provide evidence that this was originally an oral tale? What are the elements in this story that are common to most folktales?

3. Why do you think the sons really invited their mother to come live with them?

4. Explain what the narrator means by "Although Rose and Kathy were well enough to eat, they were not well enough to cook."

5. Locate examples of irony in this story.

6. Identify the turning point and climax in this story. Is the climax effective?

7. Although this story has "magical" elements to it (i.e., a woman who swells and shrinks inexplicably), does it still maintain a degree of realism?

8. What changes for Mabel at the end of this story?

9. Why does the author have Mabel meet "the lonely looking overweight woman at the next table"? Why does she not have her meet an eligible, lonely looking older gentleman?

Now Write

1. "Tell It to the Walls" is the retelling of a Tamil folktale that appears in A.K. Ramanujan's *Folktales from India: A Selection of Oral Tales from Twenty-Two Languages* (New York: Pantheon Books, 1992). Locate a copy of the book and the original story. Write an essay in which you highlight the similarities and outline the main differences between this original version and Diane Schoemperlen's modern retelling.

2. Read Karim Rashid's excerpt from *design your self*. How is a future based on instant gratification and ease equipped to meet the needs of others? How would Mabel Patterson fit into Rashid's view of the future? Would the services he describes in this futuristic world be relevant or helpful to individuals like Mabel? Write an essay in which you argue why or why not.

3. What are the fundamental elements we need to live happily? Do these change as we age? Write an essay in which you identify and expand on these fundamental needs of life and how these are present or absent in "Tell It to the Walls."

Jhumpa Lahiri

Jhumpa Lahiri (b. 1967) was born in London, England, and raised in Rhode Island. Although she was born outside the United States to Bengali Indian parents, Lahiri considers herself an American, having immigrated when she was just three years old, but one raised in two cultures since the family would often visit relatives in India.

Lahiri developed an early interest in writing when she and her friends would compose 10-page "novels" during recess in elementary school. She later earned multiple degrees in comparative literature, creative writing, and renaissance studies.

Her first book, *Interpreter of Maladies* (1999), was an international bestseller that won the Pulitzer Prize. The stories in this collection move from India to America, the perspectives shifting from distant to more intimate views of the lives of first- and second-generation immigrants. *The New Yorker* published three of her short stories and named her "one of the 20 best writers under the age of 40." Her first novel, *The Namesake* (2003), is set predominately in the United States and tells the story of a child of Indian immigrants who, like Lahiri herself, grows up in two worlds. Although the protagonist is born and raised in America, his parents' experiences, especially those of his father, are indelibly imprinted on his own life. *The Namesake* was also made into a feature film.

Lahiri's writing style is often described as controlled: simple and direct with just enough details to guide the reader. The topics of her work range from illness, isolation, adultery, cross-cultural love, arranged marriages, and how individuals forge identities outside the family. Her characters seem all too real and often exist in two realities—Indian and American—and are at times shown to be struggling with the traditions and beliefs of both cultures.

Recently, US President Barack Obama appointed Lahiri to the President's Committee on the Arts and the Humanities. She currently lives in New York City.

In Her Own Words

"When I sit down to write, I don't think about writing about an idea or a given message. I just try to write a story, which is hard enough."

"For that story ["The Treatment of Bibi Haldar"], I took as my subject a young woman whom I got to know over the course of a couple of visits. I never saw her having any health problems—but I knew she wanted to be married."

"That's the thing about books. They let you travel without moving your feet."

Before We Begin

1. What causes people to feel lonely? Can one feel lonely even living in a densely populated city?

2. In the novels of the English author Charles Dickens, it is often family members, those whose relation is based on blood ties, who do the most harm to each other while more trusting and meaningful emotional bonds are formed between friends and strangers. Can individuals in real life form strong family bonds without being related by blood?

3. Can a person want something so badly that he or she becomes physically ill? Explain.

✳ **Now Read**

The Treatment of Bibi Haldar

For the greater number of her 29 years, Bibi Haldar suffered from an ailment that baffled family, friends, priests, palmists, spinsters, gem therapists, prophets, and fools. In efforts to cure her, concerned members of our town brought her holy water from seven holy rivers. When we heard her screams and throes in the night, when her wrists were bound with ropes and stinging poultices pressed upon her, we named her in our prayers. Wise men had massaged eucalyptus balm into her temples, steamed her face with herbal infusions. At the suggestion of a blind Christian she was once taken by train to kiss the tombs of saints and martyrs. Amulets warding against the evil eye girded her arms and neck. Auspicious stones adorned her fingers.

Treatments offered by doctors only made matters worse. Allopaths, homeopaths, ayurvedics—over time, all branches of the medical arts had been consulted. Their advice was endless. After X-rays, probes, auscultations, and injections, some merely advised Bibi to gain weight, others to lose it. If one forbade her to sleep beyond dawn, another insisted she remain in bed till noon. This one told her to perform headstands, that one to chant Vedic verses at specified intervals throughout the day. "Take her to Calcutta for hypnosis" was a suggestion still others would offer. Shuttled from one specialist to the next, the girl had been prescribed to shun garlic, consume disproportionate quantities of bitters, meditate, drink green coconut water, and swallow raw duck's eggs beaten in milk. In short, Bibi's life was an encounter with one fruitless antidote after another.

The nature of her illness, which struck without warning, confined her world to the unpainted four-story building in which her only local family, an elder cousin and his wife, rented an apartment on the second floor. Liable to fall unconscious and enter, at any moment, into a shameless delirium, Bibi could be trusted neither to cross a street nor board a tram without supervision. Her daily occupation consisted of sitting in the storage room on the roof of our building, a space in which one could sit but not comfortably stand, featuring an adjoining latrine, a curtained entrance, one window without a grille, and shelves made from the panels of old doors. There, cross-legged on a square of jute, she recorded inventory for the cosmetics shop that her cousin Haldar owned and managed at the mouth of our courtyard. For her services, Bibi received no income but was given meals, provisions, and sufficient metres of cotton at every October holiday to replenish her wardrobe at an inexpensive tailor. At night she slept on a folding camp cot in the cousin's place downstairs.

In the mornings Bibi arrived in the storage room wearing cracked plastic slippers and a housecoat whose hem stopped some inches below the knee, a length we had not worn since we were 15. Her shins were hairless, and sprayed with a generous number of pallid freckles. She bemoaned her fate and challenged her stars as we hung our laundry or scrubbed scales from our fish. She was not pretty. Her upper lip was thin, her teeth too small. Her gums protruded when she spoke. "I ask you, is it fair for a girl to sit out her years, pass neglected through her prime, listing labels and prices without promise of a future?" Her voice was louder than necessary, as if she were speaking to a deaf person. "Is it wrong to envy you, all brides and mothers, busy with lives and cares? Wrong to want to shade my eyes, scent my hair? To raise a child and teach him sweet from sour, good from bad?"

Each day she unloaded her countless privations upon us, until it became unendurably apparent that Bibi wanted a man. She wanted to be spoken for, protected, placed on her path in life. Like the rest of us, she wanted to serve suppers, and scold servants, and set aside money in her *almari* to have her eyebrows threaded every three weeks at the Chinese beauty parlour. She pestered us for details of our own weddings: the jewels, the invitations, the scent of tuberoses strung over the nuptial bed. When, at her insistence, we showed her our photo albums embossed with the designs of butterflies, she pored over the snapshots that chronicled the ceremony: butter poured in fires, garlands exchanged, vermilion-painted fish, trays of shells and silver coins. "An impressive number of guests," she would observe, stroking with her finger the misplaced faces that had surrounded us. "When it happens to me, you will all be present."

Anticipation began to plague her with such ferocity that the thought of a husband, on which all her hopes were pinned, threatened at times to send her into another attack. Amid tins of talc and boxes of bobby pins she would curl up on the floor of the storage room, speaking in non sequiturs. "I will never dip my feet in milk," she whimpered. "My face will never be painted with sandalwood paste. Who will rub me with turmeric? My name will never be printed with scarlet ink on a card."

Her soliloquies mawkish, her sentiments maudlin, malaise dripped like a fever from her pores. In her most embittered moments we wrapped her in shawls, washed her face from the cistern tap, and brought her glasses of yogurt and rosewater. In moments when she was less disconsolate, we encouraged her to accompany us to the tailor and replenish her blouses and petticoats, in part to provide her with a change of scenery, and in part because we thought it might increase whatever matrimonial prospects she had. "No man wants a woman who dresses like a dishwasher," we told her. "Do you want all that fabric of yours to go to the moths?" She sulked, pouted, protested, and sighed. "Where do I go, who would I dress for?" she demanded. "Who takes me to the cinema, the zoo-garden, buys me lime soda and cashews? Admit it, are these concerns of mine? I will never be cured, never married."

But then a new treatment was prescribed for Bibi, the most outrageous of them all. One evening on her way to dinner, she collapsed on the third-floor landing, pounding her fists, kicking her feet, sweating buckets, lost to this world. Her moans echoed through the stairwell, and we rushed out of our apartments to calm her at once, bearing palm fans and sugar cubes, and tumblers of refrigerated water to pour on her head. Our children clung to the banisters and witnessed her paroxysm; our servants were sent to summon her cousin. It was 10 minutes before Haldar emerged from his shop, impassive apart from the red in his face. He told us to stop fussing, and then with no efforts to repress his disdain he packed her into a rickshaw bound for the polyclinic. It was there, after performing a series of blood tests, that the doctor in charge of Bibi's case, exasperated, concluded that a marriage would cure her.

News spread between our window bars, across our clotheslines, and over the pigeon droppings that plastered the parapets of our rooftops. By the next morning, three separate palmists had examined Bibi's hand and confirmed that there was, no doubt, evidence of an imminent union etched into her skin. Unsavory sorts murmured indelicacies at cutlet stands; grandmothers consulted almanacs to determine a propitious hour for the betrothal. For days afterward, as we walked our children to school, picked up our cleaning, stood in lines at the ration shop, we whispered. Apparently some activity was what the poor girl needed all along. For the first time we imagined the contours below her housecoat, and attempted to appraise the pleasures she could offer a man. For the first time we noted the clarity of her complexion, the length and languor of her eyelashes, the undeniably elegant armature of her hands. "They say it's the only hope. A case of overexcitement. They say"—and here we paused, blushing—"relations will calm her blood."

Needless to say, Bibi was delighted by the diagnosis, and began at once to prepare for conjugal life. With some damaged merchandise from Haldar's shop she polished her toenails and softened her elbows. Neglecting the new shipments delivered to the storage room, she began hounding us for recipes, for vermicelli pudding and papaya stew, and inscribed them in crooked letters in the pages of her inventory ledger. She made guest lists, dessert lists, listed lands in which she intended to honeymoon. She applied glycerine to smooth her lips, resisted sweets to reduce her measurements. One day she asked one of us to accompany her to the tailor, who stitched her a new *salwar-kameez* in an umbrella cut, the fashion that season. On the streets she dragged us to the counters of each and every jeweller, peering into glass cases, seeking our opinions of tiara designs and locket settings. In the windows of sari shops she pointed to a magenta Benarasi silk, and a turquoise one, and then one that was the colour of marigolds. "The first part of the ceremony I will wear this one, then this one, then this."

But Haldar and his wife thought otherwise. Immune to her fancies, indifferent to our fears, they conducted business as usual, stuffed together in that cosmetics shop no bigger than a wardrobe, whose walls were crammed on three sides with hennas, hair oils, pumice stones, and fairness creams. "We have little time for indecent suggestions," replied Haldar to those who broached the subject of Bibi's health. "What won't be cured must be endured. Bibi has caused enough worry, added enough to expenses, sullied enough the family name." His wife, seated beside him behind the tiny glass counter, fanned the mottled skin above her breasts and agreed. She was a heavy woman whose powder, a shade too pale for her, caked in the creases of her throat. "Besides, who would marry her? The girl knows nothing about anything, speaks backward, is practically 30, can't light a coal stove, can't boil rice, can't tell the difference between fennel and a cumin seed. Imagine her attempting to feed a man!"

They had a point. Bibi had never been taught to be a woman; the illness had left her naive in most practical matters. Haldar's wife, convinced that the devil himself possessed her, kept Bibi away from fire and flame. She had not been taught to wear a sari without pinning it in four different places, nor could she embroider slipcovers or crochet shawls with any exceptional talent. She was not allowed to watch the television (Haldar assumed its electronic properties would excite her), and was thus ignorant of the events and entertainments of our world. Her formal studies had ended after the ninth standard.

For Bibi's sake we argued in favour of finding a husband. "It's what she's wanted all along," we pointed out. But Haldar and his wife were impossible to reason with. Their rancour toward Bibi was fixed on their lips, thinner than the strings with which they tied our purchases. When we maintained that the new treatment deserved a chance, they contended, "Bibi possesses insufficient quantities of respect and self-control. She plays up her malady for the attention. The best thing is to keep her occupied, away from the trouble she invariably creates."

"Why not marry her off, then? It will get her off your hands, at least."

"And waste our profits on a wedding? Feeding guests, ordering bracelets, buying a bed, assembling a dowry?"

But Bibi's gripes persisted. Late one morning, dressed under our supervision in a sari of lavender eyelet chiffon and mirrored slippers lent to her for the occasion, she hastened in uneven steps to Haldar's shop and insisted on being taken to the photographer's studio so that her portrait, like those of other brides-in-waiting, could be circulated in the homes of eligible men. Through the shutters of our balconies we watched her; perspiration had already left black moons beneath her armpits. "Apart from my X-rays I have never been photographed," she fretted. "Potential in-laws need to know what I look like." But Haldar refused. He said that anyone who wished to see her could observe her for themselves, weeping and wailing and warding off customers. She was a bane for business, he told her, a liability and a loss. Who in this town needed a photo to know that?

The next day Bibi stopped listing inventory altogether and regaled us, instead, with imprudent details about Haldar and his wife. "On Sundays he plucks hairs from her chin. They keep their money refrigerated under lock and key." For the benefit of neighbouring rooftops she strutted and shrieked; with each proclamation her audience expanded. "In the bath she applies chickpea flour to her arms because she thinks it will make her paler. The third toe on her right foot is missing. The reason they take such long siestas is that she is impossible to please."

To get her to quiet down, Haldar placed a one-line advertisement in the town newspaper, in order to solicit a groom: "GIRL, UNSTABLE, HEIGHT 152 CENTIMETRES, SEEKS HUSBAND." The identity of the prospective bride was no secret to the parents of our young men, and no family was willing to shoulder so blatant a risk. Who could blame them? It was rumoured by many that Bibi conversed with herself in a fluent but totally incomprehensible language, and slept without dreams. Even the lonely four-toothed widower who repaired our handbags in the market could not be persuaded to propose. Nevertheless, to distract her, we began to coach her in wifely ways. "Frowning like a rice pot will get you nowhere. Men require that you caress them with your expression." As practice for the event of encountering a possible suitor, we urged her to engage in small conversations with nearby men. When the water bearer arrived, at the end of his rounds, to fill Bibi's urn in the storage room, we instructed her to say "How do you do?" When the coal supplier unloaded his baskets on the roof, we advised her to smile and make a comment about the weather. Recalling our own experiences, we prepared her for an interview. "Most likely the groom will arrive with one parent, a grandparent, and either an uncle or aunt. They will stare, ask several questions. They will examine the bottoms of your feet, the thickness of your braid. They will ask you to name the prime minister, recite poetry, feed a dozen hungry people on half a dozen eggs."

When two months had passed without a single reply to the advertisement, Haldar and his wife felt vindicated. "Now do you see that she is unfit to marry? Now do you see no man of sane mind would touch her?"

Things had not been so bad for Bibi before her father died. (The mother had not survived beyond the birth of the girl.) In his final years, the old man, a teacher of mathematics in our elementary schools, had kept assiduous track of Bibi's illness in hopes of determining some logic to her condition. "To every problem there is a solution," he would reply whenever we inquired after his progress. He reassured Bibi. For a time he reassured us all. He wrote letters to doctors in England, spent his evenings reading casebooks at the library, gave up eating meat on Fridays in order to appease his household god. Eventually he gave up teaching as well, tutoring only from his room, so that he could monitor Bibi at all hours. But though in his youth he had received prizes for his ability to deduce square roots from memory, he was unable to solve the mystery of his daughter's disease. For all his work, his records led him to conclude only that Bibi's attacks occurred more frequently in summer than winter, and that she had suffered approximately 25 major attacks in all. He created a chart of her symptoms with directions for calming her, and distributed it throughout the neighbourhood, but these were eventually lost, or turned into sailboats by our children, or used to calculate grocery budgets on the reverse side.

Apart from keeping her company, apart from soothing her woes, apart from keeping an occasional eye on her, there was little we could do to improve the situation. None of us were capable of understanding such desolation. Some days, after siesta, we combed out her hair, remembering now and then to change the part in her scalp so that it would not grow too broad. At her request we powdered the down over her lips and throat, penciled definition into her brows, and walked her to the banks of the fish pond where our children played cricket in the afternoon. She was still determined to lure a man.

"Apart from my condition I am perfectly healthy," she maintained, seating herself on a bench along the footpath where courting men and women strolled hand in hand. "I have never had a cold or flu. I have never had jaundice. I have never suffered from colic or indigestion." Sometimes we bought her smoked corn on the cob sprinkled with lemon juice, or two *paisa* caramels. We consoled her; when she was convinced a man was giving her the eye, we humoured her and agreed. But she was not our responsibility, and in our private moments we were thankful for it.

In November we learned that Haldar's wife was pregnant. That morning in the storage room, Bibi wept. "She says I'm contagious, like the pox. She says I'll spoil the baby." She was breathing heavily, her pupils fixed to a peeling spot on the wall. "What will become of me?" There was still no response to the advertisement in the newspaper. "Is it not punishment enough that I bear this curse alone? Must I also be blamed for infecting another?" Dissent within the Haldar household grew. The wife, convinced that Bibi's presence would infect the unborn child, began to wrap woolen shawls around her tumid belly. In the bathroom Bibi was given separate soaps and towels. According to the scullery maid, Bibi's plates were not washed with the others.

And then one afternoon, without word or warning, it happened again. On the banks of the fish pond, Bibi fell to the footpath. She shook. She shuddered. She chewed her lips. A group encircled the convulsing girl at once, eager to assist in whatever way possible. The opener of soda bottles pinned down her thrashing limbs. The vendor of sliced cucumbers attempted to unclasp her fingers. One of us doused her with water from the pond. Another wiped her mouth with a perfumed handkerchief. The seller of jackfruits was holding Bibi's head, which struggled to toss from side to side. And the man who cranked the sugarcane press gripped the palm fan that he ordinarily used to chase away flies, agitating the air from every conceivable angle.

"Is there a doctor in the crowd?"

"Watch that she doesn't swallow her tongue."

"Has anyone informed Haldar?"

"She's hotter than coals!"

In spite of our efforts, the tumult persisted. Wrestling with her adversary, wracked with anguish, she ground her teeth and twitched at the knees. Over two minutes had passed. We watched and worried. We wondered what to do.

"Leather!" someone cried suddenly. "She needs to smell leather." Then we remembered; the last time it had happened, a cowhide sandal held under her nostrils was what had finally freed Bibi from the clutches of her torment.

"Bibi, what happened? Tell us what happened," we asked when she opened her eyes.

"I felt hot, then hotter. Smoke passed before my eyes. The world went black. Didn't you see it?"

A group of our husbands escorted her home. Dusk thickened, conch shells were blown, and the air grew dense with the incense of prayers. Bibi muttered and staggered but said nothing. Her cheeks were bruised and nicked here and there. Her hair was matted, her elbows caked with dirt, and a small piece of one front tooth was missing. We followed behind, at what we assumed to be safe distances, holding our children by the hand.

She needed a blanket, a compress, a sedative tablet. She needed supervision. But when we reached the courtyard Haldar and his wife would not have her in the flat.

"The medical risk is too great for an expectant mother to be in contact with a hysterical person," he insisted.

That night Bibi slept in the storage room.

Their baby, a girl, was delivered by forceps at the end of June. By then Bibi was sleeping downstairs again, though they kept her camp cot in the corridor, and would not let her touch the child directly. Every day they sent her to the roof to record inventory until lunch, at which point Haldar brought her receipts from the morning's sales and a bowl of yellow split peas for her lunch. At night she ate milk and bread alone in the stairwell. Another seizure, and another, went unchecked.

When we voiced our concern, Haldar said it was not our business, and flatly refused to discuss the matter. To express our indignation we began to take our shopping elsewhere; this provided us with our only revenge. Over the weeks the products on Haldar's shelves grew dusty. Labels faded and colognes turned rank. Passing by in the evenings, we saw Haldar sitting alone, swatting moths with the sole of his slipper. We hardly saw the wife at all. According to the scullery maid she was still bedridden; apparently her labour had been complicated.

Autumn came, with its promise of the October holidays, and the town grew busy shopping and planning for the season. Film songs blared from amplifiers strung through trees. Arcades and markets stayed open all hours. We bought our children balloons and coloured ribbons, purchased sweetmeats by the kilo, paid calls in taxis to relatives we had not seen throughout the year. The days grew shorter, the evenings colder. We buttoned our sweaters and pulled up our socks. Then a chill set in that made our throats itch. We made our children gargle with warm saltwater and wrap mufflers around their necks. But it was the Haldar baby who ended up getting sick.

A doctor was summoned in the middle of the night and commanded to reduce the fever. "Cure her," the wife pleaded. Her shrill commotion had woken us all. 'We can give you anything, just cure my baby girl." The doctor prescribed a glucose formula, crushed aspirins in a mortar, and told them to wrap the child with quilts and covers.

Five days later the fever had not budged.

"It's Bibi," the wife wailed. "She's done it, she's infected our child. We should never have let her back down here. We should never have let her back into this house."

And so Bibi started to spend her nights in the storage room again. At the wife's insistence Haldar even moved her camp cot up there, along with a tin trunk that contained her belongings. Her meals were left covered with a colander at the top of the stairs.

"I don't mind," Bibi told us. "It's better to live apart from them, to set up house on my own." She unpacked the trunk—some housecoats, a framed portrait of her father, sewing supplies, and an assortment of fabrics—and arranged her things on a few empty shelves. By the week's end the baby had recuperated, but Bibi was not asked to return downstairs. "Don't worry, it's not as if they've locked me in here," she said in order to set us at ease. "The world begins at the bottom of the stairs. Now I am free to discover life as I please."

But in truth she stopped going out altogether. When we asked her to come with us to the fish pond or to go see temple decorations she refused, claiming that she was stitching a new curtain to hang across the entrance of the storage room. Her skin looked ashen. She needed fresh air. "What about finding your husband?" we suggested. "How do you expect to charm a man sitting up here all day?"

Nothing persuaded her.

By mid-December, Haldar cleared all the unsold merchandise off the shelves of his beauty shop and hauled them in boxes up to the storage room. We had succeeded in driving him more or less out of business. Before the year's end the family moved away, leaving an envelope containing three hundred rupees under Bibi's door. There was no more news of them.

One of us had an address for a relation of Bibi's in Hyderabad, and wrote explaining the situation. The letter was returned unopened, address unknown. Before the coldest weeks set in, we had the shutters of the storage room repaired and attached a sheet of tin to the doorframe, so that she would at least have some privacy. Someone donated a kerosene lamp; another gave her some old mosquito netting and a pair of socks without heels. At every opportunity we reminded her that we surrounded her, that she could come to us if she ever needed advice or aid of any kind. For a time we sent our children to play on the roof in the afternoons, so that they could alert us if she was having another attack. But each night we left her alone.

Some months passed. Bibi had retreated into a deep and prolonged silence. We took turns leaving her plates of rice and glasses of tea. She drank little, ate less, and began to assume an expression that no longer matched her years. At twilight she circled the parapet once or twice, but she never left the rooftop. After dark she remained behind the tin door and did not come out for any reason. We did not disturb her. Some of us began to wonder if she was dying. Others concluded that she had lost her mind.

One morning in April, when the heat had returned for drying lentil wafers on the roof, we noticed that someone had vomited by the cistern tap. When we noticed this a second morning as well, we knocked on Bibi's tin door. When there was no answer we opened it ourselves, as there was no lock to fasten it.

We found her lying on the camp cot. She was about four months pregnant.

She said she could not remember what had happened. She would not tell us who had done it. We prepared her semolina with hot milk and raisins; still she would not reveal the man's identity. In vain we searched for traces of the assault, some sign of the intrusion, but the room was swept and in order. On the floor beside the cot, her inventory ledger, open to a fresh page, contained a list of names.

She carried the baby to full term, and one evening in September, we helped her deliver a son. We showed her how to feed him, and bathe him, and lull him to sleep. We bought her an oilcloth and helped her stitch clothes and pillowcases out of the fabric she had saved over the years. Within a month Bibi had recuperated from the birth, and with the money that Haldar had left her, she had the storage room whitewashed, and placed padlocks on the window and doors. Then she dusted the shelves and arranged the leftover potions and lotions, selling Haldar's old inventory at half price. She told us to spread word of the sale, and we did. From Bibi we purchased our soaps and kohl, our combs and powders, and when she had sold the last of her merchandise, she went by taxi to the wholesale market, using her profits to restock the shelves. In this manner she raised the boy and ran a business in the storage room, and we did what we could to help. For years afterward, we wondered who in our town had disgraced her. A few of our servants were questioned, and in tea stalls and bus stands, possible suspects were debated and dismissed. But there was no point carrying out an investigation. She was, to the best of our knowledge, cured.

F.Y.I.

salwar-kameez: an outfit worn by both men and women in South Asia and Central Asia. Traditionally, the *salwar* is a loose-fitting pant much like pyjama bottoms, and the *kameez* is a long shirt that comes down to either the middle of the thigh or the top of the knee.

Vedic verses: words from the Vedas, a word derived from Sanskrit for "wisdom" and the root, "to know." These verses form a body of sacred texts from ancient India.

Words to Build on

allopaths: those who treat people by conventional medical methods, using drugs to treat symptoms

almari: Hindi word for cabinet or commode

armature: framework

assiduous: showing great care and perseverance

auscultation: the action of listening to sounds from the heart, lungs, or other organs, typically with a stethoscope, as part of a medical diagnosis

bane: a cause of great distress or annoyance

bitters: alcohol flavoured with bitter plant extracts

conjugal: relating to marriage or the relationship between husband and wife

disconsolate: very unhappy and unable to be comforted

girded: to encircle a part of the body

gripes: minor complaints

jute: rough fibre made from the stems of a tropical plant, usually used for making rope or fibre woven into sacking or matting

malaise: a general feeling of discomfort, illness, or unease whose exact cause is difficult to identify

mawkish: sentimental in an exaggerated or false way

mottled: covered by an irregular arrangement of spots or patches of colour

parapet: a low protective wall along the edge of a roof

paroxysm: a sudden attack or outburst of a particular emotion or activity

petticoat: a woman's light, loose undergarment hanging from the shoulders or the waist, worn under a skirt or dress

polyclinic: an independent clinic where both general and specialist examinations and treatments are available to outpatients

propitious: giving or indicating a good chance of success

rancour: a long-standing bitterness or resentfulness

relations: sexual intercourse

spinster: a woman, especially an older one, thought unlikely to marry

sullied: damage the purity or integrity of

throes: intense pain or torment

tumid: swollen

Tricks of the Trade

Character

Climax

Conflict

In Your Own Words: Comprehension

1. What is the setting of this story?

2. Who is telling this story? What is the narrative point of view?

3. Describe Bibi Haldar.

4. Describe Bibi Haldar's daily life in the first half of the story.

5. What is Bibi Haldar's illness?

6. What are the treatments prescribed to Bibi Haldar at the start of the story, and how do these differ from the "new" treatment?

7. How do Haldar and his wife feel about the new treatment? Why do they feel this way?

8. How do the townspeople treat Bibi Haldar? Does the way they view her change throughout the story?

9. Why does Haldar believe Bibi has "sullied" his family's name?

10. What happened to Bibi Haldar's parents? What was Bibi's relationship with her father?

In Your Own Words: Analysis

1. What are the roles of Indian women as shown in this story? How are women portrayed?

2. Do you know anyone like Bibi Haldar? What about this character makes her seem real?

3. Bibi Haldar states: "The world begins at the bottom of the stairs. Now I am free to discover life as I please." Explain what she means by these two statements.

4. Does Bibi's life change for the better by the end of the story? Explain.

5. Explain what the narrator means by "For years we wondered who in our town had disgraced her."

6. In what span of time does the story take place?

7. How would you describe Jhumpa Lahiri's writing style?

8. Does Bibi Haldar really want to be married? Support your view with evidence from the story.

9. Explain the title of this story.

✳ Now Write

1. Research the topic of hysteria and its history. What are the beliefs physicians used to have about hysteria and how did these theories affect views about women? How do such views relate to the story "The Treatment of Bibi Haldar"?

2. Select one other story by another writer in this book (Marquez, Boyden, Govier) that focuses on the portrayal of community and the individual. Compare this story to "The Treatment of Bibi Haldar."

3. Why are people sometimes afraid of or wish to avoid people who live with illness or face physical challenges? What does Jean Vanier say about this in the excerpt from *Becoming Human*, and how are these views and reactions demonstrated in "The Treatment of Bibi Haldar"?

Joseph Boyden

Joseph Boyden (b. 1966) was born in Willowdale, Ontario, and is of Irish, Scottish, and Metis heritage. The short story "Legless Joe versus Black Robe" is taken from his first short story collection, *Born with a Tooth* (1998). In 2008, Boyden won the Giller Prize for his novel *Through Black Spruce*, which was the follow up work to his first and best-selling novel, *Three Day Road* (2005). Both focus on the lives of Cree soldiers who become snipers for the Canadian military during World War I. Boyden drew upon the narratives of the men in his own family who served during the Great War. Fans of Boyden have commented on how much they enjoy the way he often revisits characters in subsequent books, fleshing out more about their personal journeys.

Boyden has taught communications in Northern College's Aboriginal program. He currently lives in both Northern Ontario and Louisiana, where he teaches writing at the University of New Orleans. His website, www.josephboyden.com, lists biographical details, readings, and upcoming publications.

In His Own Words

"Most of the time I feel more Indian than white."

"More and more over the last many years—really, all my life—I've had an Anishinabe vision of the world...We have a way in the West of looking at man as the top of the food chain—we control the world. Well, the Ojibway view is completely opposite: even rocks are higher on the scale than us, because you need a rock to build a fire. You need a rock to build a house. You need deer to eat. You need moose to eat. We are reliant on everything. But none of these things need to rely on us. We should be looking at ourselves as in debt to our natural world."

"I was never a soldier, I am not Moose Cree, and, to the best of my knowledge, I've never been a woman, but if I, as a writer, were to let these concerns overwhelm me, I would never have been able to write a book. To write about a person or culture that isn't completely your own means that you have to treat your subject with real care and respect."

Before We Begin

1. Have you ever made a snap judgment about a person based on externals only to find out that you were wrong about this person? How did you come to learn the truth about the person?
2. What do you know about the history of First Nations reserves and residential schools in Canada?
3. Was there ever a time when you were made to feel ashamed or embarrassed about something to do with your culture?

 **Now Read**

Legless Joe versus Black Robe

No roads connect Sharpening Teeth to the rest of the world. But we got roads here on the reserve, thin and covered in dirt like my nephew Crow. Four streets that form a square. In my dream a motorcycle gang, a bunch of hairy bikers, ugly bastards, roars down First Street, makes a left on Wabun, roars down Wabun, makes a left on Takan Road, roars down Takan Road, makes a left on Maheegan Street, roars down Maheegan and ends up right back on First. They pass like clockwork, every three minutes or so, never able to get out of second gear, getting madder and madder. Bikers would get bored pretty fast on a reserve like this, I tell you. They'd tear this town up quick.

It used to be the reserve was so small it couldn't even fit a full-time drunk. But then the economy worsened and the government shrank Indian benefits and most of the tourists quit coming here in summer and my wife left me. It got so bad I was a sad country song. I started my own little gang of serious drinkers. They call us the Cold Duck Four.

Booze affects a body in all sorts of ways. You might not eat nothing because you save all your money for a bottle, but still you get a paunchy stomach and soft face. I do, anyways. The other weird effect is that when I started drinking, I began growing black whiskers on my face, enough now for a scraggly little goatee and funny long patches on my cheeks. Before I was a drinker my face was smooth as a woman's ass. My theory is that Cold Duck wine is a ploy of the white man to get us Indians drinking and at the same time to get us looking more like them. It seems to be working. The bastards. But one thing that drinking hasn't affected is my dreams.

I've dreamed all my life. Most do. But me, I try to live by my dreams. To act in waking hours as I do in sleep. To believe what they tell me. I can't always act the way I do in my dreams, obviously. I'm not about to wrestle giant, beautiful women with great hunting abilities whose clothes tear off effortlessly. But I try to get meaning from the dreams, to trust them. That's why, when I dreamt my niece Linda was dead last night, I knew she really was when I woke this morning. She killed herself, I knew. So I walked to her mother's, my sister's, to find out how.

"She ate pills" is all my sister tells me with red eyes. My sister won't let me hug her. I know how bad I smell. Linda was all by herself at school in Timmins, and that's when she did it.

"Let me help you with the funeral," I say. There is a purpose for me in the sadness. I stand taller and hold my chest out in order to battle the sobbing that is building inside of me. "I'll drum with the singers for my niece." I was once the best. A powwow circuit legend. Lead drummer with Black Water Singers.

"Father Jimmy doesn't allow drumming," my sister says and then tells me to leave.

I leave and look for Father Jimmy. This funeral will be Indian with the Catholic. I think of my sad niece Linda who slept with boys so they'd like her or because she was too drunk to say no, who ate too much to smother her guilt. She was a pretty little kid whose laugh made my breath hitch in my throat, her laugh was so clean.

The priest is smoking cigarettes and drinking coffee at the Sky Ranch, staring at Elise the waitress, my relation, who he calls Pocahontas.

"My niece is dead and I want the Black Water Singers at her wedding," I tell him soon as I sit down across the table. The wide-eyed look of fear settles back quickly into his squinty eyes. I've always frightened Father Jimmy with my stinky, big body and long black hair.

"So if she's dead, why does she want to get married?" the priest asks me. He hasn't shaved in a while and his round face is speckled with sharp grey hairs. My tongue grows thick so that I'm worried I won't be able to breathe. I get up quickly and leave, half as big as when I walked in.

People on the reserve tell me I'm a wino. I am known as Legless Joe the Wino. So what if I got legs? What's in a name? Actually, I got my nickname back in my biker days, on a bad acid trip one night. I convinced myself and the rest of my buddies that my legs had melted off. We cried and wailed about the horrible accident for hours, until somebody muttered, "Poor Joe. Poor Legless Joe Cheechoo." Needless to say, that got somebody giggling, and before you know it we're all laughing so hard, a few of us threw up. The name stuck. Now it precedes me. That story was one of Linda's favourites.

Drinking isn't an easy career, considering the price of a bottle of Cold Duck and the three lousy bums I hang with always trying to steal sips off me. My girl Cindy, she's one of the gang. She loves me. I call her my fly girl. I heard that in one of those music videos before and immediately I thought of her because she's pesky and likes to get into shit. Henry's so white he's yellowy coloured like an old newspaper and he's always trying to get into Cindy. He came up clearing bush for the railway years ago and stayed. He liked the speed of life around here, of living on Indian time. Henry's got some mighty weepy cold sores, but that's only half the reason I don't like him sipping my Duck. You can't overlook he's a white man. A good white man, mind you. But haven't white men taken enough from us? Silent Sam, the fourth Cold Duck, his mind has been surrounded by a fog not unlike the kind you see on a river in early morning. This is due, I believe, to his over-drinking and is where all of us will be in a few years.

A lot of white people here on the reserve find it easier to blame my drinking on the fact I was buggered in residential school up in Fort Albany when I was a boy. I let them think this is the reason, if it makes their life any easier. But lots of Indians around here were, and most of them don't drink at all. A government commission travelled up here a few years ago to chase down allegations and I was one of the only ones who would speak to them. Made me high profile. Father Jimmy said that being able to say out loud that I been buggered is a part of healing. I told him it made me feel like buggering him. But that was a year ago when he first come up to take over the church from the crazy old priest who called us heathens and swore more than me and went berserk during mass one Sunday.

On this sad morning that Father Jimmy makes fun of me at the Sky Ranch, I leave and head back into the bush to our summer place on the river, away from people. The bad news is already travelling the reserve. Everybody will know by noon. My girlfriend, Cindy, is still sleeping. I can hear her snoring 10 metres away from our blue tarp teepee. Bottles and cans are scattered all around, glittering in the sun. I sit down and stare at the river and think about my niece Linda when she was just a skinny little kid with feet too big for her, slapping around town in rain boots. I can see her round face looking up to me, framed by messy braids, her asking me for a quarter to get a Popsicle at the store. Hard as I try, I can't see her face as an adult. Something inside won't let me. I hum an old song to myself, and bang time on my lap. It is the Death Song, the Funeral Song, sung by the Grandfathers long before they ever knew of white men or Cold Duck.

It is an Indian summer this year, but still the mornings are cold when I wake up, and soon it will be time to make winter plans. The last three years running I've mostly been able to do small things like steal food or break windows, so the band constables are forced to keep me in a warm cell and feed me three times a day. Last year all of the Cold Duck Four was in jail at the same time for a solid month, waiting for the Crown attorney and judge to fly up and condemn us.

We'd broken into the Meechim Store late at night and ate potato chips and white bread and drank pop until we threw up. Cindy stayed in the cell next to me and Henry and Silent Sam and I communicated with her by tapping a quarter on the wall. It would have been easier to shout back and forth, but tapping felt good and it was a nice break from her gravelly voice.

The Crown said time served was enough punishment and our lawyer agreed with him, so the next day we were forced by the cold wind to break into the Meechim Store again. We sat there all night, eating and getting bored, waiting for the band cops to show. Finally we fell asleep, and we weren't discovered until the store opened the next morning. That got us through the rest of the winter. But the judge talked a long time about the three-strikes policy and it makes me think this winter I should be more care-ful or I'll end up in a maximum security joint down south somewhere, for the winter and summer and next couple of winters and summers too.

When Cindy and Henry and Silent Sam wake up, I tell them about my niece. Cindy begins to cry and holds me to her, wetting the shoulder of my shirt. Linda was one of the few people in my family who still talked to me and Cindy. Henry and Silent Sam sit side by side and look out to the river, not sure what to say. Sam has been a part of my life so long that we are brothers. This is the first time in a long time that I've seen my words actually make it through the thick haze surrounding his brain. He's crying too when he turns around to look at me.

"We got to drum for her at her funeral," he says. I nod. Me and Sam used to ride together in a motorcycle gang in our youth. There were 11 of us, called the Apostles. Hard as we tried, we could never find that twelfth member. We agreed to be communistic about the whole thing—no general, no lieutenants, no hierarchy. We rode around the north in summertime, drinking a lot and doing acid, having religious visions and helping people out who were in trouble. Stranded motorists, old ladies with flat tires, lost tourists. We put the fear of God into all of them when we pulled up, and left them with the love of Jesus in their hearts when we pulled away.

We were into our own Indian Catholic thing, all of us long-haired like the Man and treating others as we liked to get treated. You never saw so many back rubs and good words and rounds of beer bought without complaint as in our motorcycle club. But our gig didn't last long. We were too nice. Nobody would take the reins. When I think back on those days now, I realize that I was trying to make sense out of the bad part of my youth—wanting to believe that we should love one another, but not in the way adults I trusted at residential school sometimes loved me. Linda loved those stories of my biker days. They always made her laugh hard.

By the afternoon we're at our picnic table drinking.

"My niece was a good one," I say. The other three nod solemn. "She didn't need to die." The other three nod again. "Her mother's heart is broken for good," I say. "It is a bad day for the Cheechoo family."

Father Jimmy walks out of the Meechim Store, pretending not to notice us. But then he turns around and walks straight to me.

"There'll be no drums or chanting at Linda's funeral," he says to me. "This is a Catholic mass." I turn my head away from him. I can feel the anger like a heat coming from him. He thinks I'm a devil, that we're all devils. "It is hard enough on her mother that she committed suicide. You know what the Church says about suicides," he whispers, his face close to mine. "For the sake of the living, don't even show up at the church, Joe Cheechoo." He turns and walks away quickly. Cindy makes a twisted face at his back and sticks her tongue out at him.

I look over to Silent Sam. "He smells like Father McKinley back in Fort Albany," I say. Sam just looks away. Sam has the same recurring dream. He told me once. The scrapes of Father McKinley's feet as he climbs the stairs to our dormitory room, my eyes wide with the fear he would pick me again that night.

It is night and I'm drunk by the time I decide to go to my sister's house to help her prepare for the wake and the funeral. When I walk in the door, the number of people standing and sitting in the house makes me very nervous. Linda's brothers stand around, their hair out of ponytails. They talk to one another and sway to some music only they can hear. They are drunk too, which surprises me. But Crow, my youngest nephew, Linda's little brother, is nowhere to be seen. He was sitting in the reserve jail last I heard, charged with one thing or another. Friends and neighbours stand everywhere, most choosing to ignore me, but I get dirty looks from some of the old ladies. The house is so crowded it is like the whole reserve is here. Someone mentions that Linda's funeral won't be for almost a whole week, time for faraway relatives to get to Sharpening Teeth. I hear someone else say that Linda's body is in a freezer down in Timmins, and that they will fly it up in a couple of days.

My grandfather, Linda's great-grandfather, stands in the kitchen by himself. He is an old, old man now who spends much of his time talking to stray dogs and to birds. He sees me and smiles kindly. I'm a little shocked. He is the first person in a long time to do so.

I make my way through the crowd and see my sister sitting on the couch with Father Jimmy. He is holding her hand. He stands up when he sees me.

"You're not welcome here right now," he says. "You gave up the right to your sister's house when you picked up the bottle." My sister won't look at me. Everyone knows that Father Jimmy's favourite drink is Scotch on the rocks. His face is red from it now.

"I'm here to talk to my sister, not to you," I tell him, trying to hold in the shouting that hisses up from my stomach and burns my throat.

"You're here to try and talk your sister into a past that is gone for ever," Father Jimmy says.

"Talk to me, sister," I say. She doesn't look up. "Talk to me, sister." Everyone is quiet, looking down at their feet. My sister won't look at me. I turn and leave.

There is nothing in me for a while, maybe two or three days. My insides are a hot, black cave. I lie in the blue tarp teepee and refuse to talk or eat. I only accept the half-finished bottles of Cold Duck that Cindy brings. I can smell autumn in the air and I know the leaves will change their colour overnight very soon. Whenever my eyes close in this blue teepee and I fall into sleep, I dream my autumn dream. I am on the back of a huge snow goose high over the swampy muskeg. I can feel the power of this goose as it flaps its wings. Below us I see a hunter aim his shotgun. He fires and the snow goose begins to fall to earth like a spinning feather. I hold onto its neck and wait for the impact. I see my frightened face reflected in the snow goose's black eye.

By the third day I know what I must do. I call a meeting. "What we're going to do," I tell my little gang, "will put us away for the winter, probably longer. You don't have to do it, but I'm going to." They ask me what, so I tell them. Cindy and Silent Sam agree but Henry is scared.

"I won't join you in this one," he says. "What about the third strike?" He is afraid of a big white prison. "I left the south and I don't want to go back," he says. But me, I no longer care.

When I commit a crime, I hear music. It's music I heard in a spy movie once, slinky sounding, with lots of drums and pianos.

Me and Cindy and Sam try to bust the church basement window quietly. There is no moon tonight, and in two days when it begins coming back, all my relations will be here and the funeral will begin and end. The window doesn't want to give so I kick it as quietly as I can but it smashes, cracking, then tinkling onto the basement floor. The police station is next door and I'm surprised they don't hear it. It's a sign I'm doing right. The three of us slide in, clumsy but safe.

All the excitement gets Cindy going. Soon as Sam makes his way upstairs, she pulls me to her and starts whispering unchurchy thoughts in my ear. She knows this might be our last chance for a very long time. But this church basement brings back memories of another church basement long ago and my throat gets tight. I whisper, "Can't," and push my way upstairs.

Sam has already found the sacristy and the Halo Vino and we thank the Lord the bottle caps twist off. It's no Cold Duck but it does the trick and within an hour we're talking and laughing. We know this is the party of the season and soon it will be over so we go hard.

I'm pretty drunk when I put on Father Jimmy's vestments. I lead Cindy and Sam to the altar and say a few words. I get rolling into my sermon with a bottle in one hand and it's not long before they're rolling in the aisles and I'm shouting out that they're blast-femurs and devil's spunk and children of the corn. "In the name of your father," I say, "and the sun, and the holy mackerel, bend over, because this priest is going to drive."

The more they laugh and the more we drink and carry on, the more hard thinking I do. Maybe it's because we're drinking red wine and I'm not used to it, or maybe it's because I know this is my last night of freedom for a long time, but suddenly I realize that this collar and black robe and the golden chalice and the white Host are like a costume an actor uses in a movie to make himself fit the part. All my life I been told that these things are what gives a priest his power, that they're his medicine. But that's not it at all. What you got, good or bad, comes from inside. A simple realization, I admit, but it makes me start looking in a new light at what a long-ago priest did to me. He wasn't the Church. He was a bad man acting like he was good. As for Father Jimmy, all I can say for him, standing here looking down from where he normally stands, is that he really believes what he does and says is right.

Oh, drinking the Halo Vino and sermonizing to Cindy and Sam, I really did begin feeling the warmth of that righteous light. Maybe I wasn't ready to forgive the world for all its sins, but I got a glimpse into the understanding, the thinking behind forgiveness. There's these two nuns that live by Father Jimmy, who help him with his work and cook and clean for him besides. A good deal if ever I heard of one. Sister Jane, she can swear like a sailor, and Sister Marie is all fat and smiles. It used to be I'd sit long hours and chat with them, back before Father Jimmy came to the reserve. We'd sit on my picnic table by the Meechim Store and soak up the sun and talk. They're good women. I'm sad we don't see each other much any more. But it was them who first talked to me about it being impossible to be perfect, to instead try to be like God wants us to be, which is always trying to be better. Suddenly I know how to end my sermon.

"Pass me another bottle, Cindy, and I will sermonize thee further," I say from the pulpit. Cindy struts up, trying to do a sexy wiggle, flashing me her saggy breasts after she hands me a fresh bottle. She goes to sit back down with Sam.

"There are many things us priests know," I begin. "There are many secrets of the world we possess, secrets like how to get into boy-sized pairs of underwear." Cindy and Sam hoot at that one. "We know things you don't know. We got a direct phone line to God." I take a gulp of wine. "I will keep this short so we can socialize after mass. As Jesus said, wherever two or three of you Indians gather in my name, get loaded. What I must tell you is that man makes mistakes. He is not perfect. Look at Father Jimmy.

Look at you and me. We get drunk, we fall down. We do bad things, we've got to take the fall for doing them. In other words, man is fallable. But God, *Gitchi-Manitou*, the Great Spirit, now there's someone who is perfect, who knows everything, who makes no mistakes. Hey, way up in those clouds, he can't afford to fall, because it's a long way down to earth. So God's gotta keep his balance. In other words, God's pretty much infallable."

Cindy and Sam nod respectfully as I walk from the pulpit. "Drink to me and I'll drink to thee," I shout at the bottom of the altar, tipping my head and drinking as much of the red liquid as I can. I smash the bottle on the ground, and it feels as good as anything I've done in a long time. God knows I'm not dishonouring Him. Sam and Cindy and me head back to the sacristy to drink more and wait for the law.

But they don't come. We drink and shout and drink some more. Bottles lie everywhere. We've smelled the place up, so I open a window for air. Cindy nods off. In a rare mood he saves just for me, Sam sings me a Cree song he learned from his grandmother when he was little. His voice carries me up to somewhere soft and I lie back and let it hold me.

I dream a good dream, a strange one. There are many images, lots of dreams swirling around one another like the northern lights do at this time of year, just above your head so that you feel you can jump up and touch them. At one point there's me and Sam and Henry and Cindy and Linda and a half-dozen other Indians, including some of my old motorcycle gang members, sitting around a long wooden table with the Man Himself with his long hair and robe. He's not saying who he is, but he's got nobody fooled. There's a halo on his head. There's no mistaking him. We're all about to eat. He picks up a big silver lid in the middle of the table and a Canada goose pops out and struts about the table, ruffling its feathers. The goose stops in front of Linda and honks and Linda stands up. I'm happy I can picture her face again. She climbs onto the table and begins to grow small, shrinking before our eyes. She climbs up on the goose's back and it flaps its wings and flies off as Linda looks back at us, smiling and waving.

We all feel good and Jesus mutters, "Goddamn, that was a big goose." Then he looks at me and says, "Legless Joe—can I call you Legless Joe? This is a pretty easy dream to read, I mean your niece flying off into the sky on the back of a goose. You don't need too much of a tricky mind to figure that one out. I know you are mad at me for some past wrongs done to you in my name, but let me tell you not to lie there sleeping any longer, because that Father Jimmy, he's a prick, and he'll make sure you go up the river for a long time. So in my name, get up, walk, be free. Hit the road before dawn."

Jesus turns his head to look up at the sky and Linda is still in the picture, on the goose's back, getting smaller and smaller, looking over her shoulder every once in a while, smiling shyly and waving. Then Jesus walks to his waiting helicopter and climbs in. The blades start turning in a *thump-thump-thump* and I wake up to the thumping of the sacristy window we opened for air last night banging in the wind. I get up quick and grab Father Jimmy's robe and begin wiping off all the bottles and doors and the altar, the spy music pounding in my head. I'm not too worried about fingerprints. Sometimes I think the police around here couldn't find the river if they had to. I wake up Sam and Cindy and scoot them downstairs and help push them through the basement window. I use a chair for a boost and the sun is just starting to break as we make our way to the school where we can get out of the cold for a while and drink a cup of coffee.

It's been two days and I haven't had a drink in that whole time. The elders tell me that alcohol and drumming are like a hard frost and a flower, or a cock and ice water. Father Jimmy knows I'm responsible for the break-in but can't prove it. Last night I found my grandfather and asked him to do a sweat lodge with me, to purify me. Then I sat by the river and drummed a long time.

All my relations are here and I walk into the church carrying my big drum in both arms and sit down at the back. Everyone is turning their heads and looking at me. Linda's casket is in the middle of the aisle, up front, by the same altar I preached at two nights ago. It arrived later the same morning we got safely out of the church. The whole reserve turned out at the airfield, and we watched as her casket was unloaded off the plane and we all followed the chief's big red pickup as it drove her slow from the runway to my sister's house. It was the most powerful, quiet thing I ever saw, that long line of people walking behind her. They had the official wake that evening, but I stayed away, sat on the river with my grandfather, drumming and thinking.

Father Jimmy enters from the sacristy followed by two altar boys. He blesses everyone and says some prayers and reads from scripture. When he's done that, he starts his sermon.

"All of you know by now the crime committed against this church the other night. Most of us have a good idea who's responsible." I can tell by the way Father Jimmy says this that he doesn't even realize I'm here. "This crime has put a further damper on our community. I came close to not being able to perform this funeral mass today, I was so upset." The whole congregation's eyes are looking at the floor. He doesn't even realize that he speaks to them like little children, I see.

"The Church has taken your hand and led you a long way," he continues. "But there are those among us who would take your other hand and pull you in the opposite direction. You get nowhere that way. You must decide on your path and stick to it. Do not become tempted by Satan, for he can only lead you to harm. Satan comes in all forms, in the bottle, in the drum, in the form of premarital sex, in drugs. Look for him, and be on guard against him." The congregation continues staring at the floor, everyone but me, it seems. I stare up at Father Jimmy.

"In her depression and drug- and alcohol-induced haze, Linda Cheechoo committed a mortal sin," Father Jimmy says. "She took the life God gave her and threw it back in His face. Without realizing what she was doing, she spat on Him. I tell you with a sad heart that this is precisely the behaviour that bars a person's admission into the Kingdom of Heaven."

I see my sister's head move, way up front in the first row. It turns up to look at Father Jimmy.

"I thought long and hard about what to say to you today in this time of great sorrow. You all know me to speak my mind, and know that I believe in tough love. I offer you all a warning." Other heads rise up to look at Father Jimmy. My grandfather's, my nephews', my aunts' and uncles'. "What Linda has done is reprehensible." He says this word carefully. "It was an act of cowardice." More heads turn up to him. "Yes, I am a believer in tough love, and these are tough words and, if we are to believe scripture, Linda must now spend eternity in purgatory as payment for her sins." Everyone is now looking up at Father Jimmy. "If all of you take this as a hard-earned lesson, the hardest lesson you will ever learn, and live your lives according to the Bible, you can still enter heaven. Poor Linda Cheechoo will only be able to peer through the gates like a child outside an amusement park, desperately wanting to get in but having no admission ticket. You must live God's Law or suffer His consequences."

I lift my big drum up from the seat beside me and carry it to the centre of the aisle at the back of the church so that it is lined up with Linda on the other side. I kneel by it, lift my stick and bang the drum once, hard. It echoes in the quiet church. Father Jimmy looks back to me, his face turning red. He shouts, "There will be no blasphemy here, Joe Cheechoo!" but I cut him off with another hammer of the drum. It travels well in here, like a strong heart.

I bang again and then pick up a rhythm, the rhythm of the river. My funeral song. Father Jimmy rushes from the pulpit. In the aisle he is cut off by Linda's brothers and my uncles and my grandfather and some cousins as they make their way back to me.

They kneel around my drum in a circle just as I begin my best wail. It is pure and true and rises to the rafters and sends a shiver down my back. The others join in the drumming, picking up the beat with hands or shoes tugged off their feet. I constrict my throat more and the song sails higher, bringing others in the church to stand in a circle around us. My grandfather answers my wail and the others in the circle join us too, eyes closed and throats tight. We sing high and drum hard. We sing for Linda's *uchak,* her soul, our voices rising to pull it from her quiet body at the front of the church and carry it, protected by her relations, to its resting place.

Father Jimmy retreats to his pulpit, his face flushed, a look of fear in his eyes. He turns and goes back to the sacristy. The rhythm comes faster and I think hard of Linda, of her as a little girl running around wearing rain boots too big for her little feet. I think of her flower-patterned dress, of her red bike, of her drinking one night with me, of her laugh, the sadness that dulled her eyes the last time I saw her. I look up to see my sister, her mother, looking down at me. Her eyes are Linda's, a little of the spark returned.

F.Y.I.

Cree: part of the Algonquin linguistic family and the largest group of First Nations people in North America. In Canada the Cree Nation is divided into eight groups that live from the east coast to the Rocky Mountains.

Host: the bread consecrated in the Eucharist

Indian benefits: Under Canada's federal Indian Act, any person who is a registered "Indian" is entitled to receive benefits. Historical treaties signed with the Crown (Canada) entitle an Aboriginal person to certain rights and benefits, including services and financial compensation.

Pocahontas: a Native woman born in Virginia circa 1595. She was the daughter of a powerful chief who met, and some say protected, an English colonist named John

Smith. Although books and films often portray them as being lovers, there is no historical proof of such a relationship. She is one of the most famous Native Americans, and her life has been the subject of biographies and fictional retellings in books and films.

powwow: a traditional time of reunion and honouring ancestors when Aboriginal peoples join in certain ceremonies, dancing, singing, and drumming. Powwow traditions continue today for the purpose of celebrating and renewing friendships and cultural ties with other groups.

pulpit: a lectern or raised platform in a church from which a priest or preacher delivers a sermon

Reserve: land set aside by the federal government for the use and occupancy of a First Nations group or band. Legal title for the land rests with the Crown (government).

residential school: various institutions or boarding schools maintained by the Canadian government for over 100 years. In 1867, the Canadian government passed an Act that began the process of formally assimilating Aboriginal people into white culture. By 1920 it became compulsory for Aboriginal children aged 7–15 to attend these schools. The children were taken by government representatives and police officers, and the schools were run by the Catholic church. Many Aboriginal children experienced physical, emotional, and sexual abuse while at these schools. The last federally run school closed in 1996. In 2008, Prime Minister Stephen Harper stood in Parliament and offered a formal apology to Aboriginal people who were forced into residential schools. Monetary compensation followed.

sacristy: a room in a church or chapel where religious or sacred items are kept

sweat lodge: a structure used by some First Nations groups as part of religious tradition; it is used for spiritual healing and also for medical purposes

teepee: a conical tent used by Plains Aboriginal peoples, made of skins, cloth, or canvas on a frame of poles

vestments: official robes worn by the Christian clergy to perform divine services for the Church

Words to Build on

buggered: slang term for the act of sodomy

heathens: derogatory term used for an irreligious person or someone who does not belong to a widely held religion, especially one who is not Christian, Jewish, or Muslim

muskeg: a swamp or bog in northern North America, consisting of a mixture of water and partly dead vegetation

paunchy: a word used to describe when the belly or stomach protrudes

Tricks of the Trade

Catharsis

Irony

Symbol

In Your Own Words: Comprehension

1. Who is telling the story? Can this voice or person be trusted as a narrator? What details reveal when and where the story takes place?

2. Based on this story, what are your impressions of life on a reserve?

3. Explain what the narrator means when he claims, "[t]here is a purpose for me in the sadness."

4. Why does Father Jimmy not allow the narrator to drum or chant at his niece Linda's funeral?

5. In the beginning the community accepts that there will be no drumming at Linda's funeral. However, by the end of story they are all gathered around Joe Cheechoo. What causes them to change their minds?

In Your Own Words: Analysis

1. What are society's attitudes toward suicide? How is suicide dealt with in this story?

2. Is Joe Cheechoo a sympathetic character? Provide reasons why he is or is not.

3. Explain why this story is titled "Legless Joe versus Black Robe."

4. Dreams and dream interpretation are respected in many First Nations cultures. How does the narrator feel about his dreams? Explain the role of dreams in this story.

5. After one of his dreams, Joe Cheechoo stops drinking. Is this a permanent change he has made in his life? Give evidence to support whether this change will last.

6. Are all white Christian characters in this story negative? Name the non-Native characters who have a positive influence on Joe Cheechoo and/or this community. Explain how these characters demonstrate this influence.

7. Explain what Joe Cheechoo means when he states, "The elders tell me that alcohol and drumming are like a hard frost and a flower, or a cock and ice water."

❄ Now Write

1. What are some stereotypes of Aboriginal people? Write an essay in which you explain how this story reflects and/or challenges any of these stereotypical views?

2. Joe Cheechoo tells his friends, "What I must tell you is that man makes mistakes. He is not perfect . . . We get drunk, we fall down. We do bad things. We've got

to take the fall for doing them. In other words, man is fallible." Think about how and when people today use the common expression "nobody's perfect." Is this what Joe Cheechoo's words mean? Explain what he means with references to the story.

3. Loss is a theme in this story. What are the different forms of loss presented in the story? Write an essay explaining the positive elements that can come from loss with reference to Boyden's "Legless Joe versus Black Robe."

Thomas King

Thomas King (b. 1943) was born in Sacramento, California. He is of Cherokee, Greek, and German ancestry. He earned his PhD in English and American Studies from the University of Utah. King worked for many years as chair of American Indian Studies at the University of Minnesota. He has published novels, short stories, poems, and essays to great acclaim and is a unique voice in Canadian literature. His style is characterized by his use of humour, clever dialogue, and oral storytelling influences. His first novel, *Medicine River* (1989), was later turned into a television movie starring Graham Greene and Tom Jackson. King's most popular writing is a collection of short stories *One Good Story, That One*, and he won a Governor General's Literary Award for his second novel, *Green Grass, Running Water* (1993). In the 1990s King was also involved in writing and performing on a popular comic radio series for the CBC called *The Dead Dog Café Comedy Hour*. King is also the first Massey Lecturer of Aboriginal descent.

His story, "The Baby in the Airmail Box," showcases not only his signature wit and penchant for the absurd, but it also addresses the more serious topics of history, colonialism, and racism. He currently teaches Native literature and creative writing at the University of Guelph and is now a Canadian citizen.

In His Own Words

"The truth about stories is that that's all we are."

"One of the surprising things about Indians is that we're still here. After some 500 years of vigorous encouragement to assimilate and disappear, we're still here."

Before We Begin

1. Is it important that a child of a certain ethnic or religious background be adopted or raised by parents of the same background? Why or why not?

2. Can any subject, no matter how serious or sacred, be treated with humour? Can humour be used to help people deal with tragic happenings or events?

3. Do you know what a residential school is? The purpose of these schools was to "educate" and "westernize" Aboriginal children. Generations of children were removed from their parents' homes and abused in these schools. Learn more about the history of Canada's residential school system by visiting http://www.cbc.ca/news/canada/story/2008/05/16/f-faqs-residential-schools.html.

4. Will a story that is meant to be spoken be the same when it is written down on paper? Is something lost when a story is put in writing?

 **Now Read**

The Baby in the Airmail Box

Okay, so on Monday

The baby arrives in a cardboard box with a handful of airmail stamps stuck on top and a label that says, "Rocky Creek First Nations."

Orena Charging Woman brings the box to the council meeting and sets it in the middle of the table. "All right," she says, after all of the band councillors have settled in their chairs, "who ordered the baby?"

"Baby?" says Louis Standing, who is currently the chief and gets to sit in the big chair by the window. "What baby?"

Orena opens the airmail box and bends the flaps back so everyone can get a good look.

"It's a baby, all right," says Jimmy Tucker. "But it looks sick."

"It's not sick," says Orena, who knows something about babies. "It's White."

"White?" says Louis. "Who in hell would order a White baby?"

And just then

Linda Blackenship walks into Bob Wakutz's office at the Alberta Child Placement Agency with a large folder and an annoyed expression on her face that reminds Bob of the various promises he has made Linda about leaving his wife.

"We have a problem," says Linda, who says this a lot, and she holds the folder out at shoulder level and drops it on Bob's desk. Right on top of the colour brochure for the new Ford trucks.

"A problem?" says Bob, which is what he says every day when Linda comes into his office and drops folders on his desk.

"Mr. and Mrs. Cardinal," says Linda.

When they were in bed together, Bob could always tell when Linda was joking, but now that they've stopped seeing each other (which is the phrase Bob prefers) or since they stopped screwing (which Linda says is more honest) he can't.

"Have they been approved?"

"Yes," says Linda.

"Okay," says Bob, in a jocular sort of way, in case Linda is joking. "What's the problem?"

"They're Indian," says Linda.

Bob pushed the truck brochure to one side and opens the file. "East?"

"West."

"Caribbean?"

"Cree."

"That's the problem?" says Bob, who can't remember if giving babies to Indians is part of the mandate of the Alberta Child Placement Agency, though he is reasonably sure, without actually looking at the regulations, that there is no explicit prohibition against it.

Linda stands in front of Bob's desk and puts her hands on her hips. "They would like a baby," she says, without even a hint of a smile. "Mr. and Mrs. Cardinal would like a White baby."

Meanwhile

Orena takes the baby out of the airmail box and passes it around so all the councillors can get a good look at it.

"It's White, all right," says Clarence Scout. "Jesus, but they can be ugly."

"They never have any hair," says Elaine Sweetwater. "Got to be a mother to love a bald baby."

Now, the baby in the airmail box isn't on the agenda, and Louis can see that if he doesn't get the meeting moving, he is going to miss his tee time at Wolf Creek, so when the baby is passed to him, he passes it directly to Orena and makes an executive decision.

"Send it back," he says.

"Not the way it works," says Emmett Black Rabbit. "First you got to make a motion. Then someone has to second it."

"Who's going to bingo tonight?" says Ross Heavy Runner. "I could use a ride."

"Maybe it's one of those free samples," says Narcisse Good. "My wife gets them all the time."

"Any chance of getting a doughnut and a cup of coffee?" says Thelma Gladstone. "I didn't get breakfast."

"We can't send it back," says Orena, "There's no return address."

"Invoice?" asks Louis.

"Nope," says Orena.

"All right," says Louis, who is not happy with the start of his day, "who wants a baby?"

"Got four of my own," says Bruce Carving.

"Three here," says Harmon Setauket.

"Eight," says Ross Heavy Runner, and he holds up nine fingers by mistake.

"You caught up on those child support payments yet?" Edna Hunt asks him.

"Coffee and doughnuts?" says Thelma, "Could we have some coffee and doughnuts?"

"Could someone come up with an idea?" Louis checks his watch.

"What about bingo?" says Ross.

"Perfect," says Louis. "Meeting adjourned."

At the same time

Bob Wakutz is shaking hands with Mr. and Mrs. Cardinal. "Would you like some coffee?" he says. "Maybe a doughnut?"

"Sure," says Mr. Cardinal. "Black, no sugar."

"Thank you," says Mrs. Cardinal. "One cream, no sugar."

Bob smiles at Linda.

Linda smiles back.

"Maybe we should get down to business first," says Bob, and he opens the file. "I see you've been approved for adoption."

"That's right," says Mrs. Cardinal.

"So, when can we expect to get a baby?" says Mr. Cardinal.

Bob looks at Linda. He still finds her attractive, and, if he's being honest with himself, he has to admit that he misses their get-togethers. "Don't we have several Red babies ready for immediate placement?"

"Yes, we do," says Linda, who has no idea what she saw in Bob.

"Perfect," says Bob.

"That's nice," says Mr. Cardinal, "but we don't want a Red baby."

"No," says Mrs. Cardinal, "what we want is a White baby."

"That's understandable," says Bob. "White babies are very popular."

Indeed

"White babies are very popular," says Louis.

"That's a dumb idea," says Orena, who has heard plenty of dumb ideas in her life, mostly from men.

"Everybody comes to bingo, don't they," says Louis, who has heard plenty of dumb ideas in his life, too, mostly from politicians.

"You can't give the baby away as a bingo prize."

"Why not?"

"Nobody wants to win a baby," says Orena. "Babies are a dime a dozen."

"This isn't just any baby," says Louis, who knows this is the best idea he is going to come up with. "This is a White baby. You make up the posters. I'll call the newspapers."

While

Bob has to get the coffee and the doughnuts himself. Black with no sugar and one cream with no sugar.

"We try to match our babies with our families," says Bob. He folds his hands in front of his face so he can smell his fingertips. "I think you can see why."

"Sure," says Mrs. Cardinal. "But lots of White people have been adopting Red babies."

"Yes," says Mr. Cardinal. "You see Black babies with White parents, too."

"And Yellow babies with White parents," says Mrs. Cardinal.

"Don't forget Brown babies with White parents," says Mr. Cardinal.

"That's true," says Bob, who is trying to remember why his left index finger smells the way it does. "And my administrative assistant Ms. Blackenship can tell you why."

"Sure," says Linda, who is particularly grumpy today and who has never liked the thing that Bob does with his fingers. "It's because we're racist."

Which explains why

Louis is late for his golf game and has to drive the golf cart to the third hole at speeds well above the posted limit. He arrives just as Del Weasel Fat hooks his drive into the trees.

"Where the hell you been?" says Vernon Miller, who tells people his handicap is 18 when it's really 10.

"Council meeting," says Louis. "Usual game?"

"Dollar a hole," says Moses Thorpe. "Greenies, sandies, and snakes. What's in the box?"

"Baby," says Louis, and he grabs his driver.

"Baby what?" says Del, who is thinking about using one of his three mulligans on this hole.

"Baby baby," says Louis. "Everybody hit?"

Moses looks in the box. "Jesus, it is a baby. But it's White."

So everyone has to have a look, and Louis can't hit until everyone is finished looking.

"This one of yours?" asks Vernon.

"Of course not," says Louis. "It came in the mail."

"Are we going to play golf, or what?" says Del, who has decided against taking a mulligan so early in the round.

Louis hits his drive straight down the fairway. He hits the green with his second shot. And then, with everyone looking, he sinks a 35-foot putt for a birdie. By the time they finish the front nine, Louis is up seven dollars.

"Jesus," says Vernon, "damn thing must be a rabbit's foot."

"Hope you plan to feed it," says Del. "'Cause I don't want it crying on the back nine."

"You know what White babies eat?" says Moses, trying to remember a really good joke he heard last week.

"Put on a few more pounds," Vernon tells Louis, "and you'll be able to nurse it yourself."

Everybody has a good laugh, even Moses who can't remember the rest of the joke.

"Come out to bingo tonight," says Louis, holding up seven fingers just to remind everyone how well he's playing. "Maybe you'll get lucky."

But

"We're not racist," says Bob. "It's simply a matter of policy."

"So, race isn't a consideration?" asks Mr. Cardinal.

"Absolutely not," says Bob. "We're not allowed to discriminate on the basis of race, religion, or sexual orientation."

"So," says Mrs. Cardinal, "how do you discriminate?"

"Economics and education," says Bob.

"Well," says Mr. Cardinal, "we're rich."

"Great," says Bob. "We're always looking for rich parents."

"And we're well educated," says Mrs. Cardinal. "Mr. Cardinal has a master's in business administration and I have a doctorate in psychology."

"Terrific," says Bob. "I'm a college graduate, too."

"We love children," says Mrs. Cardinal. "But we also want to make a contribution."

"To society," says Mr. Cardinal. "White people have been raising our babies for years. We figure it's about time we got in there and helped them with theirs."

"Admirable," says Bob.

"Both of us speak Cree," says Mrs. Cardinal. "Mr. Cardinal sings on a drum, and I belong to the women's society on the reserve, and we know many of the old stories about living in harmony with nature, so we have a great deal we can give a White baby."

Bob chats with the Cardinals, who reassure him that they would make sure that a White baby would also have ample opportunities to participate in White culture.

"We'd sign up for cable," Mr. Cardinal tells Bob.

"Spectacular," says Bob, and he assures the Cardinals that their case is his number-one priority. "Call me in a week."

After the Cardinals have gone, Linda comes into the office with a fax and drops it on Bob's desk from shoulder level. "There's a big bingo game on the reserve this weekend."

"Fabulous," says Bob, who is running out of adjectives and who is sorry that Linda has started dropping things from shoulder level instead of bending over the way she used to when she wanted him to look at her breasts.

"One of the prizes," says Linda, "is a White baby."

So

When Louis gets to the bingo hall that night with the baby in the airmail box, there's not a single seat left. "I told you this was a good idea," he tells Orena.

"They came for the truck."

"Isn't the truck next week?"

"No," say Orena, "the truck is this week."

"So we have a truck and a White baby tonight."

"Technically," say Orena, "that's correct."

"Okay, so we double up and put the baby with the truck," say Louis, who is pleased to have come up with this without even thinking.

Orena is about to tell Louis that this is another one of his bad ideas, when she sees Bob Wakutz and his administrative assistant, Linda Blackenship, come into the bingo hall.

"Did I tell you I shot an 81 today," says Louis. "Maybe you should give The Herald a call."

"Forget golf," says Orena. "We've got a problem."

Yes

"We've got a problem," Linda tells Bob. "If you move this way a little and look to the right of the stage, you'll see a heavy-set Indian guy in a gold golf shirt standing next to an Indian woman in jeans and a white top, who is, if I'm not mistaken, related to that Indian woman from Red Deer whose baby we apprehended last month and are in the process of putting up for adoption."

Bob has never been fond of long, compound/complex sentences, but he does support the use of neutral terms such as "apprehended" and non-emotional phrases such as "in the process of putting up for adoption." However, he does not like problems.

"Claimed we had the wrong family," says Linda. "How many times have we heard that one?"

"Hey, look," says Bob. "The grand prize is a new Ford truck."

"What about the baby?" says Linda.

"We'll apprehend it right after the game for the truck," says Bob, and he puts the warrant back in his pocket, stops one of the bingo girls, and buys four cards.

While

Orena and Louis stand by the truck with the baby in the airmail box.

"Those are the two assholes from the Alberta Child Placement Agency who took my cousin's little boy," says Orena. "They must be here for the White baby."

"Problem solved," says Louis.

"You can't give them the baby," says Orena.

"Why not?" says Louis.

"Precedence," say Orena. "We can't let government agencies kidnap a member of the tribe."

"The baby's a member of our tribe?"

"That's probably why it was sent to us," says Orena.

"It doesn't look Indian," says Louis, even though he knows that not all Indian babies look Indian.

"Maybe it's part Indian," says Orena.

"Just great," says Louis. "Things were certainly easier when we were in harmony with nature."

And then

Linda turns to Bob and says, "What if I were to tell you that that baby was ours."

Bob knows that there is a right answer to this question, but he can't remember what it is.

"The White baby?"

"Yes."

"You're kidding," he says, and he's pretty sure that this is not the right answer.

"What if I were to tell you that you got me pregnant," says Linda, "and that, after I gave birth, I mailed it to the reserve in order to punish you?"

Bob puts his fingers in his nose and takes a deep breath.

"Our child?"

"What would you say?"

"Wonderful," says Bob, who hasn't run out of adjectives after all. "Look, there's the truck you can win. God, is it gorgeous!"

"Yes," said Linda. "That's exactly what I thought you would say."

And just then

The game begins. Louis hands the baby in the airmail box to Orena and goes to the microphone to drum up business.

"All right," he says. "Here's the game you've been waiting for. Blackout bingo. First prize is . . . a brand new Ford pickup and a White baby. Any questions?"

Martha Red Horse holds up her hand. "Is there a cash equivalent for the baby?"

"Good luck," says Louis, and he signals Bernie Strauss to start the game before someone else can ask a question.

Linda nudges Bob. "We better do something."

"Linda," says Bob, and he says this in a fatherly way without the hint of reprimand, "look around."

"What's that supposed to mean?" says Linda.

"We're surrounded by Indians."

And with that

Bob sits down next to Mr. and Mrs. Cardinal, who have 20 bingo cards spread out between them.

"Hello," says Mr. Cardinal. "I'll bet you came for that new Ford pickup."

"Hi," says Bob, trying to sound nonchalant. "You here for the truck, too?"

"No," says Mrs. Cardinal.

Bob taps Linda on the hip, though it's more of a pat than a tap. "Look who's here."

"Wish us luck," says Mrs. Cardinal.

And quick as you please

Bernie Strauss begins calling numbers. At first Bob doesn't get any, but then he hits a run of numbers, and before he knows it, he has only two left. Three of Mr. and Mrs. Cardinal's cards also have two numbers left and one of their cards has only one number left. And then one of Bob's numbers is called and he has only one to go.

Even Linda is getting excited.

Okay

"Okay," Louis says to Orena, as he watches the number come up on the big board, "what's the worst that can happen?"

This is a question that Louis asks all the time. This is the question that Louis asks when he hasn't a clue how bad things can get. And this time, he asks it just as a squad of RCMP comes storming into the hall.

"Oh, great," says Orena. "Now you've done it."

"B-8," Bernie shouts.

"Bingo!" shouts Bob, and he leaps out of his chair. "Bingo, bingo, bingo!"

And then

The RCMP confiscate the new Ford pickup.

"You don't have a permit," the RCMP tells Louis. "If you don't have a permit, this is an illegal gambling activity."

"It's my truck," says Bob, holding up his card. "See, I have a bingo."

"We have a permit," Louis tells the RCMP, but when he turns to find Orena to ask her to show the RCMP the permit, he finds that she is gone.

"We also heard that you were giving away a White baby," says the RCMP.

"I suppose we need a permit for that, too," says Louis.

"What about my truck?" says Bob. "What about my truck?"

Well, then

Two weeks after the raid on the bingo game, Orena's cousin calls to thank her for the White baby. "Where in the world did you get it?"

"In the mail."

"And they say we don't know how to look after our kids."

"You can keep it if you want," Orena tells her cousin.

"We've filed a suit against the Alberta Child Placement Agency," says Orena's cousin. "The idiots had me mixed up with a woman in Medicine Hat. Should have my son back by the weekend."

"So, you don't want the White baby?" says Orena.

"Come on, cuz," says Orena's cousin. "You know any skins who want a White baby?"

"It's tough," says Orena. "They just aren't that appealing."

"I suppose you can get used to them," says Orena's cousin. "What do you want me to do with it?"

"Drop it in the mail," says Orena. "I'll figure out something."

In the meantime

Bob gets out of jail, while the Crown reviews the case. "Can you believe it," he tells Linda. "They take my truck, and they arrest me."

"You hit an RCMP officer."

"I didn't hit him," says Bob. "I stumbled into him by mistake."

"Is that what you tell your wife?" says Linda, who is not ready to let bygones be bygones.

"I'm going to leave her," says Bob, who finds that he is sexually aroused by Linda's reluctance and condemnation. "You just have to be patient."

"And what about that White baby?"

"What about my truck?" says Bob. "The White baby thing was probably just a gimmick to get people to come to bingo."

Okay, so on Monday

F.Y.I.

greenies, sandies, and snakes: all names that refer to golf terms

Words to Build on

jocular: given to, characterized by, intended for, or suited to joking or jesting

mulligan: a golf term meaning a shot not counted against the score, permitted in unofficial play to a player whose previous shot was poor.

Tricks of the Trade

Character

Irony

Literature of the absurd

Satire

In Your Own Words: Comprehension

1. Who is telling the story? What type of voice is present here?

2. What do the council members decide to do with the baby in the airmail box?

3. What is the relationship between Linda and Bob?

4. Describe Mr. and Mrs. Cardinal.

5. How does the adoption agency assess potential parents in this story?

6. What is the climax of this story?

7. Who wins the bingo game and what happens to the winner?

8. What happens to the baby in the airmail box?

In Your Own Words: Analysis

1. Is there any character in this story that is free of racism or prejudice?

2. Are there any sympathetic characters?

3. What are some of the attitudes towards babies in this story? Give specific examples to support your answers.

4. Do the Cardinals provide a good reason for wanting to adopt a child? Explain.

5. The statement "White babies are very popular" is repeated in this story. Is this an accurate statement today in terms of baby adoption? Is there any proof given in the story to support this statement?

6. Some have criticized King for presenting First Nations characters as caricatures, "clowns," or "buffoons." Is this the case in "The Baby in the Airmail Box"?

7. In this story King presents two "bureaucratic systems": the Rocky Creek First Nations council and the Alberta Child Placement Agency. How is each system represented? Compare the ways the two systems handle the situation of the baby in the airmail box.

❈ Now Write

1. Thomas King has stated that his writing is influenced by an older storytelling style that is part of First Nations tradition. What makes good storytelling and what elements of oral storytelling can be found in "The Baby in the Airmail Box"?

2. If parents are to adopt a child from a different ethnic or religious group, what are the responsibilities that parents have towards the child beyond that child's basic needs?

3. Compare and contrast the narrative voice in Thomas King's "The Baby in the Airmail Box" with the voice telling the story in Austin Clarke's "A Wedding in Toronto."

4. Are a stereotype and a racist image the same thing? At what point does a stereotype become a racist image? Provide examples from "The Baby in the Airmail Box."

Stephen Marche

Stephen Marche (b. 1976) was raised in Edmonton, has lived in the United States, but currently resides in Toronto. He has written for several US and Canadian newspapers and magazines, such as *Esquire*, *The Globe and Mail*, and the *National Post*. He writes on a wide variety of topics, including politics, art, pop culture, and celebrity. He has written two critically acclaimed novels, *Raymond + Hannah: A Love Story* (2005) and *Shining at the Bottom of the Sea* (2007). His latest book is called *How Shakespeare Changed Everything* and is about Shakespeare's impact on world history. More information about Marche and his books, with samples of his articles, is available at his website, www.stephenmarche.com.

In His Own Words

"Writing matters more in small countries, and Canada is a small country."

"The possibilities for writing in Toronto right now seem boundless to me: we have barely scratched the surface of our radical multiculturalism, barely touched the potential. All we have done so far is write nineteenth-century English novels about the various ethnicities that have congregated here. The result has been the masses of pedestrian exotica that win literary prizes. But what is going to happen when we start to integrate the history of the world's styles into our writing?"

"This novel [*Lucy Hardin's Missing Period*, Marche's interactive novel] began with a simple idea, that in novels the future is predetermined, but the future in real life isn't. I wanted a way of capturing how life splits apart and how people have many possibilities inside them."

Before We Begin

1. What is science fiction? Do you read it? If so, what do you like about this genre? If not, what is you don't like about this genre?
2. Do you believe that one group of people might eventually control everyone (i.e., become our "overlords") on the planet? Who might this be?
3. Should there be limits to what science/medicine/surgeons should be allowed to experiment or perform on humans?

✳ **Now Read**

The Crow Procedure

The surgery to give Mr. Dapple the wings of a crow was scheduled to take 12 minutes. Chief Resident Riel, the youngest surgeon at the Kweskatisowin Hospital, which was the largest rural hospital in Iiyiyuushii, had already upped the anaesthesia. Dapple had ordered the most expensive unconsciousness available, a full and clean f-trip with a personalized fantasia. Professor Enoch Samaritan—arriving late from his Montreal commute—entered the operating theatre just as Riel was putting the dream in the man's head through the earworm, and tried to smile. He couldn't bring himself to apologize, though. Riel was his least favourite resident—good looking, always in full war paint and headdress, and early to every metamorphosis. His youth was tiring just to look at. "Any guesses?" Riel asked his elder, who he noticed was wearing the same jeans and feather-collared strut as the day before.

"Guesses about what?"

"The fantasia."

"You know you're not supposed to look at the contents of a patient's fantasia, Riel. It's illegal."

"He's chosen a dream where he becomes a crow," Riel said. "Can you believe it? A crow flying over a forest. Talk about a limited imagination."

Before his senior colleague even had a chance to check the cleanliness of the sight-lines, Riel began pushing the patient into the allscan, the rubbery grey tube that would sheathe the patient for the duration of the procedure. He resented a workday longer than half an hour. Nonetheless, he guided the body into the machine slowly and carefully. Dapple's flesh was soft from multiple surgeries, and his back had been pre-broadened and pre-rippled, though the nervous system at his bio-age was no doubt robonecrotic anyway. Samaritan approved of Riel's vigilance. It was the one remaining characteristic that distinguished a top surgeon.

Once the patient was inside, Riel set the tarp under the allscan. He reached for the g-drones on the side table, and handed a cup of them to Dr. Samaritan, who unceremoniously poured the container over the patient's back. The robotic goo spread over every square micron of the exposed back, dripping in oily streams down and along Mr. Dapple's thick sides.

Corvine transplant was a boring metamorphosis. The whole of the back needed to be droned, and it left the two surgeons with a few minutes of dead time, and nothing to do with their hands.

"Did I ever tell you about the day I made *kiwew*?" Riel asked. "The day I crossed the border?"

Enoch sighed. "You didn't."

"I left LA. You know that. This crazy party the night before. My friend Malinka bought all these slave boys, and we used their hair for napkins. The dragon festival was on that night, and the greens beat the reds. Every promise biomechanics ever made written in dragon letters all over the sky. My friends all wondered, and I wondered a bit, too, that night, why am I moving to Iiyiyuushii?"

"They didn't know you were Cree?"

Riel laughed at the old-fashioned word. "Out there, the whole idea that you would be tied to a place—it's absurd to them. It's like saying that you're going to marry a building, that you're going to sign your will over to a rock. I was the only one who cared that I was *nehiyawi*."

Riel leaned over to check on the g-drones. They were dripping glacially across the musculature, like streams of grey sand, tearing through the nerve lines and interstitial tissue, and then plopping like concrete jelly onto the tarp below. Everything as it should be.

"And then I arrived at the border. With all my papers. They had proof I'm *nehiyawi*. Know what they did?"

"What did they do?" Samaritan asked.

"They searched me. They took off all my clothes. They searched me with their fingers."

"Well, they have to be careful," Samaritan said. Two of his nephews worked at the border control. "They don't want any synthetic material…"

"I'm far from disapproving, Professor," Riel interrupted. "Real fingers. No scanners. They searched my body with their actual hands."

"So?"

"So I knew I had returned home. I knew that I was a human being again, with hands and fingers. A person among other people."

"I see."

"I won't even tell you about my first walk in the forest. Real trees. That was the real *kiwew*, the real return."

"Is there a reason you're telling me this, Riel?"

Riel sighed. "Now I'm metamorphosing a man into a crow. Every morning, I wake up and wreck nature. Yesterday it was a peregrine. Tomorrow a dove."

"Tomorrow's a sea eagle."

"I mean, why don't we wake up tomorrow morning and go and cut down some trees? Why don't we go massacre some aspens? Like we were living 200 years ago. Let's go hack down some trees and make toilet paper and wipe our asses with it."

The g-drones interrupted Riel with the soft and high bleating of their conclusion. The patient's back was clear. Under the scanner, the tarp had collected all 285 million nanobots, leaving the patient prepped for the incisions and transplant.

Professor Samaritan leaned over and sliced the back in two exactly parallel lines each exactly 50 centimetres long. (The automatic surgeon ensured the precision of the measurements while giving the human moderator some illusion of control.)

Then it was time for the wings. The prefabricated black pair of crow's wings lowered down automatically from the overcooler. They were huge, two metres long each. Samaritan placed them precisely into the incisions. Riel lifted the tarp and poured the leftover g-drones over the patient's back again, and refixed the tarp under the scanner. Again, more waiting, the silence disturbed only by the microscopic rustling of the millipede healers busy attaching the biologies of crow and human.

Samaritan didn't like to engage too closely with the residents at the hospital—some of the other surgeons went so far as to join bonds with their wards—because engagement was so much work and he already had enough work. But if he didn't say anything to Riel now, he realized, he was going to have these conversations until his retirement four years from now.

"Can I ask you, Riel, how long you've been here?" he asked.

"Six years nearly."

Samaritan hated confrontation. "You know you're my blood, one way or the other, but I don't want to hear about you not liking the surgeries anymore."

"Metamorphoses don't fit our ways. They're the opposite of our ways."

"Riel, you know what Iiyiyuushii used to be called?"

"Quebec."

"And before then?"

"Canada."

"And you know how we got it back?"

"Louis Riel Samson's leadership and the bounty of nature."

Samaritan laughed nastily, startling his colleague. The Senior Professor was usually so unflappably mild. He had five daughters at home. "Is that how they put it on your *nehiyawi* identity exam? 'The bounty of nature?' We bought it back and we lawed it back. Louis Samson took French credits from the aft-zone and bought every scrap back, so let's not pretend—"

"I'm not—"

"Listen. I'm not blaming you. I'm saying that you shouldn't blame yourself for turning people into tigers, and don't blame me for turning this outsider into a crow. We're good at it and it's how we pay for the overlamp fields and the woods." The g-drones bleated again, the wings attached. "Go for a walk. Think about it. I'll finish."

"Professor Samaritan," Riel began apologetically.

"Go for a walk. I can teach this stupid bastard how to fly."

Samaritan turned back to check the readings on the allscan. Riel wasn't in a position to refuse, even if he wanted to. He was only a resident, now a sheepishly relieved resident happy to be excused for the day. He hadn't expected the rebuke, but he was ashamed and grateful for it in equal measure, like the time he had been expelled from introductory rhetoric in middle school.

The red exit button flashed in the shadowy half-zone of the antechamber, and the hot, acidic breath passed over his body, removing the skin-against-skin. Then the half-zone curved behind him and he was on the plains, barefoot, in buckskin. It was mid-August. The sky swirled thick and dark, rife with the possibility of rain. The long grass underfoot spread without interruption into the distance, except for a stand of aspens on the horizon. Riel waded toward them, never looking back, the hospital and its business instantly forgotten.

The allscan bleated again. The autosurgeon popped and gurgled out the sound of congratulations. The corvine graft had been successful. All that remained was waiting for the f-trip to wear off. Dr. Samaritan could break the patient's fantasia without risk, but he found that interruption often delayed comfort with the new appendages. Better to let Mr. Dapple land in his mind first. It's easier to wake up with wings after gliding to ground in a dream.

Samaritan half-curiously inspected the sleeping body as it emerged from the scanner. The man's face was scarred in a pattern popular a decade earlier—"the tiger claw"— four rough stripes across each cheek. Dapple had chosen to maintain the oozing effect. Tight was now the style. To Samaritan's surprise, Dapple's torso presented only a single tattoo, a cross over his heart in the Coptic style. The full matching scarification ran down both legs, rough and ragged, nearly down to the bone. And he was a eunuch, his groin a smooth flap that buttoned behind him. He must have had that done in Rome. The Romans were the best at castration. They were the only surgeons whose eunuchs never smelled like urine. Nonetheless, the flesh of the abdomen had softened. No one had figured out a way to prevent that side effect.

The f-trip ended gently. Dapple's blue-within-blue eyes opened abruptly. "Am I awake?" he asked.

"You are a crow," Samaritan replied.

"Has it taken?"

"It's taken."

"Wondrous."

Dapple tried to sit up, but unaccustomed to the weight of his enormous wings his legs shot in the air. He looked like an overturned beetle. "You'll learn," Samaritan said. "You'll learn. It's best to start on the edges. The force comes from the scapulars, but try moving those great primary coverts first."

The huge tips of the crow wings fluttered minutely.

"Good. A bit more?"

The spasms of the huge wings pressed Dapple back onto the operating table. Samaritan lifted him into a sitting position. With a sudden snap, like the shutting of an enormous fan, Dapple closed his wings behind his back. "Perfectly wondrous," he said.

"I'll bring you a mirror."

The autosurgeon lowered a mirror from the ceiling. The half-man, half-crow paused before his reflection, black wings framing his elegant scars, his smooth torso, his glowing azure eyes. He snapped his wings open and snapped them shut. A smile cut his face horizontally, and his left eye flicked up and to the right. It meant the final transfer of payment.

"Perfection," Dapple said. "It's like your motto said. Just like. 'Why should reality deny you the truth?' Spent the final dribidrabs of my aunt's second pension on this knify, but how worth it."

"Tear down your house and build a boat," Samaritan added.

"Perfection. May I ask you something?"

"Sure."

"Why are your people so good at these surgeries?"

Professor Samaritan told the standard and humiliating lie that kept the hospital running. "We here in Iiyiyuushii live naturally. We understand the crow. A few of us can speak with the crow."

"And is it true that you don't scar, don't even tattoo?"

"It's against the law here."

Curiosity drifted across the narcotic, transfixing blue-within-blue of Dapple's eyes. "Can I pay to see you naked?" Dapple whispered.

"No, but I am going to teach you how to fly."

Samaritan placed his hand gently on the oversized black wing and guided Dapple out the door of the operating theatre. The antechamber shadow zone brushed away the skin-against-skin with the familiar acidic scent that always relaxed the surgeon, the warm odour of a day's work ending. The sky was grey and the wind was up. Dapple shaded his gaze, even though the sun was hidden. His eyes must have been expensive.

It was the perfect day for learning how to fly, if it didn't rain. The key was hopping and flapping in rhythm for the takeoff, and then gliding into the landing. The takeoff usually required an hour to learn. The landing took three or four tumbles.

Riel was sitting on a mossy stone among the aspens, practising tranquility. An elder had taught him. By deepening his breath, he could lower his heartbeat, and by lowering his heartbeat he was able to blend into the forest. A beaver had once walked up to him and sat in his lap. A cardinal had once perched on his shoulder.

Today—a herd of wild horses. They began as a faint vibration, a growing rumble in the distance like a night terror from beyond the trees, and then, rushing past him, furious, gorgeous, as if the sky were driving them wild, as if their turgid muscle foam were a reflection of the sky. Then gone, gone, leaving peace in their wake. It could have been 50,000 years ago or 50,000 years from now.

Into their silence, behind him, the sound of giant wings, but Riel didn't turn his face to look at the Dapple crow rising through the evening sky.

F.Y.I.

Cree: a member of the North American First Nations peoples, living from the east coast to the Rocky Mountains, and forming the largest Aboriginal group in Canada. Cree also refers to the linguistic family of this people. The Cree language, which belongs to the Algonquian linguistic family group, consists of Mi'kmaq, Naskapi, Montagnais, Algonquian, Chippewa, and Ojibway; the language also spreads south of the Canadian border. The term "Cree" originates from the short form of a variation of the Ojibway word *kistanowak* (people of the north) and the Canadian French word *Cris* (earlier *Cristianaux*) from Algonquian. This led to the Nehiyawak being called the *kris* (Crees). The proper term in the Plains Cree language is *nehiyawak*. Marche's characters Samaritan and Riel use the word "Cree" and the earlier pre-conquest term *nehiyawi* in "The Crow Procedure."

Riel: Louis Riel (1844–1885), Canadian politician and leader of the Metis, through whose work the Manitoba Act was passed, which established the province. Riel was subsequently executed by the government for his part in the Red River incident (1869–1870). Riel is regarded as a folk hero for his defence of Metis rights and culture. For more on Riel, go to www.gov.mb.ca/february_holiday/biography.html.

Words to Build on

biomechanics: the study of the mechanical laws relating to the movement or structure of living organisms

bleating: a weak or wavering cry or sound

buckskin: clothes or shoes made from the skin of a male deer

corvine: of or like a raven or crow

coverts: a feather covering the base of a main flight or tail feather of a bird

eunuch: a man that has been castrated

glacially: describing an action that is done extremely slowly

graft: a piece of living tissue that is transplanted surgically

interstitial tissue: tissue that lies in spaces between nerves, muscles, and so on

metamorphosis: the process of transformation from an immature form to an adult form in two or more distinct phases

musculature: the system or arrangement of muscles in a body, part of a body, or an organ

nanobots: a hypothetical, extremely small, self-propelled machine with the ability to reproduce and act autonomously

peregrine: a powerful falcon used for falconry

prepped: to have been prepared for an event

rebuke: an expression of sharp disapproval or criticism

rife: full of

scapulars: relating to the shoulder or shoulder blades, but can also be a type of feather

sheathe: to encase in a close-fitting or protective cover

turgid: swollen and distended

unceremoniously: describing an action that is done roughly or abruptly

unflappably: describing a state that cannot be agitated or provoked

Tricks of the Trade

Conflict

Imagery

Literary allusion/Historical allusion

Setting

In Your Own Words: Comprehension

1. What is the setting for this story?
2. Who are the main characters in the story?

3. List the words Marche has invented for this story. Can you guess at what some may mean?

4. What procedures has Mr. Dapple had done to himself?

5. What other human–animal hybrids have the surgeons created?

6. Who performs these "metamorphosis" procedures and why?

7. Why does Chief Resident Riel not like performing these procedures?

8. Explain what Dr. Enoch Samaritan means when he states, "is that how they put it on your *nehiyawi* identity exam? 'The bounty of nature?' We bought it back and we lawed it back. Louis Samson took French credits from the aft-zone and bought every scrap back, so let's not pretend . . . "?

9. Where does Chief Resident Riel go to after Dr. Enoch Samaritan excuses him from Mr. Dapple's surgery?

In Your Own Words: Analysis

1. What is the significance of Chief Resident Riel and Dr. Enoch Samaritan's names?

2. Why does Mr. Dapple want to become a crow?

3. Would you have such a procedure done? Why or why not?

4. Does this story make the future sound like a utopia or dystopia? Explain.

5. Where does the climax occur in the story?

6. Why does Marche choose a crow as the metamorphosis procedure performed in the story? Is this particular animal symbolic or significant?

7. How do the two surgeons feel about these procedures? Whom do you agree with?

8. What has happened to Canada in this story? Is this in the realm of possibility?

9. Define the word "authenticity." Is there anything "authentic" in the realm portrayed in this story?

10. What type of animals do people request to become in this story? Why do you think they want to become these animals?

❄ Now Write

1. Research aspects or common features of the science fiction genre. Write an essay in which you explain how Marche's story fits or veers away from these features or characteristics.

2. Look up the definitions for "utopia" and "dystopia." In an essay, argue whether Marche's version of the future is utopian or dystopian in nature.

3. In "The Crow Procedure," the motto of the Kweskatisowin Hospital is "Why should reality deny you the truth?" Write an essay using references from the story that illustrates the multiple meanings and complexities of this statement.

Appendix

Sample Student Essays

The following are excerpts from essays written by students. Sample Essay #1 focuses on responding to a work of fiction and is an analysis of Margaret Laurence's short story "The Loons." Sample Essay #2 focuses on responding to a work of non-fiction and offers a critique of Lawrence Solomon's essay "Homeless in Paradise."

When we teach essay writing, we focus on four principles that are outlined in our LOCS system: Language, Organization, Content, and Style (see the Prologue for more detailed information on LOCS). When students can control all of these areas, not only will their essays succeed in meeting the professor's criteria and the assignment outcomes, but the essays will be sound and effective arguments in their own right.

Read these two essays, paying special attention to the comment boxes which highlight, outline, and explain the strengths and the areas that need improvement for each piece of writing. NOTE: The essays are meant to be short samples that highlight key areas students should focus on, such as the introduction, thesis statement, and body paragraph structure; they are not complete essays.

SAMPLE ESSAY #1

Original Topic/Question: Compare the characters of Piquette and Vanessa to show how Vanessa's character reveals the extent to which Piquette is trapped in her tragic circumstances.

Introduction

Use of second-person personal pronoun

Informal expression

Weak connection between opening 'hook' and lead-in to essay topic

Most times when you see someone reaching out to someone else, you think

about how nice that person is. You feel that if you were the one in need and

someone reached out to you, you would be so grateful. Well, sometimes

the one on the receiving side is not always willing to accept help. In the

Vague pronoun usage—who is 'we' referring to here?

Style/redundancy

story "The Loons, written by Margaret Laurence, we see that this is the

case. A young girl named Piquette is taken to her doctor's cottage for the

Style: wordy

Invention of words/illness

Analysis: Misinterpretation of character's motivation

Announcement: reference to essay is redundant; weak link to thesis

summer to rest her tubercular leg. Piquette intrigues Vanessa but cannot

understand why Piquette is so rude and obnoxious to her. Throughout this

essay it will be shown how Vanessa's and Piquette's lives and characters are

Punctuation: apostrophe misuse

Redundant and vague: what is the "piece of information"?

quite different. Using the story and a secondary piece of information it will

Missing word

shown that comparing Vanessa's hard times made Piquette's life seem that

Analysis: illogical statement

much more depressing. The tree main topics that will be discussed in this

Redundant/ announcement

Spelling

essay are, the difference between their duties in the household, the positive

Vague

Punctuation: comma misuse

or negative attention they are receiving at home, and the way in which

important role models in each of their lives have died.

Verb tense error

Body Paragraph

Punctuation: apostrophe misuse

Thesis needs rewriting: has no focus and lacks parallelism; the third point is too weak to construct a third body paragraph

Opening sentence is a fragment

It is brought to the readers attention very early on in the story "The Loons"

Style: wordy

Misspelling of main character's name

when Venessa's grandmother expresses her feelings at the thought of the

young Matis accompanying them to their cottage in Diamond Lake. "If that

Misspelling of main character's ethnicity

half-breed youngster (Piquette) comes along—I'm not going" elaborates on

Dropped quote

the stereotypes that have revolved around the Metis peoples in the eyes of

Generalization and weak logic

Capitalization

the english society obviously for quite some time, as the older generation

Misspelling of main character's name

(Venessa's grandmother) harbours these views towards the young Matis.

Misspelling of main character's ethnicity

Even before Piquette was born these negative preconceived notions about

Vague: what does this mean? Which society are you referring to here?

her people were prevalent, she was in essence born into a society that she

could not belong to. She was "doomed to disaster no matter what she does"

Piquette is trapped to live her life around the predisposed notions of those

around her. *Generalization: statement without proof or adequate support; repetition of "around" reinforces generalizations.; confusing*

Conclusion

The society, in which Piquette lived, greatly influenced her life, to a point where she had no choice but to face a tragic end. Piquette tried everything she could to change this, but the influence of an entire town was far too big for her.

CONCLUSION is underdeveloped; it contains imprecise wording and makes no reference to major points. No planning and no final thought. Conclusion is trite and incomplete

SAMPLE ESSAY #2

Original Topic/Question: Analyze and comment on the effectiveness of Lawrence Solomon's plans and solutions for addressing and solving the problem of homelessness.

Introduction

On September 2, 2006, an article appeared in The Globe and Mail with the headline, "Time to try a home remedy for the homeless." In the article, Gary Mason states that Vancouver, with a crisis similar to the one in Toronto, is going through a "raging debate" about the homeless crisis. Mason mentions that New York is starting to offer supportive housing to the homeless and, in our country, British Columbia has realized that "taxpayers saved about $12,000 a year for every homeless person moved into supportive housing." In "Homeless in Paradise" Lawrence Solomon states Canadians should "require housing for those unable to properly look after themselves." While no one would disagree with this statement, the "solutions" he gives in support of a plan to combat homelessness are inadequate when compared with the reality of this serious urban issue. Solomon's plan to reduce homelessness is not feasible due to unrealistic

Essay begins with an interesting and relevant quote on the topic of homelessness. This sets the tone for the reader.

Reading that is being discussed is mentioned in the introduction along with a relevant quote

housing arrangements, a voucher program that lacks immediate incentives and housing deregulation that would lead to more problems than solutions.

Body 1

Introduction logically and smoothly leads to the thesis statement. Strong three-part or "blueprint" thesis that outlines the three body paragraphs

The topic or opening sentence prepares the reader for the paragraph's content

First of all, a housing arrangement where a homeless person resides with friends or family would not be beneficial to either party. The cost of keeping a poor person living with a family would outweigh the benefits in many situations. Solomon himself states that "welfare recipients who doubled up with family members faced benefit reductions" and so the poor would be receiving fewer benefits from the government because they are partly supported by the family, and thus not in as much need of the kind of government support as if they were living on their own. The government can offer retraining and/or counselling programs, as they do for unemployment benefit earners, to help those who are in need, something family and friends cannot offer. Further, family and friends have trouble setting limits and timelines regarding how money can be spent and gauging whether the person staying with them is working towards becoming somewhat independent. In addition, the family would have to

Paragraph includes logical supporting examples

take on a large burden to support an additional person whose support may be a challenge because, unlike most middle-class citizens, citizens living in poverty often lack "work skills and social skills" that would allow them to enter into the workforce and eventually become capable of supporting themselves. Housing support from friends or family may often prove too

Good use of transition words that help link ideas and statements

costly for both parties while housing vouchers may not make homeless individuals attractive potential tenants. Furthermore, the deregulation of the housing market is impractical and can lead to unsafe living conditions.

Body 2

Secondly, the other option Solomon puts forward, the use of a voucher program, does not go far enough in terms of clearly discussing both the short-term and long-term benefits of this program and who would benefit. Housing vouchers are coupons given to the landlord by a homeless individual in exchange for a room; this voucher can later be redeemed for money from the government as opposed to a regular rent payment. This concept raises the question of how such a voucher can be beneficial to a landlord. Why should a landlord give occupancy to a risky tenant who is uncertain about paying rent and could even be potentially destructive to property, when he/she can have a "risk-free" tenant? The voucher system as described here seems to ensure payment to the landlord and not the security and independence of the renter. Further, it would be a real challenge for a government to develop a system of checks-and-balances in place to ensure that there is not a rise in "fake" vouchers or to protect from the misuse of vouchers, such as their being purchased illegally and used by those who do not need of this type of assistance.

The beginning of the second body paragraph refers to the thesis statement's second main point

Writer provides valid supporting examples to support claim made in topic sentence

The Writer's Toolbox
Tricks of the Trade

American realism: **Kate Chopin**'s story is one of the earliest examples of this genre. Broadly defined as an accurate representation of reality, it is also a technique that rejects nostalgia and idealization. Characteristics of the genre include the setting in the here-and-now, characters grappling with ethical problems and everyday experiences, and the reality of social class.

Argumentative essay: an argumentative essay's purpose is to show that the author's position on a subject is stronger or more truthful than another position. To write an argumentative essay well, the author must formulate reasons, create connections, draw conclusions, and then apply them to the topic being discussed.

Atmosphere: this term relates to the emotions triggered in not only the characters but the readers as well. The atmosphere or mood in a story is created by setting, dialogue, and description. In **Angela Carter's** "The Company of Wolves," the setting of the medieval wood and village is infused with feelings of dread, unease, gloom, terror, and danger. **Gabriel Garcia Marquez's** "The Handsomest Drowned Man in the World" shows how a skilful writer can evoke a strong sense of atmosphere for the reader without needing to give names to places and characters.

Autobiography versus memoir: the word "autobiography" comes from the Greek words αυτός (*autos,* self), βίος (*bios,* life), and γράφειν (*graphein,* to write). Memoir is a French word, but originally comes from the Latin word for memory, *memoria.* Although both involve the retelling of one's own life (i.e., memoir is essentially autobiographical writing), an autobiography may span the writer's entire life, while memoir is focused on remembering or illuminating in greater detail and perhaps more intimately a particular period of the writer's life. The French writer Marcel Proust's *Remembrance of Things Past* is a good example of a memoir, since it maps out the stages of his life and is highly detailed and intimate.

Caricature: although a French word, it comes from the Italian *caricatura,* which in turn comes from the Italian word *caricare* meaning "to overload or exaggerate." A caricature is a literary or visual representation of a subject in which the author or artist has taken a distinctive feature or idiosyncrasy and distorted or exaggerated it to produce either a comic or grotesque effect. A literary caricature is done by exaggerating certain characteristics or traits of a person or place while oversimplifying others. The literary caricature is also used to ridicule and criticize the positions, platforms, and actions of governments, institutions, organizations, and movements. Writers such as Aristophanes, **Jonathan Swift**, Charles Dickens, and **Flannery O'Connor** have all used caricature in their works.

Catharsis: refers to an emotional purging or release an audience experiences when watching a drama or tragedy; its origin is in the Greek theatre tradition. For the Greeks, tragedy was not seen as "depressing." Aristotle claimed that there is a purpose to the tragic elements in a story since they are meant to produce a feeling of release in the same way that comedy provides relief through laughter. The reader experiences catharsis when reading the story of a hero or protagonist who experiences the same emotional release.

Character: a person in a story or drama created out of the writer's imagination. The writer bases this person on some recognizable type of person. In order to flesh out a character, a writer uses both direct methods (description of qualities) and indirect methods (actions, speech, appearance) to create multidimensional personages or characters. These methods allow the reader to participate in the active visualization or creation of a character. In literary criticism there is a distinction between "flat" (predictable and unchanging) characters versus "round" (changing, dynamic, complex) characters. In some fiction, even non-human and inanimate objects/structures become characters when the writer infuses them with human-like qualities. The main character in a story or novel is called a protagonist, which comes from the Greek word πρωταγωνιστής, literally "first in the fight." The origin of the word, however, comes from ancient Greek theatre and means one who "plays the first part" or is the "chief actor."

Climax: a moment of great intensity or the point in the story when the audience is able to discern the outcome of the conflict. The climax happens at the point of maximum interest or turning point, when the reader senses the highest tension in the plot of a story, play, or film. The climax signals the beginning of the end of a story. The conflict is resolved at the climax, and the outcome of the plot becomes clear.

Closing technique: a good conclusion is important in essay writing since this is the writer's final thought on the topic or subject and encompasses the last thing the reader will read. It is a good idea to put thought into how to conclude a paper. Most readers expect to see the thesis or main idea restated in some form in the conclusion. Here are some techniques a student can use to end his or her essay: (1) conclude with a thought-provoking statement, question, quotation, or fact; (2) remind the reader of the significance of your topic and how it relates to the reader's life or the life of society in general; (3) summarize your key point, albeit in different words so as not to bore the reader; (4) come full-circle and remind the reader of an idea or statement from the essay's introduction. Do

not, under any circumstances, begin your conclusion with the words "in conclusion," since this is redundant and insulting to the reader.

Conflict: conflict is crucial to most forms of fiction since its presence contributes to the formation of complex and interesting characters; conflict also helps the writer create plausible plots and moves the action of a story forward. There are typically four types of conflict: (1) human versus human, (2) human versus nature, (3) human versus him or herself, and (4) human versus society. The opposition of forces within a character or the struggles between characters or between characters and other elements (both natural or supernatural) create conflict. Often more than one type of conflict can be taking place in a story.

Dialect: this word comes from the Greek *dialektos,* meaning "ordinary talk or conversation," and refers to the language of a specific place, class, or people, including the spelling, grammar, diction, and sounds that distinguish it from other regions or districts. Writers often use this characterization technique to help illustrate the differences between characters in regards to education, social, regional, or class status. It can even be used to help with setting, mood, tone, and authenticity. Writers such as William Shakespeare, John Steinbeck, George Eliot, Mark Twain, D.H. Lawrence, and **Flannery O'Connor** have used various dialects in their works.

Eroticism/Erotic literature: can be broadly defined as literature where sex and sexuality has a dominant presence. However, unlike pornography and other erotica, eroticism as a literary feature is not meant to sexually arouse the reader.

Essay: a piece of writing in prose that explores a subject/idea or proposes an argument. The word "essay" is derived from the French term *essai,* meaning a "try" or "attempt" at expressing an opinion. The word was coined by the French writer Michel de Montaigne in the title of his *Essais* (1580), the first modern example of the form.

Francis Bacon's *Essays* (1597) began the tradition of essay writing in English.

Foil: a character who serves as a contrast to another perhaps more primary character, so as to point out specific traits of the primary character and make this central character stand out.

Foreshadowing: a technique a writer uses to give hints about things to come in later plot developments. These hints can be very general and clear to the reader, or they can be more obscure and involve the use of symbols that are later connected to plot turns.

Grotesque: although the word is often used in everyday conversation to mean ugly, disgusting, or disturbing, in literature the term "grotesque" refers to a character, place, or situation that invokes not only a feeling of uncomfortable distaste but of pity or empathy as well. Stock characteristics or traits of the grotesque are physical deformities or mental deficiencies, for example, the Monster in Mary Shelley's *Frankenstein* or the Phantom in Gaston Leroux's *The Phantom of the Opera*. Both are horribly disfigured, mentally disturbed, and murderous sociopaths, but readers do not consider them outright monsters; in fact, readers hope that they will be able to overcome their darker natures and redeem themselves. The grotesque can also come in the form of repugnant personal qualities such as extreme arrogance, self-righteousness, egotism, or even racial/religious intolerance. These are the characteristics that define the grotesque that is identified with Southern Gothic. The Misfit in **Flannery O'Connor's** "A Good Man Is Hard to Find" is an example of a grotesque character. Writers such as William Shakespeare, Victor Hugo, Tobias Smollett, Edgar Allen Poe, Franz Kafka, William Burroughs, and Hunter Thompson have incorporated the grotesque in their works.

Historical allusion: an allusion is a reference to another work of literature, a film, or a real event. The writer uses this to draw attention to a situation and give meaning to the situation or event

being written about. In the excerpt from *In the Skin of a Lion,* **Michael Ondaatje** recreates the building of the Bloor Street Viaduct, including the historical figures who played a part in the history of the bridge. The title *In the Skin of a Lion* alludes to *The Epic of Gilgamesh* when the hero states "And after you he will let his body bear a filthy mat of hair, will don the skin of a lion and roam the wilderness" (Table VII).

Imagery: a visual description using language that appeals to the senses (sight, taste, sound, touch, hearing) and creates a sensory experience. This helps the reader form a picture of people, places, objects, and even moments described in a story. This is such an important technique in fiction that when writers create clichéd or unintentionally absurd descriptions of character and place, the quality of the story suffers. **Kate Chopin's** "The Story of an Hour" uses imagery to reflect or reinforce the protagonist's state of mind: the narrator speaks in terms of natural and material things that convey a sense of openness or freedom. **Michael Ondaatje** is so poetic in his use of imagery that many of his stories are seen by directors as being highly filmable.

Introductory essay techniques: The way a writer begins an essay is just as important as an essay's conclusion. After all, the introduction gives the reader a "first impression" of the writer's ideas. Here are some techniques to consider when writing an introduction for an essay: (1) start with an attention-grabbing fact or statistic that will prepare the reader for the evidence that will appear in the body of the essay; (2) write an interesting anecdote or "little story" that relates to the thesis or topic of the essay; (3) begin with a thought-provoking question; (4) start with a commonly held opinion and proceed to challenge it in your introduction. Finally, a good tip to keep in mind when writing introductions is to not write your introduction until the body of the essay is complete. A good introduction may come to mind naturally; if not, don't force it. Concentrate on writing the body paragraphs and even the conclusion. Once that work is done, return to writing an introduction that will adequately prepare the reader for the contents of the essay.

Irony: from the Greek word *eironia*, which dates to 423 BCE. The term, which is now a major narrative mode, first appeared in drama, philosophy, and political oratory. Because context is everything, the reader must "read between the lines" in a story to discover the irony that is formed through a hidden meaning or message. There are three types of irony: (1) verbal irony is when someone says one thing, means the opposite, and everyone knows he means the opposite; (2) situational irony is when the opposite of what is expected to happen happens, and it still makes sense; (3) dramatic irony is when the audience knows something a character doesn't. Irony is often used by writers and poets to create humour or to point out some less obvious truth, which is why irony is often subtle and indirect. Irony is not the same as sarcasm, since when a person is being sarcastic he or she is direct, blunt, and malicious.

Literary allusion/Historical allusion: an allusion is a reference to another work of literature, a film, or a historic person or event. Allusions are often indirect or brief references to well-known characters or events; these can be used to summarize broad and complex ideas by using one all-encompassing or powerful image The writer uses this to draw attention to and meaning out of the situation or event being written about.

Literature of the absurd: a term coined by Martin Esslin in 1961 that was used to describe the work of writers such as Albert Camus, Samuel Beckett, Joseph Heller, Harold Pinter, and Edward Albee. These works depict the absurd aspects of the human experience. Often these stories and plays lack traditional plots and present isolated characters who are engaged in circular, purposeless conversations.

Magic realism: a German phrase originally used to describe the works of German painters in the

1920s. In time, this label came to be used for prose that featured a mix of realism with fantastic and dream-like elements. Magic realists also often incorporate myth and fairy tales into their writing. It is distinct from "fantasy literature," which forsakes reality. The term has often been applied to the works of Central American writers such as **Jorge Luis Borges, Gabriel Garcia Marquez,** and Isabel Allende. Magic realism can also be found in the works of novelists such as Italo Calvino, Salman Rushdie, and Banana Yoshimoto. The 2001 film *Amelie* presents many elements of magic realism: talking lamps and paintings and a protagonist who literally "melts" when her love interest leaves the café where she works without asking her for a date.

Metaphor: a comparison between two unlike things that is not announced by "like" or "as". In a metaphor, a word or phrase that applies to one thing or idea is linked to another seemingly dissimilar thing or idea without making this comparison explicit or overtly obvious. For instance, if one says "his room is a disaster area," the metaphoric word "disaster" is applied to the literal word "room." The technique is used by writers to help the reader move from what is easily visualized and familiar to the non-familiar or abstract.

Modernism: a general term used for many literary styles and trends of the early twentieth century that often involved a rejection of nineteenth-century styles and techniques. Writers and poets whose works reflect modernist traits are James Joyce, Virginia Woolf, Franz Kafka, T.S. Eliot, and **Jorge Luis Borges.** These works are often characterized by themes of cultural and urban alienation and dislocation, the use of multiple points of view, and disjointed narrative trajectories.

Motif: a theme or idea that is repeated or woven through a story. Motifs are often so powerful and recognizable that they reappear in many writers' works. Some popular motifs are the age as seasons motif (spring time for youth), the saviour motif, and the innocence to experience motif.

Narrative point of view/Narrative voice: another term for the persona telling the story. The narrative voice sets the tone and can change the meaning of what is being said. The author's persona of a fictional narrative can help or hinder the success of the story. There are three types of narrative voice or points of view: (1) first-person recounts events from the "I" perspective and is immediate and direct; (2) third-person recounts the events from the "he," "she," and "they" perspective and is broader and considered to be a more objective perspective on characters and events; (3) second-person recounts events from the "you" perspective and is rarely used. It is important to remember that even with a third-person, nameless, omniscient narrator, the voice is a persona and not the author. The persona that the author creates depends on the type of story the author is trying to tell and the type of atmosphere that best compliments the story.

Narrative structure: consists of content and form. These two parts of narrative structure can best be described as story and plot. To analyze narrative structure, the reader can use "who," "what," and "where" questions to examine the story or content of a narrative fiction. "How" and "when" questions are used to study plot structure.

Naturalism: a school of writing related to realism, since naturalism also uses details to help the reader see the forces involved in shaping a character, such as his or her environment, social status, and heredity. The naturalistic writing style seeks to be a mirror of everyday reality and was a reaction against romanticism and surrealism, which tend to treat subjects idealistically or fantastically. Naturalism has general characteristics and themes: pessimism, detachment (use of non-emotional language and nameless characters), determinism, and the twist ending. Determinism refers to the notion that a character has no free will since outcomes are controlled by other forces. The twist ending is an unexpected turn of events that causes the reader to re-examine or re-evaluate previous notions about the story and characters.

Originally, the twist ending that was used by naturalist writers such as **Guy de Maupassant** was quite subtle.

Oral storytelling/Orature: the tradition within many global cultures that transmits stories orally or through telling by word-of-mouth from one generation to the next. Examples of narratives that began in the oral tradition are songs, ballads, long poems, fables, folktales, and fairytales. The tradition has certain features in common that include repetition, numerology, trickster figures, and common repeated themes.

Persuasive essay: a persuasive essay's purpose is not just to explain something or show the validity of the writer's opinion. An effective persuasive essay includes specific rhetorical techniques that convince the reader (if he or she disagrees with the writer's main idea) to "switch sides" and agree with the writer's thesis or opinion on a given topic. This type of essay may even involve rousing the reader to take some sort of action in relation to an issue or cause.

Rhetorical strategies (methods of persuasion/ types of appeal): there are numerous rhetorical devices in speaking and writing that date back thousands of years. However, some of the most common ones in writing that are used by the essay writers in this text or ones that you may use are as follows: (1) **allusion** refers to people, places, events, or excerpts from literary works with the assumption that the reader will already know or have heard about them; (2) **anecdote** is from the Greek word for "little story," as it is a brief and entertaining retelling of a personal or biographical event or situation; (3) **appeal to authority** is the use of information from experts or professionals in a given field of study to help strengthen an argument; (4) **appeal to emotion** involves using information that is likely to connect to the reader's fears, hopes, dreams, prejudices, and biases to strengthen the writer's position or argument; (5) **contrast** is when the writer draws attention to striking differences between subjects or concepts to demonstrate a particular point or position; (6) **logical reasoning** is when a writer uses sound or correct reasoning to form an argument, which can be done by putting forth an outcome or expected result based on what has gone on or happened before; (7) **parallelism** is the use of the same grammatical structure in a series or list, which is especially helpful in a thesis statement; (8) **repetition** is when a writer repeats words or phrases throughout an essay to emphasize a point; (9) a **rhetorical question** is when a writer posits an effective question on a topic to get the reader's attention or get him or her thinking about a topic without expecting a response.

Realism: broadly defined as an accurate representation of reality, it is also a technique that reflects a particular kind of subject matter. The style is a reaction against romanticism and the influence of rational philosophy and scientific method. **Margaret Laurence** valued this in other forms of literature as she praised Somali literature for its realism, "a realism that recognizes the presence of both good and evil in the world and in the individual" (Patricia A. Morely, *Margaret Laurence*, p. 50). **Leo Tolstoy** is known as one of the masters of nineteenth-century realism, or more specifically "poetic realism," which is fluid but also a style that relays events and describes characters without idealization and any romantic flourish. Elements of realism that are reflected in Tolstoy's work include characters who are ordinary and drawn from everyday life as well as a focus on characters who suffer and whose efforts to relieve those earthly pressures are ineffective or futile.

Revisionist literature: a term that is used not just for rewriting stories, but rather for a "reimagining" or "reinventing" so the reader sees the work in a new way. This technique alters the stories themselves, thereby altering the way readers read them. For instance, a writer can take an innocent heroine from a traditional story and re-envision the same heroine as someone who evolves into a stronger, experienced, and capable woman. **Angela Carter** does this in her short story

collection *The Bloody Chamber*, but for another strong example, see Emma Donoghue's *Kissing the Witch*.

Satire: a style of writing that showcases human weaknesses so as to ridicule them and show their absurdity. Two common vehicles for delivering satire are irony and burlesque (parody or lampoon). This scorn or mockery exhibited towards the focus or "butt" of satire is done to bring attention to a situation for the purpose of creating dialogue that leads to improvements or change. Satire is also found in film and television as well as the visual arts and political cartoons.

Setting: the time, place, physical details, and circumstances in which a situation or story takes place. Setting includes the background, atmosphere, and environment in which characters live. Setting can help the reader gain a better understanding of the characters and their actions. For many writers, the geography that was part of their youth helped shape their fictional creations: Charlotte Bronte, Thomas Hardy, D.H. Lawrence, and **Margaret Laurence** have been called "regional novelists." Margaret Laurence's works feature Canadian women in rural settings; she has used the same town as a setting in her novels and stories so much so that critics refer to these collected works as "the Manawaka Cycle." Of using this town as a setting she has said, "The name Manawaka is an invented one. Manawaka is not my hometown of Neepawa—it has elements of Neepawa, especially in some of the descriptions of places, such as the cemetery on the hill or the Wachakwa valley through which ran the small brown river of my childhood. In almost every way, however, Manawaka is not so much any one prairie town as an amalgam of many prairie towns. Most of all, I like to think, it is simply itself, a town of the mind, my own private world… which one hopes will ultimately relate to the other world which we all share" ("A Place to Stand On"). **Katherine Alexander's** "A Bit of Magic" is set during the Great Depression (1929–1939) when Canada's unemployment rate was at 30 per cent;

small businesses went bankrupt and there was a widespread shortage of work. Families were poverty-stricken and the level of economic, social, and psychological instability experienced by most Canadians went beyond what could be measured by official statistics. In **Garcia Marquez's** "The Handsomest Drowned Man in the World," the physical setting is an unnamed island on which the characters seem removed from time.

Southern Gothic: The writer Tennessee Williams characterized Southern Gothic as a literary style that captured "…an intuition of an underlying dreadfulness in modern experience." This literary style is unique to American literature and a sub-genre of the Gothic writing style. Created in the twentieth century, this fictional genre maintains the supernatural, ironic, and bizarre elements of the Gothic style but uses them not merely as a way to create an atmosphere of suspense and foreboding. It uses these elements to explore and comment on cultural and social issues such as race and religion in the southern United States. Southern Gothic takes the archetypes of Gothic literature and reinvents them through the use of realism. For example, the classic maiden in peril trapped in a castle of nineteenth century Gothic stories becomes a bitter and eccentric maiden aunt who never leaves her bedroom in the Southern Gothic tradition. Because it uses its characters as opportunities to further comment on or highlight objectionable facets of American southern culture, Southern Gothic also incorporates an element called the grotesque, which allows the author to create a character, place, or situation that is repugnant or cringe-inducing but still able to elicit empathy from the reader. The author can then address certain topics without coming across as too moralistic or literal. **Flannery O'Connor's** story, "A Good Man Is Hard to Find" is considered a classic example of Southern Gothic. Other authors associated with this style are Tennessee Williams, William Faulkner, and Eudora Welty.

Supporting evidence: essay writers typically use four types of supporting evidence for their writing: (1) statistics, (2) facts, (3) examples and observations, and (4) quotations. Statistics are numerical data such as dates, amounts, and percentages that help strengthen points or statements because they offer some quantifiable proof. Facts are statements that can be objectively verified or proven. Examples and observations make ideas concrete by offering further proof to support an idea; they can be relayed in one sentence or expanded into several sentences. Examples should not be based on personal observations (a writer's own family and relations), but any piece of information or verifiable proof that can support a statement. Quotations are taken from another source (an article, story, essay, poem, play) and are used to illuminate or support an idea. This last type of evidence is also referred to as "argument from authority" since quotations can be taken from experts or authorities in a specific field of study.

Symbol: a character, place, object, or word that represents something more or means something beyond its literal meaning. In stories, symbols can have universal meanings but they can also be cultural, contextual (specific to that text), or personal (relating to one specific writer or artist). Think, for example, of the ring in J.R.R. Tolkien's novels as a symbol of an extreme lust for power.

Thesis statement: the "main idea" sentence of an essay, often boiled down to one arguable statement. The word "thesis" comes from the Greek *thesi,* which means "seat" or "position," hence a thesis statement is the writer's position or opinion on a given topic. There is no need for the writer to include "I think," "I believe," or "In this essay I will show" since it is implied that the thesis statement *is* the writer's opinion. A well-constructed thesis is an absolute necessity in any good essay. Typically, the thesis statement appears at the end of the introductory paragraph of an essay, with several sentences leading the reader to the thesis. However, not all writers follow this pattern, especially when the topic or opinions expressed are controversial; in this case, the writer will position his or her thesis later in the essay so as to allow the reader to consider all the supporting evidence beforehand. When evaluating a thesis statement's effectiveness, a writer should ask the following questions: Is it grammatically correct? Is it specific and supportable? Is it persuasive?

Tone: speaking tone and tone in writing are two very different things. In speaking, tone is most obviously communicated through the speaker's facial expression and tone of voice. In writing, tone is communicated primarily through word choice and sentence structure. Tone is important in writing since it conveys to the reader the general mood of a work. For example, the tone within a work can be identified as being formal or informal, ironic, humorous, sentimental, or serious.

Turning point: also called the crisis, a turning point is a point of great tension or a moment in the story when the course of events change and this change helps determine how the action will come out.

Types of essays: there are six common types of essays college and university students are expected to write:

(1) **Exemplification/Example/Illustration essay:** all essays depend on having good examples and use them for support, but examples are often not the main focus. In an exemplification or illustration essay, the body of the essay contains extended and expanded examples to support the thesis.

(2) **Persuasive essay:** involves leading the reader to not only see the validity of the writer's argument, but to convince readers to change their own position and even urge them to some form of action.

(3) **Argumentative essay:** does not have an agenda or involve having the audience appreciate the validity of a writer's points or argument.

(4) **Cause and effect essay:** focuses on presenting the "reasons" or causes for a situation, condition, or specific issue and the "results" or effects that are the logical outcome of these causes.

(5) **Comparison and contrast essay:** a comparison essay focuses on presenting similarities while a contrast essay focuses on presenting differences. The writer may focus on both differences and similarities or focus exclusively on one or the other. There should be an understanding that the writer has a clear and definite purpose for comparing and contrasting the two subjects.

(6) **Definition essay:** definitions help us understand basic concepts but also more difficult abstract ideas. This type of essay is an expanded version of what one reads in a dictionary. Definition essays include objective and/or subjective details.

Credits

NON-FICTION

Oscar Wilde. Excerpt from *De profundis*, from *The Collected Works of Oscar Wilde* (14 vols), ed. Robert Ross (London: Methuen and co., 1908): vol. 11.

Emily Carr. 'Mother', pp. 5–13 of *Growing Pains: The Autobiography of Emily Carr* (Toronto: Oxford University Press, 1946).

Martin Luther King, Jr. 'The Purpose of Education', pp. 123–124 of *The Papers of Martin Luther King, Jr*, ed. Clayborne Carson (Berkeley, CA: University of California Press, 1992).

Maxine Hong Kingston. 'No Name Woman' from *The Woman Warrior*, copyright © 1975, 1976 by Maxine Hong Kingston. Used by permission of Alfred A. Knopf, a division of Random House, Inc.

Deborah Tannen. 'Sex, Lies and Conversation; Why Is It So Hard for Men and Women to Talk to Each Other', p. C3 in *The Washington Post* (24 June 1990).

Margaret Visser. 'High Heels', pp. 37–41 from *The Way We Are* © 1994 by Margaret Visser. Published by HarperCollins Publishers Ltd. All rights reserved.

Kenneth J. Harvey. 'Virtual Adultery', pp. 55–57 in *Everyone Hates a Beauty Queen: Provocative Opinions and Irreverent Humour* (Toronto: Exile Editions Limited, 1998).

Pat Capponi. Selection from 'Dispatches from the Poverty Line', pp. 78–85 in *Dispatches from the Poverty Line* (Toronto: Penguin Books, 1997).

Drew Hayden Taylor. 'Introduction: Pretty Like a White Boy', pp. 9–14 in *Funny, You Don't Look Like One: Observations from a Blue-eyed Ojibway* (Penticton, BC: Theytus Books, 1996).

Jean Vanier. 'Loneliness', excerpt from *Becoming Human*, copyright © 1998 by Jean Vanier. A CBC Massey Lecture. Reproduced with permission from House of Anansi Press, Toronto. Copies of the complete work can be bought online at www.anansi.ca or www.amazon.com

Lawrence Solomon. 'Homeless in Paradise', online, at Urban Renaissance Institute (http://urbanrenaissanceinstitute.wordpress.com/): http://urban.probeinternational.org/housing/rent-controls-wreckage

Stephen King. Selection from *On Writing: A Memoir of the Craft*. Reprinted with permission of Scribner, a Division of Simon & Schuster, Inc. Copyright © by Stephen King. All rights reserved.

Vandana Shiva. 'Two Myths that Keep the World Poor', online, at *Ode Magazine* (www.odemagazine.com), November 2005: http://www.odemagazine.com/doc/28/two_myths_that_keep_the_world_poor/

Rex Murphy. 'A Saint Sorely Taxed', 'Ego Warriors', and 'There's Something about Cassandra', excerpted from *Canada and Other Matters of Opinion*. Copyright © 2009 Rex Murphy Communications Inc. Reprinted by permission of Doubleday Canada.

Timothy N. Hornyak. Selection from 'Loving the Machine: The Art and Science of Japanese Robots', pp. 90–98 in *Loving the Machine: The Art and Science of Japanese Robots* (Tokyo: Kodansha, 2006).

David Sedaris. From *Me Talk Pretty One Day* by David Sedaris. Copyright © by David Sedaris. By permission of Little, Brown and Company.

George Orwell. 'Politics and the English Language', pp. 252–265 of *Horizon* (13, 76), April 1946.

Jonathan Swift. 'A Modest Proposal', pp. 439–446 in *Jonathan Swift: Gulliver's Travels and Other Writings*, ed. Louis A. Landa (Boston: Houghton Mifflin, 1960)

Karim Rashid. 'The New You', pp. vi–6 in *Design Your Self: Rethinking the Way You Live, Love, Work, and Play* (New York: HarperCollins, 2006).

Henry David Thoreau. 'Civil Disobedience'.

FICTION

Leo Tolstoy. 'God Sees the Truth but Waits', pp. 108–116 in *Master and Man and Other Stories* (Penguin, 2005). ISBN 9780140449624

Guy de Maupassant. 'Butterball', pp. 3–52 in *Butterball* (Hesperus Press).

Kate Chopin. 'The Story of an Hour', pp. 756–758 in *Kate Chopin: Complete Novels and Stories* (New York: The Library of America, 2002).

Jorge Luis Borges. 'Streetcorner Man', from *Collected Fictions* by Jorge Luis Borges. Copyright © Maria Kodama, 1998. Translation and notes copyright © Penguin Putnam Inc., 1998. Reprinted by permission of Penguin Group (Canada), a Division of Pearson Canada Inc.

Flannery O'Connor. 'A Good Man is Hard to Find', from *A Good Man is Hard to Find and Other Stories*, copyright 1953 by Flannery O'Connor and renewed 1981 by Regina O'Connor, reprinted by permission of Harcourt, Inc.

James Baldwin. 'Sonny's Blues' © 1957, originally published in *Partisan Review*. Copyright renewed. Collected in *Going to Meet his Man*, published by Vintage Books. Reprinted with the permission of the James Baldwin Estate.

Margaret Laurence. 'The Loons' from *A Bird in the House* © 1963, 1964, 1965, 1966, 1967, 1970. New Canadian Library edition 1987, 2010. Published by McClelland & Stewart Ltd. Used with permission of the publisher.

Joseph Boyden. 'Legless Joe versus Black Robe' from *Born with a Tooth*, copyright © 2001 by Joseph Boyden. Used by permission of Cormorant Books Inc.

Katherine Govier. Excerpted from *The Immaculate Conception Photography Gallery*, copyright © 1994 by Katherine Govier. Reprinted by permission.

Austin Clarke. "A Wedding in Toronto" copyright © 1971. First published in *When He Was Free and Young and He Used to Wear Silks* in Canada by Anansi in 1971. Reprinted by permission of the author via The Bukowski Agency.

Angela Carter. 'The Company of Wolves', pp. 212–220 in *Burning Your Boats: The Collected Short Stories*. Copyright © 1995 Estate of Angela Carter. Reproduced by permission of the Estate of Angela Carter c/o Rogers, Coleridge & White Ltd., 20 Powis Mews, London W11 1JN.

Gabriel Garcia Marquez. Selection from 'The Handsomest Drowned Man in the World' from *Leaf Storm and Other Stories*. Copyright © 1971 by Gabriel Garcia Marquez. Reprinted by permission of HarperCollins Publishers.

Michael Ondaatje. Excerpt from *In The Skin of a Lion*, © 1987. Published by McClelland & Stewart Ltd. Used with permission of the Author and the Publisher.

Katherine Alexander. 'A Bit of Magic', pp. 70–84 in *Children of Byzantium* (Toronto: Cormorant Books, 1987).

Thomas King. 'The Baby in the Airmail Box', pp. 34–49 in *A Short History of Indians in Canada* © 2005 by Dead Dog Café Productions Inc. Published by HarperCollins Publishers Ltd. All rights reserved.

Stephen Marche. 'The Crow Procedure', online, at www.walrusmagazine.com, *The Walrus*, July 2009.

Jhumpa Lahiri. 'The Treatment of Bibi Halder' from *Interpreter of Maladies*. Copyright © 1999 by Jhumpa Lahiri. Reprinted by permission of Houghton Mifflin Harcourt Publishing Company. All rights reserved.

Diane Schoemperlen. 'Tell It to the Walls' © Diane Schoemperlen 1995, first published by HarperCollins Canada in the anthology *The Monkey and Other Stories*. Diane Schoemperlen is the author of three novels and several story collections, including the Governor-General's Fiction Award winner, *Forms of Devotion*.

Dorothy Parker. 'A Telephone Call', from *The Portable Dorothy Parker*, edited by Marion Meade, copyright 1928, renewed © 1973, 2006 by the National Assoc. for the Advancement of Colored People. Used by permission of Viking Penguin, a division of Penguin Group (USA) Inc.

Leonid Andreyev. 'The Marseillaise', pp. 211–215 in *The Little Angel (and Other Stories)* (New York: Dedalus/Hippocrene, 1989).

Index of Themes

Education

NON-FICTION

FICTION

Family and Community Dynamics/ Family Relationships/Domestic Life

NON-FICTION

FICTION

Fashion/Social Trends

NON-FICTION

FICTION

Illusion vs. Reality (Truth vs. Fiction)

NON-FICTION

FICTION

Immigrant Experience

NON-FICTION

FICTION

Lookism

NON-FICTION

Sexual Politics and Gender

NON-FICTION

FICTION

Spirituality/Faith

NON-FICTION

FICTION

Technology

NON-FICTION

FICTION

Tone/Style and Narrative Techniques (Oral Storytelling)

NON-FICTION

FICTION

The Writing Process/Creation of Ideas

NON-FICTION

Index of Authors and Works